MAREVA INJUNCTIONS
AND
RELATED INTERLOCUTORY ORDERS

Also by the same author:

The Law of Private Companies (1994)

For my wife Aileen
and daughter Alison

Mareva Injunctions

AND
Related Interlocutory Orders

by

Thomas B. Courtney

B.A., LL.B., Solicitor

Butterworths

Ireland	Butterworth (Ireland) Ltd, 26 Upper Ormond Quay, DUBLIN 7
United Kingdom	Butterworths a Division of Reed Elsevier (UK) Ltd, Halsbury House, 35 Chancery Lane, LONDON WC2A 1EL and 4 Hill Street, EDINBURGH EH2 3JZ
Australia	Butterworths, a Division of Reed International Books Australia Pty Ltd, Chatswood, NEW SOUTH WALES
Canada	Butterworths Canada Ltd, Markham, ONTARIO
India	Butterworths India, NEW DELHI
Malaysia	Malayan Law Journal Sdn Bhd, KUALA LUMPUR
New Zealand	Butterworths of New Zealand Ltd, WELLINGTON
Singapore	Butterworths Asia, SINGAPORE
South Africa	Butterworths Legal Publishers (Pty) Ltd, DURBAN
USA	Lexis Law Publishing, Charlottesville, VIRGINIA

© Thomas B. Courtney 1998

A CIP Catalogue record for this book is available from the British Library.

ISBN 1 85475 1077

Printed in Ireland by Sciprint Ltd, Shannon, Co Clare

Foreword

The growth of the Mareva injunction in the various common law jurisdictions, including Ireland, has been a remarkable feature of civil litigation in recent decades. Until the new doctrine emerged in the English Court of Appeal in 1975, it had been assumed that the law could offer no redress to a plaintiff with a good cause of action who pursued what was frequently expensive litigation only to find that there were no assets to meet his claim. The jurisdiction in admiralty to order the arrest of a ship whose owners were being sued for maritime debts was a somewhat exotic exception to this general principle. For a court to say that it had such a jurisdiction to freeze the defendant's assets in advance of any judgment in favour of the plaintiff would be, said Lord Hatherly, LC (in *Mills v Northern Railway of Buenos Aires Company* [1870] 5 Ch App 621,) to assume "a fearful authority". That anxiety has long been dispelled, but concerns remain as to the boundaries which the law should set so as to ensure that this powerful weapon for remedying injustice does not itself become a source of oppression.

The appearance of the first comprehensive Irish study of this important and developing branch of the law is thus timely and welcome. Some years ago, I had the pleasure of contributing a foreword to Tom Courtney's book on *The Law of Private Companies* and marvelled that a busy practising solicitor could find the energy in what spare time he had to produce so impressive and comprehensive a contribution to legal literature. His industry and commitment has now resulted in a further addition to Irish legal studies which will be of great benefit to judges, barristers and solicitors alike. This is a field of the law in which even the most diligent practitioner is likely to find that decisions of considerable importance have not been reported and it is one of the great merits of Mr Courtney's book that he draws attention to a number of such cases, including the orders made by the High Court in recent times granting "worldwide" Mareva injunctions, an area of the law which may still continue to provoke controversy.

Mr Courtney's work also contains extremely helpful practical advice for solicitors and counsel intending to apply to the court for this form of relief and the legal advisers of the defendant or other third parties, such as financial institutions, who may find themselves affected by the order if it is granted. In an era when, with a greatly expanded bar, there is the ever present danger of a dilution in professional standards, it is to be hoped that practitioners will take to heart the many salutary warnings delivered by judges both here and in the United Kingdom as to the necessity for a full and frank disclosure to the court of all the relevant circumstances when a judge is being asked to assume this "fearful authority" in the necessary absence of the other party.

The consequences of invoking that jurisdiction where it is not warranted were trenchantly described by my colleague, Mr Justice O'Flaherty, in *Re John Horgan Livestock Ltd; O'Mahony v Horgan* [1995] 2 IR 411 at 422 in these terms:

> "... t needs to be emphasised that the Mareva injunction is a very powerful remedy which if improperly invoked will bring about an injustice, something that it was designed to prevent. It may put a person or a company out of business. It may contribute to delay in bringing litigation to a head. It may be used as a diversionary tactic and be a part of the skirmishes that increasingly incur in much litigation. It may - as is the case here - take on a life of its own while the main litigation is becalmed ..."

Legal mariners negotiating these sometimes hazardous waters will find Mr Courtney's work a sure and steady guide. I wish it every success.

Ronan Keane,
The Supreme Court,
Four Courts,
Dublin.

7 July 1998

Preface

It was in 1985 that, as a student in what was then University College Galway, I first heard of the Mareva injunction, which was at that time a mere ten years' old. Later that year I was given my first opportunity to learn more about this extraordinary jurisdiction when Professional Books was kind enough to give an impecunious student a voucher to the value of £100; the catch was that it was only redeemable in return for their books. One of the books I chose was by DG Powles, *The Mareva Injunction and Associated Orders*, (1985). Ironically, Professional Books was subsequently acquired by Butterworths and so, one may surmise, there was foresight in its sponsorship of student prizes.

Even the most accomplished prognosticator could not, in 1985, have foreseen the extraordinary development of the original Mareva jurisdiction. Whilst by then it had developed to being available to restrain domestic defendants from dissipating their assets within the State, the ability of the courts to grant so-called worldwide Mareva injunctions was, in 1985, not even a gleam in Lord Denning's eye.

The Mareva injunction is one of those things which make the law exciting. In an appropriate case, a deserving plaintiff can, without notice to a defendant, apply to a judge of the Circuit or High Court - outside of hours - for an order to "freeze" a defendant's assets. The plaintiff will have no legal or beneficial claim to the defendant's assets; his claim against the defendant will be one merely for damages. The Mareva injunction is remarkable because it recognises the exigencies of justice and provides a remedy in circumstances where no remedy heretofore existed.

Extraordinarily powerful remedies are capable of bringing about an injustice which, as O'Flaherty J has said, is something which the Mareva injunction was designed to prevent: *Re John Horgan Livestock Ltd; O'Mahony v. Horgan* [1995] 2 IR 411 at 422. It must always be remembered that a Mareva injunction is not available to all litigants - it will only be granted to those who can satisfy its rigorous proofs. Although a Mareva plaintiff is required to establish a number of proofs, in Ireland, the most important is that he establish a likelihood that a defendant will remove his assets from the State or otherwise dissipate them *with a view to evading the plaintiff's judgment and frustrating the anticipated order of the court*. The need to establish a nefarious intention - which was conclusively identified by the Supreme Court in its seminal decision on the Mareva injunction in *Re John Horgan Livestock Ltd; supra* - sets the Mareva remedy in Ireland apart from other strains of the Mareva injunction as it exists in other common law jurisdictions.

There are over 90 applications to both the High Court and Circuit Court noted in this book in which written judgments were not given and the only record of their existence is a report in *The Irish Times*; notwithstanding the frequency of Mareva applications before the Irish courts there are fewer than a dozen written decisions on asset freezing orders. It was this fact which persuaded me of the utility of reference to applications for Mareva relief which have been reported in the newspapers, particularly, *The Irish Times*. These cases, which because it was impossible to verify the facts of each and every one are referred to in traditional family law citation style, are *not* held out by me as precedents or authorities. They are, however, held out as factual examples of the practice and procedure of both the High Court and Circuit Court and are illustrative of the myriad of circumstances in which Mareva injunctions have been granted and refused.

In addition to treating the Mareva injunction and related interlocutory orders such as asset disclosure orders, Anton Piller orders, orders under the Bankers' Books Evidence Acts 1879 to 1989, I have also included statutory asset freezing orders. Accordingly, the relevant asset freezing provisions of the Criminal Justice Act, 1994, Proceeds of Crime Act, 1996, Family Law Act, 1995 and Family Law (Divorce) Act, 1996 are treated.

This book has been ten years in the offing - albeit punctuated by writing *The Law of Private Companies*. There are a great many people to whom I owe an enormous debt of gratitude. First and foremost comes my wife Aileen not only for her comments and critique of this book which have greatly enhanced it but also for her unstinting encouragement and support. On a personal level I would also thank my mother Susan Courtney and my friends, Niall O'Brien, solicitor and Pat Hanley, Head of Credit with ACC Bank plc for their encouragement. This book is dedicated to my wife Aileen and my darling baby daughter, Alison.

William Johnston, partner with Arthur Cox and author of *Banking and Security Law in Ireland* kindly read and commented upon all of this book. Reading another book was probably the last thing which William needed after he completed his own *magnum opus*. His encouragement, support and tempered constructive criticism are, once again, greatly appreciated. He was not the only friend to read and comment upon this book: my oldest friend, Hugh Garvey, partner with LK Shields, Solicitors (whose spare time must surely be measured in nano-seconds) made very many useful comments which have saved me embarrassment and have added to whatever benefit this book may be to practitioners. I also wish to thank John Trainor SC who willingly gave of what little free time his busy practice allows and again his comments added immeasurably to this book. I also thank Shane Murphy BL for his helpful and authoritative comments on Ch 3, *Statutory Jurisdictions to Freeze Assets* and Vincent Power, partner with A&L Goodbody and author for his critique of Ch 1, *The Mareva Injunction in Context* and, in particular, the section on admiralty law. Finally, in this regard, I would like to express my sincere gratitude and appreciation to Mr Brendan Reedy, Senior Chancery Registrar of the High Court for giving up some of his vacation and making very many practical suggested improvements to Ch 8, *Applying for a Mareva Injunction* and also for reading and approving in principle the precedent orders in the Appendices to this book. This is not to mention the members of the judiciary, the Bar and the Law Society (many of whom are mentioned throughout the book) for providing me with copies of Mareva orders and other documents where there were no written judgments otherwise available. I would also like to pay special thanks to Margaret Byrne, Mary Gaynor and, in particular, to Eddie Mackey of the Law Society's library for diligently and consistently keeping me abreast of case law - often before even the judge's ink was dry on the transcript.

Mr Justice Ronan Keane is owed a special thanks, not only for contributing his perceptive foreword to this book, but also for reading the first draft of this book and making some very pertinent and helpful suggestions at improvement.

I also thank my publishers, Butterworths and especially Gerard Coakley and Lousie Leavy for their encouragement, assistance and constant support. In this regard I also include Professor JCW Wylie who read the first two chapters of this book and urged me to continue. I also acknowledge my appreciation to Max Harvey, formerly of Butterworths who first suggested I write this book. I would also like to thank Julitta Clancy for producing what I believe, and trust you will find, is a superb index to this book.

I have tried to state the law on Mareva injunctions in Ireland as at 31 July 1998. No legal responsibility can be accepted for the contents hereof and all readers are urged to consider their specific cases in the light of particular legal advice. I would ask all practitioners who have occasion to be involved in applications for the reliefs considered in this book to send me copies of any orders or other documentation which they think might add to a greater understanding of this topic.

Thomas B. Courtney
Blackrock,
Co Dublin
31 July 1998

Contents

Chapter 4   A Substantive Cause of Action

Chapter 9   The Mareva Order and Its Effects

Chapter 10 Ancillary Orders

Appendices

Table of Statutes

Constitution of Ireland

England and Wales

Statutory Instruments (Ireland)

Statutory Instruments (UK)

Table of Cases

B

C

E

F

L

N

O

S

U

V

W

Chapter 1

The Mareva Injunction in Context

[1.01] Given the extensive international judicial examination of the jurisdiction to grant Mareva relief, it is remarkable that the Mareva injunction only came of age in 1996, that being the year of its twenty first birthday.¹ The recent origins of the Mareva injunction stand in stark contrast to other equitable remedies; hundreds of years of jurisprudence and judicial pronouncements on the availability of most legal and equitable remedies are available to guide legal practitioners. Remedies such as the general interlocutory injunction, specific performance, rectification, recission, and the declaration are well documented in the standard textbooks² and legal encyclopaedia such as *Halsbury's Laws of England* and *The English and Empire Digest*. In such reference works one can find commentary upon all aspects of such remedies, supported by judicial authorities, some dating back hundreds of years. Not so on the Mareva injunction, the development of which is inextricably linked to modern technological advances which facilitate the swift transfer of funds from one jurisdiction to another. In *Targe Towing Ltd v The Owners and All Persons Claiming an Interest in the Vessel "Von Rocks"*³ Keane J compared times past with times present, saying of the former that then:

> "... the assets of a debtor within the jurisdiction were regarded as being more readily available to satisfy creditors. In an age of greatly enhanced electronic communications, that is not always the case and hence the remarkable development of the *Mareva* injunction in recent years."

[1.02] The purpose of this book is to identify and to examine the Irish law and practice on Mareva injunctions and related interlocutory orders such as asset disclosure orders,⁴ Anton Piller orders⁵ and injunctions to restrain persons from

---

¹· So named after the second reported case where this jurisdiction was asserted, *Mareva Compania Naviera SA v International Bulkcarriers SA, The Mareva* [1975] 2 Lloyd's Rep 509, [1980] 1 All ER 213. The first such injunction was made in *Nippon Yusen Kaisha v Karageorgis* [1975] 3 All ER 282.

²· Such as, in Ireland, Keane, *Equity and the Law of Trusts in the Republic of Ireland*, (1988) Butterworths, Wylie, *Irish Land Law*, (1997) Butterworths, Wylie, *A Casebook on Equity and Trusts in Ireland*, (2nd ed 1998) Butterworths and Delany, *Equity and the Law of Trusts in Ireland*, (1996) Roundhall Sweet & Maxwell.

³· [1998] 1 ILRM 481 at 493.

⁴· See Ch 10, *Ancillary Orders*, para **[10.03]** *et seq.*

⁵· *Ibid* para **[10.38]** *et seq.*

leaving the jurisdiction.[6] Moreover, to provide as complete a picture as possible of the circumstances in which a person's assets can be frozen, the recent statutory jurisdictions to freeze assets under the Criminal Justice Act 1994, the Proceeds of Crime Act 1996, the Family Law Act 1995 and the Family Law (Divorce) Act 1996 are also treated.[7]

[1.03] This chapter is divided into three sections: Section [A] which provides an overview of the Mareva jurisdiction; Section [B] where the freezing of assets in *proprietary claims* is distinguished from Mareva relief; and Section [C] where the jurisdiction in admiralty law to arrest ships is considered and distinguished from Mareva relief.

[A] OVERVIEW OF THE MAREVA JURISDICTION

[1.04] In over-viewing the jurisdiction to grant Mareva injunctions in Ireland, the following scheme is adopted:

1.   The Mareva Injunction Defined;

2.   The Purpose of a Mareva Injunction;

3.   General Features of the Mareva Injunction;

4.   An Overview of the Development of the Mareva Injunction;

5.   The Proofs Required on a Mareva Application.

The Mareva Injunction Defined

[1.05] A Mareva injunction may be defined as a (pre-judgment or post-judgment[8]) court order which restrains a defendant from removing from the State, or otherwise disposing[9] of his own assets,[10] whether generally, or up to a specified amount,[11] until further order of the court or until the trial of the matter. It is an essential feature of the Mareva jurisdiction in Ireland that there is evidence that a defendant is likely to remove or dispose of his assets *with the intention*[12] of evading his obligations to the plaintiff and frustrating the

---

6.   See generally Ch 11, *Restraining Defendants from Leaving the State.*

7.   See Ch 3, *Statutory Jurisdictions to Freeze Assets.*

8.   *Orwell Steel (Erection & Fabrication) Ltd v Asphalt & Tarmac (UK) Ltd* [1985] 3 All ER 747 recognised that a Mareva injunction could be used as an aid to post-judgment execution. See Ch 4, *A Substantive Cause of Action*, para **[4.28]** *et seq.*

9.   Mareva orders typically prevent defendants from disposing of, reducing, charging or dealing with their assets. See Ch 9, *The Mareva Order and Its Effects*, para **[9.06]**.

10. See Ch 7, *The Defendant's Assets.*

11. See Ch 9, *The Mareva Order and Its Effects*, para **[9.09]**.

12. In Ireland it must be established to the satisfaction of the Court that a Mareva defendant has an intention to frustrate a Mareva plaintiff's future judgment: see *Re John Horgan Livestock Ltd* [1995] 2 IR 411, considered in detail in Ch 6, *The Risk of Removal or Disposal of Assets*, para **[6.18]**.

anticipated order of the court. A Mareva injunction is available where a plaintiff does not have, or claim to have, a proprietary interest in the defendant's assets which are "frozen" by the order;[13] it operates *in personam* against a defendant's person and does not act *in rem* against a defendant's assets.[14] An applicant for a Mareva injunction must, ordinarily, have a currently actionable substantive cause of action within the jurisdiction.[15]

The Purpose of a Mareva Injunction

[1.06] The essential purpose of a Mareva injunction is two-fold: first, to prevent a defendant from evading his obligations to a plaintiff; and secondly to prevent a defendant from frustrating the anticipated order of the Court. The means employed to achieve these purposes is to freeze temporarily a defendant's assets by ordering him to desist from dealing with them. Lord Donaldson MR in *Polly Peck International plc v Nadir (No 2)*[16] identified one of the basic principles underlying the Mareva jurisdiction to be:

> "So far as it lies in their power, the courts will not permit the course of justice
> to be frustrated by a defendant taking action, the purpose of which is to render
> nugatory or less effective any judgment or order which the plaintiff may
> thereafter obtain.".

Recently, the High Court of Australia most aptly described the Mareva injunction as "the paradigm example of an order to prevent the frustration of a court's process": *Patrick Stevedores Operations No 2 Pty Ltd v Maritime Union of Australia.*[17] A Mareva injunction seeks to ensure that a plaintiff's judgment against a defendant is satisfied. There are many reasons why a plaintiff might be denied satisfaction of a judgment which he has obtained against a defendant eg the defendant might have insufficient resources to begin with, or the defendant might pay other creditors first and have insufficient resources left to pay the plaintiff etc. However, it is not the purpose of a Mareva injunction to ensure that a plaintiff's judgment is satisfied in all circumstances. In Ireland, not only must the *effect* of a defendant's conduct tend to stultify an anticipated judgment - that effect must also be the defendant's *intention*. So it was held by the Supreme Court in *Re John Horgan Livestock Ltd*[18] that a Mareva plaintiff must adduce evidence of:

---

13. See para **[1.08]** *et seq infra.*
14. See Ch 9, *The Mareva Order and Its Effects*, para **[9.36]** *et seq.*
15. See, generally, Ch 4, *A Substantive Cause of Action*; *cf* the Jurisdiction of Courts and Enforcement of Judgments Acts 1988 and 1993 para **[4.50]** *et seq.*
16. [1992] 4 All ER 769 at 785g.
17. [1998] HCA 30 at 35 of the transcript of the judgment.
18. [1995] 2 IR 411.

"... an intention on the part of the defendant to dispose of his assets with a view to evading his obligation to the plaintiff and to frustrate the anticipated order of the court. It is not sufficient to establish that the assets are likely to be dissipated in the ordinary course of business or in the payment of lawful debts."[19]

It can therefore be seen that the mischief which a Mareva injunction is designed to prevent is the deliberate and intentional evasion of legal obligations and the frustration of the court's process by devious defendants.

General Features of the Mareva Injunction

(a) Mareva injunctions act in personam

[1.07] The primary effect of a Mareva injunction is to restrain a defendant from moving his assets out of the jurisdiction or disposing of, or otherwise dealing with his assets within the jurisdiction save to the extent that his assets exceed his liabilities to the Mareva-plaintiff. A Mareva injunction primarily binds the person to whom it is directed (ie the defendant in an action) although it can also affect third parties.[20] A Mareva injunction operates *in personam*: *ie* it binds the defendant to whom it is directed but it does not create any interest in that defendant's assets, which are only indirectly "frozen".[21] Mareva injunctions are, therefore, a modern day example of the old rule that Equity operates on a defendant's conscience.[22] Of course, should a defendant breach a Mareva injunction, the remedies of attachment, committal and fine will affect more than his conscience.[23] As shall be considered in Chapter 7, *The Defendant's Assets*, the extension of the Mareva jurisdiction to restrain a defendant from dealing with his assets which are situated outside of the jurisdiction of the court making the injunction was facilitated by the fact that the injunction operates *in personam*.[24] It follows that, although it is common to hear it said of Mareva injunctions that they "freeze" a defendant's assets, this is a misnomer since it is only a defendant who is *directly* bound by the injunction; a defendant's assets are affected only *indirectly* by the injunction.

---

19. [1995] 2 IR 411 at 419.
20. See Ch 9, *The Mareva Order and Its Effects*, para **[9.43]** *et seq*; and Ch 12, *Enforcing Mareva Injunctions and Other Orders*, para **[12.31]** *et seq*.
21. See Ch 9, *The Mareva Order and Its Effects*, para **[9.36]** *et seq*.
22. See Keane, *Equity and the Law of Trusts in the Republic of Ireland,* (1988) Butterworths, Ch 2 and para 2.12 in particular. See also Meagher, Gummow & Lehane, *Equity Doctrines & Remedies*, (3rd ed; 1992) Butterworths at Ch 1 for an interesting Commonwealth perspective on the history and development of Equity.
23. See Ch 12, *Enforcing Mareva Injunctions and Other Orders*, para **[12.51]** *et seq*.
24. See Ch 7, *The Defendant's Assets*, para **[7.26]** *et seq*.

(b) A *Mareva* plaintiff does not need a proprietary interest in the assets which he seeks to have "frozen"

[1.08] The Mareva injunction is a novelty in the common law world because it restricts a defendant in dealing with his own assets. A successful Mareva plaintiff will have neither (a) a proprietary right or interest (legal or beneficial) in the assets which a defendant is restrained from dealing with, nor, (b) established in a court of law (ie by obtaining a judgment or declaration) that a defendant is liable to give his assets, or their monetary value, to the plaintiff. The old principle of law which said that a person who could not bring himself within either of the conditions at (a) or (b) was not entitled to an injunction preventing another person from dealing with his own assets is known as the rule in *Lister & Co v Stubbs*.[25]

[1.09] For the greater part of a century the rule in *Lister & Co v Stubbs* was construed as an absolute rule: a defendant could not be restrained from dealing with his own assets before judgment was obtained against him.[26] Since the original landmark cases of *Nippon Yusen Kaisha v Karageorgis*[27] and *Mareva Compania Naviera SA v International Bulkcarriers SA*[28] the position has changed and the rule in *Lister & Co v Stubbs*, thought not entirely obsolete,[29] is today far from absolute. One must not lose sight of the importance of the *Lister* principle: it is undoubtedly a sound principle of law that a defendant in an action should not, ordinarily, be restricted by interlocutory order of the court from dealing with his property until after the case against him is proved. However, as recognised by Keane J in *Targe Towing Ltd v The Owners and All Persons Claiming an Interest in the Vessel "Von Rocks"*,[30] the law must keep pace with other developments and especially "enhanced electronic communications" which facilitate the worldwide dispersal of funds. In short, the

---

[25.] (1890) 45 Ch D 1. In that case (at 12) Cotton LJ said: "... I know of no case where, because it was highly probable that if the action were brought to hearing the plaintiff could establish that a debt was due to him from the defendant, the defendant has been ordered to give security until that has been established by the judgment or decree." This is considered in detail in Ch 2, *The Jurisdiction to Grant Mareva Relief*, para **[2.04]** *et seq.*

[26.] Note, however, that there have been occasional statutory inroads into the rule in *Lister & Co v Stubbs*. For example, s 118 of the Companies Act 1862 facilitated the seizing the goods of a contributory to a company who was absconding although no judgment had been obtained against him; see the modern equivalent, s 247 of the Companies Act 1963 which is considered in Ch 11, *Restraining Defendants from Leaving the State*, para **[11.42]**.

[27.] [1975] 3 All ER 282.

[28.] [1980] 1 All ER 213.

[29.] See the comments of McWilliam J in *Fleming v Ranks (Ireland) Ltd* [1983] ILRM 541 at 546, 547. See further, Ch 2, *The Jurisdiction to Grant Mareva Relief*, para **[2.17]**.

[30.] [1998] 1 ILRM 481. See para **[1.01]** *supra.*

court must attempt to find a just balance between the rights of the defendant and those of the plaintiff.

[1.10] It follows that where an injunction causes a defendant's assets to be frozen in circumstances where the plaintiff does claim to have a proprietary interest in those assets, such an injunction is *not* a Mareva injunction and is not subject to the same proofs. An application for an injunction to preserve property in which a plaintiff claims to have a proprietary interest will be determined by the standard criteria for an interlocutory injunction[31] which amounts to a less onerous test than that applied to Mareva injunctions. "Proprietary" injunctions are considered below.[32]

(c) A Mareva injunction does not create rights in the assets "frozen"

[1.11] An adjunct to the fact that a Mareva-plaintiff does not claim to have a proprietary interest in a defendant's assets is that, when granted, a Mareva injunction does not create any interest in or right to a defendant's assets.[33] It follows that a plaintiff who obtains a Mareva injunction has no better claim to a defendant's assets than any other creditor and where a Mareva-defendant is insolvent, a Mareva-plaintiff will, *per se*, rank *pari passu* with all other unsecured creditors.

(d) Mareva relief can be draconian

[1.12] The Mareva injunction is an extraordinarily powerful pre-emptive remedy and, for this reason, judicial discretion to grant Mareva relief is exercised sparingly. In *Production Association Minsk Tractor Works and Belarus Equipment (Ireland) Ltd v Saenko*[34] McCracken J said:

> "I would emphasise that a Mareva injunction is an extremely drastic remedy. In some civil law countries there is provision for the freezing of assets pending the outcome of a claim. There is no such provision in our law, and a Mareva injunction cannot be used to attain this purpose. The Court must look very carefully at any application to ensure that it is justified on the principles set out above."[35]

[31.] See Ch 5, *A Good Arguable Case*, para **[5.03]** *et seq.*
[32.] See para **[1.16]** *et seq, infra.*
[33.] See Ch 9, *The Mareva Order and Its Effects*, para **[9.36]**.
[34.] High Court, unrep, 25 February 1998 (McCracken J).
[35.] At p 5 of the transcript. The principles to which McCracken J was referring were those set out in *Third Chandris Shipping Corporation v Unimarine SA* [1979] QB 655 which were quoted with approval by the Supreme Court in *Re John Horgan Livestock Ltd; O'Mahony v Horgan* [1995] 2 IR 411. On the proofs required, see para **[1.15]** *infra* and generally, Ch 7, *Applying for a Mareva Injunction.*

The Mareva injunction has been properly described as one of the law's nuclear weapons.[36] It restricts a person's right to deal *with his own property*. Save in the case of post-judgment Mareva injunctions, Mareva relief can be granted to a plaintiff who has not yet established to the satisfaction of a court that the defendant is legally liable to pay him money; all that a plaintiff has to show is that he has "a good arguable case" against a defendant.[37] The justification for restricting a defendant's right to deal with his property is the likelihood, based upon the evidence adduced by the plaintiff, that he will anticipate defeat and divest himself of his property with the result that the judicial process is frustrated and the plaintiff's victory is pyrrhic. As noted above, the Mareva injunction attempts to balance the rights of defendants, plaintiffs and the courts. This balancing of rights shall be returned to when considering the constitutionality of the Mareva injunction.[38]

An Overview of the Development of the Mareva Injunction[39]

[1.13] The first case in which a Mareva injunction was granted was *Nippon Yusen Kaisha v Karageorgis*;[40] the second case was *Mareva Compania Naviera SA v International Bulkcarriers SA, The Mareva*.[41] Both judgments were delivered after *ex parte* applications.[42] In the early years of its development, the Mareva injunction was a remedy directed at foreign defendants which restrained them from removing their assets from the jurisdiction. Over the last two decades there have been substantial developments such as, its application to domestic defendants, the disposal of assets within the jurisdiction and the disposal of assets worldwide, which have transformed the Mareva injunction into what it is today: a remedy which is technically available against all defendants in all causes of action.

[1.14] Mareva injunctions have been granted by the Irish courts, at least, since the early 1980s and since then have been granted in a wide variety of cases: by a widow against her daughter over the proceeds of sale of the widow's home;[43] by a student nurse against a company in circumstances where she had suffered

---

36. *Per* Lord Donaldson in *Bank Mellat v Nikpour* [1985] FSR 87 at 92.
37. See Ch 5, *A Good Arguable Case*.
38. See Ch 2, *The Jurisdiction to Grant Mareva Relief*, para **[2.24]** *et seq*.
39. For a first hand account of the introduction and development of the Mareva injunction, see Lord Denning, *The Due Process of Law*, (1980) Butterworths, pp 133-151; see further Ch 2, *The Jurisdiction to Grant Mareva Relief*.
40. [1975] 3 All ER 282.
41. [1980] 1 All ER 213.
42. The first *inter partes* hearing of a Mareva injunction application was *Rasu Maritima SA v Perusahaan Pertambanga Miyak Dan Gas Bumi Negara* [1978] QB 644; see further Ch 2, *The Jurisdiction to Grant Mareva Relief*.
43. *O v K, The Irish Times*, 19 September 1991 (Johnson J).

personal injuries after a fall at a discotheque;[44] by a widow, whose husband was shot dead by the defendant who was a prisoner in Mountjoy;[45] by the Minister for Social Welfare to prevent an insurance company paying part of a settlement to a man who had sued a food manufacturer and supermarket after allegedly finding part of a mouse in a savoury pie;[46] and by companies against their former chief executive officers whom, it was alleged, had acted in breach of their duties.[47] The origins and development of the Mareva jurisdiction in Ireland are considered fully in Chapter 2, *The Jurisdiction to Grant Mareva Relief.*

The Proofs Required on a Mareva Application

[1.15] In order to obtain a Mareva injunction a plaintiff must meet certain basic conditions:

1. A plaintiff must have a substantive right which is capable of being enforced against a defendant (eg a currently actionable cause of action);[48] a claim *in personam* will suffice;[49]

2. The strength of a plaintiff's case against a defendant must be a "good arguable case";[50]

3. There must be a risk that a defendant will remove his assets from the jurisdiction or otherwise dispose of them with the intention of defeating his obligations to a plaintiff and frustrating the anticipated court order;[51]

4. The defendant must have assets which are capable of being frozen (whether those assets are inside or outside of the jurisdiction);[52]

5. The balance of convenience must favour granting the injunction.[53]

Each of these prerequisites are considered in detail in the chapters which follow. In addition, there are certain ancillary, procedural, proofs which a Mareva plaintiff must establish. These are identified and considered in detail in Chapter 8, *Applying for a Mareva Injunction.*

---

44. *C v X Ltd, The Irish Times,* 25 September 1990 (Blayney J).
45. *K v F, The Irish Times,* 30 May 1990 (Costello J).
46. *Minister for Social Welfare v M, The Irish Times,* 21 February 1991 (Murphy J).
47. See, for example, *Countyglen plc v Carway* [1995] 1 IR 208 and *Bula Resources (Holdings) plc v Stanley, The Irish Times,* 7 August 1998 (O'Higgins J).
48. See Ch 4, *A Substantive Cause of Action.*
49. A substantive cause of action in the nature of a claim *in rem* may give rise to the right to claim an ordinary injunction to preserve the plaintiff's property in the defendant's possession: see para **[1.16]** *et seq, infra.*
50. See Ch 5, *A Good Arguable Case.*
51. See Ch 6, *The Risk of Removal or Disposal of Assets.*
52. See Ch 7, *The Defendant's Assets.*
53. See Ch 8, *Applying for a Mareva Injunction,* para **[8.55]** *et seq.*

[B] PROPRIETARY CLAIMS DISTINGUISHED FROM MAREVA RELIEF

[1.16] There is nothing new *per se* about injunctions which have the effect of restraining a person from dealing with property. The novelty of a Mareva injunction lies in the fact that a defendant can be restrained in his use of *his own assets*, notwithstanding that a plaintiff has no proprietary right in or claim to those assets. This section considers the circumstances in which a plaintiff who has or claims to have a proprietary interest in assets which are in a defendant's possession may obtain an ordinary interlocutory injunction to restrain the defendant from dealing with such assets. The following issues arise:

1. The Nature of a Proprietary Claim.
2. Preserving the Subject Matter of a Cause of Action: Ord 50, r 4 of the RSC.
3. Tracing Claims.
4. Claims by Receivers.
5. Disclosure Orders in Proprietary Claims.
6. Summary of the Conditions for a "Proprietary" Injunction to Freeze Assets.

The Nature of a Proprietary Claim

[1.17] In *Republic of Haiti v Duvalier*[54] Staughton LJ usefully distinguished proprietary claims eg a tracing claim[55] from *in personam* claims, eg a claim for a monetary judgment. He said:

> "A proprietary claim is one by which the plaintiff seeks the return of chattels or land which are his property, or claims that a specified debt is owed by a third party to him and not to the defendant."[56]

A plaintiff with a proprietary claim will be more readily afforded relief to preserve or freeze the subject matter of his claim. As Staughton LJ said:

> "A plaintiff who seeks to enforce a claim of that kind will more readily be afforded interim remedies in order to preserve the asset which he is seeking to recover, than one who merely seeks a judgment for debt or damages. But if the asset has been converted into some other form or property, the question of tracing arises. If the defendant stole the plaintiff's peas, sold them and bought beans with the proceeds, the plaintiff claims that the beans are his property. Or if the defendant misappropriated the plaintiff's credit balance with bank X, and established a credit with bank Y from the proceeds, the plaintiff claims that the

---

[54.] [1989] 1 All ER 456.
[55.] On tracing claims, see para **[1.21]** *infra*.
[56.] [1989] 1 All ER 456 at 464g.

debt due from bank Y is his property. In that last case, if the proceedings are brought by the plaintiff against the defendant only, the relief claimed can be no more than a declaration, and an injunction against interference with the plaintiff's property. Ultimately the right must be enforced against the debtor, in my example bank Y."[57]

In that case, as in many others, the plaintiff's proprietary and personal claims were intertwined.[58]

Preserving the Subject Matter of a Cause of Action: Ord 50, r 4 of the RSC

[1.18] Order 50, r 4 of the Rules of the Superior Courts 1986 ("the RSC") makes express provision for the granting of interlocutory injunctions for the preservation or inspection of any property or thing which is the subject matter of a cause or matter. It provides:

> "The Court, upon the application of any party to a cause or matter, and upon such terms as may be just, may make any order for the detention, preservation, or inspection of any property or thing, being the subject matter of such cause or matter, or as to which any question may arise therein, and for all or any of the purposes aforesaid may authorise any person to enter upon or into any land or building in the possession of any party to such cause or matter and for all or any of the purposes aforesaid may authorise any samples to be taken or any observations to be made or experiment to be tried, which may be necessary or expedient for the purpose of obtaining full information or evidence."

This rule reflects the fact that for a considerable time there has been a jurisdiction to make an injunction ordering the "detention, preservation or inspection" of property which is the subject matter of a cause of action. An injunction or order made pursuant to Ord 50, r 4 of the RSC is very different to a Mareva injunction because in the case of a Mareva injunction the assets which are indirectly affected by the injunction will not be the subject matter of the cause or matter in litigation.[59]

[57.] At 464h-j.

[58.] Staughton LJ said (at 465c) of the nature of their claims that: "... I would not go so far as to say that the action in France, in aid of which these proceedings are said to be brought, is itself a proprietary or tracing claim. It does not presently assert ownership of any of the assets expected to be revealed by orders in the English proceedings. But I am confident that ownership will be asserted when and where the assets are found. This is then something of a hybrid situation; and one should perhaps consider it on the basis that interim relief is sought in aid of a monetary claim only, without any claim to ownership of the Duvaliers' assets."

[59.] See also Ord 50, r 1 of the RSC which provides: "When by any contract a *prima facie* case of liability is established, and there is alleged as matter of defence a right to be relived wholly or partially from such liability, the Court may make an order for the preservation or interim custody of the subject-matter of the litigation, or may order that the amount in dispute be brought into court of otherwise secured."

[1.19] An example of a cause of action in which it might be considered necessary to detain, preserve or inspect specific property would be an action in conversion or detinue.[60] Such injunctions are notoriously difficult to obtain and where the plaintiff can be adequately compensated in damages, the courts have been inclined to refuse to grant them.[61] Such was the case in *Magee v Darcy*[62] where the plaintiff applied for an interlocutory order to restrain the defendants from selling or removing ten Connemara ponies pending the trial of the cause. It was alleged by the plaintiff that the horses had been purchased by one of the defendants "under colour of an invalid sale in execution of a civil bill decree against the plaintiff", the amount of which decree the plaintiff contended had been satisfied by him. In that case Dowse B held that there was jurisdiction to make such an order pursuant to s 28 of the Supreme Court of Judicature (Ireland) Act 1877[63] and also under General Order 51, r 3, which was in all material respects identical to the present Ord 50, r 4. He declined, however, to exercise the jurisdiction in that case. He said:

> "I am inclined to think that the subject matter of this action is within the section, and that it is within the General Order ... at all events that is the assumption upon which I shall deal with this case. But though I hold this opinion, I do not consider this is a proper case in which to exercise the powers conferred upon me either by the stature or by the Rules ... In this writ there is a claim founded in detinue as well as a claim in trover, and consequently a return of the chattels is sought. The chattels are ten Connemara ponies; and having carefully listened to the affidavits, I fail to see, notwithstanding the claim for detinue, that the plaintiff cannot be adequately compensated in damages for any wrong done him, and I am convinced any other ponies, or a sum representing their value, would do him just as well as the interesting group of animals on whose wrongs [the plaintiff's counsel] was so eloquent. No irreparable injury will be done to anybody if these ponies are sold, and if their price is forthcoming. There is no allegation in any of the affidavits that the

---

60. On conversion and detinue, see McMahon & Binchy, *Irish Law of Torts*, (2nd ed, 1990) Butterworths at pp 528 *et seq*.
61. Orders for simple "inspection" under Ord 50, r 4 are more easily granted: see *Morris v Howell* (1888) LR (Ir) 77 where an order was made permitting the plaintiff and his foreman to enter a ship for the purpose of inspecting the timber with which it was being filled. In *Wymes v Crowley* High Court, unrep, 27 February 1987, (Irish Company Law Reports (1963-1993) 610) Murphy J made the order for inspection sought by the plaintiffs, quoting with approval the following passage in *Bennitt v Whitehouse* (1860) 28 Beav 119: "Wherever it appears that a person has power to make use of his land to the injury of another, and there is *prima facie* evidence of his doing so, though it is contradicted, still, as the only way of ascertaining the fact is by an inspection, the court will always allow it, if it can be done without injury to the defendant".
62. (1879) LR (Ir) 312.
63. See Ch 2, *The Jurisdiction to Grant Mareva Relief*, para **[2.02]** where the text of s 28 is set out.

defendants are not substantial men, and that they will not be able to pay any damages that may be recoverable against them, and the costs of the action."[64]

The observation that there was nothing to suggest that the defendants were not "substantial men" and that there was no allegation that they would not be able to pay any damages are interesting from the point of view of the Mareva jurisdiction since both matters will often be relevant factors in deciding whether to grant or refuse relief.[65] Irrespective of this, it is important to note that the sole justification for making an asset preservation order in cases of this kind is because the assets themselves form the subject matter of the plaintiff's substantive cause of action against the defendant.[66]

[1.20] Where a plaintiff claims a proprietary right to, or interest in, property which is the subject matter of the application for an injunction, the basis of such a claim will often be grounded on a trust - express, implied, resulting or constructive. Some examples of the types of action which may give rise to such an application for an injunction would be tracing claims,[67] a claim by a receiver in respect of a company's assets,[68] and a claim by a trustee to protect the assets of an estate.[69]

Tracing Claims

[1.21] The right of an owner to trace assets, of which he has been wrongfully deprived, into the hands of another is one which exists both at common law and

---

[64.] At 314, 315.

[65.] See Ch 6, *The Risk of Removal or Disposal of Assets*, para **[6.35]** *et seq.*

[66.] For a recent application, which would seem to have been brought under Ord 50, r 4, see *F v G, The Irish Times*, 23 October 1997 (Costello P). There it was reported that the plaintiff obtained an interim injunction restraining the defendant from "parting with a greyhound whose prodigy, "Tom's the Best", recently won the Irish Derby at Shelbourne Park, Dublin". The plaintiff's claim was in the nature of a proprietary claim in which he claimed ownership of a bitch called Lady's Guest.

[67.] *Polly Peck International plc v Nadir (No 2)* [1992] 4 All ER 769.

[68.] *Rex Pet Foods Ltd v Lamb Brothers (Dublin) Ltd* High Court, unrep, 26 August 1982.

[69.] *Re the Estate of Maurice Hickey, decd; Provincial Bank of Ireland v Hickey* (1891) LR (Ir) 65. The converse situation - where someone claims that particular assets are not part of a deceased's estate - may also ground such an injunction. So, in *O'Brien v O'Brien* noted at [1983] ILRM 600, the plaintiff widow of the 17th Baron of Inchiquin sought an injunction to restrain the defendant, who was the Baron's nephew, from disposing of a valuable herd of cattle and sheep and a quantity of valuable farm implements and equipment. The plaintiff's claim was based upon a partnership agreement between her and her husband under which it was provided that upon the death of either the assets of the partnership would accrue to the surviving partner. The defendant claimed ownership of the chattels by virtue of the deceased's will and or a family settlement dating back to the 1940s. It was reported that Costello J granted the plaintiff an interlocutory injunction which restrained the defendant from disposing of the stock or implements and permitting the plaintiff to do so and that he held that the plaintiff had established that the stock and equipment were part of the partnership assets and did not pass under the deceased's will or under the family settlement.

in equity.[70] Whilst it is clearly beyond the scope and purpose of this work to consider the remedy of tracing, it may be noted that the right to trace at common law is only available where the property, of which a plaintiff has been wrongfully deprived, can still be identified and has not been mixed-up with a defendant's own property. Tracing in equity is, however, available where a plaintiff's property has been converted into moneys and inter-mingled with a defendant's own property, provided that the property is in the hands of a person who is in a fiduciary relationship with the plaintiff.[71] In such cases, a plaintiff will seek to establish a proprietary right to the property in question often by seeking a declaration; the tracing remedy is only available to a person who has proprietary rights, ie rights *in rem*, to specific property. Where a plaintiff has, or is asserting, a proprietary right to property in a defendant's hands he can apply for an ordinary interlocutory injunction, as opposed to a Mareva injunction, to restrain the person who has control over the property in question.

[1.22] In *Polly Peck International plc v Nadir (No 2)*[72] the Court of Appeal made it clear that an injunction to preserve funds, to which the plaintiff made a proprietary claim, should be brought on the basis of Ord 29, r 2 of the English Rules of the Supreme Court, 1965; Ord 29, r 2 is similar, in all material respects, to the Irish Ord 50, r 4.[73] In that case the administrators of the insolvent plaintiff company alleged that the first defendant, Mr Nadir, was responsible for the misapplication of £371m of the plaintiff's funds and that another defendant, a Northern Cyprus bank (NC) controlled by Mr Nadir, was responsible for the misapplication of £142m of the plaintiff's funds. The plaintiff claimed that the £142m was transferred to an account in a London bank in the name of NC; and

---

70. See generally, Keane, *Equity and the Law of Trusts in the Republic of Ireland*, (1988) Butterworths at Ch 20; Bell, *Modern Law of Personal Property in England and Ireland*, (1989) Butterworths at Ch 20; Collins, 'Tracing Into A Vanishing Asset: High Expectations and Equitable Remedies', (1994) CLP 211 and Ashe & Reid, 'Equity and the Pursuit of Hot Money - Warning to Banks', (1997) CLP 188.

71. *Sinclair v Brougham* [1914] AC 398; *Re Hallett's Case* (1880) 13 Ch D 696; *Re Diplock* [1948] Ch 465; *Shanahan's Stamp Auctions Ltd v Farrelly* [1962] IR 386.

72. [1992] 4 All ER 769.

73. For the wording of Ord 50, r 4, see para **[1.18]** *supra*. Ord 29, r 2 of the English Rules of the Supreme Court, 1965 provides: "(1) On the application of any party to a cause or matter the Court may make an order for the detention, custody or preservation of any property which is the subject-matter of the cause or matter, or as to which any question may arise therein, or for the inspection of any such property in the possession of a party to the cause or matter. (2) For the purpose of enabling any order under paragraph (1) to be carried out the Court may by the order authorise any person to enter upon any land or building in the possession of any party to the cause or matter. (3) Where the right of any party to a specific fund is in dispute in a cause or matter, the Court may, on the application of a party to the cause or matter, order the fund to be paid into Court or otherwise secured. (4) An order under this rule may be made on such terms, if any, as the Court thinks fit...".

that *circa* £44m of this had been transferred to the account of another defendant, the Central Bank of Northern Cyprus (the Central Bank) in return for Turkish lira, and in some cases, sterling had been credited to NC's account with the Central Bank. The administrators claimed that the transfer of the plaintiff's funds was either in breach of Mr Nadir's fiduciary duties to the plaintiff company, of which he was a director, or a dishonest means of diverting the plaintiff's funds in circumstances that put the Central Bank on inquiry and thereby gave rise to a constructive trust. In addition to seeking Mareva relief[74] ancillary to their *in personam* claim, the administrators also sought an interlocutory injunction restraining the disposal of £8.9m, ancillary to their tracing and constructive trust claim.

[1.23] In the Court of Appeal Lord Donaldson MR said of the application for an injunction ancillary to the tracing claim:

> "This is a wholly different basis for an injunction, namely an application under RSC Ord 29, r 2 for an order for the interim preservation of property which is the subject matter of the cause or matter. If at the trial the plaintiffs can make good their tracing claim, they will be in the position of secured creditors to the extent, but very probably *only* to the extent, that the £8.9m has not meanwhile been removed from the jurisdiction. In this context, unlike those of a Mareva injunction, *American Cyanamid* principles do apply."[75]

Applying the *American Cyanamid* test to the plaintiff's application for a proprietary injunction, Scott LJ said:

> "First, PPI must show an arguable case. If an arguable case is shown then the balance of convenience should be applied. If the scale appears very evenly balanced it is then legitimate to take into account the strength or weakness of PPI's case."[76]

Scott LJ refused to grant the injunction on foot of the tracing claim. He found the balance of convenience to be very evenly balanced: on the one hand freezing £8.9m was likely to be damaging to the Central Bank's credibility and would put it in difficulties if a run were to develop; on the other hand if the injunction was not granted "the £8.9m may disappear as a traceable fund, leaving PPI merely with its claim for monetary compensation".[77] Moreover, Scott LJ was clearly influenced by the weakness of the plaintiff's tracing claim: the statement of claim did not plead facts from which a tracing claim could be recognised and the

---

[74]. As to which see Ch 5, *A Good Arguable Case*, para **[5.11]**.
[75]. [1992] 4 All ER 769 at 787a-b.
[76]. At 784g.
[77]. At 784j.

claim itself only emerged in a recognisable form at a late stage in the proceedings.

[1.24] Where a plaintiff obtains interlocutory relief in defence of a proprietary claim, the question arises as to whether a defendant should be permitted to expend what might be shown to be a "trust fund" in discharge of his living, legal and business expenses. As one judge has said, in the context of legal expenses: "The litigant is entitled to be heard and have his day in court. The question for me is at whose expense should he have that day?".[78] The potential injustice to a plaintiff was expressed thus by Michael Burton QC in *United Mizrahi Bank Ltd v Doherty*:[79]

> "there might be a distinction between cases where there was an injunction based on a remedy in damages and cases where the injunction was based in whole or in part on some proprietary claim. In the latter case not only could it be said that the expenditure, pending trial, on living expenses and legal costs might deplete the only available pot for execution by the plaintiff (the purpose of the Mareva being to preserve so much as possible pending trial), but, further, if the plaintiff succeeded in establishing in whole or in part a proprietary remedy at trial not only might there be noting left, but the money that would have been expended in the meanwhile would have been the plaintiff's own money; thus to add insult to injury, if the defendant on that basis were unsuccessful, he would not only have committed originally some conversion or breach of trust against the plaintiff, but then even that part of the plaintiff's property which was still left at the outset of proceedings would have been dissipated by the time it came to the trial; and the legal costs expended by the defendant in making it more difficult for the plaintiff to obtain his eventual successful judgment would have been paid for by the plaintiff, out of the plaintiff's own money."[80]

The attitude of the English courts to this question has been mixed. On the one hand is the following observation of Scott LJ in *Polly Peck International plc v Nadir (No 2)*[81] on the nature of an injunction ancillary to a tracing claim:

> "This would not be a Mareva injunction. It would not be subject to provisos enabling the use of the money for normal business purposes, or for the payment of legal fees, or the like. There is, in general, no reason why a defendant should be permitted to use money belonging to another in order to pay his legal costs or other expenses".[82]

---

78. *Chandles v Church*, English High Court, unrep, 21 December 1987 (Harman J).
79. [1998] 2 All ER 230.
80. At 233e-h.
81. [1992] 4 All ER 769.
82. At 784f.

He also said that one of the objections he had to granting a Mareva injunction in respect of the *in personam* claim - that it was wrong in principle to grant a Mareva injunction which interferes with the normal course of the defendant's business - "does not apply to an injunction to preserve a fund that, in the contention of PPI, belongs to PPI".[83] In subsequent decisions the English Court of Appeal has not set its face so firmly against the insertion of such provisos into injunctions in defence of proprietary claims. In *Sundt Wrigley & Co Ltd v Wrigley*[84] Bingham MR held that it was only in an exceptional case, where the Court was satisfied that the proprietary claim was so strong as to be demonstrated to be well founded at an interlocutory stage, that a defendant should not be free to draw enjoined funds to finance his legal expenses. He said:

> "A careful and anxious judgment has to be made in a case where a proprietary claim is advanced by the plaintiff as to whether the injustice of permitting the use of the funds by the defendant is outweighed by the possible injustice to the defendant if his is denied the opportunity of advancing what may turn out to be a successful defence."

A very pragmatic approach was taken by Ferris J in *Cala Cristal SA v Emran Al-Borno (Mubarak Abdulaziz al Hassawi, third party)*.[85] Although he permitted the defendant to draw funds from what appeared to be a frozen "trust fund" in order to discharge his legal expenses, he did so subject to three safeguards: first, the defendant was required to undertake to make good, out of funds in which the plaintiff had no proprietary claim, sums spent on costs which were ultimately found to be the proceeds of property in which the plaintiff had a proprietary interest; secondly, the defendant was required to give security to the plaintiff over a property in which it seemed that the plaintiff had no proprietary interest; and thirdly, the plaintiff was given leave to attend the taxation of the defendant's solicitor's costs. However, even where a legal expenses proviso is inserted into an injunction in aid of a proprietary claim, this will be no guarantee that the defendant's solicitor who is paid these moneys will be able to avoid a claim of constructive trust where the plaintiff subsequently establishes a proprietary claim against the defendant.[86] Where a plaintiff can assert a claim *in rem* he might be well advised to give due consideration to applying for an "ordinary" interlocutory injunction as opposed to a Mareva injunction.

[83.] At 784f-g.

[84.] (1993) CA Transcript 685.

[85.] (1994) *The Times* 6 May 1994.

[86.] This was the decision in *United Mizrahi Bank Ltd v Doherty* [1998] 2 All ER 230. In view of the fact that the plaintiff in that case was asserting a proprietary claim to the defendant's assets it is, questioned by this writer whether it was accurate to describe the injunction granted as a Mareva injunction and, more importantly, whether such a proviso ought to have been inserted into the order.

Claims by Receivers

[1.25] Where a receiver is appointed, by a debentureholder, over the property of a company, he will usually have sufficient standing to apply for an ordinary injunction to prevent the disposal of company property which is in the hands of unauthorised others. This is because a common form debenture will, almost invariably, deem the receiver to be the company's agent. A receiver was granted such an injunction in *Rex Pet Foods Ltd and Murphy v Lamb Brothers (Dublin) Ltd and another.*[87] In that case the plaintiff company and the receiver who had been appointed to the company sought an injunction restraining the defendants from disposing of certain goods which had been produced by the plaintiff and were then in the possession of one or other of the defendants or, in the alternative, an injunction preventing such goods from being disposed of until trial otherwise on terms that the proceeds of sale of the goods should be held in a suspense or trustee account pending the outcome of the trial of the substantive issues. The plaintiffs' substantive cause of action was a declaration that the defendant companies' assets were the first plaintiff's assets and a declaration that the defendant companies were trading as a single entity.

[1.26] It was held by Finlay P that the principles upon which he had to decide the interlocutory application were clear, well settled and to be found in the decision of the Supreme Court in *Education Company of Ireland v Fitzpatrick*[88] and the House of Lords in *American Cyanamid Co v Ethicon Ltd.*[89] In respect of the plaintiffs' cause of action, Finlay P noted the plaintiffs' claim that if they were given the two declarations sought, the products in the defendants' possession would be part of the assets which the receiver was entitled to have access to for the purpose of the receivership *ie* that a proprietary interest would exist. Finlay P found on the facts that there was a "serious question to be tried"[90] and furthermore held that the "balance of convenience" favoured the granting of the injunction. The making of the injunction was predicated on the basis that the first plaintiff company claimed a proprietary interest in the goods which the defendants were restrained from selling, otherwise than by lodging the proceeds thereof to a trust or suspense account.[91]

---

[87] High Court, unrep, 26 August 1982 (Finlay P); Irish Company Law Reports (1963-1993) 549.
[88] [1961] IR 323.
[89] [1975] AC 396.
[90] See Ch 5, *A Good Arguable Case*, para **[5.08]** *et seq.*
[91] At the trial of the substantive issues in *Rex Pet Foods Ltd and Murphy v Lamb Brothers (Dublin) Ltd (No 2)* High Court, unrep, 5 December 1985 (Costello J); Irish Company Law Reports (1963-1993) 585, the plaintiffs were refused the declarations sought and it was held, *inter alia*, that the first plaintiff had no title in the property which was the subject matter of the earlier injunction. Liberty was given to the defendants to apply in respect of the plaintiffs' undertaking as to damages.

Disclosure Orders in Proprietary Claims

[1.27] The courts are more inclined to make an order for disclosure of assets in a proprietary claim than in a personal, or purely monetary, claim. In appropriate cases third-party disclosure has been permitted even in the absence of a procedure in the Rules of the Superior Courts.[92] For example in *Bankers Trust Co v Shapira*[93] the Court of Appeal held that a Court was entitled to order a bank to disclose the state of, and documents and correspondence relating to, the account of a customer who was *prima facie* guilty of fraud, for the purpose of giving effect to a defrauded plaintiff's equitable right to trace his money.

[1.28] In *A v C*[94] Robert Goff J was asked to make an order which required the disclosure of assets in aid of (a) Mareva injunctions, obtained on foot of a monetary claim for damages, and (b) an ordinary interlocutory injunction, obtained on foot of a proprietary claim in the nature of a tracing order. In relation to the proprietary claim, Robert Goff J said, after citing several authorities:[95]

> "Now these cases provide ample authority that, in an action in which the plaintiff seeks to trace property which in equity belongs to him, the court not only has jurisdiction to grant an injunction restraining the disposal of that property; it may in addition, at the interlocutory stages of the action, make orders designed to ascertain the whereabouts of that property. In particular, it may order a bank (whether or not party to the proceedings) to give discovery of documents in relation to the bank account of a defendant who is alleged to have defrauded the plaintiff of his assets; and it may make orders for interrogatories to be answered by the defendants of their employees or directors."[96]

Disclosure orders against defendants and third parties in the context of Mareva injunctions are considered in Chapter 10, *Ancillary Orders*.[97]

Summary of the Conditions for a "Proprietary" Injunction to Freeze Assets

[1.29] In order to obtain an interlocutory injunction to restrain a defendant from dealing with assets to which a plaintiff asserts a proprietary claim, it is necessary for a plaintiff to show that:

[92.] However, see Ord 31, r 29 of the RSC which now allows third-party disclosure. See Ch 10, *Ancillary Orders*, para **[10.13]**.

[93.] [1980] 3 All ER 353. See Ch 10, *Ancillary Orders*, para **[10.16]**.

[94.] [1980] 2 All ER 347.

[95.] *London and County Securities Ltd v Caplan* 26 May 1978 (Templeman J) and *Mediterranea Reffineria Siciliana Petroli SpA v Mabanaft GmbH* [1978] Court of Appeal Transcript 816.

[96.] [1980] 2 All ER 347 at 351.

[97.] See Ch 10, *Ancillary Orders*, para **[10.03]** *et seq.*

1. He has, or has reasonable grounds for claiming, a proprietary interest in the property which is in the defendant's possession, ie that the property forms the subject matter of the proceedings;

2. There is a "fair" or "serious question to be tried";[98]

3. The "balance of convenience" favours the making of the injunction, which test will involve a consideration of whether the property is likely to be disposed of by the defendant, and whether the property is either unique and irreplaceable or the defendant is likely to be unable to make good the monetary value of the property.

It can immediately be seen that the proofs for such an injunction are not nearly as onerous as those applicable in an application for a Mareva injunction. For this reason, and those given above,[99] where a plaintiff can reasonably assert a claim to a proprietary interest in the assets in the defendant's possession, close consideration should be given to applying for an ordinary interlocutory injunction.

[C] ARREST OF SHIPS IN ADMIRALTY LAW

[1.30] The treatment of the arrest of ships in admiralty law which follows is by no means exhaustive. The purpose of this section is to distinguish the *in personam* Mareva injunction from the *in rem* arrest of ships by examining the jurisdiction to arrest ships in admiralty jurisdiction. The issues considered here are:

1. Arrest of Ships: An *In Rem* Jurisdiction;
2. The Circumstances When Ship Arrest is Possible;
3. An Overview of the Practice and Procedure in Arresting a Ship.
4. Mareva Relief Ancillary to the Arrest of a Ship.

Arrest of Ships: An *In Rem* Jurisdiction

[1.31] A Mareva injunction operates *in personam*: it is the defendant who is directly affected by the injunction, and not his assets. The arrest of a ship is an action *in rem*; it is the ship which is *directly* affected by the court order, and not its owners. Kelly J writing before his appointment to the bench made the following observations on the arrest of ships:

"To understand the form of arrest which is available in an Admiralty action it should be realised that in the ordinary way claims in court are claims which are made *in personam*. That is to say they are purely personal claims which must

---

98. See Ch 5, *A Good Arguable Case*, para **[5.03]** *et seq.*
99. See, for example, para **[1.24]** *supra.*

first be established before the court and only after judgment can the successful plaintiff, the judgment creditor as he is called, seize so much of the defendant's property as is necessary to satisfy his debt. In the old Court of Admiralty this procedure was found to be unsatisfactory for a variety of reasons. The owner of a vessel against whom a claim was being brought might be out of the jurisdiction; his financial standing might be unknown; the courts of the country of registry might be inefficient or expensive to approach. Accordingly, the idea of the action *in rem*, that is to say a right of action against the ship itself, was conceived which now forms part of the law of this country. The purpose of an arrest of a vessel is to secure its continued presence and to prevent her from slipping away so as to ensure that at the end of the day when the plaintiff has pursued his action to judgment an asset will be available against which that judgment can be enforced."[100]

The jurisdiction of the Court of Admiralty was previously exercised both by proceedings *in rem* and *in personam*. As Henchy J said, in his dissenting judgment, in *RD Cox Ltd v The Owners of MV "Fritz Raabe"*:[101]

"The action *in rem* in the High Court of Admiralty was developed for the purpose of establishing that Court's right to arrest a ship or other *res* (such as cargo or freight) connected with a ship, and thereby to enforce its judgment against the *res*. This was done on the theory that a pre-existing maritime lien attached to the *res* from the time the claim arose, a maritime lien being a privileged claim on the *res* for service done to it or injury caused by it. The distinctiveness, and importance, of an admiralty action *in rem*, as compared with an action *in personam*, is that the Court's order operated directly against the *res*, so that by process served on the *res* it could be detained, by arrest, within the Court's jurisdiction and, if necessary, sold to satisfy the claim; and the Court's disposition of the matter was then binding against anyone in any part of the world: see *Castrique v Imrie* (1870) LR 4 HL 414."[102]

Certain maritime claims, however, such as claims for personal injury[103] or assault and battery "on the high seas" could be brought in the Court of Admiralty but could only be pursued by proceedings *in personam*.

---

[100] Kelly, 'How Can One Arrest A Ship', paper delivered to the Irish Maritime Law Association, October 1983.

[101] Supreme Court, unrep, 1 August 1974 (Walsh J; Griffin J concurring; Henchy J dissenting).

[102] At p 4 of the transcript. In his, majority judgment, (at pp 7, 8 of the transcript) Walsh J said: "The mode of adopting proceedings *in personam* was one where it was desired to enforce a personal contract or to obtain redress for a wrong when there was no question of a lien upon a piece of property. For obvious reasons, the jurisdiction *in personam* was not frequently invoked as in the case of ships proceedings *in rem* offered a far more satisfactory remedy as most cases in admiralty involved situations which created a lien upon a ship such as claims arising in respect of derelicts, piracy, salvage, pilotage, bottomry, repairing damage to a ship, towage."

[103] Note, however, that ship arrest for personal injuries claims was permitted by the Ship Owners' Negligence (Remedies) Act 1905.

The Circumstances When Ship Arrest is Possible

[1.32] For several hundred years the law has recognised the general right to apply to court for an order to have a ship arrested in admiralty jurisdiction.[104] As Walsh J said in *RD Cox Ltd v The Owners of MV "Fritz Raabe"*:[105]

> "Prior to the Judicature Act there was a Court of Admiralty in Ireland whose existence goes back to about the 14th Century. The Court appears to have originated independently of statute and was distinguished from the Court of Admiralty in England.
>
> ... The Admiralty Court (Ireland) Act 1867, did not set up the High Court of Admiralty in Ireland but purported to extend the jurisdiction and alter and amend the procedure and practice of the High Court of Admiralty in Ireland already established and to make certain other changes."[106]

Notwithstanding the Admiralty Court (Ireland) Act 1867, the jurisdiction of the High Court in admiralty matters also derives from the law and practice of centuries of application and indeed the inherent jurisdiction of the Court, as suggested by Walsh J in *The Fritz Raabe*.[107] The practice and procedure relating to admiralty is contained in Ord 64 of The Rules of the Superior Courts 1986 ("the RSC"). In addition, the Jurisdiction of Courts (Maritime Conventions) Act 1989 has extended the jurisdiction to arrest ships by providing that the Irish courts shall give effect to the application of the International Convention Relating to the Arrest of Seagoing Ships (1952), signed at Brussels. Here, the following structure is adopted in this overview of the law of admiralty in Ireland:

(a) The inherent jurisdiction to arrest ships;

(b) The Admiralty Court (Ireland) Act 1867 and other statutes;

(c) The Jurisdiction of Courts (Maritime Conventions) Act 1989.

[1.33] Order 64, r 1 of the RSC provides that the expression "admiralty action" means any proceedings for the determination of any of the following claims or questions:

(a) a claim or question in respect of which the High Court of Admiralty in Ireland formerly had jurisdiction;

(b) a claim for the sale of a ship or any share therein;

[104.] See Yale, 'A Historical Note on the Jurisdiction of the Admiralty in Ireland', (1968) Ir Jur 146.

[105.] Supreme Court, unrep, 1 August 1974 (Griffin J concurring; Henchy J dissenting).

[106.] At pp 8-9 of the transcript.

[107.] At p 12 of the transcript. See generally, Moloney, 'When Can One Arrest A Ship', (1983) paper delivered to the Irish Maritime Law Association, October 1983. See also Doherty, 'Ship Arrest in Ireland', (1996) CLP 232.

(c) a claim to prohibit any dealing with a ship or any share therein;

(d) a claim in respect of a mortgage of, or charge on, a ship or any share therein;

(e) a claim arising out of bottomry;

(f) a claim for the forfeiture of any ship or her tackle, apparel or furniture, or the restoration thereof after seizure, or for costs or damages in respect of the seizure or detention thereof;

(g) a claim in the nature, or arising out, of pilotage;

(h) a claim arising out of a general average act;[108]

(i) a claim arising out of Article 1(1) of the First Schedule to the Jurisdiction of Courts (Maritime Conventions) Act 1989;

(j) a claim arising out of Article 1(1) of the Second Schedule to the Jurisdiction of Courts (Maritime Conventions) Act 1989;

(a) The inherent jurisdiction to arrest ships

[1.34] In Ireland, historically, only certain maritime claims, which gave rise to maritime liens, could ground proceedings *in rem*. These included:[109]

(a) derelicts;

(b) piracy;

(c) salvage on the high seas;

(d) pilotage;

(e) bottomry;

(f) repairing damage to a ship;

(g) towage;

(h) by a ship or cargo owner for collision damage.

Referring to (a) to (g) of the foregoing types of claims, Walsh J said in *The Fritz Raabe*:

> "The maritime lien which existed in respect of the types of proceedings I have already listed did not require possession of the ship but rested on the basis that the lien travelled with the ship into whoever's possession it came and could be

---

[108.] Defined by s 66(2) of the Marine Insurance Act 1906 as "any extraordinary sacrifice or expenditure ... voluntarily and reasonably made or incurred in time of peril for the purpose of preserving the property imperilled in the common adventure".

[109.] See judgment of Walsh J (at p 8 of the transcript) in *RD Cox Ltd v The Owners of MV "Fritz Raabe"* Supreme Court, unrep, 1 August 1974 (Griffin J concurring; Henchy J dissenting). Walsh J noted (at p 8 of the transcript) that "prize money or prize commissions never arose in the Irish Admiralty Court for the simple reason that Ireland never had a navy distinct from that of Great Britain."

realised by proceeding *in rem*. The lien related back to the period when it first attached.".[110]

Maritime liens are different to other liens in that they are not based on possession of the thing to which the lien attaches.[111]

[1.35] The High Court is the sole court of first instance in Ireland with jurisdiction to hear and determine admiralty actions. Formerly, there was one local Admiralty Court in Ireland, ie the Cork Local Admiralty Court which had jurisdiction over the County of Cork and adjoining waters. The admiralty jurisdiction of the Cork Local Admiralty Court (under s 23 of the Courts (Supplemental Provisions) Act 1961) was, however, repealed by s 14 of the Jurisdiction of Courts (Maritime Conventions) Act 1989.

[1.36] It may be noted that, as a general rule, ships which are in the ownership of a foreign sovereign state are immune from arrest except where they are engaged in non-sovereign, (eg commercial) activity. In *Zarine v The Owners of the SS "Otto"*[112] Hanna J held that the immunity for state ships under public international law does not apply to those vessels which are used for private trading purposes and that immunity from arrest for state ships other than those *publicis usibus destinata* is only granted where the ships are either owned or in the physical possession of the sovereign state claiming the immunity. On appeal to the Supreme Court a further point was raised, namely, that intrinsic to a successful claim of sovereign immunity was that the sovereign state claiming such immunity was recognised by the Irish government. In that case it was held that since Ireland did not then recognise the USSR as a sovereign independent state, whether *de jure* or *de facto*, state immunity could not be claimed.[113]

(b) The Admiralty Court (Ireland) Act 1867 and other statutes

[1.37] The Admiralty Court (Ireland) Act 1867 ("the 1867 Act") was passed with the express purpose of extending "the jurisdiction, [to] alter and amend the procedure and practice, and to regulate the establishment of the Court of Admiralty in Ireland". Although admiralty jurisdiction does not have its origins in the 1867 Act, the Act is significant because it extended the jurisdiction to proceed *in rem* against ships in respect of all of the maritime claims referred to therein. It is important to note that although there were many diverse types of

---

[110.] At p 8 of the transcript.

[111.] See Moloney, 'When Can One Arrest A Ship', (1983) paper delivered to the Irish Maritime Law Association, October 1983.

[112.] [1942] IR 148.

[113.] See also, *The "Eolo"* [1918] 2 IR 78 where it was held that when a private vessel is employed under the orders of a sovereign state for its service, that vessel will be a requisitioned ship and will not be liable to arrest.

admiralty action, as noted above,[114] not all were considered to be claims *in rem*, and many were only capable of being pursued *in personam*; such claims could not ground the arrest of a ship. Section 38 of the 1867 Act provides, however, that:

> The jurisdiction conferred by this Act may be exercised either by proceedings *in rem* or by proceedings *in personam*.

The effect of s 38 of the 1867 Act was to give the Court of Admiralty the power to arrest a ship in circumstances other than where a purely *maritime lien* arose. As a result, the following additional claims became capable of grounding an action for the arrest of a ship:

(a) claims for salvage: performed on the high seas or within the body of any county or partly in the one place and partly in the other and whether the wreck is found at sea or cast upon the land or partly on land and in sea;[115]

(b) claims for towage: whether on the high seas or within the body of a county;[116]

(c) claims for damage done by a ship whether within the body of a county or not;[117]

(d) claims for the building, equipping or repairing of a ship;[118]

(e) claims for necessaries supplied to any ship elsewhere than in the port to which the ship belongs;[119]

(f) questions arising between co-owners which touch upon the title or ownership, possession, employment and earnings of a ship registered in any port in Ireland or any share thereof;[120]

(g) claims by seamen for wages earned on board any ship and claims by ships' masters for wages earned and disbursements made;[121]

(h) claims in respect of any mortgage duly registered under the Merchant Shipping Act 1854;[122]

(i) claims by the owner or consignee or assignee of any bill of lading of any goods carried into port in Ireland in any ship for damage done to

---

[114] See para **[1.31]** *supra*.
[115] Section 27 of the Admiralty Court (Ireland) Act 1867.
[116] *Ibid*, s 28.
[117] *Ibid*, s 29.
[118] *Ibid*, s 30.
[119] *Ibid*, s 31.
[120] *Ibid*, s 32.
[121] *Ibid*, s 33.
[122] *Ibid*, s 34.

the goods by the negligence, misconduct or breach of duty or contract of the owner, master or crew of a ship;[123]

Those claims which may now ground an admiralty action are not maritime liens.[124] Other statutes too have extended the jurisdiction to arrest a ship on foot of other claims.[125] For example, claims in connection with the storing or discharging of cargo or the trimmings of coal, under the Merchant Shipping (Stevedores and Trimmers) Act 1911 and claims for personal and fatal injuries by a wrongful act, neglect or default of owners, charterers or the master, officers or crew or person employed by the owner of a ship under the Ship Owners' Negligence (Remedies) Act 1905.

[1.38] Section 34 of the 1867 Act created a new right to arrest a ship in favour of the holder of a registered mortgage. This would lead one to believe that the holder of an unregistered mortgage would not have sufficient standing to ground an admiralty action or to seek the arrest of a ship.[126] The converse was, however, held to be the case by a majority of the Supreme Court in *RD Cox Ltd v The Owners of MV "Fritz Raabe"*.[127] In that case the question which fell to be determined was whether the German holders of an unregistered mortgage over a ship could bring proceedings *in rem* in the High Court. The facts were that the plaintiff, RD Cox Ltd, carried out repairs to *The Fritz Raabe* and supplied materials necessary to make her capable of putting to sea. When it was not paid the plaintiff issued proceedings *in rem* (the repairs constituted the supply of "necessaries") and obtained judgment which condemned the ship in the amount of the judgment without prejudice to other claims and reserving all questions as to priority. The plaintiff successfully sought an order for the sale of the ship and, ultimately, the proceeds of sale were lodged in court. The German banks who held the two unregistered mortgages issued admiralty proceedings *in rem* in the High Court and claimed against the proceeds of the ships. The other claimants argued that the High Court had no jurisdiction to entertain the German banks' claims, contending that unregistered mortgages could not ground an admiralty

---

123. *Ibid*, s 37.

124. See *The Indian Endurance (No 2); Republic of India v India Steamship Co Ltd* [1997] 4 All ER 380 at 385 where Lord Steyn said in the House of Lords: "In the nineteenth century it was believed that an admiralty action could only be brought in respect of a maritime lien (*Harmer v Bell, The Bold Buccleugh* (1850) 7 MooPCC 267, 13 ER 884). By statute, actions *in rem* were subsequently permitted in new categories. But only after the Judicature Acts was it established that the new categories did not involve maritime liens (*Northcote v Henrich Bjorn (owners), The Henrich Bjorn* (1886) 11 App Cas 270)".

125. See Moloney, 'When Can One Arrest A Ship', (1983) paper delivered to the Irish Maritime Law Association, October 1983.

126. As to ship mortgages, see generally, Holohan, 'The Ranking of the Mortgagee of an Arrested Ship in Ireland', paper delivered to the Irish Maritime Law Association.

127. Supreme Court, unrep, 1 August 1974 (Griffin J concurring; Henchy J dissenting).

action *in rem*. The High Court held that the German banks were entitled to maintain a claim on foot of their unregistered mortgages and this was appealed to the Supreme Court. The grounds put forward in support of the appeal were that the High Court in exercising its admiralty jurisdiction could not entertain an action *in rem* in respect of an unregistered mortgage and that if it was to be entertained it should not have priority to the claim for necessaries.

[1.39] In the course of his judgment Walsh J traced the origins and nature of the jurisdiction in admiralty claims *in rem* and concluded, *inter alia*, that until the passing of the Admiralty Court (Ireland) Act 1867, the High Court of Admiralty in Ireland had no jurisdiction in mortgage suits and that s 34 of the 1867 Act contained the only jurisdiction which the Court could exercise in relation to mortgage suits and that that jurisdiction was confined to mortgages registered according to the provisions of the Merchant Shipping Act 1854.[128] As to the jurisdiction of the High Court of Admiralty, Walsh J noted that it became vested in the Supreme Court of Judicature in Ireland by virtue of the provisions of the Supreme Court of Judicature (Ireland) Act 1877. In accordance with Article 34 of the Constitution the High Court is vested with a universal original jurisdiction in all matters of fact and of law and Walsh J held that that original jurisdiction embraces all justiciable controversies related to rights connected with ships and shipping. He held, however, that the present High Court is not the old Court of Admiralty "amended, extended or otherwise redressed" when exercising this jurisdiction but a new Court established by the Oireachtas under the authority of the Constitution.[129] On the question of the jurisdiction of the High Court, Walsh J stated:

"Whether the proceedings are proceedings *in rem* or by way of proceedings *in personam* in respect of a particular justiciable controversy is simply a matter of procedure and the procedure itself is not to be confused with the justiciable controversy. The fact that particular procedures were or were not available in courts of limited jurisdiction which formerly existed is beside the point. Equally, the fact that in former times courts of limited jurisdiction, such as the Admiralty Court, had no jurisdiction in certain types of justiciable controversies does not in any way restrict the jurisdiction of the High Court to adjudicate in any justiciable controversy. The Act of 1867 dealt with the practice and procedure as well as the jurisdiction of the Court of Admiralty which was a court of limited jurisdiction. The fact that s 34 of the Act excluded from its jurisdiction claims in respect of mortgages or ships which were not registered under the Merchant Shipping Acts was a limitation as to jurisdiction. It could scarcely be argued that the High Court could not adjudicate in a claim

128. At p 11 of the transcript.
129. Citing *Quinn and White v Stokes and Quirk* [1931] IR 558 and *The People (AG) v Bell* [1969] IR 24.

26

in respect of a mortgage of a ship which was not registered simply because the old Court of Admiralty could not have done so."[130]

Walsh J then observed that s 14(2) of the Courts (Supplemental Provisions) Act 1961 provides that the jurisdiction exercisable by the High Court "shall be exercised so far as regards pleadings, practice and procedure generally, including liability as to costs, in the manner provided by the Rules of Court, and, where no provision is contained in such Rules and so long as there is no Rule with reference thereto, it shall be exercised as near as possible in the same manner as it might have been exercised" by the former High Court of Justice. Walsh J then pointed out that Ord 64, r 1 of the then RSC of 1962[131] defined the expression "admiralty action" to include, *inter alia*, (a) a claim or question in respect of which the High Court of Admiralty in Ireland formerly had jurisdiction *and* (d) a claim in respect of a mortgage of or a charge on a ship or any share therein. From this Walsh J held that (d) made it quite clear that the Rules were setting out procedure in respect of claims over which the High Court of Admiralty in Ireland formerly had no jurisdiction. Having held that the claims by the holder of an unregistered mortgage was an "admiralty action" and that the High Court had jurisdiction to hear same, Walsh J went on to hold that the jurisdiction was exercisable by proceedings *in rem*. Although the point was not addressed in that case it would seem to follow that the holder of an unregistered mortgage on a ship or any share therein has an admiralty action which can support the arrest of the ship which is the subject matter of the claim.

[1.40] It should be noted that the decision of the Supreme Court was by majority and that a dissenting judgment was delivered by Henchy J. He found that an unregistered mortgagee of a ship was not entitled to recover his mortgage debt in an admiralty action *in rem* and, by analogy, did not have the right to seek the arrest of a ship in those circumstances. It is thought that it is improbable that the majority decision of the Supreme Court will not be followed, no matter how compelling the judgment of Henchy J might be.[132]

[130.] At pp 12, 13 of the transcript.

[131.] Order 64, r 1 of the current RSC is identical in this respect.

[132.] Henchy J said: "... an admiralty action *in rem* in respect of the mortgage of a ship, whether in Ireland or England, is a creature of statute, and in this State the statutory provisions confine the action to a mortgage registered under the Mercantile Marine Act 1955. If it is to be extended to other mortgages, the extension must be made by statute. Section 8 of the Courts (Supplemental Provisions) Act 1961, does not affect the position, for it merely vests in the present High Court the jurisdiction that was exercisable by the previous High Court. Neither do the Rules of the Superior Courts effect any change, for even if that had sought to enlarge the admiralty jurisdiction of the High court - which, in my view, they do not purport to do - they would be to that extent *ultra vires*, for their function is confined to regulating matters of "pleading, practice and procedure generally, including liability to costs": s 14(2) of the Courts (Supplemental Provisions) Act 1961".

[1.41] Where a ship is arrested and the ship owner or other person claiming an interest in the ship disputes the validity of the arrest it is open to him to apply for discharge of the arrest warrant under s 47 of the Admiralty Court (Ireland) Act 1867. This section provides:

> The party at whose instance any property is arrested under a warrant of the High Court of Admiralty shall be liable to be condemned in all costs and expenses occasioned thereby, and in damages for the detention of the property, unless he shows to the satisfaction of the Court that he could not, without such arrest, have obtained bail or other security for the sum in which the cause is instituted, or that he had otherwise good and sufficient reason for having caused the issue and execution of the warrant of arrest.

This section was subjected to scrutiny by Barr J in *The MV "Blue Ice"; Agra Trading Ltd v The Owners and All Persons Claiming an Interest in the Vessel, MV "Blue Ice"*.[133] There the claimant had secured the arrest of the MV *Blue Ice* on foot of an alleged breach of a performance guarantee. The defendant contended that there was no contract between the parties and that, accordingly, there was nothing to justify the arrest of the vessel and, that pursuant to s 47 of the 1867 Act, the Court should discharge the warrant of arrest. Barr J said that the point at issue was whether the plaintiff had "established to the reasonable satisfaction of the Court that it had "good and sufficient reason" for applying for and obtaining the arrest warrant".[134] Barr J held that:

> "In assessing the circumstances which gave rise to the arrest of the vessel, it is not the function of the Court to resolve the issue between the parties as to the existence or otherwise of a valid contract of carriage between them. I am satisfied that the Court is required only to decide whether or not the plaintiff has established that it has *a fair statable case in support of its contention* that there was a concluded contract between the parties which has not been honoured by the defendant in consequence of which the plaintiff has suffered loss."[135]

On the facts of this case Barr J held that the plaintiff had discharged its obligation to establish a fair statable case and also that there were sufficient grounds for arrest; Barr J also said, however, that if the defendant successfully contested the action on the grounds that there was no contract between the parties, then the defendant would be entitled to recover for such loss as was sustained by the plaintiff's conduct. The Supreme Court[136] entertained an appeal for clarification and held that if the defendants won the substantive action they

---

[133.] High Court, unrep, 21 March 1997 (Barr J).
[134.] At p 4 of the transcript.
[135.] At p 4 of the transcript. Italics added.
[136.] Supreme Court, unrep, 18 February 1998.

could make a claim for such loss as they may have sustained by reason of the arrest of the ship and that the application of s 47 of the 1867 Act would be a matter for the trial judge.

(c) The Jurisdiction of Courts (Maritime Conventions) Act 1989

[1.42] One of the most significant changes in Irish law relating to the arrest of ships was introduced by the Jurisdiction of Courts (Maritime Conventions) Act 1989 ("the 1989 Act") which gave force of domestic law[137] to two[138] conventions, the most significant one being the International Convention Relating to the Arrest of Seagoing Ships (1952) signed at Brussels ("the Convention"). In *The MT "Marshal Gelovani"; Intergraan BV v The Owners and All Persons Claiming an Interest in the MT "Marshal Gelovani"*[139] Barr J said:

"The Convention is an agreement between the States which have subscribed to it;[140] the purpose of which may be broadly stated to be the codification of maritime law as to the arrest of ships within the jurisdiction of Contracting States."[141]

[1.43] The treatment of the 1989 Act is as follows:

(i)   The jurisdiction of the High Court;

(ii) The definitions of "arrest" and "ship" under the 1989 Act;

(iii) "Maritime claims" which ground arrest;

(iv) The power of arrest - Article 2 of the Convention;

[137.] Section 4(1) of the 1989 Act provides that "subject to the provisions of this Part, the Convention shall have the force of law in the State and judicial notice shall be taken of it".

[138.] The 1989 Act also implemented the International Convention on Certain Rules Concerning Civil Jurisdiction in Matters of Collision (1952).

[139.] High Court, unrep, 2 June 1994 (Barr J).

[140.] As at the end of January 1998, those countries which were "contracting states" to the Convention were: Brazil, France, Spain, Switzerland, Monaco, Nicaragua, Haiti, Costa-Rica, Egypt, Saint-Siege, Republic Khmere, Portugal, France, Benin, Cameroon, Comores Islands, Congo, Ivory Coast, Dijbouti, Gabonese Republic, Republic of Guinea, Burkina Faso, Mauritania, Niger, Central African Republic, Republique Malcache, Senegal, Sudan, Chad, Togo, Great Britain and Northern Ireland, Gibraltar, Hong Kong, British Virgin Islands, Bermuda, Cayman Islands, Montserrat, Anguilla, St Helena, Turks and Caicos Islands, Guernsey, Falkland Islands, Belgium, Sarawak, Borneo Septentrional, Fiji, Guyana, Maurice, Seychelles, Nigeria, Algeria, Antigua & Barbuda, Bahamas, Dominican Republic, Grenada, Nevis, St Lucia, St Vincent & the Grenadines, Belize, Kiribati, Solomon Islands, Tuvalu, Greece, Zaire, Yugoslavia, Paraguay, Syrian Arab Republic, Germany, Pologne, Tonga, Italy, Netherlands, Cuba, Denmark, Ireland, Maroc, Luxembourg, Croatia, Sweden, Estonia, Slovenia, Norway, Romania, Finland. The writer acknowledges the assistance of the Legal Division, Department of Foreign Affairs in providing the foregoing information.

[141.] At p 4 of the transcript.

> (v)   The arrest of "sister ships" - Article 3 of the Convention;
>
> (vi)   Miscellaneous provisions of the Convention.

(i) The jurisdiction of the High Court

[1.44] A ship may only be arrested under the Convention by the authority of a Court or of the appropriate judicial authority of the Contracting State in which the arrest is made.[142] Section 5(1) of the 1989 Act gives jurisdiction to the High Court to hear and determine in admiralty proceedings *in rem* any of the claims mentioned in Article 1(1) of the Convention for the purposes of the 1989 Act *and the Convention.* Accordingly, while the 1989 Act extends the jurisdiction of the High Court it does so for the express purpose of giving effect to the provisions of the 1989 Act and the Convention. The fact that s 5(1) does not extend the High Court's jurisdiction generally is borne out by Article 8(4) of the Convention which provides:

> Nothing in this Convention shall modify or affect the rules of law in force in the respective Contracting States relating to the arrest of any ship within the jurisdiction of the State of her flag by a person who has his habitual residence or principal place of business in that State.

To the extent that the 1989 Act enlarges the jurisdiction of the High Court in admiralty proceedings *in rem*, such enlargement has no application to ships flying the Irish flag in respect of claims brought by a person who is habitually resident in Ireland or has his principal place of business in Ireland. Neither, however, does the 1989 Act take from the jurisdiction of the High Court existing prior to the passing of the 1989 Act. Section 5(3) of the 1989 Act provides that nothing in s 5(1) "shall deprive the High Court of any jurisdiction to hear and to determine a claim connected with ships exercisable by the High Court otherwise than by virtue of this section".[143] As has been observed elsewhere, it would not appear that s 5(3) was intended to preserve the High Court's jurisdiction over ships flying the flag of states which ratify the Convention.[144]

[1.45] The procedural rules relating to the arrest of a ship are governed by the law of the Contracting State in which the arrest was made or sought.[145] In Ireland, the rules of procedure relating to the arrest of ships are to be found in Ord 64 of the RSC which was amended by statutory instrument to make express provision for the provisions of the 1989 Act.[146]

[142.] Article 4 of the Convention; First Schedule to the 1989 Act.

[143.] Article 9 of the Convention provides that nothing in the Convention shall be construed as creating a right of action which, apart from the provisions of the Convention, would not arise under the law applied by the Court which has seisin nor as creating any maritime liens which do not exist in that law.

[144.] See Doherty, 'Ship Arrest in Ireland', (1996) CLP 232 at 234.

[145.] Article 6.

[146.] SI 143/1990. See O'Floinn, *Practice and Procedure in the Superior Courts*, (1996) Butterworths at p 458 *et seq.*

(ii) Definitions of "arrest" and "ship" under the 1989 Act

[1.46] "Arrest", for the purposes of the Convention, and therefore the 1989 Act, is defined by Article 1(2) of the Convention as meaning "the detention of a ship by judicial process to secure a "maritime claim" (see para **[1.48]** below) but is expressly defined so as not to include the seizure of a ship in execution or satisfaction of a judgment.

[1.47] "Ship" is defined by s 13(2) of the 1989 Act to include "every description of vessel used in navigation" and "vessel" is defined to include "any ship or boat, or any other description of vessel used in navigation". These definitions received judicial scrutiny in *Targe Towing Ltd v The Owners and All Persons Claiming an Interest in the Vessel "Von Rocks"*.[147] There it had been held in the High Court by Barr J that, whilst the definitions were "inclusive and non-exhaustive", a dredger was still not a "ship" or "vessel" within the meaning of s 13(2) of the 1989 Act.[148] Barr J had held that for a craft to be capable of being used in navigation it must be capable of determining its own course and future course, be capable of free and ordered movement and be intended to do its work upon the seas - the craft in question was a dredger which, when in operation, was a rigid platform with dredging machinery attached; it had no capacity for movement when set up for work and had to be towed to its next position or site. Barr J found that a craft which has no capacity for self-propulsion, is unmanned and has no rudder or steering mechanism cannot be regarded as "being used for navigation"; he also likened a dredger to an oil rig and was of the view that neither were oil rigs, "ships".[149] Moreover, the fact that dredgers might be registered as ships did not mean that they were ships. For these reasons Barr J held that the dredger in question was not a "ship", ought not to have been arrested and, accordingly, ordered its release.

The decision of the High Court was, however, reversed by the Supreme Court. Giving the unanimous judgment of the Court, Keane J held that the dredger in question was a "ship" within the meaning of the arrest Convention and s 13(2) of the 1989 Act. Beginning with the definition of "ship" and "vessel" in s 13(2) he observed that the word "includes" indicated that the definitions were not intended to be exclusive or exhaustive and also that "ship" was defined to include "boat". He went on to find that to come within the definition of "ship", it was not essential that a craft should be capable of self-propulsion;[150] whilst the presence of a rudder and the manning of the craft with crew was an important

---

[147.] [1998] 1 ILRM 481.

[148.] [1997] 1 IR 236.

[149.] As to the meaning of "navigation" Barr J referred to *Steedman v Scofield* [1992] 2 Lloyd's Rep 163 and *Polpen Shipping Company Ltd v Commercial Union Assurance Company Ltd* [1943] 1 All ER 162.

[150.] Here ([1998] 1 ILRM 481 at 491) Keane J cited *The "Mac"* [1882] Aspinall's Maritime Law Cases 555 where a barge was found to be a "ship" despite the absence of any means of self-propulsion.

factor, it was not itself conclusive;[151] the fact that the carriage of cargo or passengers is not the exclusive or even the primary object for which the craft is being used is not a decisive consideration;[152] that for a craft to come within the category of a "ship" it was not necessary that its purpose must be "to go from one place to another"; and that even though a craft may not be "used in navigation" in the conventional sense, it might nonetheless be regarded as a "ship" for the purposes of the non-exhaustive definition in s 13(2) of the 1989 Act. As to what was necessary for a craft to fall to be defined as a "ship", Keane J held that:

> "The preponderance of judicial opinion would support the view that, provided the craft was built to do something on water and, for the purpose of carrying out that work, was so designed and constructed as to be capable of traversing significant water surfaces and did in fact regularly traverse them, it is capable of being classified as a "ship", despite the absence of any form of self-propulsion or steering mechanism, such as a rudder."[153]

Accordingly, it was held that the *Von Rocks*, whilst undoubtedly lacking some of the characteristics one would normally associate with a "ship", was still to be regarded as a "ship" within the meaning of the Convention.

(iii) "Maritime claims" which ground arrest

[1.48] The claims which the High Court has jurisdiction to hear and determine under s 5(1) of the 1989 Act are those "maritime claims" set out in Article 1(1) of the Convention. These are:

(a) damage caused by any ship either in collision or otherwise;

(b) loss of life or personal injury caused by any ship or occurring in connection with the operation of any ship;

(c) salvage;[154]

(d) agreement relating to the use or hire of any ship whether by charterparty or otherwise;

[151.] *Merchants' Marine Insurance Company Ltd v North of England Protection and Indemnity Association* [1926] 26 Lloyd's Rep 201 and *The Queen v St John Ship Building and Dry Dock Company Ltd* [1981] 126 DLR (3d) 353. At 491 Keane J quoted with approval the following passage from the judgment of Urie J in the latter case: "While it appears that she was not capable of navigation herself and was not self-propelled, these facts do not detract from the fact that she was built to do something on water requiring movement from place to place".

[152.] *Hanley v Kerry County Council* High Court, unrep, 3 March 1986 (Barr J).

[153.] [1998] 1 ILRM 481 at 491, 492.

[154.] "Salvage" is defined by s 2(4) of the 1989 Act to *include* "a reference to such claims for services rendered in saving life from a ship or in preserving cargo, apparel or wreck as, under ss 544 to 546 of the Merchant Shipping Act 1894, are authorised to be made in connection with a ship (including in the case of cargo or wreck salvage claims in respect of cargo or wreck found on land)".

(e) agreement relating to the carriage of goods in any ship whether by charterparty or otherwise;

(f) loss or damage to goods including baggage carried in any ship;

(g) general average;

(h) bottomry;

(i) towage;

(j) pilotage;

(k) goods or materials whenever supplied to a ship for her operation or maintenance;

(l) construction, repair or equipment of any ship or dock charges and dues;

(m) wages of Masters,[155] Officers, or crew;

(n) Master's disbursements, including disbursements made by shippers, charters or agents on behalf of a ship or her owners;

(o) disputes as to the title to or ownership of any ship;[156]

(p) disputes between co-owners of any ship as to the ownership, possession, employment or earnings of that ship;[157]

(q) the mortgage or hypothecation of any ship.[158]

It is readily apparent that Article 1(1) provides an extensive list of maritime claims which are justiciable under the Convention and the 1989 Act.

(iv) The power of arrest - Article 2 of the Convention

[1.49] Where a plaintiff can bring one or more of the foregoing maritime claims against a ship flying the flag of a Contracting State, he can bring proceedings *in rem* against that ship; moreover, as shall be considered next, he can, in particular circumstances, bring proceedings against a "sister ship". The primary power of arrest is contained in Article 2 of the Convention which provides:

> A ship flying the flag of one of the Contracting States may be arrested in the jurisdiction of any of the Contracting States in respect of any maritime claim, but in respect of no other claim; but nothing in this Convention shall be deemed

---

[155.] "Master" is defined by s 2(4) of the 1989 Act to *include* "every person (except a pilot) having command or charge of a ship".

[156.] Section 2(2)(a) of the 1989 Act provides that Article 1(1)(o) "shall be construed as including disputes as to possession of a ship". Article 10(a) of the Convention permits Contracting States to exclude claims under this head but the 1989 Act made no such provision.

[157.] Article 10(a) of the Convention permits Contracting States to exclude claims under this head but the 1989 Act made no such provision.

[158.] Section 2(2)(b) of the 1989 Act provides that Article 1(1)(q) "shall be construed as including the mortgage or hypothecation of any share in a ship".

to extend or restrict any right or powers vested in any Governments or their Departments, Public Authorities or Dock or Harbour Authorities under their existing domestic laws or regulations to arrest, detain or otherwise prevent the sailing of vessels within their jurisdiction.

Some important points emerge. First, the power of arrest arises in respect of a "ship", as defined above,[159] which is flying the flag of one of the Contracting States to the Convention and which is within the jurisdiction of any of the Contracting States.[160] Secondly, the power of arrest will only arise under Article 2 where the person bringing the proceedings has a "maritime claim" within the meaning of the Convention, as defined above.[161] Thirdly, it is only a "maritime claim" within the meaning of Article 1(1) which will ground an arrest under Article 2.

[1.50] Although only ships flying the flag of Contracting States can be arrested under Article 2, the Convention also makes provision for the arrest of ships flying the flag of non-Contracting States. Article 8(2) provides:

A ship flying the flag of a non-Contracting State may be arrested in the jurisdiction of any Contracting State in respect of any of the maritime claims enumerated in Article 1 or of any other claim for which the law of the Contracting State permits arrest.

For example, a ship flying the flag of a non-Contracting State, may be arrested in the jurisdiction of Ireland on foot of any of the maritime claims in Article 1(1). Article 8(3) permits a derogation insofar as a Contracting State is entitled wholly or partly to exclude from the benefits of the Convention any Government of a non-Contracting State or any person who has not, at the time of the arrest, his habitual residence or principal place of business in one of the Contracting States.[162]

(v) The arrest of "sister ships" - Article 3 of the Convention [163]

[1.51] Until the passing of the 1989 Act, the concept of the arrest of a "sister ship" was unknown to Admiralty law in Ireland. For the purposes of the Convention, a *"sister ship"* means a ship (other than the particular ship in

---

159. See para **[1.47]** *supra.*

160. Moreover, Article 8(1) provides that the provisions of the Convention "shall apply to any vessel flying the flag of a Contracting State in the jurisdiction of any Contracting State.

161. See para **[1.48]** *supra.*

162. Article 8(4) provides that nothing in the Convention shall modify or affect the rules of law in force in the respective Contracting States relating to the arrest of any ship within the jurisdiction of the State of her flag by a person who has habitual residence or principal place of business in that State.

163. See generally, McGovern, 'Arrest of Sister Ships After the Jurisdiction of Courts (Maritime conventions) Act 1989', paper delivered at a seminar of the Irish Maritime Law Association.

respect of which the maritime claim arose) which is owned by the person[164] who was, at the time the maritime claim arose, the owner of the particular ship in respect of which the maritime claim arose. Article 3(1) facilitates the arrest of sister ships by a claimant[165] in certain circumstances where a maritime claim exists in respect of another ship. It provides:

> Subject to the provisions of paragraph (4) of this Article and of Article 190, a claimant may arrest either the particular ship in respect of which the maritime claim arose, or any other ship which is owned by the person who was, at the time when the maritime claim arose, the owner of the particular ship, even though the ship arrested be ready to sail; but no ship, other than the particular ship in respect of which the claim arose, may be arrested in respect of any of the maritime claims enumerated in Article 1(1) (o), (p) or (q).

Central to the power to arrest a sister ship is that it, and the particular ship in respect of which the maritime claim arose, were owned by the same person *at the time when the maritime claim arose*. Article 3(2) deems ships to be in the same ownership "when all the shares therein are owned by the same person or persons". Section 2(3)(b) of the 1989 Act provides that for the purposes of Article 3(2) "ownership shall be construed as including beneficial ownership". The operative time for looking at ownership is the time when the maritime claim arose; this means that where two ships (A and B) were owned by the same owner, and a maritime claim arises in respect of A, Article 3(1) gives rise to the power to arrest B even though the owner has, at the time of the arrest, disposed of his interest in A. Section 2(3)(a) of the 1989 Act provides that:

> For the purpose of determining under Article 3(1) or 3(4) whether a right exists to arrest a ship other than the particular ship in respect of which the maritime claim arose the owner of the other ship shall be taken to be its owner at the time of the issue of proceedings against it.

[1.52] It is important to note that not all maritime claims within the meaning of Article 1(1) will give rise to the power to arrest a sister ship. By its very terms, Article 3(1) excludes the following maritime claims: disputes as to the title to or ownership of any ship (Article 1(1)(o)); disputes between co-owners of any ship as to the ownership, possession, employment or earnings of that ship (Article 1(1)(p)); or, the mortgage or hypothecation of any ship (Article 1(1)(q)).

[1.53] Article 3(3) of the Convention provides that a ship shall not be arrested, nor shall bail or other security be given more than once in any one or more of the jurisdictions of the Contracting States in respect of the same maritime claim by

---

[164.] Article 1(3) defines "person" to include "individuals, partnerships and bodies corporate, Governments and their Departments, and Public Authorities".

[165.] Article 1(4) defines "claimant" to mean "a person who alleges that a maritime claim exists in his favour".

the same claimant. Moreover, it is provided that if a ship has been arrested in any one of such jurisdictions or bail or other security has been given in such jurisdiction either to release the ship or avoid a threatened arrest, any subsequent arrest of the ship or a sister ship shall be set aside and the ship released unless the claimant can satisfy the Court that the bail or other security has been finally released before the subsequent arrest or that there is other good cause for maintaining that arrest.

[1.54] Another control on the arrest of sister ships is provided for in Article 3(4) of the Convention. This provides that in the case of a charter by demise of a ship, where the charterer and not the ship's registered owner is liable in respect of a maritime claim relating to that ship, the claimant may arrest such ship or sister ship in the ownership of the charterer by demise, but no other ship in the ownership of the registered owner shall be liable to arrest in respect of such maritime claims.[166]

[1.55] The arrest of ships which do not fly the flag of a Contracting State is facilitated by Article 8(2). This does not, however, permit the arrest of a sister ship which does not fly the flag of a Contracting State. In *The MT "Marshal Gelovani"; Intergraan BV v The Owners and All Persons Claiming an Interest in the MT "Marshal Gelovani"*[167] Barr J held that neither the 1989 Act nor the Convention gave jurisdiction to arrest the sister ship of a ship which did not fly the flag of a Contracting State. The facts in that case were that the *Marshal Gelovani* and the *Komandarm Fetko* were sister ships and were both registered at Batumi in the Republic of Georgia, formerly, a state of the Soviet Union. The common registered owner was the Georgian Shipping Company of Batumi which was owned by the State of Georgia. The plaintiff was a Dutch company, registered at Rotterdam which contended that there had been a breach of a charterparty agreement by the common owner in respect of the *Komandarm Fetko*; the dispute was the subject matter of an arbitration in London. When the sister ship, the *Marshal Gelovani*, was in Limerick the plaintiff successfully applied to Kinlan J, sitting as a vacation judge, to have it arrested. It was against this order that the common registered owner appealed. In his judgment Barr J began by pointing out that the Republic of Georgia was not a Contracting State to the Convention. The first question raised was a "net point" - whether there was an entitlement under the Convention to arrest a ship in respect of a maritime claim against a sister ship where both vessels flew the flag of a non-Contracting State and both were in common registered ownership?

[166.] It is provided that the provisions of this paragraph "shall apply to any case in which a person other than the registered owner of a ship is liable in respect of a maritime claim relating to that ship".

[167.] High Court, unrep, 2 June 1994 (Barr J).

[1.56] Barr J noted that Article 3 of the Convention gave rise to the power to arrest a sister ship where it flew the flag of a Contracting State; and that Article 8(2) facilitated the arrest of a ship flying the flag of a non-contracting State in respect of a maritime claim against that particular ship. He noted that the Convention did not provide for the arrest of a sister ship in circumstances where it is flying the flag of a non-Contracting State and the 1989 Act did no more than formally to adopt into Irish law the Convention as it stands. In relation to the Convention and the arrest of sister ships, Barr J said:

"... a practice authorised by the laws of many Contracting States which permitted sister ship arrest was adopted by all and incorporated into the Convention, but only insofar as the ships of Contracting States are concerned. The Convention, being in the nature of an international treaty, is a creature of public international law and is bound by the provisions thereof. It is a long established general principle in that sphere of law, which is enshrined in the Vienna Convention on the Law of Treaties 1961, that any State which is not a party to an international treaty of convention cannot be bound by it."[168]

As to the effect of Article 8(2), Barr J said that he was satisfied that it is no more than a restatement of the pre-existing maritime law whereby a ship flying the flag of a non-Contracting State may be arrested in the jurisdiction of a Contracting State in respect of the same maritime claims whereby the ships of Contracting States may be arrested. In discharging the order for the arrest of the *Marshal Gelovani* Barr J held:

"I do not perceive any incongruity or inconsistency in excluding the arrest of sister ships of non-contracting States, otherwise permitted by Article 3, and I apprehend that that was the intention of the framers of the Convention. It could not have been otherwise having regard to the general principles of public international law to which I have already referred and with which the framers of the Convention were obliged to conform."[169]

[1.57] This decision was followed by the Supreme Court in *The MV "Kapitan Labunets"; Constante Trading Ltd v The Owners and All Persons Claiming an Interest in the MV "Kapitan Labunets"*.[170] There, the plaintiff was owed money by the defendant registered owner of the *Kapitan Labunets*, in respect of bunking of some of its ships - but not in respect of the *Kapitan Labunets* which was registered in the Republic of the Ukraine, a non-Contracting State for the purposes of the Convention. The plaintiff successfully applied to the High Court for the arrest of the *Kapitan Labunets* when it was in the port of Castletownberehaven. The registered owner successfully applied to Barr J for

---

168. At p 5 of the transcript.
169. At p 6 of the transcript.
170. [1995] 1 ILRM 430.

the release of the ship and it was against his decision that the plaintiff appealed to the Supreme Court. Again, the basis of the plaintiff's contention was (i) Article 8(2) gives the High Court jurisdiction to arrest a ship flying the flag of a non-Contracting State; (ii) the Convention applies to non-Contracting States and so the provisions on the arrest of sister ships in Article 3(1) should apply; and (iii) if all the provisions of the Convention did not apply to non-Contracting States, then Article 8(3) could not be explained.

[1.58] It was held by the Supreme Court that the arrest of a sister ship flying the flag of a non-Contracting State was not permitted under the Convention or the 1989 Act. Blayney J, who delivered the judgment of the Supreme Court, held, *inter alia*, that Article 8(2) could not be construed as extending to the arrest of sister ships and that the meaning of "arrest" there could not be deducted from the context of Article 3(1) which governs the arrest of sister ships but that "arrest" fell to be defined by Article 1(2).[171] He also held that Article 8(1) made clear, albeit by omission, that the provisions of the Convention do not apply to ships flying the flag of non-Contracting States, a fact emphasised by Article 8(2) which makes the first reference to non-Contracting States. Finally, he held that Article 8(3) was perfectly comprehensible when read in conjunction with Article 8(1). It would seem therefore that the matter of the arrest of sister ships which fly the flag of a non-Contracting State has now been put beyond all question.

(vi) Miscellaneous provisions of the Convention

[1.59] Provision is made for the release of an arrested ship upon sufficient bail or other security, except where arrest was on foot of maritime claims under Article 1(1)(o) and (p) of the Convention.[172] Whether a claimant is liable in damages for the wrongful arrest of a ship or for the costs of bail or other security furnished to release or prevent the arrest of a ship will be determined by the law of the Contracting State in whose jurisdiction the arrest was made or applied for, as will the rules of procedure relating to arrest etc.[173] Article 7 of the Convention deals with the jurisdiction to determine the substantive claim which gives rise to arrest.

An Overview of the Practice and Procedure in Arresting a Ship[174]

[1.60] Admiralty actions are heard by a judge who is specifically assigned, by the President of the High Court, to hear such actions.[175] The current judge so

---

[171.] See para **[1.46]** *supra*.

[172.] Article 5.

[173.] Article 6.

[174.] See Kelly, 'How Can One Arrest A Ship?', (1983) paper delivered to the Irish Maritime Law Association; Doherty, 'Ship Arrest in Ireland', (1996) CLP 232.

[175.] Order 64, r 5 of the RSC.

assigned is Mr Justice Robert Barr. Proceedings are usually commenced by way of a plenary summons, although Ord 64, r 3 of the RSC provides that a special summons may be adopted in a claim by a mortgagee of a ship or a share therein for the sale thereof or otherwise to enforce his security or by a mortgagor for redemption of the mortgage or a claim for the sale of a ship or any share therein in pursuance of s 47 of the Mercantile Marine Act 1955.[176]

[1.61] Proceedings *in rem* are directed against "the owners of the ship and all persons claiming an interest in the said ship".[177] It has been said that "the action *in rem* is an action against the ship itself"[178] as opposed to an action *in personam* against the ship's owners. This theory, the so-called "personification theory" has fallen into decline and has generally been superseded by the "procedural theory".[179] One question which arises from this distinction is whether a statutory provision which prevents the same issue being litigated afresh between the same parties would prevent a person taking an action *in rem* where they have already taken an action *in personam*. In *The Indian Endurance (No 2); Republic of India v India Steamship Co Ltd*[180] the House of Lords held that s 34 of the UK's Civil Jurisdiction and Judgments Act 1982 had the effect of barring an action *in rem* by the plaintiffs against the defendant where the plaintiffs had already obtained a foreign judgment *in personam* against the defendant.[181] Lord Steyn said:

"... for the purposes of s 34 an action in rem is an action against the defendants from the moment the Admiralty Court is seized with jurisdiction. The jurisdiction of the Admiralty Court is invoked by the service of a writ, or where a writ is deemed to be served, as a result of the acknowledgement of the issue of the writ by the defendant before service ... From that moment, the defendants are parties to the proceedings *in rem*."[182]

[176.] A special summons may be used in any other admiralty action where all parties consent to such.

[177.] See Appendix J, forms 1, 2 and 3 of the RSC as referenced by Ord 64, r 2 for the form of an originating summons in an admiralty action.

[178.] *The Burns* [1907] P 137 at 149.

[179.] See *The Indian Endurance (No 2); Republic of India v India Steamship Co Ltd* [1997] 4 All ER 380 at 385, 388, 389 where *The August 8* [1983] 2 AC 450 and *The Deichland* [1989] 2 All ER 1066 were quoted with approval. In *The Deichland* (at 1086) Sir Denys Buckley said that "In reality, distinguished from formal aspects, the instant action is, in my judgment, as much a suit against Deich as would be an action *in personam* ...".

[180.] [1997] 4 All ER 380.

[181.] Section 34 of the 1982 Act provides: "No proceedings may be brought by a person in England and Wales ... on a cause of action in respect of which a judgment has been given in his favour in proceedings between the same parties, or their privies ... in a court of an overseas country, unless that judgment is not enforceable or entitled to recognition in England and Wales ...".

[182.] [1997] 4 All ER 380 at 391f.

It may be noted that Article 21 of the Convention on Jurisdiction and Enforcement of Judgments in Civil and Commercial Matters, implemented in Ireland by the Jurisdiction of Courts and Enforcement of Judgments Acts 1988 and 1993, provides:

> Where proceedings involving the same cause of action and between the same parties are brought in the courts of different Contracting States, any court other than the court first seised shall of its own motion decline jurisdiction in favour of that court ...[183]

It was held in *The Maciej Rataj* case[184] that no importance attached to the fact that proceedings may be of a different nature under the civil procedural law of one or other of the states concerned and that what was important was "whether or not the substantive issues which the court is called upon to examine are the same".[185] It was noted by Lord Steyn in *The Indian Endurance (No 2)* that there was a "striking similarity in language" between Article 21 and s 34 of the UK's 1982 Act.

[1.62] A warrant for the arrest of a ship or other property (eg cargo) in admiralty actions *in rem* for claims arising under Ord 64, r 1(a) to (h) of the RSC, inclusive,[186] must be in the Form No 8 in Appendix J of the RSC and may be issued by the Master of the High Court; the matters which must be addressed in the supporting affidavit are detailed in Ord 64, r 6(1). A warrant for the arrest of a ship on foot of claims arising under Ord 64, r 1(i) or (j) (ie under the 1989 Act)[187] must also be in the Form No 8 in Appendix J to the RSC and may *only* be issued by a judge of the High Court, not the Master; again, the matters which must be addressed in the supporting affidavit are detailed in Ord 64, r 6(2) of the RSC.[188]

[1.63] After a warrant of arrest issues it must be served. Except in cases where a defendant's solicitor agrees to accept service and undertakes[189] in writing to

---

[183.] Note that in *Intermetal Group Ltd and Trans-World (Steel) Ltd v Worslade Trading Ltd* High Court, unrep, 12 December 1997, O'Sullivan J noted that the effect of Article 21 (although not actually citing Article 21) was that "So long as an action remains alive in any of the contracting States, then the same action will not be maintained in another contracting State and for this purpose I think it is proper to treat all contracting States as comprising one jurisdiction".

[184.] C-406/92; [1995] All ER (EC) 229.

[185.] At 242, para 19.

[186.] See para **[1.33]** *supra*.

[187.] *Ibid.*

[188.] In an application for a warrant for arrest under Ord 64, r 6(1) or r 6 (2) a warrant may be issued notwithstanding that all of the required particulars are not mentioned in the affidavit: r 7.

[189.] Failure to comply with the undertaking renders the solicitor liable to be attached: on attachment and committal of contemnors, see Ch 12, *Enforcing Mareva Injunctions and Other Orders*, para **[12.52]** *et seq.*

enter an appearance,[190] service of the warrant of arrest against a ship, freight or cargo must be effected by nailing or affixing the original warrant[191] for a short time on the main mast or on the single mast of the vessel or other conspicuous part thereof and on taking off the warrant, leaving a true copy thereof nailed or affixed in its place.[192] Warrants of arrest are served by the Admiralty Marshal or his substitute and after service are filed in the Central Office of the High Court.[193]

Mareva Relief Ancillary to the Arrest of a Ship

[1.64] A Mareva injunction is as available to a maritime plaintiff as it is to a plaintiff in any civil action. Although the arrest of a ship takes effect *in rem* and is, therefore, a stronger remedy, a maritime plaintiff may have no choice but to seek Mareva relief where the value of an arrested ship is insufficient to compensate him for his claim.[194] A practical situation where this might arise is where a plaintiff's maritime claim does not give rise to the power to arrest a sister ship pursuant to Article 3(1) of the International Convention Relating to the Arrest of Seagoing Ships.[195] In *The Rena K*[196] Brandon J said:

> "The questions of a plaintiff obtaining a Mareva injunction in respect of several ships, or of combining an arrest of one ship in proceedings *in rem* with the obtaining of a Mareva injunction in respect of one or more other ships in proceedings *in personam*, do not arise for consideration in this case. I would, however, just say that the prospect of a plaintiff being able to obtain several kinds of security cumulatively in respect of the same claim, if the size of such claim justifies it, is not one which fills me with any consternation or dismay."

More recent *obiter dictum* support for this position can be seen in the Australian decision of Sheppard J in *Patrick Stevedores No 2 Pty Ltd v MV "Skulptor Konenkov", Enso-Gutzeit OY* .[197]

[190.] Order 64, r 8 of the RSC.
[191.] The procedure is the same for service of a summons.
[192.] Order 64, r 10 of the RSC; r 11 deals with the service of a summons or warrant of arrest of cargo or freight which is landed or transhipped; r 12 provides that if cargo is in the custody of a person who will not allow access to it, service may be made upon such person.
[193.] Order 64, r 9 of the RSC.
[194.] *The Rena K* (1979) QB 337.
[195.] See para **[1.51]** *et seq.*
[196.] (1979) QB 337 at 409, 410.
[197.] [1996] FCA (23 February 1996).

Chapter 2

The Jurisdiction to Grant Mareva Relief

[2.01] It was not without some initial difficulty that, in 1975, the English Court of Appeal first asserted the Mareva jurisdiction. In this chapter the jurisdictional basis for making a Mareva injunction is first examined in Section [A]. Section [B] then examines the difficulties associated with granting Mareva relief where there is no discernible cause of action against a defendant; these difficulties typically arose in situations where police forces tried to restrain alleged criminals from disposing of their assets. It may be noted that although recently enacted statutory provisions now facilitate the freezing of alleged criminals' assets (see Chapter 3, *Statutory Jurisdictions to Freeze Assets*) it still remains instructive to consider the jurisdictional issues raised in a case where an applicant for Mareva relief appears not to have a cause of action.

[A] THE MAREVA JURISDICTION[1]

[2.02] In Ireland the jurisdiction to grant a Mareva injunction is to be found in the general jurisdiction to make an interlocutory injunction. Section 28(8) of the Supreme Court of Judicature (Ireland) Act 1877[2] provides:

> A mandamus or an injunction may be granted or a receiver appointed by an interlocutory order of the court in all cases in which it shall appear to the court to be just or convenient that such order shall be made, and any such order may be made either unconditionally or upon such terms and conditions as the court shall think just.[3]

Moreover, Ord 50 r 6(1) of the Rules of the Superior Courts 1986, ("the RSC") which regulate the practice and procedure of the High and Supreme Courts, provides:

[1.] See generally, Ough & Flenley, *The Mareva Injunction and Anton Piller Order*, (2nd ed, 1993) Butterworths, pp 9-10; Capper, *Mareva Injunctions*, (1988) SLS/Sweet & Maxwell, pp 9-22; Powles, *The Mareva Injunction and Associated Orders*, (1985) Professional Books, pp 1-12; Keane, *Equity and the Law of Trusts in the Republic of Ireland*, (1988) Butterworths, pp 234-236; Baker & Langan, *Snell's Equity*, (29th ed, 1990) Sweet & Maxwell, p 670; Spry, *Equitable Remedies*, (4th ed, 1990) Sweet & Maxwell, pp 504-506.

[2.] As applied to the present High Court by ss 8(2) and 48(3) of the Courts (Supplemental Provisions) Act 1961.

[3.] Cited by O'Flaherty J in *Re John Horgan Livestock Ltd; O'Mahony v Horgan* [1995] 2 IR 411.

> The court may grant ... an injunction ... by an interlocutory order in all cases in which it appears to the court to be just or convenient so to do.

Accordingly, in Ireland, there is no specific statutory "Mareva jurisdiction", unlike the position in the United Kingdom where there is, since 1981, an express statutory power to grant Mareva injunctions. In Ireland,[4] the Mareva injunction has the same jurisdictional basis as any other form of interim or interlocutory injunction.[5]

[2.03] In this section the following issues in the jurisdiction to grant a Mareva injunction are considered:

1. The Principle in Lister & Co v Stubbs.

2. The Basis, Origins and Development of the Mareva Jurisdiction.

3. The Acceptance of the Mareva Jurisdiction in Ireland.

4. The Inherent Jurisdiction to Grant a Mareva Injunction.

5. The Constitutionality of the Mareva Jurisdiction.

6. The Prerequisites to Exercising the Mareva Jurisdiction.

The Principle in *Lister & Co v Stubbs*

[2.04] For nearly a century it had been thought that there was no jurisdiction to grant an injunction to restrain a defendant from dealing with his own property prior to a plaintiff obtaining judgment against him.[6] As James LJ said in *Robinson v Pickering*[7] "you cannot get an injunction to restrain a man who is alleged to be a debtor from parting with his property".[8] This rule of law has

---

4. See para **[2.16]** *et seq*, *infra*.

5. Section 22 of the Courts (Supplemental Provisions) Act 1961 empowers the Circuit Court to grant an injunction where the rateable valuation of the property does not exceed £200. In the Circuit Court the proceedings in respect of which a Mareva injunction can be ancillary relief will usually be either a Civil Bill or an Equity Civil Bill. Ord 17 r 2 of the Rules of the Circuit Court 1950 facilitates application for an *ad interim* injunction. This provides: "Applications in connection with any of the matters hereinafter mentioned may be made to the Judge by any party, without notice to any other party, on lodging with the County Registrar an *ex parte* docket and filing an affidavit in support of the application." Although there are no reported judgments where the Circuit Court granted a Mareva injunction, such injunctions have been consistently granted by the Circuit Court.

6. *Cf* where the plaintiff claims a proprietary interest in the property sought to be affected by an injunction in, for example, a tracing action: see Ch 1, *The Mareva Injunction in Context*, para **[1.16]** *et seq*.

7. (1881) 16 Ch D 660 at 663.

8. This remark was made by James LJ to the plaintiff's counsel. In that case the plaintiff was owed over £436 by the second defendant, the wife of the first defendant on foot of goods which he had supplied on credit. In seeking to charge her property (of which she and her husband were both trustees) the plaintiff sought and obtained an injunction to restrain both defendants from dealing with their property. On appeal, the injunction was discharged.

come to be known as the *"Lister* principle" or the rule in *Lister & Co v Stubbs*.[9] The facts in that case were that Stubbs was a foreman in the plaintiff's manufacturing company. His work involved the purchase of materials used in the dyeing of silk-spinners. Stubbs placed large orders for raw materials with one particular firm (Varley & Co) and in return received large commissions, some of which he invested. On learning of the secret profits paid to Stubbs, the plaintiff company brought an action claiming, *inter alia*, the commission and damages. After instigating the action, the plaintiff company sought, *inter alia*, an interlocutory injunction to restrain Stubbs from dealing with land which had been purchased in part with the commission. At the initial hearing of the application Stirling J refused the injunction sought.

[2.05] The Court of Appeal, *per* Cotton LJ and Lindley LJ upheld Stirling J's judgment. Cotton LJ said:

> "... [I]n my opinion the moneys which under this corrupt bargain were paid by Messrs Varley to the defendant cannot be said to be the money of the plaintiff's before any judgment or decree in some such action has been made. I know of no case where, because it was highly probable that if the action were brought to hearing the plaintiff could establish that a debt was due to him from the defendant, the defendant has been ordered to give security until that has been established by the judgment or decree."[10]

Cotton LJ concluded his judgment by saying:

> "... if we were to order the defendant to give the security asked for, it would be introducing an entirely new and wrong principle - which we ought not to do, even though we might think that, having regard to the circumstances of the case, it would be highly just to make the order."[11]

The judgment of Lindley LJ followed this approach, stating that the Court would do "a great mischief" were it to accede to the application.[12] The *"Lister* principle" was thus stated. It is interesting to note that the Court of Appeal gave no consideration to the risk of removal of assets from the jurisdiction, whether the defendant may have had the intention of frustrating the Court's future judgment, and, further, assumed that the Court was being asked to require the

---

[9.] (1890) 45 Ch D 1. Although the "general rule" has been traced to earlier cases (see, eg, Lord Denning MR's judgment in *Rasu Maritima SA v Perusahaan Pertambangan* [1977] 3 All ER 324 at 332 and his reference to *Mills v Northern Railway of Buenos Ayres Co* (1870) 5 Ch App 621, *Robinson v Pickering* (1881) 16 Ch D 660, *Newton v Newton* (1885) 11 PD 11, *Jagger v Jagger* [1926] P 93 and *Scott v Scott* [1950] 2 All ER 1154) *Lister & Co v Stubbs* is considered as the most important in this old line of authority.

[10.] At 12.

[11.] At 14.

[12.] At 15.

defendant to provide security by paying money into court.[13] Strongly influenced by the significance of the trustee-*cestui que trust* relationship, which (had it existed in that case) would have permitted the remedy of tracing and the *prima facie* right to an injunction to protect a proprietary right,[14] the Court of Appeal rejected the plaintiff's application for an injunction to prevent the defendant from dealing with the money. Whilst the existence of the "*Lister* principle" continues to be acknowledged,[15] as shall be considered next, the practical effect of the Mareva injunction has been to relegate it from being the general rule to now being the exception.

The Basis, Origins and Development of the Mareva Jurisdiction

[2.06] In Ireland, the acknowledged jurisdictional basis of the Mareva injunction is s 28(8) of the Supreme Court of Judicature (Ireland) Act 1877[16] and, in the United Kingdom, at the time when the Mareva jurisdiction was first asserted, it was the materially identical s 45(1) of the Supreme Court of Judicature (Consolidation) Act 1925.[17] Both provide that an interlocutory injunction may be granted in all cases where it shall appear to the Court "to be just or convenient". This does not, however, give the Court an unfettered discretion to grant interlocutory relief and an injunction can only be granted in defence of a plaintiff's legal or equitable right.[18] The judgment in *The North London Railway Company v The Great Northern Railway Company*[19] made it clear that an injunction will not be granted to a person who has no legal or equitable right. In that case it had been argued that the passing of the Judicature Act 1873, upon which the later Irish Act was based, expanded the power of the court to grant injunctive relief, even where no legal right was capable of being enforced. This was firmly, and categorically, rejected by Cotton LJ when he said:

---

13. Cotton LJ said, at 14: "... if the money sought to be recovered is not the money of the plaintiffs, we should be simply ordering the defendant to pay into court a sum of money in his possession because there is a *prima facie* case against him that at the hearing it will be established that he owes money to the plaintiffs".

14. See Ch 1, *The Mareva Injunction in Context*, para **[1.16]** *et seq.*

15. See, for example, the judgments of McWilliam J in *Fleming v Ranks (Ireland) Ltd* [1983] ILRM 541 at 546, 547 and *Powerscourt Estates v Gallagher & Gallagher* [1984] ILRM 123 at 126. See para **[2.17]** *infra.*

16. See the Supreme Court decision in *Re John Horgan Livestock Ltd; O'Mahony v Horgan* [1995] 2 IR 411.

17. Now, s 37(3) of the Supreme Court Act 1981 confers a specific statutory jurisdiction to grant Mareva relief. See fn 4, *supra.*

18. In *Day v Brownrigg* (1878) Ch D 294 the Court of appeal refused the plaintiff an injunction to restrain his defendant-neighbour from calling his house the same name as the plaintiff's house as the plaintiff had no right to enforce.

19. (1883) QBD 30.

"Great reliance was placed upon the words 'An injunction may be granted by an interlocutory order of the court in all cases in which it shall appear to the court to be just or convenient that such order should be made' ... In my opinion, all that was done by this section was to give to the High Court power to give a remedy which formerly would not have been given in that particular case, but still only a remedy in defence of or to enforce rights which according to law were previously existing and capable of being enforced ... In my opinion the sole intention of the section is this: that where there is a legal right which was, independently of the Act, capable of being enforced either at law or in equity, then, whatever may have been the previous practice, the High Court may interfere by injunction in protection of that right."[20]

Earlier, in *Beddow v Beddow*,[21] Jessel MR had said that:

"I have unlimited power to grant an injunction in any case where it would be right or just to do so; and what is right or just must be decided, not by the caprice of the judge, but according to sufficient legal reasons or on settled legal principles."

[2.07] In summary, an interlocutory injunction cannot be granted unless it is granted in defence of a plaintiff's legal or equitable rights. In the context of Mareva injunctions, this principle of law translates into the requirement that a Mareva-plaintiff must have a *substantive right*, usually, a cause of action against a Mareva-defendant.[22] Here the following matters are considered:

(a) The initial assertion of the Mareva jurisdiction - in *ex parte* hearings;

(b) Confirmation of the Mareva jurisdiction on *inter partes* hearing;

(c) The acceptance of the Mareva jurisdiction in other countries.

(a) The initial assertion of the Mareva jurisdiction - in ex parte hearings

[2.08] The first Mareva injunction was made following *ex parte* application where only the applicant's counsel was heard by the court. In what is accepted to be the first modern case where a Mareva injunction was granted, *Nippon Yusen Kaisha v Karageoris*,[23] Lord Denning MR explained why the jurisdiction to grant an ordinary interlocutory injunction[24] also empowered the court to grant a Mareva injunction:

---

20. At 39, 40.
21. (1878) 9 Ch D 89 at 93.
22. See Ch 4, *A Substantive Cause of Action* and, in particular, para **[4.46]** where the difficulties associated with so-called statutory causes of action are examined. See also para **[2.32]** *et seq*, *infra*.
23. [1975] 3 All ER 282.
24. Then contained in s 45(1) of the Supreme Court of Judicature (Consolidation) Act 1925, which was in all material respects identical with s 28(8) of the Supreme Court of Judicature (Ireland) Act 1877.

"There is no reason why the High Court or this court should not make an order such as is asked for here. It is warranted by s 45 of the Supreme Court of Judicature (Consolidation) Act 1925 which says the High Court may grant a mandamus or injunction or appoint a receiver by an interlocutory order in all cases in which it appears to the court to be just or convenient so to do. It seems to me that this is just such a case. There is a strong *prima facie* case that the hire is owing and unpaid. If an injunction is not granted, these moneys may be removed out of the jurisdiction and the shipowners will have the greatest difficulty in recovering anything."[25]

In that case the Japanese plaintiff had issued proceedings against the defendant Greek charterer for failure to pay moneys allegedly due by way of hire of three ships which had been chartered by the plaintiff shipowner to the defendant charterer. The plaintiff was aware that the defendant had moneys in England and, fearful that they would be removed from the jurisdiction, sought an injunction to prevent this so as to ensure that funds would be available to satisfy the plaintiff's judgment against the defendant. The High Court refused the injunction sought but this decision was reversed by the Court of Appeal which granted the relief.

[2.09] Four weeks later, in the case which gave the injunction its name, *Mareva Compania Naviera SA v International Bulkcarriers SA, The Mareva,*[26] Lord Denning MR had again the opportunity to consider this novel jurisdiction. The facts in *The Mareva* were that the plaintiff company had issued a writ claiming unpaid hire and damages for the repudiation of a charterparty. On the *ex parte* application of the plaintiff an interim injunction was granted preventing the defendant from removing money, which it had on deposit with a London bank, out of the jurisdiction. However, the High Court refused the plaintiff's application to extend the interim injunction and the plaintiff appealed to the Court of Appeal. In the Court of Appeal, s 45(1) of the English Supreme Court of Judicature (Consolidation) Act 1925 was again considered. Lord Denning MR reviewed cases such as *Beddow v Beddow,*[27] *The North London Railway Co v Great Northern Railway Co*[28] and the authority of *Halsbury's Laws of England*[29] and concluded that there was jurisdiction to grant a Mareva injunction. In the course of his judgment he said:

[25.] [1975] 3 All ER 282 at 283g-h.

[26.] [1980] 1 All ER 213.

[27.] (1878) 9 Ch D 89.

[28.] (1883) 11 QBD 30.

[29.] *Halsbury's Laws of England* (3rd ed) Vol 21 p 348, para 729, where the following passage was quoted as a summary of the effect of s 45(1) of the Supreme Court of Judicature (Consolidation) Act 1925: "... now, therefore, whenever a right, which can be asserted either at law or in equity, does exist, then, whatever the previous practice may have been, the Court is enabled by virtue of this provision, in a proper case, to grant an injunction to protect that right."

"In my opinion that principle applies to a creditor who has a right to be paid the debt owing to him, even before he has established his right by getting judgment for it. If it appears that the debt is due and owing, and there is a danger that the debtor may dispose of his assets so as to defeat it before judgment, the court has jurisdiction in a proper case to grant an interlocutory judgment so as to prevent him from disposing of those assets."

The plaintiff's "legal or equitable right" was identified as being the right to be paid the debt owing. Although Lord Denning MR acknowledged the principle in *Lister & Co v Stubbs*, he did not expressly overrule or distinguish it. Lord Roskill LJ, however, did, and in so doing made the crucial distinction between the Court's *jurisdiction* and past *practice*. Acknowledging that the application for the injunction had been made *ex parte* he said:

"If the charterers were represented, it would no doubt be said on their behalf that the decision of this court in *Lister & Co v Stubbs* precludes this court, not as a matter of jurisdiction but as a matter of *practice,* from granting this injunction."[30]

So, the principle in *Lister & Co v Stubbs* was distinguished on the ground that the Court had not, until that date, been challenged with suitable facts.

(b) Confirmation of the Mareva jurisdiction on **inter partes** *hearing*

[2.10] In *Rasu Maritima SA v Perusahaan Pertambangan Minyak Dan Gas Bumi Negara (Pertamina) and the Government of Indonesia* (as interveners)[31] the Court of Appeal in England was presented with the first opportunity, on an *inter partes* hearing, to consider the Mareva jurisdiction. Again, it was Lord Denning MR who was at the helm of the Court of Appeal. After making a short historical and comparative survey of the jurisdiction to freeze a defendant's assets before final judgment,[32] Lord Denning MR turned to consider what was then the present law and after citing the *Lister & Co v Stubbs* line of cases, said:

"I do not think they should be applied to cases where a defendant is out of the jurisdiction but has assets in this country. To those cases, at least, I think we should apply the principle which was applied by the customary courts in olden times and by the courts of the continent today. We should do it by means of the modern procedure of granting interlocutory injunction. It is ready to hand in a statute of wide import. In 1873 parliament decreed: 'A mandamus or an injunction may be granted or a receiver appointed by an interlocutory order of the court in all cases in which it shall appear to the court to be just or convenient ...'. ... Those words give to the court a wide discretion to grant an interlocutory injunction whenever it appears to the court to be just or

---

[30.] [1980] 1 All ER 213 at 215. Italics added.
[31.] [1977] 3 All ER 324.
[32.] At 331.

convenient. The statute was so interpreted by Jessel MR in *Beddow v Beddow* (1878) 9 Ch D 89 at 93. In 1883 this court in *North London Railway Co v Great Northern Railway Co* made statements limiting the discretion. But later decisions have made it clear that when a statute gives a discretion the courts must not fetter it by rigid rules from which a judge is never at liberty to depart. It was so held in the House of Lords in *Blunt v Blunt* [1943] 2 All ER 76 and followed by this court sitting as a full court in *Ward v James* [1965] 1 All ER 563 at 568. In those cases the courts departed from a long line of previous opinions as to the way in which discretion should be exercised, in one case in granting a divorce, in the other case ordering trial by jury."[33]

Lord Denning viewed the earlier cases of *Nippon Yusen Kaisha* and *The Mareva*, which had both held that it had been "just or convenient" to prevent the defendants in those cases from removing their assets from the jurisdiction, as being part of the evolutionary process.[34] It is interesting to note that the principal justification for distinguishing the Mareva jurisdiction from the *Lister & Co v Stubbs* line of authorities - that the defendant was a foreigner - was subsequently dropped as a requirement for the exercise of the Mareva jurisdiction. This does not, however, mean that the jurisdictional basis has changed. On the contrary, the power of the court to grant an interlocutory injunction which is "just or convenient" to protect a plaintiff's right to enforce his anticipated judgment continues to be the jurisdictional basis for the Mareva. The fact that it was initially restricted to where the defendant was a foreigner,[35] where there was a risk that assets would be removed from the jurisdiction[36] and where a defendant had assets within the jurisdiction[37] are all examples of initial limits or conditions which were placed on the exercise of that jurisdiction.

(c) The acceptance of the Mareva jurisdiction in other countries

[2.11] Before considering the acceptance of the Mareva jurisdiction in Ireland it is worth considering its reception in a selection of other common law jurisdictions.[38] Although the reaction was mixed, the Mareva jurisdiction has been accepted in the vast majority of jurisdictions. Australasia and Canada provide interesting examples of their courts' attitude to the Mareva jurisdiction,

---

33. At 333.
34. Indeed, at 333 Lord Denning MR observed, that "so just and so convenient, indeed is the procedure that it has been constantly invoked since in the commercial courts with the approval of all the judges and users of that court."
35. See Ch 6, *The Risk of Removal or Disposal of Assets*, para **[6.03]** *et seq*.
36. *Ibid*, para **[6.09]** *et seq*.
37. See Ch 7, *The Defendant's Assets*, para **[7.22]** *et seq*.
38. One of the most extensive comparative treatments of the Mareva injunction is contained in Hoyle, *The Mareva Injunction and Related Orders*, (3rd ed, 1997) Lloyd's of London Press, pp 151-168.

containing as they do a number of cases where jurisdiction was both accepted and declined.

(i) New Zealand

[2.12] In New Zealand the courts have accepted that there is jurisdiction to grant Mareva relief. In *Hunt v BP Exploration Company (Libya) Ltd*[39] Barker J held that the Mareva injunction was available to plaintiffs in New Zealand. In that case, after reviewing some of the earlier New Zealand authorities, Baker J held that the jurisdiction to grant such an injunction had been recognised in other cases,[40] and said:

> "I consider that this Court does have a *Mareva* jurisdiction. I do not accept the view that this jurisdiction is in the nature of legislating in an area forbidden to the Courts. I am not impressed by the 'assumption of fearful authority' line of cases. There appears to have been an old English procedure of 'foreign attachment' which provides a perfectly respectable ancestry for the procedure. The fact that this procedure accords with that in European countries is, for a New Zealand Court, a matter of coincidence.
>
> The court has to approach modern problems with the flexibility of modern business. In former times, as Lawton LJ pointed out,[41] it would have been more difficult for a foreign debtor to take his assets out of the country. Today, vast sums of money can be transferred from one country to another in a matter of seconds as a result of a phone call or a telex message. Reputable foreign debtors of course have nothing to fear; the facts of the reported Mareva cases indicate that the jurisdiction is wholesome; the sheer number of Mareva injunctions granted in London indicates that the jurisdiction is fulfilling a need."[42]

In *Mayall v Weal*[43] Prichard J (in the New Zealand High Court of Hamilton) refused a Mareva injunction not because of any absence of jurisdiction, but because, in that case, the prerequisites necessary for Mareva relief had not been proved: it was held that there was no evidence that the defendant would remove his assets from the jurisdiction.

(ii) Australia

[2.13] The initial attitude of the Australian courts towards granting Mareva injunctions was diverse across the various territories. The courts in South Australia were at first the most set against accepting the jurisdiction to grant

---

[39.] [1980] 1 NZLR 104.
[40.] See *Systems & Programs (NZ) Ltd v PRC Public Management Services (Inc)* [1978] NZ Recent Law 264; *Mosen v Donselaar* [1980] 1 NZLR 115.
[41.] In *The Third Chandris* [1979] 2 All ER 972 at 985, 986.
[42.] [1980] 1 NZLR 104 at 119.
[43.] [1982] 2 NZLR 385.

Mareva relief and in *Pivovaroff v Chernabaeff* [44] the Supreme Court (*per* Bray CJ) declined to follow the Mareva line of cases and held that there was no jurisdiction to make such an order. In that case an infant was suing the defendants by his father and next-friend for personal injuries sustained when his hand was caught in an onion sorting machine which he was operating on a market garden property. Three of the defendants carried on the business of market gardeners and were alleged to be the owners of the land on which the business was situated; the other defendants were alleged to have lent or hired the onion sorting machine to them and it was claimed that the machine was in a dangerous condition. When it came to the next-friend's attention that the land on which the business was carried out had been advertised for sale, he applied for an injunction to restrain the sale. His affidavit claimed that he believed that, upon the sale of the land, the vendor-defendants might move to the USA, where their parents resided. The trial judge, King J, made the order sought pursuant to s 29(1) of the Australian Supreme Court Act 1981 [45] which he accepted conferred jurisdiction to grant a Mareva injunction. This was, however, overruled by the South Australia Court of Appeal in a judgment given by Bray CJ. Referring to the English Court of Appeal's decision in *Nippon Yusen Kaisha v Karageorgis* [46] he said:

> "In my opinion, the decision of the Court of Appeal was revolutionary. It departed from a settled rule more than a century old. It would, perhaps, be an idle exercise in semantics to discuss whether the question involved was a question of jurisdiction or a question of practice, but certainly the granting of the injunction was no mere change of practice in the ordinary and limited sense, such as a change in listing procedures or in the form of documents." [47]

After reviewing the subsequent cases of *Mareva Compania Naviera* [48] and *Rasu Maritima SA* [49] he noted that in both cases the defendants had been outside of the jurisdiction whereas in the case in hand they were within it. However, Bray CJ went further than simply to decline jurisdiction on that ground alone saying that he was "far from satisfied that even in the case of a defendant outside the jurisdiction with assets within it it would be proper to issue an injunction of the type in question here". [50] He went on to give six reasons for this. First, that there was strong authority for the proposition that "you cannot get an injunction to

---

[44.] (1978) 16 SASR 329

[45.] Section 29(1) provided: "The Court may grant a mandamus, or an injunction, or appoint a receiver, by an interlocutory order in all cases in which it appears to the Court to be just or convenient so to do."

[46.] [1975] 3 All ER 282.

[47.] [1978] 16 SASR 329 at 335.

[48.] [1980] 1 All ER 213.

[49.] [1977] 3 All ER 324.

[50.] [1978] 16 SASR 329 at 338.

restrain a man who is alleged to be a debtor from parting with his property" and that there was no exception to this in the case of non-resident defendants.[51] Secondly, that it was inappropriate to introduce, in however modified a form, some version of the European practice of *saisie conservatoire* as "it is a great stretch of power to tie up a man's assets indefinitely pending the trial of an action against him which may not succeed, particularly when the amount of any judgment he may obtain is entirely at large and may be far less than the value of the frozen assets".[52] Thirdly, that Australia had not joined the Common Market nor was it bound by the Treaty of Rome. Fourthly, that s 29(1) of Australia's Supreme Court Act 1981 was "purely a machinery section" and did not alter the principles upon which the court acted in granting injunctions, and by providing for interlocutory orders alone it would not permit the making of a post-judgment Mareva injunction[53] and that interlocutory injunctions, "broadly speaking", have always, he thought, had some connection with the subject matter of the suit.[54] Fifthly, that whilst the Court has a discretion, there was a great difference between the ambit of a discretion and the exercise of a discretion - the words of s 29(1) had been construed for a least a century so as not to authorise a Mareva type order. Sixthly, that given that the legislature had in s 35 of the Australian Supreme Court Act 1981 (modelled on s 6 of the English Debtors Act 1869; s 7 of the Debtors Act (Ireland), 1872) legislated for absconding debtors and also the existence of the writ of *ne exeat regno*,[55] it "would seem unlikely that an alternative process of summary execution in anticipation of judgment, available for unliquidated damages as well as for liquidated debts due and payable, should have been slumbering unsuspected for over a century in the interstices of s 29(1) and its predecessor and its analogues."[56] This was indeed an unequivocal denial of the existence of the Mareva jurisdiction.

[2.14] Notwithstanding the initial view taken by the Court of South Australia, the jurisdiction to grant Mareva injunctions has subsequently been recognised in that territory[57] and indeed by the Courts in Victoria,[58] Western Australia,[59]

---

51. *Robinson v Pickering* (1881) 16 Ch D 660 at 661; *Scott v Scott* [19512] P 193; *Burmester v Burmester* [1913] P 76; and *Bradley Bros (Oshaw) Ltd v A to Z Rental Canada Ltd* (1970) 14 DLR (3d) 171.
52. [1978] 16 SASR 329 at 339.
53. *Cf* Ch 4, *A Substantive Cause of Action*, para **[4.28]** *et seq*.
54. Halsbury, *Laws of England*, (3rd ed) Vol 21, para 729 p 348; Kerr on *Injunctions* (5th ed, 1914), p 6; Meagher, Gummow & Lehane, *Equity - Doctrines and Remedies*, (1975), pp 452-454, paras 2112-2114.
55. See generally, Ch 11, *Restraining Defendants from Leaving the State*.
56. [1978] 16 SASR 329 at 340.
57. See, eg, *Brew v Crouch; Dionysus Pty Ltd* [1998] 6633 SCSA (23 April 1998) where, although a Mareva injunction was refused in that case, it was accepted that there was jurisdiction, in appropriate cases, to grant such relief.
58. *Praznonsky v Sablyack* [1977] VR 114.
59. *Sanko Steamship Co Ltd v DC Commodities (A'Asia) Pty Ltd* [1980] WAR 51.

Queensland,[60] and New South Wales.[61] Moreover, the High Court of Australia recognised the jurisdiction to grant a Mareva injunction in what is the leading Australian case on the Mareva injunction, *Jackson v Sterling Industries Ltd*.[62]

(iii) Canada

[2.15] In *BP Exploration Co (Libya) Ltd v Hunt*[63] the Supreme Court of the Northwest Territories in Canada, *per* Tallis J, held that there was jurisdiction to grant a Mareva injunction.[64] Indeed, in *Mooney v Orr*[65] the Supreme Court in British Columbia not only accepted the basic Mareva jurisdiction but also granted worldwide Mareva relief. In that case Newbury J said:

"On the question of jurisdiction, then, I regard this Court as having the authority, in an appropriate case, to restrain a party who is properly subject to the jurisdiction of the Court, from transferring or dealing with assets, including assets *ex juris*, where necessary to prevent his frustrating an order or possible future order of this court."[66]

Other territories, where the jurisdiction to grant Mareva relief was accepted, include Ontario[67] and Manitoba.[68]

[60.] *Hunt v BP Exploration Co (Libya) Ltd* (1980) 54 ALJR 205.

[61.] *Balfour Williamson (Australia) Pty Ltd v Douterluingne* [1979] 2 NSWLR 884; *Turner v Sylvester* [1981] 2 NSWLR 295; and *Reily McKay Pty Ltd v McKay* [1982] 1 NSWLR 264. *Cf Ex parte BP Exploration Co (Libya) Ltd; Re Hunt* [1979] 2 NSWLR 406 where Powell J declined jurisdiction, following the decision of Bray CJ in *Pivovaroff v Chernabaeff* [1978] 16 SASR 329.

[62.] (1987) 162 CLR 612.

[63.] (1980) 114 DLR (3d) 35.

[64.] See also *Liberty National Bank & Trust Co v Atkin* (1981) 121 DLR (3d) 160.

[65.] [1994] BCJ No 2322.

[66.] At p 10 of the Lexis transcript. On worldwide Mareva injunctions, see Ch 7, *The Defendant's Assets*, para **[7.21]** *et seq*. Other decisions from British Columbia where the jurisdiction to grant Mareva relief was accepted (if not always exercised) include: *Cussons v Slobbe* Supreme Court of British Columbia, unrep, 9 October 1996 (de Weerdt J) (worldwide Mareva relief granted); *Inayat N Pirani Inc v Global Pacific Capital Corporation* Supreme Court of British Columbia, unrep, 19 January 1996 (relief granted) (Baker J); *Schaefer v Fisher* Supreme Court of British Columbia, unrep, 13 February 1997 (Santanove J) (relief refused on grounds that prerequisites to relief not satisfied); *Dudley Kill & Sons Ltd v Coldstream Products Corporation*, Supreme Court of British Columbia, unrep, 20 August 1997 (Santanove J) (relief refused on grounds that prerequisites to relief not satisfied); and *Cinnamon v McLean* Supreme Court of British Columbia, unrep, 15 December 1997 (McKinnon J) (relief refused on grounds that prerequisites to relief not satisfied). All of the foregoing cases are available through the internet at http://www.courts.govbc.

[67.] *Liberty National Bank & Trust Co v Atkins* (1981) 121 DLR (3d) 160; *Quinn v Marrsta Cession Services Ltd* 133 DLR (sd) 109; and *Chitel v Rothbart* 141 DLR (3d) 268.

[68.] *Aetna Financial Services Ltd v Feigelman* 15 DLR (4th) 161. For other territories, such as Alberta, New Brunswick, Nova Scotia, and Quebec, see Hoyle, *op cit*, p 164.

The Acceptance of the Mareva Jurisdiction in Ireland

[2.16] Mareva injunctions have been granted by the Irish courts since the early 1980s.[69] The most authoritative Irish endorsement of the Mareva jurisdiction is the Supreme Court decision in *Re John Horgan Livestock Ltd; O'Mahony v Horgan*.[70] In the course of the main judgment of the Court, Hamilton CJ, said:

> "The common law, traditionally, expressed the principle that the plaintiff is not entitled to require from the defendant, in advance of judgment, security to guarantee satisfaction of a judgment that the plaintiff may eventually obtain. This position was altered in the United Kingdom by two decisions of the Court of Appeal in 1975, *viz Nippon Yusen Kaisha v Karagerogis* [1975] 1 WLR 1093 and *Mareva Compania Naviera SA v International Bulkcarriers SA* [1980] 1 All ER 213."[71]

The Chief Justice went on to note that such injunctions had come to be known as Mareva injunctions; that a Mareva injunction was an *in personam* order which restrains a defendant "from dealing with assets in which the plaintiff claims no right whatsoever";[72] that a Mareva-plaintiff has no precedence over other creditors with respect to the frozen assets; and that because of the draconian nature of a Mareva injunction certain criteria had been set down which must be established before such an injunction is granted.[73] Although Hamilton CJ clearly quoted with approval a number of English Mareva decisions,[74] he did not expressly accept the Court's jurisdiction to grant such relief. However, his acceptance of the existence of the jurisdiction to grant Mareva relief is implicit by his ruling as to the criteria which must be met before a Court should exercise its discretion to grant such an injunction.[75]

[2.17] Hamilton CJ quoted with approval from the judgment of McWilliam J in *Fleming v Ranks (Ireland) Ltd*[76] where the existence of the jurisdiction to grant a Mareva injunction in Ireland was clearly recognised. In this, one[77] of the first

---

69. See *H v H*, High Court, unrep, 7 April 1982 (O'Hanlon J), noted by Charleton (1982) 4 DULJ (ns) 114 and considered in Ch 4, *A Substantive Cause of Action*, para **[4.49]**.

70. [1995] 2 IR 411.

71. [1995] 2 IR 411 at 417, 418.

72. At 418.

73. See generally, Ch 8, *Applying for a Mareva Injunction*, para **[8.30]** *et seq.*

74. *Third Chandris Shipping Corporation v Unimarine SA* [1979] QB 645; *Z Ltd v A-Z and AA-LL* [1982] 1 QB 558; *Barclay-Johnson v Yuill* [1980] 1 WLR 1259; and *Polly Peck International plc v Nadir (No 2)* [1992] 4 All ER 769.

75. See also ([1995] 2 IR 411 at 422) the comments of O'Flaherty J as to the development of the jurisdiction to grant Mareva relief and the care which should be taken in that regard.

76. [1983] ILRM 541.

77. The first written judgment appears to be the decision of McWilliam J in *Powerscourt Estates v Gallagher and Gallagher* [1984] ILRM 123, which though reported in 1984 was actually handed down on 18 May 1982. See para **[2.18]** *infra*.

written judgments on the availability of Mareva relief in Ireland, McWilliam J had observed that:

> "The jurisdiction to grant such injunctions in England was, prior to 1981, based on provisions similar to those contained in s 28(8) of the Judicature (Ireland) Act 1877. The relevant part of this subsection is as follows: 'an injunction may be granted by an interlocutory order of the court in all cases in which it shall appear to the court to be just or convenient that such order shall be made'.
>
> *I am satisfied that there is jurisdiction to grant such an injunction* and that the cases in which it may be granted are not confined to cases in which a defendant is resident outside the State."[78]

Later, McWilliam J said:

> "I would accept as correct the statement of Sir Robert Megarry, VC at p 1266 of the *Barclay Johnson*[79]case, where he said "I would regard the Lister principle as remaining the rule, and the Mareva doctrine as constituting a limited exception to it". 'The Lister Rule' refers to the case of *Lister & Co v Stubbs* mentioned above, and is that the court will not grant an injunction to restrain a defendant from parting with his assets so that that may be preserved in case the plaintiffs' claim succeeds."[80]

This passage was quoted with approval by Hamilton CJ in *Re John Horgan Livestock Ltd; O'Mahony v Horgan*.[81] In the earlier case of *Powerscourt Estates v Gallagher & Gallagher*[82] McWilliam J had said:

> "Sir Robert Megarry, VC, in the *Barclay-Johnson* case refers to two lines of authority with regard to such injunctions. The older, which he calls the *Lister & Co v Stubbs* [1890] 45 Ch D 1, CA line establishes the general proposition that a plaintiff cannot prevent a defendant from disposing of his assets *pendente lite* merely because he fears that by the time he obtains judgment in his favour the defendant will have no assets against which the judgment can be enforced. The newer, called the Mareva line, establishes that such an injunction may be granted where it is just and reasonable to do so. The Vice-Chancellor appears to discard any distinction between foreigners and citizens as defendants except in so far as either circumstance increases the probability of property being removed from the jurisdiction. Furthermore he says, at p 1266 'The Mareva prohibition against disposition of the assets within the country is a normal ancillary of the prohibition against removing the assets from the country ...'
>
> The progress of the Mareva line of cases seems to lead to the conclusion that the injunction may be granted where it appears to the court that dispositions are

---

[78.] At 546. Italics added.
[79.] [1980] 3 All ER 190.
[80.] At 546, 547.
[81.] [1995] 2 IR 411 at 419.
[82.] [1984] ILRM 123.

likely to be made for the purpose of preventing a plaintiff from recovering the amount of his award, as distinct from conducting the normal business or personal affairs of the defendant."[83]

It is important to distinguish between the actual jurisdiction to grant a Mareva injunction and the conditions attaching to the exercise of the jurisdiction. The foregoing passage goes further than merely acknowledging the existence of the jurisdiction: it prescribes the circumstances in which that jurisdiction should be exercised. Similarly, by detailing the circumstances in which jurisdiction to grant Mareva relief should be exercised, the Supreme Court's decision in *Re John Horgan Livestock Ltd*[84] goes further than merely acknowledging the existence of such jurisdiction. It is clear, therefore, that the Supreme Court has adopted a more pragmatic approach to Mareva relief than say the Supreme Court of South Australia in *Pivovaroff v Chernabaeff*, considered above. By contrast, the Supreme Court has accepted that there is jurisdiction to grant Mareva relief but has ensured that it will only be exercised where specific prerequisites, which are detailed below,[85] are met.

[2.18] In a short concurring judgment, O'Flaherty J recognised the need for and desirability of the Mareva jurisdiction, saying:

> "The absence of any remedy for a creditor against a debtor who was prepared to depart the country or dissipate his assets in defiance of the creditor's rights was a serious defect in our law twenty years or so ago. Practitioners had been very conscious of the injustices that were often perpetrated because no remedy had been developed to meet this situation".[86]

O'Flaherty J went on to observe that at around the same time as the Mareva jurisdiction was first asserted by the Court of Appeal, the same remedy was allowed in the Irish courts by the invocation of s 28(8) of the Supreme Court of Judicature (Ireland) Act 1877, quoted at the outset of this chapter.[87]

An Inherent Jurisdiction to Grant a Mareva Injunction

[2.19] Apart from the statutory jurisdiction (contained in s 28(8) of the Supreme Court of Judicature (Ireland) Act 1877) to grant a Mareva injunction, there is authority for the view that the court possesses an inherent jurisdiction to make any order which it deems necessary to protect, vindicate and safeguard its authority.[88] The basis of this inherent jurisdiction is this: where a plaintiff has

---

[83.] At 126.

[84.] [1995] 2 IR 411.

[85.] See para **[2.31]** *infra*.

[86.] At 421.

[87.] At 421, 422. See para **[2.02]** *supra*.

[88.] See *Riley McKay Pty Ltd v McKay* [1982] 1 NSWLR 264; *Turner v Sylvester* [1981] 2 NSWLR 295; and *Pacific Centre Sdn Bhd v United Engineers (Malaysia) Bhd.*(1984) 2 MLJ 143.

initiated proceedings against a defendant against whom he has a good arguable case and there is evidence that the defendant is likely to take steps to dispose of his assets with the intention of frustrating the plaintiff's future judgment, the Court has a compelling interest in ensuring that its authority is not circumvented or usurped.[89]

[2.20] The clearest judicial exposition of the courts' inherent jurisdiction to make a Mareva order is seen in the decision of the New South Wales Court of Appeal in *Riley McKay Pty Ltd v McKay*.[90] There, after reviewing the divergence of opinion in the Australian states and in New Zealand as to the question of the jurisdiction to grant Mareva relief[91] and the possible basis of and objections to such jurisdiction,[92] the Court of Appeal decided that it had the jurisdiction to grant a Mareva injunction, and that this arose from statute or, alternatively, the Court's inherent powers. The statute in question cited by the Court was s 23 of the New South Wales Supreme Court Act 1970 which provided:

> The Court shall have all jurisdiction which may be necessary for the administration of justice in New South Wales.

Commenting on this provision, the Court said:

> "It may be that there is some difference between this provision and the inherent jurisdiction of the court but we doubt it, and if there is, it would seem to be irrelevant for present purposes. The court exercises from time to time a great many powers which are not the subject of any explicit statutory provision or rule, the exercise being based on the court's inherent powers. As it seems to us, those powers are recognised and exercised because they are necessary for the administration of justice in New South Wales. On this view s 23 confirms the existence of the Court's inherent powers but does not increase them. However the inherent jurisdiction could not exceed what is necessary for the administration of justice, and the jurisdiction conferred by the section would not be less than the inherent jurisdiction."[93]

After identifying the two principal challenges to the existence of the Mareva jurisdiction, the Court rejected both. First, as to the law's reluctance to interfere with a debtor's assets before judgment and the fact that such a jurisdiction had not been propounded before 1975, the Court found that times had changed and

---

[89.] It may even be that this is the only jurisdiction for the making of a post-judgment Mareva injunction: see Ch 4, *A Substantive Cause of Action*, para **[4.28]** *et seq.*

[90.] [1982] 1 NSWLR 264. For comment, see Hodgekiss, 'Mareva Injunctions - Recent Australian Developments', [1983] LQR 7.

[91.] At 268, 269.

[92.] At 269-276.

[93.] [1982] 1 NSWLR 264 at 270.

money can be spirited away far more easily than in times past and, moreover, the Mareva line of cases indicated that the jurisdiction to interfere with a debtor's assets must "be exercised in circumstances which are significantly different from the ordinary creditor/debtor position."[94] Secondly, the Court rejected that the Mareva jurisdiction flew in the face of the legislature's intention, finding that there was nothing to substantiate the view that the legislature intended "to preclude the courts from the remedy in question".[95]

[2.21] On the question of the Court's inherent jurisdiction to grant Mareva relief, the Court in *Riley McKay Pty Ltd v McKay* came to the following conclusions which are worth quoting *in extenso*:

> "We have come to the conclusion that jurisdiction does exist and that it derives from the Supreme Court Act, s 23, or from the Court's inherent power. The basis of jurisdiction is founded on the risk that the defendant will so deal with his assets that he will stultify and render ineffective any judgment given by the court in the plaintiff's action, *and thus impair the jurisdiction of the court and render it impotent properly and effectively to administer justice* in New South Wales. As has appeared, the jurisdiction to grant the injunction is not to be exercised simply to preclude a debtor from dealing with his assets, and in particular to prevent him from using them to pay his debts in the ordinary course of business. It is directed to dispositions which do not fall within this category and which are intended to frustrate, or have the necessary effect of frustrating, the plaintiff in his attempt to seek through the court a remedy for the obligation to which he claims the defendant is subject.
>
> Assuming that the jurisdiction is exercised with due caution, it seems to us that it is necessary for the administration of justice in this State that the court should have power to prevent a defendant who would otherwise have assets to satisfy a judgment from setting the court and its procedures at naught by making sure that its judgment will be a mere *brutum fulmen*. The whole sense and purpose of the inherent powers, as well as the powers which s 23 confers, are to ensure the effective administration of justice. The analysis of the "Mareva" injunction which has occurred during the years of growth show that it is designed to prevent conduct inimical to the administration of justice. The reported decisions show that a "Mareva" injunction will be granted where necessary to ensure that justice is effectively administered ... We conclude accordingly that the Court has jurisdiction."[96]

It is submitted that the sentiment contained in the foregoing passage[97] is very closely mirrored by the finding of the Supreme Court in *Re John Horgan*

---

94. At 272.
95. At 272-276.
96. At 276. Italics added.
97. With the exception, that is, of the Court's acknowledgement that relief may be granted where the *effect* of the disposition is to frustrate the plaintiff's claim. The Irish Supreme Court has made it clear that, in Ireland, the defendant's *intention* is paramount. See Ch 6, *The Risk of Removal or Disposal of Assets*, para **[6.16]** *et seq*.

Livestock Ltd[98] that it is necessary to establish the likelihood that the disposal of a defendant's assets is "with a view to evading his obligation to the plaintiff and to frustrate the anticipated order of the court."[99] Indeed, Lord Donaldson MR in *Polly Peck International plc v Nadir (No 2)*[100] made it clear that the courts would do all in their power to prevent the course of justice from being frustrated and judgments of the courts rendered nugatory.[101]

[2.22] It is thought that the reasoning in *Riley McKay Ltd* would be attractive to the courts in Ireland[102] which have been consistent in diligently guarding their independence, authority and integrity. In *People (DPP) v Walsh and Conneely*,[103] for example, the Supreme Court held that the High Court had jurisdiction to try persons summarily, without a jury, on charges of contempt involving the "scandalising of the court".[104] In that case O'Higgins CJ said:

> "... under the Constitution it is the solemn duty of judges to see that justice is administered in the Courts. Surely the imposition of this duty carries with it both the power and the corresponding duty to act in protection of justice, if its fair or effective administration is endangered or threatened. In my view, the judicial power of government (which, in accordance with Article 6[105] of the Constitution, is exercisable only by or on the authority of the Courts as the organ of State established by the Constitution for that purpose) is sufficiently

---

98. [1995] 2 IR 411.
99. At 419. See also the decision of Rogers J in *Turner v Sylvester* [1981] 2 NSWLR 295 at 304 where, accepting the Court's inherent jurisdiction to grant Mareva relief, he said: "whilst the nature of the abuse apprehended on the part of the defendant is of an unusual kind, the court should be astute in ensuring that its judgement is not stultified by the deliberate acts of a defendant. I am of the view that Mareva injunctions may be properly supported by this head of jurisdiction".
100. [1992] 4 All ER 769.
101. At 785 he said: "So far as it lies in their power, the Courts will not permit the course of justice to be frustrated by a defendant taking action, the purpose of which is to render nugatory or less effective any judgment or order which the plaintiff may thereafter obtain".
102. See Capper, *Mareva Injunctions*, (1988) SLS/Sweet & Maxwell, para 2.07 where he surmises that whilst not mentioned in any English decision, "it is most probable that the courts in this country have been influenced by a desire to prevent their process being abused in this way". This is indeed borne out by the statement to that effect by Lord Donaldson MR in *Polly Peck International plc v Nadir (No 2)* [1992] 4 All ER 769 at 785, last quoted.
103. [1981] IR 412. See also *Buckley v Attorney General* [1950] IR 67.
104. In that case *The Irish Times* published an article which attributed a statement to the respondents, who were members of an association called the Association for Legal Justice, to the effect that the Special Criminal Court had "so abused the rules of evidence as to make the court akin to a sentencing tribunal".
105. Article 6.1 of the Constitution provides: "All powers of government, legislative, executive and judicial, derive, under God, from the people, whose right it is to designate the rulers of the State and, in final appeal, to decide all questions of national policy, according to the requirements of the common good"; Article 6.2 provides: "These powers of government are exercisable only by or on the authority of the organs of State established by the Constitution."

extensive to authorise the Courts to take any action that is necessary for the due administration of justice."[106]

The author submits that, upon it being shown that a defendant is intent upon frustrating the administration of justice by putting his assets beyond its reach, and to say "Oh dear, Oh dear, how very awkward there is nothing we can do,"[107] would be to fail to defend both a plaintiff's rights *and* those of the courts charged, by Article 38 of the Constitution of Ireland, with the administration of justice.[108]

[2.23] Not all commentators have welcomed the "inherent jurisdiction" approach. Most critical have been Meagher, Gummow and Lehane, in *Equity - Doctrines and Remedies*.[109] On the question of an "inherent jurisdiction", they say that it could not be submitted that disposing of one's assets could be:

> "... an interference with the administration of justice: it permits justice to be administered, but attempts to evade the effect of its administration. Indeed, if such a disposition of assets were an interference with the administration of justice it would constitute a contempt of Court, since that is the definition of contempt; but no judge, however avid to amplify his jurisdiction, has ever suggested that such conduct is contemptuous."[110]

It is submitted that the distinction between interfering with the administration of justice and evading its effects is contrived and unsustainable. The direct effect of disposing of one's assets with the intention of frustrating a future judgment or order of the Court is to stultify the administration of justice. Where a judgment is obtained which is incapable of being enforced, the administration of justice is rendered a waste of time as the plaintiff is afforded no remedy for the wrong which the Court has found to have been perpetrated against him. Whether such conduct be categorised as being either direct or indirect, it is submitted that it clearly interferes with the administration of justice. In such cases, the appropriate means to prevent an interference with the administration of justice is the Mareva injunction.

The Constitutionality of the Mareva Jurisdiction

[2.24] It is trite to say that a Mareva injunction interferes with a defendant's property rights; nevertheless, this must be the starting point in any review of the

---

[106.] [1981] IR 412 at 426.

[107.] *Per* Harman J in *Re Oriental Credit Ltd* [1988] 1 All ER 892 at 895 in the context of the need to make a Bayer injunction to restrain the respondent from leaving the jurisdiction. See generally, Ch 11, *Restraining Defendants from Leaving the State*.

[108.] See para **[2.24]** *infra* where the constitutionality of the Mareva injunction is further considered.

[109.] (3rd ed, 1993) Butterworths, pp 613, 614; para [2190].

[110.] *Ibid*.

constitutionality of the Mareva jurisdiction. The question is this: is such interference unconstitutional or is it a justifiable interference with property rights? The Constitution of Ireland contains two separate references to property rights: Article 43 and Article 40.3.2°. Both Articles must be read in conjunction so as to give full effect to the provisions of each.[111] Article 43 provides:

> 1.1 The State acknowledges that man, in virtue of his rational being, has the natural right, antecedent to positive law, to the private ownership of external goods.
>
> 2° The State accordingly guarantees to pass no law attempting to abolish the right of private ownership or the general right to transfer, bequeath, and inherit property.
>
> 2.1 The State recognises, however, that the exercise of the rights mentioned in the foregoing provisions of this Article ought, in civil society, be regulated by the principles of social justice.

In addition, Article 40.3.1° provides:

> The State guarantees in its laws to respect, and, as far as practicable, by its laws to defend and vindicate the personal rights of the citizen.

Can it then be said that Mareva injunctions, *per se*, breach defendants' constitutional property rights? It is submitted that the answer is a definite "no" and that the Mareva injunction is, rather, a permissible delimitation of a defendant's property rights in the interests of the common good, as permitted by Article 43.

[2.25] A Mareva injunction involves the rights of three parties: a plaintiff's right to have access to the courts to redress a wrong done to him and in some cases his right to private property, a defendant's right to private property and the court's right to uphold its own authority and the administration of justice.[112] It always falls to the court to decide whether or not to grant a Mareva injunction. In declining or acceding to an application for a Mareva injunction, the court must balance competing constitutional rights. Freezing a defendant's assets could in certain circumstances be an unjust attack on his property rights; yet for a plaintiff to have suffered loss and to be refused the relief required to safeguard his rights may be a failure to defend those rights. For a court not to ensure that a defendant does not thwart the effective administration of justice would be anathema to the Constitution which gives life to the courts.

[2.26] The only reported case in which the constitutionality of the Mareva jurisdiction was specifically mentioned was *Countyglen plc v Carway*, the facts

---

[111.] See *Dreher v Irish Land Commission and the Attorney General* [1984] ILRM 94 and *O'Callaghan v Commissioners of Public Works* [1985] ILRM 364.

[112.] Article 34 of the Constitution of Ireland.

of which are considered below.[113] There, Murphy J observed that counsel on behalf of the respondents had asserted that "a Mareva injunction must of necessity impinge upon a defendant's constitutional rights in relation to private property and his or her right to earn his livelihood."[114] The judge went on to say, however, that that argument:

> "... merely relates to the existence of the rights and the likelihood of some measure of inconvenience. Whether that inconvenience has any degree of significance cannot be assessed without the assistance of the respondents. It may be that the assets of the respondents in the State far exceed the amount which the applicant seeks to freeze. At the other end of the scale the respondents may have no assets available to them within the jurisdiction. In either case, the actual hardship or inconvenience would be little or none. If the respondents disclose the existence of some asset within the jurisdiction of this court, then it might be anticipated in accordance with the guidelines indicated in the English cases and the practice adopted in this jurisdiction that *the Mareva injunction, if granted, would be fine-tuned to ensure that the interest of the applicant would be protected without any unnecessary hardship to the respondents.*"[115]

Whilst the Mareva jurisdiction has the *potential* to be an unjust attack on a defendant's property rights it can, in other circumstances, amount to a vindication of a plaintiff's property rights. There is no more appropriate a forum than the courts nor better decision makers than the judiciary to decide where the proper balance lies in any given case. As Murphy J acknowledged in *Countyglen* it is always open to the courts to fine-tune the Order ie it can use a *local*, as distinct from a *general*, anaesthetic when *freezing* a defendant's assets so as to minimise any unnecessarily harsh effects. The employment of the "maximum sum", "ordinary living expenses", "ordinary business expenses" and "legal expenses" provisos[116] are the means used to mitigate the unacceptable effects of a Mareva injunction and their almost universal usage is indicative of the judiciary's concern that Mareva injunctions are tailored to meet only the necessities of the case.

[2.27] The constitutionality of two statutory provisions which provide for the freezing of a defendant's assets have been considered in two cases.[117] In the first

---

[113.] [1995] 1 IR 208. See Ch 5, *A Good Arguable Case*, para **[5.22]**.

[114.] At 217.

[115.] At 217, 218. Italics added.

[116.] See Ch 9, *The Mareva Order and Its Effects*, para **[9.12]** *et seq.*

[117.] See Casey, *Constitutional Law in Ireland*, (2nd ed, 1993) Sweet & Maxwell, p 545, written before the Proceeds of Crime Act 1996 or Criminal Justice Act 1994 were passed where the view is taken that "... the freezing by court order of assets pending trial on relevant criminal charges would arguably be valid."

case, *Clancy and McCarthy v Ireland & the Attorney General*[118] certain provisions of the Offences Against the State (Amendment) Act 1985 ("the 1985 Act") were under review. Section 2(1) of the 1985 Act provides:

> On production to any bank of a document purporting to be signed by the Minister[119] and bearing the seal of the Minister and stating -
>
> (i) that, in the opinion of the Minister, moneys described in the document and held by the bank would, but for the operation of section 22 of the Principal Act,[120] be the property of an unlawful organisation and that those moneys stand forfeited to and vested in the Minister by virtue of the said section 22, and
>
> (ii) that the Minister requires the bank to pay those moneys, or so much of them as are held by the bank at the time of the production to it of the document, into the High Court on a specified day or not later than a specified day and, in the meantime, to refrain from doing any act or making any omission inconsistent with that requirement and to notify as soon as may be thereafter the person or persons in whose name or names the moneys are held by the bank of their payment into that Court,
>
> the bank shall comply with the requirement.

The facts in the *Clancy* case were that the Minister for Justice ordered the Bank of Ireland to pay over £1.75 million, standing to the credit of the plaintiffs' account, into the High Court. The plaintiffs sought the return of the money claiming that they had been wrongly and unconstitutionally deprived of their ownership of the money. In the course of his judgment, Barrington J said:

> "The 1985 Act admittedly provides for the freezing of a bank account and the payment of the funds in it into the High Court without notice to the account holder but it does not confiscate his property or deprive him of a fair hearing. He is entitled to claim the funds in the High Court and he is entitled to a fair hearing there though, admittedly, the onus of proof is on him to establish his title. In the event of a mistake having been made there is provision for the payment of compensation."[121]

Barrington J held that the 1985 Act was presumed to be constitutional and that its provisions amounted to a permissible delimitation of property rights in the interests of the common good.[122]

[118.] [1989] ILRM 670. For a commentary see de Burca, 'Constitutional Law - Seizure of Funds and Fair Procedures', [1989] DULJ 132.

[119.] Defined by s 1(1) of the 1985 Act as the Minister for Justice.

[120.] Defined by s 1(1) of the 1985 Act as the Offences Against the State Act 1939.

[121.] [1989] ILRM 670 at 676.

[122.] See also *Cox v Ireland* [1992] 2 IR 503 where the constitutionality of s 34 of the Offences Against the State Act 1939 was considered.

[2.28] Like the 1985 Act, a Mareva injunction does not involve the confiscation of property; it confers no security on the Mareva-plaintiff; the grant of a Mareva injunction does not deprive a person of a fair hearing and Mareva injunctions invariably make provision for compensation, in the form of the plaintiff's undertaking as to damages which may be called upon by the Court should it transpire that the injunction ought not to have been granted.[123] Unlike the 1985 Act, a Mareva injunction does not act *in rem*, against a defendant's assets, but only operates against his person and a defendant is not obliged to pay his assets into Court. In both respects, a Mareva injunction is a far lesser interference with a civil defendant's property rights than an order made pursuant to the 1985 Act.

[2.29] In the second case to consider the constitutionality of statutory asset-freezing provisions, *Gilligan v Criminal Assets Bureau*,[124] it was the constitutionality of the Proceeds of Crime Act 1996 which came under scrutiny by McGuinness J.[125] In that case, the defendant contended, *inter alia*, that in enacting the Proceeds of Crime Act 1996 ("the 1996 Act") the State had failed to protect his property rights from unjust attack and in this regard relied upon Articles 40.3.2° and 43 of the Constitution. In dismissing the constitutional challenge McGuinness J said, in relation to this ground, that:

> "It appears to me that the State has a legitimate interest in the forfeiture of the proceeds of crime. The structure of the Act, in a similar way to ordinary civil injunction proceedings, allows for the temporary freezing of assets and for various actions to be taken on an interlocutory basis. The respondent at any time may intervene to show good title to the assets. If he does so not only must they be returned, but the Court may order the State to pay compensation to him. It is also provided at s 3 that the Court shall not make an interlocutory order 'if it is satisfied that there would be a serious risk of injustice'...
>
> While the provisions of the Act may, indeed, affect the property rights of a respondent it does not appear to this Court that they constitute an 'unjust attack' under Article 40.3.2°, given the fact that the State must in the first place show to the satisfaction of the Court that the property in question is the proceeds of crime and that thus, prima facie, the respondent has no good title to it, and also given the balancing provisions built into ss 3 and 4 [of the Proceeds of Crime Act 1996].
>
> The Court would also accept that the exigencies of the common good would certainly include measures designed to prevent the accumulation and use of assets which directly or indirectly derive from criminal activities. The right to private ownership cannot hold a place so high in the hierarchy of rights that it protects the position of assets illegally acquired and held."[126]

[123.] See Ch 8, *Applying for a Mareva Injunction*, para **[8.58]** *et seq.*
[124.] High Court, unrep, 26 June 1997 (McGuinness J).
[125.] See generally, Ch 3, *Statutory Jurisdictions to Freeze Assets*, para **[3.32]** *et seq.*
[126.] At p 71 of the transcript.

In the case of a Mareva injunction the assets which a defendant may be restrained from dealing with will be his own assets. The rationale for restraining the dealing in assets formulated by McGuinness J - ie because they derive from the proceeds of crime - is substituted, in the case of a Mareva injunction, with the need to show that a defendant's intention in removing or disposing of his assets is with a view to frustrating the plaintiff's claim and the Court's anticipated order. Again, there are parallels between freezing orders under the 1996 Act and Mareva injunctions: first, "compensation" under the 1996 Act is paralleled by the ability to compensate a Mareva-defendant by reliance upon a Mareva-plaintiff's undertaking in damages; secondly, the "risk of serious injustice" condition for making an order under the 1996 Act may be seen as paralleled by the need to establish to the court's satisfaction that the onerous pre-conditions to the grant of Mareva relief exist.[127]

[2.30] In summary, it is submitted that for the various reasons set out above, there can be no doubt but that the Mareva jurisdiction, *per se*, is constitutional. Indeed, in *Gilligan v Criminal Assets Bureau*,[128] McGuinness J said:

"The procedure provided for by ss 2 and 3 of the 1996 Act is very similar in many respects to the familiar power of the Courts in other civil proceedings to grant on an *ex parte* basis interim Freezing Orders, followed by interlocutory hearings on affidavit and subsequently final adjudications as to respective legal rights and liabilities in regard to property. It can often happen that such Freezing Orders are sought in circumstances where the allegations made against defendants involve fraud or other conduct which would be in breach of the criminal law. *It has never been seriously suggested that such procedures are unconstitutional*".[129]

The Prerequisites to Exercising the Mareva Jurisdiction

[2.31] The jurisdiction to grant a Mareva injunction in Ireland has been clearly established. As has been alluded to above,[130] the most vexed question is when will a Court see fit to *exercise* the Mareva jurisdiction, since it is not in every application for a Mareva injunction that the criteria for its grant will be found by a Court to exist. The criteria which must be satisfied before a Court will accede to an application for a Mareva injunction have been set out in the previous chapter.[131]

---

[127] See Ch 1, *The Mareva Injunction in Context*, para **[1.15]**.
[128] High Court, unrep, 26 June 1997 (McGuinness J).
[129] At p 58 of the transcript. Italics added.
[130] See para **[2.18]** *supra*.
[131] See Ch 1, *The Mareva Injunction in Context*, para **[1.15]**.

[B] JURISDICTION TO GRANT MAREVA RELIEF WHERE THERE IS NO DISCERNIBLE CAUSE OF ACTION

[2.32] One of the essential proofs[132] for the grant of a Mareva injunction is that a plaintiff has a substantive right which is capable of being enforced (eg typically a cause of action)[133] against a defendant. This is a basic prerequisite to the foundation of the jurisdiction to grant a Mareva injunction since every injunction is always ancillary to some substantive right and cannot in and of itself be a substantive cause of action. Very often government agencies such as the police or other public officials will not have a substantive cause of action in civil law against persons, suspected of criminal activity, whose assets they wish to freeze.[134] Whilst the legislatures in both the United Kingdom[135] and Ireland[136] have now provided a remedy in most such cases by passing specific legislation which permits application to be made to the High Court to have a defendant's assets frozen, it remains useful to consider how the courts dealt with this issue prior to the enactment of such legislation. After all, it is conceivable that where specific statutory jurisdictions have not envisaged particular scenarios, the courts may again be asked to grant Mareva relief.

[2.33] A number of cases[137] have considered the difficulties associated with public officials, such as Chief Constables in the United Kingdom, applying to court for injunctive relief without having a substantive civil cause of action against a defendant.[138] Where the courts did accept that there was jurisdiction to

---

[132.] See Ch 8, *Applying for a Mareva Injunction*, para **[8.45]** *et seq.*

[133.] *Caudron v Air Zaire* [1986] ILRM 10. See, generally, Ch 4, *A Substantive Cause of Action*.

[134.] Sometimes the State will have a civil cause of action against a person allegedly involved in criminal activity. In the *Criminal Assets Bureau v H*, *The Irish Times*, 30 January 1997 (Costello P) the High Court granted a Mareva injunction restraining the defendant from reducing his assets in Ireland below £475,000 or from disposing of two properties in Co Clare. In this case the defendant had left Ireland "hurriedly" on 20 July 1993 before the arrest of his yacht, *The Brime*, on which cannabis resin worth £20 m was found. The defendant was subsequently arrested in the UK and was imprisoned in Bristol. The Mareva injunction was subsequently extended: *The Irish Times*, 11 February 1997 (Costello P). The cause of action in that case, which permitted the granting of Mareva relief, was an income tax demand which the defendant had failed to pay. See also *Criminal Assets Bureau v E*, *The Irish Times*, 20 December 1997 where a Mareva injunction was obtained on foot of income tax assessments against a man suspected of being involved in the Brinks-Allied robbery in Dublin in 1995.

[135.] See the English Drug Trafficking Offences Act 1986 and the Criminal Justice Act 1988. See generally Ch 3, *Statutory Jurisdictions to Freeze Assets*.

[136.] See the Offences Against the State (Amendment) Act 1985, para **[2.27]** *supra*, and the Criminal Justice Act 1994 and the Proceeds of Crime Act 1996 which are considered in Ch 3, *Statutory Jurisdictions to Freeze Assets*.

[137.] See, for example, *Chief Constable of Kent v V* [1983] 1 QB 34; *West Mercia Constabulary v Wagener* [1982] 1 WLR 127; *Chief Constable of Hampshire v A Ltd* (1984) 79 Cr App R 30 CA; *Chief Constable of Leicestershire v M* [1989] 1 WLR 20.

[138.] See Capper, *Mareva Injunctions*, (1988) SLS/ Sweet & Maxwell, p 108.

grant Mareva relief in these circumstances, they usually[139] did so on either of three grounds: (1) by finding that the public official had a "sufficient interest" to obtain the injunction;[140] (2) by finding that the public official had a "legal or equitable right";[141] or (3) by finding that the public official was entitled to Mareva relief on the basis of a "statutory" cause of action. It is undoubtedly the case that some of the applications for Mareva relief which are next considered were misguided. Nobody can have any legitimate interest in freezing another person's assets, by means of a Mareva injunction, for the sake of it - it is intrinsic in any grant of Mareva relief that the sole purpose is to preserve a defendant's assets so as to permit a plaintiff to satisfy a future judgment. In the absence of the possibility of there being a future judgment or, perhaps, future fine, there can be no justification for restraining a person from dealing with his own assets.

The "Sufficient Interest" Basis for Jurisdiction

[2.34] The "sufficient interest" basis for the jurisdiction to grant Mareva relief to public officials was promulgated by Lord Denning MR in *Chief Constable of Kent v V.*[142] Whilst accepting that the Chief Constable had no substantive civil cause of action and that such was required for an injunction to be granted under s 45(1) of the English Supreme Court of Judicature (Consolidation) Act 1925, Lord Denning MR held that the wording of its replacement, s 37(1) of the English Supreme Court Act 1981,[143] changed this and allowed the court to grant an interlocutory injunction even where there was no cause of action. He went on to find that all that was required was that the Chief Constable show that he had a "sufficient interest" to apply for the injunction and that it was just and convenient that an injunction be granted. This reasoning could not, clearly, be applied in Ireland. It is very much doubted that this reasoning would, today, be followed in the UK.[144]

---

139. In *West Mercia Constabulary v Wagener* [1982] 1 WLR 127 Forbes J held that there was jurisdiction to grant Mareva relief under O 29 r 2(1) of the English Rules of the Supreme Courts 1965 but this was emphatically rejected by the Court of Appeal in *Chief Constable of Kent v V* [1983] 1 QB on the grounds that the power to order the detention or preservation of property was ancillary to the plaintiff having a substantive cause of action.

140. *Chief Constable of Kent v V* [1983] 1 QB 34 *per* Lord Denning MR.

141. *Ibid per* Lord Donaldson LJ.

142. [1983] 1 QB 34.

143. Section 37(1) provides: "The High Court may by order (whether interlocutory or final) grant an injunction or appoint a receiver in all cases in which it appears to the court to be just or convenient to do so."

144. Lord Justice Donaldson and Lord Justice Slade in *Chief Constable of Kent v V* and a majority of the Court of Appeal in *Chief Constable of Hampshire v A* [1985] 1 QB 132 did not accept Lord Denning MR's conclusions.

A "Legal or Equitable Right"

[2.35] It is thought that the only reasonable basis for granting a Mareva injunction is where it is established that there is a "legal or equitable right" which is capable of being protected by an injunction. The existence of such a right is a clear requirement before s 28(8) of the Supreme Court of Judicature (Ireland) Act 1877 can be invoked to grant any injunction. In *Chief Constable of Kent v V*[145] Lord Donaldson MR accepted that it was necessary for a plaintiff to have a legal or equitable right but he went on to grant the relief sought after finding that, there, the Chief Constable had a common law right to detain money in a bank account where he could show that it had been obtained in breach of the criminal law.[146] In that case it had been alleged that the defendant had fraudulently written cheques from an old lady's cheque book and that he had paid the proceeds into his own bank accounts.

[2.36] This case was distinguished, however, by Hoffmann J in *Chief Constable of Leicestershire v M*.[147] There the defendant had been charged but not tried with the offence of obtaining mortgage advances by deception. It was alleged that he had used the advances to buy a number of houses which were in the process of being resold at a considerable profit. The Chief Constable sought an injunction to restrain the defendant from dissipating the profits from the sales so as to reduce the amount of money available to satisfy a contemplated substantial fine; the lenders involved would be repaid, otherwise, and so were not interested in injunctive relief. In the course of his judgment Hoffmann J distinguished the *Chief Constable of Kent* case on the grounds that there the money in question could be "traced" to the defendant's bank account whereas in the present case the money was not money "obtained from another in breach of the criminal law but profits which he would not have been able to make except by the use of the money so obtained".[148] In so holding Hoffmann J accepted that there was jurisdiction to "freeze" money where it could be directly traced from a breach of the criminal laws; it being a prerequisite that a form of proprietary right to the money be shown. This, of course, would not be an exercise of the Mareva jurisdiction which does not require the plaintiff to establish a proprietary right in the assets sought to be affected by the injunction and in these circumstances one cannot truly regard the *Chief Constable of Kent* case as an example of the exercise of the Mareva jurisdiction.

[145.] [1983] 1 QB 34.
[146.] At 47.
[147.] [1989] 1 WLR 20.
[148.] At 23.

A Statutory Cause of Action

[2.37] In *Securities and Investment Board v Pantell SA*,[149] the facts of which are detailed below,[150] Sir Nicolas Browne-Wilkinson V-C held that the court could grant a Mareva injunction as relief ancillary to a so-called "statutory" cause of action and in the course of his judgment distinguished his finding from that of Hoffmann J in *Chief Constable of Leicestershire v M*:

> "In this case the SIB itself has no beneficial interest in the moneys nor, apart from the statute, any cause of action against [the defendants]. But in my judgment the statutory right of action for the benefit of investors conferred on the SIB by s 6[151] is as much a right of action as any normal right of action in common law. It follows that in my judgment the SIB is as much entitled to apply for protection by way of Mareva relief on behalf of the investors adversely affected by breach of the Act as would an ordinary private individual be entitled in an ordinary action.
>
> Since granting the order yesterday I have considered whether my decision was inconsistent with a recent decision of Hoffmann J in *Chief Constable of Leicestershire v M* [1988] 3 All ER 1015, [1989] 1 WLR 20. In that case the judge refused interim relief by way of a Mareva injunction to the chief constable, who was seeking to restrain the defendant, a person facing a criminal trial for fraud, from disposing of property so as to ensure that there would be property available out of which a fine, if any, imposed by the criminal court could be paid. In that case the moneys in question were not those in which any person defrauded had a legal interest. There was therefore no traceable interest in any private individual. Nor in that case was there any statutory cause of action such as that conferred on the SIB by s 6 of the Act. In my judgment that is the feature which distinguishes the two cases. Parliament, by giving the Secretary of State (that is to say the SIB) a statutory cause of action, has invested the Secretary of State and the SIB with the necessary locus standi to apply for relief. In my judgment the court has the incidental powers, including the power to grant Mareva relief, necessary to prevent such statutory right of action being rendered abortive by dissipation of assets."[152]

---

[149] [1989] 2 All ER 673.

[150] See Ch 4, *A Substantive Cause of Action*, para **[4.46]**.

[151] Section 6 of the UK Financial Services Act 1986 provided, *inter alia*, that: "(2) If, on the application of the Secretary of State, the court is satisfied that a person has entered into any transaction in contravention of section 3 above the court may order that person and any other person who appears to the court to have been knowingly concerned in the contravention to take such steps as the court may direct for restoring the parties to the position in which they were before the transaction was entered into ... (4)The court may under this subsection order the person concerned to pay into court, or appoint a receiver to recover from him, such sum as appears to the court to be just ... (5) The court may under this subsection order the person concerned to pay to the applicant such sum as appears to the court to be just ...".

[152] *Ibid* at 677e-g.

In *R v Consolidated Fastfrate Transport Inc*[153] the Ontario Court of Appeal accepted that there was jurisdiction to grant a Mareva injunction in aid of criminal proceedings to freeze a defendant's assets in anticipation of a criminal conviction and fine although, on the facts of that case, it declined to exercise its jurisdiction. In the judgment of Galligan JA, it was well established that the Attorney General, as protector of the public rights and public interest, may obtain an injunction to prevent a breach of the criminal law[154] and he reasoned that:

"Once it is accepted, as I think it must, that the superior courts have jurisdiction to issue injunctions in support of, or to aid or assist the criminal law, I am unable to discern any reason why a court would have jurisdiction to restrain a person from carrying out a particular activity, but would not have the power to restrain it from disposing of its assets."[155]

While he acknowledged that there is strong English authority for the proposition that in the absence of specific statutory authority the courts do not have the power to deprive an accused person of his property pending the outcome of criminal proceedings[156] he did not think that it ought to be followed in Ontario.[157] He concluded that he was unable to accept that, if there was jurisdiction to grant injunctions in aid of the criminal law, such jurisdiction would not extend to granting a Mareva injunction *in an appropriate case* and

---

[153.] (1995) 125 DLR (4th) 1. See Epp, 'Freezing Funds for Fines and Mareva Injunctions', [1997] JBL 72.

[154.] Citing *Stoke-on-Trent City Council v B & Q (Retail) Ltd* [1984] 1 AC 754. As to injunctions in aid of public and statutory rights in Ireland, see Keane, *Equity and the Law of Trusts in the Republic of Ireland*, (1988) Butterworths, paras 15.17-15.21 and Delany, *Equity and the Law of Trusts in Ireland*, (1996) Roundhall Sweet & Maxwell, pp 413-415. The right of Attorneys General to apply for injunctions enforcing public policy was recently restated by the Court of Appeal in *Attorney General v Blake (Jonathan Cape Ltd, third party)* [1998] 1 All ER 833. There, Lord Woolf MR said (at 849): "In our judgment, the jurisdiction of the courts, on an application made by the Attorney General, is not limited, as Lord Lester submitted, to granting an injunction restraining the commission or repeated commission of a criminal offence, If, as here, a criminal offence has already been committed, the jurisdiction extends to enforcing public policy with respect to the consequences of the commission of that crime, *eg* restraining receipt by the criminal or a further benefit as a result of or in connection with that crime ... It is a case of the civil court providing, in furtherance of a recognised head of public policy, support in upholding the criminal law in an exceptional situation." In that case the defendant, a former member of Britain's secret intelligence service, who had spied for the former USSR, was restrained from receiving any further royalties from the publication of a book in which recounted his exploits.

[155.] (1995) 125 DLR (4th) 1 at 8.

[156.] Citing in *Malone v Metropolitan Police Commissioner* [1980] QB 49 and *Chief Constable of Leicestershire v M* [1989] 1 WLR 20.

[157.] Citing *Ontario (Attorney General) v Stranges* (1984) 12 CCC (3d) 455; 9 DLR (4th) 629; affirmed 13 CCC (3d) 575; 12 DLR (4th) 638.

that "exceptional circumstances" should exist. On the facts of that case, however, he held that such "exceptional circumstances" did not exist[158] and he allowed the appeal and held that the Mareva injunction ought not to have been granted in that case.

[2.38] Although every application for Mareva relief ancillary to a statutory cause of action will turn on the wording of the individual statutory provision in question, it is by no means clear that this basis for finding a plaintiff to have a substantive cause of action will be followed. Indeed in *Department of Social Security v Butler*[159] the Court of Appeal held that the English High Court has no ancillary power to grant a Mareva injunction where it has no substantive powers to enforce the statutory right in question. Although in at least one successful Irish High Court application for Mareva relief, a statutory cause of action was pleaded in the alternative,[160] it is thought that the circumstances in which the High Court would grant Mareva relief solely based on a statutory cause of action may be limited and strictly confined to where a statutory right entitles a plaintiff to seek an award of money (whether in the form of a judgment or a fine) from a defendant.[161]

Conclusion

[2.39] It is against this background that the legislatures in both Ireland and the UK have considered it necessary to pass specific legislation to provide the courts with the jurisdiction to grant Mareva-type orders where public officials do not have a substantive cause of action against the persons whose assets are sought to be frozen. The foregoing cases may still, however, be of relevance where the circumstances of future cases do not fall within the statutory jurisdictions which are considered in the chapter which next follows. It is thought, however, that the development of the Mareva jurisdiction in such cases will be limited. As Hoffmann J said in *Chief Constable of Leicestershire v M*:

---

158. Weiler JA concurred, albeit cautiously, that there was jurisdiction to grant a Mareva injunction in aid of the criminal law but found that on the facts such jurisdiction ought not to have been exercised. He said (at 30): "The injunction sought is a very grave interference with property rights. In granting a Mareva injunction, McCombs J [the trial judge] went beyond the recognised types of situations in which injunctions have been granted to the Attorney General in the public interest or to enforce a right. The exercise of judicial restraint ought to have been considered and jurisdiction ought to have been declined. *I cannot say, however, that McCombs J did not have jurisdiction to make the order in question*". (Italics added).

159. [1995] 4 All ER 193.

160. *The Minister of Social Welfare v M, The Irish Times,* 21 and 22 February 1991. For background to the application, see *The Irish Times* 13 February 1991. See generally, Ch 4, *A Substantive Cause of Action*, para **[4.44]** *ante.*

161. See, for example, *H v H*, High Court, unrep, 7 April 1982 (O'Hanlon J) where a Mareva injunction was granted as relief ancillary to the statutory right of a spouse to maintenance.

"... the decision of the Court of Appeal in *Malone v Metropolitan Police Commissioner* [1980] QB 49 contains powerful arguments against the extension on grounds of public policy of the common law powers of the court to interfere with the property of persons who have not yet been convicted of criminal offences. Those arguments have since been reinforced by the enactment of the sections in the Drug Trafficking Offences Act 1986 which make elaborate provision for enabling courts to restrain dispositions of assets suspected of being derived from dealings in drugs and the even more recent enactment of similar provisions applicable to all indictable offences in the Criminal Justice Act 1988 ... The recent and detailed interventions of parliament in this field suggest that the courts should not indulge in parallel creativity by the extension of general common law provisions".[162]

It has been recognised that the way forward in freezing the assets of suspected criminals is not by bastardising the Mareva jurisdiction, but by enacting specific legislation, permitting the police in prescribed circumstances, to apply for an order to freeze assets. The next chapter considers some of the "Mareva-type" statutory powers to freeze assets which have been enacted by the legislature in Ireland.

[162.] [1989] 1 WLR 20 at 23F-H.

Chapter 3

Statutory Jurisdictions to Freeze Assets

[3.01] In addition to the equitable jurisdiction to grant a Mareva injunction, a number of statutes, many of quite recent origin, have given the Court express statutory power to grant Mareva-type orders, the effect of which are to freeze a defendant-respondent's assets. Although the Irish legislature has not, as yet, expressly provided for a statutory Mareva jurisdiction in civil matters generally, it is interesting to note that all of the statutory enactments considered here which permit a defendant's assets to be frozen are closely modelled on the Mareva injunction. In this section the following statutes which facilitate the freezing of assets are considered:

- [A] Freezing Orders in Family Law Legislation;
- [B] Restraint Orders under the Criminal Justice Act 1994;
- [C] Interim & Interlocutory Orders under the Proceeds of Crime Act 1996;
- [D] Section 908(4) of the Taxes Consolidation Act 1997.

Although there are other isolated statutory provisions which facilitate the freezing of assets, the foregoing are the most important and frequently invoked statutory jurisdictions.[1] The first statutory provisions to facilitate the freezing of assets are concerned with civil law but confined to cases where the cause of action is rooted in family law. Both the Criminal Justice Act 1994 and the Proceeds of Crime Act 1996 facilitate the freezing of criminals' or alleged criminals' assets and were enacted because of the problems, considered in Chapter 2, where an applicant for Mareva relief does not have a substantive civil cause of action. Section 908(4) of the Taxes Consolidation Act 1997 (which replaces s 18(4) of the Finance Act 1983) provides express statutory authority to freeze a taxpayer's assets in certain specified circumstances at the behest of the Revenue Commissioners.

[A] FREEZING ORDERS IN FAMILY LAW LEGISLATION

[3.02] Family law is ripe for applications where an applicant spouse has grounds for believing that the other spouse, who may be ordered to pay to the applicant

---

[1.] See, for example, s 2(1) of the Offences Against the State (Amendment) Act 1985, considered in Ch 2, *The Jurisdiction to Grant Mareva Relief*, para **[2.27]**.

spouse, maintenance, alimony or other debts, is about to dissipate his or her assets or otherwise remove them from the jurisdiction. Whilst an ordinary Mareva injunction is available in family law cases,[2] the vast majority of applications brought by one spouse to have the assets of another spouse frozen will now be brought pursuant to either s 35(2) of the Family Law Act 1995 ("the 1995 Act") or s 37(2) of the Family Law (Divorce) Act 1996 ("the 1996 Act").[3] Application may be brought under these sections where the applicant spouse seeks relief in judicial separation or divorce proceedings, respectively.

Section 35(2) of the Family Law Act 1995

[3.03] Section 35(2) of the 1995 Act provides:

> (a) The court, on the application of a person ("the applicant") who -
>
> > (i) has instituted proceedings that have not been determined for the grant of relief,
> >
> > (ii) has been granted leave under section 23(3) to institute such proceedings, or
> >
> > (iii) intends to apply for such leave upon the completion of one year's ordinary residence in the State -
>
> may -
>
> > (I) if it is satisfied that the other spouse concerned or any other person, with the intention of defeating the claim for relief, proposes to make any disposition of or transfer out of the jurisdiction or otherwise deal with any property, make such order as it thinks fit for the purpose of restraining that other spouse or other person from so doing or otherwise for protecting the claim ...[4]

A number of points are noteworthy. First, the court's order may be directed at a person other than the respondent spouse, such as a nominee or, to use the language of the early Mareva cases, a "collaborator"[5] to whom the respondent's assets are intended to be transferred or where the respondent's assets are otherwise held by another person. Secondly, the prohibition on any "disposition" is very broadly defined as meaning "any disposition of property howsoever made other than a disposition made by a will or codicil".[6] Thirdly, the substantive "relief" sought by the applicant which will ground an application for a restraining order under s 35(2) is defined[7] to mean the financial or other

---

2. See Ch 4, *A Substantive Cause of Action*, para **[4.49]** *post*.
3. See generally, Shatter, *Shatter's Family Law*, (4th ed, 1997) Butterworths, paras [17.187]-[17.189].
4. The court is also empowered to set aside "reviewable dispositions" as defined by s 35(1): s 35(2)(a)(II). See further *JR v PR* [1996] IFLR 194 (Circuit Court); *O'H v O'H* [1990] 2 IR 558; *JD v DD* High Court, unrep, May 1997 (McGuinness J); *Sherry v Sherry* (1990) *The Times*, 28 November 1990 (CA); *Kemmis v Kemmis* [1988] 2 FLR 223; and *B v B (P Ltd intervening) (No 2)* [1995] 1 FLR 374.
5. *Barclay-Johnson v Yuill* [1980] 3 All ER 190 at 194a-j *per* Megarry V-C.
6. Section 35(1) of the 1995 Act.
7. By s 35(1) of the 1995 Act.

material benefits conferred by an order under either ss 7, 8, 9, 10(1)(a) or (b), 11, 12, 13, 17, 18 (except s 18(1)(e)), 24, 25[8] or a relief order.[9] Fourthly, references to "defeating a claim for relief" are defined by s 35(1) of the 1995 Act as references to:

(i) preventing relief being granted to the person concerned, whether for the benefit of the person or a dependant member of the family concerned;

(ii) limiting the relief granted; or

(iii) frustrating or impeding the enforcement of an order granting relief.

Fifthly, application cannot be brought for an order restraining the disposition of property where an applicant has been granted the substantive relief sought. A freezing order can only be brought where an applicant has: (a) instituted proceedings for the recognised substantive relief which have not been determined; or (b) has been granted leave to institute such proceedings; or (c) intends to apply for leave to institute such proceedings upon the completion of one year's ordinary residence in the State. The effect of the foregoing is that a post-judgment freezing order cannot be granted under s 35 of the 1995 Act. Sixthly, where an order is made under s 35(2)(a), the order shall include such provisions (if any) as the court considers necessary for its implementation (including provisions requiring the making of any payments or the disposal of property).[10] Seventhly, where neither of the conditions in s 27(1)(a) and (b)[11] is

---

8. Section 7 of the 1995 Act facilitates the making of a periodical or lump sum maintenance order pending the grant of a decree of judicial separation; s 8 facilitates the making of a periodical or lump sum order on the granting of a decree of judicial separation; s 9 facilitates the making of a property adjustment order on the granting of a decree of judicial separation; s 10(1)(a) facilitates the making of a order providing for the conferral on one spouse of the sole right to occupy the family home or directing the sale and providing for the disposal of the proceeds of the family home; s 10(1)(b) facilitates the making of an order under s 36 of the 1995 Act which relates to the determination of questions between spouses in relation to property; s 11 facilitates the making of financial compensation orders on the granting of a decree of judicial separation; s 12 facilitates the making of a pension adjustment order; s 13 facilitates the making of an order preserving pension entitlements after judicial separation; s 17 facilitates the making or retrospective periodical payments orders; s 18 facilitates the variation of certain orders; s 24 facilitates the making of a maintenance order, pending a "relief order" - see fn 9; and s 25 facilitates the making of an order providing for a spouse out of the estate of another spouse in circumstances where a marriage has been dissolved in a country outside of the State.

9. "Relief order" is defined by s 2(1) of the 1995 Act as meaning "an order under Part II made by virtue of s 23". Section 23 concerns relief orders made after divorce or separation outside of the State.

10. Section 35(3) of the 1995 Act.

11. Section 27(1)(a) provides: "either of the spouses concerned was domiciled in the State on the date of the application for an order under s 23(3) in relation to the relief order or was so domiciled on the date on which the divorce or judicial separation concerned took effect in the country or jurisdiction in which it was obtained"; and (b) provides: "either of the spouses was ordinarily resident in the State throughout the period of one year ending on either of the dates aforesaid".

satisfied, s 35(4) provides that the Court shall not make an order under s 35(2) in respect of any property other than the family home concerned.

[3.04] It is very important to recognise that a prerequisite to the court making an order restraining the disposition of property is that the respondent spouse must act "with the intention of defeating the claim for relief".[12] It should, however, be noted that the difficulties which an ordinary Mareva plaintiff may encounter in establishing an intention to defeat his claim are not entirely shared by an applicant for a restraining order under s 35(2) of the 1995 Act. Although an essential proof in a family law freezing order is that the respondent should have the intention of defeating a claim for relief as defined, in certain circumstances, a presumption is created that a respondent has such an intention. Section 35(5) of the 1995 Act provides that:

> Where an application is made under subsection (2) with respect to ... a disposition or other dealing with property that the other spouse concerned or any other person proposes to make and the court is satisfied -
>
> (a) in case the application is for an order under subsection (2)(a)(I), that the disposition or other dealing concerned would (apart from this section) have the consequence ...
>
> of defeating the applicant's claim for relief, it *shall be presumed, unless the contrary is shown, that that other spouse or other person* disposed of or otherwise dealt with the property concerned, or, as the case may be, *proposes to do so, with the intention of defeating the applicant's claim for relief.*[13]

Why an applicant for an ordinary Mareva injunction should have the full burden of proving the requisite "intention",[14] but an applicant bringing an application under s 35(2) of the 1995 Act can avail of such a presumption in satisfying this evidential burden, is not readily apparent.[15] Although Shatter, in his authoritative work on *Family Law*, refers[16] to the legislation ameliorating the difficulty of establishing a respondent's intention, this does not explain why the onus of proof shifts with the effect that an applicant under the 1995 Act is afforded preferential treatment to, perhaps, an equally deserving applicant for an ordinary Mareva injunction.

[12.] On this requirement in the case of a Mareva injunction, see Ch 6, *The Risk of Removal or Disposal of Assets*, para **[6.16]**.

[13.] Italics added. Subsection (5) is paraphrased; the remainder of the subsection deals with creating a presumption where it is sought to have a "reviewable disposition" (as defined by s 35(1) of the 1995 Act) set aside.

[14.] *Re John Horgan Livestock Ltd; O'Mahony v Horgan* [1995] 2 IR 411, considered in Ch 6, *The Risk of Removal or Disposal of Assets*, para **[6.18]** *et seq.*

[15.] The position in Ireland is similar to that in the United Kingdom. There, s 37(5) of the Matrimonial Causes Act 1973 creates a similar rebuttable presumption.

[16.] *Op cit*, para [17.188].

[3.05] Whatever the justification for alleviating the evidential burden on an applicant under s 35(2) of the 1995 Act may be, the effect is to make it relatively easier to obtain an order under s 35 than to obtain a Mareva injunction. Nevertheless, as demonstrated by English cases such as *Ghoth v Ghoth*[17] family law litigants may still apply for an ordinary Mareva injunction in circumstances where worldwide Mareva relief is sought.[18] It has been contended[19] that it would be an abuse of the Mareva injunction to invoke it in matrimonial causes because it is recognised that the specific criteria under family law legislation are not met (eg, as to a respondent's intention).[20] This commentary is, however, premised on the basis that in the United Kingdom, a Mareva plaintiff is not obliged to prove that there is a likelihood of the defendant removing or otherwise disposing of his property *with a view to frustrating the plaintiff's future judgment*. Accordingly, in the United Kingdom, an application for an ordinary Mareva injunction might be made in a family law case where there is no nefarious intention on the part of a respondent. In Ireland, however, an applicant for such an order in a family law case would not be so motivated since, here, an ordinary Mareva plaintiff must show that the defendant's intention in removing or otherwise disposing of his assets is with the intention of frustrating the plaintiff's future judgment.[21] A Mareva injunction may, however, be appropriate where an applicant has secured judgment since s 35 only permits the making of pre-judgment freezing orders.[22]

Section 37(2) of the Family Law (Divorce) Act 1996

[3.06] The procedure for obtaining an order restraining the disposition of property under s 37(2) of the 1996 Act is broadly similar to that in s 35(2) of the 1995 Act, upon which it is based. Section 37(2)(a) of the 1996 Act provides:

> The court, on the application of a person ("the applicant") who has instituted proceedings that have not been determined for the grant of relief, may -

---

[17.] [1992] 2 All ER 920; see Ch 7, *The Defendant's Assets*, para **[7.54]**.

[18.] Note, however, that it has been held in the United Kingdom in *Hamlin v Hamlin* [1986] 1 FLR 61 that an order under s 37 of the UK's Matrimonial Causes Act 1973 operated, like a Mareva injunction, *in personam* and could be invoked to prevent a respondent from dealing with property outside of the jurisdiction.

[19.] See Ashe & Rider, *International Tracing of Assets*, (1997) FT Law and Tax, Vol 1, Chapter B4 by Timothy Scott QC, "Matrimonial Law" at B4.12.

[20.] *Cf Shipman v Shipman* [1991] 1 FLR 250.

[21.] See *Re John Horgan Livestock Ltd; O'Mahony v Horgan* [1995] 2 IR 411 and, generally, Ch 6, *The Risk of Removal or Disposal*, para **[6.18]** *et seq* for a full discussion.

[22.] Note that on an applicant being granted a decree of judicial separation or divorce, the Court may order either spouse to pay to the other periodical payments or a lump sum and may require security to be given: s 8 of the 1995 Act and s 13 of the 1996 Act: see Shatter, *op cit*, para [17.11] *et seq*.

(I) if it is satisfied that the other spouse concerned or any other person, with the intention of defeating the claim for relief, proposes to make any disposition of or to transfer out of the jurisdiction or otherwise deal with any property, make such order as it thinks fit for the purpose of restraining that other spouse or other person from so doing or otherwise for protecting the claim.

As in the case of the 1995 Act's provisions, considered above,[23] a number of points arise in connection with the foregoing. First, the order may be directed at a person other than a respondent spouse. Secondly, the term "disposition" is again widely defined.[24] Thirdly, the substantive "relief" sought by the applicant, which will ground an application for a restraining order under s 37(2), is defined[25] to mean the financial or other material benefits conferred by an order under ss 12, 13, 14, 15(1)(a) or (b), 16, 17, 18, 22 (except s 22(1)(e)).[26] Fourthly, references to "defeating a claim for relief" are defined by s 37(1) in exactly the same terms as these words are defined by s 35(1), considered above.[27] Fifthly, application can *only* be brought for an order restraining the disposition of property where the applicant has "instituted proceedings, that have not been determined for the grant of relief": s 37(2)(a). Finally, it may be noted that s 37(3) of the 1996 Act replicates s 35(3) of the 1995 Act and, also, that s 37(4) of the 1996 Act shifts the burden of establishing that a respondent's intention is to defeat a claim for relief, from the applicant by creating, in the same circumstances as provided for in s 35(2) of the 1995 Act, a presumption that such is the respondent's intention.[28]

The propriety of s 37 of the 1996 Act was alluded to by McGuinness J in *Gilligan v Criminal Assets Bureau*[29] in the course of her judgment where she upheld the constitutionality of the Proceeds of Crime Act 1996. After noting the court's power, on an *ex parte* application, to freeze a spouse's assets,

---

23. See para **[3.03]** *supra*.

24. Section 37(1) of the 1996 Act which is in precisely the same terms as s 35(1) of the 1995 Act.

25. By s 37(1) of the 1996 Act.

26. Section 12 of the 1996 Act facilitates the making of a periodical or lump sum maintenance order pending the grant of a decree of divorce; s 13 facilitates the making of a periodical or lump sum order on the granting of a decree of divorce; s 14 facilitates the making of a property adjustment order on the granting of a decree of divorce; s 15(1)(a) facilitates the making of a order providing for the conferral on one spouse of the sole right to occupy the family home or directing the sale and providing for the disposal of the proceeds of the family home; s 15(1)(b) facilitates the making of an order under s 36 of the 1995 Act which relates to the determination of questions between spouses in relation to property; s 16 facilitates the making of financial compensation orders on the granting of a decree of divorce; s 17 facilitates the making of a pension adjustment order; s 18 facilitates the making of an order for provision for a spouse out of the estate of the other spouse; s 22 facilitates the variation of certain orders.

27. See para **[3.03]** *supra*.

28. See para **[3.04]** *supra*.

29. High Court, unrep, 26 June 1997 (McGuinness J), pp 57-58 of the transcript.

McGuinness J referenced the fact that s 37(4) of the 1996 Act shifts the burden of proof and said:

> "The onus of proof is clearly laid on the respondent to demonstrate that he or she did not act with the intention of defeating the other spouse's claim for relief.
>
> The corresponding provision under s 29 of the Judicial Separation and Family Law Reform Act 1989 has been frequently and widely used, in particular in the form of freezing orders made on an *ex parte* basis, and there is no reason to believe that this will not continue under the new legislation. There are many other examples of similar presumptions which may fall to be rebutted in civil proceedings ... It can often happen that such freezing orders are sought in circumstances where the allegations made against defendants involve fraud or other conduct which would be in breach of the criminal law. It has never been seriously suggested that such procedures are unconstitutional."

[B] RESTRAINT ORDERS UNDER THE CRIMINAL JUSTICE ACT 1994

[3.07] One of the primary purposes of the Criminal Justice Act 1994 ("the 1994 Act") was to provide for the recovery, by confiscation, of the proceeds of drug trafficking and other indictable offences. As a means of facilitating the making of an effective confiscation order, the 1994 Act enables the High Court to make a *restraint order*, the effect of which is to restrain a person from dealing with his property. The 1994 Act was passed following the publication of a report by the Law Reform Commission in 1991.[30] In many respects the 1994 Act is similar to the English Drug Trafficking Offences Act 1986 which has been superseded by the Drug Trafficking Act 1994 and the Criminal Justice Act 1988 and so, some of the English authorities can be of assistance in interpreting the 1994 Act. To an extent the 1994 Act has, in practice, been surpassed by the Proceeds of Crime Act 1996, considered below,[31] under which most applications to freeze suspected criminals' assets are now brought.

[3.08] Central to the High Court's power to make a restraint order is the fact that a *confiscation order* either has, or will, be made by the High Court.[32] Confiscation orders[33] can be made under the 1994 Act in either of two

---

[30] For newspaper commentary on the need for such legislation see *The Irish Times* 2 May 1991 and 31 July 1991.

[31] See para **[3.31]** *infra*.

[32] On confiscation orders under the English Drug Trafficking Offences Act 1986 (now superseded by the Drug Trafficking Act 1994), see generally, *R v Johnson* [1991] 2 All ER 428; *R v Harrow Justices, ex p DPP* [1991] 3 All ER 873; *R v Chrastny (No 2)* [1992] 1 All ER 193; *R v Richards* [1992] 2 All ER 572; *R v Redbourne* [1993] 2 All ER 753; *R v Rose* [1993] 2 All ER 761; *Re Barretto, Wadsted v Barretto* [1994] 1 All ER 447.

[33] For some recent English cases on confiscation orders under the English Drug Trafficking Offences Act 1986, see *R v Emmett* [1997] 4 All ER 737; *R v Clark* [1997] 4 All ER 803; and *R v Liverpool Magistrates' Court, ex p Ansen; Re Ansen* [1998] 1 All ER 692.

circumstances. The first, under s 4(4), is where a person has been sentenced or otherwise dealt with by a court in respect of one or more drug trafficking offences of which he has been convicted on indictment and it is determined that the convicted person has benefited from drug trafficking.[34] The second, under s 9(1), is where a person has been sentenced or otherwise dealt with by a court in respect of an offence of which he has been convicted on indictment and the court orders him to pay such sum as it thinks fit.[35]

[3.09] In considering the provisions of the 1994 Act the following issues are addressed:

1. The Jurisdiction to Make a Restraint Order.

2. Making Ancillary Disclosure Orders.

3. Circumstances when the Power is Exercisable.

4. Property Affected by a Restraint Order.

5. Legal and Living Expenses' Provisos.

6. Discharge and Variation of Restraint Orders.

7. The Power to Appoint a Receiver.

8. Registration of Restraint Orders.

9. The Insolvency of Respondents.

The Jurisdiction to Make a Restraint Order

[3.10] The 1994 Act empowers the High Court, on application being made, to freeze the assets of certain defendants in certain criminal proceedings. The power to make a restraint order under the 1994 Act arises in the context of drug trafficking and other indictable offences. Section 24(1) of the 1994 Act is the main empowering provision, which provides:

> The High Court may by order (in this Act referred to as a "restraint order") prohibit any person from dealing with any realisable property, subject to such conditions and exceptions as may be specified in that order.

---

34. Section 4(1) of the 1994 Act. On the burden and standard of proof to establish whether a defendant has benefited from drug trafficking under the English Drug Trafficking Offences Act 1986, (now superseded by the Drug Trafficking Act 1994) see *R v Dickens* [1990] 2 All ER 626. It may be noted that the Criminal Justice (No 2) Bill, 1997, as passed by Seanad Éireann proposes to amend s 4 of the 1994 Act although it is not proposed to amend subsection 4.

35. Section 9(1) of the 1994 Act. Note that here it is not mandatory that the court finds that the convict benefited from the offence; it is provided that an application may be brought by the DPP if it appears to him that the convict has benefited from the offence of which he was convicted or of that offence and another offence "of which he is convicted in the same proceedings of which the court has taken into consideration in determining his sentence": s 9(2).

Accordingly, specific jurisdiction is conferred upon the High Court to make a restraint order, the effect of which is to freeze a person's assets. The extent of the prohibition in such an order is defined in s 24(8) which provides that for the purposes of the 1994 Act, "dealing with property held by any person" includes, without prejudice to the generality of that expression:

    (a) where a debt is owed to that person, making a payment to any person in reduction of the amount of the debt, and

    (b) removing the property from the State.

In many respects, the statutory jurisdiction conferred upon the High Court is similar to the Mareva jurisdiction. In other respects it is most different. First, unlike ordinary applications to the Court for the exercise of its Mareva jurisdiction, the intentions of the person whose assets are frozen by a restraint order made under s 24 of the 1994 Act are immaterial. Secondly, unlike a Mareva injunction which operates *in personam*, a restraint order under the 1994 Act would appear to operate *in rem*. Section 24(9) provides:

> Where the High Court has made a restraint order, a member of the Garda Siochana or an officer of customs and excise may, for the purpose of preventing any realisable property being removed from the State, seize the property.[36]

Moreover, restraint orders may be registered against lands which they affect, thereby indicating that where the applicant is successful, a right over or interest in the land exists.[37] A defendant against whom a Mareva injunction is made is restrained in person from dealing with his assets, but the assets themselves are not liable to be seized.[38]

[3.11] The purpose of the English legislation was considered by the Court of Appeal in *Re Peters*[39] and alluded to in the Irish case of *Director of Public Prosecutions v EH*[40] where Kelly J said that there was no difference between it and the purpose of a restraint order which is made under the Irish 1994 Act. Kelly J also accepted the analogy between restraint orders and Mareva injunctions and quoted, with approval, the following passage from the headnote of the report in *Re Peters*:

[36.] It is provided that property seized under this subsection shall be dealt with in accordance with the court's directions. Note that in *Gilligan v Criminal Assets Bureau*, High Court, unrep, 26 June 1997 (McGuinness J), McGuinness J said (p 41 of the transcript) of the Proceeds of Crime Act 1996, considered at para **[3.31]** *et seq, infra* that "The action is strictly speaking an action *in rem* rather than *in personam*...".

[37.] See s 25 of the 1994 Act, considered at para **[3.26]** *infra*.

[38.] See Ch 7, *The Defendant's Assets*, para **[7.06]** and Ch 9, *The Mareva Order and Its Effects*, para **[9.36]**.

[39.] [1988] 1 QB 871.

[40.] High Court, unrep, 22 April 1997 (Kelly J).

"The purpose of a restraint order under the Drug Trafficking Offences Act 1986 was the preservation of assets at a time when the Court did not know whether the defendant would be convicted and was closely analogous to the Mareva jurisdiction; that the exercise of the power in accordance with the guidance given in section 13(2) of the Act of 1986 was consistent with the purpose of maintaining assets to meet a final order if one should be made, and meeting the reasonable requirements of their owner in the meantime but always subject to the legislative purpose of maintaining the value of the realisable property in order for it to be available to satisfy any confiscation order that might ultimately be made."

The freezing of a defendant's assets cannot be an end in itself. Just as in the case of a Mareva injunction, where a defendant's assets cannot be frozen unless there is a likelihood that a plaintiff will obtain a judgment against him, a restraint order should not be made unless it is likely that a confiscation order will be made.[41]

Making Ancillary Disclosure Orders

(a) Ancillary disclosure orders in aid of restraint orders

[3.12] In *Re O (disclosure order)*[42] the Court of Appeal held that the court has jurisdiction to make an order compelling a defendant to disclose his assets and income on the basis that such was ancillary to the power to make a restraint order under s 77 of the English Criminal Justice Act 1988. Glidewell LJ said:

"If a restraint order is made, but the Crown Prosecution Service (the CPS) do not know what property the defendant has, or the full extent of his property, there is no way in which the CPS can ensure that the defendant complies with the restraint order. It is for this reason that I agree that the power to make a restraint order must comprehend an ancillary power to require a defendant to disclose his assets and income."

The courts' inherent power to make a disclosure order has been recognised in Ireland, albeit *obiter dictum*, in the context of applications brought under the Proceeds of Crime Act 1996 which, in s 9, contains an express provision for the making of disclosure on affidavit.[43] It should be noted that in *Re O (disclosure order)* it was held that any disclosure was subject to the common law privilege against self-incrimination[44] and that any disclosure order must be confined to

---

[41.] See Ch 4, *A Substantive Cause of Action*, para **[4.14]**.

[42.] [1991] 1 All ER 330.

[43.] See para **[3.43]** *et seq, infra*.

[44.] See also *In Re a Defendant*, High Court (UK, unrep) 26 March 1987 (Webster J) where *Rank Film Distributors Ltd v Video Information Centre* [1982] AC 380 was distinguished on the grounds that an undertaking not to use the information as evidence in a prosecution would be given by the prosecutor and so would afford defendants sufficient protection. On the privilege against self-incrimination, see para **[3.44]** *et seq, infra* and also Ch 10, *Ancillary Orders*, para **[10.47]** *et seq* (in the context of asset disclosure orders in aid of Mareva relief) and para **[10.62]** *et seq* (in the context of Anton Piller orders).

furthering the purpose of a restraint order: to ensure that the defendant's property is preserved so as to make it available to satisfy any confiscation order. In particular, any information obtained by a disclosure order may not be used as evidence in the prosecution of the offences alleged against the defendant.[45] This reasoning has been followed in Ireland in *MM v DD*[46] and *Gilligan v The Criminal Assets Bureau*,[47] both in the context of the Proceeds of Crime Act 1996. It has also been held that upon a restraint order being discharged, the power to make a disclosure order will lapse.[48]

(b) Disclosure orders under s 7A of the Bankers' Books Evidence Acts, 1879-1989

[3.13] In addition to the foregoing powers to make a disclosure order, the Criminal Assets Bureau may have regard also to s 7A of the Bankers' Books Evidence Acts 1879-1989[49] ("the 1879-1989 Acts"). This section provides:

> If, on an application made by a member of the Garda Siochana not below the rank of Superintendent, a court or a judge is satisfied that there are reasonable grounds for believing -
>
> (a) that an indictable offence has been committed; and
>
> (b) that there is material in the possession of a bank specified in the application which is likely to be of substantial value (whether by itself or together with other material) to the investigation of the offence;
>
> a court or judge may make an order that the applicant or another member of the Garda Siochana designated by him be at liberty to inspect and take copies of any entries in a banker's book for the purposes of investigation of the offence.

In appropriate circumstances, an order under s 7A of the 1879-1989 Acts may be used to supplement a restraint order made or sought under the 1994 Act.[50] In Ireland it was considered necessary to amend the 1879 Act to expressly provide, in s 7A, that the mechanism for compelling the disclosure of the contents of bankers' books was available in criminal proceedings. In the United Kingdom it was held in *Williams v Summerfield*[51] there was sufficient jurisdiction to make

---

[45.] Lord Donaldson MR held (at 336d) that the following condition should be inserted into all orders for disclosure in aid of a restraint order: "No disclosure made in compliance with this order shall be used as evidence on the prosecution of an offence alleged to have been committed by the person required to make that disclosure or by any spouse of that person."
[46.] High Court, unrep, 10 December 1996 (Moriarty J).
[47.] High Court, unrep, 26 June 1997 (McGuinness J).
[48.] *Re K*, High Court (UK, unrep) 6 July 1990 (McCullough J).
[49.] Inserted by s 131(c) of the Central Bank Act 1989.
[50.] Application under s 7A of the 1879-1989 Acts can be brought in the District Court in accordance with Ord 38 of the District Court Rules, 1997 (SI 93/1997) as amended by the District Court (Bankers' Books Evidence) Rules, 1998 (SI 170/1998).
[51.] [1972] 2 All ER 1334.

an order under s 7 of the 1879 Act in aid of criminal proceedings. In the *Summerfield* case, and in other English cases,[52] it was stressed that great care should be exercised by a court when making an order in aid of criminal proceedings. The Bankers' Books Evidence Acts 1879-1989 are considered further in the context of disclosure in civil matters in Chapter 10, *Ancillary Orders.*[53]

Circumstances when Power to Make a Restraint Order is Exercisable

[3.14] The power of the High Court to make a restraint order under s 24(1) of the 1994 Act is expressed, by s 23(1) of the 1994 Act, only to be *exercisable,* where:

> (a)(i) proceedings have been instituted in the State against the defendant for an offence which is a drug trafficking offence or an indictable offence other than a drug trafficking offence or an application has been made in respect of the defendant under section 7, 8, 13 or 18 of this Act,

> (ii) the proceedings of the application have not or has not been concluded, and

> (iii) either a confiscation order has been made or it appears to the court that there are reasonable grounds for thinking that a confiscation order may be made in the proceedings or that in the case of an application under sections 7, 8, 13 or 18 of this Act the court will be satisfied, as the case may be, as mentioned in section 7(3), 8(4), 13(2) or 18(2) of this Act,

> or

> (b)(i) the court is satisfied that proceedings are to be instituted against a person in respect of an offence which is a drug trafficking offence in respect of which a confiscation order might be made under *section 9* of this Act or that an application of a kind mentioned in subsection 1 (a)(i) of this section is to be made in respect of a person, and

> (ii) it appears to the court that a confiscation order might be made in connection with the offence or that a court will be satisfied as mentioned in subsection 1(a)(iii) of this section.

[3.15] It is noteworthy that the power to make a restraint order is *exercisable* in two distinct sets of circumstances. The first set of circumstances (detailed in s 23(1)(a)(i)-(iii) of the 1994 Act) concern situations where proceedings have actually been instituted against a defendant for a recognised offence[54] or

---

52. See also *R v Marlborough Street Metropolitan Stipendiary Magistrate, ex p Simpson* [1980] Crim LR 305 and *R v Nottingham City Justices, ex p Lynn* [1984] Crim LR 554.
53. See Ch 10, *Ancillary Orders*, para **[10.25]** *et seq.*
54. Ie a "drug trafficking offence" or an "indictable offence other than a drug trafficking offence"; Section 3(1) defines "drug trafficking offence".

application has actually been made against the defendant under ss 7,[55] 8,[56] 13[57] or 18[58] of the 1994 Act; where those proceedings or such application has not been concluded; and where a confiscation order has been made or it appears to the court that there are reasonable grounds for thinking that a confiscation order may be made in the proceedings or on such application.

[3.16] The second set of circumstances (detailed in s 23(1)(b)(i)-(ii) of the 1994 Act) envisage a situation where proceedings have *not* as then been instituted against a defendant for a drug trafficking offence or an offence in respect of which a confiscation order may be made or an application brought under ss 7, 8, 13 or 18; and where it appears to the court that a confiscation order may be made or that a court will be satisfied that there are reasonable grounds for thinking that a confiscation order may be made in the proceedings or such application.[59] These circumstances are so wide as to make virtually anyone amenable to having their property affected by a restraint order. It is, therefore, immediately apparent that the 1994 Act has conferred on the High Court a very wide and far reaching jurisdiction.

[3.17] Section 23(3) of the 1994 Act safeguards a defendant's rights by providing that where a restraint order is made before proceedings have been instituted against a defendant, "the court shall discharge the order if proceedings in respect of an offence are not instituted or the relevant application is not made within such time as the Court considers reasonable."

Property Affected by a Restraint Order

[3.18] Restraint orders can apply to all "realisable property" held by a specified person, whether or not described in the order, and, where transferred to him after the making of the order. *"Realisable property"* is defined in s 3(1) of the 1994 Act as meaning "(a) any property held by the defendant, and (b) any property held by a person to whom the defendant has directly or indirectly made a gift caught by this Act". Accordingly, whilst the High Court is empowered by

---

55. Section 7 concerns applications by the DPP for a reassessment of whether the defendant has benefited from drug trafficking.
56. Section 8 concerns applications by the DPP for a revised assessment of the value of the proceeds of drug trafficking.
57. Section 13 applies where a person has been convicted on indictment of one or more offences and concerns application where the defendant has died or is absent.
58. Section 18 allows the DPP to apply to the High Court in cases where there is an increase in the value of realisable property.
59. Section 23(2) provides that where the power to make a restraint order under s 24 is exercisable *before proceedings have been instituted* references to "the defendant" shall be construed as references to the person referred to in s 23(1)(b)(i); and references to "realisable property" shall be construed as if, immediately before that time, proceedings had been instituted against the person involved.

s 24(1) to prohibit any person from dealing with any realisable property, the only property which may be the subject of a restraint order is property held by a "defendant" or a person to whom a "defendant" has directly or indirectly made a gift. "Defendant" is defined by s 3(1) as meaning:

> ... for the purposes of the provisions of this Act relating to confiscation, and subject to section 23(2)(a) of this Act, a person against whom proceedings for the relevant drug trafficking or other offence have been instituted.

Living and Legal Expenses Provisos

[3.19] Section 24(2) of the 1994 Act provides that:

> Without prejudice to the generality of subsection (1) of this section, a restraint order may make such provision as the court thinks fit for living expenses and legal expenses.

In this respect a restraint order can, at the High Court's discretion, be made subject to much the same sorts of provisos as can an ordinary Mareva injunction.[60] That said, there are substantial differences between the Mareva jurisdiction and the statutory power to make restraint orders. In *Re R (restraint order)*[61] it was held that there was no jurisdiction under the similar English Drug Trafficking Offences Act 1986,[62] or under the court's inherent jurisdiction, to imply a cross-undertaking in damages on the part of the prosecution as a means of indemnifying innocent third parties affected by the restraint order against any abuse of proceedings. Where a restraint order does not, *ab initio*, make provision for living expenses and legal expenses, application may be brought subsequently, under s 24 of the 1994 Act, to have the order varied.

Discharge and Variation of Restraint Orders

[3.20] A restraint order *may*, at any time, be discharged or varied by the High Court in relation to any property; however, it *shall* be discharged on the conclusion of the proceedings or application.[63] Application for the discharge or variation of a restraint order may be made by any person affected by it.[64] In *Director of Public Prosecutions v EH*[65] application was made to Kelly J to vary the terms of an order previously made against the defendant applicant by

---

60. See Ch 9, *The Mareva Injunction and Its Effects*, para **[9.12]**.
61. [1990] 2 All ER 569.
62. Note that this has been superseded by the English Drug Trafficking Act 1994.
63. Section 24(5) of the 1994 Act.
64. Section 24(6) of the 1994 Act. On the variation of restraint orders see *Re R (restraint order)* [1990] 2 All ER 569 where a landlord sought a variation of a restraint order where its tenant's interest in a three year lease had been the subject of an order under s 8 of the Drug Trafficking Offences Act 1986.
65. High Court, unrep, 22 April 1997 (Kelly J); delivered *ex tempore*.

Moriarty J. As to the purpose of s 24 of the 1994 Act, which permits an order to be varied, Kelly J said:

> "Orders made under [the 1994 Act] have far reaching effects which are rather similar to the effects of the Mareva type orders which have been granted in ordinary litigation in this jurisdiction for a number of years.
>
> The Mareva orders were always subject to being varied by the Court so as to allow a defendant to draw down from the frozen fund or assets, money sufficient to discharge legal and living expenses. The legislature, in enacting section 24, expressly recognised that the restraint which might be imposed pursuant to orders made under that section could also be subject to variation so as to provide for living expenses and legal expenses (see subsection (2) of section 24)".[66]

In reviewing the principles applicable to applications to vary restraint orders so as to provide for living or legal expenses, Kelly J considered the decision of the English Court of Appeal in *Re Peters*[67] and accepted the analogy drawn there between restraint orders and Mareva injunctions and he found that the purposes of the Irish and the English legislation were no different.[68] In *Re Peters* it was held by the Court of Appeal that variation of a restraint order to allow payment of school fees so as not to disrupt the education of the defendant's son and to allow payments for the defendant's clothing and defence were permissible variations; however, it was also found that the anticipatory discharge of other liabilities which could be expected to arise, only after the outcome of the trial was known, was contrary to the underlying purpose of the English Act. Kelly J said that that case did not itself answer the question as to the approach which the court should take on this or similar applications and in so finding, he said that assistance could be gleaned from the decision of Robert Goff J in *A v C*.[69] He quoted the following passage from the headnote in that case, saying that Robert Goff J had held:

> "Although the Court had jurisdiction to qualify a Mareva injunction where the defendant satisfied the Court that assets subject to the injunction were required for a purpose which did not conflict with the policy underlying the Mareva jurisdiction, in order to satisfy that burden the defendant has to go further than merely to state that he owed money to someone and had to show that he did not have any other assets available out of which the debt would be paid. Since the defendants had failed to adduce evidence to show that they had no other assets out of which they could pay their legal costs, their application was dismissed".

[66.] At p 1 of the transcript.

[67.] [1988] 1 QB 871.

[68.] See para **[3.11]** *supra*.

[69.] [1981] 2 All ER 126. On the variation of Mareva injunctions, see generally, Ch 9, *The Mareva Order and Its Effects*, para **[9.31]** *et seq.*

Turning to the facts of the case before him, Kelly J noted that the defendant had sought permission to spend approximately £735 per month in respect of living expenses. Although he found that this figure was not unreasonable for a person who has to provide for a partner and three children, he noted that the evidence established that since the defendant's release from Garda custody, sums amounting to £17,500 had, prior to the making of the restraint order by Moriarty J, been withdrawn by the defendant from bank accounts under his control. Approximately £12,000 remained unaccounted for. Kelly J found that the defendant's explanation that he had used that money to repay a business associate or associates was unsatisfactory; that the payment to such third party or parties remained a mystery; that such third parties may not even have existed; and that if the defendant still had such moneys under his control, they would be sufficient to pay monthly expenses for a period well in excess of one year. Kelly J expressly adopted the following test prescribed by Robert Goff J in *A v C*:

> "In order to satisfy the burden placed upon a defendant who seeks such a variation he has to go further than merely to state that he owes money to someone, he has to show that he does not have other assets available out of which the debt would be paid."[70]

In applying this test Kelly J refused the defendant's application to vary the original restraint order: the defendant merely claimed to have paid the money to someone but he could not or would not say who that person was.[71]

[3.21] Although it is undoubted that restraint orders are clearly analogous to Mareva injunctions, it is thought that the same principles which apply to the variation of a Mareva injunction are not necessarily the same as those which govern the variation of a restraint order under the 1994 Act. In its purest form a Mareva injunction affects assets which are beneficially owned by a defendant and, in this respect, a Mareva injunction may be distinguished from an injunction granted on foot of a proprietary claim, such as a tracing action where a plaintiff claims to have a beneficial interest in the property, the subject matter of the injunction.[72] In an application to vary a Mareva injunction it must always be remembered that a defendant should not be restricted in dealing with his *own assets* save as is absolutely necessary to protect a plaintiff's legitimate interests and to defend the court's authority. It is for this reason that Mareva orders are invariably varied so as to permit the discharge of living, legal and business expenses.[73] It must be questioned, however, whether the same principle applies

---

70. At p 5 of the transcript.
71. *Cf Customs and Excise Commissioners v Norris* [1991] 2 QB 293 where a pre-conviction restraint order under the UK's drug trafficking legislation was varied to allow the defendant to fund an appeal against conviction for a drug trafficking offence and confiscation order.
72. See Ch 1, *The Mareva Injunction in Context*, para **[1.08]** *et seq*.
73. See generally, Ch 9, *The Mareva Order and Its Effects*, para **[9.12]** *et seq*.

in the case of either certain restraint orders or injunctions which restrain the disposal of assets in aid of a proprietary claim. If the assets affected by a proprietary injunction or a restraint order were themselves misappropriated from somebody else, the defendant can have no right to dissipate them for any reason, even to discharge his necessary living expenses. In the case of restraint orders under the 1994 Act a further distinction must be drawn between orders affecting assets or money which were clearly stolen by the defendant from an identifiable victim and orders affecting assets or money which were "earned" by the defendant through illegal activities and which truly represent the proceeds of criminal activity, eg profits earned from supplying controlled drugs etc. It is thought that, in the former case, variation to permit the discharge of expenses should not be permitted, and that in the latter case the application of the Mareva variation-test is appropriate.[74] Moreover, a variation to facilitate the discharge of legal expenses will rarely be justified because of the existence of both civil and criminal legal aid.[75]

[3.22] The position in relation to the variation of restraint orders on the application of third parties thereby affected is different. In *Re K (restraint order)*[76] a restraint order had been made against the defendant under the English Drug Trafficking Offences Act 1986.[77] This had the effect of freezing the defendant's deposit and overdraft accounts. The defendant had a deposit account with the Bank of India which had granted her an overdraft facility on the security of an express right of set-off against the deposit account following

---

[74.] See further, para **[3.62]** *infra*, where s 6 of the Proceeds of Crime Act 1996 is considered.

[75.] See, eg, *DPP v Felloni*, High Court, unrep, 18 December 1997 (Shanley J) where an application to vary a freezing order to facilitate the payment of legal fees was refused. There, the applicants claimed that the Department of Justice had refused to pay their counsel's fees notwithstanding that the defence had been granted a criminal legal aid certificate. It was reported that, in refusing to vary the order, Shanley J said that there was a valid legal aid order which had not been appealed or quashed and that it seemed to him that the criminal proceedings in the case did not conclude until the issue of confiscation had been determined. It was found that the legal aid certificate was perfectly appropriate and would be extremely difficult to impugn and, moreover, the applicants could still apply for civil legal aid and still have the barrister of their choice; and there were no grounds for believing they would be prejudiced if their original solicitor did not continue to act on their behalf. It should also be noted that the variation was also refused on the grounds that the applicants had failed to disclose six *ex juris* accounts containing circa £115,000. In *Criminal Assets Bureau v H, The Irish Times*, 13 June 1998 (Shanley J) it was reported that H, who was serving a 20 year jail sentence on drug charges, was granted free legal aid by the High Court to fight a tax demand for more than £240,000. It was, however, stated in the report that Shanley J said that it was open to the Criminal Assets Bureau, at the time of the full hearing, to raise the question of whether or not it was correct to grant legal aid and that if H lost, there would be judgment against him in the sum of the legal aid involved.

[76.] [1990] 2 All ER 562.

[77.] Now superseded by the English Drug Trafficking Act 1994.

combination and consolidation of all accounts. If the bank paid off the overdraft facility (£380,000) a credit balance (£320,000) would have been left in the deposit account. The bank applied to have the order varied to permit the consolidation and set-off. Whilst the bank acknowledged that the money in the deposit account could be assumed to be the proceeds of drug trafficking, it contended that this did not affect its right to combine and set-off the accounts. The bank was successful in its application for a variation of the restraint order. Otton J held:

> "In my judgment the right of a bank to combine is well established and is fundamental to the bank/customer relationship. It is a means of establishing the indebtedness of the customer to the bank and the bank to the customer. In exercising this right a bank is not asserting a claim over the moneys, nor is it in conflict with the claims of the Crown. It is merely carrying out an accounting procedure so as to ascertain the existence and amount of one party's liability to the other.
>
> ... the process of setting off the moneys due by the bank to the customer against the liability incurred by the customer is not 'disposing of or diminishing' the assets and the words 'or in any way dealing with any ... assets' must be construed as a class formed by the words 'disposing' and 'diminishing'. The chose in action is not unencumbered: it is subject to the contractual right of set-off. In short, neither the combination nor contractual set-off would amount to a disposal or diminution of the assets and in my judgment can be so exercised."[78]

Central to Otton J's reasoning was that there was a presumption that the rights of a third party which had acted in good faith and in ignorance of the tainted source of the deposited money should not be prejudiced.[79] It is submitted that should such a question arise for determination by the Irish High Court, the decision in *Re K (restraint order)* should be followed. There can be no justification for a windfall to the exchequer which is at the expense of a bona fide third party.

The Power to Appoint a Receiver

[3.23] Section 24(7) of the 1994 Act also empowers the High Court to appoint a receiver where it has made a restraint order.[80] Any such receiver appointed may take possession of any realisable property and, in accordance with the Court's directions, manage or otherwise deal with any property in respect of which he is appointed.

[78.] [1990] 2 All ER 562 at 567. *Cf Re W, The Times*, 15 November 1990 (Buckley J) where it was held that a restraint order made under the English Criminal Justice Act 1988 had priority over a bona fide third-party judgment creditor.

[79.] See also *Re Peters* [1988] 3 All ER 46.

[80.] A receiver may also be appointed under s 20(2) of the 1994 Act.

[3.24] Section 26(2) of the 1994 Act provides that the *powers* of a receiver appointed under ss 24(7) or 20(2)[81] :

> ... shall be exercised with a view to making available, for satisfying the confiscation order or, as the case may be, any confiscation order that may be made in the defendant's case, the value for the time being of realisable property held by any person by the realisation of such property.

Where realisable property is held by a person to whom the defendant has, directly or indirectly, made a gift caught by the 1994 Act, a receiver's powers shall be exercised "with a view to realising no more than the value for the time being of the gift."[82] Section 26(4) provides that a receiver's powers shall also be exercised with a view to allowing any person, other than the defendant or the recipient of such a gift, to retain or recover the value of the property held by him. It is also provided that in exercising the powers no account is to be taken of any obligations of the defendant or the recipient of the gift which conflict with the obligation to satisfy the confiscation order. It is thought that this must be construed strictly so as not to prejudice the rights of third parties.[83]

[3.25] Section 27 of the 1994 Act exempts a receiver from liability to any person in respect of any loss or damage caused, except by the receiver's negligence, where he takes action in relation to property which is subsequently found not to be "realisable property". A receiver will, however, only be exempted from liability where he would have been entitled to take the action which he took, were the property "realisable property" and also provided that he believes, on reasonable grounds, that he is entitled to take that action.

Registration of Restraint Orders

[3.26] Section 25 of the 1994 Act facilitates the registration of restraint orders in a series of governmental registries. Application can be made for the registration of an inhibition in the Land Registry,[84] and of a notice in both the Registry of Deeds[85] and in the Companies Registration Office.[86] The procedure also provides for the registration of the discharge or variation of a restraint order and upon the relevant Registrar receiving notice that a restraint order has been discharged or varied he is obliged to either cancel or vary the entry made as appropriate. The fact that restraint orders can be registered in, say, the Land Registry, underscores their *in rem* nature. The extent to which, if any, such

---

[81.] And also the powers of the High Court under ss 20 or 24 of the 1994 Act.
[82.] Section 26(3) of the 1994 Act.
[83.] See para **[3.22]** *supra*.
[84.] Section 25(1)-(3) of the 1994 Act.
[85.] *Ibid s* 25(4)-(6).
[86.] *Ibid s* 25(7)-(9).

registration will affect the rights of third parties who subsequently acquire interests in such "realisable property" remains to be seen.

The Insolvency of Respondents

[3.27] Section 28 of the 1994 Act deals with the situation where a person who holds "realisable property" is adjudicated bankrupt. In such an eventuality, property held by him which is the subject of a restraint order made before the order adjudicating him bankrupt, and, any proceeds of property realised under ss 20(5), 20(6) or 24(7) in the hands of a receiver is excluded from the property of the bankrupt for the purposes of the Bankruptcy Act 1988.[87] Where a person is adjudicated bankrupt and has directly or indirectly made a gift caught by the 1994 Act, s 28(3)(a) provides that no decision as to whether the gift is void shall be made under ss 57, 58 or 59 of the Bankruptcy Act 1988 in three specific circumstances. First, at any time when proceedings for an offence in respect of which a confiscation order might be made have been instituted against the bankrupt but have not been concluded. Secondly, at any time when an application has been made in respect of the defendant under ss 7, 8, 13 or 18 of the 1994 Act and has not been concluded. Thirdly, at any time when property of the person to whom the gift was made is subject to a restraint order. Section 28(3)(b) goes on to provide that where a bankrupt has made a gift any decision as to whether it is void made under the Bankruptcy Act 1988 after the conclusion of the proceedings or application must take into account any realisation, under the 1994 Act, of property held by the person to whom the gift was made.

[3.28] Section 29 of the 1994 Act contains certain safeguards for the Official Assignee or trustee in a bankruptcy where he seizes or disposes of any property which is subject to a restraint order. Where, at the time of the seizure or disposal of such property, the Official Assignee or trustee believes, on reasonable grounds, that he is entitled to seize the property, he shall not be liable to any person in respect of any loss or damage resulting from the seizure or disposal except where caused by his negligence. This section also provides that the Official Assignee or trustee shall have a lien over the property or over its proceeds of sale for expenses incurred in connection with the bankruptcy or other proceedings in relation to which the seizure or disposal purported to take place and such of his remuneration as may be reasonably assigned to his acting in such proceedings. Section 29(2) provides that where the Official Assignee or trustee does not know, and has no reasonable grounds for knowing, that property

---

[87.] *Ibid s* 28(1). Note that sub-s (4) modifies sub-s (1) to include references to earlier legislation where a petition in bankruptcy was presented or an adjudication in bankruptcy was made before 1 January 1989.

is the subject of a restraint order he is entitled to payment of his expenses under s 22 of the 1994 Act whether or not he has seized or disposed of the property so as to have a lien.

[3.29] Section 30 of the 1994 Act deals with the situation where "realisable property" is held by a company which is in the course of being wound up.[88] Where an order for the winding up of a company has been made or a resolution has been passed by the company for a voluntary winding up the functions of the liquidator or provisional liquidator shall not be exercisable in relation to property which is subject to a restraint order made before the "relevant time",[89] and, the proceeds of property realised by virtue of s 20(5) or (6) or s 24(7) of the 1994 Act for the time being in the hands of a receiver.

[3.30] Where an order has been made or a resolution passed for the winding up of a company the powers conferred on the High Court or a receiver by ss 20 or 24 of the 1994 Act shall not be exercisable in relation to any "realisable property" held by the company to which the functions of the liquidator are exercisable so as to inhibit him from exercising those functions for the purpose of distributing the company's property to its creditors or so as to prevent the payment out of any property or expenses[90] properly incurred in the winding up in respect of the property.

[C] INTERIM & INTERLOCUTORY ORDERS UNDER THE PROCEEDS OF CRIME ACT 1996

[3.31] The Proceeds of Crime Act 1996 ("the 1996 Act") was passed by the Oireachtas on 4 August 1996[91] following the drug-gang related murder of Ms Veronica Guerin, an investigative crime reporter with Independent Newspapers who had exposed the identities of numerous alleged criminals involved in drug dealing.[92] The 1996 Act gives jurisdiction to the High Court[93] to make either an

---

88. "Company", in this context, is defined as meaning "any company which may be wound up under the Companies Acts, 1963-1990. See generally, Courtney, *The Law of Private Companies*, (1994) Butterworths at Ch 18.
89. "Relevant time" is defined by s 30(3) as meaning "(a) where no order for the winding up of the company has been made, the time of the passing of the resolution for voluntary winding up, (b) where such an order has been made and, before the presentation of the petition for the winding up of the company by the court, such a resolution had been passed by the company, the time of the passing of the resolution, and (c) in any other case where such an order has been made, the time of the making of the order."
90. Including the remuneration of the liquidator or provisional liquidator.
91. For an overview of the operation of the 1996 Act, see *Gilligan v The Criminal Assets Bureau* High Court, unrep, 26 June 1997 (McGuinness J).
92. For this reason the 1996 Act has sometimes been referred to in the media as "the Guerin Act".
93. The "Court" is defined as "the High Court": s 1(1) of the 1996 Act.

interim or interlocutory order against a person in possession or control of "property" which directly or indirectly constitutes the "proceeds of crime". The effect of either an interim or interlocutory order is to prohibit:

> ... the person or any other specified person or any other person having notice of the order from disposing of or otherwise dealing with the whole or, if appropriate, a specified part of the property or diminishing its value ....[94]

If a restraint order made under the 1994 Act can be said to be merely similar to a Mareva injunction,[95] an interim or interlocutory order made under the 1996 Act can be said to be its statutory codification in a criminal law context. An interim order, made under s 2(1) lasts for a maximum period of 21 days from the making of the order. It is envisaged that an interlocutory order, made under s 3(1) will endure for over seven years, as s 4(1) facilitates the making of a disposal order where an interlocutory order has been in force for not less than seven years. Applications for relief under the 1996 Act are invariably brought by the Criminal Assets Bureau.

The Constitutionality of the 1996 Act

[3.32] The constitutionality of the 1996 Act was strongly challenged, but staunchly vindicated by the High Court in *Gilligan v The Criminal Assets Bureau*.[96] In that case it was contended by the plaintiff that the 1996 Act was unconstitutional for the following reasons:

(1) by failing to protect the right to a fair trial and the right to fair procedures by assuming, without charge, indictment, trial or conviction, the existence of a criminal offence;

(2) by requiring the plaintiff to prove on affidavit that he is not a criminal and that his assets are not the proceeds of crime;

(3) by forcing the plaintiff to account for his assets;

(4) by failing to protect the privilege against self-incrimination and right to silence;

(5) that by assuming, without due process of law, that the plaintiff is guilty of a criminal offence the Act failed to uphold the presumption of innocence;

(6) by giving the court a discretion as to whether to allow funds to be released for legal expenses, the Act was in breach of Article 40.3;

[94.] Section 2(1) (in the case of an *interim* order) and s 3(1) (in the case of an *interlocutory* order) of the 1996 Act. See paras **[3.39]** and **[3.41]**, respectively.

[95.] See *Director of Public Prosecutions v EH* High Court, unrep, 22 April 1997 (Kelly J): see para **[3.11]** *supra*.

[96.] High Court, unrep, 26 June 1997 (McGuinness J).

(7) by failing to protect the plaintiff's property rights from unjust attack and particularly by permitting the appointment of a receiver and the possible disposal of the plaintiff's assets;

(8) by failing to protect the plaintiff's rights under EU law, Article 6 of the European Convention on Human Rights and Article 1 of the First Protocol of the said Convention; and

(9) by having retrospective effect.

[3.33] The constitutionality of the 1996 Act was upheld by McGuinness J in a comprehensive and lengthy judgment. The essential findings of the High Court were:

(1) that proceedings under the 1996 Act were civil and not criminal and that the forfeiture proceedings therein were civil and not criminal in nature and that there was no constitutional bar on the determination in civil or other proceedings of matters which may constitute elements of criminal offences;[97]

(2) that the "reversal of proof" in requiring a respondent to establish that property frozen pursuant to ss 2 or 3 of the 1996 Act did not breach Articles 38.1 or 40.3 of the Constitution as the shifting of the onus of proof in either criminal or civil proceedings has been found to be permissible;[98]

(3) that the 1996 Act did not *per se* infringe a respondent's privilege against self-incrimination, although an undertaking from the Director of Public Prosecutions of the kind sought by Moriarty J in *MM v DD*[99] would be essential in virtually every case where a discovery order under s 9 is granted;[100]

(4) that the fact that the Court had a discretion under s 6 of the 1996 Act as to whether to make payments to provide for legal expenses did not encroach upon a respondent's constitutional rights to access to the Court and to legal aid and, moreover, it must be presumed that the

---

[97.] *Melling v O'Mathghamhna and the Attorney General* [1962] IR 1; *Goodman v Hamilton (No 1)* [1992] 2 IR 542; *O'Keeffe v Ferris* Supreme Court, unrep, 19 February 1997; *Attorney General v Southern Industrial Trust Ltd and Simons* (1960) 94 ILTR 161; and *Clancy v Ireland* [1988] IR 326 considered.

[98.] *MM v DD* High Court, unrep, 10 December 1996 (Moriarty J); *Hardy v Ireland* [1994] 2 IR 550; *O'Leary v Ireland* [1995] 1 IR 254; and Section 37 of the Family Law (Divorce) Act 1996 (as to which see para **[3.06]** and **[3.04]** on s 35(2) of the Family Law Act 1995 *ante*).

[99.] High Court, unrep, 10 December 1996 (Moriarty J). See para **[3.44]** *infra*.

[100.] *MM v DD* High Court, unrep, 10 December 1996 (Moriarty J); *Re O (a disclosure order)* [1991] 2 QB 520; *Istel Ltd v Tully* [1993] AC 45; *R v Thomas (a disclosure order)* [1992] 4 All ER 814; and *Heaney v Ireland* [1996] 1 IR 580 considered.

Court will use its discretion in a constitutional way and that persons will not be wrongfully deprived of legal representation;[101]

(5) that the 1996 Act did not infringe a respondent's private property rights under Articles 40.3.2° and 43 of the Constitution since, *inter alia*, the State has a legitimate interest in the forfeiture of the proceeds of crime and because the exigencies of the common good include measures designed to prevent the accumulation of assets which directly or indirectly derive from criminal activities;[102] and

(6) that the operation of the 1996 Act was not retrospective, notwithstanding the definition of "proceeds of crime" in s 1(1) of the 1996 Act,[103] since the legislature had not declared any act to be an infringement of the law which was not so at the time of its commission.

McGuinness J went on to find that the 1996 Act, as a whole, was a proportionate response by the legislature to the threat to society posed by the operations of major criminals.[104] Just as in *MM v DD*[105] where Moriarty J acknowledged the phenomenon of organised crime, so too did McGuinness J, saying:

"... the Court has before it the evidence of two very senior police officers who have many years of experience of criminal investigation work. Both of them, as earlier outlined, paint a picture of an entirely new type of professional criminal who organises, rather than commits, crime and who thereby renders himself virtually immune to the ordinary procedures of criminal investigation and prosecution. Such persons are able to operate a reign of terror so as effectively to prevent the passing on of information to the Gardai. At the same time their obvious wealth and power causes them to be respected by lesser criminals or would-be criminals.

---

[101] *MacAuley v Minister for Post and Telegraphs* [1966] IR 345; and *State (Healy) v Donoghue* [1976] IR 325 considered.

[102] *Cox v Ireland* [1992] 2 IR 503 and *Clancy v Ireland* [1988] IR 326 considered.

[103] See para [**3.38**] *post*.

[104] On this point the learned judge cited the following passage from Costello J in *Heaney v Ireland* [1994] 3 IR 593: "In considering whether a restriction on the exercise of rights is permitted by the Constitution, the Courts in this country and elsewhere have found it helpful to apply the test of proportionality, a test which contains the notions of minimal restraint on the exercise of protected rights, and of the exigencies of the common good in a democratic society. This is a test frequently adopted by the European Court of Human Rights (see for example *Kearns Newspapers Ltd v United Kingdom* (1979) 2 EHRR 245) and has recently been formulated by the Supreme Court in Canada on the following terms. The objective of the impugned provision must be of sufficient importance to warrant overriding a constitutionally protected right. It must relate to concerns pressing and substantial in a free and democratic society. The means chosen must pass a proportionality test. They must: - (a) be rationally connected to the objective and not be arbitrary, unfair or based on irrational considerations; (b) impair the right as little as possible; (c) be such that their effects on rights are proportional to the objective; *Chaulk v R* [1990] 3 SCR 1303 at 1335 and 1336."

[105] High Court, unrep, 10 December 1996 (Moriarty J).

... in the context of a relatively small community, the operations carried out by major criminals have a serious and worsening effect. This is particularly so in regard to their importation and distribution of illegal drugs, which in its turn leads to a striking increase in lesser crimes carried out by addicts seeking to finance their addiction.

In theory this type of threat to public order and the community at large may seem less serious than the threat posed to this State by the operation of politically motivated illegal organisations. In practice major and minor drug-related crime is probably perceived by ordinary members of the community as more threatening and more likely to affect the every day lives of themselves and their children."[106]

[3.34] In this consideration of the provisions of the 1996 Act, the following issues are considered:

1. "Property" which may be Affected.
2. The Definition of "Respondents".
3. "Dealing" in Relation to "Property".
4. Interim Orders.
5. Interlocutory Orders.
6. Discovery and Disclosure Orders.
7. Evidence and Procedures for Interim and Interlocutory Orders.
8. Ancillary Orders which the High Court can Make.
9. Notice of Interim and Interlocutory Orders.
10. Duration, Discharge and Variation of Interim and Interlocutory Orders.
11. The Power to Appoint a Receiver.
12. Disposal Orders.
13. Registration of Interim and Interlocutory Orders.
14. Insolvency of Persons Affected.
15. Compensation for Persons Affected.

"Property" which may be Affected

[3.35] It was necessary to assign statutory definitions to the key words used in the 1996 Act. So, "property", which can be affected by either an interim or interlocutory order, is defined as *including*:

[106.] At pp 76, 77 of the transcript. McGuinness J went on to quote from O'Mahony, *Criminal Chaos - Seven Crises in Irish Criminal Justice*, (1996) Roundhall Sweet & Maxwell at pp 204. 205 as an example of the effects of drug abuse on a community.

money and all other property, real or personal, heritable or moveable, including choses in action and other intangible or incorporeal property and references to property shall be construed as including references to any interest in property.[107]

Moreover, the word "interest" in relation to "property" is defined to include "right".[108] The value of "property" is also highly material because there is a *de minimus* provision. Accordingly, before the High Court can make either an interim order under s 2 or an interlocutory order under s 3, it must be satisfied that the value of the property in a person's possession or control, which constitutes or was acquired with the proceeds of crime, is not less than £10,000.[109]

The Definition of "Respondents"

[3.36] Those who may be prohibited from dealing in property by an interim order under s 2 of the 1996 Act are persons in possession or control of "property", as defined above, or any other specified person or any other person having notice of the order.[110] Moreover, s 3(1) of the 1996 Act (which deals with interlocutory orders) refers to "respondent" which is defined by s 1(1) as meaning:

> a person in respect of whom an application for an interim order or an interlocutory order has been made or in respect of whom such an order has been made and includes any person who, but for this Act, would become entitled, on the death of the first-mentioned person, to any property to which such an order relates (being an order that is in force and is in respect of that person).

The important point here is that *any* person can be made directly subject to either an interim or interlocutory order, the essential determinant being that they are in possession or control of "property", as defined in s 1 of the 1996 Act.

[3.37] A degree of protection against suit is afforded to banks, building societies, other financial institutions and any other third parties who are given notice of an order and act on foot of it. Section 14 provides that no action or proceedings shall lie against such persons "in respect of any act or omission done or made in compliance with an order" under the 1996 Act.

[107.] Section 1(1) of the 1996 Act. In *Criminal Assets Bureau v T, The Irish Times* 23 May 1998 (Shanley J), it was reported that a house (which had been decorated to a high standard and included a jacuzzi and gymnasium) and a Honda Civic motor car were accepted to constitute the proceeds of crime.

[108.] *Ibid.*

[109.] Section 2(1)(b) and s 3(1)(b) of the 1996 Act.

[110.] Section 2(1) of the 1996 Act.

"Dealing" in relation to Property

[3.38] Although the operative part of both an interim and interlocutory order will prohibit a person from "disposing of or otherwise dealing with" specified property, the term "disposing of" is not defined, presumably because it is thought to be self-explanatory. The word "dealing" is, however, defined to *include*:

(a) where a debt is owed to that person, making a payment to any person in reduction of the amount of the debt;

(b) removing the property from the State, and

(c) in the case of money or other property held for the person by another person, paying to releasing or transferring it to the person or to any other person.[111]

The expression "proceeds of crime" is defined as meaning "any property obtained or received at any time (whether before or after the passing of this Act) by or as a result of or in connection with the commission of an offence".[112]

Interim Orders

[3.39] Section 2 of the 1996 Act gives jurisdiction to the High Court to make an interim order. Section 2(1) provides:

Where it is shown to the satisfaction of the Court on application to it *ex parte* in that behalf by a member or an authorised officer -

(a) that a person is in possession or control of -

(i) specified property and that the property constitutes, directly or indirectly, proceeds of crime, or

(ii) specified property that was acquired, in whole or in part, with or in connection with property that, directly or indirectly, constitutes proceeds of crime,

and

(b) that the value of the property or, as the case may be, the total value of the property referred to in both subparagraphs (i) and (ii), of paragraph (a) is not less than £10,000,

the Court may make an order ("an interim order") prohibiting the person or any other specified person or any other person having notice of the order from disposing of or otherwise dealing with the whole or, if appropriate, a specified part of the property or diminishing its value during the period of 21 days from the date of the making of the order.

[111.] Section 1(1) of the 1996 Act.
[112.] *Ibid.*

Moreover, s 2(2)(a) of the 1996 Act provides that an interim order may contain such provisions, conditions and restrictions as the High Court considers necessary or expedient.

[3.40] The procedure for making an interim order is by *ex parte* application. Those who can make application, grounded on affidavit, are either, a member of the Garda Siochana not below the rank of Chief Superintendent, or, an authorised officer.[113] As noted above, application for such an order will invariably be brought by a duly authorised representative of the Criminal Assets Bureau.

Interlocutory Orders

[3.41] Section 3(1) of the 1996 Act empowers the High Court to make an interlocutory order:

> Where, on application to it in that behalf by the applicant, it appears to the Court, on evidence tendered by the applicant, consisting of or including evidence admissible by virtue of section 8 -
>
> (a) that a person is in possession or control of -
>
> > (i)   specified property and that the property constitutes, directly or indirectly, proceeds of crime, or
> >
> > (ii) specified property that was acquired, in whole or in part, with or in connection with property that, directly or indirectly, constitutes proceeds of crime,
> >
> > and
>
> (b) that the value of the property or, as the case may be, the total value of the property referred to in both subparagraphs (i) and (ii) of paragraph (a) is not less than £10,000,
>
> the Court shall make an order ("an interlocutory order") prohibiting the respondent or any other specified person or any other person having notice of the order from disposing of or otherwise dealing with the whole or, if appropriate, a specified part of the property of diminishing its value, unless, it is shown to the satisfaction of the Court, on evidence tendered by the respondent or any other person -
>
> (I) that that particular property does not constitute, directly or indirectly, proceeds of crime and was not acquired, in whole or in part, with or in connection with property that, directly or indirectly, constitutes proceeds of crime, or
>
> (II) that the value of all the property to which the order would relate is less than £10,000:

[113.] "Authorised Officer" is defined by s 1(1) of the 1996 Act to mean an officer of the Revenue Commissioners authorised in writing by the Revenue Commissioners to perform the functions conferred by the 1996 Act on authorised officer.

Provided, however, that the Court shall not make the order if it is satisfied that there would be a serious risk of injustice.

Section 3(2)(a) provides that an interlocutory order may also contain such provisions, conditions and restrictions as the High Court considers necessary or expedient.

[3.42] As with an application for an interim order, those who can apply for an interlocutory order are a Garda Chief Superintendent or an authorised officer (invariably, Criminal Asset Bureau personnel). Section 3 of the 1996 Act makes it relatively easy for an applicant to obtain an interlocutory order for two reasons. First, the High Court is impelled to make such an order *unless* the respondent can prove that the particular property in question is not, or was not acquired, directly or indirectly, with the proceeds of crime or establishes that the value of the property is less than £10,000. This effectively switches the burden of proof from the applicant to the respondent: upon an applicant tendering evidence consisting of or including the kind of evidence detailed in s 8 of the 1996 Act,[114] it then falls to the respondent to show why the Court should *not* make an interlocutory order. Secondly, unlike the making of an ordinary interlocutory injunction which can only be made where it is "just or convenient" to do so, an interlocutory order under the 1996 Act *shall, inter alia*, be made under s 3 of the 1996 Act, *unless*, "there would be a serious risk of injustice". The traditional test for interlocutory relief has been stood on its head.

Discovery and Disclosure Orders

[3.43] It would be difficult to successfully apply for an order under the 1996 Act if the applicant did not have precise information as to the nature and extent of a respondent's property. Section 9 of the 1996 Act provides that at any time during proceedings commenced under either s 2 or s 3, or while either an interim or interlocutory order is in force, the High Court[115] may by order direct the respondent to file an affidavit in the Central Office of the High Court specifying:

    (a) the property of which the respondent is in possession or control, or

    (b) the income, and the sources of the income, of the respondent during such period (not exceeding ten years) ending on the date of the application for the order as the Court may specify, or both.

In this regard the 1996 Act goes further than the Criminal Justice Act 1994 which was silent as to the court's power to order the disclosure of assets, although, as seen above,[116] the courts in England have held that such a power was inherent in the court's jurisdiction.

[114.] See para **[3.49]** *infra*.

[115.] In the case of an appeal, the Supreme Court may make such an order.

[116.] See para **[3.12]** *supra*.

[3.44] One of the first cases to examine the power to direct that an affidavit be filed by a respondent, under s 9 of the 1996 Act, was *MM v DD*.[117] That case concerned an application which contested an order for discovery that had been made against the respondent pursuant to s 9 of the 1996 Act. Earlier, an interim order under s 2 had been made against the respondent. The respondent's counsel raised three specific grounds of objection[118] to the making of the order under s 9, the second of which is considered here: that the relief sought, if granted, would offend against the respondent's privilege against self-incrimination. In rejecting this contention Moriarty J began by noting that even in circumstances where the court had no express power to order disclosure or discovery, it had been held in England in *AJ Bekhor & Co Ltd v Bilton*[119] that "the Court had an inherent power to make all such ancillary orders, including an order for discovery, as appeared to the Court to be just and convenient to ensure that the exercise of the Mareva jurisdiction was effective to ensure its purpose".[120] Moriarty J said that:

> "With regard to the present case, this decision is relevant insofar as it demonstrates that a Court may be willing to give an Order of the nature contemplated by section 9 of the 1996 Act, even in the absence of an express power, so that it may be argued that *a fortiori*, a Court with an express statutory power ought clearly to exercise it in appropriate cases."[121]

As to the contention that the exercise of the statutory power to order discovery might infringe the defendant's privilege against self-incrimination, Moriarty J noted that this had been raised in the English case of *Re O (disclosure order)*.[122] In that case the Court of Appeal had said that since the English Act did not abrogate the common law rule against self-incrimination a party could decline to comply with a disclosure order if there was a risk of self-incrimination but that the use to which discovered information could be put may be attached to the order. In that case Lord Donaldson MR said that the following condition should be inserted in all orders for disclosure in aid of a restraint order under the English Criminal Justice Act 1988:

---

[117] High Court, unrep, 10 December 1996 (Moriarty J).

[118] The three grounds were: (a) that the nature and standard of proof advanced on affidavit against the respondent were unsatisfactory and inadequate to warrant the grant of the relief sought and in particular offended against the hearsay rule; (b) that the relief sought if granted would offend against the respondent's privilege against self-incrimination; and (c) that there was a possible retrospection under the 1996 Act.

[119] [1981] 2 All ER 565; [1981] 1 QB 923. See generally, Ch 10, *Ancillary Orders*, para **[10.04]** *et seq.*

[120] At p 6 of the transcript.

[121] At pp 6, 7 of the transcript.

[122] [1991] 1 All ER 330; [1991] 2 QB 520, considered at para **[3.12]** *supra.*

"No disclosure made in compliance with this order shall be used as evidence on the prosecution of an offence alleged to have been committed by the person required to make that disclosure or by any spouse of that person."[123]

In that case, the Crown Prosecution Service was a party to the proceedings and consented to the order on these terms. Moriarty J noted that in the subsequent case of *Istel Ltd v Tully*,[124] a case which involved the granting of an Anton Piller order[125] ancillary to civil fraud proceedings, the defendant had appealed to the House of Lords on the grounds that compliance with the order would infringe his right against self-incrimination. He noted that in that case, although the Crown Prosecution Service was not a party to the proceedings, a letter was received which said that the agency undertook not to profit from any disclosure in the current proceedings and that it would only rely upon evidence obtained independently of the proceedings. Moriarty J held that:

"Applying this judgment to the present case, I am satisfied that, noting the degree of nexus between the applicant and the office of the Director of Public Prosecutions, it will be necessary if discovery is ordered that an undertaking be given by the Director of Public Prosecutions similar to that given by the Crown Prosecution Service in *Istel Ltd v Tully*, in order to prevent possible prejudice in any future criminal proceedings. Such a course was indeed conceded in argument...".[126]

[3.45] It may be noted that in *MM v DD* Moriarty J declined to follow *R v Thomas (a disclosure order)* [127] where it was said by Leggett LJ that disclosure of assets did not amount to self-incrimination, but merely facilitated an assessment of the amount to be recovered from a defendant who had benefited from drug trafficking.

[3.46] In *Gilligan v The Criminal Assets Bureau*[128] the privilege against self-incrimination was also addressed in the context of an overall challenge to the constitutionality of the 1996 Act. There, McGuinness J reviewed Moriarty J's decision in *MM v DD* and the Supreme Court's decision in *Heaney v Ireland*.[129] Although finding that the Supreme Court in the latter case had made it clear that "the privilege against self-incrimination, or the right to silence, is by no means absolute"[130] McGuinness J said that:

[123.] [1991] 1 All ER 330 at 336d.
[124.] [1993] AC 45.
[125.] See Ch 10, *Ancillary Orders*, para **[10.38]**.
[126.] At p 8 of the transcript.
[127.] [1992] 4 All ER 814.
[128.] High Court, unrep, 26 June 1997 (McGuinness J). See para **[3.32]** *supra*.
[129.] [1996] 1 IR 580.
[130.] At p 65 of the transcript.

"In order to minimise any encroachment on the citizen's rights and in order to operate the procedures under the Act in a way which is in accordance with constitutional justice, it seems to me that the Court would need to take particular care in deciding whether to make an Order under section 9 requiring disclosure. This is especially so when one bears in mind the wide scope of the discovery which may be ordered ... It appears to me that the type of undertaking sought by Moriarty J in the *MM v DD* case would be essential in virtually every case where an Order under section 9 is granted. Even then there may well be difficulty in operating such an undertaking in a secure and watertight manner."[131]

McGuinness J's concerns over s 9 were repeated at the conclusion of her judgment.[132] It is thought, however, that provided an undertaking of the sort envisaged by Moriarty J in *MM v DD* is given, s 9 of the 1996 Act is indeed workable without unnecessarily infringing a respondent's privilege against self-incrimination.

[3.47] The retrospective operation of s 9 of the 1996 Act, in requiring disclosure of income and property going back ten years, formed the third ground of objection to the disclosure order in *MM v DD*.[133] After noting the decisions in *Chestvale v Glackin*,[134] *Hamilton v Hamilton*[135] and *Re Hefferon Kearns*,[136] Moriarty J applied the reasoning of the Supreme Court in *Heaney v Ireland*[137] which concerned the constitutionality of s 52 of the Offences Against the State Act 1939. That section required a person detained under that Act to give an account of his movements during any specified period on demand by the Garda Siochana. There, the Supreme Court concluded that there was proper proportionality in the section between any infringement of the citizen's rights and the State's entitlement to protect itself. Moriarty J said:

"In the context of the foregoing, whilst conscious of the presumption that a statute shall be prospective rather than retrospective, I am of the view that section 9 should be held to enable discovery of property or income held or enjoyed by a respondent for a maximum period of ten years prior to application."[138]

---

131. *Ibid.*
132. At p 79 of the transcript.
133. High Court, unrep, 10 December 1996 (Moriarty J).
134. [1992] ILRM 221.
135. [1982] IR 471.
136. [1993] 3 IR 177.
137. [1996] 1 IR 580.
138. At p 13 of the transcript.

[3.48] In *Gilligan v The Criminal Assets Bureau*[139] the same issue was again considered by the High Court, albeit in the context of the 1996 Act generally, as opposed to s 9 in particular. McGuinness J held that the operation of the 1996 Act was not retrospective, notwithstanding that the definition of "proceeds of crime" contained in s 1(1) provides that it means any property obtained or received at any time (whether before or after the passing of the 1996 Act) because the Oireachtas had not declared any act to be an infringement of the law which was not so at the time of its commission. As McGuinness J said:

> "The acquisition of assets which derive from crime was not a legal activity before the passing of the 1996 Act and did not become an illegal activity because of the 1996 Act".[140]

Accordingly, McGuinness J held that it was permissible to require a respondent to disclose the existence of his assets.

Evidence and Procedures for Interim and Interlocutory Orders

[3.49] Section 8 of the 1996 Act contains certain provisions on evidence and proceedings taken under the Act. Section 8(1) provides that the statement by a member of the Garda Siochana or an authorised officer, whether on affidavit[141] or in oral evidence,[142] that he believes either or both:

(i)   that the respondent[143] is in possession or control of specified property and that the property constitutes, directly or indirectly, proceeds or crime,

(ii) that the respondent is in possession of or control or specified property and that the property was acquired, in whole or in part, with or in connection with property that, directly or indirectly, constitutes proceeds of crime,

and that the value of the property or, as the case may be, the total value of the property referred to in both paragraphs (i) and (ii) is not less than £10,000 ..."

then, if the court is satisfied that there are reasonable grounds for his belief, his statement will be evidence of those matters.

[3.50] Section 8(2) of the 1996 Act provides that in respect of all applications under the 1996 Act, the standard of proof "required to determine any question" is that applicable in civil proceedings ie the balance of probabilities.[144] In *MM v*

[139.] High Court, unrep, 26 June 1997 (McGuinness J).

[140.] At p 72 of the transcript.

[141.] In an application for an interim order under s 2 of the 1996 Act.

[142.] In an application for an interlocutory order under s 3 of the 1996 Act or an interim order, as aforesaid, where such is directed by the High Court.

[143.] See para **[3.36]** *supra*.

[144.] Section 8(5) provides that a document purporting to authorise a person who is described therein as an officer of the Revenue Commissioners to perform the functions conferred on authorised officers by the 1996 Act and to be signed by a Revenue Commissioner "shall be evidence that the person is an authorised officer".

DD,[145] a contested discovery application under s 9 of the 1996 Act, the respondent's counsel contended that the nature and standard of proof advanced against the respondent were unsatisfactory and inadequate to warrant the grant of the relief sought and in particular offended the rule against hearsay. This contention was rejected by Moriarty J. After noting the provisions of s 8 and in particular the requisite standard of proof, he said:

> "It seems to me that I am clearly entitled to take notice of the international phenomenon, far from peculiar to Ireland, that significant numbers of persons who engage as principals in lucrative professional crime, particularly that referable to the illicit supply of controlled drugs, are alert and effectively able to insulate themselves against the risk of successful criminal prosecution through deployment of intermediaries, and that the Act is designed to enable the lower probative requirements of civil law to be utilised in appropriate cases, not to achieve penal sanctions, but to effectively deprive such persons of such illicit financial fruits of their labours as can be shown to be proceeds of crime. I am not concerned with construing the Act as a whole, but it is noteworthy that, whilst its scheme indeed introduces significant innovations, a wide discretion is entrusted to the Court to ensure compliance with the "*audi alteram partem*" rule and other precepts of natural justice, and to ensure that injustice is not perpetrated against meritorious respondents, for example by the compensation provisions comprised in section 16 of the Act."[146]

As to the contention that the hearsay rule was offended, Moriarty J said:

> "Clearly also, the Act adopts a procedure broadly analogous to Mareva applications, and it is the established usage of the Courts that some appreciable measure of hearsay evidence is considered acceptable in affidavits filed on behalf of parties."[147]

Moriarty J found that, in the case in hand, the evidence tendered on affidavit was outside the realm of mere hearsay, speculative or otherwise inadequate evidence but he reserved for another occasion consideration of the hypothesis of how to address a case in which hearsay proof of suspicion alone is tendered. He did acknowledge concern that significant circumspection and care for a respondent's entitlements may need to be exercised and that "a generalised advertence to "the innocent who have nothing to fear" would not appear to in any realistic sense satisfy the requirements of sections 2 or 3 of the Act".[148]

[145.] High Court, unrep, 10 December 1996 (Moriarty J).

[146.] At pp 3,4 of the transcript.

[147.] At p 4 of the transcript. In support Moriarty J noted the Supreme Court's decisions in *McKeon v DPP* Supreme Court, unrep, 1995 and *DPP v Henry Doherty* Supreme Court, unrep, 26 February 1993 which he said acknowledged that hearsay could be relied upon in exceptional cases. On the drafting of affidavits in Mareva applications, see Ch 8, *Applying for a Mareva Injunction*, para **[8.26]** *et seq*.

[148.] At p 5 of the transcript.

[3.51] Section 8(3) provides that proceedings for an interim order "shall be heard otherwise than in public", and other proceedings under the 1996 Act may also be held *in camera* where the court considers this to be proper. Moreover, s 8(4) provides that the High Court may, if it considers it appropriate to do so, prohibit the publication of such information as it may determine in relation to proceedings under the 1996 Act including information in relation to applications for the making or refusal of and the contents of orders under the Act and the person to whom they relate. It will be observed that many of the judgments on foot of the 1996 Act, which have been referred to here, have been expurgated and reported in traditional family law format.

Ancillary Orders which the High Court can Make

[3.52] Section 5(1) of the 1996 Act empowers the High Court, on application being made, to make "such orders as it considers necessary or expedient to enable the order aforesaid to have full effect". This power arises at any time when an interim or interlocutory order is in force. The applicant is obliged to serve notice of the application on (a) the respondent - unless the court is satisfied that it is not reasonably possible to ascertain the respondent's whereabouts - and (b) any other person in relation to whom the Court directs that notice be given.[149]

Notice of Interim and Interlocutory Orders

[3.53] Section 2(2)(b) of the 1996 Act provides that an interim order (and s 3(2)(b) provides that an interlocutory order) *shall* provide for notice of the order to be given to the respondent and any other person who appears to be or is affected by it unless the High Court is satisfied that it is not reasonably possible to ascertain his whereabouts.

Duration, Discharge and Variation of Interim and Interlocutory Orders

[3.54] Here the following issues are considered:

    (a) Interim orders: duration, discharge and variation;

    (b) Interlocutory orders: duration, discharge and variation;

    (c) Forfeiture and confiscation orders;

    (d) Applications to permit the discharge of living expenses etc.

(a) Interim orders: duration, discharge and variation

[3.55] The prohibition on disposing of or otherwise dealing with specified property in an interim order made under s 2 of the 1996 Act is expressed to last for a period of 21 days from the date upon which the order is made.[150] Subject to

---

149. Section 5(2) of the 1996 Act.
150. Section 2(1) of the 1996 Act.

the order not being discharged or varied during that time, s 2(5) provides that an interim order shall:

> continue in force until the expiration of the period of 21 days from the date of its making and shall then lapse unless an application for the making of an interlocutory order in respect of any of the property concerned is brought during that period and, if such an application is brought, the interim order shall lapse upon -
>
> (a) the determination of the application,
>
> (b) the expiration of the ordinary time for bringing an appeal from the determination,
>
> (c) if such an appeal is brought, the determination or abandonment of it or of any further appeal or the expiration of the ordinary time for bringing any further appeal,
>
> whichever is the latest.

Accordingly, where an interim order has been made and is in force and where an interlocutory order is applied for, the interim order shall not lapse, notwithstanding that the period of 21 days has elapsed, until the application for the interlocutory order has determined and the appeal process for or against the making of an interlocutory order has determined. This provision was necessary to avoid the creation of a window whereby property could lawfully be disposed of during the period between the lapsing of an interim order and the making of an application for and grant of an interlocutory order.

[3.56] Notwithstanding that an interim order shall ordinarily last for a period of 21 days from the making of the order, application may be brought within that period to have the interim order discharged or varied. Section 2(4) of the 1996 Act provides that where the applicant, in practice, the Criminal Assets Bureau, seeks to have an interim order discharged the High Court shall discharge the order. An application brought under s 2(4) requires the applicant to give notice to a respondent (unless the Court is satisfied that it is not reasonably possible to ascertain his whereabouts) and also to such other person as the High Court directs.[151]

[3.57] Section 2(3) of the 1996 Act empowers a respondent or other person affected by the order, to make application for its discharge or variation. It provides:

> Where an interim order is in force, the Court, on application to it in that behalf by the respondent or any other person claiming ownership of any of the property concerned may, if it is shown to the satisfaction of the Court that -

---

[151.] Section 2(6) of the 1996 Act.

(a) the property concerned or a part of it is not property to which subparagraph (i) or (ii) of subsection (1)(a) applies, or

(b) the value of the property to which those subparagraphs apply is less than £10,000,

discharge or, as may be appropriate, vary the order.

The grounds for discharge or variation under s 2(3)[152] are two-fold: (1) where the "property" in question is not in fact the "proceeds of crime" or has not been acquired with the proceeds of crime; and (2) where the value of the property is less than £10,000. In essence, s 2(3) envisages an application being brought to discharge or vary the interim order in cases where a respondent challenges the very basis upon which the order was made by the Court on the grounds that the essential proofs were not satisfied. An application brought under s 2(3) requires the respondent or other person seeking a discharge or variation to give notice to the applicant and such other persons as the High Court directs.[153]

(b) Interlocutory orders: duration, discharge and variation

[3.58] The ostensible purpose of a freezing order under the 1996 Act is to preserve property so as to make it amenable to a subsequent disposal order under s 4. Accordingly, an interlocutory order, made under s 3(1) of the 1996 Act, has the potential to last for over 7 years, as s 4(1) does not permit the making of a disposal order unless an interlocutory order has been in force for not less than 7 years. Section 3(5) of the 1996 Act provides:

Subject to subsections (3) and (4), an interlocutory order shall continue in force until -

(a) the determination of an application for a disposal order in relation to the property concerned,

(b) the expiration of the ordinary time for bringing an appeal from that determination,

(c) if such an appeal is brought, it or any further appeal is determined or abandoned or the ordinary time for bringing any further appeal has expired,

whichever is the latest, and shall then lapse.

In this respect an interlocutory order made under s 3(1) is very different, and infinitely more draconian, than an ordinary Mareva injunction which will normally only last until the trial of the substantive cause of action, although it can be continued thereafter in aid of execution.[154]

[152.] As to applications for variation of either interim or interlocutory orders to enable the respondent or others discharge certain expenses or conduct his business, see para **[3.61]** *infra*.
[153.] Section 2(6) of the 1996 Act.
[154.] See Ch 4, *A Substantive Cause of Action*, para **[4.28]**.

[3.59] Section 3(4) of the 1996 Act provides that where the applicant Criminal Assets Bureau, seeks to have an interlocutory order discharged, the High Court shall discharge the order. An application brought under s 3(4) requires that notice be given to a respondent - unless the Court is satisfied that it is not reasonably possible to ascertain his whereabouts - and to such other person as the High Court directs.[155]

[3.60] Section 3(3) of the 1996 Act facilitates applications for the discharge or variation of an interlocutory order by a respondent or some other party. This provides:

> Where an interlocutory order is in force, the Court, on application to it in that behalf at any time by the respondent or any other person claiming ownership of any of the property concerned, may, if it is shown to the satisfaction of the Court that the property or a specified part of it is property to which paragraph (I) of subsection (1) applies, or that the order causes any other injustice, discharge or, as may be appropriate, vary the order.

Where application is brought under this provision a respondent or other person seeking a discharge or variation must give notice to the applicant and also to such other persons as the High Court directs.[156] There are only two grounds upon which the Court can discharge or vary an interlocutory order. The first is where it is shown to the satisfaction of the Court that the property, or a specified part thereof, does not constitute, directly or indirectly, the proceeds of crime nor was it acquired in whole or in part with, or in connection with, property that, directly or indirectly, constitutes the proceeds of crime. So, money obtained legitimately, eg, being compensation paid to a respondent in respect of a road traffic accident, would not be covered by the order.[157] The second, more nebulous ground, is where it is shown to the satisfaction of the Court that an interlocutory order "causes any other injustice". In the absence of judicial interpretation any suggestion as to what might come within the second ground must be speculative, but it is opined that if "Equity's darling"- the *bona fide* purchaser for value without actual notice of an interim or interlocutory order - was to be affected by such an order, he should be given relief under this ground.

[155.] Section 3(6) of the 1996 Act.

[156.] Section 3(6) of the 1996 Act.

[157.] See *F v Governor of Mountjoy, The Irish Times* 2 May 1998 (Shanley J) where it was reported that F was successful in his application that the Governor of Mountjoy be ordered to return certain cash to him which was the proceeds of a road traffic accident; it was reported that in ordering that the money be released, Shanley J had said that the money in question was not covered by an interlocutory freezing order since that order related to property which F was alleged to have received in connection with drug-trafficking.

(c) Forfeiture and confiscation orders

[3.61] Section 3(7) of the 1996 Act provides for the discharge or variation of an interim or interlocutory order where a forfeiture order or confiscation order under the Criminal Justice Act 1994[158] or a forfeiture order under the Misuse of Drugs Act 1977 relates to property affected by an order under the 1996 Act. In such a case the interim or interlocutory order under the 1996 Act will stand discharged if it relates only to the specified property or it will stand varied by the exclusion of the specified property if it also relates to other property.

(d) Applications to permit the discharge of living expenses etc

[3.62] Section 6(1) of the 1996 Act allows the High Court, on application being made by a respondent[159] or any other person affected by either an interim or interlocutory order, to make such orders as it considers appropriate in relation to any of the property concerned if it considers it essential to do so for the purpose of enabling:

(a) the respondent to discharge the reasonable living and other necessary expenses (including legal expenses in or in relation to proceedings under this Act) incurred or to be incurred by or in respect of the respondent and his or her dependants, or

(b) the respondent or that other person to carry on a business, trade, profession or other occupation to which any of that property relates.

Any order made by the High Court under this provision may contain such conditions and restrictions as the Court considers necessary or expedient to protect the value of the property and to avoid any unnecessary diminution in the value of the property.[160] At first sight this provision resembles the High Court's practice of granting Mareva injunctions which restrain the disposal of assets subject to certain exceptions, which take the form of "provisos", as to living expenses, legal expenses and ordinary business expenses.[161] However, in the case of a Mareva injunction, the assets affected by the order are a defendant's own assets and the plaintiff will neither have, claim to have nor acquire any proprietary interest in them. The difference, however, is that whilst such provisos are almost standard in Mareva injunctions, under s 6 of the 1996 Act the High Court can only make such an order "if it considers it *essential* to do so" for either of the two stated purposes. Even where it is essential to a respondent that he discharges his legal and living expenses, it must be questioned whether he should be allowed to utilise what are accepted by the Court as being "the

---

158. See para **[3.08]** *supra.*
159. Any such application shall be on notice to the applicant-Criminal Assets Bureau and any other person to whom the High Court directs notice be given: s 8(3).
160. Section 8(2) of the 1996 Act.
161. See Ch 9, *The Mareva Order and Its Effects*, para **[9.12]** *et seq.*

proceeds of crime" to discharge such expenses. The State already has in place a safety net to help those in need with social welfare for "living expenses" and with free legal aid for the impecunious who are charged with criminal offences or otherwise affected by a freezing order.[162] It is submitted that the circumstances in which the High Court will accede to applications under s 6 will be exceptional and due regard will be had to the qualifying words, "if it considers it essential to do so".

The Power to Appoint a Receiver

[3.63] Section 7(1) of the 1996 Act also empowers the High Court to appoint a receiver where it has made an interim[163] or interlocutory order.[164] This power is thought to be similar to the appointment of a pre-judgment receiver in aid of a Mareva injunction.[165] Subject to such exceptions and conditions (if any) as the High Court may specify, any such receiver appointed by the court may take possession of any property to which such order relates and, in accordance with the Court's directions, manage or otherwise deal with any property over which he is appointed. Moreover the Court may require any person having possession or control of property in respect of which the receiver is appointed to give up possession to the receiver. One example of where a receiver was appointed is *Criminal Assets Bureau v X*.[166] The newspaper report stated that this was the first case in which a receiver had been appointed under the 1996 Act to dispose of a two-bedroom property on Dublin's quays and a Victorian house in Fairview which had been converted into flats. It was reported that gardaí believed that the man who owned the property had driven the motorcycle from which a gunman alighted and had shot dead the journalist, Ms Veronica Guerin.[167]

[162.] See, eg, *F v Criminal Assets Bureau*, *The Irish Times*, 19 December 1997 (Shanley J) which concerned an application for the variation of an order made under the Criminal Justice Act 1994, in order to facilitate the payment of legal expenses. See para **[3.21]** *supra*.

[163.] In *Criminal Assets Bureau v B*, *The Irish Times* 4 November 1997 (O'Sullivan J) where it was reported that following the making of an interim order restraining the disposal of the respondent's property a receiver had been appointed. It was reported that the present application was for an interlocutory injunction and that it was contended by the respondent's counsel that this was misconceived since the money in question had been lodged to the account of the receiver and the respondents were not in control of the property and that the Criminal Assets Bureau had applied prematurely for the appointment of a receiver. The report concluded by saying that the application was adjourned to enable instructions to be taken.

[164.] As to the appointment of receivers generally, see Ch 10, *Ancillary Orders*, para **[10.69]** *et seq*.

[165.] See Ch 10, *Ancillary Orders*, paras **[10.72]**-**[10.76]**.

[166.] *The Irish Times* 25 January 1997.

[167.] See also *Criminal Assets Bureau v Gilligan*, *The Irish Times* 13 February 1997 where it was reported that Morris J refused the respondent's application to prevent the appointment of a receiver.

[3.64] Section 7(2) of the 1996 Act exempts a receiver from liability to any person in respect of any loss or damage caused, except by the receiver's negligence. This applies in cases where a receiver takes action in relation to property which is not in fact the subject of an interim or interlocutory order. In such an event, a receiver will not be liable, provided that he would have been entitled to take such action were the property subject to an order and also provided that he believes, and has reasonable grounds for believing, that he was entitled to take that action.

[3.65] It should also be noted that by s 15(1) of the 1996 Act, where an order is in force, a member of the Garda Siochana or an officer of Customs and Excise may seize the property for the purpose of preventing it from being removed from the State.[168]

Disposal Orders

[3.66] The purpose of an interim or interlocutory order is ostensibly to make the property, which is affected by such orders, amenable to a disposal order. The effect of a disposal order is to deprive the respondent of his rights in or to the property because upon the making of the order "the property shall stand transferred to the Minister or other person to whom it relates".[169]

[3.67] Section 4(1) of the 1996 Act, which governs the making of a disposal order, provides:

> Subject to subsection (2), where an interlocutory order has been in force for not less than 7 years in relation to specified property, the Court, on application to it in that behalf by the applicant, may make an order ("a disposal order") directing that the whole or, if appropriate, a specified part of the property be transferred, subject to such terms and conditions as the Court may specify, to the Minister or to such other person as the Court may determine.[170]

Where application[171] for a disposal order is made, the High Court is obliged to make the order, unless:

> it is shown to its satisfaction that that particular property does not constitute, directly or indirectly, proceeds of crime and was not acquired, in whole or in

---

168. Section 15(2) provides that property so seized shall be dealt with in accordance with the directions of the court.
169. Section 4(4). The Minister for Finance may then sell or otherwise dispose of the property so transferred and the proceeds of the disposal and any money transferred to him shall be paid into or disposed of for the benefit of the Exchequer: s 4(5).
170. The "Minister" refers to the Minister for Finance: s 1(1) of the 1996 Act.
171. The applicant is obliged to give notice to the respondent (unless the Court is satisfied that it is not reasonably possible to ascertain his whereabouts) and to such other persons as the Court directs: s 4(3) of the 1996 Act.

part, with or in connection with property that, directly or indirectly, constitutes proceeds of crime.[172]

In deciding whether or not to make a disposal order, the Court must give:

> an opportunity to be heard by the Court and to show cause why the order should not be made to any person claiming ownership of any of the property concerned.[173]

Provided that the High Court is satisfied that there would be no "serious risk of injustice" it may make a disposal order.[174] In the interests of justice the High Court may, on its own initiative, adjourn the hearing of the application for a disposal order for up to two years.

Registration of Interim and Interlocutory Orders

[3.68] Section 10 of the 1996 Act provides for the registration of interim and interlocutory orders in a series of governmental registries. Accordingly, an applicant can apply for the registration of an inhibition in the Land Registry[175] and of a notice in both the Registry of Deeds[176] and the Companies Registration Office.[177] Section 10 also provides for the registration of the discharge or variation of an interim or interlocutory order and upon the relevant Registrar receiving notice that an order has been discharged or varied he is obliged to either cancel or vary the entry made as appropriate.[178] The comments made in relation to s 25 of the 1994 Act equally apply here.[179]

Insolvency of Persons Affected

[3.69] Section 11 of the 1996 Act deals with the situation where a person who is in possession or control of property which is the subject of an interim, interlocutory or disposal order is adjudicated bankrupt. Where such orders are made *before* a person is adjudicated bankrupt, then such property is excluded from the property of the bankrupt for the purposes of the Bankruptcy Act 1988.[180] Where a person has already been adjudicated bankrupt, the High Court is precluded from making an interim, interlocutory or disposal order.[181]

[172.] Section 4(2) of the 1996 Act.

[173.] *Ibid*, s 4(6).

[174.] *Ibid*, s 4(8).

[175.] *Ibid*, s 10(1).

[176.] *Ibid*, s 10(4).

[177.] *Ibid*, s 10(7).

[178.] *Ibid*, s 10(2), (5) and (8) (variation of orders) and s 10(3), (6) and (9) (discharge).

[179.] See para **[3.26]** *supra*.

[180.] Section 11(1). Note that sub-s (3) modifies sub-s (1) to include references to earlier legislation where a petition in bankruptcy was presented or an adjudication in bankruptcy was made before 1 January 1989.

[181.] Section 11(2) of the 1996 Act.

[3.70] Section 12 of the 1996 Act contains certain safeguards for the Official Assignee or trustee in bankruptcy where he seizes or disposes of any property which is subject to an interim, interlocutory or disposal order. Provided that at the time of the seizure or disposal he believes, on reasonable grounds, that he is entitled (whether in pursuance of an order of the court or otherwise) to do so, he shall not be liable to any person in respect of any loss or damage resulting from the seizure or disposal except where caused by his negligence. The section also provides that the Official Assignee or trustee shall have a lien on the property or its proceeds of sale for expenses incurred in connection with the bankruptcy or other proceedings in relation to which the seizure or disposal purported to take place and such of his remuneration as may be reasonably assigned to his acting in such proceedings. Section 12(2) provides that where the Official Assignee or trustee does not know and has no reasonable grounds for knowing that property is the subject of an order under the 1996 Act, whether or not he has seized or disposed of the property so as to have a lien, he is entitled to payment of expenses incurred in respect of the property.

[3.71] Section 13 of the 1996 Act deals with the situation where property affected by an interim, interlocutory or disposal order is held by a company which is being wound up. Where an order for the winding up of a company has been made or a resolution has been passed by the company for a voluntary winding up, the functions of the liquidator or provisional liquidator shall not be exercisable in relation to corporate property which is subject to an interim, interlocutory or disposal order made before the "relevant time".[182]

[3.72] Where an order has been made or a resolution has been passed for the winding up of a company the powers conferred on the High Court to make an interim or interlocutory order pursuant to ss 2 or 3 shall not be exercisable in relation to any property held by the company to which the functions of the liquidator are exercisable so as to inhibit him from exercising those functions for the purpose of distributing the company's property to its creditors or so as to prevent the payment out of any property or expenses[183] which are properly incurred in the winding up in respect of the property.[184]

[182.] "Relevant time" is defined by s 13(3) as meaning "(a) where no order for the winding up of the company has been made, the time of the passing of the resolution for voluntary winding up, (b) where such an order has been made and, before the presentation of the petition for the winding up of the company by the court, such a resolution had been passed by the company, the time of the passing of the resolution, and (c) in any other case where such an order has been made, the time of the making of the order."

[183.] Including the remuneration of the liquidator or provisional liquidator.

[184.] Section 13(2) of the 1996 Act.

Compensation for Persons Affected

[3.73] Section 16 of the 1996 Act provides a procedure whereby the High Court can award compensation to persons wrongly affected by an interim, interlocutory or disposal order.[185] An application for compensation can only arise where:

(a) an interim order is discharged or lapses and an interlocutory order in relation to the matter is not made or, if made, is discharged (otherwise than pursuant to section 3(7)),

(b) an interlocutory order is discharged (otherwise than pursuant to section 3(7) or lapses and a disposal order in relation to the matter is not made or, if made, is discharged,

(c) an interim order or an interlocutory order is varied (otherwise than pursuant to section 3(7) or a disposal order is varied on appeal.[186]

In such circumstances a person may be awarded compensation where it can be shown to the satisfaction of the High Court that the person: (a) is the owner of property to which an order referred to in s 16(1)(a) or (b) related or an order referred to in s 16(1)(c) had related but by reason of its being varied by a Court has ceased to relate; and (b) the property does not constitute, directly or indirectly, proceeds of crime or was not acquired, in whole or in part, with or in connection with property that, directly or indirectly, constituted the proceeds of crime. The actual compensation payable is determined by the High Court on the basis of what it considers to be just in the circumstances, in respect of any loss incurred by the person by reason of the order concerned.[187]

[D] SECTION 908(4) OF THE TAXES CONSOLIDATION ACT 1997

[3.74] Before concluding this treatment of statutory jurisdictions to freeze assets, it is worth mentioning one other statutory power by which the Revenue Commissioners can make application to court to have a taxpayer's assets frozen. Section 908(4) of the Taxes Consolidation Act 1997 ("the 1997 Act") (or, in its original manifestation, s 18(3) of the Finance Act 1983) empowers the High Court to make an order requiring certain financial institutions[188] to furnish to an authorised officer of the Revenue Commissioners such particulars and information as may be specified in the order, in relation to a taxpayer.[189] Section

---

[185.] As Moriarty J observed, in *MM v DD*, High Court, unrep, 10 December 1996, (p 4 of the transcript), s 16 of the 1996 Act is one of the ways of ensuring that injustice is not perpetrated against meritorious respondents.

[186.] Section 16(1) of the 1996 Act.

[187.] The Minister for Finance must be given notice of, and is entitled to be heard in, any proceedings for compensation: s 16(2) of the 1996 Act.

[188.] As defined by s 18(1) of the 1983 Act. This is considered in detail in Ch 10, *Ancillary Orders*, para **[10.32]** *et seq*.

[189.] *Ibid*.

908(4) of the 1997 Act augments the power to obtain information by permitting the "freezing" of money held by a financial institution for a taxpayer. It provides:

> Where a judge makes an order under this section, he or she may also, on the application of the authorised officer concerned, make a further order prohibiting, for such period as the judge may consider proper and specify in the order, any transfer of, or any dealing with, without the consent of the judge, any assets or moneys of the person to whom the order relates that are in the custody of the financial institution at the time the order is made.

It may be surmised that the reason for giving the High Court an express statutory power to make an order which is, in all but name, a Mareva injunction, was because of the doubts over the Revenue Commissioners' standing to apply for Mareva relief without having a substantive cause of action.[190] It is mandatory that the hearing of an application for a disclosure order or freezing order under s 908 of the 1997 Act and any appeal in connection therewith be held *in camera*.[191]

[3.75] An order made pursuant to s 908(4) of the 1997 Act operates in a way which is fundamentally different to a Mareva injunction. So, whilst a Mareva injunction operates *in personam* against a defendant, a s 908(4) type freezing order is directed at the "third party" ie the financial institution where a taxpayer has deposited his money.

[3.76] An order can only be made under s 908 of the 1997 Act against an individual and cannot be made against a company. This is because s 908(4) refers to the assets or moneys of "the person to whom the order relates" and s 908(1) assigns the same meaning to "person" as in s 907 which defines "person" (other than in the definition of "financial institution") to mean "an individual who is ordinarily resident in the State". The reference in the definition of "person" to "individual" clearly excludes companies within the meaning of s 2 of the Companies Acts 1963-1990 or, indeed, any other body corporate, wheresoever and howsoever incorporated.

[190.] See Ch 2, *The Jurisdiction to Grant Mareva Relief*, para **[2.32]**.

[191.] Section 908(6) of the 1997 Act provides that applications for discovery or freezing orders or appeals in connection therewith: "... *shall* be held in camera." Italics added.

Chapter 4

A Substantive Cause of Action

[4.01] A Mareva injunction, like any other interim or interlocutory injunction, is not (and cannot be used as) an end in itself. Mareva relief is a form of ancillary relief, ie ancillary to a substantive right which will usually be a cause of action.[1] The first proof[2] in any application for a Mareva injunction is that a plaintiff has a substantive right, which is enforceable in Ireland, against a defendant. Whereas when the Mareva jurisdiction was first asserted, the paradigm type of cause of action was breach of contract, this is now no longer the case and the circumstances in which Mareva relief will be granted are not fettered by the type of cause of action pursued by a plaintiff. The only exception to the rule that a plaintiff must have a substantive right which is enforceable in Ireland is where a plaintiff is entitled to seek protective measures under the Brussels Convention[3] or the Lugano Convention.[4] In this chapter the following issues are considered:

[A] The Necessity for a Substantive Right or Cause of Action.

[B] The Causes or Actions which Can Ground Mareva Relief.

[C] The Jurisdiction of Courts and Enforcement of Judgments Acts 1988 and 1993.

[A] THE NECESSITY FOR A SUBSTANTIVE RIGHT OR CAUSE OF ACTION

[4.02] Mareva relief is and can only ever be ancillary relief. Being interlocutory or interim relief, it cannot be granted in the absence of a currently[5] enforceable substantive right or cause of action against the defendant. Lord Diplock put the matter thus:

> "A right to obtain an interlocutory injunction is not a cause of action. It cannot stand on its own. It is dependant on there being a pre-existing cause of action

---

1.   See *Channel Tunnel Group Ltd v Balfour Beatty Construction Ltd* [1993] 1 All ER 664 at 686 *per* Lord Mustill; see para **[4.09]** *infra*.
2.   See Ch 8, *Applying for a Mareva Injunction*, para **[8.45]**.
3.   Expressed to have been given force of law in Ireland by the Jurisdiction of Courts and Enforcement of Judgments (European Communities) Act 1988.
4.   Expressed to have been given force of law in Ireland by the Jurisdiction of Courts and Enforcement of Judgments Act 1993.
5.   See para **[4.10]** *et seq, infra*.

against the defendant arising out of an invasion, actual or threatened, by him of a legal or equitable right of the plaintiff for the enforcement of which the defendant is amenable to the jurisdiction of the court. The right to obtain an interlocutory injunction is merely ancillary and incidental to the pre-existing cause of action. It is granted to preserve the status quo pending the ascertainment by the court of the rights of the parties and the grant to the plaintiff of the relief to which his cause of action entitles him, which may or may not include a final injunction."[6]

Therefore, unless a plaintiff has a substantive right (usually, but not invariably, a cause of action) a Mareva injunction cannot be granted.[7] In this section the following issues are considered:

1. A Substantive Cause of Action

2. A Currently Actionable Cause of Action.

3. Mareva Injunctions and "Third Parties".

4. An Anticipated Cause of Action.

5. Post-Judgment Mareva Injunctions - Substantive Rights.

A Substantive Cause of Action

[4.03] The Supreme Court's decision in *Caudron v Air Zaire*[8] is the leading Irish authority for the proposition that Mareva relief cannot stand alone and must always be ancillary to a substantive cause of action. In that case the plaintiffs were ex-employees of the first-defendant company who were owed substantial sums for arrears of salary, loss of pension rights and, in some cases, breach of contract. None of the plaintiffs' grievances gave rise to a cause of action which was capable of sustaining proceedings in Ireland because their causes of action had arisen in Belgium. The plaintiffs' actions against the defendants in the Belgian courts were successful at trial but set aside on appeal because the plaintiffs' contracts of employment contained exclusive jurisdiction clauses which conferred jurisdiction on the Zairian courts. The attraction provided by Ireland to the plaintiffs was that the first defendant's Boeing 737 had been reposited in Dublin airport for repairs by Aer Lingus. The aircraft was in fact being detained by Aer Lingus which had asserted a lien over it to secure sums due, arising from its servicing and repair of the aircraft. The plaintiffs initiated

---

6. *Owners of cargo lately laden on board the vessel Siskina v Distos Compania Naviera SA, The Siskina* [1977] 3 All ER 803 at 824f-h.

7. See also *Caudron v Air Zaire* [1986] ILRM 10, considered in the following paragraph. See also *Siporex Trade SA v Comdel Commodities Ltd* [1986] 2 Lloyd's Rep 428 at 436 where Bingham J said: "I take it to be clear law, both on principle and authority, that a Mareva injunction will not be granted to an applicant who has no cause of action against the defendant at the time of application ...".

8. [1986] ILRM 10.

proceedings against the defendants and sought and obtained leave to serve the plenary summons outside of the jurisdiction. The plaintiffs also applied for a Mareva injunction to restrain the defendants from removing the aircraft from Ireland. This application was resisted by the defendants and they brought a motion seeking an order[9] to set aside the decision of Costello J which had given the plaintiffs liberty to issue an originating plenary summons.

(a) The High Court decision of Barr J in Caudron v Air Zaire

[4.04] The High Court granted the relief sought by the plaintiffs. Barr J held that the court had jurisdiction under s 28(8) of the Supreme Court of Judicature (Ireland) Act 1877 to grant a Mareva injunction to the plaintiffs. He observed that Ord 11, r 1(g) of the Rules of the Superior Courts 1962 provided that the High Court may allow service of an originating summons out of the jurisdiction - or *ex juris* - where:

> "... any injunction is sought as to anything to be done within the jurisdiction or any nuisance within the jurisdiction, is sought to be prevented or removed, whether damages are or are not also sought in respect thereof;"[10]

Barr J acknowledged that the issues before him resolved themselves into one central issue: does the right to a Mareva injunction, and nothing more, bring a claimant within the ambit of r 1(g) and thereby entitle the Court to make an order for service out of the jurisdiction. Counsel for the defendants sought to rely upon the unanimous House of Lords decision in the leading English authority, *The Siskina*[11] where it had been held that a Mareva injunction was only ancillary relief and could not, *per se*, be a substantive cause of action. Counsel for the plaintiffs relied upon the judgment of Denning MR in the Court of Appeal in *The Siskina*, arguing that Mareva injunctions were not just ancillary relief, but were in fact substantive in nature and were similar to an admiralty claim *in rem*.[12] It was also argued that the English RSC were materially different to the Irish RSC.

[4.05] The House of Lords judgment in *The Siskina* was distinguished by Barr J from *Caudron v Air Zaire* on the basis that the English rules contained a materially different wording.[13] In the course of his judgment Barr J said:

---

9. Pursuant to Ord 12 r 26 of the Rules of the Superior Courts 1962, now Ord 12 r 26 of the Rules of the Superior Courts, 1986 ("the RSC").
10. This provision has been replaced by Ord 11 r 1(g) of the RSC 1986.
11. [1977] 3 All ER 803 considered at para **[4.07]** *infra*.
12. It may be noted that Barr J did not accept the submission that a Mareva injunction was analogous to a claim *in rem* in admiralty jurisdiction. As to admiralty jurisdiction to arrest ships, see Ch 1, *The Mareva Injunction in Context*, para **[1.30]** *et seq*.
13. The English rule in issue in *The Siskina* provided: "If in an action begun by the writ an injunction is sought ordering the defendant to do or refrain from doing anything within the jurisdiction (whether or not damages are also claimed ...)".

"... it seems to me that there are crucial distinctions between the latter case and that under consideration. The most important of these is the difference between the wording of the Irish and English rules ... The incorporation of the phrase 'an injunction' for 'any injunction' are material alterations which support the interpretation of Lord Diplock and are relied upon by him as part of the basis for his rejection of the majority judgments in the Court of Appeal."[14]

In so holding Barr J held he was satisfied that the plaintiffs were entitled to the order permitting service out of the jurisdiction. He went on to review the principles applicable to the granting of a Mareva injunction and he granted an interlocutory order to the plaintiffs.[15] The defendants appealed this decision to the Supreme Court.

(b) The Supreme Court decision in Caudron v Air Zaire[16]

[4.06] The Supreme Court reversed the High Court decision of Barr J. The decision of the Supreme Court was given by Finlay CJ. The appellant-defendants' contentions were succinctly set out by him as being:

"... firstly, that in order for the court to have jurisdiction to issue and serve notice of an originating summons out of the jurisdiction, the injunction sought therein would have to be the substantive or part of the substantive relief claimed and not a relief of an interlocutory or ancillary nature and, secondly, and in the alternative, that, even if it was within the jurisdiction of the court to give liberty to issue and serve out of the jurisdiction in cases where a summons sought an interlocutory or ancillary injunction, it could not do so in any case where there was added to that claim in the originating summons any other claim which was not of itself within one of the sub-rules of O 11 r 1 capable of being the subject matter of an order giving liberty to serve out of the jurisdiction."[17]

In reversing the High Court decision of Barr J, Finlay CJ held in favour of the defendants. He said:

[14.] [1986] ILRM 10 at 16,17.

[15.] See Ch 5, *A Good Arguable Case*, para **[5.21]** where the judgment of Barr J on this point is considered.

[16.] See generally, Binchy, *Irish Conflicts of Law*, (1988) Butterworths, pp 153-156 and Gill, 'Order XI, 'Mareva Injunctions' and the Jurisdiction of the Irish Courts in Private International Law', (1986) 4 ILT 70.

[17.] [1986] ILRM 10 at 20. The plaintiff's contention was that "once the injunction by way of Mareva injunction is *bona fide* sought by them, then irrespective of whether it is temporary or ancillary in nature as distinct from being a substantive part of their claim, it brings their originating summons within Ord 11 r 1(g) and that being so they are automatically entitled to add as a further claim to be determined on that summons their claim for damages for breach of contract": also at 20.

"When, in O 11 r 1(g), the phrase 'any injunction is sought' is used it must, in my view, be interpreted in the light of the provisions of O 11 r 1 itself which provide for service out of the jurisdiction of an originating summons or notice of an originating summons. The injunction sought, referred to in sub-rule (g) must, therefore, on the interpretation of the order and rule, freed from any authority, be an injunction necessarily and properly sought in the originating summons, which is the document with the issue and service of which outside the jurisdiction the entire order is concerned. It cannot, in my opinion, be an injunction which is properly sought not as part of the endorsement of claim on the summons but rather by means of a motion *ex parte* or on notice.

The real relief sought by the plaintiffs in this action by way of injunction is...a temporary injunction pending the determination of the action only."[18]

Finlay CJ followed the reasoning of the House of Lords in *The Siskina*,[19] which he acknowledged, had reinforced his own view.

(c) The English approach in **The Siskina**

[4.07] The facts in *The Siskina* were that certain cargo-owners claimed damages from the owners of a ship for an alleged breach of the terms of a bill of lading contract. A conflict of laws arose: the contract provided that the courts of Genoa in Italy had exclusive jurisdiction; the breach of contract allegedly happened in Cyprus; the ship in question had sank after the alleged breach of contract and the ship-owner's only asset was the proceeds of an insurance policy held by a London agent. As with the plaintiffs in the *Air Zaire* case, the plaintiffs in *The Siskina* were keen to institute proceedings in the jurisdiction which offered them the only opportunity of enforcing their judgment against the defendant's assets. To this end the plaintiff-cargo owners instituted proceedings in the English courts against the defendant-ship owners for breach of contract/duty and sought a Mareva injunction to restrain the ship owners from disposing of the proceeds of the insurance policy and from removing them out of the jurisdiction. On an *ex parte* application, leave was granted to serve notice of the writ outside of the English jurisdiction. Leave was subsequently set aside upon the defendant's application to the High Court, but once more reinstated on further appeal to the Court of Appeal. The defendants appealed to the House of Lords.

[4.08] The House of Lords reversed the Court of Appeal[20] on the grounds that the applicants sought merely an interlocutory injunction: they did not and could

---

18. [1986] ILRM 10 at 21.
19. [1977] 3 All ER 803; [1979] AC 210.
20. In his book, *The Due Process of Law* (1980) Butterworths, Lord Denning, who had given the decision in the Court of Appeal does not hide his dissatisfaction over the decision of the House of Lords. At p 141 he says: "I have suffered many reversals but never so disappointing as this one. Particularly because I felt that their decision was unjust."

not apply for a perpetual injunction because they did not have a justiciable cause of action in England and Wales. Lord Diplock held:

> "In the instant case the cargo owners have no legal or equitable right or interest in the insurance moneys payable to the shipowners in respect of the loss of the Siskina which is enforceable here by a final judgment of the High Court. All that they have is a claim to monetary compensation arising from a cause of action against the shipowner which is not justiciable in the High Court without the shipowners' consent - which they withhold. To argue that the claim to monetary compensation *is* justiciable in the High Court because *if it were justiciable* it would give rise to an ancillary right to a Mareva injunction restraining the shipowners doing something in England pending adjudication of the monetary claim, appears to me to involve the fallacy of *petitio principii* or, in the vernacular, an attempt to pull oneself up by one's own bootstraps."[21]

(d) Substantive cause of action or substantive right?

[4.09] Although the House of Lords has not subsequently overruled its decision in *The Siskina*[22] it has clarified[23] the *ratio decidendi* of that judgment. So in the case of *Channel Tunnel Group Ltd v Balfour Beatty Construction Ltd*[24] Lord Mustill said:

> "... the doctrine of *The Siskina*, put at its highest, is that the right to an interlocutory injunction cannot exist in isolation, but is always incidental to and dependant on the enforcement of a substantive right, *which usually although not invariably takes the shape of a cause of action.*"[25]

This analysis better explains how Mareva injunctions are available to judgment creditors, a matter considered in some detail below.[26] A more radical departure from the rationale of *The Siskina* was taken by Lord Nicholls in his dissenting judgment in the Privy Council decision in *Mercedes-Benz AG v Leiduck*.[27] There, he viewed Mareva injunctions as being different to all other forms of interim and interlocutory relief and as not requiring a pre-existing cause of action. In Lord Nicholls' view this "is inconsistent with the analysis of the Mareva injunction as ancillary to a prospective right of enforcement".[28] It is thought that this goes too far and that an applicant for a Mareva injunction must

---

21. [1977] 3 All ER 803 at 824, 825.
22. *Owners of cargo lately laden on board the vessel Siskina v Distos Compania Naviera SA, The Siskina* [1977] 3 All ER 803; [1979] AC 210.
23. *Cf R v Consolidated Fastfrate Transport Inc* (1995) 125 DLR (4th) 1 at 26, 27 where Weiler JA suggests that *The Siskina* has been attenuated by the *Channel Tunnel* case.
24. [1993] 1 All ER 664.
25. At 686. Italics added.
26. See para **[4.28]**.
27. [1995] 3 All ER 929.
28. At 949h.

have some substantive right (legal, equitable or even constitutional) against the defendant which can give rise to an award of damages. As Lord Mustill said in the *Channel Tunnel* case, that right will usually take the shape of a cause of action; it may also be the right to enforce a judgment which has been obtained.

A Currently Actionable Cause of Action

[4.10] Not only must a Mareva plaintiff have a substantive right (eg a cause of action) against a defendant, but his right must also be immediately enforceable eg his cause of action against a defendant must be currently actionable. So, a plaintiff's substantive action (to which the Mareva injunction is ancillary relief) must not be statute barred or otherwise incapable of being immediately proceeded with by the plaintiff.

[4.11] A statute may prohibit the taking of proceedings against certain parties in certain circumstances. This is best illustrated by an example. Section 5(3) of the Companies (Amendment) Act 1990 provides, *inter alia*, that when a company is under the protection of the court, no proceedings may be commenced against the company, save with the leave of the court.[29] In *Re Goodman International*,[30] an application brought by *Banque Paribas of London*, it was reported by *The Irish Times* that Hamilton P refused leave to issue proceedings against a number of subsidiary companies in the Goodman Group of companies which were, at that time, under the protection of the court. Furthermore, he refused to grant a Mareva injunction which had been sought to freeze the assets of the companies. Although the plaintiff may have had a substantive cause of action, the effect of the companies being under the protection of the court meant that no proceedings could be issued, and accordingly no ancillary Mareva relief could be granted.[31]

[4.12] Another example is to be found in s 54(1) of the Consumer Credit Act 1995 ("the 1995 Act") which provides that a creditor or owner of goods shall not enforce a provision of a consumer credit agreement (other than a housing loan) unless he has first served on the consumer, at least 10 days before he proposes to take any action, a notice specifying certain matters, which include, "a statement of the action he intends to take to enforce the term of the agreement, the manner

---

[29.] Section 5(3) of the Companies (Amendment) Act 1990 states: "Subject to subsection (2), no other proceedings in relation to the company may be commenced except by leave of the court and subject to such terms as the court may impose and the court may on the application of the examiner make such order as it thinks proper in relation to any proceedings including an order to stay such proceedings."

[30.] *The Irish Times*, 20 October 1990 (Hamilton P).

[31.] See generally, Courtney, *The Law of Private Companies*, (1994) Butterworths, para [17.036]. The international comity of courts will not always mean that a Mareva injunction will not be granted against a company which is under the protection of a foreign court. So in *Felixstowe Dock & Railway Co v United States Lines Inc* (1989) 1 QB 360 Hirst J refused to discharge a Mareva injunction affecting the English assets of a company undergoing Chapter 11 reconstruction in the United States.

and circumstances in which he intends to take such action and the date on or after which he intends to take such action".[32] One effect of this provision is to temporarily displace a creditor's or owner's right to sue a consumer ie although he may well have a cause of action it may not be currently actionable. It is important to note, however, that following an amendment to the provision contained in the original Bill[33] it is now possible for a creditor or owner to apply to court, under s 54(4) of the 1995 Act, to have the provisions of the section dispensed with "where the court is satisfied that it would be just and equitable to do so". Where a creditor or owner can satisfy the court that Mareva relief should be granted it is thought that this should *ipso facto* satisfy the court that it is just and equitable to dispense with the provisions of s 54 of the 1995 Act. It is submitted that a creditor or owner anxious to obtain Mareva relief could bring an *ex parte* application under s 54(4) of the 1995 Act contemporaneous to making application for Mareva relief on the usual undertakings to stamp, issue and serve the originating proceedings.

[4.13] Section 5(3) of the Companies (Amendment) Act 1990 and s 45(1) of the Consumer Credit Act 1995 are but two examples of situations where an otherwise valid cause of action may be rendered temporarily ineffective;[34] in other cases a once justiciable cause of action may be rendered permanently ineffective.[35]

Mareva Injunctions and "Third Parties"

[4.14] The question of whether a Mareva injunction can be granted against a third party is fraught with confusion.[36] Indeed, before there can be any

---

[32.] Section 54(1)(v) of the Consumer Credit Act 1995. See also subsection (2) which provides, *inter alia*, that a creditor or owner cannot by reason of any breach by a consumer of an agreement, (a) determine the agreement, (b) demand early payment of any sum, (c) recover possession of the goods, (d) treat any right conferred on the consumer by the agreement as determined, restricted or deferred, or (e) enforce any security, unless he has served on the consumer not less than 10 days before he proposes to take any action, a notice specifying certain matters. See Bird, *Consumer Credit Law* (1988) Roundhall Sweet & Maxwell, pp 336-343.

[33.] See Editorial, (1994) *Commercial Law Practitioner* 66 where the original wording was objected to on the basis that it prevented a creditor or owner from seeking Mareva relief.

[34.] For example, where a plaintiff has a cause of action but the defendant is immune from suit by reason of, say, the Diplomatic Relations and Immunities Act 1967; see generally, Brown, 'Diplomatic Immunity: State Practice under the Vienna Convention on Diplomatic Relations', (1988) 37 ICLQ 53.

[35.] For example, causes of action barred pursuant to the Statute of Limitations 1957. See generally, Brady & Kerr, *The Statute of Limitations*, (2nd ed; 1994) Law Society of Ireland.

[36.] Some of the cases where this issue has arisen include: *SFC Finance Co Ltd v Masri* [1985] 2 All ER 747; *TSB Private Bank International SA v Chabra* [1992] 2 All ER 245; *Mercantile Group (Europe) AG v Aiyela* [1994] 1 All ER 110; *LED Builders Pty Ltd v Eagle Homes Pty Ltd*, [1997] 826 FCA (22 August 1997); *Mercedes-Benz v Leiduck* [1995] 3 All ER 929; *International Credit and Investment Co (Overseas) Ltd v Adham* [1998] BCC 134. See also, Ch 7, *The Defendant's Assets*, para **[7.16]** *et seq*.

meaningful analysis of this topic, one must first nail one's colours to the mast and define what one means by the expression "third party". By "third party" this writer means (a) a person against whom a plaintiff does not have a cause of action or other, currently enforceable, substantive right *eg* a person who is not a defendant or co-defendant, and/or (b) a person other than an agent, collaborator or nominee of a defendant eg a person who does not hold assets as trustee for a defendant. It is this writer's contention that there is no jurisdiction to grant a Mareva injunction which directly restrains a "third party", thus defined, from dealing with his own assets.

A Mareva injunction should never be granted against a person who is truly a "third party" because where a plaintiff does not have a substantive right or cause of action against a person he cannot ever hope to mark judgment against him; there is, therefore, no rationale for making an order to restrain him from disposing of his assets with a view to evading his obligations to the plaintiff and frustrating the anticipated order of the court.[37] A defendant's agent is not, on this writer's analysis, a true "third party" and an agent, through his holding of assets in trust for a defendant, may be made the subject of a declaration or other order which is capable of being marked against him by a plaintiff. Since an order can be made against an agent, so too can an order be frustrated by an agent, and hence the rationale for granting a Mareva injunction directly against such a person. It is submitted that most of the cases which are held out as authorities for granting a Mareva injunction against a "third party" are not in fact such. Rather, on close inspection it will be seen that the "third party" is in fact a person who could be joined as a co-defendant, against whom a judgment could be marked. Here, the following issues are considered:

    (a) The ownership of assets - defendants' or third parties'?

    (b) Distinguishing "third parties" from "co-defendants"

    (c) Companies controlled by defendants

    (d) Ancillary to an ancillary order?

    (e) Making a "third party" a "co-defendant"

(a) The ownership of assets - defendants' or third parties'?

[4.15] Disputes often arise concerning who is the beneficial owner of particular assets.[38] The principal reason why a Mareva-plaintiff would wish to enjoin a so-called "third party" would be where the third party has assets which the plaintiff believes should be available to satisfy his future judgment. Some guidance on the principles applicable to determining disputes as to the ownership of assets is

---

[37.] *Re John Horgan Livestock. O'Mahony v Horgan* [1995] 2 IR 411.
[38.] *Fitzpatrick v Criminal Assets Bureau*, High Court, unrep, 27 February 1998 (Shanley J).

given in *SCF Finance Co Ltd v Masri*,[39] which is considered in Chapter 7, *The Defendant's Assets*.[40] Assets which are legally and beneficially owned by true "third parties" can never be available to satisfy a plaintiff's judgment. This is borne out by *Winter v Marac Australia Ltd*[41] where the New South Wales Court of Appeal said that where a Mareva injunction is sought against a third party:

> "... it must be shown that the person against whom judgment may be obtained has some right in respect of or control over or other access, direct or indirect, to the relevant assets so that they or the proceeds of their sale could be required to be applied in discharge of the judgment debt."

On the other hand, assets which are legally and/or beneficially in a defendant's ownership (if not possession) should be available to satisfy a future judgment and a person who holds such assets for a defendant will be amenable to being directly enjoined by a Mareva injunction. This is because, should a Mareva plaintiff be successful against a defendant whose assets are held by such a person, he can recover those assets in legal proceedings against that person who will not be a "third party".[42] There is, therefore, a substantive right against the "third party", if not a readily statable substantive cause of action.

[4.16] It is necessary to distinguish between assets in which a plaintiff asserts a proprietary claim and assets in which a defendant has a proprietary interest. Where a plaintiff asserts a proprietary claim to assets which he fears are likely to be removed from the State, or otherwise disposed of, his remedy is an ordinary interlocutory injunction and not a Mareva injunction.[43] On the other hand, it is submitted, that a Mareva injunction can only be granted against a person who is not a primary defendant where he holds assets in which a defendant has a proprietary interest. In this regard the writer disagrees with the recent decision of the Federal Court of Australia in *LED Builders Pty Ltd v Eagle Homes Pty Ltd*[44] which rejected the view that a Mareva injunction is only available against a person (other than the defendant) where that person holds legal title to an asset which is beneficially owned by the defendant. The facts in that case were that

---

[39.] [1985] 2 All ER 747.

[40.] At para **[7.17]**.

[41.] (1986) 6 NSWLR 11 at 12, cited by the trial judge in *LED Builders Pty Ltd v Eagle Homes Pty Ltd* [1997] 826 Federal Court of Australia, hereafter, "FCA" (22 August 1997), considered *post*.

[42.] A plaintiff could, in such a case, obtain a declaration that the assets belonged to the defendant and should therefore be available to satisfy the plaintiff's claim; indeed, the plaintiff could apply to have a receiver by way of equitable execution appointed to such assets or apply for a garnishee order: see Ch 10, *Ancillary Orders*, para **[10.77]** and **[10.83]** respectively.

[43.] *Polly Peck International plc* v *Nadir (No. 2)* [1992] 4 All ER 769 and, generally, Ch 1, *The Mareva Injunction in Context*, para **[1.16]** *et seq*.

[44.] [1997] 826 FCA (22 August 1997).

the plaintiff-applicant ("LED") had successfully sued the defendant-respondent ("Eagle") for infringement of LED's copyright in certain floor plans for project homes and had elected for an account of profits. Pending the taking of profits LED applied for a Mareva injunction against Eagle and certain "third parties". The third parties were a Mr and Mrs C and a company controlled by them called Ultra Modern Developments Pty Ltd ("Ultra"). LED contended that Mr and Mrs C would take steps designed to deprive it of sufficient assets to satisfy the taking of the account and relied upon the declaration of substantial dividends in Eagle in favour of Mr and Mrs C. LED also contended that there had been an informal transfer of much of Eagle's business to Ultra. The evidence showed that Eagle's business had been wound down which would indicate that, to an extent at least, LED's application for Mareva relief was too late since the party against whom it would be able to recover moneys after the account for profit, had already disposed of much of its assets. The primary judge, granted the relief as against Eagle but refused to grant a Mareva injunction against Mr and Mrs C and Ultra, and LED appealed to the Federal Court of Australia.

The Federal Court of Australia granted the appeal; the joint-judgment of Beaumont and Branson JJ held that:

> "... we cannot accept, as the primary judge appears to suggest, that it is an ingredient of the Mareva jurisdiction that the debtor has a specific proprietary interest in the third party's assets (see *eg Mercedes-Benz AG v Leiduck* [1996] 1 AC 284; [1995] 3 All ER 929 where (at 300; 937) Lord Mustill emphasises that Mareva relief takes effect *in personam* only and distinguishes tracing and other such remedies protecting proprietary rights). It is sufficient, for present purposes, that the assets of the defendant and the third parties are 'mixed up' and 'controlled', in the sense explained by Kiefel J in *Tomlinson* above".[45]

It is submitted that this reasoning is fundamentally flawed. Of course a Mareva injunction only operates *in personam* against a defendant's person, but that has nothing whatsoever to do with establishing whether or not a Mareva defendant has a beneficial interest in assets in the hands of a third party. The purpose of such an inquiry is merely to establish whether such assets can, ultimately, be utilised to satisfy a plaintiff's future judgment; the answer to this depends entirely upon whether the assets belong to a defendant *ie* a person against whom a plaintiff can mark judgment.[46] This is not to say, however, that a Mareva injunction ought not to have issued against the "third party" in this case. Indeed, there is evidence to suggest that Ultra and Mr and Mrs C were not true "third

---

[45.] The *Tomlinson* case refers to *Tomlinson v Cut Price Deli Pty Ltd* [1995] FCA (22 June 1995) (Kiefel J). See para **[4.17]** *infra*.

[46.] Leave to appeal the decision of the Federal Court of Australia was granted on 1 May 1998 in *Cardile v LED Builders Pty Ltd*, (1998) High Court, unrep, Australia (Brennan CJ, Gummow and Callinan JJ).

parties", as that term is used here; it may have been possible for LED to bring proceedings against the prospective respondents for a declaration or to have the dispositions set aside and, in such event, LED would have had a substantive right or cause of action against the prospective respondents to which the Mareva injunction would have been ancillary relief. It is submitted that this must be the central enquiry in any application to have a person, who appears to be a non-defendant, directly enjoined by a Mareva injunction.

(b) Distinguishing "third parties" from "co-defendants"

[4.17] It is submitted that collaborators, nominees and defendants' agents are not true "third parties" to an action between a plaintiff and a defendant.

Indeed, a person who conspires with a defendant to deprive a plaintiff of his rights may be liable to be sued personally by a plaintiff, and therefore, to becoming a co-defendant.[47] A Mareva injunction can properly be granted against a person to whom a defendant transfers his assets so as to deliberately evade the effects of a Mareva injunction. In the case of a transfer of assets by a company to a third party with the effect of defrauding the company's creditors a *quia timet* Mareva injunction may be granted in contemplation of an eventual application under s 139 of the Companies Act 1990 to have the assets returned: see para **[4.27]** below. In the Australian case of *Tomlinson v Cut Price Deli Pty Ltd*[48] it was alleged that the first defendant ("CPD") had assigned its principal assets to another company, Cut Price Deli (Aust) Pty Ltd (Aust) during the currency of the plaintiffs' proceedings against CPD with the deliberate intent of placing its assets beyond the plaintiffs' reach. It was also claimed that unless the so-called "third party" was restrained by a Mareva injunction, steps would be taken to further distance or encumber CPD's property. Kiefel J held that there was jurisdiction to grant a Mareva injunction against a "third party" where:

> "... the third party has actively participated in the deliberate removal of assets, as here alleged. In effect the further injunction is simply recognising that a party such as CPD and those associated with it effectively controls Aust (or the same people in any event control both entities) and makes clear that they are not to act through Aust to further deal with or encumber the assets."

The decision in *Tomlinson* can be seen as an example of where the courts have, in granting a Mareva injunction against a third party, "lifted the corporate veil", a matter considered below.[49] It is thought, however, that this case illustrates a

---

[47] On the tort of conspiracy, see McMahon & Binchy, *Irish Law of Torts*, (1989) Butterworths, p 574.

[48] [1995] FCA (22 June 1995) (Kiefel J).

[49] See para **[4.20]** *infra*.

bigger principle and that a non-corporate so-called "third party" collaborator could equally be made directly subject to a Mareva injunction.

[4.18] A person who holds assets on behalf of a defendant is not a "third party". This point is borne out by *Mercantile Group (Europe) AG v Aiyela*.[50] There, the plaintiff had commenced proceedings seeking $US1.8m from the first defendant ("Mr A") and the fourth defendant ("Mrs A") and certain companies. Mr A and two of the companies admitted liability and undertook to pay $US2.2m, whereupon the actions against the other defendants, including Mrs A, were abandoned. When it became clear that Mr A would only pay $388,000 the plaintiff entered judgment for the balance. The plaintiff was successful in obtaining Mareva relief against Mr A and, subsequently, a Mareva injunction was also granted against Mrs A, against whom an asset disclosure order had also been made. It was against these orders that Mrs A appealed. It was held by the Court of Appeal that the court had jurisdiction to make both a disclosure order and a Mareva injunction against Mrs A. Hoffmann LJ said:

> "In this case, the plaintiff's substantive right is a judgment debt owed by Mr [A]. The Mareva injunction against Mrs [A] is incidental to and in aid of the enforcement of that right."[51]

On this analysis, the jurisdictional basis for granting Mareva relief against Mrs A was that it was "ancillary to ancillary relief".[52] A different basis was, however, asserted by Steryn LJ who said:

> "The relevant part of the December order was a Mareva injunction over sums in Mrs [A's] account at the Midland Bank, Tolworth. It was accepted by Mrs [A] for the purposes of the hearing before Hobhouse J that there was an arguable case that Mrs [A] held these sums upon trust for her husband. In these circumstances, there was jurisdiction to make a direct order against Mrs [A]. In upholding these orders we are not departing from any relevant authority which spells out the scope of the court's jurisdiction. It is also just and convenient that the court should have jurisdiction to make such orders".[53]

Accordingly, it is clear that there was an arguable case[54] that Mrs A held moneys on trust for Mr A and so it was possible for the plaintiff to satisfy his future judgment debt with the assets, in Mrs A's name, which were frozen by the

---

[50.] [1994] 1 All ER 110.

[51.] At 116e.

[52.] See para **[4.24]** *infra*.

[53.] At 117c-e.

[54.] At 114f Hoffmann LJ said of Mrs A that "Her counsel accepted that there was evidence to suggest that Mr [A] was determined to frustrate execution of the judgment against him, that Mrs [A] had no independent financial means and that moneys emanating from her husband or companies which he controlled had been paid into bank accounts in her name".

injunction. It is equally clear that, in these circumstances, Mrs A was not a true "third party" as defined herein at para **[4.14]**.

[4.19] The Supreme Court of South Australia in *Brew v Crouch; Dionyus Pty Ltd*[55] identified the following "common thread running through" *LED Builders*,[56] *Tomlinson*,[57] *Australian Competition Consumer Commission v Top Snack Foods Pty Ltd*[58] and the earlier case of *Vereker v Choi*:[59]

> "Leaving aside any obvious proprietary interest of the defendant in the assets, in each case there was a transfer to a person or body over whom the immediate defendant had no apparent control, but who or which was related in some way to the defendant. In other words, there was ultimately some common control or beneficial ownership, and the transaction could be seen as a device to transfer beneficial ownership or rights to indemnity away from the defendant in the proceedings. In that way, if the defendant were made bankrupt or placed in liquidation by the plaintiff, the assets would not be available to the judgment creditor ...
>
> In this case there is no suggestion that any of the assets of the defendant have been transferred to Dionysus in a similar manner in order to frustrate the plaintiff's ability to recover a judgment against the defendant. Similarly, there is no suggestion that Dionysus holds any such assets on trust for the defendant."

D had not been disposing of its assets, the defendant had not transferred his assets to D to frustrate the plaintiff's judgment and there did not seem any way in which the plaintiff could ever mark judgment against D. Bleby J refused to grant a Mareva injunction against D which was, in these circumstances, a true third party.

(c) Companies controlled by defendants

[4.20] The question of whether a Mareva injunction can be granted against a so-called "third party" often becomes most vexed where a defendant and a third party are director/shareholders and closely-held private company, respectively. The Irish courts have, on a number of occasions, restrained a company from disposing of its assets in circumstances where it was controlled by the primary defendant-director/shareholder;[60] moreover, a director/shareholder has been restrained from disposing of his own personal assets in circumstances where it

---

[55] [1998] 6633 SASC (23 April 1998).
[56] [1997] FCA 862 (22 August 1997).
[57] *Tomlinson v Cut Price Deli Pty Ltd* [1995] FCA (22 June 1995) (Kiefel J).
[58] [1997] FCA (7 November 1997).
[59] (1985) 4 NSWLR 277.
[60] Frequently, however, it is unclear as to whether the assets in question are beneficially owned by the defendants of the companies which they are alleged to control.

appears that the substantive relief was only claimed against the company.[61] It is thought that the only legal basis for granting a Mareva injunction in such cases is that the plaintiff has a substantive right or cause of action against all of the parties directly bound by the injunction which would entitle him to mark judgment against them. Often it will be alleged that the person, who might be termed a third party, holds assets in trust for the primary defendant, which assets may be utilised in satisfaction of a judgment against the defendant director/ shareholders.

[4.21] In a number of English cases where Mareva relief has been granted against so-called "third parties" it has not been clear that the principles set out in the preceding paragraph have been complied with. One such example is *TSB Private Bank International SA v Chabra*.[62] In that case the plaintiff ("TSB") advanced £1.5m to a borrower on the strength of a guarantee from the first defendant. When the borrower failed to repay the loan TSB instituted proceedings against the first-defendant ("C") and obtained a Mareva injunction which restrained C from removing his assets from the jurisdiction or otherwise disposing of his assets. C's assets included a majority shareholding in a company called Beverley Hotels (London) Ltd (BHL). The Mareva injunction also restrained C from dealing with BHL's assets within the jurisdiction, and in particular the proceeds of sale of its hotel and restaurant interests and a property used by C as his residence, which was reputedly owned by BHL. C had left the jurisdiction by the time the injunction was granted.

TSB made application for, and the court permitted, BHL to be added as a party to the action. TSB also obtained a Mareva injunction against BHL. BHL applied for the writ against it to be struck out on the ground that there was no cause of action against BHL and for the Mareva injunction to be discharged as there was no cause of action to which it could be ancillary. Mummery J held that the court was entitled to join BHL and further held that it had jurisdiction in an appropriate case to grant a Mareva injunction against a co-defendant even

---

61. In *T v A Ltd & F, The Irish Times*, 10 December 1997 (Kelly J) it was reported that the plaintiff obtained a Mareva injunction against the second defendant, an individual who was controlling shareholder and director in the first defendant company, in circumstances where it appears, from the newspaper report at least, that the plaintiff's cause of action was one for personal injuries against his former employer, the first defendant company. Apart from the fact that the land upon which the first defendant's factory plant was situate was owned by the second defendant and his wife, it is unclear from the newspaper report what cause of action the plaintiff had against the second defendant. See also, eg, *E&E v HIT Ltd & O'D, The Irish Times*, 1 May 1991 (Barron J) where the plaintiff investors obtained Mareva injunctions against the defendant-investment company and two others (who appeared from the report to be its controller-directors) in circumstances where monthly payments to the plaintiffs of interest derived from the investment of their life savings had dried up without sufficient reason.

62. [1992] 2 All ER 245.

though a plaintiff had no cause of action against the co-defendant.

TSB accepted the it had no cause of action against BHL. BHL had not executed the guarantee which formed the basis of the proceedings against C. However, TSB argued that the assets of BHL belonged to C. TSB also alleged that C had organised his affairs through a complex structure of companies which held all of his assets in the United Kingdom. Mummery J accepted that there was great uncertainty as to the ownership of certain assets. It was not clear whether or not these were owned by C or by BHL. In the circumstances, Mummery J felt it was in order to join BHL as it fell within the broad provisions of Ord 15, r 6(2)(b)(ii) of the UK's Rules of the Supreme Court 1965.[63] Of course, by joining BHL in the proceedings, it could no longer be considered to be a third party as it was then a co-defendant: judgment could be marked against BHL.

[4.22] In some cases where Mareva injunctions have been granted against a company in an action against a director/shareholder or against a director/shareholder in an action against a company the courts have clearly "lifted the corporate veil". In *Re A Company*[64] certain plaintiff-companies brought an action, by their liquidator, against the defendant alleging deceit and breach of trust. There was evidence that the defendant had arranged his personal affairs so that his personal assets were held by a network of companies, both English and foreign, the effect of which was to conceal his beneficial interests. On the plaintiffs' application discovery by interrogatories was ordered and the defendant was restrained from disposing of shares in his foreign companies or interests under trusts or shares in English or foreign companies which were entitled to English assets. The defendant was restrained from procuring the disposition of English assets by any such trusts or companies. The defendant appealed against these orders on the ground, *inter alia*, that he merely owned shares in certain companies and there was no evidence that he had any entitlement to those companies' assets.

The Court of Appeal dismissed the appeal on all grounds. The plaintiffs' evidence was accepted that, by using nominees to hold shares, an appearance was given that the defendant's assets were legally and beneficially held by others and that there was a strong *prima facie* case that the whole structure was only a facade behind which the defendant controlled and manipulated the company directors and trustees. Cumming-Bruce LJ held that:

---

63. This provides that there could be joined as a party - "any person between whom any party to the cause or matter there may exist a question or issue arising out of or related to or connected with any relief or remedy claimed in the cause or matter which in the opinion of the Court it would be just and convenient to determine as between him and that party as well as between the parties to the cause or matter." See Ord 15, r 13 of the Irish RSC, considered at para **[4.25]** *infra*.

64. [1985] BCLC 333.

"... the Court will use its powers to pierce the corporate veil if it is necessary to achieve justice irrespective of the legal efficacy of the corporate structure under consideration ...

We hold that the evidence sufficiently establishes that over a period of years the servants or agents of the first defendant have on the first defendant's instructions brought into existence the sophisticated and intricate network of interrelated English and foreign companies and foreign trusts as a mechanism through which the first defendant could at will dispose of his English assets. The evidence sufficiently establishes that when, after the fraud alleged in the statement of claim, the first defendant realised that insolvency of the plaintiffs was in sight, he either then arranged that his English assets should disappear into the network of interrelated English and foreign legal structures of such complexity that only he and/or his agents could disentangle his personal interest, or in the case of some English assets, he had already achieved this confusion against the contingency of future judgment. In either case we hold that there is ample evidence to justify the orders now sought by the plaintiffs...".[65]

The courts will only ever "lift the corporate veil" in exceptional circumstances. This was recognised by Cumming-Bruce LJ who said the order made was "exceptional in its characteristics" and was "exceptional because the facts are exceptional". The effect of lifting the corporate veil is to make a person amenable to the court's jurisdiction by joining them as a party to the proceedings.

[4.23] *International Credit and Investment Co (Overseas) Ltd v Adham*[66] shows just how far a court may go to ensure that its orders are obeyed. In that case a worldwide Mareva injunction had been granted against certain persons which restrained them not only from dealing with assets directly in their beneficial ownership but also from dealing with assets of companies which they directly or indirectly controlled. When it became apparent that the Mareva orders might not be obeyed, application was successfully brought to have a receiver appointed over certain assets which were the subject of the orders. Robert Walker J said:

"... a Mareva injunction may indeed, in appropriate circumstances, operate as an order *in rem*, and such an order may be justified and indeed necessary where parties have the ability to switch real assets from one shadowy hand to another in such a way that it is difficult to keep track of where they are. That is the justification for orders which look through offshore companies in order to find real assets - or which do, if you look, pierce the corporate veil, to use the vivid but imprecise metaphor which is sometimes used."[67]

[65.] At 338.
[66.] [1998] BCC 134.
[67.] At 137.

As imprecise a metaphor as "lifting or piercing the corporate veil" is, it is submitted that it is heretical to consider Mareva injunctions in terms of operating *in rem*. Whilst Mareva injunctions may sometimes appear to have an *in rem* effect, they operate *in personam* against a defendant and not against his assets.[68] So, assets in the hands of a corporate third party may be indirectly affected by a Mareva injunction where the court believes that they are beneficially owned by a defendant. It is, however, the corporate third party which is the subject of the order, not the assets, and the joining of the corporate third party may be facilitated by the lifting of the corporate veil on grounds, for example, of fraud,[69] avoidance of existing legal obligations[70] or agency.[71]

(d) Ancillary to an ancillary order?

[4.24] In *TSB Private Bank International SA v Chabra*[72] Mummery J also distinguished *The Siskina*[73] so as to permit him to grant an injunction in circumstances where it did not appear that there was a cause of action against BHL. The distinction made was this: whereas in *The Siskina* the plaintiff had no cause of action against anyone, in the *TSB* case, there were two parties and the plaintiff had a good cause of action against one of them. Mummery J concluded:

> "The claim for an injunction to restrain disposal of assets by Mr Chabra is ancillary and incidental to that cause of action. In my judgment, the claim to a similar injunction against the company is also ancillary and incidental to the claim against Mr Chabra and the court has power to grant an injunction in an appropriate case. It does not follow that, because the court has no jurisdiction to grant a Mareva injunction against the company, if it were the sole defendant, the court has no jurisdiction to grant an injunction against the company as ancillary, or incidental, to the cause of action against Mr Chabra: see *eg Vereker v Choi* (1985) 4 NSWLR 277 at 283. I agree that such a course is an

---

68. See Ch 9, *The Mareva Order and Its Effects*, para **[9.36]** *et seq.*
69. As in the cases of *Re Darby* [1911] 1 KB 95, *Re Bugle Press Ltd* [1961] Ch 270, *Re Shrinkpak Ltd*, High Court, unrep, 20 December 1989 (Barron J). See Courtney, *The Law of Private Companies* (1994) Butterworths, para [4.005] *et seq.*
70. As in the cases of *Cummings v Stewart* [1911] 1 IR 236, *Jones v Lipman* [1962] 1 All ER 442 and *Guilford Motor Co Ltd v Horne* [1933] Ch 939. However, in *Adams v Cape Industries plc* [1990] Ch 433 the Court of Appeal held that it was not right to disregard the separate legal personality of a company merely to avoid prospective or future obligations. See generally, Courtney, *op cit*, para [4.001] *et seq.*
71. *Smith, Stone and Knight v Birmingham Corporation* [1939] 4 All ER 116, *Firestone Tyre and Public Co v Llwellin* [1957] 1 All ER 561 and *Re FG (Films) Ltd* [1953] 1 All ER 615. Again, see generally, Courtney, *op cit*, para [4.006] *et seq.*
72. [1992] 2 All ER 245. See also Ch 5, *A Good Arguable Case*, para **[5.32]**.
73. [1977] 3 All ER 821. At 824 Lord Diplock said: "A right to obtain an interlocutory injunction is not a cause of action. It cannot stand on its own. It is dependent on there being a pre-existing cause of action against the defendant arising out of an invasion, actual or threatened, by him of a legal or equitable right of the plaintiff for the enforcement of which the defendant is amenable to the jurisdiction of the court. The right to obtain an interlocutory injunction is merely ancillary and incidental to the pre-existing cause of action".

exceptional one, but I do not accept that it is one that the court has no jurisdiction to take".[74]

This basis for granting Mareva relief against supposed "third parties" has recently been accepted by the Federal Court of Australia in *LED Builders Pty Ltd v Eagle Homes Pty Ltd*[75] and *Tomlinson v Cut Price Deli Pty Ltd*.[76] It is submitted that such a basis can only ever be justified where there is a reasonable prospect that a plaintiff will be able to enforce his judgment against the enjoined "third party"; and, where this is the case, it is submitted that he cannot truly be said to be a third party and must, in fact, be a co-defendant.

(e) Making a "third party" a "co-defendant"

[4.25] Where a defendant's ownership of assets is in question and there is doubt as to whether he or a third party is the beneficial owner, it will often be appropriate to join the third party in the proceedings.[77] This was in fact what was done in *TSB Private Bank International SA v Chabra*.[78] In Ireland too the RSC facilitate the joining of third parties. Ord 15 r 13 provides:

> ... The Court may at any stage of the proceedings, either upon or without the application of either party, and on such terms as may appear to the Court to be just, order...that the names of any parties, whether plaintiffs or defendants, who ought to have been joined, or whose presence before the Court may be necessary in order to enable the Court effectually and completely to adjudicate upon or settle all the questions involved in the cause or matter, be added ...

This rule recently received consideration in *Allied Irish Coal Supplies Ltd v Powell Duffryn International Fuels Ltd*[79] where the Supreme Court upheld the earlier High Court decision of Laffoy J who had refused to join a third party called Powell Duffryn plc ("PLC") in the proceedings between the plaintiff and defendant ("PDIF"). In that case PDIF was a subsidiary of PLC and the plaintiff contended that it and PLC were a single economic entity and that this justified the lifting of the veil.[80] On the facts it was held by the Supreme Court that there was no justification whatsoever for disregarding PLC's and PDIF's separate

---

[74.] *Op cit* at 255,256.

[75.] [1997] 826 FCA (22 August 1997).

[76.] [1995] FCA (Kiefel J), (22 June 1995). See also *McIntyre v Pettit* (1988) 90 FLR 196.

[77.] *SFC Finance Co Ltd v Masir* [1985] 2 All ER 747; *cf Tomlinson v Cut Price Deli Pty Ltd* [1995] FCA 22 June 1995 (Kiefel J) where it is suggested that sometimes, to join a third party, would be a mere formality.

[78.] [1992] 2 All ER 245. See para **[4.21]** *supra*.

[79.] [1997] 1 ILRM 306 (HC); [1998] 2 ILRM 61 (SC).

[80.] In the High Court Laffoy J noted that, in support of this last proposition, the plaintiff had relied upon Courtney, *The Law of Private Companies* (1994, Butterworths), paras [4.001]-[4.006], the authorities referred to therein and in particular *Power Supermarkets Ltd v Crumlin Investments Ltd* High Court, unrep, June 22, 1981 (Costello J).

corporate personalities. Unlike many of the Mareva cases considered over the previous pages, there was absolutely no suggestion of fraud, collusion or that PLC held assets to which PDIF was beneficially entitled. For that reason the following passage from the judgment of Murphy J should be read in context. During the course of the majority judgment Murphy J said:

> "On the pleadings as drafted and the amendments as proposed the plaintiff's contractual and legal rights are asserted as against PDIF and refuted by that company. That is the issue and not a question as to what assets would be available to meet a judgment if and when obtained.
>
> In my view it would be inappropriate for the Court in the exercise of its discretion to add a defendant to a cause or action solely for the purpose of enabling the plaintiffs to have a determination as to the extent of the assets which would be available to him in the event of his being successful in that cause or action. For that reason alone I believe that the application was rightly refused."[81]

Where there is evidence that a defendant has deliberately transferred his assets to a third party so as to evade a Mareva injunction or where there is evidence that a third party was a corporate facade for a defendant, it would be open to a court to take a different line. In such circumstances the presence of the third party may well be necessary in order to effectually and completely adjudicate the questions in the cause of action and, accordingly, it could very well be appropriate to join a third party in the action. The fact that the plaintiff was, by virtue of the Statute of Limitations, 1957, out of time in instituting proceedings against PLC was, it is thought, also influential to the court in refusing the order brought under Ord 15 r 13.[82] Finally, it should be noted that it was recently held by the English Court of Appeal in *Ord v Belhaven Pubs Ltd*[83] that, although widely drafted, the similar English Ord 15, r 7(2) was not wide enough to cover a situation where a plaintiff wished to substitute, in place of a defendant, either a company which was in the same ownership as a defendant or a company which was the shareholder of a defendant company.

An Anticipated Cause of Action

[4.26] An "anticipated" or apprehended tort or breach of contract or other anticipated substantive cause of action will generally be an insufficient basis for invoking the Mareva jurisdiction. This rule can be seen as flowing from the requirement that there must be a currently actionable substantive cause of action

---

[81.] [1997] 2 ILRM 61 at 69, 70.

[82.] See also *Southern Mineral Oil Ltd v Cooney*, High Court, unrep, 11 May 1998 (Shanley J) where the more recent decision of the Supreme Court in *Allied Irish Coal Supplies Ltd v Powell Duffryn International Fuels Ltd* was followed in preference to the earlier decision of the Supreme Court in *O'Reilly v Granville* [1971] IR 90 where the Court there allowed the plaintiff to add a defendant although the limitation period had expired as against that defendant.

[83.] [1998] TLR 228.

in existence before a Mareva injunction can be granted. In *Zucker v Tyndall Holdings plc*[84] the plaintiffs were minority shareholders in a Swiss company and were also parties to a shareholders' agreement with the majority shareholders under which the plaintiffs were entitled to exercise an option to sell their shares. The plaintiffs exercised their option to sell but, when this was challenged, they sought a declaration from the Swiss courts to the effect that they had in fact validly exercised their option. They also sought an order that the defendant pay them 6 million Swiss Francs in respect of the shares. Subsequently the plaintiffs issued a writ against the defendant in the English courts claiming specific performance of the shareholders' agreement and a Mareva injunction to restrain the defendant from disposing of its assets. The Mareva injunction was granted following an *ex parte* application but was discharged on the *inter partes* hearing. The plaintiffs appealed unsuccessfully to the Court of Appeal.

[4.27] The Court of Appeal in the *Zucker* case reaffirmed the principle in *The Siskina*. It was held that the relief sought by the plaintiffs was merely declaratory and, in such circumstances, there were no grounds for granting a Mareva injunction. Neill LJ said:

> "As I understand the present law, it is that a Mareva injunction cannot be granted unless there is an existing cause of action which can be immediately enforced. An order for specific performance which is granted before the time of performance has arrived is ... really in two parts: first of all the declaratory part and secondly the part where consequential directions might be given.
>
> ... there has been no failure to pay the sum of 6 million Swiss Francs. It is true that ... the attitude taken by the respondent company is that the circumstances which would give rise to the valid exercise of the put option have not arisen. But it is not suggested that there has been any failure to pay the money at this stage when [the due date] is still six weeks away and there has been no repudiatory breach. The appellants have the right to be paid, but, in the words of Lord Diplock , there has been no invasion of that right. The word 'invasion' is the word used by Lord Diplock in *The Siskina* [1977] 3 All ER 803 at 824. In the earlier case to which Lord Diplock referred, *North London Rly Co v Great Northern Rly Co* (1883) 11 QBD 30, Cotton LJ referred to a legal or equitable right 'being interfered with'.
>
> It seems to me that, as the law stands at present, for the purposes of a Mareva injunction it is necessary to demonstrate that a legal or equitable right has been interfered with or invaded or that such an invasion or interference is threatened, though, it is certainly true...that interlocutory relief can be obtained in certain circumstances to protect an equitable interest even before the time for performance under a contract has arisen."[85]

However, to say that there is *no* jurisdiction to grant *quit timet* Mareva relief (*ie*

[84.] [1993] 1 All ER 124.

before a substantive cause of action is currently actionable) may be to go too far.[86] A Mareva injunction might be justified as a *quia timet* injunction where there is a real threatened breach of an obligation which is presently enforceable.[87] Extreme cases could arise where no existing substantive cause of action against a defendant appears to exist but where the circumstances are so compelling as to justify a court granting Mareva relief.[88] Even in such extreme situations it may be found to be the case that the substantive cause of action is not readily statable, rather then non-existent.

Were a defendant company to dispose of its property so as to defraud its creditors, a plaintiff might be able to claim a *quia timet* Mareva injunction against the person to whom the property was given on the basis that if the company were put into receivership or wound up, application could be brought under s 139 of the Companies Act 1990 to order the return of the property. In that an application could not, until the company was being wound up or in receivership, be brought under s 139, the cause of action would be anticipatory and any injunction granted, *quia timet*.

Post-Judgment Mareva Injunctions - Substantive Rights

[4.28] A pre-judgment Mareva plaintiff must have a currently actionable substantive cause of action. It has been established, however, that Mareva relief is available as an aid to execution and that it is sufficient that a post-judgment Mareva plaintiff has an enforceable substantive right to recover an award from a defendant. One of the first cases to establish this was *Orwell Steel (Erection and Fabrication) Ltd v Asphalt & Tarmac (UK) Ltd*[89] where Farquharson J concluded that:

> "There is ... in my judgment, power to grant an interlocutory injunction between final judgment and execution.[90]

---

85. [1993] 1 All ER 124 at 131. See also *Veracruz Transportation Inc v VC Shipping Co Inc, The Veracruz* [1992] 1 Lloyd's Rep 353; *Steamship Mutual Underwriting Association (Bermuda) Ltd v Thakur Shipping Co Ltd* [1986] 2 Lloyd's Rep 439, *Siporex Trade SA v Comdel Commodities Ltd* [1986] 2 Lloyd's Rep 428 and *The Niedersachsen* [1984] 1 All ER 398.
86. In *Zucher v Tyndall Holdings plc* [1993] 1 All ER 124 at 132 Staughton LJ said: "One example that has occurred is what I call the poisoned pill case, where the plaintiff is bound by his contract to pay money to the defendant against delivery of a chattel, and accompanies his cheque with a Mareva injunction granted a day or two earlier, anticipating that the chattel, when delivered, will be defective in breach of contract. That is not permitted."
87. See *Zucher v Tyndall Holdings plc* [1993] 1 All ER 124 at 132 *per* Staughton LJ.
88. A clearer case could be stated for a *quia timet* ordinary injunction to protect a proprietary claim *eg* where a fiduciary (broker, solicitor, accountant) announcing that he is intent upon putting trust moneys on a horse in the Grand National and thereafter intent upon leaving for Antigua might be sufficient grounds for causing a court to accede to a beneficiary's request for *quia timet* injunctive relief.
89. [1985] 3 All ER 747.

If there is such a power, there seems to be no logical reason why a Mareva injunction should not be used in aid of execution. Indeed, in one sense it could be said that there is greater justification for restraining a defendant from disposing of his assets after judgment than before any claim has been established against him. It is true that there are a variety of methods for enforcing execution as set out in [the Rules of the Supreme Court] and once the plaintiff has obtained judgment it may be said that he should pursue the remedies provided by the rules rather than extend the application of Mareva injunctions still further. The answer to that objection is that, as has been frequently pointed out, the Mareva injunction acts *in personam* on the defendant and does not give the plaintiff any rights over the goods of the defendant or involve any attachment of them. In this context it would have the effect of preserving the defendant's goods until execution could be levied on them; and the remedies of injunction and execution can take effect side by side."[91]

In that case the plaintiff had obtained judgment against the defendant. The decree was successfully appealed by the defendant. A stay was placed on the order, provided that the defendant paid the sum awarded into court. The defendant failed to do so and the plaintiff became entitled to enforce the judgment. The plaintiff obtained a writ of *fieri facias* but this was ineffective. The plaintiff feared that the defendant would transfer certain assets to another company to avoid execution of the judgment. The plaintiff successfully obtained a Mareva injunction, preserving the defendant's goods until execution could be levied upon them.[92] In so holding Farquharson J relied upon the decision of Baggallay LJ in *Smith v Cowell*[93] where he had said:

"Section 25, subs (8) of the Judicature Act 1973, provides that 'a mandamus or injunction may be granted, or a receiver appointed by an interlocutory order of the Court,' in all cases in which it shall appear just and convenient; and the defendant's contention is that the Court has no power under that section to make an order for a receiver in an action after judgment, for the words 'interlocutory order' mean an order prior to final judgment. But with that contention I cannot agree. The interpretation of the word 'interlocutory', as

---

90. On the authority of *Smith* v *Cowell* (1880) 6 QBD 75 and Ord 29 r 1 of the English Rules of the Supreme Court 1965.
91. [1985] 3 All ER 747 at 749h-750a.
92. See also *Stewart Chartering Ltd* v *C & O Managements SA, The Venus Destiny* [1980] 1 All ER 718, where Goff J continued a Mareva injunction granted before judgment, in aid of execution. In *TDK Tape Distributor (UK) Ltd* v *Videochoice Ltd* [1985] 3 All ER 345 at 349c-d where Skinner J said: "It seems to me that a Mareva injunction is looking to the future and is dealing with a situation between the obtaining of the judgment and its eventual execution ...". See also *Babanaft International Co SA* v *Bassatne* [1989] 2 WLR 232 where a worldwide Mareva injunction was granted in aid of execution and *Mercantile Group (Europe) AG v Aiyela and others* [1994] 1 All ER 110.
93. (1880) 6 QBD 75.

used in the sub-section, is to be found later on in the sub-section itself, which provides that 'if an injunction is asked either before, or at, or after the hearing of a cause', it may be granted etc. But it is only by an interlocutory order that the Court has power under this section to grant an injunction. In the case of an injunction therefore, the section clearly contemplates an interlocutory order being made after the hearing of a cause, or in other words, after judgment."[94]

Although Farquharson J held that the matter was, at that time, concluded in England by reason of their Ord 29, r 1 of the Rules of the Supreme Court, 1965[95] it is thought that Baggallay LJ's interpretation of s 25(8) of the English Supreme Court of Judicature Act 1873 can equally be applied to our s 28(8) of the Supreme Court of Judicature (Ireland) Act 1877.[96]

[4.29] In *Jet West Ltd v Haddican*[97] Lord Donaldson MR considered this matter again. He said that he would produce direct authority that:

> "... a Mareva injunction can be granted or can be continued in support of any judgment or order of the Court for the payment of money, whether or not the exact sum which will be payable has been quantified at the date of the order and the date at which the Mareva injunction is sought".[98]

Lord Donaldson MR expressly approved of the judgment of Robert Goff J in *Stewart Chartering Ltd v C & O Managements SA, The Venus Destiny*.[99] In that case Robert Goff J had relied upon the court's inherent jurisdiction as the basis for granting Mareva relief to a judgment-creditor. In the course of his judgment (being part of the passage quoted with approval by Lord Donaldson MR), Goff J had said:

> "The solution to this problem lies, in my judgment, in the inherent jurisdiction of the court to control its own process, and in particular to prevent any possible abuse of that process. If the plaintiffs were unable to obtain a judgment in the present case without abandoning their Mareva injunction, it would be open to a defendant to defeat the very purpose of the proceedings simply by declining to enter an appearance. Such conduct would be an abuse of the process of the

---

94. At 77.
95. Order 29 r 1 provides: "An application for the grant of an injunction may be made by any party to a cause or matter before or after the trial of the cause or matter, whether or not a claim for the injunction was included in that party's writ, originating summons, counterclaim or third party notice, as the case may be."
96. Note, though, that s 28(8) of the 1877 Act provides: "... if an injunction is asked, either before, or at, or after the hearing of any cause or matter, *to prevent any threatened or apprehended waste or trespass*, such injunction may be granted ...". Whether the words in italics qualify the significance of the words which precede them is an arguable point. On balance, it is thought that the real significance of the reference is that, whatever the specific circumstances, s 28(8) of the 1877 Act envisages the granting of "interlocutory" injunctions after judgment.
97. [1992] 2 All ER 545, citing *Faith Panton Property Plan Ltd v Hodgetts* [1981] 2 All ER 877.
98. *Ibid* at 548.
99. [1980] 1 All ER 718.

court; and in my judgment the court has power to take the necessary steps, by virtue of its inherent jurisdiction, to prevent any such abuse of its process. The appropriate action to be taken by the court in such circumstances is, in my judgment, to grant leave to the plaintiffs, in an appropriate case to enter judgment in default of appearance, notwithstanding that the writ is indorsed with a claim for an injunction. If the court so acts, it can also order that the Mareva injunction continue in force until after the judgment, in aid of execution. The purpose of the Mareva injunction is to prevent a defendant from removing his assets from the jurisdiction so as to prevent the plaintiff from obtaining the fruits of his judgment; from this it follows that the policy underlying the Mareva jurisdiction can only be given effect to if the court has power to continue the Mareva injunction after judgment in aid of execution."[100]

It is thought that this rationale applies equally to situations where a judgment-creditor only seeks Mareva relief for the first time after obtaining judgment against a defendant.

[4.30] A different rationale was advanced for post-judgment Mareva injunctions by the English Court of Appeal in *Mercantile Group (Europe) AG v Aiyeal*.[101] There, Hoffmann LJ interpreted *The Siskina* as requiring a plaintiff to have a substantive cause of action or other *substantive right*; an example of such a substantive right is a judgment debt and a Mareva injunction can be granted as relief ancillary to that right.

[4.31] In Ireland it has also been accepted that there is jurisdiction to grant post-judgment Mareva relief. This was made clear by Carroll J in *Elwyn (Cottons) Ltd v Pearle Designs Ltd*.[102] There she held that the Master of the High Court had no discretion and was obliged to grant Mareva relief where a judgment creditor applied for protective measures pursuant to s 11(1) of the Jurisdiction of Courts and Enforcement of Judgments (European Communities) Act 1988 because "... a Mareva-type injunction ... is a protective measure which the High Court would have power to grant in respect of proceedings within its jurisdiction."[103]

[4.32] In view of the acceptance of the existence of the jurisdiction to grant a pre-judgment Mareva injunction, it seems almost perverse to raise a question as to the existence of a jurisdiction to grant a post-judgment Mareva injunction. In addition to the inherent jurisdiction basis for granting post-judgment Mareva relief it has been argued that s 28(8) of the 1877 Act empowers the court to grant post-judgment Mareva relief because an order made pursuant to that section may be considered to be "interlocutory" in the sense that all of the matters in dispute between the parties have not been finally determined.[104]

[100.] At 719.
[101.] [1994] 1 All ER 110.
[102.] [1989] IR 9; [1989] ILRM 162; (1989) ITLR 6 March 1989.
[103.] At 12. See further para **[4.59]** *et seq, infra.*

[4.33] An old Irish case where an injunction was granted restraining a judgment debtor from, *inter alia*, realising any part of a sum of money about to be paid to her, is the 1942 Circuit Court case of *Hyland v Fox*.[105] In that case the plaintiff, who had obtained judgment against the defendant in respect of arrears of rent, successfully obtained an injunction which prevented the defendant and her solicitors from realising any part of a sum paid to the defendant by the Department of Finance as compensation for "war damage". The defendant had had her furniture destroyed by German aircraft in January 1941. The plaintiff had sought an order of garnishee directing the Minister for Finance to pay the compensation to him. Judge Davitt held that a garnishee order would not lie against the Minister for Finance but held that he could grant an injunction which, *inter alia*, restrained the defendant and her solicitors from realising the amount of the draft to be paid to her.

[4.34] Post-judgment Mareva relief has also been granted in Ireland on a number of occasions in more recent times. In *W v H*[106] Blayney J is reported as having granted the plaintiff a Mareva injunction which restrained the defendants from disposing of the proceeds of sale of a house, or removing such proceeds from the State, save where those proceeds exceeded £75,000. The newspaper report states that the plaintiff had some years previous obtained a judgment in the High Court for £20,000 with costs. One of the defendants was at the time of the injunction proceedings in prison, serving a sentence for his part in attempting to smuggle arms into the State on board the Eksund. It was also reported that the defendant's home had been put up for sale and that although it was in the first defendant's sole name, it had purportedly been transferred into the second defendant's name. It was alleged that the first defendant, against whom the earlier judgment had been obtained, was denuding himself of the only asset to which his creditors could look. In *Ulster Bank Ltd v H*[107] Carney J was reported to have granted a Mareva injunction to the plaintiff bank in respect of the defendant's National Lottery windfall. The bank had two years earlier obtained judgment for £234,038 against the defendant and his father which remained unsatisfied.

[B] THE CAUSES OR ACTIONS WHICH CAN GROUND MAREVA RELIEF

[4.35] The most basic prerequisite to obtaining a Mareva injunction is that a plaintiff has a substantive cause of action against a defendant. However, when the Mareva jurisdiction was first mooted it was synonymous with a *particular type* of cause of action, namely, breach of contract in commercial cases. Since then, however, the circumstances in which a Mareva injunction will be granted have been extended and today, Mareva relief is generally available in all civil causes of action. Here we consider:

[104.] See Capper, *Mareva Injunctions*, (1988) SLS/Sweet & Maxwell, p 56, para 4.03. See further at pp 73-75, paras 5.33-5.38.

[105.] (1943) Ir Jur Rep 35.

[106.] *The Irish Times*, 2 July 1992, (Blayney J).

[107.] *The Irish Times*, 6 June 1992, (Carney J).

(1) Contractual and commercial causes of action,

(2) Tortious causes of action, and

(3) Statutory causes of action.

Contractual Causes of Action

[4.36] The original paradigm cause of action to which the Mareva injunction was ancillary relief was a breach of contract in a commercial case involving liquidated damages. One could be even more specific and point to disputes which involved charterparties.[108] An action for breach of contract which involves a claim for liquidated damages is, perhaps, the ideal cause of action. In a case involving an alleged breach of a commercial contract it will often be more readily possible to establish whether there has in fact been a breach and Mareva relief will be a proportionate measure to preserve the *status quo*. The Mareva jurisdiction has, however, developed into a general private law remedy and Irish and other courts have consistently granted Mareva relief in cases alleging both large[109] and small[110] breaches of contract. An example of a case involving an alleged breach of a non-commercial contract which came before the High Court is *P v T*.[111] In that case a married couple were successful in obtaining an interim *ex parte* Mareva injunction against the builder from whom they had purchased their house, and whom they wished to prevent "selling up" and leaving the

---

[108.] *Nippon Yusen Kaisha v Karageorgis* [1975] 3 All ER 282, *Mareva Compania Naviera SA v International Bulkcarriers SA* [1980] 1 All ER 213, *Rasu Maritima SA v Perusahaan Pertambangan Minyak Dan Gas Bumi Negara; The Pertamina* [1977] 3 All ER 324 and *The Siskina* [1977] 3 All ER 803 all involved alleged breaches of charterparty. See generally, Denning, *The Due Process of Law*, (1980) Butterworths, p 133 *et seq* for an interesting first-hand account of the development of the Mareva jurisdiction.

[109.] See, for example, *B,W & S v N, The Irish Times*, 4 September 1997 (Geoghegan J) where the newspaper report states that the plaintiffs were granted "Mareva orders freezing almost £1m of [the defendant's] assets in Ireland", ancillary to their claim for breach of contract of service/ contract for services relating to advising on property purchase, overseeing the running of racing stables and stud farms and the purchase of bloodstock in Ireland and abroad for the defendant. The newspaper report went on to state, *inter alia*, that it was alleged that commission on the purchase of a horse, amounting to £145,000 was never paid, that funds were not made available to the first plaintiff to buy yearlings and other bloodstock and that the defendant had instructed the first plaintiff to sell a property which was alleged to be his principal asset in Ireland; the plaintiffs feared that the estimated proceeds thereof which amounted to an estimated £1m would be taken to Japan.

[110.] Mareva relief, ancillary to contractual causes of action, are quite common in the Irish High Court. These range from alleged failure to pay commission on the sale of Lamborghini cars: *F v LMI Ltd, The Irish Times*, 5 February 1991 (Blayney J) and 5 March 1991 (Blayney J); to alleged simple breach of contract for services (house refurbishment): *PPHS Ltd v Vonk, The Irish Times*, 31 May 1995 (Circuit Court; Judge Cyril Kelly); to alleged breach of contract for the sale of goods (sale of cigarettes to vending machine businessman): *GC & Co Ltd v F, The Irish Times*, 3 August 1995 (Flood J); to alleged failure to repay sums due to a Bank: *Bank of Ireland v N, The Irish Times*, 12 March 1991 (Costello J), *Allied Irish Banks, plc v Two Solicitors, The Irish Times*, 3 June 1992 (Costello J); to alleged breach of the terms of a contract for sale of a castle: *IC Ltd v CC Ltd, The Irish Times*, 26 February 1991 (Keane J).

[111.] *The Irish Times*, 16 May 1989.

country. The proceedings related to an allegedly defective septic tank which, it was claimed, did not work and leaked raw sewage. The newspaper report stated that the plaintiffs had been told that the house had been built in accordance with planning permission and that it had an adequate and working septic tank; it is presumed that the action was taken in contract. Barrington J is reported as having granted the plaintiffs interim Mareva relief, the effect of the order being to restrain the defendant from reducing his assets within the State below £63,272.25. The order was, however, discharged following an *inter partes* hearing.[112] It is clear, however, that in contractual disputes where the subject matter can range from ships to septic tanks, Mareva relief is available.

Tortious Causes of Action

[4.37] The foregoing paragraphs have already recounted the development of the Mareva injunction from being, initially, a remedy in commercial disputes to being now available in all contractual disputes. However, the extension of the remedy to non-contractual, particularly tort actions, was a more far-reaching development by reason of the fact that a plaintiff's claim in tort will almost invariably involve unliquidated damages. Although this development has been recognised by the Irish Supreme Court in *Re John Horgan Livestock Ltd; O'Mahony v Horgan*,[113] a note of regret is seen in the concurring judgment of O'Flaherty J who said:

> "In its original manifestation, the remedy was used in clear cases where a debt was established and the debtor was about to abscond or to dissipate his assets.
>
> As the jurisdiction developed, it appears now to be sufficient to establish that the plaintiff has a good arguable case and for a diverse series of cases. I would have preferred that the remedy should have been confined to situations where there was a clear case involving a claim for a definite sum of money or, otherwise, for some tangible object - where the claim was more or less certain, in so far as there is ever certainty in any litigation. It may now be too late to put that particular clock back."[114]

It is thought that it is, indeed, too late to turn back the clock and to disallow Mareva relief in cases involving contentious claims for unliquidated damages. It must be the case, however, that in tortious actions judges will exercise the Mareva jurisdiction more sparingly and more discerningly than in a clear-cut case involving a claim for a definite sum. A review of some of the instances where the Irish High Court has granted Mareva relief will, it is thought, satisfy most objective commentators that where the Irish courts have granted Mareva relief in tortious causes of action, such was justified.

---

[112] *The Irish Times*, 27 May 1989 (Barrington J).
[113] [1995] 2 IR 411.
[114] At 422.

(a) Personal injuries actions[115]

[4.38] One of the first, and most tragic, applications for Mareva relief in a tortious cause of action was *Allen v Jambo Holdings Ltd*.[116] In that case, the plaintiff's husband was decapitated by the propeller of the defendant company's aeroplane. The plaintiff issued proceedings claiming damages under the English Fatal Accidents Act 1976 and sought a Mareva injunction to prevent the defendant company from removing the offending aircraft from England as that was its only asset within the jurisdiction. The injunction was granted *ex parte* but subsequently discharged. The plaintiff appealed against the discharge to the Court of Appeal. One issue before the court was whether it was appropriate to grant a Mareva injunction in a case involving a non-commercial cause of action. The Court of Appeal unanimously held that there was jurisdiction in an appropriate case to grant a Mareva injunction as ancillary relief in a non-commercial cause of action. As to the novelty of the application, it was said that as recently as 1975 the Mareva injunction itself was "something of an innovation in regard to mercantile transactions".[117] However, Templeman LJ held:

"So far as the question of jurisdiction is concerned, I can see no difference between a Mareva injunction in a commercial action and a Mareva injunction for personal injury or any other cause of action save this, that in the kind of actions in which Mareva injunctions have been granted, where the contest is between two big commercial concerns, there is usually very little argument about the value of the cross-undertaking in damages, and there are freely available methods of security."[118]

Although the plaintiff's claim was by no means bound to succeed the Court of Appeal considered it appropriate to grant a Mareva injunction.[119]

[4.39] While, to date, there is no written judgment where the Irish High Court has granted a Mareva injunction as ancillary relief in a tortious cause of action, the newspaper reports abound with examples of cases where such applications have been successful. In *C v X Ltd*[120] it was reported that a student nurse suffered a leg injury at a discotheque held in an hotel owned by the defendant company.

[115.] See generally, Courtney, 'Mareva Injunctions in Personal Injuries Actions', (1995) Dli - The Western Law Gazette 107.

[116.] [1980] 2 All ER 502. The case is considered by Lord Denning in *The Due Process of Law*, (1980) Butterworths, page 148, under the sub-heading, "A man is decapitated".

[117.] At 506b per Shaw LJ

[118.] At 506g. On undertakings in Mareva injunctions see Ch 8, *Applying for a Mareva Injunction*, para **[8.57]** *et seq.*

[119.] As to the limited value of the plaintiff-widow's undertakings, see Ch 8, *Applying for a Mareva Injunction*, para **[8.64]**.

[120.] *The Irish Times*, 25 September 1990 (Blayney J).

Proceedings had been issued by the plaintiff for personal injuries. The plaintiff claimed that the hotel was being sold to an American company and that if this happened the defendant company would have no further assets within the jurisdiction. The plaintiff's counsel was reported as saying that the defendant company had not entered an appearance to the plaintiff's claim and, further, that he was instructed that the individual co-defendant had considerable business interests in America. Blayney J is reported to have granted an interim Mareva injunction restraining the defendants from reducing their assets within the State below £175,000 and from removing assets up to that amount out of the jurisdiction.

[4.40] A similar set of facts grounded the application for a Mareva injunction in *C v M*[121] where it was reported that the plaintiff had been injured in an accident at the defendant's public house in June 1992 and had instituted proceedings against the defendant. The report stated that it was heard that the defendant was alleged to be working as a street musician in Cyprus and that the defendant was alleged to have sold the public house for £128,000. It was also alleged that the defendant did not have public liability insurance at the time of the plaintiff's accident. The plaintiff had expressed a fear that the defendant would distribute the proceeds of sale of the public house outside of the jurisdiction. It was reported that Johnson J granted a Mareva injunction restraining the defendant from reducing his assets within the State below £35,000, which sum was, presumably, an estimate of the plaintiff's claim and costs.[122]

[4.41] Another, unusual example, is the application in *K v F*,[123] where a widowed mother of four children successfully obtained a Mareva injunction against the man who had killed her husband and who was incarcerated in Mountjoy, whilst serving a 10 year sentence. The plaintiff had issued civil proceedings against the defendant and had subsequently heard it rumoured that he might be attempting to dispose of his farm to avoid payment of any damages which the High Court might award. It was reported that Costello J granted the plaintiff an interlocutory Mareva injunction which prevented the defendant, his servants or agents, from disposing of his farm or any other assets owned by him.

[4.42] The only written judgment of the Irish High Court to concern a Mareva injunction in a personal injuries action is *Moloney v Laurib Investments Ltd*.[124]

[121.] *The Irish Times*, 10 September 1994 (Johnson J).
[122.] See also *C v C Ltd*, *The Irish Times*, of 3 July 1997 (Circuit Court; Judge Devally) where again the plaintiffs were taking a number of personal injuries actions against an hotel. There it was reported that the hotel premises was the defendant's only asset and it was feared that if it was sold the assets might be dissipated so as to be unavailable to meet any court judgment. Maximum sum orders were granted of up to £30,000 in each case.
[123.] *The Irish Times*, 30 May 1990 (Costello J).
[124.] High Court, unrep, 20 July 1993 (Lynch J); (1993) *Irish Times, Law Report* 6 December 1993.

In that case the plaintiff - a minor suing by her mother and next friend - unsuccessfully applied for a Mareva injunction. The tragic facts of the case were that the plaintiff had suffered serious personal injuries after allegedly falling through an unguarded opening on a floor of an unfinished building. Her injuries indicated that she would remain a paraplegic and would be confined to a wheelchair. Lynch J accepted that the plaintiff had a statable case against the defendant, that the defendant also had a statable defence but he said that it was not appropriate to require that anything more regarding the issue of liability be established on the hearing of a Mareva application. On the facts of the case, which are considered in detail below,[125] Lynch J refused to grant a Mareva injunction, giving the following as reasons:

> "... the absence of any worthwhile undertaking on behalf of the plaintiff as to damages; also to the interference which an injunction would involve in normal development projects by the defendant company; also to the interference with creditors' prospects of repayment of their debts by the defendant company; *also to the wholly unliquidated tortious nature of the plaintiff's claim* and to the fact that it is doubtful if the grant of an injunction would in any event improve significantly or at all the plaintiff's prospects of enforcing a judgment in her favour against the defendant company ...".[126]

It is thought that the reference to the "wholly unliquidated tortious nature of the plaintiff's claim" was but one small factor in Lynch J's decision to refuse to exercise his discretion in favour of granting the Mareva relief sought by the plaintiff. Indeed, the most decisive factor in Lynch J's decision would appear to be the fact that the risk of dissipation of the defendant's assets was not accompanied by the intention to frustrate any future judgment of the plaintiff.[127] Whilst courts rightly exercise more caution in personal injuries cases, as was reluctantly recognised by O'Flaherty J in *Re John Horgan Livestock Ltd*,[128] it is now accepted that Mareva relief is available, in appropriate circumstances, in tortious causes of action.[129]

[125.] See Ch 6, *The Risk of Removal or Disposal of Assets*, para **[6.26]**.

[126.] At p 6 of the transcript. Italics added.

[127.] See Courtney, 'Mareva Injunctions in Personal Injuries Actions', (1995) Dli - The Western Law Gazette 107 at 108,109.

[128.] [1995] 2 IR 411.

[129.] See also *T v A Ltd & F, The Irish Times*, 10 December 1997 (Kelly J). In that case the plaintiff was granted Mareva relief restraining the second defendant from reducing his assets below £2m. The first defendant had already given the Court an undertaking not to reduce his assets below £2m. The plaintiff was alleged to have suffered extensive personal injuries whilst working for the first defendant when a fat machine exploded as a result of which he was rendered a paraplegic. The newspaper report states that in granting the relief sought, Kelly J said that he was satisfied that the plaintiff "had fulfilled the criteria set down by the Supreme Court for the granting of such an injunction including giving an undertaking for damages".

(b) General actions in tort

[4.43] Mareva injunctions are generally available as ancillary relief in all tortious causes of action. Indeed, at present, it can be said that if there is a paradigm cause of action which grounds Mareva relief, it would be in actions taken in tort for conversion, fraudulent conversion and conspiracy to defraud.[130] *Countyglen plc v Carway*[131] and *Re John Horgan Livestock Ltd*[132] are the main Irish Mareva decisions where allegations of fraud or misappropriation have been made. Moreover, the newspaper reports abound with examples of instances where the courts have granted Mareva relief where the plaintiff has alleged fraud. Indeed, in such cases, the requirement that a Mareva plaintiff adduce evidence of the defendant's intention to frustrate judgment is thought to be more easily satisfied.[133]

[4.44] Alleged social welfare fraud has proved to be a sufficient cause of action to justify the High Court to exercise its Mareva jurisdiction. The case of *The Minister for Social Welfare v M*[134] was an especially interesting example of the use of the Mareva jurisdiction. The background facts[135] to this successful

---

[130.] See generally Ch 6, *The Risk of Removal or Disposal of Assets*, para **[6.46]** *et seq* where the cases of *Irish Press Newspapers Ltd v Malocco & Kileen, The Irish Times*, of 30 March 1995; *Re TSD Ltd; D v O'D&O'D, The Irish Times*, 31 January 1992 (Costello J); see also *The Irish Independent* 4 February 1992 and *Re Mark Synnott (Life and Pensions) Brokers Ltd*, For newspaper coverage of the *Synnott Case* see *The Irish Times*, 15, 18, 19, 25, 27 June; 3, 4, 6, 9, July; 6, 7, 8, 9 November 1991.

[131.] [1995] 1 IR 208.

[132.] [1995] 2 IR 411.

[133.] In *PS Ltd and PS(T) Ltd v C, The Irish Times*, 22 March 1996 (McCracken J) where the plaintiff was successful in obtaining Mareva relief in circumstances where it alleged that the defendant employee had been "systematically defrauding the two [plaintiff] companies". In *D v M, The Irish Times*, 8 June 1996 (McCracken J) the plaintiff obtained a maximum sum Mareva injunction restraining the defendant from reducing her assets below £73,000. The defendant was a part time baby-sitter for the plaintiff and was also employed to package change for the plaintiff's cigarette machine business. When the plaintiff noticed a shortfall he reported the matter to the Gardai who, he claimed, installed a concealed camera in the room where she packed the change; he alleged that he was told by Gardai that the video recorded the defendant taking the money. In *JRB&SLtd v E, The Irish Times*, 18 February 1998 (Kelly J) it was reported that a Mareva injunction was granted to the plaintiff cash-and-carry against a once valued customer whom, it was alleged, had stolen up to £300,000 worth of cigarettes. As in the case of *D v M* the defendant in this application too had been recorded in the act of conversion by a specially installed concealed surveillance camera.

[134.] *The Irish Times*, 21 ("Department seeks bite of award") and 26 ("Judge extends order cutting pie pay-out") February 1991. The writer acknowledges with gratitude the assistance provided by counsel for both parties, Peter Charleton SC and RAM Robbins SC and the solicitors for both parties, Stuart Coonan of the Chief State Solicitors' Office and Sean Costello of Frank Ward & Co, for their valuable assistance.

[135.] For the background facts, see *The Irish Times*, 13 February 1991.

Mareva application could be said to be quite "unsavoury". The defendant, M, began to eat a tin of steak and kidney pie which his wife had bought in a supermarket when, having consumed about two-thirds, thought he was eating cotton wool and spat it out. On taking the meal away his wife showed him what appeared to be the hind legs of a mouse, with part of its tail. The defendant was immediately sick and, thereafter, his appetite suffered greatly, and it was reported that the defendant became resigned to a diet of milk and Guinness. M subsequently sued the supplier and the manufacturer.[136] In the course of a High Court hearing, it was reported that M had been "signing on the dole" whilst, contemporaneously, working on a casual basis for his brother in a fruit and vegetable business in the Dublin markets. *The Irish Times* reported subsequently, that M was alleged to have received £35,000 in settlement of his High Court action.[137]

By coincidence, or perhaps prompted by the wide-spread media interest in M's encounter with the mouse, a staff officer of the Department of Social Welfare attended in the public gallery for the hearing of the action in the High Court before Egan J. Subsequently, the Minister for Social Welfare instituted proceedings against M under s 151 of the Social Welfare (Consolidation) Act 1981[138] and sought damages for conversion, fraudulent conversion and negligence. The staff officer's affidavit averred, *inter alia*, to the foregoing causes of action, the fact that there were assets available (the alleged settlement of £35,000) and claimed that the defendant had no answer to the claims made and that he would make himself "judgment proof".[139] It was reported in *The Irish Times* that Murphy J granted the Mareva injunction sought by the Minister for Social Welfare and restrained the defendant from reducing the amount of the settlement below the sum of £16,996.[140]

[4.45] A number of cases which have centred on alleged conversion have involved family members. In *O v K*[141] an 80 year old widow was successful in obtaining a Mareva injunction which restrained her daughter from transferring or dealing with any assets she may have held except in so far as they exceeded

---

[136.] It was reported in *The Irish Times*, 26 February 1991 that the manufacturer of the pie claimed that it played no active part in the High Court proceedings, that the pie in question was produced in England by an English company and that M's complaint had been dealt with by an insurance company.

[137.] See *The Irish Times*, 21 February 1991.

[138.] See para **[4.48]** *infra*.

[139.] On the evidence adduced that the defendant would make himself "judgment proof" see also Ch 6, *The Risk of Removal or Disposal of Assets*, para **[6.53]**.

[140.] An insurance company was also enjoined from paying the defendant more than half of the alleged settlement sum of £35,000. The court's order was subsequently extended on consent by Keane J: *The Irish Times*, 26 February 1991.

[141.] *The Irish Times*, 19 September 1991 (Johnson J).

£65,574. The widow was sole legatee of her late husband's estate. Upon the sale of their family home the widow was alleged to have endorsed the cheque, at the behest of her daughter, on the understanding that it would be lodged in their joint names. It was heard that this had not happened; that the widow had went to live with her daughter but that she had been forced to leave to live with another daughter; and that she had not received the originals of her own solicitor's letters advising her as to the best use to which she could put the money. It was reported that the daughter claimed that the money was given to her as a gift, that she had invested the money for her mother's maintenance and that if necessary she would submit accounts to the court showing disbursements of all funds. It was subsequently reported in *The Irish Times* that the proceeds of sale had been lodged in court.[142] *H v H & C*[143] involved similar facts. In that application the first defendant's parents had earlier obtained a Mareva injunction preventing their daughter from dissipating her assets below £10,000. It was alleged that the parents had lent their daughter £7,570 on an undertaking that she would repay them from the proceeds of a personal injuries action. The report in *The Irish Times* stated that it was alleged by the daughter that she had been given the money as a gift, that she had been harassed by her parents, that her husband had been attacked with a hammer and that she and her husband were living in a tent as her parents' action had prevented them from buying a house. It was also reported that the defendants had taken every step they possibly could to avoid service of documents and to conceal their whereabouts and that the judge is reported to have continued the Mareva injunction until the trial of the action.[144]

Statutory Causes of Action

[4.46] In the present context "statutory cause of action" means a right of action which does not exist at common law or in equity and which is created by an Act of the Oireachtas.[145] An English example of a Mareva injunction which was granted as relief ancillary to a statutory cause of action was *Securities and Investment Board v Pantell SA*, which has been considered previously.[146] In that

---

[142] *The Irish Times*, 26 September 1991 (O'Hanlon J).

[143] *The Irish Times*, 30 July 1994 (Circuit Court; Judge Cyril Kelly).

[144] In *The Irish Times*, 28 October 1994 it was reported that the plaintiffs' action was successful, that the defendants were ordered to repay the sum of £7,570 and that Judge James Carroll continued the Mareva injunction post judgment.

[145] Many statutes create private causes of action which entitle various persons to institute proceedings, foreign to the common law, against various persons. On example is the various statutory causes of action created under the Companies Acts 1963-1990 such as ss 297, 297A and 298 of the Companies Act 1963 and s 204 of the Companies Act 1990 which grounded the liquidator's cause of action in *Re John Horgan Livestock Ltd; O'Mahony v Horgan* [1995] 2 IR 411. As to actions commenced by notice of motion (as opposed to actions commenced by summons) see Ch 8, *Applying for a Mareva Injunction*, para **[8.19]**.

[146] [1989] 2 All ER 673. See Ch 2, *The Jurisdiction to Grant Mareva Relief*, para **[2.37]**.

case the UK Securities and Investment Board (SIB) obtained a Mareva injunction against the defendant which froze its London bank account, pending the outcome of its investigation into alleged contravention of the UK Financial Services Act 1986.[147] The circumstances of the prosecution were that the defendant company had, from Switzerland, advertised investment advice in the United Kingdom. The defendant had stressed its own impartiality and went on to commend the shares in a particular company (which it said were listed) and described it as the "share of 1988": in fact it was unlisted and its president was one of the defendant's two directors. After the Swiss authorities had taken action against the defendant for breaches of Swiss banking laws, the British SIB was told that the defendant had sent cheques, which it had received from English investors, to a bank account in its name in London. It was this account which the SIB sought to freeze.

[4.47] In the *Pantell* case no cause of action existed against the defendant at common law. Sir Nicholas Browne-Wilkinson V-C held, however, that the court could grant a Mareva injunction as relief ancillary to a statutory cause of action. In the course of his judgment he said:

> "In the ordinary case the court grants Mareva relief (ie injunctions restraining the dissipation of assets pending trial of an action) at the suit of an individual who has a private right to damages or other relief (that is to say a private cause of action): see *Siskina (cargo holders) v Distos Cia Naviera SA, The Siskina* [1977] 3 All ER 803, [1979] AC 210. In this case the SIB itself has no beneficial interest in the moneys nor, apart from the statute, any cause of action against [the defendants] But in my judgment the statutory right of action for the benefit of investors conferred on the SIB by s 6 is as much a right of action as any normal right of action in common law. It follows that in my judgment the SIB is as much entitled to apply for protection by way of Mareva relief on behalf of the investors adversely affected by breach of the Act as would an ordinary private individual be entitled in an ordinary action."[148]

This decision is open to criticism, in particular, for circumventing the principle in *The Siskina*, to wit, that before a plaintiff can obtain a Mareva injunction he must have a currently actionable substantive right or cause of action against a Mareva defendant.[149] One commentator[150] has challenged the decision, saying:

> "It is doubtful that the court had jurisdiction to grant the Mareva in the first place. The SIB personally had no cause of action to satisfy the *Siskina*

[147.] See generally, Crighton, 'Pantell (No 1) Mareva Injunctions: Isolated Incursion into the Field of Public Law or Part of a Strategic Plan?', [1994] JBL 8.
[148.] *Ibid* at 677e-g.
[149.] See para **[4.02]** *et seq, supra*.
[150.] See Creighton, *op cit*, [1994] JBL 8 at 26.

precondition; it was necessary therefore for the Vice-Chancellor to create a new right in the form of a statutory or public cause of action. Justice and expediency have been found to be insufficient grounds for usurping the function of the legislature. The inadequacies of the [Financial Services Act] should not have been rectified by judicial lawmaking."

The dangers of public bodies applying for a Mareva injunction in circumstances where they do not have a civil cause of action against a person are obvious. There is a very strong case for arguing that public bodies, being instruments of the State, ought to have a civil cause of action if they are to avail of an equitable civil remedy. The State, being the master of public bodies, may enact such legislation as it desires to bolster the remedies available to its organs.[151] It is one thing for the court to be sympathetic to an ordinary citizen and tempted to stretch the concept of justice and equity where no remedy is clearly available; it is another matter entirely for the court to exercise its equitable discretion to shore up a gap in the statutory remedies available to a public body where this is the result of legislative inaction or neglect. Different considerations entirely exist where a private individual has a statutory right to bring an action to, say, obtain an order that a sum of money be paid to him or her eg to seek an order for maintenance as in the case of *H v H*,[152] considered below.[153]

[4.48] As noted above, some statutes provide public bodies with causes of action which more readily afford a remedy. In *The Minister of Social Welfare v M*[154] Murphy J granted a Mareva injunction against the defendant who, it was alleged, had been "signing on the dole" whilst contemporaneously working for a wage. The plaintiff's proceedings were brought under s 151 of the Social Welfare (Consolidation) Act 1981 ("the 1981 Act") and also for conversion, fraudulent conversion and negligence. Section 151(1) of the 1981 Act provides:

> Every payment of unemployment assistance received by any person while he was disqualified from receiving unemployment assistance or was disqualified from receiving unemployment assistance or the statutory conditions were not complied with by him or which he was otherwise disentitled to receive shall be repayable by such person to the Minister on demand made in that behalf by a

---

[151.] For example, s 74 of the Central Bank Act 1997 expressly authorises the Central Bank to seek an injunction to prevent an unauthorised person from acting as a credit institution. It is interesting to note that s 74 was enacted some time after primary and secondary legislation criminalising such activity was enacted. *Cf R v Consolidated Fastfrate Transport Inc* (1995) 125 DLR (4th) 1 and Epp, 'Freezing Funds for Fines and Mareva Injunctions', [1997] JBL 72 considered in Ch 2, *The Jurisdiction to Grant Mareva Relief*, para **[2.37]** where it was held that the Attorney General has standing to seek an injunction to restrain a breach of the criminal law.

[152.] High Court, unrep, 7 April 1982 (O'Hanlon J); noted by Charleton, (1982) 4 DULJ 114.

[153.] See para **[4.49]** *infra*.

[154.] *The Irish Times*, 21 and 22 February 1991. For background to the application, see *Irish Times*, 13 February 1991. See para **[4.44]** *supra*.

deciding officer and, if not repaid, may be recovered by the Minister as a simple contract debt in any court of competent jurisdiction or by deduction from any payment or payments of unemployment assistance to which such person subsequently becomes entitled.

Although a Mareva injunction was granted against the defendant, it is not clear whether Murphy J granted it as relief ancillary to the cause of action in s 151 of the 1981 Act or, as the grounding affidavit invited, on foot of the claim for conversion. It is thought, however, that even in the absence of the Minister's common law action for conversion and/or fraudulent conversion, there was jurisdiction to grant Mareva relief ancillary to the statutory cause of action in s 151(1) of the 1981 Act. It is thought that the decision to state the Minister's claim "in-double-harness" may have indicated a nervousness to place sole reliance upon the statutory cause of action as the sole platform for Mareva relief.

[4.49] The substantive cause of action which grounded the plaintiff's application for a Mareva injunction in *H v H*[155] was her statutory right, as a spouse, to maintenance under s 5(1) of the Family Law (Maintenance of Spouses and Children) Act 1976.[156] The facts[157] of the application were that the plaintiff had previously obtained a barring order and an interim maintenance order against the defendant. Before the second hearing to determine the final amount of maintenance to be paid to the plaintiff, her solicitor wrote to the defendant's employers seeking a statement of his earnings, whereupon it was learned that, after 20 years' employment with the same employer, he had opted to take voluntary redundancy and was due a sum in excess of £9,000, being one year's salary. At the second hearing the initial order of £60 per week was confirmed and the defendant-husband did not try to argue that he was then unemployed and that his only asset was his redundancy lump sum. In such circumstances the plaintiff successfully obtained a Mareva injunction from O'Hanlon J in the High Court which restrained the defendant from:

> "disposing of, or dissipating his assets whether real or personal, whether within the jurisdiction of this Honourable Court or without in such a manner as would diminish the defendant's property so as to entitle him, before the period of one year elapses after the making of such an order in the terms of this paragraph, to apply to the District Court for an Order varying the Maintenance Order as made by Rathfarnham District Court on the _____ day of _____ 1981 on the grounds that such aforesaid asset has been disposed of or diminished".[158]

[155.] High Court, unrep, 7 April 1982 (O'Hanlon J); noted by Charleton, (1982) 4 DULJ 114.
[156.] See para **[4.46]** *et seq, supra*.
[157.] The facts of the application are only available from Charleton's case note, *op cit*.
[158.] *Ibid*, p 115.

Nowadays, pre-judgment Mareva relief in family law cases will invariably be sought under either s 35 of the Family Law Act 1995[159] or s 37 of the Family Law (Divorce) Act 1996.[160]

[C] THE JURISDICTION OF COURTS AND ENFORCEMENT OF JUDGMENTS ACTS, 1988 AND 1993

[4.50] The principle that a plaintiff must have a substantive right or cause of action, justicable in Ireland, before he can apply for a Mareva injunction was greatly distorted, first, by the Jurisdiction of Courts and Enforcement of Judgments (European Communities) Act 1988 ("the 1988 Act") and, then by the Jurisdiction of Courts Enforcement of Judgments Act 1993 ("the 1993 Act") which are collectively known as the Jurisdiction of Courts and Enforcement of Judgments Acts, 1988 and 1993 ("the 1988 and 1993 Act").[161] It is now the case that application for a Mareva injunction can be made in Ireland, even if a plaintiff has no cause of action against a defendant in Ireland, provided that he does have a cause of action which is justicable in a Contracting State to the Brussels Convention or the Lugano Convention.[162] The RSC were amended to take account of the 1988 Act by the Rules of the Superior Courts (No 1) 1989 (SI 14/1989).[163]

[4.51] At the time of writing it is proposed to consolidate the provisions of the 1988 and 1993 Act by the enactment of the Jurisdiction of Courts and Enforcement of Judgments Bill 1998 ("the 1998 Bill").[164] As far as the granting of protective and provisional measures such as Mareva injunctions are concerned, there is no substantive change proposed. If enacted as currently drafted, s 13 of the 1998 Bill will, in all material respects, mirror s 11 of the

---

[159.] Formerly s 29 of the Judicial Separation and Family Law Reform Act 1989.

[160.] See Ch 3, *Statutory Jurisdictions to Freeze Assets*, para **[3.02]** *et seq.*

[161.] See Gill, 'Mareva Injunctions and the Brussels Convention', (1989) ILT 156.

[162.] Section 3 of the 1993 Act amended s 1 of the 1988 Act by stating that "contracting state" means - "(a) one of the original parties to the 1968 Convention (Belgium, the Federal Republic of Germany, France, Italy Luxembourg and the Netherlands), or (b) one of the parties acceding to the 1968 Convention under the 1978 Accession Convention, the 1982 Accession Convention or the 1989 Accession Convention (the State, Denmark, the United Kingdom, the Hellenic Republic, Spain, and the Portuguese Republic), being a state in respect of which, as may be appropriate, the 1978 Accession Convention has entered into force in accordance with Article 39 of that Convention or the 1982 Accession Convention has entered into force in accordance with Article 15 of that Convention or the 1989 Accession Convention has entered into force in accordance with Article 32 of that Convention".

[163.] See generally, Hogan and O'Reilly, *Guide to Changes in the Rules of the Superior Courts 1986 As A Consequence of the Coming Into Operation of the Jurisdiction of Courts and Enforcement of Judgments (European Communities) Act 1988.*

[164.] References herein to the 1998 Bill are to the draft as passed by Seanad Éireann, dated 13 May 1998.

1988 Act which currently facilitates the granting of Mareva relief. The reader's attention shall be drawn to the precise new proposed wording contained in s 13 of the 1998 Bill when we review the current wording in s 11 of the 1988 Act. The matters which require to be addressed in this section are broken down as follows:

1. Articles 24 of the Brussels and Lugano Conventions.

2. Pre-Judgment Mareva Relief under the Conventions.

3. Post-Judgment Mareva Relief under the Conventions.

Articles 24 of the Brussels and Lugano Conventions

[4.52] In *Babanaft International Co SA v Bassatne*[165] Kerr LJ said of the Brussels Convention that:

> "... it contains the most extensive code evidencing international reciprocity in the recognition and enforcement of judgments and orders issued in foreign jurisdictions, and...it includes art 24 dealing with provisional and protective measures. The forerunner of the European Judgments Convention had been a network of bilateral conventions, and among the original six member states nearly all of these had included a provision corresponding to art 24 ...".[166]

Article 24 of the Brussels Convention provides:

> Application may be made to the courts of a Contracting State for such provisional, including protective, measures as may be available under the law of that State, even if, under this Convention, the courts of another Contracting State have jurisdiction as to the substance of the matter.

Article 24 of the Lugano Convention is in precisely the same terms.

Their effect is to reverse in part the decision of the Supreme Court in *Caudron v Air Zaire* and of the House of Lords in *The Siskina*,[167] to the extent that now, a plaintiff may apply to the Irish courts for Mareva relief where he has no cause of action justicable in Ireland, *provided* that he has a cause of action in one of the Contracting States to the Brussels Convention or the Lugano Convention. It is important to state that a plaintiff with a cause or action which is only justicable

---

[165] [1989] 1 All ER 433. See further, Ch 7, *The Defendant's Assets*, para **[7.27]** *et seq.*

[166] At 442d.

[167] Note that the jurisdiction of the English High Court has been further extended by the Civil Jurisdiction and Judgments Act 1982 (Interim Relief) Order 1997, SI 1977/302 (UK) which came into force on 1 April 1997. The effect of this statutory instrument is to extend the effect of s 25 of the UK's Civil Jurisdiction and Judgments Act 1982 to non-Convention countries and to proceedings outside the scope of either the Brussels Convention or Lugano Convention. As Millett LJ said in *Credit Suisse Fides Trust v Cuoghi* [1997] 3 All ER 724 at 728: "The position has now been reached, therefore, that the High Court has power to grant interim relief in aid of substantive proceedings elsewhere of whatever kind and wherever taking place".

in a non-Contracting State cannot apply for Mareva relief and the principle laid down in *Caudron v Air Zaire* will, in such a case, continue to apply.

[4.53] One of the leading decisions of the European Court of Justice[168] on the Brussels Convention is *Denilauler v SNC Couchet Freres*.[169] In that case a French court was seised of a contractual cause of action, and in the course of the proceedings made an order, the effect of which was to authorise the freezing of the defendant's assets which were moneys in a bank account in Germany. The defendant resisted the plaintiff's application to enforce the order on the grounds that he, the defendant, had had no notice of the order before it was made; on this basis a German court referred the matter to the European Court of Justice. The European Court of Justice held:

> "The courts of the place or, in any event, of the contracting State, where the assets subject to the measures sought are located, are those best able to assess the circumstances which may lead to the grant or refusal of the measures sought or to the laying down of procedures and conditions which the plaintiff must observe in order to guarantee the provisional and protective character of the measures ordered. The Convention has taken account of these requirements by providing in Article 24 that application may be made to the courts of a Contracting State for such provisional, including protective, measures as may be available under the law of that State, even if, under the Convention, the courts of another contracting State have jurisdiction as to the substance of the matter."[170]

[4.54] The 1988 and 1993 Act "domesticated" the principles and provisions contained in both the Brussels and Lugano Conventions. Two separate jurisdictions are established. Section 11(1) of the 1988 Act concerns pre-judgment relief and gives the High Court the discretion to grant provisional and protective measures, including Mareva injunctions. Section 11(3) of the 1988 Act concerns post-judgment relief and, as considered below, contains measures which direct the Master of the High Court to grant Mareva relief.[171] Although the focus here is on Mareva injunctions, it is important to recognise that "provisional, including protective measures" would also include asset disclosure orders,[172] Anton Piller orders,[173] and even injunctions to prevent a defendant from leaving the State.[174]

[168.] See *de Cavel v de Cavel [143/79]* [1979] ECR 1055.

[169.] Case 125/79; [1981] 1 CMLR 62.

[170.] [1981] 1 CMLR 62 at 81.

[171.] It should be noted that whilst both subsections (1) and (3) of s 11 of the 1988 Act allow for relief other than Mareva injunctions the treatment of these provisions here is confined to Mareva relief.

[172.] See further, Ch 10, *Ancillary Orders*, para **[10.03]** *et seq.*

[173.] *Ibid*.

[174.] See Ch 11, *Restraining Defendants from Leaving the State*.

Pre-Judgment Mareva Relief under the Conventions

[4.55] Section 11 of the 1988 Act empowers the High Court to make provisional measures and protective measures where a plaintiff has a cause of action in any of the States which are Contracting States to the Brussels Convention. Section 11 of the 1993 Act applies ss 5 to 14 of the 1988 Act to the application of the Lugano Convention in the State and so application for provisional and/or protective, measures under the Lugano Convention are brought under s 11 of the 1988 Act in exactly the same manner as provisional and/or protective measures under the Brussels Convention. Provisional measures are those which are interim or interlocutory and so not final. Protective measures are those which preserve a defendant's assets so as to have them available to satisfy the plaintiff's judgment. In Ireland, and other common law countries, the Mareva injunction is the best example of a protective measure; in civil law countries the French *saisie conservatoire* or German *pfandungsbeschluss* are examples of similar remedies.

[4.56] Section 11(1) of the 1988 Act provides that provisional, including protective measures, may be granted in Ireland by the High Court in circumstances where an applicant has not obtained a final judgment against the respondent. Pre-judgment relief is governed by s 11(1) of the 1988 Act which provides:

> Where -
>
> (a) proceedings have been commenced or are to be commenced in a Contracting State other than the State, and,
>
> (b) they are or will be proceedings whose subject-matter is within the scope of the 1968 Convention as determined by Article 1 (whether or not the 1968 Convention has effect in relation to the proceedings),
>
> the High Court may, on application to it pursuant to Article 24, grant provisional, including protective, measures of any kind that the Court has power to grant in proceedings that, apart from this Act, are within its jurisdiction.[175]

[175.] The 1998 Bill, as drafted, provides the following new s 13(1): "On application pursuant to Article 24 of the 1968 Convention, the High Court may grant any provisional, including protective, measures of any kind that the Court has power to grant in proceedings that, apart from this Act, are within its jurisdiction, if - (a) proceedings have been or are to be commenced in a Contracting State other than the State, and (b) the subject matter of the proceedings is within the scope of the 1968 Convention as determined by Article 1 (whether or not that Convention has effect in relation to the proceedings)." Whilst the High Court's power to grant provisional including protective measures in s 13(1) of the 1998 Bill is ostensibly confined to the Brussels Convention, s 20, somewhat cumberously, applies the power in s 13(1) to applications, pursuant to Article 24 of the Lugano Convention.

Next we consider (a) the prerequisites to seeking relief; (b) the High Court's discretion; and (c) the procedure in applying for relief.

(a) The prerequisites to seeking relief

[4.57] The first prerequisite to seeking a Mareva injunction from the High Court under s 11(1) of the 1988 Act is that the plaintiff has commenced proceedings (or proceedings are to be commenced) in a State other than Ireland, which is a "Contracting State" to the Brussels or Lugano Conventions.[176] Accordingly, one effect of s 11(1) of the 1988 Act is to overrule to an extent the Supreme Court's requirement in *Caudron* that, to obtain a Mareva injunction, a plaintiff must have a substantive cause of action in Ireland. It is, however, very important to note that the rule in *Caudron* remains good law as far as non-Contracting States are concerned. The commencement of proceedings in England will entitle a plaintiff to apply for a Mareva injunction in Ireland; but s 11(1) of the 1988 Act will not save a plaintiff from the effects of *Caudron* where he has commenced proceedings in, say, the United States of America.

[4.58] Under s 11(1) of the 1988 Act the High Court may only grant provisional, including protective, measures in respect of an action within the scope of the Brussels Convention or the Lugano Convention. Articles 1 of both the Brussels and Lugano Conventions provide that they apply in civil and commercial matters, whatever the nature of the court or tribunal but do not extend in particular to revenue, customs or administrative matters. Moreover, the Conventions do not apply to:

1. The status or legal capacity of natural persons, rights in property arising out of a matrimonial relationship, wills and succession;
2. Bankruptcy, proceedings relating to the winding-up of insolvent companies or other legal persons, judicial arrangements, compositions and analogous proceedings;
3. Social security;
4. Arbitration.

In respect of such causes of action, no reliance can be placed upon s 11(1) of the 1988 Act and where Mareva relief is sought from the Irish courts, such causes of action must be actionable *per se* before the Irish courts.

(b) The High Court's discretion

[4.59] Section 11(1) of the 1988 Act empowers the High Court to make a provisional, including protective, order where a substantive cause of action is pending in another Contracting State . Central to the High Court's jurisdiction is

---

[176.] See s 1 of the 1988 Act as amended by s 3 of the 1993 Act: see para **[4.50]** *supra*.

that the granting of any relief is entirely discretionary. Section 11(1) is couched in permissive as opposed to imperative language, to wit the use of the words "the High Court may".[177] The High Court's discretion to refuse relief is further underscored by s 11(2) which provides:

> On an application under subsection (1) of this section, the High Court may refuse to grant the measures sought if, in the opinion of that Court, the fact that that Court has not jurisdiction, apart from this section, in relation to the subject-matter of the proceedings in question makes it inexpedient for that Court to grant such measures.[178]

Section 11(1) does not confer jurisdiction upon the High Court to grant Mareva relief *per se*; the only reason why the High Court can grant a Mareva injunction on foot of a s 11(1) application is because it already has that power under s 28(8) of the Supreme Court of Judicature (Ireland) Act 1877.[179] As Carroll J said in *Elwyn (Cottons) Ltd v Pearle Designs Ltd*:[180]

> "... a Mareva-type injunction ... is a protective measure which the High Court would have power to grant in respect of proceedings within its jurisdiction."

Section 11(1) does not *confer* the jurisdiction to grant Mareva relief or any other relief on the High Court; it merely removes one of the proofs usually required for Mareva relief, ie, that the plaintiff has a substantive right or cause of action which is justiciable in Ireland.[181]

[4.60] One of the first occasions when the High Court exercised its discretion to grant a Mareva injunction under s 11(1) of the 1988 Act was in *Granada Group plc v H*, in an application reported in *The Irish Times*.[182] There, the plaintiff sought an order from the High Court to prevent the defendant Englishman from reducing his assets in Ireland below £4.5m. Lynch J was reportedly told that proceedings had been started in London by the plaintiffs, arising out of a share acquisition agreement. It was claimed that the defendant, by the production of false accounts, had received sums while a director of the company concerned. A

[177.] See also Ord 42A r 3: "The Court may make *ex parte* any interim order pursuant to s 11(1) of the 1988 Act ...".

[178.] Section 13(2) of the 1998 Bill proposes the following new wording: "On an application under subsection (1), the High Court may refuse to grant the measures sought if, in its opinion, the fact that, apart from this section, that Court does not have jurisdiction in relation to the subject matter of the proceedings makes it inexpedient for it to grant those measures."

[179.] See Ch 2, *The Jurisdiction to Grant Mareva Relief*, para **[2.02]** *et seq.*

[180.] [1989] IR 9 at 12.

[181.] In *Republic of Haiti v Duvalier* [1989] 1 All ER 456 at 463e where Staughton LJ said: "... art 24 expressly refers to 'measures ... available under the law of that State', and does not attempt to lay down what those measures must be. However, it seems to me that the convention *requires* each contracting state to make available, in aid of the courts of another contracting state, such provisional and protective measures as its own domestic law would afford if its courts were trying the substantive action. That would be harmonisation of jurisdiction, although not of remedies."

[182.] *The Irish Times*, 27 October 1988.

Mareva injunction had been made in England. The plaintiff's application was for a similar order from the Irish court since the defendant reputedly owned a stud farm in Ireland. Lynch J is reported as having granted the relief sought, making an interim maximum sum Mareva injunction, preventing the defendant from reducing his assets in Ireland below £4.5m.[183]

[4.61] In exercising its discretion under s 11(1) of the 1988 Act the High Court will have regard to whether the applicant has established, to the satisfaction of the Court, the existence of all Mareva proofs,[184] other than that he has a substantive cause of action which is justicable in Ireland. In particular the Court must be satisfied that the defendant is intent upon disposing of his assets (or removing them from the jurisdiction) with a view to evading his obligations to the applicant and frustrating a future judgment of a court or other competent tribunal.[185] There are few other limitations on the exercise of the High Court's discretion. In *X v Y and Y Establishment*[186] the defendant had tried to argue that the power to grant a Mareva injunction under s 25 of the English Civil Jurisdiction and Judgments Act 1982 ("the 1982 Act") was only exercisable where either proceedings could be served on the defendant in England or where service was permitted under the English Rules of the Supreme Court. This contention was rejected by the English High Court which held that it was sufficient that proceedings have, or are about to be, commenced in a "Contracting State". Indeed, as with s 25 of the 1982 Act, s 11(1) of the 1988 Act expressly provides that the court's powers are only exercisable where the proceedings have been commenced in a Contracting State other than Ireland.[187]

[183.] See also *Brink's-Mat Ltd v S, The Irish Times*, 4 and 11 July 1989 (Costello J). Here Costello J (on 3 July 1989) continued an interim Mareva injunction against S and others, preventing the removal of circa IR£4m from an account with Bank of Ireland Finance Ltd. It was alleged that the first-defendant was known to have had association with an individual who had been convicted of dishonest handling of the proceeds of the infamous Brink's-Mat robbery. It was reported that the High Court heard that 3,000kg of gold bullion was stolen from Brink's-Mat Ltd's premises in November 1983. Subsequently, deposits were made in Bank of Ireland's Croydon branch and later transferred to Bank of Ireland Finance Ltd, Dublin. Costello J (on 10 July 1989) made an interlocutory Mareva injunction.

[184.] See Ch 8, *Applying for a Mareva Injunction*, para **[8.31]**.

[185.] See Ch 6, *The Risk of Removal or Disposal of Assets*, para **[6.18]** *et seq.*

[186.] (1989) *Financial Times Law Reports* 16 May 1989; and see Gill, 'Mareva Injunctions and the Brussels Convention', (1989) ILT 156.

[187.] In the context of the enforcement of a foreign judgment it was said by Blayney J in *Rhatigan v Textiles Confecciones Europeas SA* [1989] IR 18 at 24 that he accepted that "... it had to be proved not only that the 1968 Convention was in force in the State at the time the application was made, but also that it was in force in the United Kingdom at the time the proceedings were instituted there ...". *Cf Alltrans Inc v Interdom Holdings Ltd (Johnson Stevens Agencies Ltd, third parties)* [1991] 4 All ER 458 where the Court of Appeal construed s 25 of the Civil Jurisdiction and Judgments Act 1982 as allowing interim Mareva relief where proceedings had been commenced in a country which at the time proceedings had been commenced was not a "Contracting State" but which was, at the time of the application for interim relief, a "Contracting State"; and that the Brussels Convention did not prevent s 25 of that Act having a wider effect than required to implement Article 24 of the Convention.

[4.62] Whether or not it would be "inexpedient" to make an order is also a factor within the discretion of the High Court and, in this regard, it has recently been stated by the English Court of Appeal that a worldwide Mareva injunction[188] may be granted pursuant to s 25 of the 1982 Act where such would not be inexpedient. In *Credit Suisse Fides Trust SA v Cuoghi*[189] the plaintiff company had commenced proceedings in Switzerland[190] against the defendant, whom it alleged was complicit in the misappropriation of US$21.66m by one of the plaintiff's employees, and the plaintiff sought from the English court a worldwide Mareva injunction as a provisional and protective measure, ancillary to its Swiss cause of action. The defendant appealed to the Court of Appeal against the High Court's decision to grant the relief sought on the grounds that a worldwide Mareva injunction should only be made in very exceptional circumstances. This was rejected by the Court of Appeal which held that where application is made under s 25 of the 1982 Act, s 25(2)[191] of that Act made it plain that the focus of the court's attention was whether it would be expedient to make the order in view of its lack of jurisdiction over the substantive cause of action: it was immaterial to an application brought under s 25 that the circumstances of the case were exceptional or very exceptional. In this regard Millett LJ distinguished *Rosseel NV v Oriental Commercial Shipping (UK) Ltd*[192] where it had been held that worldwide Mareva relief should only be granted in exceptional circumstances on the basis that, *inter alia*, it was not concerned with s 25 of the 1982 Act. Millett LJ declined to follow the decision of the same (albeit differently composed) Court in *S & T Bautrading v Nordling*[193] where Saville LJ had followed the *Rosseel NV* case and held that the Court would not make an order which extended beyond its own territorial jurisdiction, save in an exceptional case. Millett LJ said of Saville LJ's decision that:

> "No consideration appears to have been given by the court to the terms of s 25(2) or to the question whether the making of a worldwide order would have been inexpedient; and no account appears to have been taken by the court that

[188.] See generally, Ch 7, *The Defendant's Assets*, para **[7.21]** *et seq.*
[189.] [1997] 3 All ER 724.
[190.] A party to the Lugano Convention on Jurisdiction and the Enforcement of Judgments in Civil and Commercial Matters 1988 which extended the principles of the Brussels Convention to its Contracting States.
[191.] It should be noted that s 25(2) of the 1982 Act is, in all material respects, identical in substance to the Irish s 11(2) of the 1988 Act. See para **[4.59]** *supra.*
[192.] [1990] 3 All ER 545. See further, Ch 7, *The Defendant's Assets*, para **[7.54]**.
[193.] [1997] 3 All ER 718.

the defendants were domiciled in England or of the absence of any question of conflicting jurisdictions".[194]

Millett LJ said that he found it regrettable that a gloss had been placed on the words of s 25(2) of the 1982 Act and went on to say:

> "The question for consideration is not whether the circumstances are exceptional or very exceptional, but whether it would be inexpedient to make the order. Where an application is made for *in personam* relief in ancillary proceedings, two considerations which are highly material are the place where the person sought to be enjoined is domiciled and the likely reaction of the court which is seised of the substantive dispute. Where a similar order has been applied for and has been refused by that court, it would generally be wrong for us to interfere. But where the other court lacks jurisdiction to make an effective order against a defendant because he is resident in England, it does not at all follow that it would find our order objectionable."[195]

Applying these considerations to the facts of the case in hand Millett LJ found that the defendant was both resident and domiciled in England; and, moreover, that the Swiss court could not make an order against the defendant because he was not resident there. On this reasoning it would be open to the Irish High Court under s 11(1) of the 1988 Act to make a worldwide Mareva injunction and an asset disclosure order in aid of proceedings taken in another Contracting State where the defendant is resident or domiciled in Ireland and thereby amenable to the court's jurisdiction where the courts of the State seised on the substantive proceedings have not declined to make such an order on grounds of principle.[196]

(c) The procedure in applying for relief

[4.63] The procedure pertaining to an application under s 11(1) of the 1988 Act is set out in Ord 42A of the RSC.[197] An application for provisional, including protective measures, must be made *ex parte* and grounded upon affidavit, specifying the measures sought.[198] In addition to setting out the basic information and exhibiting all necessary supporting documents, the affidavit must:

[194.] [1997] 3 All ER 724 at 731j-732a.

[195.] At 732b.

[196.] On worldwide Mareva relief, see further, Ch 7, *The Defendant's Assets*, para **[7.21]** *et seq.*

[197.] As inserted by SI 14/1989, Rules of the Superior Courts (No 1) 1989. See generally, O'Floinn, *Practice and Procedure in the Superior Courts* (1996) Butterworths, p 338.

[198.] Order 42A rules 1 and 2. An originating plenary summons is necessary: see Hogan, *Additional Notes on the Jurisdiction of Courts and Enforcement of Judgments (European Communities) Act 1988*, which followed on from Hogan & O'Reilly, *Guide to Changes in the Rules of the Superior Court 1986 as a Consequence of the Coming into Operation of the Jurisdiction of Courts and Enforcement of Judgments (European Communities) Act 1988*, (1989).

(a) state the nature of the proceedings or intended proceedings and exhibit a certified true copy of the document or documents used or proposed to be used to institute the proceedings;

(b) specify the Contracting State (other than the State) in which the proceedings have been commenced or are to be commenced; and

(c) state the particular provision or provisions of the 1968 Convention by which the Court of the Contracting State (other than the State) has assumed jurisdiction or, in the case of intended proceedings, would be entitled to assume jurisdiction.[199]

[4.64] Order 42A provides that the High Court may make, *ex parte*, any interim order pursuant to s 11(1) of the 1988 Act "upon such terms as to costs or otherwise or subject to such undertaking, if any, as the court may think just", and, moreover, any party affected by such an order may apply to the court to set it aside. On the other hand, the RSC provide that where an application is made for an interlocutory order, it is necessary to proceed by notice of motion.[200]

Post-Judgment Mareva Relief under the Conventions

[4.65] In Ireland, post-judgment provisional and protective orders under the Brussels and Lugano Conventions are governed by s 11(3) of the 1988 Act. Section 11(3) provides that:

> Subject to Article 39, an application to the Master of the High Court for the enforcement of a judgment and an application to the High Court for the enforcement of an instrument or settlement referred to in Title IV of the 1968 Convention may include an application for the granting of such protective measures as the High Court has power to grant in proceedings that, apart from this Act, are within its jurisdiction and, where an enforcement order is made in relation to a judgment or such an instrument or settlement, the order shall include a provision granting any such protective measures as aforesaid as are applied for as aforesaid.[201]

Section 5 of the 1988 Act empowers the Master of the High Court to make an order, enforcing a judgment obtained in another Contracting State.[202] Where an order is made for the enforcement of a judgment obtained in another Contracting

---

[199.] *Ibid*, rule 2.

[200.] *Ibid*, rule 3.

[201.] Section 13 of the 1998 Bill, as drafted, proposes new sub-ss (3) and (4) to replace s 11(3) of the 1988 Act: "(3) Subject to Article 39 of the 1968 Convention, an application to the Master of the High Court for an enforcement order respecting a judgment may include an application for any protective measures the High Court has power to grant in proceedings that, apart from this Act, are within its jurisdiction. (4) Where an enforcement order is made, the Master of the High Court shall grant any protective measures referred to in *subsection (3)* that are sought in the application for the enforcement order."

[202.] See *Rhatigan v Textiles y Confecciones Europeas SA* [1989] IR 18.

State, the imperative wording of s 11(3) of the 1988 Act and Article 39(2) of the Brussels and Lugano Conventions make it clear that the Master of the High Court has no discretion to refuse to make an order for protective measures.[203] Accordingly, where an order for the enforcement of a judgment is made, protective measures *must* be granted by the Master, if these are sought by the applicant. This was confirmed by Carroll J in *Elwyn (Cottons) Ltd v Pearle Designs Ltd.*[204] There, the Master of the High Court had refused to grant a Mareva injunction notwithstanding that he had, pursuant to s 5 of the 1988 Act, made an order enforcing a foreign judgment which had been obtained in a Contracting State. On appeal to the High Court Carroll J held that the Mareva injunction sought by the applicant was a protective measure which the High Court had power to grant in respect of proceedings within its jurisdiction. Accordingly, it was held that the Master of the High Court had no discretion to refuse the protective relief sought. Carroll J held:

> "According to the wording of s 11(3), if the Master of the High Court was satisfied that the protective measure sought was relief which the High Court had power to grant in proceedings within its jurisdiction, then once the enforcement order was made, it should have included a provision granting the protective measure."[205]

Moreover, an applicant has a right to have protective measures granted at the same hearing as the hearing on the enforcement of the judgment. A second decision from another court is not required. Carroll J quoted from the ECJ's decision in *Capelloni and Acquilini v Pelkmans*:[206]

> "As the Commission has correctly stated, the effect of Article 39 is that a party who has obtained authorisation for enforcement is under no obligation to obtain specific and separate judicial authorisation in order to proceed with protective measures during the period mentioned in that article, even though such authorisation may normally be required by the national procedural law of the court in question.
>
> That conclusion follows from the very wording of the second paragraph of Article 39 which states that the decision authorising enforcement "shall carry with it" the power to proceed with protective measures, That expression indicates that the right to proceed with such measures derives from the decision

---

[203.] Section 11(3) provides, *inter alia* that the order "*shall include* a provision granting any such protective measures"; Article 39(2) of the Convention also provides that "The decision authorising enforcement *shall carry* with it the power to proceed to any such protective measures". Italics added in both instances.

[204.] [1989] IR 9; [1989] ILRM 162; (1989) ITLR of 6 March 1989.

[205.] At 12.

[206.] [1985] ECR 3147.

allowing enforcement and therefore that a second decision, which could not in any event undermine that right, would not be justified.

It must therefore be stated in reply to the second question submitted by the national court that by virtue of Article 39 of the Convention a party who has applied for and obtained authorisation for enforcement may, by virtue of that article and during the period mentioned therein, proceed directly with protective measures against the property of the party against whom enforcement is sought and is under no obligation to obtain specific authorisation."[207]

As to the appropriate remedy available to an applicant who had been refused protective relief, Carroll J held that the appropriate course of action was to seek an order of *mandamus* because there was no procedure whereby an applicant could appeal a refusal of the Master to refuse protective relief.

[4.66] In the subsequent case of *Elwyn (Cottons) Ltd v The Master of the High Court*[208] the applicant's petition for judicial review was decided by O'Hanlon J. He considered that there were two issues to be decided. On the first he concurred with the earlier reasoning of Carroll J and held that the Master of the High Court had no jurisdiction to refuse protective measures where he had made an order enforcing a judgment under s 5 of the 1988 Act. On the second issue he held that there was jurisdiction to make an order of mandamus against the Master of the High Court[209] and granted the order of mandamus. The new, replacement, wording for s 11(3) of the 1988 Act proposed in s 13(3) and (4) of the 1998 Bill (as passed by Seanad Éireann) will not alter this position.

[4.67] One interesting aspect of s 11(3) of the 1988 Act is that it discriminates grossly between a "domestic" judgment creditor who applies in the ordinary way for post-judgment Mareva relief and a "foreign" judgment creditor who seeks Mareva relief as a protective measure, under s 11(3) of the 1988 Act. Whereas a foreign judgment creditor can insist upon post-judgment Mareva relief as of right, his domestic counterpart must establish to the satisfaction of a judge of the Circuit or High Courts, that the various proofs have been met, including that the judgment-debtor has the requisite "nefarious intent".[210] Whether a successful constitutional challenge could be mounted on this basis remains to be seen.

[207.] At 3160, paras 24, 25 and 26.

[208.] [1989] IR 14.

[209.] Citing *State (Gallagher Shatter & Co) v Toirleach de Valera (A Taxing Master)* High Court, unrep, 9 December 1983 (Costello J).

[210.] See Ch 6, *The Risk of Removal or Disposal of Assets*, para **[6.16]**.

Procedure in the Master's Court

[4.68] Upon an application for the enforcement of a judgment under s 5 of the 1988 Act an applicant must, by *ex parte* application, state on affidavit the protective measures (if any) which he seeks.[211] Furthermore Ord 42A r 5 of the RSC provides that the applicant must exhibit:

(1) The judgment which is sought to be enforced or a certified or otherwise duly authenticated copy thereof;

(2) In the case of a judgment given in default, the original or a certified copy of the document which establishes that the party in default was served with the document or documents instituting the proceedings or with an equivalent document or documents in sufficient time to enable him to arrange his defence;

(3) Documents which establish that, according to the law of the state in which it has been given, the judgment is enforceable and has been served;

(4) Where appropriate, a document showing that the applicant is in receipt of legal aid in the state in which the judgment was given.

In addition, Order 42A r 6 provides that the grounding affidavit must also state the following:

(1) Whether the said judgment provides for the payment of a sum or sums of money;

(2) Whether interest is recoverable on the judgment or part thereof in accordance with the law of the state in which the judgment was given, and if such be the case, the rate of interest, the date from which interest is recoverable, and the date on which interest ceases to accrue;

(3) An address within the State for service of proceedings on the party making the application and, to the best of the deponent's knowledge and belief, the name and usual or last known address or place of business of the person against whom judgment was given;

(4) The grounds on which the right to enforce the judgment is vested in the party making the application;

(5) As the case may require, that at the date of the application the judgment has not been satisfied, or if the judgment has not been fully satisfied, the part or amount in respect of which it remains unsatisfied.

Where an applicant does not produce the documents referred to in rr 5 or 6, the Master of the High Court may, if he sees fit, adjourn the application to enable their production, or alternatives, or he may dispense with their requirement.[212]

[211.] Order 42A, rule 5. See generally, O'Floinn, *Practice and Procedure in the Superior Courts*, (1996) Butterworths, p 338.

[212.] *Ibid*, rule 7.

[4.69] It would seem that an applicant seeking protective measures under s 11(3) of the 1988 Act cannot be compelled to give the usual form of undertaking as to damages[213] which would be normal where the court grants injunctive relief.[214] This follows from the fact that the Master of the High Court has no discretion to refuse protective measures where an applicant seeks same on getting an order for the enforcement of a judgment and therefore he cannot grant relief subject to a condition that the applicant gives an undertaking as to damages. The position is, however, different where an applicant seeks pre-judgment relief under s 11(1) of the 1988 Act as in such cases the High Court can exercise its discretion and grant a Mareva injunction subject to an applicant giving an undertaking as to damages where the court thinks such an undertaking is just.[215]

[213.] *Cappellone v Pelkmans* [1985] ECR 3147; *Brennero v Wendel* [1984] ECR 3971 and see generally, Hogan & O'Reilly, *op cit* at fn 198.

[214.] On undertakings as to damages, see further Ch 8, *Applying for a Mareva Injunction*, para **[8.58]** *et seq.*

[215.] Order 42A of the RSC. See para **[4.64]** *supra.*

Chapter 5

A Good Arguable Case

[5.01] It is not sufficient that a Mareva plaintiff simply has a substantive cause of action against a defendant; he must also satisfy the court as to the quality and strength of his case against the defendant. Accordingly, the second essential prerequisite to the granting of a Mareva injunction is that a plaintiff has a "good arguable case" against a defendant.[1] In an application for a Mareva injunction it has been established beyond doubt in the United Kingdom that the required strength of a plaintiff's case is that he must have "a good arguable case" against a defendant. In Ireland, however, acceptance of the "good arguable case" test has been mixed, with some suggestions that the test for an ordinary interlocutory injunction, namely, whether there is "a serious or fair question to be tried", is also applicable in an application for Mareva relief.[2]

[5.02] In this chapter the following specific issues are considered in the context of the requirement that a Mareva plaintiff has "a good arguable case":

1. The Serious/Fair Question Test in Ordinary Interlocutory Injunctions.

2. The "Good Arguable Case" Test in Applications for Mareva Injunctions.

3. The Meaning of "Good Arguable Case".

4. Establishing a "Good Arguable Case".

5. "Good Arguable Case" or "Serious Question to be Tried" - A Difference?

The Serious/Fair Question Test in Ordinary Interlocutory Injunctions

[5.03] Before considering the test applicable to the exercise of the court's discretion in an application for a Mareva injunction it is useful to first examine the test applicable in an application for an ordinary interlocutory injunction. The basic rationale of any interlocutory injunction is to preserve the status quo

---

[1.] See generally, Ough & Flenley, *The Mareva Injunction and Anton Piller Order*, (2nd ed, 1993) Butterworths, pp 96-99; Goldrein & Wilkinson, *Commercial Litigation: Pre-Emptive Remedies*, (2nd ed, 1991) Sweet & Maxwell, pp 171-175; Capper, *Mareva Injunctions*, (1988) SLS/Sweet & Maxwell, pp 31-35; Powles, *The Mareva Injunction and Associated Orders*, (1985) Professional Books, pp 20-23.

[2.] For example, by Murphy J in *Countyglen plc v Carway* [1995] 1 IR 208. See para **[5.22]** *infra*.

between the parties from the time the injunction is granted to the trial of the substantive issue.[3] Interlocutory injunctive relief is needed because of the inevitable delays involved between the time when a plaintiff is wronged and the time when a plaintiff is finally granted relief by the courts. Moreover, as Lord Diplock pointed out in *American Cyanamid Co v Ethicon Ltd*,[4] an interlocutory injunction will be necessary where the "wrong" done to a plaintiff cannot be compensated by the payment of damages:

> "The object of the interlocutory injunction is to protect the plaintiff against injury by violation of his right for which he could not be adequately compensated in damages recoverable in the action if the uncertainty were resolved in his favour at the trial."[5]

For a plaintiff to be wronged, for the wrong to continue and for him to have no relief for a period of up to two years, would indeed be a great injustice. For this reason, the courts of equity have afforded relief to plaintiffs by granting an interlocutory prohibitory or mandatory order to preserve the status quo pending trial of the substantive cause of action. The jurisdiction of the court in equity to grant interlocutory injunctions in all cases in which it is just or convenient so to do was extended to all superior courts when the jurisdiction was enshrined in statute by s 28(8) of the Supreme Court of Judicature (Ireland) Act 1877.

[5.04] While the jurisdiction to grant an ordinary interim[6] and interlocutory injunction is beyond question,[7] all interlocutory injunctive relief is discretionary, and the circumstances in which the court will exercise its discretion are quite varied. One difficulty faced by a court to which an application for an interlocutory injunction is made, is how far to go, at an interlocutory hearing, in investigating the issues in dispute. A court cannot, and will not, attempt to resolve all issues at an interlocutory hearing: such a detailed examination is reserved to the actual trial of the matter. As O'Sullivan J commented in *Intermetal Group Ltd and Trans-World (Steel) Ltd v Worslade Trading Ltd*,[8] an

---

3. Keane J in his book *Equity and the Law of Trusts in the Republic of Ireland*, (1988), para [15.22] says that an interlocutory injunction is granted by the court "to preserve the status quo until the plaintiff's claim for a perpetual injunction has been granted". Often, however, the granting of an interlocutory injunction will determine the matter and, moreover, interlocutory injunctions will rarely be sought with a view to obtaining a perpetual injunction.
4. [1975] 1 All ER 504.
5. At 509c-d.
6. As Meagher, Gummow & Lehane, *Equity Doctrines and Remedies*, (3rd ed, 1992) Butterworths say (p 605): "An interim injunction is really best viewed as a type of interlocutory injunction; it may be issued before or after writ, *ex parte* or *inter partes*. It is an injunction granted until a named day or further order, not (as is the real interlocutory injunction) until the hearing or further order. The principles applicable to interlocutory injunctions also apply to it".
7. See Ch 2, *The Jurisdiction to Grant Mareva Relief*, at para **[2.16]** *et seq*.
8. High Court, unrep, 12 December 1997 (O'Sullivan J).

application for, *inter alia*, a worldwide Mareva injunction, which entailed a three and a half day hearing before the High Court:

> "I do not think it is either possible or appropriate to attempt to summarise at this stage the several conflicts and inconsistencies that have arisen between the parties in these and several further affidavits".[9]

Whether a court grants or declines to grant an application for injunctive relief it is still making a decision. If an injunction is granted, which should not have been granted, the defendant is likely to be prejudiced; if an injunction is not granted, which should be granted, the plaintiff is likely to be prejudiced. It is against this background that one must consider the difficulties faced by a court in the formulation of the appropriate test for injunctive relief. In an application for a Mareva injunction the far-reaching and potentially draconian effects on a defendant need to be weighed against the futility of a plaintiff's pyrrhic victory where a defendant successfully renders himself judgment-proof.

[5.05] Until 1975 in the United Kingdom, and until 1983 in Ireland, the test applicable to the grant of an ordinary interlocutory injunction was considered to be whether a plaintiff could establish that he had a *prima facie* case against the defendant in the action. In *Esso Petroleum Co (Ireland) Ltd v Fogarty*[10] the Supreme Court appeared to favour various formulations of this test which was generally considered to be difficult to pass. In that case O'Dalaigh CJ said: "The court before stripping him [a defendant] of this right must be satisfied that the probability is in favour of the defendant's case ultimately failing in the final issue of this suit".[11] This was indeed a very difficult test to pass.

[5.06] Today, in Ireland and the United Kingdom, the test which a plaintiff must ordinarily pass in order to be granted an interlocutory injunction is that there is a fair or serious question to be tried at the trial of the action between the plaintiff and the defendant.[12] The case responsible for this change was *American Cyanamid Co v Ethicon Ltd*[13] which concerned an alleged patent infringement;

---

9. At p 11 of the transcript. Later, at p 12 of the transcript, O'Sullivan J said: "In dealing with an interlocutory application which is of extreme urgency, I can do no more than record my initial view that I am attracted on balance more by the arguments supporting the retention of a residual discretion". See paras **[5.21]** and **[5.27]** *infra*.

10. [1965] IR 531. See also *JT Strarford and Sons v Lindley* [1965] AC 269.

11. At 539.

12. See *Campus Oil Ltd v The Minister for Industry and Energy* [1983] IR 88 where the Supreme Court accepted the test promulgated by the House of Lords in *American Cyanamid Co v Ethicon Ltd* [1975] 1 All ER 504. See generally, Keane, *Equity and the Law of Trusts in the Republic of Ireland*, (1988), para [15.22] *et seq*, Delany, *Equity and the Law of Trusts in Ireland*, (1996) Roundhall Sweet & Maxwell, p 390 *et seq* and Kerr & Whyte, *Irish Trade Union Law*, (1985) Professional Books, p 319 *et seq*.

13. [1975] 1 All ER 504.

the plaintiff had a patent for an absorbable surgical suture and the defendant, a rival company, proposed to introduce its own type of artificial suture. The plaintiff claimed that the defendant's suture would infringe its patent and successfully applied for an interlocutory injunction to prevent the alleged infringement. The trial judge had found, on the evidence, that the plaintiff had made out a strong *prima facie* case against the defendant and he had held that the balance of convenience favoured the granting of an interlocutory injunction to preserve the status quo pending the trial of the issues between the parties. The defendant successfully appealed to the Court of Appeal where it was held, on the evidence, that the plaintiff had not established a *prima facie* case of the infringement of the patent. The Court of Appeal held that it was well established in law that before a court would grant an interlocutory injunction, or even consider the question of where the balance of convenience between the parties lay, it must be satisfied that, on the balance of probabilities, the plaintiff would succeed in establishing his right to a permanent injunction at the trial of the action. It was against this decision of the Court of Appeal that the plaintiff appealed to the House of Lords.

[5.07] The House of Lords in *American Cyanamid Co v Ethicon Ltd*[14] allowed the appeal. Lord Diplock's summary of the reasons for the Court of Appeal's decision are worth quoting since it puts the old and new tests in context. He said that the Court of Appeal:

> "... considered that there was a rule of practice so well established as to constitute a rule of law that precluded them from granting any interim injunction unless on the evidence adduced by both parties on the hearing of the application the applicant had satisfied the court that on the balance of probabilities the acts of the other party sought to be enjoined would, if committed, violate the applicant's legal rights. In the view of the Court of Appeal the case which the applicant had to prove before any question of balance of convenience arose was *'prima facie'* only in the sense that the conclusion of law reached by the court on that evidence might need to be modified at some later date in the light of further evidence either detracting from the probative value of the evidence on which the court had acted or proving additional facts."[15]

This formulation was emphatically rejected by Lord Diplock. After reviewing the authorities he said:

> "The use of such expressions as 'a probability', 'a *prima facie* case', or 'a strong *prima facie* case' in the context of the exercise of a discretionary power to grant an interlocutory injunction leads to confusion as to the object sought to

---

[14.] [1975] 1 All ER 504.
[15.] [1975] 1 All ER 504 at 508.

be achieved by this form of temporary relief. The court no doubt must be satisfied that the claim is not frivolous or vexatious; in other words, that there is a serious question to be tried.

It is no part of the court's function at this stage of the litigation to try to resolve conflicts of evidence on affidavit as to facts ... So unless the material available to the court at the hearing of the application for an interlocutory injunction fails to disclose that the plaintiff has any real prospect of succeeding in his claim for a permanent injunction at the trial, the court should go on to consider whether the balance of convenience lies in favour of granting or refusing the interlocutory relief that is sought."[16]

The test set out by Lord Diplock has been described[17] as being similar to a "multi-requisite" test in that "he sets out a series of hurdles which have to be cleared sequentially"; ie, the court must be satisfied that there is a serious question to be tried and then go on to consider whether the balance of convenience favours the granting of interlocutory relief.[18]

[5.08] The leading Irish authority on the test applicable on an application for an interlocutory injunction is the Supreme Court's decision in *Campus Oil Ltd v Minister for Industry and Energy*[19] ("*Campus Oil*") where O'Higgins CJ said that he entirely agreed with the final paragraph from Lord Diplock's decision, last quoted. The facts in this case were that the plaintiff sought a declaration from the High Court that the Fuels (Control of Supplies) Order 1982 ("the Order") was invalid under Articles 30 and 31 of the Treaty of Rome. The Order imposed an obligation upon importers of petroleum oils to purchase a certain proportion of oils from a state-owned refinery. The question whether the Order was invalid under the Treaty of Rome was referred to the European Court of Justice and whilst the question was being resolved the defendants sought a mandatory interlocutory injunction to compel the plaintiff to comply with the terms of the Order. In the High Court Keane J granted the injunctive relief sought and in so doing rejected the view that an applicant for an interlocutory injunction had to establish the probability of success at the trial of the substantive action. He held:

"... it seems open to this court to apply the test propounded by Lavery J in the *Education Company* Case[20] and to determine the person seeking the relief has shown that there is a fair question raised to be decided at trial. I respectfully agree with the view of Mr Justice Murphy ([1983] ILRM 258) that this, in all material respects, is the same as the test propounded by Lord Diplock ...".[21]

---

16. At 510.
17. Kerr & Whyte, *op cit*, at p 322.
18. See generally, Gray, 'Interlocutory Injunctions Since Cyanamid', [1981] CLJ 307.
19. [1983] IR 88.
20. *Education Company of Ireland Ltd v Fitzpatrick* [1961] IR 323.
21. [1983] IR 88 at 95.

The Supreme Court's decision in *Education Company of Ireland Ltd v Fitzpatrick* ("*Fitzpatrick*") was, however, open to a number of interpretations and was indeed generally considered to be an authority for the proposition that the plaintiff was required to show a fair *prima facie* case ie that on the balance of probabilities he was likely to succeed at the trial of the substantive issue.[22]

[5.09] The decision of Keane J in *Campus Oil* was appealed to the Supreme Court where the main judgment of the court was given by O'Higgins CJ with a concurring judgment from Griffin J. In dismissing the appeal, and upholding the decision of Keane J, O'Higgins CJ said:

> "In my view, the test to be applied is whether a fair *bona fide* question has been raised by the person seeking the relief. If such a question has been raised, it is not for the court to determine that question on an interlocutory application: that remains to be decided at trial. Once a fair question has been raised, in the manner in which I have indicated, then the court should consider the other matters which are appropriate to the exercise of its discretion to grant interlocutory relief. In this regard, I note the views expressed by Lord Diplock, with the concurrence of the other members of the House of Lords, at p 407 of the report of *American Cyanamid v Ethicon Ltd*. I merely say that I entirely agree with what he said."[23]

Earlier, O'Higgins CJ had rejected the existence of the probability test which he said had not found favour in the *Fitzpatrick*[24] case and he had found that such a test would be contrary to principle.

[5.10] The concurring judgment of Griffin J in *Campus Oil* attempted to clarify the confusion caused by a number of senior judges, in a series of cases, purporting to agree with apparently conflicting principles on the circumstances in which the courts would exercise their discretion to grant interlocutory relief. After comprehensively reviewing *Fitzpatrick, Esso Petroleum Co (Ireland) v Fogarty*[25] and *American Cyanamid* and noting that it had been submitted that there were differences between the tests applied he said:

> "... any such differences are more apparent than real ... The tests applied by Lavery J ('that there is a fair question raised to be decided at the trial'), by Kingsmill Moore J ('that a serious question of law arose'), by Mr Justice Walsh ('that there is a substantial question to be tried') and by Lord Diplock ('that there is a serious question to be tried') are essentially the same ...

[22.]   Kerr & Whyte, *op cit*, pp 319, 320.

[23.]   At 107.

[24.]   He did note that there was one reference to "probability" contained in an extract from *Kerr on Injunctions* (6th ed) which was quoted by Lavery J in *Fitzpatrick* but which he held was "of doubtful significance" (at 106) and that Lavery J had laid down the proper test to be: "The plaintiffs have to establish that there is a fair question raised to be decided at the trial. The arguments, lasting three days in this Court, show I think that there is such a question to be determined."

[25.]   [1965] IR 531.

It seems to me that the passage which I have cited from the speech of Lord Diplock has much to recommend it in logic, common sense and principle. I would respectfully adopt it as being a correct statement of the law to be applied in cases of this kind."

It is notable that both O'Higgins CJ and Griffin J concluded the issue by agreeing with Keane J who had held that there was a fair question to be tried and that this was the correct test. The *Campus Oil* case and *Irish Shell Ltd v Elm Motors Ltd*[26] are taken as the leading Irish authorities for the principle that a fair or serious question must be raised by a plaintiff seeking interlocutory relief; where this is satisfied the court must then decide whether the balance of convenience favours the granting of the injunction.[27]

[5.11] Where a plaintiff seeks an interlocutory Mareva injunction, it is said that he must show that he has "a good arguable case" against a defendant.[28] This formulation would seem to have been intended to place a greater onus of proof on a Mareva applicant than on an applicant for an ordinary interlocutory injunction. In reality, there is a very fine distinction between the usual interlocutory test and the Mareva test.[29] On occasion the distinction is blurred. In *Polly Peck International plc v Nadir (No 2)*[30] Scott LJ, in considering whether he would grant an ordinary interlocutory injunction to protect a fund in which the plaintiff had asserted a proprietary claim,[31] said:

"In deciding whether or not an interlocutory injunction to protect the £8.9m should be granted, the approach prescribed by *American Cyanamid v Ethicon Ltd* ... should be followed. First, [the applicant] must show an arguable case. If an arguable case is shown then the balance of convenience should be applied."

Here Scott LJ seems to have applied the Mareva criterion to the question as to whether an ordinary injunction should be made. All the more ironic then that Lord Donaldson MR should, in the same case, have said that:

"[t]he approach called for by the decision in *American Cyanamid Co v Ethicon Ltd* ... has, as such, no application to the grant or refusal of Mareva injunctions which proceed on principles which are quite different from those applicable to other interlocutory injunctions".[32]

The question is: what difference in practice, if any, is there between these tests?

---

[26]. [1984] ILRM 595.
[27]. As to the application of the balance of convenience test in an application for a Mareva injunction, see Ch 8, *Applying for a Mareva Injunction*, para **[8.55]**.
[28]. In respect of a post-trial Mareva injunction, the good arguable case criterion is inapplicable as the plaintiff has already had his entitlement to certain sums vindicated by a court of law.
[29]. See paras **[5.14]** and **[5.34]** *infra*.
[30]. [1992] 4 All ER 769 at 784.
[31]. As to injunctions in defence of proprietary claims see Ch 1, *The Mareva Injunction in Context*, para **[1.16]** *et seq*.
[32]. [1992] 4 All ER 769 at 786.

The "Good Arguable Case" Test in Applications for Mareva Injunctions

[5.12] In considering the meaning of the "good arguable case" test and in distinguishing it from the "fair or serious question to be tried" test, the following issues are considered:

    (a) Different tests for different types of injunctions;

    (b) The emergence of the "good arguable case" test;

    (c) The "good arguable case" test in Ireland;

    (d) The "good arguable case" test in the Supreme Court.

(a) Different tests for different types of injunctions

[5.13] It seems established that the test applicable to a Mareva injunction is not the same test which is usually applicable to an ordinary interlocutory injunction, as settled by the Supreme Court in *Campus Oil Ltd v Minister for Industry and Energy (No 2)*.[33] This is not unusual. The courts in Ireland have formulated a number of different tests for different types of injunctions other than Mareva injunctions: eg,[34] injunctions to restrain a petition for the winding up of a company;[35] injunctions to restrain the publication of a defamation;[36] and injunctions to enjoin the enforcement of an Act of the Oireachtas on the basis that the legislation is unconstitutional.[37]

(b) The emergence of the good arguable case test

[5.14] It has been well established in the United Kingdom that the applicable test for the granting of a Mareva injunction is that a plaintiff must show that he has

---

[33.] [1983] IR 88.

[34.] See generally, Delany, *Equity and the Law of Trusts in Ireland*, (1996) Roundhall Sweet & Maxwell, pp 396-400.

[35.] *Truck and Machinery Sales Ltd v Marubeni Komatsu Ltd*, High Court, unrep, 23 February 1996 (Keane J). Keane J held that the principles laid down in *Campus Oil* were not necessarily applicable where an injunction was sought to restrain a petition to have a company wound up as "different considerations entirely apply where, as here, the object of the application is to prevent the respondent from exercising his right of access to the courts". It was held that the applicant for the injunction to restrain the presentation of a petition should establish "at least a *prima facie* case that its presentation would constitute an abuse of process". See generally, Canniffe, 'Restraining a Creditor's Winding Up Petition - The Position Since *Truck and Machinery Sales v Marubeni Komatsu Ltd*', (1997) CLP 30.

[36.] *Sinclair v Gogarty* [1937] IR 377 where Sullivan CJ held that "an interlocutory injunction should only be granted in the clearest cases where any jury would say that the matter complained of was libellous, and where if the jury did not so find, the court would set aside the verdict as unreasonable." See Delany, *op cit* at 397, 398.

[37.] *Crotty v An Taoiseach* [1987] IR 713. In that case Barrington J said that a greater emphasis on the term "fair question of law" would apply where it was sought to impugn the constitutionality of legislation. See also *Pesca Valentia v The Minister for Fisheries & Forestry* [1986] ILRM 68 and *Cooke v The Minister for Communications* (1989) *Irish Times Law Reports* of 20 February 1989.

"a good arguable case" against the defendant in the trial of the substantive cause of action. In the case of a Mareva injunction, the requirement that a plaintiff establish that he has a "good arguable case" is in substitution for having to establish that there is a fair or serious question to be tried. In *Derby & Co Ltd v Weldon (No 1)*[38] Parker LJ said:

> "In my view the difference between an application for an ordinary injunction and Mareva lies only in this: that in the former case the plaintiff need only establish that there is a serious question to be tried, whereas in the latter test is said to be whether the plaintiff shows a good arguable case. The difference ... is incapable of definition ...".

[5.15] The first case in which the "good arguable case" criterion in the test for a Mareva injunction appears to have been formulated was *Rasu Maritima SA v Perusahaan Pertmanbangan Minyak Dan Gas Bumi Negara; The Pertimina.*[39] In the course of his judgment Lord Denning MR said:

> "The defendant may put in an affidavit putting forward a specious defence sufficient to get him leave to defend, conditional or unconditional. But when the case actually comes to the court for trial, he throws his hand in. It is then seen that the affidavit was simply filed in order to gain time. So under this new [Mareva] procedure a defendant may put forward a specious defence just so as to remove his assets from the jurisdiction. The weakness of the defence may not appear until later. So I would hold that an order restraining removal of assets can be made whenever the plaintiff can show that he has a "good arguable case". That is a test applied for service on a defendant out of the jurisdiction ... and it is a good test in this [Mareva] procedure which is appropriate when defendants are out of the jurisdiction. It is also in conformity with the test as to the granting of injunctions whenever is it just and convenient as laid down by the House of Lords in *American Cyanamid Co v Ethicon Ltd.*"[40]

Here, the formulation of the "good arguable case" test is seen to have emanated from the test applied to service of proceedings on a defendant who was out of the jurisdiction. The case cited by Lord Denning MR as authority was *Vitkovice Hornia Hutri Tegrstvo v Korner.*[41] However, the test promulgated by the House of Lords in *Korner* was not uniform, and their Lordships' formulations included "a strong argument"[42] and "a proper ... [case] ... to be heard in our courts".[43] The *Korner* case concerned an application to set aside leave to serve proceedings out

---

[38.] [1989] 1 All ER 469 at 475.
[39.] [1977] 3 All ER 324. See generally, Powles, *The Mareva Injunction and Associated Orders*, (1985) Professional Books Ltd at p 20.
[40.] [1977] 3 All ER 324 at 334.
[41.] [1951] 2 All ER 334, [1951] AC 869. See also *Seaconsar Ltd v Bank Markazi* [1993] 4 All ER 456 and *The Canada Trust Co v Stolzenberg (No 2)* Court of Appeal, unrep, 29 October 1997.
[42.] *Per* Lord Radcliffe at 885.
[43.] *Per* Lord Simonds at 880.

of the jurisdiction[44] and this was highly influential in Lord Denning's decision that a plaintiff applying for a Mareva injunction must establish that he has a "good arguable case". This is because, originally, the Mareva injunction was seen as a procedure to bolster the position of a plaintiff whose cause of action was against a foreign defendant. Hence the rationale for the importation of a test used in connection with the service of proceedings on an *ex-juris* defendant. Since Mareva relief is now granted against domestic as well as foreign based defendants,[45] one can reasonably question whether the rationale for deploying the "good arguable case" test continues to be valid.[46]

[5.16] The requirement that a plaintiff must show that he has a "good arguable case" was again asserted in *Establissement Esefka International Anstalt v Central Bank of Nigeria*.[47] In this case the Nigerian Ministry for Defence ordered 240,000 tonnes of cement worth US$14.376m from the plaintiff, payment to be by letters of credit which issued from the Midland Bank in the UK. The cement was shipped but a question arose over 94,000 tonnes which were supposed to have been shipped on board eight vessels. Bills of lading and associated documents for these shipments, were presented to the bank for payment, which was made. There were doubts as to whether the documents were genuine and suspicions over whether they had been forged and the defendant refused to pay moneys due in respect of demurrage. The plaintiff instituted proceedings and obtained a Mareva injunction but this order was successfully appealed by the defendant. One of the grounds for discharging the Mareva injunction was the absence of a "good arguable case" against the defendant. After reviewing the evidence which suggested that the documents presented had been forged and that there was great doubt as to whether the eight ships ever existed at all, Lord Denning MR said:

> "I think I have said enough about the case to show that in regard to the claim there is a good arguable defence on account of the forged or fraudulent bills of lading to show that the claim is not well-founded ...
>
> ... I would not like to throw any doubt whatsoever upon the validity of the Mareva injunctions which have been granted since they were started year by

---

[44.] See Ord 11 of RSC 1986.

[45.] See Ch 6, *The Risk of Removal or Disposal of Assets*, para **[6.05]** *et seq.*

[46.] For a recent application of the test in *Korner* in the context of service of proceedings *ex juris*, see *Attock Cement Co Ltd v Romanian Bank for Foreign Trade* [1989] 1 WLR 1147 at 1152 *et seq.* There, Staughton LJ said (at 1155): "... I conclude that, where there is a disputed question of fact which is essential to the application of RSC Order 11, rule 1, the judge must reach a provisional or tentative conclusion that the plaintiff is probably right upon it before he allows service to stand. The nettle must be grasped, and that is what I take to be meant by a good arguable case."

[47.] [1979] 1 Lloyd's Rep 445.

year in the Commercial Court and have proved to be of the greatest value, but in order that they should operate there should at least be a "good arguable case" for the plaintiffs that the money is going to become due to them. On the material before us, it seems to me that there are many doubts in the plaintiff's claim and there is so much defence to be raised against it that it would not be a case where the plaintiffs have a really good arguable case to succeed. This is one ground on which it would not be right to grant a Mareva injunction."[48]

In that case the plaintiff did have a substantive cause of action against the defendant but the court found that the cause was not of a sufficient quality. The evidence which suggested that the cement had not been shipped and that the bills of lading had been forged was sufficient for the court to determine that the plaintiff did not have a "good arguable case" against the defendant. It is interesting to see the implicit suggestion that the existence of a "good arguable defence" is the converse to a plaintiff's "good arguable case"; it is thought, however, that proof of the latter will not necessarily be rebutted by proof of a "good arguable defence" since both can co-exist. Indeed, in *Moloney v Laurib Investments Ltd*,[49] after reviewing the circumstances of the plaintiff's claim against the defendant, Lynch J referred to the plaintiff as having "a stateable case against the defendants" and to the defendants as having "a stateable defence to the plaintiff's claim".[50]

[5.17] Another early case to focus on the requirement that a plaintiff must show that he has a "good arguable case" was *Bakarim v Victoria P Shipping Co Ltd, "The Tatiangela"*.[51] In that case the defendants had charged a ship known as the Tatiangela to a Saudi company. The plaintiff's goods were being carried on the ship when it sank. The plaintiff elected to sue the ship's owner (and not the charterer), arguing that the charterer had negotiated the charterparty of the ship on the plaintiff's behalf and that, on this basis, it was entitled to sue the defendant for breach of the charterparty because the ship was not seaworthy. In effect the plaintiff claimed that it was the undisclosed principal to the charterparty and that the charterer was merely an agent. In was on this rock that the plaintiff's claim for Mareva relief foundered and although it obtained a Mareva injunction *ex parte*, the injunction was discharged on *inter partes* hearing. After reviewing the plaintiff's evidence on the alleged agency - which consisted essentially of an affidavit from an associate legal executive employed

---

[48.] At 448. Italics added.

[49.] High Court, unrep, 20 July 1993 (Lynch J), p 2 of the transcript. See generally, Ch 6, *The Risk of Removal or Disposal of Assets*, para **[6.26]** *et seq* where the facts of this case are considered.

[50.] These comments were not, however, made in the context of either the plaintiff or the defendant having to satisfy any particular test and, accordingly, could be interpreted as merely a general comment on the relative strengths of both parties' cases.

[51.] [1980] 2 Lloyd's Rep 193.

by the plaintiff's solicitors[52] - Parker J concluded that there was insufficient evidence for finding that the charterer had in fact acted as the plaintiff's agent. He said:

"I have no doubt that the evidence presently before the court is inadequate. There is no scrap of documentary evidence of agency or of transactions which would normally flow from an agency if there was one. Nor is there any information shown to have been given by either of the parties to any oral agency or by someone present at the time. These matters are of great importance, particularly in the case of an alleged undisclosed principal where, since ratification cannot arise, the date of the alleged agency is or can be crucial. The plaintiff must, it is common ground, show a 'good arguable case'. He has not in my judgment done so and I decline the invitation to make a conditional order. Had the point been raised late, such an order or an adjournment, might well have been appropriate, but the plaintiff has had three months in which to produce adequate evidence. He has failed to do so and as his whole case depends upon his being the charterer this is sufficient to dispose of both applications for it must follow that the injunction should be discharged and the proceedings set aside."[53]

The plaintiff's substantive action against the defendant for breach of charterparty turned upon there being privity of contract; privity was sought to be established by proving an agency and because there was insufficient evidence of an agency, it was arguable that the plaintiff did not even have a substantive cause of action against the defendant, let alone a "good arguable case".

[5.18] The "good arguable case" test has not been universally accepted in all countries which have accepted the Mareva jurisdiction. So, in most of the terrritories of Canada the test applicable to the granting of a Mareva injunction is that a plaintiff must establish that he has a "strong *prima facie* case". So in *Chitel v Rothbart*,[54] MacKinnon ACJO said in the Ontario Court of Appeal that:

"Whatever the test may be regarding the granting of interlocutory injunctions generally, in my view, the granting of a Mareva injunction, under special and limited circumstances, requires that the applicant establish a strong *prima facie* case".

[52.] The affidavit stated that from the deponent's enquiries he was advised that the charterer was a trading establishment owned by an Ali Salem and that Salem and the plaintiff "have a long history of trading co-operation and sometimes undertake business in joint names" and that the charterer was acting for the plaintiff "under a verbal agreement between them": at 196.
[53.] [1980] 2 Lloyd's Rep 193 at 197.
[54.] (1982) 141 DLR (3d) 268 at 278.

As Galligan JA said in *R v Consolidated Fastfrate Transport Inc*:[55]

> "It is, therefore, settled law in [Ontario] that in order for a plaintiff to obtain a Mareva injunction the court must be persuaded that not only does the plaintiff have a *prima facie* case but that it has a strong *prima facie* case".[56]

Although some doubt existed as to the appropriate test applicable in British Columbia following the decision in *Mooney v Orr*,[57] where it seems that the "good arguable case" test found favour, it has recently been said by McKinnon in *Cinnamon v McLean*:[58]

> "It was conceded in *Mooney* that there was a 'strong *prima facie* case' and so the introduction of the lower UK test (a 'good arguable case') was of no particular interest to the parties. Subsequently in *Reynolds v Harmanis*[59] Mr Justice Esson sought to lay to rest any suggestion that the UK test had found favour in British Columbia. He said (at 366): 'The first question to be considered is whether the plaintiff has put forward a strong *prima facie* case. The test often applied in the English cases, that of establishing a "good arguable case" has not generally been adopted in this country'".[60]

[5.19] Similarly, in Australasia, the courts have tended to favour the application of the *"prima facie* case" test in Mareva applications. So in *Hunt v BP Exploration Company (Libya) Ltd*[61] Barker J in the Supreme Court of Auckland, New Zealand, made reference to the need for a plaintiff to normally have a *prima facie* case. It would seem that the *"prima facie* case" test also applies in Australia. In *Patterson v BTR Engineering (Aust) Ltd*[62] Meagher JA said that a plaintiff must prove that he has a *prima facie* case against the defendant.[63]

(c) The good arguable case test in Ireland

[5.20] Notwithstanding the reservations expressed above[64] as to the present justification for the original rationale for requiring a Mareva plaintiff to show

---

[55.] (1995) 125 DLR (4th) 1 at 12. The strong *prima facie* test was also accepted by Estey J in the Supreme Court of Canada in *Aetna Financial Services Ltd v Feigelman* (1985) 15 DLR (4th) 161 at 178.

[56.] This test was also accepted as being that applicable to the grant of Mareva injunctions in Ontario by Weiler JA in his concurring judgment.

[57.] (1994) 100 BCLR (2d) 335 (Huddart J).

[58.] (1997) Supreme Court of British Columbia, 15 December 1997 (McKinnon J).

[59.] (1995) Supreme Court of British Columbia, 16 May 1995 (Esson CJSC).

[60.] See also *Inayat N Pirani Inc v Global Pacific Capital Corporation* (1996) Supreme Court of British Columbia, unrep, 19 January 1996 (Baker J).

[61.] [1980] 1 NZLR 104 at 121.

[62.] (1989) 18 NSWLR 319 at 321, 326.

[63.] See generally, Meagher, Gummow and Lehane, *op cit*, at p 611. See also *LED Builders Pty Ltd v Eagle Homes Pty Ltd* [1997] 826 FCA (22 August 1997) Federal Court of Australia.

[64.] See para **[5.15]** *supra*.

that he has got a "good arguable case", the fact remains that the courts in both England and Ireland continue to apply the "good arguable case" test. The first Irish judicial acceptance of this test was in *Fleming v Ranks (Ireland) Ltd*[65] where McWilliam J stated that a Mareva plaintiff "must show that he has a good arguable case". This was the first of many Irish applications where the need for a Mareva plaintiff to prove that he has a "good arguable case" against the defendant has been referred to by the courts.[66]

[5.21] One of the next Irish judgments, where a written judgment was given, to consider the requirement that a Mareva plaintiff have a "good arguable case" was the High Court judgment in *Caudron v Air Zaire*.[67] Although Barr J's decision was reversed by the Supreme Court, his observations on the need to show that there was a "good arguable case" were not addressed by the Supreme Court which non-suited the plaintiffs' application on the far more fundamental basis that they had no substantive cause of action which was cognisable by the Irish courts.[68] In assessing the strength of the plaintiffs' claim against the defendants, Barr J began his judgment by recognising that the test to be applied in deciding whether to grant an interlocutory injunction was that adopted by Keane J in *Campus Oil Ltd v Minister for Industry and Energy (No 2)*[69] and he quoted the following passage from the headnote of the case as reported in *The Irish Reports*:

> "An application for an interlocutory injunction, to be successful, must establish, first, that there is a fair question (to be determined at the trial of the action) concerning the existence of the right which he seeks to protect or enforce by the injunction and, secondly, that the circumstances are such that the balance of convenience lies on the side of the granting of the injunction.

After noting that this test was approved of by the Supreme Court, Barr J went on to find that the test applied by Kerr LJ in the context of an application for a Mareva injunction in *The Niedersachsen*[70] was:

[65.] [1983] ILRM 541 at 546.

[66.] For example, in *P v MM Ltd*, *The Irish Times*, 1 August 1989, (Blayney J) it is reported that Blayney J said that "a good arguable case" was one of the necessary proofs required in order to obtain Mareva relief; in *B v C and JPC & Co Ltd*, *The Irish Times*, 27 June 1991 (Barron J) counsel for the defendant is reported as having said that one of the requirements for Mareva relief was that a Mareva plaintiff show that he has "a good arguable case"; and in *H v IAS Ltd*, *The Irish Times*, 6 August 1992 (Morris J) it was reported that Morris J dismissed an application for a Mareva injunction on the grounds that the plaintiff had failed to satisfy him that he had a case which was likely to succeed or that he had a strong arguable case.

[67.] [1986] ILRM 10.

[68.] See generally, Ch 4, *A Substantive Cause of Action*, para **[4.06]** *et seq*.

[69.] [1988] IR 88.

[70.] [1984] 1 All ER 398. See para **[5.25]** *infra*.

"In our view the test is whether, on the assumption that the plaintiffs have shown at least 'a good arguable case', the court concludes, on the whole of the evidence then before it, that the refusal of a Mareva injunction would involve a real risk that a judgment or award in favour of the plaintiffs would remain unsatisfied."[71]

Barr J held that he respectfully adopted that test "as being a logical development of the law where the particular type of relief sought is a Mareva injunction". Applying these principles to the case in hand Barr J found that the plaintiffs had satisfied the test. He noted that it had been conceded that substantial sums of money were due to the plaintiffs, that the only asset available to satisfy their claims was the aircraft which the plaintiffs sought to have "frozen" by the Mareva injunction, that any judgment which they might obtain in Zaire would be of no value to them and that the only question remaining was whether "there is a fair question raised therein for determination". Barr J said:

"It is not part of my function at this interlocutory stage of the proceedings to consider whether or not the employees are likely to succeed in their action against the airline if tried in this jurisdiction. I have to be satisfied only that there is a fair arguable case to be made in support of the employees' claims and that the balance of convenience favours the making of the order sought."[72]

After referring to two possible defences which the defendants could have raised (sovereign immunity and an exclusive jurisdiction clause) Barr J concluded by saying:

"In the light of the facts of the instant case, it is clear that there is a fair arguable question raised as to whether or not the airline is entitled to the benefit of the exclusive jurisdiction clause in the employees' contracts of service."[73]

That Barr J chose to mix his words and refer to "a fair arguable question" is not too great a surprise since, after all, the Irish courts' interpretation of the test for even an ordinary interlocutory injunction has, in the past, been varied.[74]

[5.22] The need for a Mareva plaintiff to show that he has a "good arguable case" was again considered in Ireland in *Countyglen plc v Carway*.[75] The background to this case was that in January 1994 the High Court had made an order (pursuant to s 8 of the Companies Act 1990) appointing an inspector to Countyglen plc for the purpose of investigating its affairs. The inspector produced an interim report in July and a final report in October of 1994.

---

71. [1986] ILRM 10 at 16.
72. [1986] ILRM 10 at 17.
73. *Ibid.*
74. See paras **[5.08]-[5.10]**, *supra*.
75. [1995] 1 IR 208.

Subsequent to the final report the company instituted proceedings against the respondents claiming various declarations and seeking to recover the loss sustained by the company or, alternatively seeking an order under s 12 of the Companies Act 1990. In addition the company sought ancillary relief against the respondents in the form of a Mareva injunction to preserve their assets pending the hearing of the substantive action. The High Court made an interim Mareva injunction on the basis of the company's undertaking as to damages and by the agreement of the parties this was continued until the hearing of the interlocutory application.

On the interlocutory hearing the applicants contended that the applicable test for a Mareva injunction was that set out in *Campus Oil Ltd v Minister for Industry and Energy (No 2)*, ie "whether a fair *bona fide* or serious question had been raised to be decided at the trial by the party seeking relief".[76] The respondents, on the other hand, contended that "something more [was] required where a Mareva injunction [was] sought". Murphy J noted the decisions in *Mareva Compania Naviera SA v International Bulkcarriers SA, The Mareva,*[77] *Rasu Maritima SA v Perusahaan Pertambangan Minyak Dan Gas Bumi Negara, The Pertamina*[78] in which Denning MR referred to the need to show "a good arguable case". Referring to *Z Ltd v A-Z and AA-LL,*[79] Murphy J quoted the following extract from the judgment of Kerr LJ:

> "It follows that in my view Mareva injunctions should be granted, but granted only, when it appears to the court that there is a combination of two circumstances. First, when it appears likely that the plaintiff will recover judgment against the defendant for a certain or approximate sum. Secondly, when there are also reasons to believe that the defendant has assets within the jurisdiction to meet the judgment, in whole or in part, but may well take steps designed to ensure that they are no longer available or traceable when judgment is given against him."[80]

Murphy J expressly acknowledged that there were conflicting tests from which one could choose in deciding a Mareva application. He answered the question which must have been asked by all who have tried to reconcile the different approach to Mareva injunctions as opposed to ordinary interlocutory injunctions (ie which test?), saying:

---

76. [1995] IR 208 at 214.
77. [1980] 1 All ER 213.
78. [1978] QB 644.
79. [1982] QB 558.
80. [1995] IR 208 at 215. Murphy J also noted McWilliam J's endorsement for the need for the plaintiff to show "a good arguable case" in *Fleming v Ranks (Ireland) Ltd* [1983] ILRM 541: see para **[5.20]** *supra*.

"I doubt that there is any significant difference between the expressions 'good arguable case' and a 'substantial question to be tried' but if such a distinction exists, I would prefer the latter criterion as the one approved by the Supreme Court in *Campus Oil Ltd v The Minister for Industry and Energy (No 2)* [1983] IR 88, although not specifically related to the Mareva type injunction. What I reject emphatically is that a plaintiff seeking a Mareva injunction must establish as a probability that his claim would succeed. This 'probability' test was rejected by the Supreme Court in *Campus Oil Ltd v The Minister for Industry and Energy (No 2)* [1983] IR 88 as a matter of precedent and principle".[81]

Murphy J concluded that it was entirely inappropriate for the court, on an interlocutory application, to review such of the evidence as is available to it and to attempt to forecast the outcome of the proceedings as a matter of probability or likelihood. He said: "[w]hat can and should be done is to determine that there is a fair, serious, question to be tried". Turning to the case before him he said:

"In the present case there is evidence to support the serious allegations of fraud and breach of trust made against the defendants. At the same time I recognise that in the voluminous affidavits sworn by Mr John Carway the validity of this evidence and the weight to be attached to it has been challenged on numerous grounds and that those issues too are serious and *bona fide*. It is not my task, however, to assess which case is likely to prevail.

It is in relation to the risk of the defendants' assets being dissipated in advance of any judgment in the matter with a view to defeating the same and also with regard to the general balance of convenience that considerations different from those pertaining in relation to the conventional injunctions arise."[82]

Accordingly, whilst Murphy J held that the plaintiff in the *Carway* case had satisfied the requirement to show "a good arguable case" or, had established that there were serious and *bona fide* issues to be tried, he found that such a test was in practice little different to the hurdle which an applicant for any interlocutory injunction had to clear. The case did not turn on the plaintiff satisfying this test, but rather, the considerably more difficult test of whether there was a risk that the defendants' assets would be dissipated with a view to defeating the plaintiff's future judgment.[83] The fact that the risk of removal or disposal of assets by the defendants is with a view to frustrate a future judgment has, in Ireland, been elevated above all other proofs in an application for a Mareva injunction and must, in consequence, be seen to colour the "good arguable case" test.[84]

---

[81] *Ibid.*
[82] At 216.
[83] See generally, Ch 6, *The Risk of Removal or Disposal of Assets*.
[84] See para **[5.35]** *infra*.

(d) The "good arguable case" test in the Supreme Court

[5.23] Undoubtedly, the case of *Re John Horgan Livestock Ltd*[85] is primarily an authority for the proposition that, in Ireland, it is necessary for a Mareva plaintiff to establish to the court's satisfaction that the defendant is likely to remove his assets from the jurisdiction, or otherwise dissipate them within the jurisdiction, with a view to evading his obligations to the plaintiff and frustrating the expected order of the court.[86] However, in this, the most authoritative and detailed examination of the law and practice applicable to the granting of Mareva relief in Ireland, the Supreme Court recognised the importance of the "good arguable case" proof in Irish Mareva applications. After quoting the exact passage from Kerr LJ in *Z Ltd v A-Z and AA-LL*[87] which had also been quoted by Murphy J in *Countyglen plc v Carway*[88] Hamilton CJ said:

> "Consequently a Mareva injunction will only be granted if there is a combination of two circumstances established by the plaintiff ie (i) that he has an arguable case that he will succeed in the action, and (ii) the anticipated disposal of a defendant's assets is for the purpose of preventing a plaintiff from recovering damages and not merely for the purpose of carrying on a business or discharging lawful debts".[89]

Accordingly, it must be taken as established that a person seeking Mareva relief in Ireland must satisfy the court that he has a "good arguable case".

The Meaning of "Good Arguable Case"

[5.24] Since its initial formulation the expression "good arguable case" has been almost bandied about in some judgments. In few cases has the test been actually examined and explained. It has become, rather, a catch phrase of the Mareva era, where those who use it appear to know what they mean but decline to distinguish its practical effect from that of the "serious or fair question to be tried" test.

[5.25] In *The Niedersachsen*[90] Mustill J laboured with the meaning of the expression "good arguable case". In the course of his judgment he said:

[85.] [1995] IR 411.

[86.] See Ch 6, *The Risk of Removal or Disposal of Assets*, para **[6.16]** *et seq*.

[87.] [1982] 1 QB 558.

[88.] [1995] 1 IR 208.

[89.] [1995] 2 IR 411 at 418. The Chief Justice went on to quote with approval McWilliam J's judgment in *Fleming v Ranks (Ireland) Ltd* [1983] ILRM 541 at 546 where he referenced the need for a "good arguable case": see para **[5.20]** *supra*. Note also that the judgment of O'Flaherty J acknowledged the requirement that a plaintiff establish that he "has a good arguable case for a diverse series of cases".

[90.] *Ninemia Maritime Corp v Trave Schiffahartsgesellschaft mbh & Co KG, The Neidersachsen* [1984] 1 All ER 398.

"... the *Pertimina* case is the foundation authority, and the test of 'a good arguable case' was adopted by the Court of Appeal ... so it seems appropriate to adopt it here. But what exactly does the expression mean? ... it appears that the following propositions are justified.[91]

(1) The plaintiff must do more than make a bare assertion of facts which would give the court jurisdiction.

(2) The question whether the plaintiff has shown a prima facie case is not an appropriate test, at least where the respondent has adduced evidence in opposition.

(3) The court cannot, and should not attempt to, try the issues at an interlocutory stage.

(4) Nor does the expression 'made sufficiently to appear' mean that the court should apply the same standard of proof as will be appropriate at the trial ...

(5) ... the speeches use a variety of terms to express the same concept: 'satisfied', 'a proper one to be heard in our courts', 'a good arguable case', 'a strong argument', 'a strong case for argument'. These expressions suggest that the plaintiff has to do substantially more than show that the case is merely 'arguable': a word which to my mind at least connotes that, although the claim will not be laughed out of court, the plaintiff will not be justified in feeling any optimism. On the other hand, if I am right on proposition (4), the plaintiff need not go so far as to persuade the judge that he is likely to win ...[92]

In these circumstances, I consider that the right course is to adopt the test of a good arguable case, in the sense of a case which is more than barely capable of serious argument, and yet not necessarily one which the judge believes to have a better than 50% chance of success."[93]

A Mareva plaintiff must satisfy the court, hearing the application, that his case against the defendant is not spurious. To say that his case must be "arguable" does not mean, as Mustill J made clear, that the plaintiff must be likely to succeed in the final analysis of the substantive issues.

[5.26] In *The Canada Trust Co v Stolzenberg (No 2)*,[94] Waller LJ said of the meaning of the "good arguable case" test, in the context of an application for service of proceedings, as opposed to an application for a Mareva injunction, that:

"It is also right to remember that the 'good arguable case' test, although obviously applicable to the *ex parte* stage, becomes of most significance at the

---

[91.] Note that the indentation to the passage quoted from the decision of Mustill J is added.

[92.] At this point in his judgment, Mustill J considered the judgment of Kerr LJ in *Z Ltd v A* [1982] 1 All ER 556 (considered *infra*) and concluded that "he was doing no more than reiterate that the plaintiff must always demonstrate a likelihood of success, and was not prescribing the degree of likelihood".

[93.] [1984] 1 All ER 398 at 403, 404.

[94.] Court of Appeal, unrep, 29 October 1997.

inter partes stage where two arguments are being weighed in the interlocutory context which, as I have stressed, must not become a 'trial'. 'Good arguable case' reflects in that context that one side has a much better argument on the material available. It is the concept which the phrase reflects on which it is important to concentrate ie of the court being satisfied or as satisfied as it can be having regard to the limitations which an interlocutory process imposes that factors exist which allow the court to take jurisdiction."[95]

Applying this test in the context of a Mareva application means that the court is required to be satisfied that "factors exist" which would allow the court to grant interlocutory relief for a plaintiff's benefit and, implicitly, to the defendant's detriment.

Establishing a "Good Arguable Case"

[5.27] Whether or not a plaintiff has a "good arguable case" will obviously depend upon the facts in any given case.[96] Although the courts have consistently said that it is inappropriate, at an interlocutory hearing, to resolve difficult conflicts of evidence or to decide substantive points of law,[97] some examination of the issues is necessary where the court has to establish the strength of a plaintiff's case.[98] In *Production Association Minsk Tractor Works and Belarus Equiptment (Ireland) Ltd v Saenko*[99] the plaintiffs applied for a Mareva injunction to restrain the defendants from, *inter alia*, disposing of or dealing with their assets below the sum of £300,000. The plaintiffs had alleged that the

---

[95.] At p 5 of the transcript. At p 4 he said: "It is I believe important to recognise ... that what the court is endeavouring to do is to find a concept not capable of very precise definition which reflects that the plaintiff must properly satisfy the court that it is right for the court to take jurisdiction".

[96.] Note *H v IAS Ltd*, *The Irish Times*, 6 August 1992 (Morris J). There, Morris J is reported as having dismissed an application by a former vice-president of a company to have more than £700,000 worth of assets of the aircraft leasing company frozen. It was reported that the defence claimed that the application was intended to bring the respondent to the negotiating table and was "the nearest to an abuse of a very useful jurisdiction of the commercial courts". It was reported that Morris J in dismissing the application said that the applicant had failed to satisfy him that he had a case which was likely to succeed or that he had a strong arguable case.

[97.] See paras **[5.04]** and **[5.21]** *supra* and further, *Derby & Co Ltd v Weldon (No 1)* [1989] 1 All ER 469.

[98.] Note that in *Polly Peck International plc v Nadir (No 2)* [1992] 4 All ER 769 Scott LJ took over 6 pages to review the evidence as to whether the plaintiff's case was "good arguable" or speculative. See also the decision of Saville J in *Boobyer v Holman & Co Ltd and the Society of Lloyd's (No 2)* [1993] 1 Lloyd's Rep 96. Both decisions have been used as support for the suggestion that "there is some reason to believe that the courts are beginning to engage in a stricter scrutiny of the merits of the plaintiff's case at the interlocutory stage": see Ough & Flenley, *The Mareva Injunction and Anton Piller Order*, (2nd ed, 1993) Butterworths, para 5.11.5.

[99.] High Court, unrep, 25 February 1998 (McCracken J).

first defendant had misappropriated moneys from the second plaintiff and that he had defrauded the second plaintiff. McCracken J recognised that the plaintiffs had made very serious allegations and went on to state that fraud "must be pleaded with great particularity"[100] and that he did not have the sort of particulars of the claim which will eventually have to be given. On the question of the strength of the plaintiffs' case, McCracken J said:

> "I realise this is an interlocutory application made at an early stage and I do believe, having regard to all the affidavits filed, that the plaintiffs have shown a good arguable case that at least some monies may have been misappropriated. I emphasise I am not making any finding that this is so, only that an arguable case has been made out ...".[101]

The plaintiffs' application failed on the ground that there was no evidence to establish an intention on the part of the defendants to evade their obligations to the plaintiffs or to frustrate the anticipated order of the court.[102]

[5.28] In *Polly Peck International plc v Nadir (No 2)*[103] Scott LJ made reference to the interaction between the consequences of a Mareva injunction for a defendant with the requirement that a plaintiff should have a "good arguable case". After noting that the appeal concerned the strength of the plaintiff's case, the potential effect of the injunction on the defendant and the potential effect on the plaintiff of discharging the injunction, he said:

> "I must consider each of these matters in turn. But, in their bearing on the result of this appeal, they are not independent of one another. A Mareva injunction could not ever be justified unless at least a fair arguable case for liability could be shown. But the strength of the case sufficient to support the grant of a Mareva injunction is dependent to some extent on the consequences to the defendant of the injunction, as well, of course, as on the consequences to the plaintiff if an injunction is not granted."[104]

In that case Scott LJ concluded that the plaintiff did have a claim against the defendant but, "though a possible one, is at present based on little more than speculation".[105] Addressing the other two issues quoted above he found, secondly, that a Mareva injunction would seriously interfere with the defendant bank's normal course of business and could quite possibly destroy the bank and thirdly, that lifting the injunction would make it possible that a judgment

---

[100.] At p 2 of the transcript.

[101.] At p 2 of the transcript.

[102.] See Ch 6, *The Risk of Removal or Disposal of Assets*, para **[6.47]**.

[103.] [1992] 4 All ER 769. See Zuckerman, 'Mareva and Interlocutory Injunctions Disentangled', [1992] LQR 559.

[104.] At 775.

[105.] At 784c.

obtained by the plaintiff would be worthless. He concluded by holding that the balance came down against continuing the Mareva injunction for two reasons:

> "First, I regard [the plaintiff's] present claim against the Central Bank as no more than speculative. Second, it is, in my opinion wrong in principle to grant a Mareva injunction so as, before any liability has been established, to interfere with the normal course of business of the defendant. To impose a Mareva injunction that will have that effect in order to protect a cause of action that is no more than speculative is not simply wrong in principle but positively unfair."[106]

[5.29] In finding that the plaintiff's claim was no more than speculative, Scott LJ found that a "good arguable case" had not been established. Although this case is considered elsewhere in this book, a review of the facts in *Polly Peck International plc v Nadir (No 2)*[107] will be instructive at this point, so as to see what led Scott LJ to the conclusion that the plaintiff had not established a "good arguable case". The administrators of the insolvent plaintiff company had alleged that the first defendant, Mr Nadir, was responsible for the misapplication of £371m of the plaintiff's funds and that another defendant, a Northern Cyprus bank (NC), controlled by Mr Nadir, was responsible for the misapplication of £142m of the plaintiff's funds. The plaintiff claimed that the £142m was transferred to an account in a London bank in the name of the NC; and that approximately £44m of this was transferred to the account of another defendant, the Central Bank of Northern Cyprus (the Central Bank) in return for Turkish lira, and in some cases, sterling being credited to NC's account with the Central Bank. The plaintiff sought, *inter alia*, Mareva relief against the Central Bank. The nature of the plaintiff's claim in this regard was that a constructive trust existed. It was alleged that the constructive trust arose out of the £44m being transferred to the Central Bank. Scott LJ noted that the critical question was whether the Central Bank "knew or must be treated as having known that the funds transferred were [the plaintiff's] funds and were being misapplied".[108] Scott LJ said that he found it difficult to accept that the Central Bank must have known that the funds were likely to be mainly belonging to the plaintiff and, moreover, found that the transfer of funds did not give the Central Bank cause to suspect improprieties. Although he acknowledged that at trial, direct evidence and discovery could bring to light matters from which one could infer knowledge or suspicion of impropriety, Scott LJ did not consider that a "good arguable case" was established and for these reasons considered the claim to be speculative. Moreover, Scott LJ said that he did "not regard the case thus rested

---

[106.] At 784e.
[107.] [1992] 4 All ER 769.
[108.] At 776h.

as likely to succeed in the absence of some further explanation from the bank" and thought that the reverse was the case.[109]

[5.30] One situation where plaintiffs have been found not to have a "good arguable case" is in cases of alleged breach of contract where there are doubts as to whether a plaintiff has any cause of action against the defendant.[110] In *Bidgood v Setzer*[111] the plaintiff sought Mareva relief against the defendants. The plaintiff's cause of action was for breach of an alleged contract between the plaintiff and the defendants. It was not disputed that there were three management agreements between each of the defendants and a company called Moveclass Ltd. These agreements provided for management services to be carried out for Moveclass Ltd by the plaintiff personally. However, the agreements were with Moveclass Ltd and only it was entitled to sue on foot of a breach of the agreements. The plaintiff claimed that in furtherance of a tax scheme, and by novation, he was personally substituted for Moveclass Ltd as the manager under the management agreements. Parker LJ found that the plaintiff's replies to the defendants' particulars referred to intentions and understandings but nothing that amounted to a straightforward plea that there was an oral agreement in the terms alleged. Although an unsigned draft agreement was produced and it was asserted by the plaintiff's counsel that there was an oral agreement in the terms of the draft, Parker LJ said that the plaintiff's affidavit did not assert or depose to there being any agreement in the terms of the draft agreement. In upholding the decision of Otton J that the plaintiff had not shown a "good arguable case", Parker LJ concluded:

> "[The plaintiff's counsel] drew our attention to a number of matters in the documents which she contends, with considerable force, are more consistent with the version advanced by her than with the version advanced by the defendants. But that is not sufficient. Before she can be entitled to obtain for her client a Mareva injunction, it is necessary to satisfy the court that she has a 'good arguable case' for the existence of an agreement upon which her client is entitled to sue. It may be that in the process of discovery, documentary or by interlocutories, or by evidence at the trial, she will ultimately establish that there is such an agreement giving her client the right to sue, to recover commission and to recover damages, but for my part I am quite unable, giving

---

[109.] At 781d. In *Polly Peck International plc v Nadir (No 3)*, (1993) TLR 159 (CA 22 March 1993) the Court of Appeal overturned the refusal of Knox J to discharge an order giving leave to serve the Central Bank out of the jurisdiction on the ground that the plaintiff had not shown a sufficiently strong case against the Central Bank.

[110.] See also was *Bakarim v Victoria P Shipping Co Ltd, 'The Tatiangela'* [1980] 2 Lloyd's Rep 193, considered at para **[5.17]** *supra*.

[111.] UK decision of the Court of Appeal, unrep, 9 October 1984 (Lexis transcript).

full weight to all of the matters which she raises, to see that the required standard of proof has been achieved."[112]

As in *"The Tatiangela"* the Court of Appeal chose to deal with the issue as one concerning the quality or strength of the plaintiff's cause of action. It is thought, however, the in both cases the strength of the plaintiff's case was incidental to the more serious question of whether the plaintiff had a cause of action at all.[113]

[5.31] The question as to whether a plaintiff had, on the evidence, a "good arguable case" sufficient to justify Mareva relief was again addressed in *Aiglon Ltd & L'Aiglon SA v Gau Shan Co Ltd; Gau Shan Co Ltd v Aiglon Ltd*.[114] This case concerned a dispute under a contract for the sale of raw cotton by Aiglon Ltd ("the first plaintiff"), to the defendant, Gau Shan Co Ltd. After the dispute was referred to arbitration, an award was made in favour of the defendants against the plaintiff and L'Aiglon SA ("the second plaintiff"). On foot of the arbitration award the defendant obtained a worldwide[115] Mareva injunction and an asset disclosure order against both plaintiffs, the only substantive claim against the second plaintiff being the defendants' counterclaim for an order under s 26 of the English Arbitration Act 1950 granting leave to enforce the award against them and to enter judgment against them. The defendants also added an Irish company and a Mr K to the counterclaim. The defendants claimed that the transfer of all of the first plaintiff's assets to the Irish company was effected at the instigation of Mr K with the intention, on the part of all concerned, of making the first plaintiff judgment-proof. It was also alleged that this transfer was either for no consideration or, alternatively, at an undervalue. The second plaintiff successfully applied to have the Mareva injunction and disclosure order set aside on the basis that the defendants had not established that they had a "good arguable case" against it and that there was insufficient evidence to establish that the second defendant was party to the original contract of sale.

[5.32] Subsequent to this decision, the defendants brought a fresh application to have the Mareva injunction and disclosure order extended against the second plaintiff on fresh grounds. The defendants sought to establish a claim against the second plaintiff on three grounds: first, under s 423 of the English Insolvency

---

[112.] At p 2, 3 of the Lexis transcript.

[113.] In *Dynawest International Ltd v Margate Resources Ltd*, UK decision unrep, 9 November 1984 (CA) (*Lexis transcript*), Ackner LJ said: "... in order to make out a *prima facie* case for a Mareva injunction the plaintiffs had in the first instance not only to show a good arguable case that there had been a breach of contract by the defendants, but also that they had a good arguable case that they were entitled to recover damages flowing from that breach to the extent of US$2m"; p 5 of the transcript.

[114.] [1993] 1 Lloyd's Rep 164.

[115.] See generally, Ch 7, *The Defendant's Assets*, para **[7.21]** *et seq*.

Act 1986 on the basis that it was party to the "asset stripping" of the first plaintiff; secondly, under s 238 of the English Insolvency Act 1986 on the basis that since the first plaintiff was a shell company without assets a liquidator could apply to reverse the disposal of assets; and thirdly, on foot of fresh arbitration proceedings which asserted that the second plaintiff was indeed party to the contract for the sale of the cotton. Hirst J accepted that the first and second new grounds established a "good arguable case" but rejected that the third ground established such. In respect of the first ground, s 423 gave the court power to, *inter alia*, restore the position to what it would have been had the transaction at an undervalue not taken place and it was the case that the defendants had a direct claim against the second plaintiff under this section. Hirst J accepted that such a claim had been substantiated by the defendants. In respect of the second ground Hirst J acknowledged that the defendants did not have a direct claim against the second plaintiff under s 238 of the Insolvency Act 1986 but he found that there was jurisdiction to grant a Mareva injunction against a third party where this was ancillary to the relief sought against the first defendant;[116] and he held that the defendants had established a "good arguable case" in this regard on the basis that there was "credible evidence that the assets of [the second plaintiff] may in part be the assets of [the first plaintiff], who have as a result of the asset-stripping operation clearly put it out of their own power to meet the arbitration award".[117] It is thought that, again, the court's judgment in this case intermingles the strength of the case with the existence of a substantive cause of action.

[5.33] The issue to be resolved in the case of *Page v Combined Shipping and Trading Co Ltd*[118] was whether the plaintiff should be granted Mareva relief in circumstances where he claimed compensation for suffering "damage" within the meaning of Reg 17(7) of the UK's Commercial Agents (Council Directive) Regulations 1993.[119] The background facts were that the plaintiff had entered into an agency agreement with the defendant company under which he was obliged to buy and sell commodities on the defendant's behalf in return for half of the net profit and this agency agreement was to continue for four years. On being informed by the defendant that its South African parent company had decided to close down its trading activities the plaintiff terminated the agency agreement alleging that the defendant's conduct constituted a repudiatory breach of the agency agreement. The plaintiff sued the defendant, alleging that

---

[116.] On the authority of *TSB Private Bank International SA v Chabra* [1992] 2 All ER 245; see generally, Ch 4, *A Substantive Cause of Action*, para **[4.21]**.

[117.] [1993] 1 Lloyd's Rep 164 at 170.

[118.] [1997] 3 All ER 656.

[119.] For Ireland, see the European Communities (Commercial Agents) Regulations 1994 (SI 33/1994) and generally, O'Mara, 'New Regulations Establish Protection for Commercial Agents', (1994) CLP 162.

he had suffered "damage" within the meaning of Reg 17(7), on the basis that the plaintiff had been deprived of commission, and that he was entitled to compensation under Reg 17(6) of the UK's 1993 Regulations. The plaintiff's application for a Mareva injunction to restrain the defendant from removing assets worth approximately £300,000 from the UK to South Africa was refused initially on the basis that he did not have an arguable case to recover a significant sum as compensation under Reg 17 of the UK's 1993 Regulations; the basis for this finding was that the defendant could have operated the agency agreement for the remainder of the term of four years and the plaintiff would have received no commission and so suffered no loss by the premature termination.

On appeal to the Court of Appeal it was, however, held that the plaintiff did have a "good arguable case" for recovering a substantial sum and that he was entitled to a Mareva injunction. Staughton LJ reviewed the purpose of the UK's 1993 Regulations and found that their purpose was to improve the position of commercial agents and to harmonise the law of the Member States within the EU. On this basis he found that it was arguable that the compensation provisions in Reg 17 would apply to a loss of commission caused by the defendant's failure to ensure that there was "proper performance" of the agency agreement. Although Staughton LJ consistently used the expression "good arguable case" it is interesting to note that Millett LJ, in his concurring judgment, held that "[i]t is, in my judgment, plain that there is a serious question to be tried".[120] This judgment is of interest in that it illustrates two points about the "good arguable case" test: first, the fact that the trial judge and the Court of Appeal judges could reach two entirely different conclusions on the same set of facts as to whether the plaintiff had a "good arguable case" and, secondly, that even within the same court, one judge should express himself satisfied that there was a "good arguable case" whilst another judge should find that there was "a serious question to be tried"!

"Good Arguable Case" or "Serious Question to be Tried' - A Difference?

[5.34] The requirement that a Mareva plaintiff must demonstrate that he has a "good arguable case" is beleaguered by semantics. The essence of what the plaintiff must prove in an application to the Irish High Court is that he has a serious question to be tried. Indeed in *The Canada Trust Co v Stolzenberg (No 2)*[121] Nourse LJ said:

> "... there may well at times have been a measure of confusion between 'good arguable case' and 'serious question to be tried' or the like, perhaps because

---

[120.] [1997] 3 All ER 656 at 661j.
[121.] Court of Appeal, unrep, 29 October 1997.

these expressions can mean different things to different minds and, to some at some rate, there cannot be a serious question to be tried if the plaintiff does not have a 'good arguable case'".[122]

Neither case law, nor Irish newspaper reports of High Court applications for Mareva relief, indicate that any applicant has been refused relief where he has shown that he had a serious question to be tried as opposed to a good arguable case. Although in *Re John Horgan Livestock Ltd*[123] the Supreme Court endorsed the requirement that a Mareva plaintiff must establish that he has a "good arguable case",[124] it did not actually explain what that meant, let alone distinguish (if that be possible) that test from the "serious or fair question to be tried" test applicable to ordinary interlocutory injunctions.

[5.35] Establishing the strength of a plaintiff's case is but one of a number of factors to be considered by a court in deciding whether to grant Mareva relief. In *The Niedersachsen*[125] Kerr LJ said:

> "A 'good arguable case' is no doubt the minimum which the plaintiff must show in order to cross what the judge rightly described as the 'threshold' for the exercise of the jurisdiction. But at the end of the day the court must consider the evidence as a whole in deciding whether or not to exercise this statutory jurisdiction."

In practice, it is thought that provided a plaintiff's case is not obviously spurious, the Irish courts have tended to focus their attention on the requirement that there must be evidence to suggest that a defendant is likely to remove or dispose of his assets with a view to evading his obligations to the plaintiff or frustrating a future order of the court.[126] It has been suggested[127] that the authorities in other jurisdictions, such as Australia and New Zealand, have found that the strength of a plaintiff's case depends largely on other factors relevant to the grant of Mareva relief, the risk of dissipation of assets and the overall balance of convenience being cited. It is thought that this is broadly correct, save that, in the light of the Supreme Court decision in *Re John Horgan (Livestock) Ltd*, this writer would ascribe a fundamental importance to a defendant's intentions in dealing with his assets. Where there is clear and compelling evidence of such an intention that itself would tend to confirm that a plaintiff has a "good arguable case", or that there is "a fair or serious question to

---

[122.] At p 20 of the transcript.

[123.] [1995] IR 411.

[124.] See para **[5.23]** *supra*.

[125.] [1984] 1 All ER 399 at 415e-f. The reference to a "statutory jurisdiction" was because Kerr LJ had just quoted s 37(3) of the UK's Supreme Court Act 1981.

[126.] See Ch 6, *The Risk of Removal or Disposal of Assets*, at para **[6.16]** *et seq*.

[127.] Capper, [1995] 17 DULJ (ns) 110 at 114,115.

be tried" or, otherwise, that the plaintiff's cause of action is of sufficient quality. Where the evidence of a nefarious intention on the part of a defendant is less than compelling, there will be a greater focus on the strength of the plaintiff's case before the court will grant Mareva relief.[128] Of course where there is no direct or inferred evidence of a nefarious intention on the part of the defendant to remove or dispose of his assets, Mareva relief will not be justifiable even if the plaintiff could be said to have "an open and shut" case in respect of his substantive cause of action against the defendant.

[128.] As Capper, *op cit*, has said: "Where the plaintiff's case appears strong less will be required on these other factors and where it is relatively weak more will be required."

Chapter 6

The Risk of Removal or Disposal of Assets

[6.01] Following the Supreme Court's decision in *Re John Horgan Livestock Ltd; O'Mahony v Horgan*,[1] the need to prove that a defendant's intention in disposing of his assets is to evade his obligations to the plaintiff and to frustrate the future judgment of the court has become the paramount factor in whether a court will exercise its discretion to grant a Mareva injunction. As a result of that decision, in Ireland, one of the most important proofs[2] for a Mareva injunction is that there is evidence of a risk that a defendant will remove his assets from the jurisdiction or otherwise dispose of his assets with the intention of evading his obligation to the plaintiff and to frustrate the anticipated order of the court. Indeed, it can be said that a defendant's nefarious intention has become the *raison d'être* of the Mareva jurisdiction in Ireland.

[6.02] This chapter commences by tracing the evolution of the Mareva jurisdiction from being a remedy primarily designed to prevent foreign defendants from removing their assets out of the jurisdiction to a remedy which now can prevent a domestic defendant from disposing of his assets within the jurisdiction. Next will be considered the requirement that a Mareva plaintiff must establish a likelihood of a risk that a defendant's assets will be removed from the jurisdiction, or otherwise disposed of within the jurisdiction, with the intention of evading his obligation to the plaintiff and to frustrate the anticipated order of the court. The following issues are addressed in this chapter:

1. The Original Mischief: *Ex Juris* Removal of Assets by Foreigners;

2. Removal of Assets from the Jurisdiction by Domestic Defendants;

3. Restraining the Disposal of Assets Within the Jurisdiction;

4. An Objective Test in the United Kingdom - The Focus on "Effect";

5. A Subjective Test in Ireland - The Focus on "Intention";

6. Establishing the "Requisite Intention".

[1.] [1995] 2 IR 411. See para **[6.18]** *infra*.

[2.] See Ch 8, *Applying for a Mareva Injunction*, para **[8.31]**.

The Original Mischief: *Ex Juris* Removal of Assets by Foreigners

[6.03] The removal of assets from the jurisdiction by a "foreign" defendant so as to make himself judgment-proof was the original mischief which the Mareva jurisdiction sought to prevent. This is clear from the early cases, such as *The Mareva*[3] itself. In the early applications for Mareva relief it so happened that the defendants tended to be foreign nationals or foreign corporations. As a result, the courts initially drew a distinction between foreign and domestic defendants.

[6.04] The distinction between foreign and domestic defendants was noted by Lord Hailsham in *The Siskina*,[4] the first House of Lords decision to consider, albeit peripherally, the Mareva injunction. There, Lord Hailsham said:

> "One cannot help contrasting the comparatively favourable position accorded in the Mareva cases to the plaintiff suing a foreign based defendant with assets in England to whom RSC Ord 11 can apply contrasted with that of a similar plaintiff with a claim against an English based defendant served in the ordinary way ... I believe the truth to be that sooner or later the courts or the legislature will have to choose between two alternatives. Either the position of a plaintiff making a claim against an English based defendant will have to be altered or the principle of the Mareva cases will have to be modified. In any event it is clear that Mareva injunctions cannot be allowed to flourish independently in the Arcadia of the commercial list without being applied in the High Court generally in all cases where plaintiffs and defendants are comparably placed."[5]

It was primarily because the early Mareva cases concerned foreign defendants that, on their facts, they were easily distinguished from the *Lister* principle, considered earlier.[6] The tendency of courts to allude to a defendant's foreigness when exercising the jurisdiction was probably more of an attempt to justify the fledgling jurisdiction than a principled objection to its extension to domestic defendants.

Removal of Assets from the Jurisdiction by Domestic Defendants

[6.05] As Lord Hailsham predicted in 1977, it was inevitable that attention would sooner or later focus on devious domestic defendants, who could remove their assets from the jurisdiction with impunity.[7] The case which most forcefully

---

3. *Mareva Compania Naviera SA v International Bulkcarriers SA* [1980] 1 All ER 213, [1975] 2 Lloyd's Rep 509; *Nippon Yusen Kaisha v Karageorgis* [1975] 3 All ER 282. See Ch 2, *The Jurisdiction to Grant Mareva Relief*, para **[2.08]** *et seq.*
4. *Owners of cargo lately laden on board the vessel Siskina v Distos Compania Naviera SA, The Siskina* [1977] 3 All ER 803.
5. *Ibid* at 829a-d.
6. See Ch 2, *The Jurisdiction to Grant Mareva Relief*, para **[2.04]** *et seq.*
7. *Chartered Bank v Daklouche* [1980] 1 All ER 205 was one of the first cases to mark this milestone. See Lord Denning, *The Due Process of Law*, (1980) Butterworths, p 147.

dispelled the distinction between foreign and domestic defendants was *Barclay-Johnson v Yuill*.[8] The facts there were that the plaintiff and the defendant jointly purchased, renovated and eventually sold a penthouse apartment. The resale realised a profit of £3,300. This sum was lodged into a bank account in the defendant's name. The plaintiff alleged that the defendant owed her £2,000. During negotiations the plaintiff discovered that the English defendant had sold his own apartment, had gone abroad and was cruising on an ocean-going yacht. The plaintiff was aware that, previously, the defendant had gone to live abroad when he had encountered financial difficulties. No doubt mindful of his past record the plaintiff feared that the defendant would transfer his assets abroad to defeat her claim. The plaintiff applied for a Mareva injunction, *inter alia*, to restrain the defendant from removing the proceeds of the resale out of the jurisdiction. An interim Mareva injunction was granted but on application for an extension, the defendant joined in issue and claimed that the court could not grant a Mareva injunction against a, so-called, domestic defendant.

[6.06] The task of dispelling the distinction between foreign and domestic defendants fell to Megarry V-C. He began by reviewing the two lines of authority: the *Lister* principle and the Mareva jurisdiction. Despite the defendant's nationality and domicile, he granted the injunction. Megarry V-C's dictum is worth quoting *in extenso*:

> "It seems to me that the heart and core of the Mareva injunction is the risk of the defendant removing his assets from the jurisdiction and so stultifying any judgment given by the courts in the action. If there is no real risk of this, such an injunction should be refused; if there is a real risk, then if the other requirements are satisfied, the injunction ought to be granted. If the assets are likely to remain in the jurisdiction, the plaintiff, like all others with claims against the defendant, must run the risk common to all, that the defendant may dissipate his assets, or consume them in discharging other liabilities, and so leave nothing with which to satisfy any judgment. On the other hand, if there is a real risk of the assets being removed from the jurisdiction, a Mareva injunction may prevent their removal. It is not enough for such an injunction merely to forbid the defendant to remove them from the jurisdiction, for otherwise he might transfer them to some collaborator who would then remove them; accordingly the injunction will restrain the defendant from disposing of them even within the jurisdiction ...
>
> If, then, the essence of the jurisdiction is the risk of the assets being removed from the jurisdiction, I cannot see why it should be confined to 'foreigners', in any sense of that term. True, expressions such as 'foreign defendants'... and 'foreign based defendants' ... appear in the cases, and for the most part the cases have concerned those who may fairly be called foreigners...Naturally the

---

8. [1980] 3 All ER 190.

risk of removal of assets from the jurisdiction will usually be greater or more obvious in the case of foreign-based defendants, and so the jurisdiction has grown up in relation to them. But I cannot see why this should make the requirement of foreignness a prerequisite of the jurisdiction."[9]

Whilst it may be more likely that foreign defendants would have fewer qualms that domestic defendants about making themselves judgment-proof, it would be naive to think that devious domestic defendants would not also be inclined to spirit their assets out of the jurisdiction (or secrete them within the jurisdiction) in circumstances where it seemed likely that judgment would be marked against them. It is, therefore, only proper that the court should have jurisdiction to prevent this abuse of its process, by directing its order to wherever that threat may come.

[6.07] In *Prince Abdul Rahman Bin Turki Al Sudairy v Abu-Taha*[10] it was again emphasised that it was merely a matter of probability that there was a greater likelihood that a foreign defendant would remove his assets from the jurisdiction as compared to a domestic defendant. This time the enlarged jurisdiction was sanctioned by the Court of Appeal. In this case the plaintiff prince negotiated with the defendants to buy an Aston Martin Lagonda motor car for £34,000. The plaintiff later sued for breach of this agreement and sought a Mareva injunction to restrain the defendant from moving out of the jurisdiction or otherwise disposing within the jurisdiction any of his assets, save insofar as they exceeded £34,000. Again the defendant was resident within the jurisdiction. Referring explicitly to the comments of Lord Hailsham in *The Siskina*, Lord Denning MR said:

> "The courts are now faced with the two alternatives. We have to make the choice. I have no doubt what our choice should be. We must not modify 'the principle of the Mareva cases'. It has proved of such great value to the Commercial Court that it must be retained intact. So we must 'alter the position of a plaintiff making a claim against an English based defendant'. We must do it by putting all defendants on the same footing, no matter whether they be foreign based or English based. The same principle applies to both."[11]

After quoting the dictum of Megarry V-C, quoted above, Lord Denning MR concluded that there was jurisdiction to make a Mareva injunction against a domestic defendant:

> "So I would hold that a Mareva injunction can be granted against a man even though he is based in this country if the circumstances are such that there is a danger of his absconding, or a danger of the assets being removed out of the

---

9.   *Ibid* at 194a-j.
10. [1980] 3 All ER 409.
11. *Ibid* at 411f-g.

jurisdiction or disposed of within the jurisdiction, or otherwise dealt with so that there is a danger that the plaintiff, if he gets judgment, will not be able to get it satisfied."[12]

As stated by Lord Denning MR in the foregoing passage, the circumstances of each case are crucial. The Mareva injunction is a remedy available in all circumstances where an abuse of the courts' process is likely. The status of a defendant as foreign or domestic is irrelevant.

[6.08] The extension of the Mareva jurisdiction from foreign to domestic defendants was followed in Ireland by McWilliam J in *Fleming v Ranks (Ireland) Ltd*[13] who expressly adopted the reasoning of Megarry V-C in *Barclay-Johnson*. McWilliam J said:

"I am satisfied that there is a jurisdiction to grant such an injunction and that the cases in which it may be granted are not confined to cases in which a defendant is resident outside the State."[14]

Although one eminent jurist has urged caution,[15] it is submitted that it is proper and correct for a court to exercise the Mareva jurisdiction in such circumstances. Indeed, the recent emphasis upon defendants' intentions and in particular upon the necessity to establish a likelihood that assets will be disposed of with a nefarious intent, seen in *Re John Horgan Livestock Ltd*,[16] is thought to be more than sufficient protection for defendants.

Restraining the Disposal of Assets Within the Jurisdiction

[6.09] Originally, the Mareva injunction was directed at the removal of assets out of the jurisdiction but, as already seen, the jurisdiction has been enlarged with the passage of time. At first the disposal to "collaborators" alone was enjoined, but gradually the jurisdiction was claimed to prevent the disposal or dissipation of assets within the jurisdiction where this was done with the intention of rendering a prospective judgment worthless.

[6.10] The first revision was to extend the prohibition to the transfer of assets by the defendant to a "collaborator". In *Barclay-Johnson v Yuill*[17] Megarry V-C

---

12. At 412a.
13. [1983] ILRM 541.
14. At 546. Other countries in which the Mareva jurisdiction has been recognised have also accepted this extension (and the extension to prohibiting the disposal of assets within the jurisdiction, considered next at para **[6.09]**). See, for example, the early Australian cases of *Riley McKay Pty Ltd v McKay* [1982] 1 NSWLR 264 and *Australian Iron & Steel Pty Ltd v Buck* [1982] 2 NSWLR 889.
15. See Keane, *Equity and the Law of Trusts in the Republic of Ireland*, (1988) Butterworths para 15.41.
16. [1995] 2 IR 411. See para **[6.18]** *infra*.
17. [1980] 3 All ER 190.

recognised that the value of a Mareva injunction could be entirely nullified were a defendant to transfer his assets to a collaborator. In the course of his judgment he said:

> "... if there is a real risk of the assets being removed from the jurisdiction, a Mareva injunction will prevent their removal. It is not enough for such an injunction merely to forbid the defendant to remove them from the jurisdiction, for otherwise he might transfer them to some collaborator who would then remove them: accordingly the injunction will restrain the defendant from disposing of them even within the jurisdiction."[18]

This was the first extension to the scope of the Mareva injunction. The fullness of time brought further extension.

[6.11] It would seem that Lord Denning MR always considered that the Mareva injunction had a wider scope than that which it initially appeared to have. In *Prince Abdul Rahman Bin Turki Al Sudairy v Abu-Taha*[19] he said:

> "... I would hold that a Mareva injunction can be granted against a man even though he is based in this country if the circumstances are such that there is a danger of his absconding, or a danger of the assets being removed out of the jurisdiction or disposed of within the jurisdiction, or otherwise dealt with so that there is a danger that the plaintiff, if he gets judgment, will not be able to get it satisfied."[20]

It has long been accepted in Ireland that there is jurisdiction to grant a Mareva injunction to restrain a defendant from disposing of his assets within the State; in no case has it been suggested that Mareva relief is confined to cases where there is a risk of assets being removed from the State. In *Powerscourt Estates v Gallagher & Gallagher*[21] the plaintiff sued the defendants on foot of personal guarantees entered into by them in support of a loan made by the plaintiff to a borrower-company. After the borrower-company failed to repay the sums owed, the plaintiff then called upon the defendants to pay the outstanding sums which were in excess of £588,000. The plaintiff obtained an interim Mareva injunction and in the instant proceedings sought an interlocutory Mareva injunction. The plaintiff claimed that there were substantial grounds for believing that the defendants were likely to dispose of their personal assets, by creating a charge over them, so as to frustrate the plaintiff's claim. The defendants opposed the interlocutory application and claimed that a Mareva injunction could only issue where a defendant was a foreign national or had a foreign domicile and where he was likely to take his property out of the jurisdiction. On the question of whether

18. *Ibid* at 194e-f.
19. [1980] 3 All ER 409.
20. At 412a.
21. [1984] ILRM 123.

a Mareva injunction could be granted otherwise than in circumstances where a defendant was about to remove his assets from the jurisdiction, McWilliam J said:

> "The progress of the Mareva line of cases seems to lead to the conclusion that the injunction may be granted where it appears to the court that dispositions are likely to be made for the purpose of preventing a plaintiff from recovering the amount of his award, as distinct from conducting the normal business or personal affairs of the defendant."[22]

[6.12] Mareva injunctions are typically couched in terms similar to the following:

> **"IT IS ORDERED THAT**
>
> The defendant, his servants or agents or any person acting on behalf of them and any person having knowledge of the making of this Order or otherwise be restrained until [after the ____ day of _____ 199__][23] [or further order] from removing from the State[24] or in any way disposing of, reducing, transferring, charging, diminishing the value thereof, or otherwise dealing with all or any of his assets which are in the State[25] save in so far as the value of said assets shall exceed the sum or value of IR£___."[26]

It is difficult to know exactly (for it is nowhere recorded) how early in the development of the Mareva injunction in Ireland the Irish courts accepted that there was jurisdiction to restrain a defendant from disposing of his assets within the jurisdiction, as distinct from removing them from the jurisdiction.

An Objective Test in the United Kingdom - The Focus on "Effect"

[6.13] In the United Kingdom, and some other jurisdictions which have accepted the Mareva jurisdiction, the authorities have tended to suggest that the motives of the defendant in disposing of assets or removing them from the jurisdiction are irrelevant. This was certainly the opinion of Kerr LJ in *The Niedersachsen*[27] who rejected the contention that a defendant must possess a nefarious intention. In that case Kerr LJ said:

---

22. At 126.
23. This is appropriate in the case of an *ex parte* interim order; in the case of an interlocutory order - which will invariably be *inter partes* - alternative wording might be "... until judgment in the substantive cause of action between the Plaintiff and the Defendant ...".
24. Or, "Ireland" or "the jurisdiction of this court".
25. A "general" freezing order would stop after "... State"; as considered in Ch 9, *The Mareva Order and Its Effects*, para **[9.08]** by far the most common and appropriate restriction is the inclusion of a "maximum sum" order.
26. See further Appendix 1.
27. *Ninemia Maritime Corp v Trave Schiffahrtgesellschaft mbh & Co KG* [1984] 1 All ER 398 at 419f-h.

"Since the origin of this jurisdiction, the authorities clearly show that in order to obtain a Mareva injunction, a plaintiff must show that he would suffer some prejudice as a result of ... a 'dissipation of assets' in the event of the injunction being refused. The issue is as to the test which the plaintiff must satisfy. We were told on this appeal that there is a difference of judicial opinion whether the test is ... 'that the defendant will deal with his assets with the object, and not just with the effect, of putting them out of the plaintiff's reach'. To some extent this difference appears to have arisen from a phrase in an obiter passage in my judgment in *Z Ltd v A* [1982] 1 All ER 566 at 572, [1982] QB 558 at 585 that a defendant may 'take steps designed to ensure that these [assets] are no longer available or traceable when judgment is given ...'. Thus we were referred to an unreported judgment of Bingham J in *Home Insurance Co v Administratia Asicurarilor de Stat* (29 July 1983) in which these words were interpreted "as a requirement that one must show nefarious intent". However, this interpretation of the emphasised words goes much further than the tenor of the authorities to which we refer below.[28] We also consider that the distinction mentioned by the judge in the present case, which he did not in fact find it necessary to resolve, between 'object' and 'effect', is not the right basis for providing the appropriate test. In our view the test is whether, on the assumption that the plaintiff has shown at least 'a good arguable case', the court concludes, on the whole of the evidence then before it, that the refusal of a Mareva injunction would involve a real risk that a judgment or award in favour of the plaintiff would remain unsatisfied."

This view is based on objective criteria and has no regard to a defendant's intentions or purposes; all that is important is the objective effect of a defendant's actions. Such is the diversity[29] of opinion on this point in the United Kingdom that one cannot say with complete certainty that Kerr LJ's dictum in *The Niedersachsen* is the preferred view of the English judiciary.[30] So, for example, in *Polly Peck International plc v Nadir (No 2)*[31] Lord Donaldson MR set out five principles which underlie the Mareva jurisdiction, the first two being:

[28.] *Establissement Esefka International Anstalt v Central Bank of Nigeria* [1979] 1 Lloyd's Rep 445 at 448; *Third Chandris Shipping Corp v Unimarine SA, The Pythia, The Angelic Wings, The Genie* [1979] 2 All ER 972 at 985 and 987; *Montecchi v Shimco (UK) Ltd* [1979] 1 WLR 1180 at 1183; *Barclay-Johnson v Yuill* [1980] 3 All ER 190 at 195; *Prince Abdul Rahman Bin Turki Al Sudairy v Abu-Taha* [1980] 3 All ER 409 at 412.

[29.] See Capper, *Mareva Injunctions*, (1988) Sweet & Maxwell at p 46 where the author cites authorities for the two streams of judicial opinion on the question of whether or not the plaintiff has to show that the disposal of assets is intended to frustrate judgment.

[30.] In *Ashtiani v Kashi* [1986] 2 All ER 970 Dillon LJ said (at 978g-h) that: "In the present case, however, it is *a fortiori* not appropriate to grant leave to freeze or seize the defendant's assets overseas, as on the facts of this case ... it is quite wrong to draw the inference that the removal of assets from the jurisdiction by the defendant was anything to do with avoiding this or any other claim. See Capper, 'Mareva Injunctions: A Distinctively Irish Doctrine?', (1995) 17 DULJ (ns) 110 at 118.

[31.] [1992] 4 All ER 769.

"(1) So far as it lies in their power, the courts will not permit the course of justice to be frustrated by a defendant taking action, *the purpose of which* is to render nugatory or less effective any judgment or order which the plaintiff may thereafter obtain. (2) It is not the purpose of a Mareva injunction to prevent a defendant acting as he would have acted in the absence of a claim against him. Whilst a defendant who is a natural person can and should be enjoined from indulging in a spending spree undertaken *with the intention of dissipating or reducing his assets before the day of judgment*, he cannot be required to reduce his standard of living with a view to putting by sums to satisfy a judgment which may or may not be given in the future. Equally no defendant, whether a natural or a juridical person, can be enjoined in terms which will prevent him from carrying on his business in the ordinary way or from meeting his debts or other obligations as they become due prior to judgment being given in the action."[32]

It is thought that the foregoing references to a defendant's "purpose", "intention" and even to "dissipating"[33] cannot be squared with the passage from Kerr LJ's judgment last quoted and for this reason some doubt must exist as to whether, in the United Kingdom, it is sufficient that the effect of a defendant's conduct is to frustrate future judgment.

[6.14] The Federal Court of Australia has recently addressed the effect/intent debate in *Hayden v Teplitzky*[34] and has come down on the side of effect being sufficient. There, Lindgren J posed the following question and made the following comments on the alternatives:

"What is the ground of the court's jurisdiction to grant Mareva relief? In particular, is it a threatened dissipation of assets as an objective fact, or is it a subjective purpose, objective or aim of the defendant to render irrecoverable any judgment which the plaintiff may obtain? If the former reflects the position, payment of a defendant's only funds to discharge a debt will give jurisdiction, albeit the creditor is unrelated to the defendant, the genuineness of the debt is unassailable, and the proposed payment would have been made in the exercise of the discretion whether to grant relief. The defendant's purpose would, however, be relevant to the exercise of the discretion whether to grant relief. If, on the other hand, purpose is an essential element of the ground of jurisdiction, it is difficult to conceive of circumstances in which Mareva relief would be withheld in the exercise of discretion."[35]

---

[32] At 785g-h. Italics added.

[33] "Dissipating" is not a neutral word to describe the action of expending money or assets. Its literal meaning is to "squander" or "fritter away" and where used, implies that the person engaged in dissipating is disposing of their assets in a less than frugal manner.

[34] [1997] 230 FCA (9 April 1997) (Lindgren J).

[35] At p 22 of the transcript.

Lindgren J reviewed the Australian authorities in *Reily McKay Pty Ltd v McKay*,[36] *Jackson v Sterling Industries Ltd*[37] and *Patterson v BTR Engineering (Aust) Ltd*[38] which he found equivocal. He found that the question in issue was directly addressed in Australia in *Glenwood Management Group Pty Ltd v Mayo*,[39] *Beach Petroleum NL v Johnson*,[40] and *Northcorp Ltd v Allman Properties (Australia)*[41] which clearly came down in favour of the applicable test being objective, ie a Mareva injunction can be granted where there is evidence that the effect of a defendant's conduct is such as to frustrate judgment. He concluded:

> "The ground of jurisdiction in the present case is, therefore, whether [the defendant] intends to do acts which will have the effect of rendering a judgment for damages obtained against it by the applicants in the present proceedings wholly or partly ineffective".[42]

If one follows the "effect" test through to its logical conclusion absurdity and injustice can result. So, for example, in *Reches Pty Ltd v Tadiran Ltd*,[43] the question posed was:

---

36. [1982] 1 NSWLR 264. There the reference to the Mareva jurisdiction being "directed to dispositions ... which are intended to frustrate, *or have the necessary effect of frustrating*, the plaintiff in his attempt to seek through the court a remedy ..." (italics added) was equivocal.

37. (1987) 162 CLR 612. There too Deane J's comment (at 625) that the purpose of the Mareva injunction was "... to prevent a defendant from disposing of his actual assets ... *so as to* frustrate the process of the court by depriving the plaintiff of the fruits of any judgment ..." was equivocal. (Italics added). As Lindgren J said in *Hayden* (p 24 of the transcript) "The words "so as to" in these passages are equivocal: they may refer to the purpose or the effect of frustration". He went on to note that the other two judgments in that case do not favour one view or the other.

38. (1989) 18 NSWLR 319. Lindgren J found that the judgment of Gleeson CJ was "not inconsistent with an insistence upon the presence of a purpose of defeating the plaintiff" (at p 24 of the transcript).

39. [1991] 2 VR 49. There, Young CJ said: "... in the only case, so far as I am aware, where the question has been asked, does the plaintiff have to show that the disposal of assets is intended to frustrate a judgment, the answer given was "No". The court is concerned with the effect rather than purpose: see *The Niedersachsen* [1983] 1 WLR 1421".

40. (1992) 9 ACSR 404. There, von Doussa J held (at 405) that "... it is not necessary for the applicants to show an active intent on the part of the respondent to defeat the applicants from recovering the judgment".

41. [1994] 2 Qd Rep 405. There the Queensland Court of Appeal held that a plaintiff seeking Mareva relief does not have "to show that the purpose of the defendant's disposition, occurring or apprehended, is to prevent recovery of the amount of any judgment" (at 407).

42. At p 25 of the transcript. Italics added. *Cf LED Builders Pty Ltd v Eagle Homes Pty Ltd* [1997] 826 FCA (22 August 1997) (minority concurring judgment of Tamberlin J). After finding that the defendant's assets were at risk, Tamberlin J reached his decision to grant Mareva relief on evidence that the defendants "have deliberately engaged in a scheme calculated to remove assets from the reach of the" plaintiff (at p 13 of the transcript).

43. [1998] 666 FCA (11 June 1998).

"... whether it is appropriate to restrain a respondent which is a foreign corporation from removing or depleting its sole asset within Australia, in circumstances where: (a) the removal or depletion is in the ordinary course of business, (b) the respondent is a major and profitable corporation with very substantial assets, particularly current assets, (c) there is nothing to suggest that the respondent is likely to "default": that is, to decline to pay a judgment debt and to resist, other than by grounds properly available to it under the law, enforcement of a judgment against it, and (d) the respondent resides, and principally carries on its business, in a jurisdiction where enforcement is possible under a reciprocal regime for the registration of judgments."[44]

In these circumstances it is hardly surprising that (notwithstanding the decisions just referred to) Lehane J found a way to refuse the Mareva injunction sought against the defendant-Israeli company. Lehane J accepted that any judgment obtained by the plaintiff would be more difficult to satisfy if the defendant had expatriated its only Australian asset (a chose in action). Lehane J found, however, that there was no serious risk that the court's process was likely to be frustrated; the defendant was a large and prosperous corporation, incorporated in a country which had reciprocal arrangements with Australia for the enforcement of judgments; the defendant had ample means readily available to satisfy any judgment; and the defendant bore none of the hallmarks of a likely defaulter. It would seem that Australia's reciprocal judgment-enforcement arrangements with Israel was used as an excuse to save the "effect" test from perpetrating a serious injustice.

[6.15] There are a number of difficulties, both theoretical and practical, associated with a test which is only concerned with the effect of a defendant's actions and which disregards a defendant's intentions in removing or disposing of his assets. First, to ignore a defendant's intention when exercising such a potentially draconian jurisdiction cannot be right in principle; it is thought that a defendant's intentions in disposing of his assets is the central issue in exercising the Mareva jurisdiction. Secondly, it is well established that a Mareva injunction confers on a plaintiff no extra rights or greater priority to a defendant's assets than he would otherwise have;[45] a Mareva plaintiff can neither seek specific assets to settle his personal claim, nor, can he prevent a defendant from paying other creditors or expending sums on living expenses and, accordingly, a Mareva defendant's intention in disposing of assets is again seen to be central to the question as to whether it is appropriate to grant a Mareva injunction. Thirdly, the courts have consistently recognised the importance of a defendant's intentions in dealing with his assets by inserting into Mareva orders the living

---

[44.] At p 5 of the transcript of the judgment.
[45.] See Ch 9, *The Mareva Order and Its Effects*, at para **[9.39]** *et seq.*

expenses, legal expenses, and business expenses provisos;[46] such provisos expressly permit the payment of certain expenses from a defendant's assets where such expenditure is incurred, *ipso facto*, without a nefarious intention.

It is therefore submitted that even in jurisdictions where it is sufficient to show that the effect of a defendant's conduct is to frustrate a future judgment, the reality is that *bona fide* dispositions are permitted, whether by the order itself in the form of provisos to the injunction or upon an application for variation being made.[47] The real difference between the approach in the United Kingdom and the approach taken by the Irish courts, considered next, is that in the United Kingdom Mareva relief will be granted without the need to demonstrate a "nefarious intention" on the part of a defendant but there must be evidence that there is some risk that assets will be disposed of or removed from the jurisdiction.[48] In both jurisdictions, however, defendants are not prevented from making lawful *bona fide* disbursements from their assets.

A Subjective Test in Ireland - The Focus on "Intention"

[6.16] In Ireland it is not sufficient that an applicant for a Mareva injunction merely prove that there exists a risk that a defendant's assets are likely to be removed from, or dissipated within, the jurisdiction. The judgments of the Irish High Court have made it clear that an applicant for a Mareva injunction must also establish a likelihood that a defendant will remove his assets from, or dissipate his assets within, the jurisdiction with the intention of evading his obligations to the plaintiff and frustrating any future order of the court.[49] Put another way, in removing or disposing of his assets, a defendant must have in mind the object, purpose or intent to frustrate judgment: he must have a "nefarious intention".

[6.17] Where a defendant removes his assets from the jurisdiction or otherwise disposes of his assets within the jurisdiction and thereby leaves himself with insufficient assets to satisfy a future judgment, the result will be that the plaintiff's judgment will go unsatisfied and thus be frustrated. Here, we closely examine the circumstances which led to the Supreme Court's finding in *Re John Horgan Livestock Ltd* that a plaintiff must show that there is a likelihood that a defendant will dispose of his assets with a nefarious intention. To this end the following points are considered:

    (a) The Supreme Court decision in *Re John Horgan Livestock Ltd*;

---

46. *Ibid*, at para **[9.12]** *et seq.*
47. As to variation, see Ch 9, *The Mareva Order and its Effects*, para **[9.31]** *et seq.*
48. This may include evidence of a "nefarious intent", but may be shown otherwise.
49. See Courtney, 'Mareva Injunctions: Proving an Intention to Frustrate Judgment', (1996) CLP 3.

(b) Restatement or clarification of the law in Ireland?;

(c) Early Irish decisions requiring proof of defendants' intentions;

(d) Has Ireland adopted a singular stance?

(a) The Supreme Court decision in **Re John Horgan Livestock Ltd**

[6.18] Ever since Irish lawyers had the benefit of the first written decisions of the Irish High Court on the Mareva jurisdiction it has been apparent that the risk of removal or dissipation of assets by a defendant must be accompanied by the intention to frustrate the enforcement of the plaintiff's judgment, ie a defendant must intend to make himself "judgment-proof".[50] For this reason the Supreme Court's decision in *Re John Horgan Livestock Ltd; O'Mahony v Horgan*[51] should have come as no major surprise to Irish lawyers. The facts in this case were that the Mareva applicant was the official liquidator of John Horgan Livestock Ltd and the defendants were its directors. The company in question, which was in the business of importing, exporting and dealing in livestock, was put into official liquidation on the petition of the Revenue Commissioners. The statement of affairs indicated an estimated deficiency of £11.653 million in the company's assets. Subsequently, the liquidator instituted proceedings against the defendants for: misfeasance (under s 298(2) of the Companies Act 1963 ("the 1963 Act")); a declaration pursuant to s 204 of the Companies Act 1990 ("the 1990 Act") that the defendants were in breach of s 202(10) of the 1990 Act and should be made personally liable for certain debts and other liabilities of the company; and a declaration pursuant to s 297 or 297A of the 1963 Act[52] that the respondents should be made personally liable for the company's debts. Upon learning of the existence of an insurance policy payable to the second defendant director, the liquidator sought an injunction to restrain him from collecting or receiving the sum of £71,000 with interest which represented the proceeds of an insurance policy, or, an injunction to restrain him from disposing of or dissipating or charging the said proceeds of the insurance policy.

[6.19] Murphy J granted the official liquidator an interlocutory Mareva injunction, the effect of which was to restrain the second named defendant from disposing of, or dissipating, or charging the sum of £71,000 with interest being the proceeds of the insurance policy. The judgment of Murphy J was *ex tempore*, but in the Supreme Court Hamilton CJ said that counsel's notes had

---

[50.] For the early Irish Mareva decisions which required plaintiffs to prove that defendants intended to frustrate a future order of the court, see para **[6.24]** *et seq, infra*; as early as 1985 the requirement that "intent" be proved in Ireland was noted by Capper, *op cit*, at p 46

[51.] [1995] 2 IR 411.

[52.] As inserted by s 138 of the 1990 Act.

been accepted by Murphy J as a proper transcript of his judgment. In the course of his judgment Murphy J had said:

> "[The liquidator], in his affidavit, avers to a significant list of wrongdoings in particular the failure to keep proper or adequate records. On the financial side, he states that he estimates the deficiency at £11.6 million and he expresses the view that loans to directors amount to £2.4 million and after certain payments the balance due on foot of these loans is £1.9 million. There are a number of other matters queried. But for all of the detail in this affidavit, the crucial topic is dealt with in Paragraph 47 where [the Liquidator] avers as follows: 'I am naturally concerned having regard to the manner in which the affairs of the company were conducted to ensure that the said sum of £71,000 should be available to meet any decree which may be made in favour of the company in liquidation against the second named respondent and apprehensive that in the absence of such order the said sums will not be available'."[53]

As to the criteria which a Mareva plaintiff must prove, Murphy J set out the five points listed by Lord Denning MR in *Third Chandris Shipping Corporation v Unimarine SA*[54] and apparently accepted that the first three points had been met by the plaintiff-liquidator, saying:

> "The real issue is whether the plaintiff has given any grounds for believing that there is any risk of dissipation. All the plaintiff has said is that he is apprehensive in this regard. That is a far cry undoubtedly from evidence of conscious abuse."[55]

The learned trial judge had concluded:

> "I have stressed the infirmities in the plaintiff's application. Counsel for the [defendant] has analysed still further the weaknesses and contradictions but without providing any affidavit in reply. It seems to be that it must be recognised that the [defendant], having been given notice and having been afforded an opportunity to adjourn the matter declined an invitation to put in such an affidavit. The [defendants] resist the applications on the basis of their submission. On the face of it, there is reason for considerable concern as to the manner in which the [defendants] have carried on the business of the company. One may criticise the lack of detail given by [the liquidator] in relation to the allegation. His computation of the directors' indebtedness to the company may be criticised. But that criticism would be entertained more readily if there was a denial on affidavit. No direct evidence is given that monies would be dissipated but in the context of the sums involved and the parties' obligations to the banks, the concern of the official liquidator has not been shown to be displaced.

[53.] High Court, unrep, 28 June 1993, *ex tempore* judgment of Murphy J, as reproduced in part in the judgment of the Chief Justice in the Supreme Court at [1995] 2 IR 411 at 415, 416.

[54.] See Ch 8, *Applying for a Mareva Injunction*, para **[8.30]**.

[55.] [1995] 2 IR 411 at 416.

On the overall complexities of the matter, the probabilities that monies will cease to be retained is likely. It seems to be that the injunction should be granted in the specific circumstances of the case."[56]

It was against this finding of the High Court that the defendant appealed. The grounds of appeal were threefold but, for present purposes, only one ground of appeal is relevant: that the trial judge had erred in law in failing to have sufficient regard to the applicable test, and in particular to the failure to give grounds supported by evidence for believing that there was a risk of the assets being removed from the State or otherwise dissipated with a view to avoiding any future payment to the liquidator.

[6.20] In the Supreme Court two judgments were delivered, the leading one by Hamilton CJ and a short concurring judgment by O'Flaherty J. The Chief Justice's judgment began by reviewing the facts of the case, the High Court's findings and the grounds of appeal. He commenced his review of the Mareva jurisdiction by reviewing the principles underlying the grant of Mareva injunctions. His starting point was "the *Lister* principle"[57] which he described in the following terms:

"The common law, traditionally, expressed the principle that the plaintiff is not entitled to require from the defendant, in advance of judgment security to guarantee satisfaction of a judgment that the plaintiff may eventually obtain."[58]

It must, of course, be remembered that modern Mareva injunctions neither require defendants to give security nor, as was sought in *Lister & Co v Stubbs*, do they direct that money be paid into court.[59] Hamilton CJ then noted that this principle was altered by the Court of Appeal's findings in *Nippon Yusen Kaisha* and *The Mareva* itself, both of which have been referred to earlier. Defining the Mareva injunction, Hamilton CJ said:

"Injunctions of this type became known as Mareva injunctions. A Mareva injunction is an *in personam* order, restraining the defendant from dealing with assets in which the plaintiff claims no right whatsoever. A Mareva order does not give the plaintiff any precedence over other creditors with respect to the frozen assets."[60]

Acknowledging the "draconian nature" of such orders, Hamilton CJ noted with approval the five criteria for the grant of a Mareva injunction which had been

---

[56.] [1995] 2 IR 411 at 416, 417.

[57.] *Lister v Stubbs* (1890) 45 Ch D 1. See further, Ch 2, *The Jurisdiction to Grant Mareva Relief*, para **[2.04]**.

[58.] [1995] 2 IR 411 at 417.

[59.] See Ch 2, *The Jurisdiction to Grant Mareva Relief*, para **[2.05]**. See also, Ch 9, *The Mareva Order and Its Effects*, at para **[9.39]** *et seq.*

[60.] At 418.

laid down by Lord Denning in *Third Chandris Shipping Corporation v Unimarine SA*[61] and that these had been set out by Murphy J in the High Court.[62] After citing with apparent approval a passage in *Z Ltd v AZ*[63] Hamilton CJ said:

> "Consequently, a Mareva injunction will only be granted if there is a combination of two circumstances established by the plaintiff ie (i) that he has an arguable case that he will succeed in the action and (ii) the anticipated disposal of a defendant's assets is for the purpose of preventing a plaintiff from recovering damages and not merely for the purpose of carrying on a business or discharging lawful debts."[64]

In this passage the Chief Justice focused upon the need for a plaintiff to show that the risk of removal of assets from the State, or dissipation within, by the respondent must be with a view to evading his obligation to the plaintiff and to frustrate the anticipated order of the court. After reviewing the decision of McWilliam J in *Fleming v Ranks (Ireland) Ltd*,[65] he said:

> "Consequently, the cases establish that there must be an intention on the part of the defendant to dispose of his assets with a view to evading his obligation to the plaintiff and to frustrate the anticipated order of the court. It is not sufficient to establish that the assets are likely to be dissipated in the ordinary course of business or in the payment of lawful debts."[66]

Hamilton CJ opted for a subjective test where the focus is firmly upon a defendant's intentions in dealing with his assets.

[6.21] The Supreme Court reversed the decision of the High Court and found that the plaintiff was not, on the evidence, entitled to Mareva relief. Hamilton CJ held that the test had not been satisfied because the liquidator had not "adduced evidence to show, or to entitle the learned trial judge to infer, that the respondent is likely to dissipate the asset ... with the intention of evading his obligation (if any) to the liquidator". Referring to the "apprehension" cited by the liquidator in his affidavit, Hamilton CJ found that the liquidator had not stated or alleged that

---

[61.] [1979] QB 645.

[62.] [1995] 2 IR 411 at 416.

[63.] [1982] 1 QB 558 where, at 585, Kerr LJ said: "It follows that in my view Mareva injunctions should be granted, but granted only, when it appears to the court that there is a combination of two circumstances. First, when it appears likely that the plaintiff will recover judgment against the defendant for a certain or approximate sum. Secondly, when there are also reasons to believe that the defendant has assets within the jurisdiction, to meet the judgment in whole or in part, but may well take steps designed to ensure that these are no longer available or traceable when judgment is given against him."

[64.] [1995] 2 IR 411 at 418. As to (i), that a plaintiff has an "arguable case", see Ch 5, *A Good Arguable Case*.

[65.] [1983] ILRM 541. See para **[6.24]** *infra*.

[66.] [1995] 2 IR 411 at 419.

the respondent would dissipate the asset with the intention of frustrating any order of the court that may be made. Again, he said:

> "The learned trial judge does not appear to have considered the question whether the apprehended dissipation of the asset was for the purpose of evading any decree that might be made in the proceedings.
>
> Before being entitled to the relief sought by him, the liquidator must establish that there was a likelihood that the assets would be dissipated with the intention that they would not be available to meet any decree or part of a decree ultimately made against the [defendant] in the proceedings.
>
> In my view, no such intention was established in this case. The entitlement of the [defendant] to the proceeds of the policy of insurance ... arose because of a fire on the [defendant's] property which destroyed a shed thereon.
>
> While the use of such proceeds to replace the shed in the ordinary course of his business as a farmer or to pay his lawful debts would mean that such asset would not be available to meet any decree which the liquidator might obtain against the [defendant], that fact does not entitle the liquidator to the injunction sought. He must further establish that such utilisation of the asset was made with the intention of evading payment to the liquidator.
>
> As no such intention was established in this case, the [defendant's] appeal in this case must be allowed on this ground."[67]

Consequently, where a plaintiff's affidavit does not adduce any evidence as to the likelihood of a defendant removing or disposing of his assets with a nefarious intention, a Mareva injunction will not be granted by an Irish court. As shall be considered below,[68] however, in the absence of any direct evidence as to a defendant's intentions, it may be possible to adduce evidence from which the "requisite intention" may be inferred.

(b) Restatement or clarification of the law in Ireland?[69]

[6.22] The Supreme Court's decision in *Re John Horgan Livestock Ltd* is a most significant development in Irish legal practice and procedure. The question which must be asked however, is whether the decision marks a radical departure in Irish jurisprudence? Is this requirement, to establish that there is a likelihood that a defendant will dispose of his assets with the intention that they will not be available to meet any court order a new requirement? In short, is the decision in *Re John Horgan Livestock Ltd* a restatement of the Irish law on Mareva injunctions? It is thought that the decision is not a "restatement"; that it may be more accurate to consider it as a "clarification" and a firm reminder that a

---

[67.] [1995] 2 IR 411 at 420, 421.

[68.] See para **[6.29]** *infra*.

[69.] See generally Courtney, 'Mareva Injunctions: Proving an Intention to Frustrate Judgment', (1996) CLP 3.

jurisdiction which has the potential to cause great injustice must be exercised sparingly. The reasons for saying this are three-fold. In the first place it represents little more than a greater emphasis on an existing evidential requirement. In the second place, in previous applications to the High Court where a defendant's intentions were not expressly referred to, the evidence for such can often be seen in the evidence tendered for proving the risk of removal or dissipation of assets, both proofs being intermingled. In the third place, the requirement that a Mareva plaintiff adduce evidence that a defendant will dispose of his assets with a nefarious intention is merely the flip-side of the existing practice which was to permit *bona fide* dispositions of assets after a Mareva injunction had been granted ie by granting a Mareva injunction but making it expressly subject to living, legal and ordinary business expenses provisos.[70]

[6.23] It has been suggested by one commentator that the Irish courts have not "been ploughing their own furrow"[71] and that:

> "It is also unlikely that an applicant for a Mareva injunction has to establish any degree of likelihood that the defendant intends to defeat judgment by the disposal of assets as opposed to disposing of them for no good reason with the likely result that any judgment or award made against him will go unsatisfied. This is the kind of abuse the Mareva injunction is directed against and is probably what Irish courts mean by the requirement that the defendant intends to defeat judgment, an intention which may be inferred from the risk that assets will be disposed of for no good reason."

To the extent that this passage plays down the importance of a defendant's objectives, intentions and purpose in removing or disposing of his assets and suggests it is sufficient that a Mareva plaintiff shows that a defendant is intent upon disposing of his assets "for no good reason", it is thought to be wrong. The Supreme Court's decision in *Re John Horgan Livestock Ltd* clearly and unequivocally requires a plaintiff to satisfy the court that a defendant is likely to dispose of his assets with a view to evading his obligation to a plaintiff and to frustrate the anticipated order of the court. There must be actual evidence of the existence of a nefarious intention;[72] the absence of good intentions is not sufficient.[73]

[70.] See Ch 9, *The Mareva Injunction and Its Effects*, para **[9.12]** *et seq.*

[71.] Capper, 'Mareva Injunctions: A Distinctively Irish Doctrine?' (1995) 17 DULJ (ns) 110 at 119.

[72.] Evidence of a nefarious intention may be direct or inferred: see para **[6.29]** *et seq, infra.*

[73.] The requirement that there be evidence before the court to establish the requisite nefarious intention was restated by McCracken J in *Production Association Minsk Tractor Works v Saenko*, High Court, unrep, 25 February 1998 (McCracken J). See para **[6.47]** *infra.*

(c) Early Irish decisions requiring proof of defendants' intentions

[6.24] In *Fleming v Ranks (Ireland) Ltd*[74] the ITGWU and the defendant entered into an agreement regarding details of compensation for various categories of employees of the defendant-company. When the defendant made redundancy proposals that were unacceptable to the ITGWU, the agreement was referred to the Labour Court. The Labour Court made recommendations which were unacceptable to the defendant. Ultimately, the ITGWU (through nominees) sought a Mareva injunction to restrain the defendant from disposing of, or dealing with, its assets so as to reduce their value below the sum of £84,000 so as to evade any obligation to the plaintiffs. McWilliam J held that although the plaintiffs had a good arguable case, he was:

> "... of opinion that, to justify such an injunction, the anticipated disposal of a defendant's assets must be for the purposes of preventing a plaintiff from recovering damages and not merely for the purpose of carrying on a business or discharging lawful debts".[75]

The Mareva injunction sought by the plaintiffs was, accordingly, refused by McWilliam J because of the absence of any intention on the part of the defendant to frustrate the plaintiffs in their recovery of any damages.

[6.25] Previously, in *Powerscourt Estates v Gallagher & Gallagher*[76] McWilliam J had also stressed the importance of showing that a defendant has a "nefarious intention". In that case the defendant directors of the Gallagher group of companies entered into a guarantee for the repayment of £500,000 plus interest which the plaintiff had loaned to a third party. Upon the third party's default the plaintiff had called upon the defendants to pay on foot of their guarantee. The defendants refused to discharge the sums due and owing and the plaintiff instituted proceedings. Having obtained interim Mareva relief, the plaintiff sought an interlocutory injunction to restrain the defendants from disposing of their assets inside or outside of the jurisdiction, or charging their assets so as to prefer certain creditors over the plaintiffs. In making the order sought, McWilliam J held that:

> "... the injunction may be granted where it appears to the court that dispositions are likely to be made for the purpose of preventing a plaintiff from recovering the amount of his award, as distinct from conducting the normal business or personal affairs of the defendant.
>
> In the present case, the reluctance of the defendants to disclose their assets and their dispositions and proposed dispositions of them combined with the fact

---

[74.] [1983] ILRM 541.
[75.] At 546.
[76.] [1984] ILRM 123.

their businesses are not personal but conducted by a group of companies, indicates that they are probably mainly interested to deprive the plaintiff of the opportunity of recovering."[77]

In this case the plaintiff was successful in obtaining the injunction, and, as in the *Ranks (Ireland)* case, the defendants' intentions were central to that outcome.

[6.26] An even clearer example of where the High Court insisted that the risk of removal of assets from the State or dissipation of assets be accompanied by the defendant's intention to frustrate the plaintiff's judgment is provided by *Moloney v Laurib Investments Ltd*.[78] In that case the infant plaintiff had suffered severe personal injuries, allegedly sustained "in the hours of darkness by falling through an unguarded opening in a floor of an unfinished building situate at Mountjoy Square"[79] which was owned by the defendant company. Pending the trial of the substantive issues the plaintiff sought a Mareva injunction to restrain the defendant from, *inter alia*, disposing of its only asset which was the building at Mountjoy Square and from reducing its assets within the State below £1 million. The defendant company had been formed to acquire the unfinished office block where the plaintiff was allegedly injured. One of the defendant's directors had advanced £280,000 to the defendant-company and another company which was owned by that director had advanced £300,000 to the defendant company to enable it to buy the building. No public liability insurance had been taken out in respect of the building. The defendant had bought the building with a view to either disposing of it at a profit or by letting it. The profitable disposal of the building was, however, dependant upon development being completed within the time limits prescribed by the Urban Renewal Act 1986. The defendant had entered into negotiations with potential partners with a view to such development. Lynch J, in the course of refusing to make the order sought, said:

"If the proposed scheme were brought to fruition it would involve the disposal of the defendant-company's only asset, namely the unfinished building, to a new entity in consideration of the work to be done and I assume the wiping out of the defendant company's debts so that thereafter the company would have neither assets nor debts. I am satisfied that these schemes were in contemplation ever before the defendant company was made aware of the plaintiff's accident and were not and are not designed to be implemented for the purpose of defeating the plaintiff's claim. They were and are designed to be implemented for the purpose of realising at last some profit from the investment in the unfinished building some fifteen and a half years' ago."[80]

---

77. At 126.
78. High Court, unrep, 20 July 1993 (Lynch J).
79. At p 1, 2 of the transcript.
80. At p 4, 5 of the transcript.

Although this was but one factor in Lynch J's reasoning in that case[81] it seems clear that the absence of any intention on the defendant's part deliberately to evade its obligations to the plaintiff or to frustrate a future order of the court was the most significant factor in the decision to refuse Mareva relief.

(d) Has Ireland adopted a singular stance?

[6.27] It is clear that there are at least two strains of the Mareva jurisdiction. The first is that seen in *The Niedersachsen*[82] where, all other things being equal, it is sufficient that the mere *effect* of a defendant's action in removing or disposing of his assets is to frustrate the future order of the court. This test does not require a Mareva plaintiff to show that a defendant *intends* or has the *objective* of deliberately frustrating the court's order and/or evading the plaintiff's claim. The second strain of Mareva relief is the Hibernian strain, as consistently dispensed by the Irish courts and conclusively defined by the Supreme Court in *Re John Horgan Livestock Ltd*.[83] Here, the very basis of the relief is to prevent a defendant from taking deliberate steps which are designed to evade his obligations to a plaintiff and to frustrate the anticipated order of the court. The test is unashamedly subjective: if a plaintiff cannot directly or indirectly establish[84] to the satisfaction of the court the likelihood of assets being disposed of or removed by a defendant with a nefarious intention, Mareva relief will not be forthcoming.[85]

[6.28] Although the Irish Supreme Court is not alone in considering the question, it is alone in its singular emphasis on a Mareva defendant's intentions in removing or disposing of his assets. A similar, though not as cherished, concern can be seen in *Aetna Financial Services Ltd v Feigelman*[86] where the Supreme Court of Canada (*per* Estey J) said after noting the Ontario Court of Appeal decision in *Chitel v Rothbart*:[87]

[81.] See Ch 4, *A Substantive Cause of Action*, para **[4.42]** *et seq.* See also *Brew v Crouch; Dionysus Pty Ltd* [1998] 6633 SASC (23 April 1998) where a similar finding was made in respect of a company which it was sought to have enjoined by a Mareva injunction.

[82.] [1984] 1 All ER 398. See para **[6.13]** *supra.*

[83.] See para **[6.18]** *supra.*

[84.] As to establishing the "requisite intention" see para **[6.29]** *et seq, infra.*

[85.] *Cf* Capper, 'Mareva Injunctions: A Distinctively Irish Doctrine?', (1995) 17 DULJ (ns) 110 at 119 where it is suggested that the Irish courts have *not* "been ploughing their own furrow". See para **[6.23]** *supra.*

[86.] (1985) 15 DLR (4th) 161.

[87.] (1982) 141 DLR (3d) 268. There MacKinnon ACJO said (at 289): "The applicant must persuade the court by his material that the defendant is removing or there is a real risk that he is about to remove his assets from the jurisdiction to avoid the possibility of a judgment, or that the defendant is otherwise dissipating or disposing of his assets, in a manner clearly distinct from his usual or ordinary course of business or living, so as to render the possibility of future tracing of the assets remote, if not impossible in fact or in law".

"In summary, the Ontario Court of Appeal recognised *Lister* as the general rule, and Mareva as a 'limited exception' to it, the exceptional injunction being available only where there is a real risk that the defendant will remove his assets from the jurisdiction or dissipate those assets 'to avoid the possibility of a judgment'...".[88]

Although it has been said that the emphasis in *Aetna* was that "dissipating assets otherwise than in the discharge of ordinary business and living expenses was the acid test",[89] the Ontario Court of Appeal in *R v Consolidated Fastfrate Transport Inc*[90] has held, by majority, that in the context of Mareva injunctions in aid of the criminal law, a defendant should be shown to have an "improper purpose". It may well be, however, that the line taken by the Irish Supreme Court is becoming increasingly attractive to courts in other jurisdictions.[91]

Establishing the "Requisite Intention"

[6.29] Proving a person's intention is always a difficult business. Proving that there is a likelihood that there is a risk that a defendant will remove his assets from the jurisdiction or otherwise dispose of his assets with the intention of evading his obligation to the plaintiff and to frustrate the anticipated order of the court can be especially difficult. Although the very fact that a defendant's intentions are relevant means that the test is essentially subjective, the evidential test for proving a defendant's intentions is an objective test ie based on the evidence before the court, is it *likely*[92] that the risk of removal or dissipation of

---

88. (1985) 15 DLR (4th) 161 at 178.
89. See Capper, 'Mareva Injunctions: A Distinctively Irish Doctrine?', (1995) 17 DULJ (ns) 110 at 118. *Cf Inayat N Pirani Inc v Global Pacific Capital Corporation*, Supreme Court of British Columbia, 19 January 1996 (Baker J) where *Aetna, Sekisui House Kabushiki v Nagashima* (1982) 42 BCLR 1 (CA) and *Mooney v Orr* (1994) 98 BCLR (2d) 318 (SC) were cited by Baker J as authorities which establish, *inter alia*, "that there is a real risk of removal or dissipation of assets by the respondent to avoid judgment" (at p 5 of the transcript).
90. (1995) 125 DLR (4th) 1.
91. In *Schaefer v Fisher*, Supreme Court of British Columbia, 13 February 1997 (Satanove J) the need to show that a Mareva defendant is trying to strip himself of assets to avoid a judgment was stressed. Satanove J recognised that it was "not just the imminent removal of assets from the jurisdiction that must be established, but also some element of "secreting away", or intention to defraud a potential judgment creditor that is required". The learned judge cited a number of authorities in support: in *Alers-Hankey v Solomon* [1994] BCJ No 1201 Melvin J found that "there should be evidence from which an inference can be drawn that the purpose for the removal of assets is to defeat a potential claim"; and in *Grenzservice Speditions v Jans* (1995) 15 BCLR (3d) 370 at 379 Huddart J said: "A Mareva injunction is not execution before judgment or a remedy *in rem*. It is granted to prevent dissipation of assets or their secretion or removal from the jurisdiction to avoid judgment, not to prevent their reasonable use in the ordinary course of a person's life or business".
92. In *Re John Horgan Livestock Ltd* [1995] 2 IR 411 at 420 Hamilton CJ spoke of "a likelihood that the assets would be dissipated with the intention that they would not be available ...".

assets is intended to frustrate the plaintiff's judgment? There is no doubt but that the best evidence would be a written acknowledgement by a defendant that he intends to remove or dissipate his assets with a view to frustrating the plaintiff's judgment. Indeed, a shrewd Mareva plaintiff may be able to provoke a careless or arrogant defendant into supporting the plaintiff's application where he can induce the defendant to say in a recordable medium that he intends to ensure that the plaintiff will never get his hands on his assets.[93] In the absence of such an acknowledgement, a Mareva plaintiff may still prove the likelihood that the removal or disposal of assets will be with the requisite intention by adducing evidence from which such can be *inferred*. The court can be invited to draw an inference from the facts and circumstances of the case and from the defendant's disposition, status and traits. For example, where a plaintiff establishes a good arguable case of fraud or other nefarious activity against a defendant, as in the cases considered below,[94] a court may be more inclined to accept that there is a likelihood that the defendant's future actions may be motivated by nefarious intentions.

[6.30] Whether or not a court accepts that there is evidence that a defendant is likely to dispose of his assets with the requisite intention will clearly depend upon the circumstances of each case. The following factors may, however, be of significance in proving or disproving the existence of the requisite intention:

    (a) Bare assertions will not suffice;

    (b) The defendant's nationality;

    (c) The defendant's personality, character and lifestyle;

    (d) Using companies to hold assets;

    (e) Where the defendant has left or is likely to leave the State;

    (f) The defendant's status, occupation or business;

    (g) Evidence of fraud or previous dishonesty.

(a) Bare assertions will not suffice

[6.31] In *The Niedersachsen*[95] Kerr LJ said that:

> "Bare assertions that the defendant is likely to put any assets beyond the plaintiff's grasp and is unlikely to honour any judgment or award are clearly not enough by themselves. Something more is required."[96]

[93.] See Hoyle, *The Mareva Injunction and Related Orders*, (3rd ed; 1997) Lloyd's of London Press at p 67. See, for example, *SIMS v Celcast Pty Ltd* [1998] 6662 SASC (5 May 1998) (Williams J).

[94.] See para **[6.46]** *et seq, infra*.

[95.] [1984] 1 All ER 398.

[96.] At 417.

In *Re John Horgan Livestock Ltd* there was no evidence that the defendant would dissipate his assets with a view to frustrating the liquidator's potential judgment and for this reason the Supreme Court declined to grant a Mareva injunction.[97] Subsequently, in *Tobin and Twomey Services Ltd v Kerry Foods Ltd and Kerry Group plc*,[98] Carroll J refused Mareva relief to the plaintiff on the grounds that there was no evidence that the defendant would dissipate its assets with a view to frustrating the plaintiff's future arbitration award. Upholding her decision the Supreme Court (*per* Blayney J) saw no reason to differ from the view expressed in Carroll J's judgment where she said:

> "As to the Mareva injunction, Mr Tobin avers that he believes the defendants intend to obstruct the plaintiff as every turn and delay payment. He says without the Mareva order the first defendant will seek to avoid any award of judgment obtained.
>
> In my view there is nothing to sustain its suspicion.
>
> There is no evidence to suggest that the first named defendant is dissipating its assets."[99]

Clearly, where there is no evidence adduced by the plaintiff of the defendant's likely intention, the court must decline Mareva relief.[100] This was, however, always the case as "bare assertions" never have been considered sufficient to ground the jurisdiction to grant a Mareva injunction.

[6.32] One consequence of the Supreme Court's emphasis on a defendant's intentions must surely be greater attention to detail in plaintiffs' grounding affidavits.[101] In the absence of direct proof that a defendant's intention is to remove or dissipate his assets with a view to frustrating a plaintiff's judgment, the plaintiff should detail facts and circumstances from which such an intention may be inferred. A large number of factors have proved to be relevant to the

---

[97] As Hamilton CJ said ([1995] 2 IR 411 at 420): "Before being entitled to the relief sought by him, the liquidator must establish that there was a likelihood that the assets would be dissipated with the intention that they would not be available to meet any decree or part of a decree ultimately made against the [respondent] in the proceedings. In my view, no such intention was established in this case."

[98] [1996] 2 ILRM 1.

[99] At 11,12.

[100] See also *Production Association Minsk Tractor Works v Saenko*, High Court, unrep, 25 February 1998 (McCracken J) where McCracken J found (at p 5 of the transcript) that there was no "evidence to establish such an intention on the part of the defendants". In *Schaefer v Fisher* Supreme Court of British Columbia of 13 February 1997 (Satanove J) a Mareva injunction was refused, the judge saying "There is no evidence from which I can infer reasonably that the defendant is trying to strip himself of assets in British Columbia to avoid a judgment here".

[101] As to the drafting of the affidavit grounding an application for Mareva relief, see Ch 8, *Applying for a Mareva Injunction*, para **[8.26]** *et seq*.

question of whether there is a likelihood that the defendant will dispose of his assets.[102] In order for it to be equitable that a Mareva injunction be granted, these factors should point to the likelihood that a defendant has or is attempting to make himself judgment-proof. In the absence of such evidence Mareva relief should not be granted.[103]

[6.33] In *The Niedersachsen*[104] Mustill J said of the evidence required in proving a risk of dissipation of assets:

"The judge who hears the proceedings *inter partes* must decide on all the evidence laid before him. The evidence adduced for the defendant will normally be looked at for the purposes of deciding whether there is enough to displace any inferences which might otherwise be drawn from the plaintiff's evidence. But I see no reason in principle why, if the defendant's evidence raises more questions than it answers, and does so in a manner which tends to enhance rather than allay any justifiable apprehension concerning dissipation of assets, the court should be obliged to leave this out of account. On the other hand the plaintiff has no right to criticise the defendant's evidence, for omissions or obscurities. The defendant is entitled to choose for himself what evidence, if any, he adduces. The less impressive his evidence, the less effective it will be to displace any adverse inferences. But there must be an inference to be displaced, if the injunction is to stand, and comment on the defendant's evidence must not be taken so far that the burden of proof is unconsciously reversed."[105]

(b) The defendant's nationality

[6.34] While it is no longer a prerequisite to the granting of a Mareva injunction that a defendant is a foreigner, where a defendant is a non-national, this may be a material factor in assessing the risk that he will remove his assets from the

---

[102] See *O'Regan v Iambic Productions Ltd* [1989] NLJR 1378 where Sir Peter Pain approved of a checklist of factors relevant in determining whether the requisite risk of dissipation of assets exists.

[103] In *H v IAS Ltd* an application reported in *The Irish Times*, 6 August 1992 (Morris J) the plaintiff sought a Mareva injunction to restrain the defendant company from reducing its assets within the jurisdiction below £707,000. The plaintiff's claim against the company for constructive or wrongful dismissal was hotly contested by the company which claimed that the purpose of the plaintiff's application was to bring the defendant to the negotiating table. It was reported that the defendant's counsel said that the plaintiff had not shown that the defendant might take steps to ensure that its assets would not be available if judgment was given against the defendant. The newspaper report concluded by saying that Morris J refused the application for Mareva relief on the basis that the plaintiff had not satisfied him that he was likely to succeed or that he had a "strong arguable case".

[104] *Ninemia Maritime Corp v Trave Schiffahrtgesellschaft mbh & Co KG* [1984] 1 All ER 398 at 419f-h.

[105] At 409f-g.

jurisdiction with the intention of frustrating judgment. In *Barclay-Johnson v Yuill*[106] Megarry V-C said:

> "... [i]n determining whether there is a real risk, questions of the defendant's nationality, domicile, place of residence and many other matters are all material to a greater or lesser degree."[107]

It was a material fact that the defendant was believed to be outside of the jurisdiction, aboard a yacht, and that he had sold his apartment. In addition to an individual defendant's nationality,[108] a corporate defendant's residence and domicile have also been held to be of relevance[109] in deciding whether there is evidence of a risk that assets will be removed from the jurisdiction. It must, of course, be remembered that a defendant's nationality is at best but a factor and clearly can never, *per se*, be conclusive evidence that he has the "requisite intention".[110]

(c) The defendant's personality, character and lifestyle

[6.35] A number of cases have held that a defendant's personality and character is an important factor in assessing the risk of removal of assets from the jurisdiction. In the *Prince Abdul Rahman* case[111] Lord Denning MR said of the defendants, who were resident in the United Kingdom that:

> "... they are most secretive about their home addresses. In their affidavits both give their addresses as '6th floor, 49 Park Lane, London'; but that is a business office. We are told that it is now empty and deserted. Neither of them gives his home address ...
> Why not? It leads me to think that they are not at all trustworthy ...".[112]

A defendant's frankness with the court has also been found to be relevant to both the initial granting of a Mareva injunction[113] and a subsequent application to have an injunction varied or discharged.[114] In addition, where there is

---

[106.] [1980] 3 All ER 190.

[107.] [1980] 3 All ER 190 at 195c-d.

[108.] See *GI v K*, *The Irish Times*, 17 and 24 September 1991, involving an application by one German national against another. See also *B, W & S v N*, *The Irish Times*, 4 September 1997 (Geoghegan J) where the defendant was a Japanese businessman.

[109.] See *Third Chandris Shipping Corporation v Unimarine SA*, *The Pythia* [1979] 2 All ER 972 at 985. See also *HKN Invest Oy v Incotrade PVT Ltd*, an application for a Mareva injunction reported in *The Irish Times*, 19 October 1991.

[110.] See, eg, *Production Association Minsk Tractor Works v Saenko*, High Court, unrep, 25 February 1998 (McCracken J) considered at para **[6.47]** *infra*.

[111.] [1980] 3 All ER 409.

[112.] *Ibid* at 410g-j.

[113.] See *Faith Panton Property Plan Ltd v Hodgetts* [1981] 2 All ER 877.

[114.] See *Re Kelly's Carpetdrome Ltd*, High Court, unrep, 9 May 1983 (Costello J) and see further, Ch 8, *Applying for a Mareva Injunction*, para **[8.44]**.

evidence that a defendant has acted in total breach of a prior agreement, the court may be inclined to infer the requisite nefarious intention. So in *QBEI&R(E) Ltd v G*,[115] the plaintiff company obtained a Mareva injunction against the defendant, a former employee, which restrained him from reducing his assets in the jurisdiction below £38,000. It was reported that the plaintiff had loaned the defendant £60,000 to enable him to relocate from Luxembourg to Ireland on condition that it would be repaid in six months from the proceeds of sale of his house in Luxembourg. When the defendant could not secure a work permit in Ireland, his employment with the plaintiff was terminated. It was reported that the plaintiff had only been repaid £29,000, that it had learnt that the defendant's property in Luxembourg had been sold some years previously, and that the defendant's Irish property had been sold at auction and that the completion was scheduled for the following week. In these circumstances it was reported that O'Sullivan J granted an interim Mareva injunction which restrained the defendant from reducing his assets in the State below £38,000.

[6.36] In *Countyglen plc v Carway*,[116] the plaintiff company was granted Mareva relief against certain of its directors. Murphy J said of the evidence adduced on affidavit that the defendants might remove assets from the jurisdiction that:

> "The actual evidence adduced by the applicants in the present case as to the nature or extent of the assets of the respondents within the jurisdiction of this court and of the danger of the respondents dissipating those assets or transferring them outside the jurisdiction is extremely limited. The only asset identified was the family home in Killaloe and whatever inference might be drawn from the statement that Mr Carway 'lives a high lifestyle and is involved in substantial business transactions'. What emerges clearly from the affidavit of [the Mareva-applicant's Chief Executive] and indeed the report of the inspector is that the nature of Mr Carway's business and his lifestyle is such as would facilitate the transfer of assets on an international basis. Indeed it is significant that Mr Carway now appears to be living in the Isle of Man whereas he was living in County Clare when the investigation by the inspector took place."[117]

Whether the evidence adduced in that case would today, in the light of the Supreme Court's pronouncements, be considered sufficient to show an intention on the defendant's part to evade obligations and frustrate judgment must be questioned. That the defendant may have had a high lifestyle which may have facilitated him in removing his assets is one thing; however, to draw an inference from that alone of a likelihood that he would remove or dissipate his

---

[115.] *The Irish Times*, 2 April 1998 (O'Sullivan J).

[116.] [1995] 1 IR 208.

[117.] At 217. The inspector referred to was an inspector appointed to investigate the affairs of the applicant company under the Companies Act 1990.

assets with the intention of frustrating judgment would, it is thought, be open to question.

(d) Using companies to hold assets

[6.37] The use of a group of companies to shield a defendant's affairs was also found to be material in establishing the requisite intent in *Powerscourt Estates v Gallagher & Gallagher.*[118] In that case McWilliam J said:

> "... the reluctance of the defendants to disclose other assets and their dispositions and proposed dispositions of them combined with the fact their businesses are not personal but conducted by a group of companies, indicates that they are probably mainly interested to deprive the plaintiff of the opportunity of recovering."[119]

The significance of conducting business through companies is that while such will usually be a perfectly legitimate and lawful means of arranging one's business affairs, it can also be used as a means of utilising the concept of separate legal personality to put one's assets beyond the reach of one's creditors.[120] Where a defendant's assets become mixed up with those of a company controlled by him, the court may, in an appropriate case, grant a Mareva injunction against the company by joining it in the action as a co-defendant.[121]

[6.38] The application for a Mareva injunction in *T v A Ltd & F*[122] is particularly interesting since, although there is no written judgment, it was heard after the Supreme Court's pronouncements in *Re John Horgan Livestock Ltd* and, moreover, the newspaper report states that in granting the injunction Kelly J said that he was satisfied that the plaintiff "had fulfilled the criteria set down by the Supreme Court for the granting of such an injunction." Here too it was claimed that the defendant-company's business had been transferred to another company controlled by nominees. In this case the plaintiff, who it was claimed was a paraplegic as a result of a fat extracting machine exploding at a rendering factory, sued the first defendant employer company and the second defendant director and controlling shareholder on whose land (jointly owned with his wife)

[118.] [1984] ILRM 123.

[119.] At 126.

[120.] In *Mooney v Orr* [1994] BCJ No 2322 Newbury J said (at p 14 of the transcript) "... the existence of the two unsatisfied judgments registered in British Columbia and the evidence of Mr Mooney's predilection and experience of the use of offshore trusts and companies to make himself "bulletproof" - are sufficient to show a relative deficiency of assets held by Mr Mooney in the province and that there is a "real risk" of his transferring or concealing significant assets elsewhere". It seems that there it was sufficient that the *effect* of a removal or transfer of assets would be to frustrate judgment.

[121.] See Ch 4, *A Substantive Cause of Action*, para **[4.20]** *et seq*.

[122.] *The Irish Times*, 10 December 1997 (Kelly J).

the first defendant's factory premises was located. In bringing an application for a Mareva injunction to restrain the defendants from reducing their assets below £2 million, the plaintiff claimed that his counsel had advised that if he was successful the plaintiff could secure an award of £2 million which was likely to represent the entire value of the defendants' assets. The newspaper report of the application states that the plaintiff claimed that the defendants had been engaged in a course of conduct motivated by a desire to put their assets beyond the reach of his claim. This was apparently substantiated by the following claims made in evidence: that the factory premises had been closed down and all workers let go except for two lorry drivers; that inspections of the factory premises had revealed that all operations at the factory had ceased and that the factory premises had been locked up; that since the proceedings had been initiated the business formerly carried on at the factory premises appeared to have been transferred to another company, of which the directors appeared to be the second defendant's son and daughter-in-law. Although it is not clear what weight in that case Kelly J attached to the plaintiff's allegation that the first defendant's business had been transferred to another company, where such a claim is substantiated and a defendant offers no reasonable explanation for such action, it is open to a court to infer that such a course of conduct is motivated by a desire to evade obligations to a plaintiff and to frustrate a subsequent order of the court.[123]

(e) Where the defendant has left or is likely to leave the State

[6.39] Where there is evidence that the defendant is likely to leave the jurisdiction without showing cause, a court may infer from this fact a nefarious intention on the defendant's part. In *Re Holbern Investment Trust Ltd*[124] it was reported that some of the evidence which persuaded the High Court to grant Mareva relief was the fact that efforts to contact one of the defendants who was alleged to be the managing director of the defendant company had failed and that there was a notice at his home which said that he had gone away. It was also said that the man had left his family home, where his wife resided, and was "not contactable".[125] Equally the converse should apply and where there is evidence

---

[123.] See also *PCII v GTF*, *The Irish Times*, 20 June 1998 (O'Sullivan J). In that case a worldwide Mareva injunction was granted to 20 plaintiffs against 12 defendants. Two defendant trust companies were restrained from reducing the value of their assets below $5 million. After reviewing the affidavit evidence the newspaper report stated that it was the view of O'Sullivan J that: "the apprehensions of the plaintiffs that the assets will be either dissipated or removed from the court's jurisdiction with a view to depriving the plaintiffs of their money was well founded".

[124.] *The Irish Times*, 7 May 1991 (Barron J).

[125.] See *Barclay Johnson v Yuill* [1980] 3 All ER 190, considered at para **[6.05]** *supra* and also, for example, *PPHS Ltd v von K*, a Circuit Court application reported in *The Irish Times*, 31 May 1995 (Judge Kelly) where a Dutch woman was reportedly enjoined from dissipating her assets below £30,000 in circumstances in which she was alleged to be leaving Ireland to escape debts. Here, the plaintiff had not been fully paid for work carried out to the defendant's house. Judge Kelly reportedly allowed service of the order by fax and telephone.

that a defendant has no intention of leaving the State[126] or where the defendant undertakes not to leave the State[127] this might result in Mareva relief being refused or justify the discharge of an existing Mareva injunction.[128]

[6.40] Where a defendant has in fact left the jurisdiction a Mareva injunction may still be appropriate relief where he still has property in the State as in the application in *C v M*[129] where the defendant publican - in whose public house the plaintiff alleged he had suffered personal injuries - had left Ireland and was working as a street musician in Cyprus. Although a defendant may not himself be amenable to the court's process, his professional advisors such as solicitors and accountants and others such as banks and estate agents have nothing to gain and all to lose if they fail to comply with a court order. Moreover, a defendant's unexplained departure from the jurisdiction will often amount to evidence from which a court could conclude that a defendant's intentions are not honourable and that there is a likelihood that he will remove or dispose of his assets with the "requisite intention". In *Bank of Ireland v N*[130] the newspaper report stated that a branch manager of the plaintiff bank gave evidence that there had been a number of newspaper reports to the effect that the defendant insurance broker, whom it was alleged, had absconded with about £500,000 and had apparently left Ireland with a secretary working in his office and had gone either to Brazil or to the Caribbean. Costello J is reported as having granted an injunction preventing his solicitor from disposing of £5,000 held for the broker.[131]

[6.41] Sometimes the risk will be that a defendant's assets alone are likely to be removed from the jurisdiction. In *P v MMs Ltd*[132] application was made by a former chief executive of the defendant company seeking to prevent the company and other companies within the group from disposing of its assets

---

[126.] See *L v H and TT Ltd, The Irish Times*, 20 March 1991 (Costello J).
[127.] In *K v L, The Irish Times*, 20 August 1988 where an interim Mareva injunction was discharged on the defendant's undertaking not to leave the jurisdiction.
[128.] *Cf* where the defendant is found to have "strong ties" to the country: see *Cinnamon v McLean*, Supreme Court of British Columbia, 15 December 1997 (McKinnon J).
[129.] *The Irish Times*, 10 September 1994 (Johnson J). See further Ch 4, *A Substantive Cause of Action*, para **[4.40]**.
[130.] *The Irish Times*, 12 March 1991 (Costello J).
[131.] Evidence that a defendant has left the jurisdiction will not *per se* justify the grant of a Mareva injunction. In *A Bishop v B Priest, The Irish Times*, 29 August 1989 (Barr J) it was reported that the plaintiff bishop sought a Mareva injunction to restrain the defendant priest from dealing with his assets in circumstances where it was alleged that a fund raising scheme under his control ran up debts of £1m. Whilst it was alleged that the defendant priest had left the jurisdiction, it was reported that Barr J refused the injunction saying that the names of the other priests who had given information to the plaintiff bishop should be disclosed and that there was no indication whether the priest had gone to America for a day, a week or a year. The newspaper report said that Barr J had remarked that "he could have gone on holidays".
[132.] *The Irish Times, inter alia*, 18 and 29 July, and 1 August 1989.

within the jurisdiction below £15.5 million. The plaintiff's claim against the defendant included, *inter alia*, damages for wrongful dismissal. The claim for the Mareva injunction was brought after the plaintiff saw an advertisement in *The Irish Times* for the sale by tender of four of the defendant's five factories. Blayney J was reported as having said that there were three issues to be considered in such an application: whether the plaintiff had an arguable case, whether there were assets in the jurisdiction and whether there was a real risk of them being dissipated and secreted. It was reported that the court had heard evidence that if a disposal of the four factories took place, the proceeds would pass outside of the jurisdiction to another company within the defendant group. Blayney J is reported as having decided that there was a real risk the assets would pass out of the jurisdiction. However, in the circumstances, the Mareva injunction granted was for a maximum sum of £2.3 million over the proceeds of sale and did not prevent the sale of the factories.[133]

(f) The defendant's status, occupation and business

(i) Solicitors

[6.42] A number of cases have considered a defendant's occupation and status to be relevant factors in deciding whether to grant or refuse Mareva relief. In *McD v C*,[134] Carroll J refused to make an order against a solicitor who was in the course of administering an estate against which the plaintiff was alleged to have had a claim. Apart from the fact that there was no evidence that the defendant was likely to dissipate the estate's assets, the newspaper report stated that Carroll J observed that, as a solicitor, the defendant was an officer of the court and, all other things being equal it was not appropriate to grant a Mareva injunction against him. The defendants' profession as solicitors and officers of the court did not, however, prevent the High Court from making a Mareva injunction where there were allegations of the fraudulent misappropriation of clients' funds in *Irish Press Newspapers Ltd v Malocco & Killeen*.[135]

[133.] See also *NBFC v W, The Irish Times*, 19 July 1988 where Carroll J gave leave to serve notice of motion for a Mareva injunction. The risk of removal of the defendant's assets from the jurisdiction was a report in *The Irish Times* suggesting that the defendant intended to remove the goods in question (allegedly subject to a bill of sale) to Northern Ireland. In *B v PS plc, The Irish Times*, 25 April 1997 an interim Mareva injunction was granted in a case where the plaintiff (who claimed to be the defendant company's operations director and vice-president) alleged that he had only received £10,000 of his £185,000 per annum salary and that the defendant company had made attempts to remove all of its assets from the jurisdiction.

[134.] *The Irish Times*, 18 December 1990 (Carroll J).

[135.] *The Irish Times*, 3 October 1991 (Denham J). In *Allied Irish Banks, plc v Two Solicitors, The Irish Times*, 3 June 1992 (Costello J), the plaintiff bank obtained a Mareva injunction against the defendant solicitors, thereby preventing them from disposing of their alleged shares in a National Lottery win. It was reported that the bank had a claim of £27,741 against the defendant-solicitors on foot of an overdrawn current account. This injunction was later discharged (see *The Irish Times*, 5 June 1992) on the basis that the plaintiff bank's grounding affidavits upon which the injunction was obtained was incorrect.

(ii) Official liquidators

[6.43] In the absence of exceptional facts, it will generally be inappropriate to grant a Mareva injunction against an official liquidator appointed by the court. In *Re Greendale Developments Ltd; McQuaid v Malone and Fagan*[136] the plaintiff liquidator to Greendale Developments Ltd sought (from the first defendant only) the recovery of two sums, £104,784 and £129,714.58, which he alleged the company was entitled to recover on a quasi-contract basis, the latter sum of money had allegedly been paid by the company in respect of the purchase of a property, the title to which was vested jointly in the defendants. As against both defendants the liquidator sought, *inter alia*, a declaration that the company had a beneficial interest in that property commensurate with its payment of £129,714.58. The liquidator had earlier obtained a monetary judgment for that amount against the second defendant pursuant to the provisions of s 298(2) of the Companies Act 1963. In the instant application before Laffoy J the defendants produced a defence and counterclaim which they sought to deliver. They claimed that the monetary judgment had been obtained by fraud and that proceedings had been instituted to have the judgment set aside. It was further proposed to plead that the company was indebted to the second defendant in the sum of £207,263 plus interest and that any liability of the defendant was subject to set-off. In addition, the defendants sought an interlocutory Mareva-type[137] injunction to restrain the liquidator from reducing the surplus assets in the liquidation below £250,000. Rejecting the application for Mareva relief against the liquidator, Laffoy J said:

> "The winding-up of the company is a winding up by the court. The liquidator's power to deal with the assets of the company other than with the sanction of the court or of the Committee of Inspection are extremely circumscribed by the Companies Acts 1963 to 1990. As I understand the position, the defendants are represented on the Committee of Inspection. Given these facts, I think this is a preposterous application and I refuse it."[138]

In an official liquidation it is clear that there is little or no risk that assets will be applied by an official liquidator to any improper purpose. Moreover, it is thought that the overriding prerequisite to Mareva relief in Ireland - that there is a nefarious intent - will, in the absence of very extreme circumstances, never be attributed to an official liquidator.[139]

[136.] High Court, unrep, 2 July 1997 (Laffoy J).

[137.] It would appear that a Mareva injunction was being sought as it does not appear that the defendants were asserting a proprietary claim against the liquidator.

[138.] At p 6 of the transcript.

[139.] In *Dudley Kill & Sons Ltd v Coldstream Products Corporation*, Supreme Court of British Columbia, 20 August 1997 (Satanove J) a Mareva injunction sought by the defendant against the plaintiff was refused on the basis that an accountant had been appointed as trustee of the plaintiff's assets under the Vancouver Bankruptcy Act and that the Judge was "confident that there exists no present risk of funds being diverted or dissipated" and that "if this has already happened, as alleged by the defendant, then a Mareva injunction will not assist".

(iii) Financial institutions

[6.44] Where the defendant is a large financial institution such as a bank, a Mareva injunction will be granted only in the most extraordinary of circumstances. Accordingly, clear and convincing evidence of a risk of dissipation or removal must be adduced by the plaintiff. In *Polly Peck International plc v Nadir (No 2)*[140] the insolvent plaintiff company's administrators sued the first defendant, its former chief executive, for misapplication of £371 million of the plaintiff's funds. The fifth defendant was a Northern Cyprus Bank which the plaintiff claimed was controlled by the first defendant and which acted as his family's private bank. It was alleged that the fifth defendant was responsible for the misapplication of £142 million of the plaintiff's moneys; that these moneys were transferred into the fifth defendant's account at a London clearing bank; and that some £45 million of this was transferred into the account of the fourth defendant, the Central Bank of Northern Cyprus, in return for either Turkish lire or sterling. The Central Bank exercised a supervisory and regulatory role for Northern Cyprus. It was contended, *inter alia*, by the plaintiff that the Central Bank either had actual knowledge that the funds had been improperly diverted from the plaintiff or the circumstances of the case ought to have put the Central Bank on enquiry. The plaintiff obtained a Mareva injunction against the Central Bank in respect of the £45 million on the basis that the court was satisfied that there was a real risk that, in the absence of the Mareva injunction, the funds might be removed from the jurisdiction. To mitigate the usual effects of such an injunction a proviso was written into the order which would enable the Central Bank to carry on its banking business in the normal way by enabling it to make payments of up to £6 million in traunches of £1 million each subject to the plaintiff's administrators' consent to such drawings.

[6.45] It was held by the Court of Appeal that only in most unusual circumstances would a court grant a Mareva injunction against a financial institution. Slade LJ said:

> "As a general principle, a Mareva injunction ought not to interfere with the ordinary course of business of the defendant. It is not intended to give the plaintiff security in advance of judgment but merely to prevent the defendant from defeating the plaintiff's chances of recovery by dissipating or secreting away assets. This principle makes the grant of a Mareva injunction against a bank, at any rate a bank carrying on a normal banking business, very difficult. A Mareva injunction ought never to prevent a defendant from paying its creditors their due debts. A bank must repay its depositors in accordance with the terms on which the deposits are held."[141]

[140.] [1992] 4 All ER 769.
[141.] At 782.

Lord Donaldson of Lymington MR expressed concern at the possibility that a Mareva injunction directed at a bank could provoke a run on the bank. While he accepted that this did not happen in this case he did say:

> "... I consider that it would be in the ordinary course of the Central Bank's business in depositing funds to take account not only of competing interest rates, but also of whether depositing funds in one country rather than another would be more likely to retain the confidence of its depositors. An injunction which inhibited the bank from taking account of such considerations would, I think, be contrary to principle.
>
> In expressing this view I am not to be taken as saying that a Mareva injunction can never be granted against a bank, but the circumstances would have to be unusual."[142]

Although the foregoing passages are useful, it is thought that an application for a Mareva injunction against a bank will require the same proofs as any other Mareva application. In *Balkanbank v Taher*[143] Barr J granted a Mareva injunction to the applicant against the respondent bank. It is submitted that the most likely reason to decline Mareva relief against a bank will be the plaintiff's failure to adduce sufficient evidence that there is risk that the assets will be removed or dissipated with the intention to frustrate the plaintiff's judgment.

(g) Evidence of fraud or previous dishonesty

[6.46] Where there is evidence of fraud or previous dishonesty by a defendant the courts are more inclined to accede to a request to exercise the Mareva jurisdiction. Although the substantive issues will not be addressed in an interlocutory or interim application, the court may be influenced by evidence which supports the contention that a defendant has been party to fraudulent behaviour as such can be suggestive of the defendant's character and the likelihood that he will have few qualms about evading his obligations to the plaintiff and frustrating the court's future order. In these cases, the fact that a plaintiff can establish that he has a good arguable case of fraud against a defendant may itself go a long way towards satisfying the court that the defendant is an untrustworthy person who is likely to take whatever steps are available to evade his obligations to the plaintiff and to frustrate any future order of the court. In the Australian case of *Patterson v BTR Engineering (Aust) Ltd*[144] Meagher JA said that in New South Wales a Mareva plaintiff had to prove two ingredients: first, a *prima facie* case against the defendant[145] and secondly, "that there is some risk of a dispersal by the defendant of his assets so as to defeat the

---

[142.] At 786.

[143.] An application reported in *The Irish Times*, 30 March 1995. See Ch 7, *The Defendant's Assets*, at para **[7.49]** *et seq.*

[144.] (1989) 18 NSWLR 319.

[145.] In Ireland, "a good arguable case" is sufficient: see Ch 5, *A Good Arguable Case*.

value of the plaintiff's victory if he ultimately wins". As to proving the latter he said:

> "... in exceptional cases ... one can infer the existence of the latter ingredient partly or wholly from proof of the former. This may well be the situation in all cases where the plaintiff's *prima facie* case against the defendant involves proof or gross dishonesty ... the trial judge was justified, in dealing with the second ingredient, to take into account that a defendant against whom it had been proved at a *prima facie* level that he was guilty of theft of $10 million of the plaintiff's property would not be likely to preserve it intact on his theft having been discovered, or indeed to preserve intact any property he may legitimately own."[146]

It is thought that such an inference is equally open to an Irish court, even though the plaintiff may[147] have only established "a good arguable case" of fraud or gross dishonesty.

A Mareva plaintiff may also seek to rely upon the contents of a statutory report, such as that of an inspector appointed under the Companies Act 1990 where the inspector has found evidence that a director or others have deliberately misled the company and where his alleged conduct can frame an action in fraud, deceit and breach of fiduciary duty.[148]

[6.47] Allegations of fraud will not, *per se*, mean that a court will inevitably infer the requisite intention on the part of a defendant. An example of this is seen in the case of *Production Association Minsk Tractor Works and Belarus Equipment (Ireland) Ltd v Saenko*.[149] In that case the plaintiffs sought a Mareva injunction to restrain the defendants from, *inter alia*, dealing with or disposing of their assets so as to reduce their value below £300,000. The first plaintiff was a body corporate established under the laws of Belarus and manufactured tractors. The second plaintiff was an Irish company which was a wholly owned subsidiary of the first plaintiff and was the distribution company for the tractors in Ireland. The first defendant was a citizen of Belarus and was managing director of the second plaintiff from 1 January 1993 to 31 July 1997; the second and third defendants were the first defendant's wife and daughter. The plaintiffs alleged that the first defendant had misappropriated moneys from the second plaintiff and had defrauded the second plaintiff. On this point McCracken J observed:

---

146. At 326. See also *LED Builders Pty Ltd v Eagle Homes Pty Ltd* [1997] 826 FCA (22 August 1997) (Tamberlin J).
147. Of course whilst a "good arguable case" is the minimum standard which a Mareva plaintiff must show, a Mareva plaintiff in a particular application may adduce evidence of a stronger case against a defendant.
148. *Bula Resources (Holdings) plc v Stanley, The Irish Times*, 7 August 1998 (O'Higgins J).
149. High Court, unrep, 25 February 1998 (McCracken J).

"These are very serious allegations. At this stage there is no Statement of Claim, and of course fraud must be pleaded with great particularity, and accordingly, I do not have the sort of particulars of the claim which will eventually have to be given. The amounts concerned are very large, almost £300,000 according to the grounding affidavit ...

I realise this is an interlocutory application made at an early stage and I do believe, having regard to all the affidavits filed, that the plaintiffs have shown a good arguable case that at least some monies may have been misappropriated. I emphasise I am not making any finding that this is so, only than an arguable case has been made out, although not for the amount claimed by the plaintiffs in the *ex parte* application."[150]

Notwithstanding his acceptance that the plaintiffs had made out an arguable case that moneys had been misappropriated, McCracken J was not so influenced as to infer an intention to the defendants to evade their obligations to the plaintiffs or to frustrate the anticipated order of the court. McCracken J said:

"... the plaintiffs make the case that the defendants are non-resident in this country and are selling their home. In fact the defendants have been resident here since 1993 and I am satisfied that they are genuinely seeking to purchase a new home here. The defendant has started a business here, a fact which again was known to the plaintiff when the interim application was made but was not disclosed to the court. I think it is unlikely in the extreme that the defendants will voluntarily return to Belarus, particularly in view of the allegations against them by a Belarus company."

Moreover, McCracken J found that there was no evidence before him to establish the requisite intention promulgated in *Re John Horgan Livestock Ltd*. It is thought that in that case the allegations of misappropriation were outweighed by the apparent absence of any other evidence which would show a nefarious intention. In these circumstances McCracken J was more influenced by the fact that the plaintiffs had breached the "golden rule" of full and frank disclosure of all material facts on an *ex parte* application.[151]

[150.] At p 2 of the transcript.

[151.] It must be recognised that not every case involving mere allegations of fraud will justify a court in granting Mareva relief. In *S Ltd v O'C, The Irish Times*, 11 July 1989 (Blayney J) the plaintiff company which dealt with the purchase and sale of animal skins and hides employed the defendant to manage one of its sub-offices. The plaintiff swore an affidavit alleging certain discrepancies: although records indicated that 1345 hides and 3316 skins had been bought, they were not to be found in storage and did not appear to have been sold; moreover, it was claimed that 18 cheques had issued to people who did not do business with the plaintiff company. It was reported that Blayney J refused to grant a Mareva injunction to the plaintiff. It was also reported that the judge found that there was no evidence that the defendant "intended to take his assets out of the jurisdiction or to dissipate them and he could not take into account the basis on which the action was brought".

[6.48] Alleged fraudulent dealings have formed the basis of a great many of the applications for Mareva relief in Ireland. In *Irish Press Newspapers Ltd v Malocco & Kileen*[152] the circumstances were that Mr Malocco, a partner in a firm of solicitors, was alleged to have misappropriated an estimated £312,000 which had been entrusted to him by his client, Irish Press Newspapers Ltd for the purpose of settling libel actions.[153] When the plaintiff learned that the books and records produced by the firm of solicitors were false, it successfully applied for a Mareva injunction to restrain Mr Malocco and his partner Mr Kileen from disposing of their assets within the jurisdiction below the sum of £500,000. The evidence before the court indicated that a fraud had been perpetrated against the plaintiff and there was also evidence that the defendants had attempted to cover their tracks by providing fraudulent documentation alleging all was well when it was not. In such cases where fraud is alleged it is tempting to infer that there is a risk that assets are likely to be removed or dissipated.[154]

[6.49] In a number of cases official liquidators of insolvent companies have successfully applied for Mareva injunctions to restrain directors and others from dealing with their assets.[155] In the application in *Re TSD Ltd; D v O'D & O'D*[156] the liquidator of a company which was in the course of being wound up successfully obtained a "maximum sum" Mareva injunction which restrained the company's directors from reducing their assets below £5 million. The newspaper report said that the liquidator had stated in his grounding affidavit that he believed that the company had operated a system of obtaining finance in respect of non-existent vehicles through the preparation of invoices containing details of non-existent vehicles and chassis' numbers. It was also reported that the directors were alleged to have been responsible for the situation and had both operated and maintained the fraudulent leasing agreements. Costello J is reported as having granted the order after he heard the liquidator's submission that, in the light of the facts to hand, he must consider the possibility that the

---

152. An application reported in *The Irish Times*, 3 October 1991 (Denham J).
153. The defendants' status as officers of the court was no bar to the making of a Mareva injunction in a case such as this where serious fraud was alleged. See para **[6.42]** *supra*.
154. Both Malocco and Kileen were subsequently charged and were separately sentenced to terms of imprisonment for their part in the fraud perpetrated on the Irish Press. Mr Malocco was ultimately jailed for five years on six charges of fraud: see *People (DPP) v Malocco*, reported in *The Irish Times*, 16 May 1995 (Judge Lynch).
155. See generally Courtney, *The Law of Private Companies* (1994) Butterworths, para [19.029].
156. *The Irish Times*, 31 January 1992 (Costello J); see also *The Irish Independent*, 4 February 1992.

defendants had either secreted the misappropriated moneys inside or outside the State.[157]

[6.50] One of the most celebrated Irish cases of broker-fraud to occur in the early 1990s was *Re Mark Synnott (Life and Pensions) Brokers Ltd.*[158] The facts, as they emerged in the newspapers' coverage were as follows. Over a number of years this brokerage business had consistently mismanaged client funds; investors had been attracted to Mr Synnott on foot of his claims to have discovered a brilliant investment strategy which could net returns of at least 20% per annum; moneys received for investment purposes were, in fact, often just put into a bank account; when a return was expected by the investor, money was simply withdrawn from the bank account and paid over to the investor; it eventually emerged that the company had been trading at a loss for at least eight years. When the discrepancies came to light a number of investors successfully applied for Mareva injunctions to restrain the company's managing director from reducing his assets below a particular amount. The newspaper report of the application stated that one of the investors, a widow, alleged on affidavit that the managing director appeared to have engaged in a deliberate and consistent pattern of extracting moneys under misrepresentation from the plaintiffs and that she believed that it was likely that he would attempt to secrete any assets to which he was personally entitled and that this would be done with the intention of frustrating the execution of any judgment against him.[159] The first in a series

---

[157.] See also *Re Europa Forklift Hire Ltd, The Irish Times*, 30 August 1991 where it was reported that a provisional liquidator obtained a Mareva injunction against a company's directors. The effect of the order made was that the company's directors were prevented from reducing their assets below IR£1.5 million. It was reported that a large number of trucks could not be traced and did not appear to have existed; of the 60 new trucks purchased earlier that year only 22 could be traced. See also *Re STC Ltd; M v F, The Irish Times*, 25 August 1995 (Barr J) where the liquidator of a company was given leave to apply for an injunction to restrain the company's two directors from reducing their assets below £250,000 and an asset disclosure order. It was reported that the liquidator's proceedings sought a declaration that some or all of the defendants had carried on the company's business with intent to defraud its creditors and for other fraudulent purposes; moreover it was said that the liquidator's affidavit stated that there were no assets left in the company. In *EW Ltd K & W v McN, The Irish Times*, 2 and 4 April 1998 (Kelly J) it was reported that the joint liquidators obtained Mareva relief against the directors of a company which operated a bonded warehouse. The injunctions restrained the directors and a company controlled by them from reducing their assets in the jurisdiction below £2 million and from reducing their shares in the company controlled by them below £2 million. It was reported that the liquidators adduced evidence that large sums of money appeared to have been misappropriated over several years and stored in a secret account in a building society; said account not having been disclosed to the company's auditors. It also appeared that in excess of £2 million was owed to the revenue commissioners.

[158.] For newspaper coverage of the *Synnott Case* see *The Irish Times*, 15, 18, 19, 25, 27 June; 3, 4, 6, 9, July; 6, 7, 8, 9 November 1991.

[159.] The fact that the newspaper report in *The Irish Times*, 15 June 1991 (Carney J) actually reported that the widow's affidavit said that "She believed it likely that he would attempt to secrete any of his assets to which he was personally entitled and that this would be done *with the intention of frustrating the execution of any judgment against him*" (italics added) is further evidence that the "requisite intent" existed as an Irish requirement for Mareva relief long before the Supreme Court's decision in *Re John Horgan Livestock Ltd*.

of Mareva injunctions in this case was, on the foregoing evidence, granted by
Carney J. It is thought that proving a likelihood of risk of dissipation of assets
(or removal of assets from the jurisdiction) with a nefarious intention is
considerably simplified in cases involving fraud as the allegations of fraud,
albeit only on affidavit evidence, will frequently permit the inference of a
likelihood of a risk of dissipation/removal of assets.[160]

[6.51] Good arguable cases of conversion by persons other than professional
advisors may also assist the court in concluding that there is a risk of removal of
assets. In the Australian case of *Praznovsky v Sablyack*[161] the plaintiff was suing
the defendant for damages for the tort of conspiracy in respect of a burglary of
the plaintiff's house. The defendant, who had been charged with a criminal
offence, was about to dispose of her house which was her only property in the
jurisdiction and the plaintiff sought an injunction to prevent this. Harris J
accepted the plaintiff's counsel's submission that he should "draw inference
against the defendant". In making an injunction preventing the defendant from
disposing of the proceeds of sale of her house other than by direction of the
court, he said:

> "The defendant herself has sworn that she intends to use the proceeds to buy
> another home.
> In my opinion, in the circumstances, it would be unsafe to rely upon the
> statements of the defendant's intention. The net proceeds of the sale of the
> defendant's property will be about $80,000 or so. With that sum in her
> possession and faced with trial on a serious criminal charge ... and as far as it is
> known, having no other property in Victoria, in my opinion, the plaintiffs run
> an appreciable risk that the defendant, if not restricted, may disappear with the
> proceeds of sale before her trial and that the plaintiffs' action against her will
> prove fruitless."[162]

An Irish example is provided by *D v M*[163] where the plaintiff, who had employed
the defendant as a baby-sitter and also to package change for his cigarette

---

[160.] See also *Bank of Ireland v K*, *The Irish Times*, 22 July 1997 and 29 July 1997 where the
plaintiff bank obtained an order preventing the defendant from disposing of his assets so as to
reduce his assets below £500,000. In that case it was reported that the defendant was an
employee of the bank and that upon his taking annual leave two customers had called to effect
transactions but that the account records produced by them could not be reconciled with the
bank's own accounts. It was also reported that the bank alleged that the defendant's solicitor
told the branch manager, *inter alia*, that the defendant understood that he would be dismissed
and that it was indicated that the defendant-employee had been "teeming and lading" accounts
of about 40 customers involving thousands of transactions over a period of three years. The
report of 22 July 1997 concluded by saying that McCracken J had, in these circumstances, said
that he believed that the bank had made a strong case for granting the order.
[161.] [1977] VR 114.
[162.] At 120.
[163.] *The Irish Times*, 8 June 1996 (McCracken J).

vending machine business, obtained an injunction restraining her from reducing her assets below £73,000 in circumstances where it was alleged that she had stolen from his house. It was said in the newspaper report that the plaintiff had contacted the Gardai who had installed a concealed camera in the room where she was to package the change and it was claimed that he had been told by the Gardai that the video recorded the defendant taking the money.[164] As in the case of allegations of fraud, evidence of conversion by the defendant may also give rise to an inference of the requisite intention.

[6.52] Applications for Mareva relief against persons suspected of being involved in serious criminal activity have been brought by the Criminal Assets Bureau. One such application was *Criminal Assets Bureau v E*[165] where a Mareva injunction was applied for as relief ancillary to proceedings to enforce a tax assessment. There, it was reported that the defendant, who was suspected of being involved in the Brinks-Allied robbery of £2.8 million, had a record of convictions for minor criminal offences including larceny, car thefts and receiving stolen property. The newspaper report also said that it was believed that the defendant was in the process of moving up to £100,000 from bank and building society accounts. A CAB officer was reported as having stated in court that it was his belief that the defendant was trying to move his assets out of the reach of the authorities. Again, it is submitted that in cases such as this, the courts are more inclined to infer a nefarious intention to a defendant.

[6.53] Where it is shown that a defendant has fraudulently obtained social welfare from the State it is thought that such may also be indicative of a disposition to frustrate a future order of the court. In *CBS (UK) Ltd v Lambert*[166] the Court of Appeal found that the defendant's conduct provided ample evidence of a likelihood that the defendant would dissipate his assets. The evidence heard that the defendant had pretended to be unemployed and had received social security benefit. In fact he was working and in the course of his work had pirated the plaintiff's musical recordings in breach of his copyright. The court heard that the defendant had expended large sums of money on expensive cars and other easily disposable goods. The Court of Appeal, in making the order sought, accepted that the defendant's conduct indicated a desire to conduct his business and financial affairs in such a manner as to make

---

[164.] See *B v C & JPC & Co Ltd, The Irish Times,* 27 June 1991 (Barron J) where it was reported that in accepting an undertaking from the defendant not to dispose of a list of property, Barron J commented that there was a very considerable list of complaints against the defendant who was accused of fraud.

[165.] *The Irish Times,* 20 December 1997.

[166.] [1983] 1 Ch 37.

himself "judgment-proof". In the *Minister for Social Welfare v M*,[167] which is considered in another chapter,[168] the basis of the plaintiff's claim was that the defendant had, over a period of time, perpetrated a fraud on the Department of Social Welfare by claiming social welfare assistance whilst, at the same time, working on a casual basis for his brother in a fruit and vegetable business in the Dublin markets. In that case the High Court granted a Mareva injunction to the plaintiff.

[167.] *The Irish Times*, 21 ("Department seeks bite of award") and 26 ("Judge extends order cutting pie pay-out") of February 1991. The writer acknowledges with gratitude the assistance provided by counsel for both parties, Peter Charleton SC and RAM Robbins SC and the solicitors for both parties, Stuart Coonan, of the Chief State Solicitors' Office and Sean Costello, of Frank Ward & Co, for their valuable assistance.

[168.] See Ch 4, *A Substantive Cause of Action*, para **[4.44]**.

Chapter 7

The Defendant's Assets

[7.01] The primary purpose of a Mareva injunction is to restrain a defendant from removing his assets from the State or otherwise disposing of them so as to make himself "judgment-proof". Accordingly, it stands to reason that the fourth essential proof[1] for a Mareva injunction must be that a Mareva plaintiff establishes the existence of some assets in the ownership of a defendant which are available to satisfy a judgment. Formerly, the jurisdiction to make a Mareva injunction was confined to cases where a defendant had assets *within* the jurisdiction of the court making the order.[2] This restriction has been conclusively dispensed with by the courts of the United Kingdom[3] and the practice of the Irish High Court[4] and the courts in other jurisdictions has been to follow suit. Accordingly, it is now the case that Mareva injunctions are granted to restrain a defendant from dealing with his assets wherever situate, *inside* or *outside* of the jurisdiction of the court making the order. The so-called *worldwide* Mareva injunction is considered in detail in Section [B]. First, however, this chapter begins by examining the types of assets which a defendant may be restrained from dealing with.

[A] THE TYPES OF ASSETS WHICH MAY BE AFFECTED

[7.02] A Mareva injunction may restrict a defendant from dealing with, or disposing of, any type of assets which are in his ownership. "Assets" include both real and personal property; a Mareva injunction can restrain a defendant from dealing with his present or future, real or personal property, whether chattels or choses-in-action. In the first section of this chapter the following types of assets which may be affected by a Mareva injunction are analysed:

1. Real Property.
2. Chattels.

---

1. See Ch 8, *Applying for a Mareva Injunction*, para **[8.53]**.
2. *Intraco Shipping Corp Ltd v Notis Shipping Corp of Liberia; The Bhoja Trader* [1981] 2 Lloyd's Rep 256 and *Ashtiani v Kashi* [1986] 2 All ER 970.
3. *Babanaft International Co SA v Bassatne* [1989] 1 All ER 433 and the other cases considered at para **[7.27]** *et seq, infra*.
4. See *Deutsche Bank Aktiengesellschaft v Murtagh & Murtagh* [1995] 2 IR 122. See also *Taher v Balkanbank* (1995) High Court, unrep, 29 March 1995 (Barr J), *The Irish Times*, 30 March 1995 and generally at para **[7.35]** *infra*.

3. Choses in Action

4. Money in Bank Accounts.

5. Future Assets.

6. Assets in Joint-Ownership and Legally in the Name of a Third Party

7. The Sufficiency of the Defendant's Assets.

[7.03] It is important to recognise that all Mareva injunctions operate *in personam* (against a defendant's person) and not *in rem* (against a defendant's assets).[5] Whilst here, as elsewhere, there is reference to assets being "the subject of", "affected by" or "frozen by" a Mareva injunction it should always be remembered that a Mareva injunction can only ever indirectly affect a defendant's assets by operating through the person of a defendant.[6] In *Derby & Co Ltd v Weldon (No 2)*[7] Lord Donaldson MR said:

> "... a Mareva injunction does not have any *in rem* effect on the assets themselves or the defendant's title to them. Nor does such an injunction have a *direct* effect on third parties. The injunction (a) restrains those to whom it is directed from exercising what would otherwise be their rights and (b) indirectly affects the rights of some, but not all, third parties to give effect to instructions from those directly bound by the order to do or concur in the doing of acts which are prohibited by the order."[8]

As Neill LJ observed in *Babanaft International Co SA v Bassatne*[9] "... the injunction has its legal operation not on the property itself but on the person who is subject to the jurisdiction of the court." Mareva injunctions affect defendants and do not directly attach to defendants' assets.

Real Property

[7.04] It is quite common for a Mareva injunction to restrain a defendant from conveying, transferring, assigning, sub-letting, mortgaging, charging or otherwise disposing of his real property.[10] Although an order which prevents a

---

5. *Cf* admiralty actions involving the arrest of ships and proprietary claims which are considered in Ch 1, *The Mareva Injunction in Context*, paras **[1.16]** and **[1.30]**, respectively.
6. See generally, Ch 9 *The Mareva Order and Its Effects*, para **[9.36]** *et seq.*
7. [1989] 1 All ER 1002.
8. At 1012.
9. [1989] 1 All ER 433 at 450d. See para **[7.27]** *infra*.
10. There are numerous examples of Mareva injunctions granted where a defendant's real property was affected. For an example of some of the orders made by the High Court which were only recorded in the newspapers, see: *P v T, The Irish Times*, 16 May 1989 (Barrington J). In that application the defendant was restrained from selling his house. The applicants had alleged that the defendant had defectively constructed their house and intended selling his own. The order was, however, subsequently discharged: *The Irish Times*, 27 May 1989. See also *LB v C*, an application recorded by *The Irish Times*, 27 June 1991 where, in lieu of making a Mareva injunction, Barron J accepted an undertaking from the defendant not to dispose of his property. In *K v F, The Irish Times*, 31 May 1990, Costello J restrained the defendant - who resided in Mountjoy prison - from disposing of his farm: see Ch 4, *A Substantive Cause of Action* para **[4.41]**.

defendant from disposing of his property will implicitly prevent him from mortgaging his property, some orders of the courts will expressly prevent a defendant from creating a mortgage over his property.[11] A Mareva injunction which is directed at a defendant's real property may seek to preserve its value by either preventing the defendant from disposing of the land,[12] or, more usually (and, one might add, more appropriately) by restraining the defendant from dealing with the proceeds of sale of the land.

[7.05] It has been observed[13] that as regards enjoining the disposal of land, "a plaintiff may have difficulty in satisfying the fourth principle of the guidelines laid down in the *Third Chandris* case, ie the risk of dissipation, because unlike money, land is less liquid".[14] Notwithstanding the foregoing, the inherent danger is that a defendant may dispose of his interest in land for market value, secrete the proceeds of sale and thereby make himself judgment-proof; alternatively, a defendant could dispose of his lands to a collaborator at an undervalue. One way in which the Irish courts have resolved the foregoing dilemma is by establishing that the sale is at arms' length, for a market consideration,[15] and then directing the order at the proceeds of sale of the land. In *P v MM Ltd*[16] Blayney J is reported as having clarified the terms of an earlier Mareva injunction which had the effect of restraining the defendant from reducing its assets below £2.3 million, saying that it did not operate to prevent the defendant from selling certain premises.[17] Similarly, in *C v CC Ltd*[18] it was reported that Keane J made

---

[11.] *Powerscourt Estates v Gallagher* [1984] ILRM 123 *Canadian Imperial Bank of Commerce v Bhattessa* (1991) *The Times* 10 September 1991 (Harman J). See also the order made in *HBC Ltd v A Ltd, The Irish Times*, 20 June 1991 where in lieu of making an order, Lardner J accepted an undertaking from the defendants not to dispose of their property by creating a mortgage without first giving notice to the court.

[12.] See the application in *P v T, The Irish Times*, 16 May 1989, considered in fn 10, *supra*.

[13.] Goldrein & Wilkinson, *Commercial Litigation: Pre-Emptive Remedies*, (2nd ed, 1991) Sweet & Maxwell at p 179.

[14.] The authors mentioned above, fn 13, cite *Naz v Kaleem* [1980] CLY 409 (Bow County Court) as an authority on this point.

[15.] Where it is established that a proposed disposal is in the ordinary course of business and for a market consideration the courts will generally deem it inappropriate to block the sale of land. For an Australian example, see *Brew v Crouch; Dionysus Pty Ltd* [1998] 6633 SASC (23 April 1998).

[16.] *The Irish Times*, 23 March 1991 (Blayney J). See further Ch 6, *The Risk of Removal or Disposal of Assets*, para **[6.41]**.

[17.] See also the Australian case of *Praznovsky v Sablyack* [1977] VR 114. There, the plaintiff sought a Mareva injunction to restrain the defendant (whom the plaintiff was suing for the tort of conspiracy in respect of a burglary of the plaintiff's house) from disposing of her house which appeared to be her only principal asset within the jurisdiction. Harris J permitted the defendant to proceed with the sale of the land in accordance with an existing contract for sale but restrained her from disposing of or dealing with the net proceeds of such sale otherwise than by order of the Court.

[18.] *The Irish Times*, 26 February 1991.

an order which restrained the defendant from reducing its assets below a specified sum, but that he also clarified the order by saying that it did not prevent the defendant from selling a castle which appeared to be its only asset within the State.[19] In *HNC Ltd v SQP Ltd*[20] Murphy J is reported as having refused to grant an order which would have had the effect of preventing the defendant from selling an hotel; it was also reported that he said that the defendant's undertaking to set aside £500,000 from the proceeds of sale was sufficient to protect the plaintiff's rights. It is thought that directing the injunction at the proceeds of sale of land is the most appropriate means of achieving the desired end, *viz* that a defendant's assets are available to meet the plaintiff's future judgment. It will often be to go too far to restrain the actual disposal of specific assets as the only legitimate interest which a Mareva plaintiff has in a defendant's assets is in maintaining their value in anticipation of executing judgment. If an applicant for an injunction has a proprietary claim to specific assets in a defendant's possession, and his interest is in recovering those specific assets, his appropriate relief is not a Mareva injunction but an injunction to protect that proprietary right or interest.[21]

[7.06] It has been held in the United Kingdom[22] that a Mareva injunction cannot be registered as a mortgage, charge or other incumbrance on unregistered property and it is submitted that this is good law in Ireland. In relation to registered land, and notwithstanding certain suggestions[23] to the contrary, it is submitted that a Mareva injunction cannot be registered as a "caution" on a Land Registry folio because a Mareva plaintiff does not, *per se*, have any interest *whatsoever* in any land which is registered in a defendant's name.[24] A caution restricts a registered owner from disposing of registered land without notice to a person who claims "any right in, to or over registered land or a

---

[19.] See also, for example, *L v H and TT Ltd, The Irish Times,* 20 March 1991 where Costello J made an order which affected the proceeds of sale of a defendant's property only; *C v X Ltd, The Irish Times,* 25 September 1990 (Blayney J), considered in Ch 4, *A Substantive Cause of Action* para **[4.39]**.

[20.] *The Irish Times,* 29 April 1989 (Murphy J).

[21.] See Ch 1, *The Mareva Injunction in Context,* para **[1.16]** *et seq.*

[22.] In *Stockler v Fourways Estates Ltd* [1983] 3 All ER 501 it was held that a pre-judgment Mareva injunction could not be registered as a charge against unregistered land.

[23.] See Ough & Flenley, *The Mareva Injunction and Anton Piller Order,* (2nd ed, 1993) Butterworths at p 11 at para 2.1.2 and Hoyle, *The Mareva Injunction and Related Orders,* (3rd ed, 1997) Lloyd's of London Press at p 89.

[24.] *Cf* "restraint orders" made pursuant to the Criminal Justice Act 1994 and interim and interlocutory orders made pursuant to the Proceeds of Crime Act 1996 which can be registered in the Land Registry, Registry of Deeds and (in the case of corporate defendants) in the Companies Registration Office (s 25 of the 1994 Act; and s 10 of the 1996 Act, respectively). See generally, Ch 3, *Statutory Jurisdictions to Freeze Assets,* para **[3.26]** and para **[3.68]**, respectively.

registered charge".[25] As noted, a Mareva injunction does not attach to a defendant's assets which comprise registered land: the injunction merely operates *in personam* and so to suggest that a Mareva plaintiff has any "right in, to or over"[26] a defendant's land is, surely, entirely fallacious.[27] The other recognised means of inhibiting dealings with registered land is through an "inhibition". Again, it is thought that it would be inappropriate for a Mareva plaintiff[28] to apply to the Registrar of Titles for an inhibition because he has no interest in a defendant's land.[29]

Chattels

[7.07] A general purpose Mareva injunction,[30] as distinct from one directed at specific assets in a defendant's possession, will affect all of a defendant's assets, including those which constitute chattels personal. In one of the earlier cases, *Rasu Maritima SA v Perusahaan Pertambangan Minyak Dan Gas Bumi Negara*,[31] Lord Denning MR said, after acknowledging that money in a bank account is one of the most appropriate assets to "freeze" indirectly:

> "... I would not limit the new procedure to money. Money can easily be changed into pictures, or diamonds, or stocks and shares or other things. The procedure should apply to goods also."[32]

Mareva injunctions have been granted which have specifically restrained defendants from dealing with a great variety of specific chattels: an aircraft;[33]

---

[25] Section 97(1) of the Registration of Title Act 1964. See generally, Fitzgerald, *Land Registry Practice*, (2nd ed, 1995) Roundhall Press, p 161 *et seq.*

[26] Note that "right" is defined by s 3(1) of the Registration of Title Act 1964 Act to include "any estate, interest, equity or power" over lands.

[27] For the *effect* of Mareva injunctions, see Ch 9, *The Mareva Order and Its Effects*, para **[9.35]** *et seq.*

[28] *Cf* an applicant for an ordinary injunction to protect a proprietary claim: see Ch 1, *The Mareva Injunction in Context*, para **[1.16]**.

[29] Although s 98 of the Registration of Title Act 1964 provides that an inhibition may be entered on the register on foot of a court order, it is thought that it would be inappropriate and not in keeping with the nature of the Mareva jurisdiction for a court to order, in aid of a Mareva plaintiff, that an inhibition be registered against registered land owned by a defendant.

[30] See Ch 9, *The Mareva Order and Its Effects*, para **[9.03]**.

[31] [1978] QB 644.

[32] At 662A.

[33] *Allen v Jambo Holdings Ltd* [1980] 2 All ER 502; and see *Societe Nationale d'Etude et de Construction de Moteurs d'Aviation v Jugoslovenski Aer Transport and Bosphorus Airways*, *The Irish Times*, 18 January 1995 where the applicant was successful in obtaining an injunction to restrain the defendants from removing from the State or disposing of a Boeing 737 which was located in Dublin Airport. See also *Visionair International Inc v Eurowatch California Inc* [1979] CAT 719 (United Kingdom).

horses;[34] a ship;[35] a ship's cargo;[36] postage stamps;[37] a motor car;[38] shares in a company[39] and even a beige box in a bank safety deposit box allegedly containing gold sovereigns and gems.[40] Again it is important to recognise that although a court order may specify particular assets in a defendant's possession, this does not mean that the plaintiff is claiming to have a proprietary interest in them; the purpose of describing specific assets in a Mareva order is simply to further the certainty of the court's order.

[7.08] A Mareva injunction cannot be used as a means of holding a defendant to ransom by preventing him from using a specific asset which he needs to use for a particular purpose. This is vividly illustrated by the Court of Appeal's decision in *Camdex International Ltd v Bank of Zambia (No 2)*.[41] In that case the plaintiff had obtained a Mareva injunction against the defendant (the Central Bank of Zambia) which was the plaintiff's judgment debtor. The injunction extended to the defendant's assets generally and therefore included a large quantity of high denomination bank notes which the defendant had arranged to be printed in the United Kingdom; notes of high denomination had been ordered because inflation was very high in Zambia. The defendant applied to have the Mareva injunction varied so as to exempt the bank notes; the basis for this application was that the notes were of no intrinsic value and were greatly needed in Zambia where they would be of great importance to the Zambian economy. The application was refused. It was held that the bank notes did have a real value because the Central Bank of Zambia would be likely to wish to re-purchase them for a considerable price and it was held that the Mareva injunction was not being used to hold the defendant to ransom. The decision not to vary the Mareva

---

[34.] In *T Ltd (in receivership) v McE & McE*, *The Irish Times*, 24 October 1989, an order was made preventing the sale or disposal of 45 horses by the defendant.

[35.] *The Rena K* [1979] 1 QB 377; *Gatoil Industries Inc v Arkwright Boston Manufacturers Mutual Insurance Co* [1985] AC 255.

[36.] *Clipper Maritime Co Ltd v Mineralimportexport* [1981] 1 WLR 1262.

[37.] *Johnson v L & A Philatelics* [1981] FRS 286.

[38.] In *N Ltd v S&CBC*, *The Irish Times*, 18 June 1992 (Blayney J) where it was reported that Blayney J granted a Mareva injunction which prevented the defendants from removing a Porsche car from the jurisdiction. *The Irish Times*, 28 July 1992 reported that the order was continued with the consent of the defendants.

[39.] In *EW Ltd; K and W v McN and McD*, *The Irish Times*, 4 April 1998 (Kelly J) the plaintiff liquidators obtained a Mareva injunction which restrained the defendant-directors of a company in liquidation from reducing their assets in the jurisdiction below £2 million and also from reducing their shares in a named company below the same amount.

[40.] In *Allied Irish Banks, plc v W*, *The Irish Times*, 21 February 1990, (Carroll J) where it was reported that Carroll J made an order which prevented the defendant from removing such a box from the jurisdiction.

[41.] [1997] 1 All ER 728.

injunction so as to release the bank notes from its scope was successfully appealed to the Court of Appeal where Bingham MR said:

> "It seems to me that in a situation such as this, it is important to go back to first principles. A Mareva injunction is granted to prevent the dissipation of assets by a prospective judgment debtor, or a judgment debtor, with the object or effect of denying a claimant or judgment creditor satisfaction of his claim or judgment debt. Here, it is plain that the defendant wants to transfer these bank notes to Zambia. In doing so it would not, as it seems to me, dissipate any asset available to satisfy the judgment debt because the asset has, in the open market, no value. It is not an asset of value to the plaintiff or other creditors of the defendant if it were put on the market and sold. It is true that the denial of this asset to the defendant would put the defendant in a position of such extreme difficulty that the defendant would seek to pay a price beyond the market value of the asset in order to recover it, but that is, as it would seem to me, what would in ordinary parlance be described as holding someone to ransom."[42]

In this case, the plaintiff had no proprietary interest in the bank notes and, therefore, could not justify restraining the defendant from moving them to Zambia. The only other basis upon which the defendant could have been restrained from moving the bank notes would be if they had a value and the effect[43] of their removal would be to frustrate the plaintiff's judgment. Because the bank notes had no intrinsic value there was no justifiable reason for restraining their removal from the United Kingdom.

[7.09] In certain exceptional circumstances an order for the delivery up of chattels to a plaintiff or a plaintiff's solicitors may be granted; such an order is not, however, a Mareva injunction.[44] In *Johnson v L & A Philatics*[45] the Mareva plaintiff claimed that the defendant owed him over £21,000 for services provided. In restraining the defendant from removing its stamps from the jurisdiction or otherwise dealing with them, Robert Goff J's order also provided that the defendant had to, *inter alia*, deliver up all stamps in their possession.[46]

[42.] At 732j-733b. Phillips LJ said (at 736b): "... it seems to me, that the Mareva is being used in relation to these bank notes not for the purpose of preserving an asset that will be of value in the process of execution, but in an attempt to pressurise the defendant into discharging part of its liability under the judgment. That is not a legitimate use of the Mareva injunction." Of course in Ireland, the defendant's intention in removing the bank notes from the jurisdiction would have been crucial and, on the facts, it would have been found that the primary intention was not nefarious. See Ch 6, *The Risk of Removal or Disposal of Assets*, para **[6.16]** *et seq.*

[43.] Note that in Ireland, it is not sufficient that the *effect* of the removal is to frustrate judgment; it must be established that the defendant's *intention* is to frustrate judgment: see *Re John Horgan Livestock Ltd; O'Mahony v Horgan* [1995] 2 IR 411 and Ch 6, *The Risk of Removal or Disposal of Assets*, para **[6.16]** *et seq.*

[44.] *CBS (UK) Ltd v Lambert* [1983] 3 WLR 746; [1982] 3 All ER 237.

[45.] [1981] FRS 286.

[46.] See further, Ch 10, *Ancillary Orders*, para **[10.66]** *et seq* and, for *Anton Piller Order*, see para **[10.38]** *et seq.*

Such an order is quite exceptional and will only be made in the most extraordinary circumstances.

Choses in Action

[7.10] Choses in action which are in a defendant's ownership can be affected by a Mareva injunction. Chose in action was defined by Channell J in *Torkington v Magee*[47] as follows:

> "'Chose in action' is a known legal expression used to describe all personal rights of property which can be claimed or enforced by action, and not by taking physical possession."

Choses in action, whether legal or equitable in nature, cannot be grasped, held or have a tangible manifestation.[48] The authors of *Snell's Equity*[49] cite debts, bills of exchange, policies of insurance, sweepstakes tickets and shares in companies as being legal choses in action; and legacies, legatees' rights in an unadministered estate, shares in a trust fund, surplus proceeds of sale in the hands of a mortgagee, and rights of relief of forfeiture of a lease for non-payment of rent as being equitable choses in action.

[7.11] It follows that debts due to a defendant from a third party can be affected by a Mareva injunction. The clearest example of a third party debt to a defendant which is commonly affected by Mareva injunctions is a defendant's bank account which, where in credit, represents a debt due by a bank to its customer.[50] The goodwill of a business can be an asset of a defendant which is also liable to be affected by a Mareva injunction.[51] Other examples of choses in action liable to be affected by a Mareva injunction are insurance policies and their proceeds[52] and even a defendant's share in a National Lottery win.[53] In *The Minister of Social Welfare v M*[54] Murphy J granted the plaintiff a Mareva injunction against

---

[47.] [1902] 2 KB 427 at 430.

[48.] One must not confuse, say, a share certificate with a share: a share certificate merely evidences title to a share; the share itself is intangible.

[49.] Baker & Langan, *Snell's Equity*, (29th ed, 1990) Sweet & Maxwell at p 71.

[50.] See para **[7.13]** *infra*.

[51.] *Darashah v UFAC (UK) Ltd* (1980) *The Times*, 30 March 1980.

[52.] *TDK Tape Distributor (UK) Ltd v Videochoice* [1985] 3 All ER 345. See para **[7.15]** *infra*. See also *Re John Horgan Livestock Ltd: O'Mahony v Horgan* [1995] 2 IR 411 where there was no objection in principle to the freezing of the proceeds of an insurance policy although, in that case, the injunction was refused on other grounds.

[53.] So, for example, in *Allied Irish Banks, plc v Two Solicitors*, *The Irish Times*, 5 June 1992 (Denham J) an injunction restraining two solicitors from disposing of their assets to as to reduce them below £30,000 was discharged after they denied being members of the previous weekend's winning National Lottery syndicate. The injunction had been granted earlier that week by Costello J.

[54.] *The Irish Times*, 21 and 22 February 1991. For background to the application, see *The Irish Times*, 13 February 1991. For the context in which the Mareva injunction was made, see Ch 4, *A Substantive Cause of Action*, para **[4.48]**.

the defendant, a social welfare recipient, the effect of which was to restrain an insurance company from paying more than half of a £35,000 settlement award to the defendant. The defendant had successfully settled an action against a department store and a food manufacturer after allegedly finding part of a mouse in a savoury pie which he had partially eaten. The matter of the settlement came to the attention of the Department of Social Welfare who alleged that the defendant had been in receipt of social welfare payments while working on a casual basis.

[7.12] It is questionable whether all choses in action should be capable of being affected by a Mareva injunction, eg a defendant's cause of action against a third party. The issue in some cases will not turn on the nature of the assets, but rather upon the policy question of whether it is appropriate to restrict a defendant in, say, litigating a cause of action. In *Normid Housing Association Ltd v Ralphs & Mansell*[55] Lloyd LJ denied Mareva relief to the plaintiff where this would have had the effect of preventing the defendant from settling an insurance claim. It is thought that it would be entirely inappropriate for a Mareva injunction to interfere with the terms of settlement of any cause of action. It would be one thing for a defendant to be intent on disposing of his cause of action with intent to frustrate a plaintiff's future judgment; it is entirely different to propose to interfere with *bona fide* settlement negotiations. The crucial point upon which a Mareva application will fail or succeed will depend upon the evidence of the defendant's intentions in disposing of the cause of action.[56]

Money in Bank Accounts [57]

[7.13] One of the most common forms which a Mareva injunction takes is to restrain a defendant from disposing of moneys held in an account with a bank or other financial institution.[58] In principle, money in a bank account is no different to any other chose in action and is capable of being made "the subject" of a Mareva injunction. Although any bank or other financial institution within the jurisdiction of the court making the order will, where it has notice of the order, be bound by the terms of the order,[59] the primary effect of the order will be to restrain the defendant account-holder from dealing with the moneys.[60] It is

---

[55.] [1989] 1 Lloyd's Rep. 265.

[56.] On the relevance of defendants' intentions, see generally Ch 6, *The Risk of Removal or Disposal of Assets*, para **[6.16]**.

[57.] For some specific issues associated with defendants' money held in bank accounts, see further, Ch 9, *The Mareva Order and Its Effects*, para **[9.47]** *et seq.*

[58.] On the nature of bank accounts see generally Hapgood, *Paget's Law of Banking*, (11th ed, 1996) Butterworths at pp 160-176.

[59.] *See Z Ltd v A-Z and AA-LL* [1982] 1 All ER 556, and generally, Ch 9, *The Mareva Order and Its Effects*, para **[9.45]** *et seq.*

[60.] Sometimes the Mareva order will be specifically directed at a bank or other financial institution where the defendant is known to have an account, see, *H v W, The Irish Times*, 13 September 1989 (Johnston J).

important that the Mareva plaintiff give as much detail of the defendant's account as possible. An account number and the branch of the bank or other financial institution where the account is kept should, where available, be supplied to the court for inclusion in its order.[61] Where such details are not known to the Mareva plaintiff, they may be procured by an order for discovery ancillary to the Mareva injunction.[62] It should be noted, however, that where a bank is asked to comply with a Mareva injunction without being given sufficient details to identify the customer concerned, the bank will be entitled to a reasonable fee for causing a search of its customers and their accounts and this will be payable by the Mareva plaintiff.[63]

[7.14] The existence of a bank account has been held to be sufficient evidence that a defendant has assets within the jurisdiction so as to justify the granting of a Mareva injunction. In *Third Chandris Shipping Corporation v Unimarine SA*[64] it was held by Lawton LJ that the existence of an overdrawn current account was sufficient proof of assets. It should, however, be noted that it appears that Lawton LJ had in mind "[l]arge overdrafts, such as commercial undertakings have, [which] are almost always secured in some way".[65] It is submitted that evidence of a current account should not invariably satisfy the requirement that a Mareva defendant has assets; and, further, it is thought that a Mareva injunction should not be made unless there is adequate evidence that the defendant has some assets which can be affected as otherwise the making of the order would be in vain.

Future Assets

[7.15] It is submitted that a Mareva injunction which restrains a defendant from disposing of his assets save insofar as they exceed a specific amount is not confined to assets which he has at the time the order is made and that, with equal force, it restrains him from dealing with assets acquired after the injunction is made ie over "future assets". There are sound reasons why this should be the case. As Colman J said in *Soinco SACI v Novokuznetsk Aluminium Plant*:[66]

> "... I am bound to say that, in my experience, the standard form of Mareva injunction has consistently been treated in the Commercial Court for many years as applicable to assets brought into the jurisdiction throughout the currency of the order but subject always to the overall monetary ceiling

---

[61.] See generally, Ch 8, *Applying for a Mareva Injunction*, para **[8.54]**.

[62.] See Ch 10, *Ancillary Orders*, para **[10.03]**.

[63.] *Z Ltd v A-Z and AA-LL* [1982] 1 All ER 556. See further Ch 9, *The Mareva Order and Its Effects*, para **[9.46]**.

[64.] [1979] 1 QB 645.

[65.] At 673.

[66.] [1997] 3 All ER 523 at 538.

incorporated in the order. If the assets of a trading company caught by the order were to be confined to those in existence at the date of the order, but subject always to dissipation in the ordinary course of business, much of the value of the Mareva jurisdiction would be destroyed. Every time further funds were received by a trading company in such a case it will be necessary to apply for another injunction. The view on this matter expressed *obiter* by Skinner J in *TDK Tape Distributors (UK) Ltd v Videochoice Ltd* reflects the assumption which has consistently been adopted in this court."

In *TDK Tape Distributors (UK) Ltd v Videochoice Ltd*[67] the plaintiff obtained a Mareva injunction against the defendants.[68] Subsequently, one of the defendants became entitled to a sum of money under an endowment insurance policy which had matured upon his wife's death. The proceeds of the policy were thereupon utilised to pay (through his solicitors) the defendant's counsels' legal fees which had been incurred in defending criminal proceedings. This policy had not been disclosed previously by the defendant who had been ordered to disclose the full value and whereabouts of all of his assets. The plaintiff applied to have the defendant and his solicitors punished for contempt of court. It was argued, *inter alia*, that neither the life policy nor its proceeds were assets or interests in assets of the defendant since the proceeds of the policy were acquired after the injunction was made. Central to the argument was that "Mareva injunctions in general, unless they spell it out specifically, do not apply to ... "after acquired" assets".[69] Skinner J held that the defendant's interest in the endowment policy was an asset which was in existence at the time the injunction was made and that, accordingly, it was unnecessary to deal with the arguments that a Mareva injunction does not attach to after-acquired assets. Skinner J's *obiter dictum* comments are, however, instructive:

> "In this particular case the asset in question was not an after-acquired asset. Second, even if it was, on the arguments presented to me, I would have found that it was caught by this particular injunction. It seems to me that it would be a negation of the purpose of that injunction if, every time the defendant acquired some new asset or property, it was up to the plaintiffs to discover it and make an application to the court that the existing injunction be extended to deal with it. It seems to me that a Mareva injunction is looking to the future and is dealing with the situation between the obtaining of the judgment and its

---

67. [1985] 3 All ER 345.
68. The terms of the injunction were that the defendant was ordered that: "... he by himself, his servants or agents or otherwise be restrained and an injunction is hereby granted restraining him until further order from disposing of or dealing with any of his assets or any interest which he may have in such assets within the jurisdiction except insofar as they may exceed the sum of £601,500 odd, save that he may spend up to £100 per week on ordinary living expenses": [1985] 3 All ER 345 at 347.
69. At 348g-h.

eventual execution, and it will cover any assets which are acquired between the granting of the order and the eventual execution of any judgment obtained in the action in question."[70]

It is submitted that the foregoing passage represents the law in Ireland on this point and that it is unnecessary for a Mareva injunction to specifically refer to future assets. The crucial point is that a Mareva injunction operates *in personam* and is, therefore, primarily directed at the defendant: the defendant's assets are, technically, a secondary consideration.[71] Where, however, a Mareva plaintiff is aware that the defendant is likely to shortly acquire valuable assets, it may well be prudent to put the matter beyond question by making this specifically part of the order.[72]

Assets in Joint-Ownership and Legally in the Name of a Third Party

[7.16] It is a prerequisite to the making of a Mareva injunction that the assets affected by the order are in the beneficial ownership of the defendant. The main difficulties which can arise here concern first, assets which are in the joint-ownership of the defendant and another party and, secondly, assets which appear to be in the sole beneficial ownership of a third party. In this context, "third party" has the same meaning as given in Chapter 4, *A Substantive Cause of Action* at para **[4.14]** and subsequent paragraphs to which the reader is referred generally.

[7.17] Where money is held jointly in a bank account, by a defendant and a third party, a Mareva injunction granted against the defendant alone ought not to prevent the third party from drawing on the account, unless such is specifically provided for in the order.[73] This is because to do otherwise would be an interference with the rights of the third-party. *SCF Finance Co Ltd v Masri*[74] concerned an application to vary the terms of a Mareva injunction. In that case, a Mareva injunction had been granted which restrained the defendant from "dealing with his assets within the jurisdiction so as to reduce them below the value of £700,000" and was expressed to apply to all accounts "held by or on behalf of the [first] defendant or by or on behalf of the [first] defendant jointly with any other persons or by nominees or otherwise howsoever at three named banks carrying on business in London."[75] It was subsequently alleged that the

---

[70.] At 349b-c.

[71.] See para **[7.03]** *supra*, and see Ch 9, *The Mareva Order and Its Effects*, para **[9.36]** *et seq*.

[72.] Sometimes, it seems, orders will specifically refer to "future assets" as in *BAD Teo v HD Co (I) Ltd*, *The Irish Times*, 15 September 1989 (Johnston J). There it was reported that the defendant was restrained from disposing of, selling or dealing with assets which it had, or which it would have, within the jurisdiction.

[73.] *Z Ltd v AZ & AA-LL* [1982] 2 WLR 288 at 299, [1982] 1 All ER 566 at 577 *per* Kerr LJ.

[74.] [1985] 2 All ER 747.

[75.] At 748g.

first defendant was continuing to trade in London by using his wife's account which was in her maiden name. As a result of this the original order was, on application, extended to specifically include the assets of the defendant's wife. In the Court of Appeal Lloyd LJ noted that the point in issue was the effect of a dispute between the plaintiff and a third party as to the ownership of assets.

[7.18] The defendant's counsel's argument was that unless the third party's claim to own the assets was obviously unsustainable the court was bound to give effect to that claim. This had been rejected at trial by Hirst J who had ordered that there be a hearing into the issue. On appeal, Lloyd LJ also rejected the defendant's submissions and held:

> "... I see no difficulty in the court's resolving any dispute which may arise between a plaintiff and a third party as to the ownership of assets to which the Mareva injunction has been applied. If that is so, then I can see no reason whatever why the court should be obliged to discharge the injunction on the mere say-so of the third party. If the court were so obliged, then the Mareva jurisdiction would be in danger of being nullified at the whim of the unscrupulous. If a court were not permitted to inquire into a third party's claim, but were bound to accept it at its face value, how could the court be satisfied that any transfer of assets to the third party had occurred before rather than after the injunction? Every consideration of policy and convenience points, in my view, against the principle which counsel for the second-defendant asserts."[76]

In concluding his judgment Lloyd LJ summarised the law applicable to the situation where there is a dispute between a plaintiff and a third party over the ownership of assets:

> "(i) Where a plaintiff invites the court to include within the scope of a Mareva injunction assets which appear on their face to belong to a third party eg a bank account in the name of a third party, the court should not accede to the invitation without good reason for supposing that the assets are in truth the assets of the defendant.
>
> (ii) Where the defendant asserts that the assets belong to a third party, the court is not obliged to accept that assertion without inquiry, but may do so depending on the circumstances. The same applies where it is the third party who makes the assertion, on an application to intervene.
>
> (iii) In deciding whether to accept the assertion of a defendant or a third party, without further inquiry, the court will be guided by what is just and convenient, not only between the plaintiff and the defendant, but also between the plaintiff, the defendant and the third party.
>
> (iv) Where the court decides not to accept the assertion without further inquiry, it may order an issue to be tried between the plaintiff and the third party in advance of the main action, or it may order that the issue await the

---

[76.] At 750g-h.

outcome of the main action, again depending in each case on what is just and convenient."[77]

It is thought that the foregoing points accurately summarise the principles of law which govern disputes between plaintiffs and third parties as to the ownership of assets.[78]

[7.19] The situation where a third party and a defendant jointly hold assets must be distinguished from cases where a third party holds assets on a defendant's behalf without having any beneficial interest in them.[79] The position of third parties was recently considered in Australia in *LED Builders Pty Ltd v Eagle Homes Pty Ltd*.[80] In that case, some confusion was evident between situations where (a) a third party holds a defendant's assets on trust for him ie the defendant has a proprietary interest in the assets held by the third party, and (b) situations where it is sought to directly enjoin a third party from dealing with his own assets in circumstances where there is a question as to whether the plaintiff has a cause of action against the third party. Both judgments of the Federal Court of Appeal rejected the notion that the *only* way in which a plaintiff could get a Mareva injunction over a third party's assets would be if the defendant has a proprietary interest in the third party's assets.

It is submitted that where a third party holds assets on behalf of a defendant, of course those assets are liable to be affected by a Mareva injunction directed at the defendant because the defendant is the equitable or beneficial owner of those assets and the third party is but a nominee. Where, however, assets are in the legal *and* equitable or beneficial ownership of a third party, such assets may only be affected by a Mareva injunction where a plaintiff has a substantive cause of action against the third party as would entitle him to mark judgment against the third party; in such a case, the "third party" will, in reality, be a co-defendant. As a matter of principle, a Mareva injunction can never be obtained against a person against whom the plaintiff can never obtain judgment.[81] Even in cases such as *TSB Private Bank International SA v Chabra*[82] and *Mercantile Group (Europe) AG v Aiyela*[83] which appear to be authorities for the proposition that a Mareva injunction can issue against third parties and freeze "their assets", the real basis for granting Mareva relief, in those cases, turned upon the strong

---

[77.] At 753c-f.

[78.] For a recent Irish decision where it was necessary to enquire into the true beneficial ownership of assets, see *Fitzpatrick v Criminal Assets Bureau*, High Court, unrep, 27 February 1998 (Shanley J).

[79.] See Ch 4, *A Substantive Cause of Action*, para **[4.14]** *et seq* where the question of Mareva injunctions and "third parties" is addressed in greater detail.

[80.] [1997] 826 FCA (22 August 1997).

[81.] See further, Ch 4, *A Substantive Cause of Action*, para **[4.14]** *et seq.*

[82.] [1992] 2 All ER 245.

[83.] [1994] 1 All ER 110.

evidence that the assets in the third parties' names were in fact beneficially owned by the defendants.[84]

The Sufficiency of the Defendant's Assets

[7.20] It is clearly the case that a Mareva injunction will not restrain a defendant from dealing with his assets over a *maximum* amount ie to the extent that they exceed the total value of the plaintiff's claim.[85] There is authority for the proposition that the value of assets sought to be frozen ought also to bear some reasonable *minimum* relation to the value of the plaintiff's claim.[86] In *Re John Horgan Livestock Ltd: O'Mahony v Horgan*[87] the plaintiff liquidator sought a Mareva injunction to restrain the second defendant director from collecting or receiving the sum of £71,000 with accrued interest, being moneys payable under a policy of insurance or, alternatively, from disposing of or dissipating or charging the said sum. In this case the statement of affairs of the company showed a deficit of £11.653 million. The plaintiff's application for a Mareva injunction was granted by Murphy J in the High Court but the second defendant's appeal was upheld by the Supreme Court. The main reason for upholding the appeal was because the plaintiff had failed to establish that there was a likelihood that the assets would be dissipated by the defendant with the intention that they would not be available to meet any judgment that the plaintiff might recover. The judgment of O'Flaherty J did, however, contain an interesting observation on the sufficiency of assets:

> "... on the facts of this case, the remedy is neither appropriate nor relevant. The amount that it is sought to freeze is but a tiny fraction of the millions of pounds that it is said are involved in the main action. It has to be reiterated that the Mareva remedy is to protect assets that may be dissipated in which case the

---

[84.] Support for this view can be taken from Ough & Flenley, *op cit*, at 2.1.4 who say, "In general, the assets must be in the legal or beneficial ownership of the defendant, although *the court may be willing to infer ownership in an exceptional case where there is a strong evidential basis for the inference*, and it is necessary to do so to protect the plaintiff", (italics added) citing the *TSB Bank case* and *The Theotokis* [1983] 2 Lloyd's Rep 204 as authority.

[85.] On maximum sum orders, see Ch 9, *The Mareva Order and Its Effects*, para **[9.09]**.

[86.] In *Sions v Ruscoe-Price* (1988) *The Independent* 30 November 1988, the Court of Appeal upheld a County Court Judge's refusal to grant a Mareva injunction to a plaintiff who was only owed £2,000. Ough & Flenley, *op cit*, at 5.6.3 where the following passage from the judgment of Woolf LJ is quoted from the Lexis transcript of the decision: "... having regard to the nature of the Mareva relief, basically it is inappropriate for use with relation to small sums of money. One can readily see that with people of modest means the costs involved in invoking the Mareva procedure, far from assisting the parties, may be prejudicial to their interests, because the amount of costs which could be incurred consequential to a Mareva order being made could be out of all proportion to the sum at stake".

[87.] [1995] 2 IR 411. See Ch 6, *The Risk of Removal or Disposal of Assets*, para **[6.18]** *et seq*.

judgment that the plaintiff gets will go unsatisfied. A Mareva injunction is not appropriate to enforce a claim to the assets themselves.

Since the assets in question here are of little or no relevance to the amount at stake - which runs into many millions of pounds - aside altogether from the fact that the case in regard to dissipation of assets has not been made out even to a *prima facie* extent - there is not here a situation where Mareva relief should be granted."[88]

Although it has long been recognised that equity should not act in vain, it is thought that this maxim should not act as an absolute fetter which would prevent a court from exercising its discretion to grant a Mareva injunction. Indeed, where all other requisite proofs have been established - particularly that there is a likelihood that the assets will be disposed of with a view to frustrating the plaintiff's judgment - it is submitted that, except in cases where a defendant has little or no assets,[89] the paucity of his assets ought not, *per se*, preclude the court from granting Mareva relief.[90]

[B] ASSETS LOCATED OUTSIDE OF THE JURISDICTION

[7.21] One of the most significant developments in the Mareva jurisdiction occurred in 1988 when the English Court of Appeal decided in a trilogy of cases that there was jurisdiction to enjoin a defendant from dealing with his assets although they were situate *outside of the jurisdiction*. These decisions were even more significant because of the fact that prior to 1988 there were express authorities for the proposition that a Mareva injunction could only be granted where a defendant had assets within the jurisdiction of the court making the order. In this section the following matters are addressed:

1. Confining Mareva Relief to Cases where Assets are Within the Jurisdiction.

---

88. At 422.

89. In *Dang v Nguyen*, (1998) Supreme Court of British Columbia, 25 February 1998 (Donald J) leave to appeal against a refusal to grant a Mareva injunction was refused on the ground, *inter alia*, that "A mortgage has been placed on the defendant's property. The plaintiff does not propose to ask this Court to set aside the transaction. Since the plaintiff is not aware of any other asset which could form the subject matter of a meaningful restraining order, and most of the defendant's interest in the property is mortgaged, the appeal would be an empty exercise." It is probably correct that Mareva relief should be refused where a defendant has no assets, unless there is a reasonably likelihood that he will soon come into money or other assets as, in such circumstances, the order would not be fruitless.

90. Indeed it is evident from O'Flaherty J's judgment that there were other issues which led him to focus in on the sufficiency of the assets sought to be affected. He said (at 422) of the application for a Mareva injunction that "It may - as is the case here - take on a life of its own while the main litigation is becalmed. I glean that a sense of urgency is not affecting the main litigation and will not do so while this side-show is running".

2. The Worldwide Mareva Jurisdiction Summarised.

3. The *Babanaft*, *Duvalier* and *Derby* Trilogy.

4. Worldwide Mareva Injunctions in Ireland.

5. Worldwide Mareva Injunctions in Other Jurisdictions.

6. The Undertaking not to Institute Foreign Proceedings.

7. The "*Babanaft* Proviso".

8. Ordering Defendants to Transfer Assets Between Jurisdictions.

9. Limitations on the *Ex Juris* Mareva Jurisdiction.

10. When is Worldwide Mareva Relief Justified?

Confining Mareva Relief to Cases where Assets are Within the Jurisdiction

[7.22] The two cases which are usually cited as examples of the courts' former attitude to making Mareva injunctions which affect assets outside of their jurisdiction are *Intraco Shipping Corp Ltd v Notis Shipping Corp of Liberia; The Boja Trader*[91] and *Ashtiani v Kashi*.[92] In *The Boja Trader* the only asset which the defendants had was a bank guarantee (equivalent to a letter of credit) which the plaintiff had given to the defendant in part consideration for a ship. The nature of the dispute was a claim for damages. The court declined to grant a Mareva injunction which would affect the defendant's bank guarantee because, in that case, it was only payable in Greece. For that reason it was held that the defendant did not have assets within the jurisdiction and, accordingly, that it was inappropriate to grant a Mareva injunction.

[7.23] In *Ashtiani v Kashi*[93] the basis of the dispute between the plaintiffs and the defendant concerned money which was allegedly owed on foot of a compromise agreement whereby the defendant had agreed to pay US$500,000 to the first plaintiff and US$750,000 to the second plaintiff. The plaintiffs claimed that the defendant had only paid US$200,000 to the second plaintiff; the defendant claimed that the agreement had been entered into as a result of misrepresentation, duress and that there was no consideration for the agreement. The plaintiffs sought and obtained a Mareva injunction. The trial judge, Hirst J, also directed the defendant to disclose the value, particulars, identity and whereabouts of his assets both within *and without* the jurisdiction. The defendant disclosed five foreign bank accounts in Guernsey, Brussels, Luxembourg, Portugal and California. Consequent to this the plaintiffs successfully applied in Guernsey, Belgium and Luxembourg for Mareva-type

---

[91.] [1981] 2 Lloyd's Rep. 256.
[92.] [1986] 2 All ER 970, noted by Gill, (1986) ILT 18.
[93.] *Ibid.*

injunctions. The defendant applied to have Hirst J's order discharged and this application was granted by Sir Neil Lawson on the defendant's undertaking not to dispose of a leasehold property in England without advance notice to the plaintiffs. It was this order which was appealed to the Court of Appeal.

[7.24] In the Court of Appeal the plaintiffs sought, *inter alia*, an extension of the Mareva injunction to attach the foreign assets. Dillon LJ noted that the argument for such extension was based:

> "... on the broad view that the function of the Mareva order is to see that a judgment when obtained will not be nugatory or fruitless for want of assets to attach...".[94]

Dillon LJ began his analysis by looking at the rule in *Lister v Stubbs*,[95] noting that the Mareva injunction was an exception to that rule and he then considered some of the authorities which seemed to require that a defendant have assets within the jurisdiction. Dillon LJ was not disposed to making a disclosure order relating to foreign assets, let alone a Mareva injunction which would affect assets situate outside of the jurisdiction. Dillon LJ gave the following reasons for refusing to extend the Mareva jurisdiction to assets situate *ex juris*:

> "In my judgment there are valid reasons why the Mareva injunction should be limited to the assets of the defendant within the jurisdiction of the court. Firstly, it could very well be oppressive to the defendant that, as a result of an order of an English court, his assets everywhere should be frozen or he should be subjected to applications for seizure orders in many other jurisdictions. Secondly, it is difficult for the English court to control or police enforcement proceedings in other jurisdictions. It is not very desirable that the English court should attempt to control such foreign proceedings, and the difficulties are underlined where, as here, the plaintiffs are not resident within the jurisdiction of the English court. Thirdly, as Lord Roskill pointed out in his speech in *Home Office v Harman* [1982] 1 All ER 532 at 552, [1982] 1 AC 280 at 323, our judicial process in requiring discovery involves invasion of an otherwise absolute right of privacy. The particular form of discovery he was concerned with there was the discovery in the course of an action and the production of relevant documents with a view to the fair trial of the action, but his comment that the order involves an invasion of privacy applies with the fullest force to an order on an individual or a company to disclose all his or its assets throughout the world. Fourthly, it has been many times laid down that the object of a Mareva injunction is not to give the plaintiff security for the amount of his claim in advance of judgment in the action; but, if there is an order for disclosure of foreign assets, that may lead to the plaintiff obtaining security in

---

[94.] At 975a.
[95.] (1890) 45 Ch D 1; [1886-90] All ER 797. See generally, Ch 2, *The Jurisdiction to Grant Mareva Relief* para **[2.04]**.

some foreign jurisdiction. For instance, in the present case an order has been obtained in Belgium. We have evidence that under Belgian law the court will not make any order attaching assets unless those assets are specifically identified. It would be necessary, for instance, in order to attach a bank account to have particulars of that account and the branch where it is kept. The defendant has been compelled by Hirst J's order to disclose and identify his bank account in Belgium. The plaintiffs have thereby been enabled to obtain an order in Belgium ...

The disclosure of foreign assets cannot be regarded as ancillary to the making of a Mareva injunction limited to the English assets. It cannot stand on its own feet as a primary exercise of jurisdiction if the Mareva exercise is limited to English assets ...".[96]

Dillon LJ held that the order for the disclosure of the defendant's foreign assets ought never to have been made.

[7.25] On first consideration, the suggestion that the courts could assert a worldwide Mareva jurisdiction could be thought of as blatant arrogance, even of judicial jingoism. What right have the courts of one country to assert an extra-territorial jurisdiction and thereby affect (albeit indirectly) assets situate in the sovereign territory of another country? The courts, however, have made it clear that the effect of a worldwide Mareva injunction is not to act *in rem* against the defendant's foreign assets;[97] its effect is, rather, to act *in personam* against the defendant and others who are present within the jurisdiction of the court making the order or who are otherwise amenable to its jurisdiction.[98] Indeed, in *Ashtiani v Kashi*, the judgment of Neill LJ which concurred with that of Dillon LJ recognised the basis upon which a worldwide Mareva injunction *could* be granted:

"This jurisdiction to protect a plaintiff against the risk that the judgment of the court will be rendered ineffective because in the meantime the defendant will have disposed of or dissipated his assets is a *jurisdiction which is exercised in personam*. It may be said, therefore, that in principle there is no reason why a court could not make an order restraining a party over whom it has jurisdiction from dealing with his assets wherever such assets may be situated."[99]

Notwithstanding this, Neill LJ found that it was clear that the practice up to that time was that Mareva injunctions would be confined to cases where the defendant had assets within the jurisdiction. The ground had, however, been turned.

[96.] [1986] 2 All ER 970 at 977e-978c.

[97.] See further, Ch 9, *The Mareva Order and Its Effects*, para **[9.36]**.

[98.] See the judgment of Nicholls LJ in *Babanaft International Co SA v Bassatne* [1989] 1 All ER 433; [1989] 2 WLR 232.

[99.] At 979h, italics added.

The Worldwide Mareva Jurisdiction Summarised

[7.26] It is now established that there is jurisdiction to make a pre-judgment or post-judgment worldwide Mareva injunction which can restrain a defendant from dealing with all of his assets, worldwide, or, indeed, specific assets situate in another jurisdiction.[100] The basis of the jurisdiction is that because Mareva injunctions operate *in personam* it is irrelevant where a defendant's assets are situate; the only relevant matter is whether the defendant is himself amenable to the jurisdiction of the court making the order.[101] The worldwide Mareva jurisdiction will, however, only be exercised in exceptional circumstances.[102] The protection of third parties is of fundamental importance in making an *ex juris* Mareva injunction and a provision, termed a *Babanaft proviso*, which protects third parties will invariably be included in the injunction.[103]

The *Babanaft*, *Duvalier* and *Derby* Trilogy

[7.27] In 1988 there was a trilogy of Court of Appeal decisions on the propriety of worldwide Mareva injunctions. Although courts in other jurisdictions appeared to have accepted prior to 1988 that there was jurisdiction to make an *ex juris* or worldwide Mareva injunction, this was the first time that the courts in England accepted the validity of such an extension to the original Mareva jurisdiction.[104] The first in the trilogy was *Babanaft International Co SA v*

[100.] In England: in *Babanaft International Co SA v Bassatne* [1989] 1 All ER 433; [1989] 2 WLR 232; *Republic of Haiti v Duvalier* [1989] 1 All ER 456, [1989] 2 WLR 261; *Derby & Co Ltd v Weldon (No 1)*[1989] 1 All ER 469, [1989] 2 WLR 276; in Ireland: *Deutsche Bank Aktiengesellschaft v Murtagh & Murtagh* [1995] 2 IR 122; *Taher v Balkanbank, The Irish Times*, 30 March 1995 (Barr J); *Clonmeen Manor House Ltd v Royal Lodge Ltd* (1994) High Court (Costello J), *The Irish Times*, 31 March 1994; *JRB&S Ltd v E, The Irish Times*, 18 February 1998 (Kelly J) where Kelly J was reported as having granted a Mareva injunction which applied to assets "within and outside the jurisdiction"; and *Bula Resources (Holdings) plc v Stanley, The Irish Times*, 7 August 1998 (O'Higgins J) where, following the publication of the report of an inspector who had been appointed to the plaintiff company under the Companies Act 1990, the plaintiff was successful in obtaining a worldwide Mareva injunction against the defendant, its former chairman and chief executive, who was resident in Moscow. See also *Intermetal Group Ltd and Trans-World (Steel) Ltd v Worslade Trading Ltd*, High Court, unrep, 12 December 1997 (O'Sullivan J) where although O'Sullivan J refused to make a worldwide Mareva injunction, he declined to do so on the evidence available and not on grounds of principal.

[101.] Worldwide Mareva injunctions have, in the UK, been given in aid of foreign proceedings under the Civil Jurisdiction and Judgments Act 1982: see *Credit Suisse Fides Trust SA v Cuoghi* [1997] 3 All ER 724, noted by Springthorpe, 'Recent Developments in Mareva Injunctions', [1998] BLR 7. See generally, Ch 4, *A Substantive Cause of Action*, para **[4.62]**.

[102.] *Derby & Co Ltd v Weldon (No 1)* [1989] 1 All ER 469 at 478g-h. See para **[7.55]** *infra*.

[103.] For the *Babanaft proviso*, see *Babanaft, Duvallier* and *Derby*; and para **[7.27]** *et seq, infra*.

[104.] See, eg, the Australian cases of *Hospital Products Ltd v Ballabil Holdings Pty Ltd* [1984] 2 NSWLR 662 and *Jackson v Sterling Industries Ltd* (1987) 162 CLR 612 considered at para **[7.42]** *infra*.

Bassatne,[105] which involved an application for a post-judgment Mareva injunction. The facts were that, having obtained judgment for $15m against the defendant, the plaintiff sought, and obtained at trial, a Mareva injunction which covered the defendants' assets outside of the jurisdiction and which restrained the defendants from dealing with their assets worldwide without first giving five days' notice to the plaintiff in every case. On foot of the injunction, the plaintiff's solicitors notified 47 entities worldwide which were thought to hold the defendants' assets. The trial judge, Vinelott J had refused the defendants' application to restrain the plaintiff from notifying banks and other institutions of the terms of the injunction. The Court of Appeal held that there was jurisdiction to make a so-called worldwide Mareva injunction in respect of the defendants' assets which were situate outside of the jurisdiction.

[7.28] In the Court of Appeal Kerr LJ noted that the injunction granted by Vinelott J had been qualified by the following proviso:

> "Nothing in this injunction shall prevent any bank or third party (not being a third party connected or associated in any way with the defendants or either of them or any relative of the defendants or either of them or any company or firm united or associated in any way with the defendants or either of them) or any relative of the defendants or either of them from exercising any right of set off it may have in respect of facilities given to the defendants or the said companies before the date of this injunction including any interest which has accrued or may hereafter accrue in respect of such facilities."[106]

Acknowledging that the foregoing was a standard type of proviso which was regularly inserted into Mareva orders, Kerr LJ said of the purpose of this proviso that it:

> "... is of course inserted for the benefit of third parties who may be affected by the freezing order. My reason for quoting it is that it illustrates that, although Mareva injunctions are orders made *in personam* against defendants, they also have an *in rem* effect on third parties. It shows that, save to the extent of the proviso, the order is binding on third parties who have notice of the injunction."[107]

Turning to the question of the propriety of Mareva injunctions which affect assets situate outside of the jurisdiction, Kerr LJ held that there was power under s 37(1) of the Supreme Court Act 1981 to make an order with *ex juris* effect. He noted that the Mareva jurisdiction was still developing and that in appropriate cases there was jurisdiction to grant a Mareva injunction against a defendant

---

[105.] [1989] 1 All ER 433; [1989] 2 WLR 232.

[106.] At 438e-f.

[107.] At 438g-h. See further, Ch 9, *The Mareva Order and Its Effects*, para **[9.36]** *et seq* and Ch 12, *Enforcing Mareva Injunctions and Other Orders*, para **[12.31]** *et seq*.

which extended to his assets which are situate outside of the jurisdiction and he found that this jurisdiction should not be limited to post-judgment relief. Kerr LJ did, however, accept that unqualified worldwide Mareva injunctions could never be justified and that third parties must be protected.

[7.29] Kerr LJ placed considerable reliance upon the Brussels Convention, saying that the key to the proper exercise of any extra-territorial jurisdiction must lie in whether there will be international reciprocity for the recognition and enforcement of the Mareva injunction.[108] For Kerr LJ, Article 24, which provides for provisional and protective measures pending judgment, was of particular significance.

[7.30] The short concurring judgment of Neill LJ is also instructive. After quoting from the judgment of Dillon LJ in *Ashtiani v Kashi* reproduced above,[109] Neill LJ acknowledged that he was a party to that decision and said that he remained of the opinion that that decision accurately reflected the exercise and development of the Mareva jurisdiction to that time. However, after conducting a short review he concluded:

> "In my judgment, the arguments against granting a Mareva-type injunction extending to assets outside the jurisdiction are much weaker in a case where judgment has been obtained than in a case where an interlocutory order is sought before trial. Indeed, I am satisfied that there will be many cases, of which the present case is one, where justice requires that, once judgment has been obtained, the successful plaintiffs should be able to obtain the protection of an injunction extending to all the assets of the defendants whether within or outside the jurisdiction of the court."[110]

Neill LJ went on to state that every worldwide Mareva injunction should contain the following proviso:

> "Provided always that no person other than the defendants themselves shall in any way be affected by the terms of this order ... or concerned to enquire whether any instruction given by or on behalf of either defendant or by anyone else, or any other act or omission of either defendant or anyone else, whether acting on behalf of either defendant or otherwise, is or may be a breach of this order ... by either defendant."[111]

[108.] See Ch 4, *A Substantive Cause of Action*, para **[4.50]** *et seq.*

[109.] See para **[7.25]** *supra.*

[110.] At 450b-c It may be noted, however, that if the jurisdiction to make worldwide Marevas was confined to post-judgment situations, this was short lived as five days later the Court of Appeal granted a pre-judgment worldwide Mareva injunction in *Duvalier*: see para **[7.32]** *infra.*

[111.] At 450f-g. Note that Kerr LJ (at 447) would have preferred to have added "unless ... [the order] is enforced by the courts of the states in which any of the defendants' assets are located."

Whilst this came to be known as the *Babanaft proviso* it is important to note that the wording was both refined and further developed in subsequent cases, considered below.[112]

[7.31] Nicholls LJ's judgment in the *Babanaft* case began by examining the nature of how equity operates and in particular the fact that it acts *in personam* against the defendant.[113] From this foundation Nicholls LJ had little difficulty in establishing the jurisdiction to grant a Mareva injunction which affected a defendant's foreign assets. His one concern was, understandably, the effect which the exercise of such a jurisdiction might have on third parties:

> "It would be wrong for an English court, by making an order in respect of overseas assets against a defendant amenable to its jurisdiction, to impose or attempt to impose obligations on persons not before the court in respect of acts done by them abroad regarding property outside the jurisdiction. That, self-evidently, would be for the English court to claim an altogether exorbitant, extra-territorial jurisdiction ...
>
> To meet this difficulty I can see no alternative but to grasp the nettle firmly, and write into the order, which applies only to property outside the jurisdiction, an express provision to the effect that nothing in the relevant part of the order is to affect any person other than the defendants personally. This will remove any extra-territorial vice which otherwise the order might have, or be thought to have.
>
> I have considered anxiously whether an order in such a form would be wrong in principle. It is certainly unattractive to make an order which, contrary to the normal position, third parties are bidden to ignore. But in this case the alternative is not to make any temporary 'holding' order at all. Given that choice, I think that justice and convenience require an order binding only on the defendants rather than no order at all. The touching concern shown by the defendants on this appeal for the integrity of banks and others overseas should not be allowed to obscure the judge's finding that these defendants would be likely to do whatever they can to frustrate execution of the judgment."[114]

The Court of Appeal in the *Babanaft* case pushed the Mareva jurisdiction further than it had ever been pushed. It is thought that this decision was correct and is good law and that provided third parties are afforded adequate protection there can be no objection to the exercise of an *ex juris* Mareva jurisdiction in appropriate cases.

[7.32] Five days after the Court of Appeal gave judgment in the *Babanaft* case it again gave judgment in a similar application in the case of *Republic of Haiti v*

[112.] See para **[7.46]** *et seq*, *infra*.
[113.] See para **[7.03]** *supra* and para **[7.35]** *infra*.
[114.] At 453e-f.

Duvalier.[115] There, a pre-judgment worldwide Mareva was sought by the Republic of Haiti against the former president of the country and his family. It was alleged that $120 million had been embezzled by the defendants and the plaintiff instituted proceedings in France, in 1986, and in England, in 1988. Upon the institution of the English proceedings the plaintiff obtained an *ex parte* Mareva injunction which (1) restrained the defendants from dealing with their assets which were the subject of the French action; (2) froze the defendants' assets within England and Wales save insofar as they exceeded $120 million; (3) ordered the defendants' solicitors to disclose the nature, location and value of the defendant's assets; and (4) gagged the defendants' solicitors by preventing them from disclosing the making of the order. Upon learning of the order the defendants appealed to have it set aside but were unsuccessful. It was against this decision that the defendants appealed to the Court of Appeal. Two main questions arose for the Court of Appeal to decide. The first concerned the *ex juris* service of a writ claiming interim relief under the Civil Jurisdiction and Judgments Act 1982 (UK) pursuant to the Rules of the Supreme Court 1965 (UK) without leave.[116] The second question concerned the court's power and discretion to make a worldwide Mareva injunction against a *non-resident* defendant and the nature of protection to be afforded to third parties.

[7.33] In relation to the jurisdiction to make a worldwide Mareva order, Slaughton LJ followed the earlier decision of *Babanaft International Co SA v Bassatne* and held that there was jurisdiction to grant a Mareva injunction pending trial over assets worldwide although he accepted that the "cases where it will be appropriate to grant such an injunction will be rare, if not very rare".[117] It had been asserted that it was wrong in principle to make an order against non-residents in relation to their possible assets situate outside of the jurisdiction but Slaughton LJ applied the rule in *Re Liddell's Settlement Trust*[118] and refused to distinguish between substantive relief and interim relief: once a person is properly served, they are amenable to the court's jurisdiction. On the question of the court's discretion, Slaughton LJ again stressed the extraordinary circumstances of the case in hand. On this point he said that what was determinative was:

> "the plain and admitted intention of the defendants to move their assets out of the reach of the courts of law, coupled with the resources they have obtained

---

[115.] [1989] 1 All ER 456, [1989] 2 WLR 261.

[116.] See Ch 4, *A Substantive Cause of Action*, para **[4.50]** *et seq.*

[117.] [1989] 1 All ER 456 at 466b.

[118.] [1936] 1 All ER 239 at 248 where Romer J said: "The moment that a person is properly served under the provisions of RSC Ord XI that person, so far as the jurisdiction of a court is concerned, is in precisely the same position as a person who is in this country".

and the skill they have hitherto shown in doing that, and the vast amount of money involved. This case demands international co-operation between all nations."[119]

It was Slaughton LJ who coined the term "*Babanaft* proviso". He made a number of changes to the proviso which had first been promulgated in *Babanaft International Co SA*, one being to provide that it did not exempt natural persons who are resident in the country where the worldwide Mareva injunction is made,[120] and another being to graft on a qualification to the proviso that the order was not to affect third parties unless and to the extent that it was enforced by the courts of the countries in which the assets were located.

[7.34] The third case in the trilogy was *Derby & Co Ltd v Weldon (No 1)*,[121] the first in a series of judgments in that particular action. There the plaintiff brought an action against the defendants alleging breach of contract, conspiracy and fraudulent breach of fiduciary duty. A Mareva injunction was granted only over assets within the jurisdiction. The plaintiff appealed to the Court of Appeal. Again the Court of Appeal granted the injunction sought over the defendants' assets worldwide, but subject to a further safeguard for the defendants. This time the injunction was made conditional upon the plaintiffs' undertakings not to apply to foreign courts to enforce the order nor to use information disclosed about overseas assets in any foreign proceedings. Parker LJ distinguished the test for a domestic Mareva injunction from the test for a worldwide Mareva injunction on the following basis:

> "The mere fact that the plaintiff shows a good arguable case and a real risk of disposal or hiding of English assets, the requisites for an internal Mareva, clearly cannot by itself be sufficient to justify an extra-territorial Mareva either worldwide or at all. Such a Mareva would clearly be unjustified if, for example, there were sufficient English assets to cover the appropriate sum, or, if the court were not satisfied that there were foreign assets or that there was a real risk of disposal of the same, or if it would in all the circumstances be oppressive to make the order."[122]

After finding that the evidence in that case was sufficient to satisfy the test for granting a worldwide Mareva injunction, Parker LJ went on to make the order but stressed the importance of safeguards:

> "... it appears to me that there is every justification for a worldwide Mareva, so long as, by undertaking or proviso or a combination of both, (a) oppression of the defendants by way of exposure to a multiplicity of proceedings is avoided,

---

119. [1989] 1 All ER 456 at 467.
120. At 468.
121. [1989] 1 All ER 469, [1989] 2 WLR 276.
122. At 474.

(b) the defendants are protected against the misuse of information gained from the ordinary order for disclosure in aid of the Mareva, (c) the position of third parties is protected."[123]

Worldwide Mareva plaintiffs' undertakings not to misuse information obtained or to commence foreign proceedings and the protection of third parties through the *Babanaft* proviso are considered below.[124]

Worldwide Mareva Injunctions in Ireland

[7.35] Ironically, in one of the first recorded Mareva injunctions granted by an Irish court, *H v H*,[125] the defendant was restrained from disposing of or dissipating his assets within or *without* the jurisdiction.[126] The primary objection to the making of a worldwide Mareva injunction is that in granting such relief the court is making an extra-territorial order which intrudes upon the jurisdiction of foreign courts. There is, however, early precedent for the granting of extra-territorial injunctive relief by an Irish Court. In *Lett v Lett*[127] an injunction was granted which restrained the defendant from prosecuting an action which had been commenced in Argentina. The plaintiff and defendant had formerly been husband and wife but had been divorced. Both then signed a consent whereby a settlement was agreed, on foot of which the plaintiff was obliged to transfer certain moneys and land to the defendant. The plaintiff then went to Argentina and prospered. Upon learning of her former husband's new wealth, the defendant threatened to institute further proceedings, seeking a larger allowance. Notwithstanding that the plaintiff had agreed to pay a further annual sum to her, the defendant instituted proceedings in Argentina. The Irish Court of Appeal upheld the trial judge's decision to grant an injunction preventing the defendant from prosecuting the proceedings. Recognising the extraordinary nature of the jurisdiction to grant such an injunction in these circumstances, Porter MR said:

> "The old and established jurisdiction of this country in reference to cases in foreign tribunals was founded not on any arrogant assumption of powers in our courts over foreign tribunals, but upon an undoubted control over the subjects of the realm, as a personal right to restrain them from committing injustice by prosecuting inequitable claims in respect of property, wherever asserted."[128]

[123.] At 475.

[124.] See para **[7.43]** and para **[7.46]**, respectively, *infra*.

[125.] High Court, unrep, 7 April 1982 (O'Hanlon J).

[126.] See Ch 4, *A Substantive Cause of Action*, para **[4.49]**.

[127.] [1906] IR 618.

[128.] *Ibid* at 629. As further support for the jurisdiction to make an injunction with extra-territorial effect, Porter MR cited as authority the House of Lords decision in *The Carron Iron Co v Maclaren* 5 HL Cas 416 and an early edition of *Kerr on Injunctions*.

Although this case has not, to the writer's knowledge, been relied upon as authority by an Irish court when exercising its extra-territorial jurisdiction it is thought to be good authority for the proposition that an Irish court has jurisdiction to make an *in personam* order against those who are subject to its authority with respect to how they deal with their assets which are situate abroad.[129]

[7.36] There have been a number of judicial comments which could lead one to think that the Irish courts have looked upon worldwide Mareva injunctions with displeasure. In *Countyglen plc v Carway*,[130] the facts of which have already been considered,[131] Murphy J confined the Mareva injunction to assets within the jurisdiction saying "that a Mareva injunction should be so restricted appears to have been established *obiter dictum* by the decision in *Allied Arab Bank Ltd v Hajjar* [1987] 3 All ER 739; [1988] QB 787".[132] It was, however, acknowledged by Murphy J that his comment was also *obiter dictum* being made in the context that the order sought in *Countyglen* was a domestic Mareva injunction. On the propriety of an order for discovery ancillary to the Mareva injunction Murphy J said:

> "With regard to discovery, there is no doubt as to the power of the court to make an order for discovery as ancillary to a Mareva injunction. In my view, it is desirable that such an affidavit should be sworn in the present case. However, it seems to me that the order in that behalf should be restricted, like the injunction itself, to the assets of the defendants within the jurisdiction of this court."[133]

---

129. See also the dictum of Lord Brougham LC in *Lord Portarlington v Soulby* (1834) My & K 104 at 108, [1824-34] All ER Rep 610 at 612 quoted by Nicholls LJ in *Babanaft International Co SA v Bassatne* [1989] 1 All ER 433 at 451g-j. In an English application for an injunction to restrain the defendant from taking proceedings in Ireland on a bill of exchange, Lord Brougham LC said: "In truth, nothing can be more unfounded than the doubts of the jurisdiction. That is grounded, like all other jurisdiction of the Court, not upon any pretension to the exercise of judicial and administrative rights abroad, but on the circumstance of the person of the party on whom this order is made being within the power of the court. If the court can command him to bring home goods from abroad, or to assign chattel interests, or to convey real property locally situate abroad if, for instance, as in *Penn v Lord Baltimore* ((1750) 1 Ves Sen 444, [1558-1774] All ER Rep 99), it can decree the performance of an agreement touching the boundary of a province in North America; or, as in the case of *Toller v Carteret* (1705) 2 Vern 494, 23 ER 916), can foreclose a mortgage in the isle of Sark, one of the channel islands; in precisely the like manner it can restrain the party being within the limits of its jurisdiction from doing anything abroad, whether the thing forbidden be a conveyance or other act *in pais*, or the instituting or prosecution of an action in a foreign court."
130. [1995] 1 IR 208.
131. See Ch 5, *A Good Arguable Case*, para **[5.22]**.
132. [1995] 1 IR 208 at 218.
133. At 218.

The decision in the *Countyglen* case contains the strongest Irish judicial pronouncement, such as it is, against the making of a Mareva injunction which restrains a defendant from dealing with assets which are situate outside of the jurisdiction. There are other judicial comments which seem not to recognise a worldwide Mareva jurisdiction, by reason of their emphasis on the requirement of proof of assets *within the jurisdiction*. So, in the Supreme Court decision of *Re John Horgan Livestock Ltd: O'Mahony v Horgan*[134] it was held by Hamilton CJ that one of the five criteria which should be established prior to a Mareva injunction being granted was that "the plaintiff should give some grounds for believing that the defendant had assets within the jurisdiction."[135] Too much cannot, however, be read into this comment because in that case the applicant for Mareva relief was looking for a "domestic" Mareva injunction; of course in the case of a domestic Mareva injunction there must be assets within the jurisdiction as otherwise the exercise of the jurisdiction would have been futile, just in the same way that a worldwide Mareva injunction should not be granted without proof that the defendant has some assets *outside* of the jurisdiction.[136]

[7.37] On the other hand there is direct authority from Costello J that the Irish courts will, in a suitable case, grant a worldwide Mareva injunction. In *Deutsche Bank Aktiengesellschaft v Murtagh & Murtagh*[137] the plaintiff German bank claimed 1 million Deutschmarks from the defendants on foot of their guarantees. The guarantees were executed in Germany, intended to be performed in Germany and Costello J recognised that they were subject to German law. The defendants entered a "without prejudice" appearance to the plaintiff's summary summons claiming that the Irish courts had no jurisdiction in the matter. On foot of the plaintiff's proceedings the plaintiff sought ancillary relief in the form of a Mareva injunction to restrain the defendants from dealing with their assets within the jurisdiction and in particular a property called "Olde Court Castle" in County Tipperary. The motion was adjourned generally on the basis of the

---

[134] [1995] 2 IR 411.

[135] At 416, *per* Hamilton CJ, quoting Murphy J who was quoting Lord Denning in *Third Chandris Shipping Corporation v Unimarine SA* [1979] QB 645. See also *Tobin and Twomey Services Ltd v Kerry Foods Ltd and Kerry Group plc* [1996] 2 ILRM 1 where the Supreme Court (per Blayney J) quoted with apparent approval a quotation from Carroll J in her High Court judgment in that case that "Indeed there is no evidence that the first named defendant has assets within the jurisdiction".

[136] Indeed in *Intermetal Group Ltd and Trans-World (Steel) Ltd v Worslade Trading Ltd*, High Court, unrep, 12 December 1997 (O'Sullivan J) O'Sullivan J declined to make a worldwide Mareva injunction saying (at p 26 of the transcript): "Even if the scope of a Mareva type injunction were limited, I do not think I have sufficient detail in relation to the defendant's assets to enable me to frame an order". See Ch 8, *Applying for a Mareva Injunction*, para **[8.54]**.

[137] [1995] 2 IR 122.

defendants' undertakings. Subsequently, a new motion was brought by the plaintiff to restrain the defendants from dealing with their "extra-territorial assets".

[7.38] After deciding that the Irish courts had jurisdiction to adjudicate on the plaintiff's claim, Costello J went on to review the history of the interlocutory applications. He noted that on 17 October 1994 the plaintiff had sought an injunction to restrain the defendants from dealing with assets within Ireland and, in particular, the "Olde Court Castle". On 24 October 1994 one of the defendants had sworn an affidavit saying that that property was subject to a charge to secure a loan of £50,000 (in favour of a building society)[138] and that it was also subject to a second charge which secured a loan of £200,000. This motion was adjourned generally on the defendants' undertakings; one of which was to swear an affidavit which identified the defendants' assets within the jurisdiction. This affidavit disclosed that the second charge was "in favour of JM of 140 Borough Road, Middlesboro, England in the sum of Stg£200,000" ranking in priority behind a building society's mortgage. Costello J observed that:

> "The plaintiff, not surprisingly, was concerned to learn about the second charge as (a) it had written a letter of demand on the 7th October 1994 and the charge had, apparently, been executed five days later on the 12th October 1994 and (b) the charge was not in favour of a financial institution but of a private individual. Accordingly, they applied for and obtained on the 22nd November 1994 an interim injunction restraining the defendants from dealing outside the State with monies received in consideration for the execution of the second charge and other relief."[139]

In what was the most dramatic extension of the breadth of the Mareva jurisdiction in Ireland since the late McWilliam J recognised in *Powerscourt Estates v Gallagher & Gallagher*[140] (the first written Irish judgment on the Mareva injunction) the very existence of that jurisdiction in Ireland, Costello J held:

> "I am satisfied that the plaintiffs are entitled to the relief they claim. In my opinion the court has jurisdiction to restrain the dissipation of extra-territorial assets where such an order is warranted by the facts. The basis on which a Mareva injunction is granted is to ensure that a defendant does not take action designed to frustrate subsequent orders of the court. It is well established in England that a Mareva injunction may extend to foreign assets and I believe

---

138. Although unclear from the judgment the subsequent reference to "the building society's mortgage" implies that this was the first charge.
139. [1995] 2 IR 122 at 131 (Emphasis added).
140. [1984] ILRM 123.

that the Irish courts have a similar power in order to avoid the frustration of subsequent orders it may make. The court has ancillary power also and in suitable cases it may grant a disclosure order requiring a defendant to swear an affidavit in respect of assets outside the jurisdiction (see *Derby & Co Ltd v Weldon (Nos 3 and 4)* [1989] 2 WLR 412'."[141]

The judgment of Costello J does not give any indication of the actual form of the order which the court made. In particular, no mention of the so-called *Babanaft* proviso was made in the judgment and there is no record of whether such was included in the actual order made.[142] Although this is the only written judgment of the High Court where worldwide Mareva relief has been granted, a number of worldwide Mareva injunctions have been made *ex tempore*[143] and many of these appear to have included a *Babanaft* proviso.

Worldwide Mareva Injunctions in Other Jurisdictions

[7.39] The acceptance of the jurisdiction to grant worldwide Mareva relief in Ireland and other jurisdictions demonstrates the willingness of courts to recognise that compelling reasons for extending the scope of Mareva relief in one jurisdiction are equally compelling in another jurisdiction. In the first Canadian case to accept the validity of worldwide Mareva relief, *Mooney v Orr*,[144] Newbury J said in the Supreme Court of British Columbia:

"The reasons for extending Mareva injunctions to apply to foreign assets are valid in British Columbia no less than in England and Australia - the notion that a court should not permit a defendant to take action designed to frustrate existing of subsequent orders of the court, and the practical consideration that in this day of instant communication and paperless cross-border transfers, the courts must, in order to preserve the effectiveness of their judgments, adapt to new circumstances. Such adaptability has always been, and continues to be, the genius of the common law. "[145]

The background circumstances to this application for a Mareva injunction which was to have effect outside of British Columbia were unusual; indeed the

---

[141.] At 131. See Conlon-Smyth, 'International Mareva Injunctions', (1996) *Practice and Procedure* 12.

[142.] On the "*Babanaft* proviso" see para **[7.46]** *infra*.

[143.] See *Taher v Balkanbank, The Irish Times*, 30 March 1995 (Barr J); *Clonmeen Manor House Ltd v Royal Lodge Ltd, The Irish Times*, 31 March 1994 (Costello J); *JRBS Ltd v E, The Irish Times*, 18 February 1998 (Kelly J); *Bula Resources (Holdings) Ltd v Stanley, The Irish Times*, 7 August 1998 (O'Higgins J); and *Intermetal Group Ltd and Trans-World (Steel) Ltd v Worslade Trading Ltd*, High Court, unrep, 12 December 1997 (O'Sullivan J) where although O'Sullivan J refused to make a worldwide Mareva injunction, he declined to do so on the evidence available and not on grounds of principal.

[144.] [1994] BCJ No 2322; noted by Cook, [1995] 2 JIBL N-54.

[145.] At p 9, 10 of the transcript, para 11 of the judgment.

application for Mareva relief was made in the middle of a complex trial which was then in its ninth week. The defendants in the trial had counterclaimed against the plaintiff (M) and had sought three specific orders from the court: first, an interlocutory injunction restraining M from disposing of or dealing with any of his assets wherever situate; secondly, an order that he disclose the full value and identify the location of his assets; and thirdly, that Coopers & Lybrand Ltd be appointed receivers to his assets and that he transfer his overseas assets to them.

[7.40] Newbury J first considered the jurisdictional question and reviewed in some detail the decision in *Babanaft International Co SA v Bassatne*.[146] In deciding whether there was jurisdiction to make a worldwide Mareva injunction Newbury J's task was not made any easier by the fact that there was direct Canadian authority against extending Mareva injunctions to foreign assets. So, in *Zellers Inc v Doobay*,[147] after considering the *Babanaft* case and the *Ashtiani* case, Melnick LJSC had said:

> "... I am of the view that the more restrictive approach in *Ashtiani* is the better one. I conclude that I do not have the jurisdiction to order a Mareva injunction to affect assets of Doobay or others in her family outside of the jurisdiction of this court".

Newbury J found that since the *Zellers* case, the reluctance of the English courts to grant worldwide Mareva injunctions had been overcome and after citing and reviewing a number of English[148] and Australian[149] authorities she concluded that she had jurisdiction to make a worldwide Mareva injunction.

> "Accordingly, I conclude that the developments I have described do constitute an evolution of the law sufficient to warrant a reconsideration of this court's ruling in *Zellers Inc v Derby* ... I believe it is open to me to depart from the conclusion reached in *Zellers* concerning the jurisdiction to grant 'worldwide' Mareva injunctions generally ... On the question of jurisdiction then, I regard this court as having authority, in an appropriate case, to restrain a party who is properly subject to the jurisdiction of the court, from transferring or dealing with assets, including assets *ex juris*, where necessary to prevent his frustrating an order of possible future order of this court".[150]

[146.] [1989] 1 All ER 433.

[147.] 34 BCLR (2d) 187.

[148.] *Republic of Haiti v Duvalier* [1989] 1 All ER 456; *Interpol Ltd v Galani* 1987] 1 All ER 981; *Maclaine Watson & Co Ltd v International Tin Council (No 2)*[1988] 3 All ER 257; *Ghoth v Ghoth* [1992] 1 All ER 920 and *Derby & Co Ltd v Weldon(No 1)* [1989] 1 All ER 469; and *(No 2)* [1989] 1 All ER 1002; and *(No 6)* [1990] 3 All ER 263.

[149.] See para **[7.42]** *infra*.

[150.] At p 10 of the transcript, para 12 of the judgment.

It is thought that the decision of Newbury J represents good law as it carefully and comprehensively reviewed previously held views of the law against the background of compelling legal developments in other jurisdictions, before coming to a well balanced conclusion.

[7.41] Having decided the "jurisdictional question" in the affirmative, Newbury J went on to consider the case at bar and whether (a) the applicant had a strong *prima facie* case; (b) there was evidence that there was an insufficiency of assets within the jurisdiction and significant assets outside the jurisdiction; and (c) there was a real risk of disposal of these assets situate outside of the jurisdiction. Newbury J held: (a) that the applicants had "a good arguable case" on their counterclaim against M;[151] (b) that M's assets in British Columbia were not sufficient to satisfy existing judgments made against M and (c) the fact that there were two unsatisfied judgments and the evidence of M's "predilection and experience in the use of offshore trusts and companies to make himself 'bullet-proof' - are sufficient to show a relative deficiency of assets ... in the province and that there is a 'real risk' of his transferring or concealing significant assets elsewhere".[152] On these facts Newbury J granted the applicant a worldwide Mareva injunction.[153] This decision has been followed on a number of occasions by other judges in the Supreme Court of British Columbia.[154]

[7.42] If there is anything surprising about the acceptance of the jurisdiction to grant worldwide Mareva relief in Canada, a country made up of several territories with separate courts having exclusive jurisdictions, it is that it took until 1995 for a written judgment to be delivered. Long before the trilogy of Court of Appeal cases, the Courts in Australia had accepted the jurisdiction to

---

[151.] Whether the judge was consciously saying that "a good arguable case" was sufficient without having to show a *"prima facie* case" is a moot point: see Ch 5, *A Good Arguable Case*, para **[5.05]**.

[152.] At p 15 of the transcript, para 21 of the judgment.

[153.] Newbury J granted the worldwide Mareva injunction subject to a modified *Babanaft* proviso (see para **[7.46]** *infra*) but modified the disclosure order by excusing M from going to the trouble of procuring expert valuation appraisals. She also limited the third order sought by providing that the receiver would not alter situs of the assets without Court approval, recognising that such could have disastrous tax implications for M.

[154.] See *Mooney v Orr* (1994) 100 BCLR (2d) 335 (Huddart J); *Cussons v Slobbe*, (1996) Supreme Court of British Columbia of 9 October 1996 (de Weerdt J); *Reynolds v Harmanis*, (1995) Supreme Court of British Columbia, 16 May 1995 (Esson CJSC); *Wong v Gray* (1998) Supreme Court of British Columbia, 18 June 1998 (Collver J). Note though that in *Delmas & Wong v Orion 2000 Technologies Ltd* (1997) Supreme Court of British Columbia, 7 April 1997 (Burnyeat J) it was said that "While I am not prepared to say that the court doesn't have jurisdiction to grant such a 'worldwide' Mareva injunction where there are no British Columbia assets and where the relief sought is to force the party to an action to firstly, create an asset and, secondly, not then to remove that asset from another jurisdiction, I am satisfied that such an order is not appropriate in this case".

grant a Mareva injunction to affect assets which were situate outside of the jurisdiction of the court making the order. So in 1984 in *Hospital Products Ltd v Ballabil Holdings Pty Ltd*[155] Rogers J said:

> "I should say at the outset that it appears to me that the purpose nominated as the *raison d'etre* for the remedy could fail to be satisfied in given circumstances if the relief is restricted to assets within the jurisdiction. To take the most simple situation, let it be assumed that a defendant, within the jurisdiction, has assets overseas against which execution could be levied in the event of judgment being obtained against the defendant within the jurisdiction. Is the court powerless to prevent such a defendant from transferring the foreign assets into the anonymity of a numbered Swiss bank account in the face of clear statements by the defendant of an intention to do so? Putting the question another way, why should the attempt of a defendant, within the jurisdiction, to make himself judgment proof in relation to foreign assets be any more permissible or less inimical to the proper administration of justice than similar action with respect to locally owned assets? ... Is there a premium to be placed on foresight in removal of assets before the grant of injunctive relief where the purpose is to render the defendant judgment proof?".[156]

The Undertaking not to Institute Foreign Proceedings

[7.43] Where worldwide Mareva injunctions have been granted the courts have been anxious to ensure that Mareva plaintiffs do not abuse information obtained from defendants about their overseas assets by utilising same to ground foreign proceedings.[157] The insistence upon a plaintiff's undertaking not to apply to foreign courts to commence foreign proceedings or to use information disclosed about foreign assets in foreign proceedings is to the fore in the safeguards employed by the courts. In *Tate Access Floors Inc v Boswell*[158] it was held that even if such an undertaking is not expressly given by an applicant for a worldwide Mareva injunction it will be *implied*.[159] In this case the first plaintiff alleged that the individual defendants (who were former employees) had defrauded the plaintiffs by incorporating companies (the corporate defendants), raising false invoices for payment by the plaintiff and then authorising said payments. This was another international case: the first plaintiff was a Maryland (USA) company, the second plaintiff was its UK subsidiary and the payments alleged to have been made to the defendant companies were through bank accounts in the Isle of Man, the Channel islands and London. The plaintiffs

---

[155.] [1984] 2 NSWLR 662 at 664.

[156.] See also *Jackson v Sterling Industries Ltd* (1987) 162 CLR 612.

[157.] See *Derby & Co Ltd v Weldon (No 1)* [1989] 1 All ER 469; [1989] 2 WLR 276.

[158.] [1990] 3 All ER 303.

[159.] On "implied undertakings" generally, see O'Floinn, 'Implied Undertakings - Valuable Safeguard or Unnecessary Obstacle?', (1997) CLP 200.

obtained worldwide Mareva injunctions and Anton Piller orders against the defendants. These orders: restrained the defendants from reducing their assets below £1 million; ordered the defendants to disclose and deliver up information and to permit the plaintiffs to enter and to search and to seize documents; and required the defendants to verify on oath the information and documents disclosed and delivered up. Subsequently, the plaintiffs instituted proceedings against the defendants in Jersey, the Isle of Man and Maryland USA. The defendants then applied to the English courts to have the Mareva and Anton Piller orders set aside on three grounds, the only one relevant for present purposes being that the Mareva injunctions did not contain an undertaking not to start overseas proceedings or use the information obtained in the UK proceedings for the purpose of overseas proceedings.[160]

[7.44] In the first place it is significant that the Court of Appeal acknowledged that worldwide Mareva relief is capable of being oppressive if plaintiffs were permitted to commence foreign proceedings against defendants. As Browne-Wilkinson V-C said:

> "... I wholly accept, that in any case where a worldwide order is made, it is capable of operating oppressively if the plaintiffs are free to start other proceedings in other jurisdictions (thereby exposing the defendants to a multiplicity of proceedings) and to use information obtained under compulsion in this jurisdiction for the purposes of pursing criminal or civil remedies in other jurisdictions. It is for that reason that the court of Appeal has laid down that, as a term of any worldwide Mareva relief, the order should contain undertakings not, without the leave of the court, to start such proceedings or use such information ...".[161]

The Court of Appeal held that whilst it would have been preferable to have included an express undertaking not to either start foreign proceedings or to use information obtained for the purpose of foreign proceedings, such an undertaking would, in any event, be *implied* into the court's order. It was pointed out that Warner J had given his consent to the plaintiffs to institute certain foreign proceedings and that it was implied that no other proceedings would be commenced without the court's consent. In relation to the non-use of information obtained in the proceedings otherwise than for the purpose of the proceedings it was held that any order for discovery imposes an implied undertaking not to use the information disclosed for a collateral or improper

---

160. The other grounds were: because the Anton Piller orders prejudiced their privilege against self-incrimination; and because the plaintiffs failed to disclose to the judge that they would start proceedings overseas and that they had improperly used information obtained in the English proceedings for the collateral purpose of bringing the Isle of Man proceedings and for claiming punitive relief in the Maryland USA proceedings.
161. [1990] 3 All ER 303 at 310.

purpose. It was held, accordingly, that the worldwide Mareva injunction was not oppressive.[162]

[7.45] In *Morris v Mahfouz*[163] it was held by Dillon LJ in the Court of Appeal that it did not automatically follow, as a matter of logic, that a worldwide Mareva plaintiff would be required to undertake not to issue fresh proceedings in a foreign court arising out of the same subject matter without first obtaining leave of the court granting the worldwide Mareva. Such an undertaking would only be required if it seemed *prima facie* oppressive that the plaintiff should be free to start further proceedings in other jurisdictions. In the instant case, and in the context of the infamous BCCI litigation where worldwide Mareva injunctions had been granted, Dillon LJ held that it was appropriate for the liquidators to undertake that they would not, without the leave of the court, commence new proceedings based on the same or similar subject matter in all other jurisdictions save one. The defendants in that case had also sought the undertakings to include the following prohibition: "(including, for the avoidance of doubt, the making of any new complaints, laying of any information or similar procedure to criminal authorities)". This was, however, refused by Dillon LJ who considered it highly undesirable for liquidators to be fettered, in providing to the appropriate authorities, material in connection with a prosecution for fraud and the enforcement of regulatory procedures simply because they had successfully obtained Mareva relief.

The "*Babanaft* Proviso"

[7.46] From the first formulation of the *Babanaft* proviso in the case which gave it its name, to the first attempt to fine-tune its wording by Slaughton LJ in *Republic of Haiti v Duvalier*, it has been clear that the protection of third parties is a paramount concern for the courts when exercising the worldwide Mareva jurisdiction. There have been further developments to the *Babanaft* proviso and the wording which is currently in use in both the English and Irish[164] courts is that which was adopted in *Derby & Co Ltd v Weldon (No 2)*.[165] There, Lord Donaldson MR devised the following wording:

> "**PROVIDED THAT**, in so far as this order purports to have any extra-territorial effect, no person shall be affected thereby or concerned with the terms thereof until it shall be declared enforceable or be enforced by a foreign

---

[162.] Note that in Ireland too, worldwide Mareva injunctions are made subject to the plaintiff's undertaking not to use information obtained for collateral purposes: see *Clonmeen Manor House Ltd v Royal Lodge Ltd & William George Saxecoburg and Gotha, The Irish Times*, 31 March 1994 and considered at para **[7.51]** *infra*.

[163.] (1993) *The Times Law Reports* 605.

[164.] See para **[7.49]** *infra*.

[165.] [1989] 1 All ER 1002.

court and then it shall only affect them to the extent of such declaration or enforcement **UNLESS** they are (a) a person to whom this order is addressed or an officer of or an agent appointed by power of attorney of such a person or (b) persons who are subject to the jurisdiction of this court and (i) have been given written notice of this order at their residence or place of business within the jurisdiction, and (ii) are able to prevent acts or omissions outside the jurisdiction of this court which assist in the breach of the terms of this order."[166]

[7.47] The purpose of the *Babanaft* proviso is to exempt, from the ambit of the worldwide Mareva order, third parties outside of the jurisdiction who might otherwise be affected. Where a third party is located *entirely outside* the jurisdiction or where a third party is situated *entirely inside* the jurisdiction, the effects of worldwide Mareva injunctions are without unjustly harsh consequences for the third parties. Where, however, a third party - such as a bank - has branches both inside and outside the jurisdiction difficulties could conceivably arise were a worldwide Mareva injunction made without any proviso. As Lord Donaldson said in *Derby & Co Ltd v Weldon (No 2)*:

> "Is action by the foreign bank to be regarded as contempt, although it would not be so regarded but for the probably irrelevant fact that it happens to have an English branch? Is action by the foreign branch of an English bank to be regarded as contempt, when other banks in the area are free to comply with the defendant's instructions ?"[167]

It was against the backdrop of the foregoing problem that Lord Donaldson formulated the current wording of the *Babanaft* proviso.

[7.48] The current proviso makes a threefold distinction between those who can be affected by a worldwide Mareva order.[168] The first category of persons recognised are the defendants or other persons who are party to the proceedings: these people are bound to obey the order. The second category of persons distinguished by the proviso are those who are subject to the jurisdiction of the court which grants the order and who have notice of the order and who may be able to prevent a defendant and others from breaching the terms of the order: again, this category of person is bound to obey any order of the court whether the order relates to activities inside or outside the jurisdiction of the court because they are amenable to the jurisdiction of the court. The third category of persons are distinguished by omission, namely, all others who are not specifically mentioned in the proviso: foreign nationals, whether human or

---

[166.] At 1013a-c.

[167.] [1989] 1 All ER 1002 at 1011, 1012. On the need to protect third parties see also *Ghoth v Ghoth* [1992] 2 All ER 920 mentioned at para **[7.54]** *infra*.

[168.] See further, Ough & Flenley, *The Mareva Injunction and Anton Piller Order*, (2nd ed, 1993) Butterworths, para 2.20.4 at p 38.

artificial persons, who are not subject to the jurisdiction of the court making the order and also those who are subject to the court's jurisdiction but who have not been given written notice of the terms of the order at their residence or place of business within the jurisdiction or who are unable to prevent acts or omissions outside of the jurisdiction which assist in the breach of the order. The persons in this third category are *not bound by the order*. It is thought that this classification strikes a good balance between a court's interests in ensuring that the administration of justice is not frustrated and that a defendant's obligations to a plaintiff are not evaded, on the one hand, as against the rights of third parties not to be concerned with the orders of foreign courts, on the other hand.

[7.49] On many occasions where the Irish High Court has granted worldwide Mareva relief, it has incorporated - in the body of the order - a *Babanaft* type proviso.[169] In *Balkanbank v Taher and Ors*[170] the parties included Balkanbank, a Bulgarian bank and Via Holdings Ltd (formerly known as Taher Investments Ltd) which were equal shareholders in Balkan International Ltd, a joint-venture company. Balkanbank issued proceedings against the defendants alleging fraud, breach of trust and breach of duty. These allegations arose primarily out of the alleged actions of T and McG (two of Via Holdings Ltd's directors who were also nominee directors of the joint-venture company and were also defendants) in causing that company to draw down a $7 million loan. The purpose to which the loan was put was also in issue. Having commenced proceedings on 3 October 1990 the plaintiff, Balkanbank, sought and obtained a Mareva injunction from the High Court which affected the defendants' assets within Ireland.[171] On 8 October 1990 Balkanbank sought and obtained from the English High Court a worldwide Mareva injunction.[172]

The Irish case was eventually tried before Blayney J in the High Court and judgment issued on 12 February 1992. Balkanbank's principal allegations of fraud failed, although two of the defendants were ordered to account for certain sums to Balkanbank. Consequently, the Irish Mareva injunction was discharged and an enquiry into damages, on foot of the plaintiff's undertaking as to damages, was ordered.[173] In support of the inquiry as to damages, the defendants were successful in obtaining a domestic Mareva injunction against Balkanbank in Ireland. The decision of Blayney J was, however, appealed to the Supreme

---

[169.] See also para **[7.50]** *et seq, infra.*

[170.] *The Irish Times*, 30 March 1995.

[171.] *The Irish Times*, 4 October 1990 (Costello J).

[172.] See *Balkanbank v Taher* [1994] 4 All ER 239. This judgment concerned the defendants' counterclaim and attempt to enforce the plaintiff's undertaking in damages following the discharge of the worldwide Mareva injunction which it had obtained on 8 October 1990.

[173.] On undertakings as to damages and their enforcement, see Ch 8, *Applying for a Mareva Injunction*, para **[8.57]** *et seq.*

Court and final judgment was delivered on 19 January 1995.[174] The Supreme Court rejected Balkanbank's appeal against Blayney J's finding in the High Court that there had been no fraud or breach of duty by the defendants. In addition, however, the Supreme Court, found that the High Court had been wrong to go outside of the proceedings and to order two of the defendants to account for certain sums to Balkanbank as this radically changed the nature of the proceedings and was not in accordance with fair procedures.

[7.50] Subsequent to the Supreme Court's decision, the defendants applied to Barr J in the High Court for a worldwide Mareva injunction against Balkanbank in support of their claim for damages as a result of Balkanbank's Mareva injunction being discharged.[175] Although there was no written judgment handed down by Barr J the order made by him[176] provided:

> "**IT IS ORDERED** that the Plaintiff/Defendant in the issue its servants or agents or anyone having knowledge of the making of this order or otherwise howsoever be restrained until after Wednesday the 5th day of April 1995 (or until further Order in the meantime) from reducing its assets within or without the jurisdiction of this court below the sum of IR£20 million or the equivalent in other currencies."

Of particular interest is the fact that the order of the High Court contained a *Babanaft* proviso in the following terms:

> "... insofar as the Order made herein purports to have any effect outside Ireland no person shall be affected by it or concerned with the terms of it until it shall have been declared enforceable or shall have been recognised or registered or enforced by a foreign court (and then it shall only affect such person to the extent of such declaration or recognition or registration or enforcement) unless that person is:
>
> (a) a person to whom this Order is addressed or an officer or an agent appointed by power of attorney of such a person or
>
> (b) a persons who is subject to the jurisdiction of this court and who
>
>   (i) have been given written notice of this Order at his or its residence or place of business within the jurisdiction
>
>   (ii) is able to prevent acts or omissions outside the jurisdiction of this court which assist in the breach of the terms of this order."[177]

[174.] Supreme Court, unrep, 19 January 1995 (Hamilton CJ) (*nem diss*)

[175.] *The Irish Times*, 30 March 1995.

[176.] The writer acknowledges with gratitude the assistance given by Mr Bryan F Fox, Solicitor (who instructed Mr Connor Maguire SC) who made available a copy of Barr J's order.

[177.] In *Clonmeen Manor House Ltd v Royal Lodge Ltd), The Irish Times*, 31 March 1994, Costello J reportedly granted a Mareva injunction which affected the defendants' assets, wherever situate and also seemed to include a *Babanaft*-type proviso. See Callanan, Strahan and Dempsey, 'The Obtaining of Mareva Injunctions in Ireland', [1994] 7 JIBL 273 at 276, 277 and 278.

Barr J also ordered that Balkanbank should disclose its assets both within and without the jurisdiction of the Irish court.[178]

[7.51] In *Clonmeen Manor House Ltd v Royal Lodge Ltd & William George Saxecoburg and Gotha*[179] the High Court granted the plaintiffs a Mareva injunction which restrained the defendants from dealing with their assets wherever situate save insofar as they exceeded £92,000. In that case the plaintiffs' claim concerned an alleged failure by the defendants, to perform agreements involving the purchase of property by the plaintiffs. The interim order of the High Court, which had been made by Flood J, restrained the defendants from:

> "... disposing of or transferring, charging, diminishing or in any way howsoever dealing with any of their assets wherever the same may be situate save insofar as the same exceed the sum or value of £92,000.00 subject to the proviso hereunder.
>
> And the court doth grant an injunction restraining the Defendants and each of them until after the 18 April 1994 or until further order in the meantime whether by them or either of them or their respective servants or agents or any persons acting on behalf of them or either of them or otherwise howsoever from disposing of or transferring, charging, diminishing or in any way howsoever dealing with any of their assets situate in any member state of the European community save insofar as the same or the value thereof shall exceed £92,000."

It is notable that both this order, and the interlocutory order, included *Babanaft* provisos which were couched in terms materially identical to the proviso in *Balkanbank v Taher*.[180] It may also be noted here that the defendants in *Clonmeen Manor House Ltd* were also ordered to disclose the nature and location of their assets and had a receiver appointed over their assets;[181] and that the order was made on the plaintiffs' undertaking "not to use any information obtained by reason ... of this order except for the purposes of these proceedings without leave of the court".

[178.] For the terms of the disclosure order made by Barr J, see Ch 10, *Ancillary Orders*, para **[10.12]**.

[179.] *The Irish Times*, 31 March 1994 where the interim injunction was granted (Flood J); the interlocutory injunction was granted on 9 May 1994 (Costello J). The writer acknowledges with gratitude the assistance of Claire Callanan, Solicitor, of Gerrard Scallan & O'Brien in providing copies of both orders which were first mentioned in Callanan, Strahan & Dempsey, *op cit*, at 276.

[180.] *The Irish Times*, 30 March 1995.

[181.] See further, Ch 10, *Ancillary Orders*, para **[10.75]**.

Ordering Defendants to Transfer Assets Between Jurisdictions

[7.52] It has also been held by the courts in at least two jurisdictions - the United Kingdom and Canada - that, in exceptional cases, there is jurisdiction to order a defendant to transfer his assets from one jurisdiction to another. The purpose of such an order is to render a defendant's assets amenable to the judicial process. In *Derby & Co Ltd v Weldon (No 6)*[182] the Court of Appeal decided that it had jurisdiction, in appropriate cases, to order a defendant to transfer assets which were affected by a worldwide Mareva injunction from one jurisdiction to another. Referring to the object of a Mareva injunction, Dillon LJ said:

> "I see no reason why that should not extend, in principle and in an appropriate case, to ordering the transfer of assets to a jurisdiction in which the order of the English court after the trial of the action will be recognised from a jurisdiction in which that order will not be recognised and the issues would have to be relitigated if ... the only connection of the latter jurisdiction with the matters in issue in the proceedings is that moneys have been placed in that jurisdiction in order to make them proof against the enforcement ... of any judgment which may be granted to the plaintiffs by the English courts in this action or indeed if the only connection with the latter jurisdiction is financial, as a matter or controlling investments".[183]

The basis of this power also lies in the *in personam* jurisdiction of the court over a defendant who is properly served with proceedings pursuant to the Rules of the Superior Courts. As Slaughton LJ said in that case, the jurisdiction to make such an order is not disputed and the real question is whether the court should *exercise* such a far-reaching jurisdiction.[184] In that case it was, however, held that it was unnecessary to order that assets be transferred from one jurisdiction to another.

[7.53] Courts must be extremely careful not to unwittingly bring financial disaster upon a Mareva defendant by ordering him to transfer his assets from one jurisdiction to another. This danger was recognised in *Mooney v Orr,*[185] where the applicants sought to appoint a receiver to M's assets outside the jurisdiction, where Newbury J said:

[182.] [1990] 3 All ER 263.

[183.] At 273f-g.

[184.] At 275c. Slaughton LJ also said (at 275, 276): "One can envisage cases which might be plain enough, for example where the actual proceeds of fraud are on board a ship on the high seas flying no national flag and subject to no country's local jurisdiction. Or they may be in a country which has no effective system of law, or one which can only be regarded as wholly uncivilised. In less obvious cases the English courts should proceed with great caution, particularly against defendants who have not been served here but abroad under Ord 11".

[185.] [1994] BCJ No 2322.

"... it is not clear to me whether the applicants intend that assets in other jurisdictions be transferred to this province. If so, I suspect that the tax consequences of such transfers could be disastrous to Mr Mooney, quite apart from the complexities of trust and corporate law that could be encountered. At this stage I propose to require that the prior approval of either this court or Mr Mooney be obtained before the receiver would be empowered to move an asset from one jurisdiction to another."[186]

As with worldwide Mareva injunctions generally, it is thought that the circumstances in which it will be appropriate to order a defendant to transfer his assets from one jurisdiction to another will be very rare indeed.

Limitations on the *Ex Juris* Mareva Jurisdiction

[7.54] The *ex juris* Mareva jurisdiction must always be exercised sparingly. While it is one thing to confirm the existence of the courts' powers to make such orders in "appropriate circumstances", it must be acknowledged that such appropriate circumstances will very rarely be found to exist. In *Rosseel NV v Oriental Commercial and Shipping (UK) Ltd*[187] Lord Donaldson MR refused to make a worldwide Mareva injunction. He said that whilst the court had jurisdiction to make a worldwide Mareva injunction in aid of foreign proceedings or arbitration awards, the jurisdiction would only be exercised in exceptional circumstances and that there were "no sufficiently exceptional features in this case to justify our exercising it."[188] It may be noted, however, that in *Credit Suisse Fides Trust SA v Cuoghi*[189] Millett LJ held that when a court is asked to grant a worldwide Mareva injunction in the context of Article 24 of the Brussels Convention, the central question was not whether the circumstances were exceptional or very exceptional, but whether or not it would be inexpedient to make the order. Notwithstanding this latter decision it is submitted by the writer that only in exceptional circumstances will an Irish court grant a worldwide Mareva injunction, whether pursuant to s 11 of the Jurisdiction of Courts and Enforcment of Judgments Acts 1988 and 1993 or otherwise.

In *Ghoth v Ghoth,*[190] after stressing that third parties who assist in the breach of an injunction are themselves guilty of contempt of court, Lord Donaldson MR adopted a cautious approach to the making of a worldwide Mareva injunction

---

186. At p 16 of the transcript, para 24 of the judgment. Newbury J added the following "proviso" to the order: "... provided however that this Order shall not be construed to require or empower the receiver to alter the situs of any of the assets which are situate outside the jurisdiction of this Court, without the prior consent or either the said [respondent] or of this Court".
187. [1990] 3 All ER 545.
188. At 457a.
189. [1998] 3 All ER 724. See Ch 4, *A Substantive Cause of Action*, para **[4.62]**.
190. [1992] 2 All ER 920.

and again noted the importance of protective clauses for the protection of such third parties.

When is Worldwide Mareva Relief Justified?

[7.55] There is clear evidence that the Irish High Court has accepted that there is jurisdiction, in an appropriate case, to grant a worldwide Mareva injunction. It is thought that the necessity for the Irish courts to make worldwide Mareva injunctions will be infrequent. In *Derby & Co Ltd v Weldon (No 1)*[191] Nicholls LJ noted that worldwide Mareva injunctions were, and should remain, very much the exception rather than the norm:

> "In my view each case must depend on its own facts. An order restraining a defendant from dealing with any of his assets overseas, and requiring him to disclose details of all his assets wherever located, is a draconian order. The risk of prejudice to which, in the absence of such an order, the plaintiff will be subject is that of the dissipation or secretion of assets *abroad*. This risk must, on the facts, be appropriately grave before it will be just and convenient for such a draconian order to be made. It goes without saying that before such an order is made the court will scrutinise the facts with particular care."[192]

It is thought that the cases where the Irish courts will be justified in granting worldwide Mareva relief will be few and far between. Whilst some cases will "cry out"[193] for a worldwide Mareva injunction, the exercise of such an extraordinary jurisdiction will only ever be justified in extraordinary circumstances, and only then with safeguards such as the *Babanaft* proviso (to protect third parties) and on a plaintiff's undertaking not to use information obtained in a manner which is oppressive to a defendant.

[191.] [1989] 1 All ER 469, [1989] 2 WLR 276.

[192.] At 478g-h.

[193.] *Per* Kerr LJ in *Babanaft International Co SA v Bassatne* [1989] 1 All ER 433 who said that some situations "... cry out - as a matter of justice to the plaintiffs - for disclosure orders and Mareva-type injunctions covering foreign assets of defendants even before judgment".

Chapter 8

Applying for a Mareva Injunction

[8.01] A Mareva injunction can be granted following an *ex parte* application without the defendant being heard (in which case it will be an *interim* injunction) or following an *inter partes* application, after both the plaintiff and the defendant have been heard (in which case it can be either an *interim* or an *interlocutory* injunction). In an application to the High Court for a Mareva injunction, a Mareva plaintiff's legal advisors will have to prepare a notice of motion[1] and also a grounding affidavit.[2] Furthermore, since Mareva relief is always ancillary relief, a Mareva plaintiff must also institute proceedings in respect of his substantive cause of action. Accordingly, if proceedings are not already in existence, a Mareva plaintiff's legal advisors must, at the time when application is being made for a Mareva injunction, also prepare an originating document (eg summons, motion or petition) so as to commence proceedings.[3] Finally, it is very important that an aspiring Mareva plaintiff recognise from the outset that the *quid pro quo* to the court granting Mareva relief will be to require him to give certain undertakings.

[8.02] In this chapter the procedural steps and documentation involved in bringing an application for a Mareva injunction are considered under four distinct headings:

[A] The Application: *Ex Parte* or *Inter Partes*, Interim or Interlocutory?

[B] Instituting Proceedings by an Originating Document.

[C] The Grounding Affidavit for a Mareva Injunction.

[D] Undertakings Required on Application for Mareva Relief.

Much of the law and practice considered here is equally applicable to injunctive relief generally, and is not exclusively confined to Mareva injunctions. By reason of the dearth of writings on civil proceedings in Ireland generally,

---

1. An *ex parte* docket is the appropriate document to be used in the case of an *ex parte* application to the Circuit Court. On *ex parte* applications, see para **[8.05]** *infra*.
2. The grounding affidavit, which will be in support of the Mareva relief, should adduce sufficient evidence of the plaintiff's entitlement to a Mareva injunction. See para **[8.25]** *et seq, infra*.
3. The nature of the plaintiff's claim against the defendant will determine the type of originating document used. As to the doubt expressed by Keane J in *Re Greendale Developments Ltd*, Supreme Court, unrep, 20 February 1997 that Mareva relief may be confined to where the plaintiff's relief is sought under a plenary summons: see para **[8.20]** *infra*.

however, it is thought necessary to visit the first principles applicable to an application for any injunction, albeit with specific reference to Mareva injunctions.

[A] THE APPLICATION: *EX PARTE* OR *INTER PARTES*, INTERIM OR INTERLOCUTORY?

[8.03] A Mareva injunction, like any other type of injunction, can be described as being either *ex parte* or *inter partes*, interim or interlocutory. The first distinction is this: where an injunction is made following an *ex parte* application it means that only the plaintiff is heard by the court; the defendant will not even be aware that a hearing has been held until he is served with (or otherwise given notice of) the injunction. By contrast, where an application for an injunction is made following an *inter partes* hearing, both sides will have been heard by the court. Injunctive relief will be granted on an *ex parte* application only in cases of real urgency. Sometimes, where there is some urgency but not, in the opinion of the court, such urgency as to justify the granting of an *ex parte* injunction, a plaintiff may on an *ex parte* application to the court, be given leave to serve short notice of motion for an interlocutory injunction.

[8.04] The second distinction is between interim and interlocutory injunctions. An interlocutory Mareva injunction will operate to restrain a defendant from removing or disposing of his assets *until the trial of the substantive cause of action*. An interim injunction,[4] on the other hand, is a type of interlocutory injunction which only lasts until a specified date (usually the return date for a notice of motion seeking interlocutory relief), or until further order of the court. Where an interim injunction is first granted it will be on foot of an *ex parte* application. The same principles of law govern the granting of both interim and interlocutory injunctions;[5] the law does, however, impose an additional duty on a plaintiff who applies for an *ex parte* injunction to make full and frank disclosure of all material facts.[6] Here, the following matters are considered:

1. Applications for *Ex Parte* Mareva Injunctions;

2. Applications on Short Notice of Motion;

3. Interlocutory Injunctions: *Inter Partes* Applications.

[4.] See Meagher, Gummow & Lehane, *Equity Doctrines and Remedies* (3rd ed, 1992) Butterworths, para [2183], p 605.

[5.] As to which, see generally, Ch 5, *A Good Arguable Case*, para **[5.04]** *et seq.*

[6.] See para **[8.32]** *infra*.

Applications for *Ex Parte* Mareva Injunctions[7]

[8.05] The general rule is that a defendant should be given adequate notice of a plaintiff's application for any injunction so as to enable him to prepare his defence. In practice, notice that an application for an injunction will be made is effected by serving a notice of motion on the defendant. As *Kerr* said in 1927:

> "No motion should be made without previous notice to the parties affected thereby. But the court or a judge may, if satisfied that the delay caused by proceeding in the ordinary way would or might entail irreparable or serious mischief, make an order for an injunction *ex parte* upon such terms as to costs or otherwise, and subject to such undertaking, if any, as the court or judge may think just, and any party affected by such order may move to set it aside".[8]

Mareva relief will very commonly take the form of an *ex parte* interim injunction which restrains the defendant from removing or disposing of his assets until a particular date - usually the return date for a motion to seek an interlocutory injunction for which short service is usually directed at the same time as the court grants the interim injunction.[9] It is hardly surprising that the *ex parte* procedure is favoured in Mareva applications since to serve notice of motion on a person (believed to be intent upon frustrating the judicial process) could conceivably be the very catalyst which might actually precipitate the removal, dissipation or other disposal of assets.[10]

[8.06] The procedural basis for an *ex parte* application is Ord 50 r 7 of the RSC which provides *inter alia*, that an application for an injunction under Ord 50 r 6[11]

[7.] See generally, Goldrein & Wilkinson, *Commercial Litigation: Pre-Emptive Remedies* (2nd ed, 1991) Sweet & Maxwell, pp 50-57.

[8.] Kerr, *Law and Practice of Injunctions* (6th ed, 1927); (reprinted 1981) Gaunt & Sons at 634.

[9.] In *Don King Productions Inc v Warren (No 2)* [1998] TLR 386 Moses J said that, ordinarily, a Mareva plaintiff is required to give due notice to the defendant of his intention to seek injunctive relief. In that case it was held, however, that an *ex parte* application was justified because one of the defendants (who was a partner of the plaintiff) had concealed receipts of large instalments of income due to the partnership and that that concealment was without any logical basis.

[10.] As Ough & Flenley, *The Mareva Injunction and Anton Piller Order* (2nd ed, 1993) Butterworths, para 5.1.1 have put it: "Applications for either Mareva injunctions or Anton Piller orders are invariable made *ex parte*. This is because it is implicit in either application that the defendant is essentially a rogue. If he is a rogue then he is likely to remove or dissipate assets or destroy evidence as soon as he knows of the proposed application. If the plaintiff were to make an *inter partes* application, giving the defendant at least two working days' notice of the proposed application, then, if he were a rogue, this would give him ample opportunity to remove assets or destroy evidence. The application should therefore be made *ex parte* and without notifying the defendant or his solicitors of the intended application."

[11.] On Ord 50, r 6 see generally, Ch 2, *The Jurisdiction to Grant Mareva Relief*, para **[2.02]**.

"may be made either *ex parte* or on notice". *Ex parte* applications, generally, are regulated by Ord 52, r 3 of the RSC which provides:

> In any case the Court, if satisfied that the delay caused by proceeding by motion on notice under this Order would or might entail irreparable or serious mischief, may make any order *ex parte* upon such terms as to the costs or otherwise and subject to such undertaking, if any, as the Court may think just; and any party affected by such order may move to set it aside.

To make an *ex parte* application for a Mareva injunction in the High Court,[12] a plaintiff's solicitor should prepare and (if time permits) have stamped: (a) an "originating document" eg summons, notice of motion or petition, as appropriate, and (b) an affidavit grounding the application for the Mareva injunction.[13] It will often be helpful to have a notice of motion ready for issue to initiate the subsequent interlocutory application. Sometimes a draft Mareva order will also be prepared.[14] Counsel will then make the application to one of the judges sitting in the Chancery Court at the first available opportunity. Where no Chancery judge is available application can be made to any sitting judge: see para **[8.09]** below. Where an *ex parte* interim order is made a return date will then be fixed to hear the *inter partes* interlocutory motion, which will usually be the subsequent Monday. An applicant for an *ex parte* order must always bear in mind the "golden rule", which is that he is under a duty to make full and frank disclosure to the court of all material matters.[15]

[8.07] In exceptional cases, justice might require that the application for an *ex parte* Mareva injunction is heard *in camera*. Whilst Article 34 of the Constitution provides that justice must be administered in public, the effects of this general rule are mitigated by the proviso, "save in such special and limited cases as may be prescribed by law". One such example is s 45(1) of the Courts (Supplemental Provisions) Act 1961 which empowers the court to hear in private "applications of an urgent nature for relief by way of ... injunction". It will sometimes be the case that, for Mareva relief to be effective, it will be necessary that there is no publicity surrounding the hearing of the *ex parte* application. A Mareva plaintiff who believes that the effectiveness of his remedy turns upon whether the application is held *in camera* or not should be

---

[12.] Order 17, r 2 of the Rules of the Circuit Court 1950 ("RCC") provides that: "Applications in connection with any of the matters hereinafter mentioned may be made to the Judge by any party, without notice to any other party, on lodging with the County Registrar an *ex parte* docket and filing an affidavit in support of the application". One of the orders listed is "an ad interim order".

[13.] See para **[8.25]** *infra*.

[14.] See generally, Ch 9, *The Mareva Order and Its Effects*. See also Appendices 1 and 2.

[15.] See para **[8.32]** *et seq*, *infra*.

prepared to adduce evidence of his apprehension of this fact to the satisfaction of the court.[16]

[8.08] Although the general rule is that proceedings must have been instituted *prior* to injunctive relief being granted, in cases of great urgency a plaintiff's solicitor may undertake to stamp and issue the documents (including the originating document)[17] which are necessary to commence proceedings against a defendant. Where there is no time to make, swear and file a grounding affidavit, application can be made on oral evidence. If at all possible, a draft of the grounding affidavit should be exhibited. In such cases, however, the leave of the court is required before any *ex parte* injunction which the court may grant can be of any force as Ord 40, r 20 of the RSC provides:

> Except by leave of the Court no order made *ex parte* in Court founded on any affidavit shall be of any force unless the affidavit on which the application was made was actually made before the order was applied for, and produced or filed at the time of making the application.

[8.09] In the case of a truly urgent application during the hours when the High Court is sitting, application can be made by a plaintiff's counsel to any sitting judge; this is done by counsel taking the first opportunity to interrupt the proceedings in train, advise the judge of the urgency of the matter and, on being given leave to proceed, making the application.

In cases of extreme urgency, an application for a Mareva injunction may even be made at a judge's home. It is this, perhaps, which makes all injunctions, and Mareva injunctions in particular, so powerful and immediate a remedy. In the case of an urgent interim application, outside of the hours when the High Court sits, a plaintiff's solicitor should endeavour to ascertain, from a High Court registrar, what High Court judge has been designated to hear urgent applications on that particular day. When the High Court judge is identified, the plaintiff's solicitor and counsel should attend, after telephoning ahead notice of their impending arrival, at the judge's home with draft proceedings and affidavit together with the undertakings mentioned in para **[8.08]**. It is also essential that arrangements be made for the duty registrar to be in attendance to administer oaths, if necessary, and to record the order.

Outside of vacation sittings the convention is that a plaintiff's counsel should contact a judge - usually the most junior - to see whether the judge is prepared to hear their application. When counsel has established the availability of a judge, counsel should then contact a registrar of the High Court, advise him that a

---

[16.] See Keane, *Equity and the Law of Trusts in the Republic of Ireland*, (1988) Butterworths, p 242, para 15.42.

[17.] As to "originating documents" see para **[8.14]** *et seq, infra*. As to stamping originating documents, see para **[8.23]** *infra*.

judge is available, and request that he attend at a designated place, usually the judge's home.

Where it is not possible to attend on a judge in person, it may even be possible to apply for an injunction over the telephone. In this regard some guidance is given by *Refson & Co Ltd v Saggers*[18] where Nourse J said:

> "In cases where relief is sought over the telephone, the material part or parts of the draft indorsement should normally be read to the judge. Only in cases of exceptional urgency should the court be asked to act without sight or hearing of the material part or parts of a draft endorsement".

The circumstances when this course of action will be appropriate are rare and very exceptional. Undeserving applicants, who make application thus, can expect, rightly, to be given short shrift.

Applications on Short Notice of Motion

[8.10] *Ex parte* injunctions are an emergency remedy and when an applicant or his legal advisers overlook this, the courts will not hesitate to remind them that the *ex parte* procedure is reserved for appropriate cases.[19] In many cases it will be more appropriate to apply for leave to serve the motion on giving shorter notice than is ordinarily required. The period of notice which is ordinarily required for a notice of motion is prescribed by Ord 52, r 6 of the RSC which provides:

> Unless the Court gives special leave to the contrary there must be at least two clear days between the service of a notice of motion and the day named in the notice for hearing the motion; provided that, where the notice of motion requires to be served personally out of Court, it shall be served not less than four clear days before the hearing of the application.

Where proceedings are in train and a defendant's solicitor is on record, the notice of motion will not be required to be served personally on the defendant and, in such a case, the ordinary rule is that there must be two clear days between the service of the notice of motion and the return day. Saturday,

---

18. [1984] 3 All ER 111 at 116.

19. Note, for example, the warning on *ex parte* applications reportedly made by Costello J: see *The Irish Times*, 14 June 1990, where the judge was reported as having refused to grant two *ex parte* injunctions and as having said that application for *ex parte* interim orders were then sought virtually automatically "and in my experience about 90% of them wrongly". The report continued that Costello J also said: "Myself and my colleagues on the bench find ourselves refusing applications for interim injunctions on a regular basis". In this regard it was reported that Costello J distinguished interlocutory applications/applications on short notice from *ex parte* applications. Where *ex parte* injunctions are sought in circumstances where the court believes they are not merited, it will order that notice of the application be served on the defendant: *Lord Byron v Johnston* 2 Mer 29.

Sunday, Christmas Day and Good Friday are excluded in calculating "clear days".[20] It is almost invariably the case that a notice of motion will be served on a Monday. However, to illustrate what is meant by "clear days" it is useful, to take as an example, the service of a notice of motion on a Thursday; in such event the return day will - unless abridged by leave of the court - be the following Tuesday, the two clear days being Friday and Monday. Where a defendant has not retained a solicitor (a common enough occurrence in Mareva applications) the RSC require that he be served personally, and so, ordinarily, 4 clear days' notice is required. So, if a notice of motion is served on a Thursday, the return day will unless abridged be the following Thursday.

[8.11] Where a plaintiff's application has some urgency, but not such as would justify an *ex parte* application, application can be made to court for leave to serve short notice of motion as permitted by Ord 52, r 6 of the RSC. The effect of being given leave to serve short notice of motion is that the defendant is given less time to prepare for the hearing of the injunction and so the court must be satisfied that, on balance, the potential prejudice to the defendant is outweighed by the necessities of the plaintiff's plight. Where a plaintiff obtains leave to serve short notice of motion on a defendant, the original will be initialled by the registrar (in England, the notice must expressly state that such leave has been given by the court[21]). It has also been noted that in the interests of fairness, copies of any affidavit upon which the plaintiff intends to rely, must be served contemporaneously on the defendant.[22]

Interlocutory Injunctions: *Inter Partes* Applications

[8.12] In an ordinary civil action, after proceedings have been commenced, matters will proceed in the manner prescribed by the RSC unless the plaintiff requires interlocutory or interim relief. As considered in the foregoing paragraphs, the general rule is that an application for an interlocutory Mareva injunction should be by way of notice of motion.[23] An affidavit, detailing the plaintiff's grounds for Mareva relief, must be drafted, stamped and served with the notice of motion once the motion has been stamped and given a return date.[24] In the notice of motion the plaintiff should include details of the matters upon which he seeks a court order or directions.[25]

[20.] Order 122, r 2 of the RSC.

[21.] *Dawson v Beeson* 22 Ch D 504.

[22.] *Succri v Gunner* [1919] WN 173.

[23.] Order 52, r 1 provides "All interlocutory applications to Court and all applications authorised by these Rules to be made to the Court shall be made by motion, save as otherwise provided by these Rules."

[24.] See para **[8.25]** *infra*.

[25.] Order 52, r 5. Rule 7 provides that all motions must contain the name and registered place of business for the solicitor serving the motion and the solicitor to be served; shall be dated the day on which they are served; and where served on or by parties appearing in person must state their names and residences or addresses for service.

[8.13] Upon the motion being heard the court may make any order or give such directions as may be just.[26] Alternatively, on the return day the court may adjourn the motion on such terms (if any) as the court thinks fit.[27] Typically, on the first return date, a defendant will ask the court for an adjournment to take instructions or to file a replying affidavit and the court will invariably accede to this request, continuing the interim injunction on the plaintiff's continued undertaking as to damages. Where the court is of the opinion that any person to whom notice has not been given ought to have had notice, it may either dismiss the motion or adjourn the hearing thereof in order that such notice may be given on such terms (if any) as the court may think fit to impose.[28] Where a person who has been served with notice of a motion fails to attend the court, the court may proceed in his absence and where this happens, such proceedings shall not be reheard unless the court is satisfied that the person who did not attend was not guilty of wilful delay or negligence and, in such case, the costs occasioned by the non-appearance shall be in the court's discretion.[29] If the court is to be asked to proceed in the absence of a notice party it will first require sufficient evidence of service of the notice of motion on the absent party; indeed, where a defendant has not entered an appearance, the plaintiff may be required to adduce evidence of service of the originating document.

[B] INSTITUTING PROCEEDINGS BY AN ORIGINATING DOCUMENT

[8.14] As has been considered in detail in Chapter 4, the first essential prerequisite to applying for a Mareva injunction is that a plaintiff has a substantive cause of action against the defendant.[30] In practice, this means that a Mareva plaintiff must have instituted *proceedings* (or must undertake to institute proceedings forthwith) against the defendant in respect of a recognised cause of action; the Mareva injunction will be claimed as ancillary relief to this "substantive cause of action". The more usual way of initiating proceedings in the High Court is by issuing a *summons* which will be one of three types: summary, special or plenary.[31] Civil proceedings in respect of certain types of actions must, however, be commenced by notice of motion and others must be commenced by petition.

---

[26] Order 122, r 5.
[27] *Ibid*, r 9.
[28] *Ibid*, r 8.
[29] *Ibid*, r 12.
[30] See, generally, Ch 4, *A Substantive Cause of Action.*
[31] Order 1, r 1 of the RSC.

Summary Summons

[8.15] Civil proceedings may be instituted in the High Court by issuing a summary summons[32] in three broad classes of claims:

1. In all actions where the plaintiff seeks to recover a debt or liquidated demand in money payable by the defendant, or on a trust;[33]

2. In actions where a landlord seeks to recover possession of land, (with or without a claim for rent or mesne profits) against a tenant whose term has expired or has been duly determined by notice to quit or for non-payment of rent;[34]

3. Claims in which the plaintiff in the first instance desires to have an account taken.[35]

Moreover, a summary summons may be adopted in any claim with the consent of all parties.[36]

[8.16] The summary summons procedure is intended for use in less contentious matters where a defendant has no real defence to a plaintiff's claim. It is on account of this that summary proceedings are generally heard on affidavit and, usually, oral evidence will not be heard.[37] If there is a paradigm cause of action which is litigated using the summary procedure, it is for a debt for an amount certain, the very type of case in which the Mareva injunction made its debut. It is, therefore, surprising that in *Re Greendale Developments Ltd*,[38] considered below,[39] Keane J questioned whether Mareva relief was available as ancillary relief in proceedings which are commenced by an originating document other than a plenary summons. It is thought that claims commenced by summary

---

[32.] An originating summons for the commencement of summary proceedings in the case of the three classes of claim mentioned in Ord 2, r 1 must be in the Form No 2 in Appendix A, Part I of the RSC.

[33.] Ord 2, r 1(1) of the RSC provides that the debt or liquidated demand payable by the defendant may be with or without interest arising on: a contract, express or implied, (to include on a bill of exchange, promissory note, cheque or other simple contract debt); or a bond or contract under seal for payment of a liquidated amount of money; or on a statute where the sum sought to be recovered is a fixed sum of money or in the nature of a debt other than a penalty; or on a guarantee, whether under seal or not, where the claim against the principal is in respect of a debt or liquidated demand only; see O'Floinn, *Practice and Procedure in the Superior Courts*, (1996) Butterworths, p 5 *et seq*.

[34.] *Ibid* Ord 2, r 1(2).

[35.] *Ibid* Ord 2, r 1(3).

[36.] *Ibid* Ord 2, r 2.

[37.] Oral evidence may be called for where there is service of a notice requiring cross-examination of the deponent on an affidavit in accordance with Ord 40, r 31 or where the matter is remitted for plenary hearing: see O'Floinn, *op cit*, p 3.

[38.] Supreme Court, unrep, 20 February 1997 (Keane J) *nem diss*.

[39.] See para **[8.20]** *infra*.

summons will often provide the "closest-fit" to the original rationale behind the Mareva jurisdiction. Indeed, O'Flaherty J's expressed preference in *Re John Horgan Livestock Ltd*[40] was that "the remedy should be confined to situations where there was a clear case involving a claim for a definite sum of money or otherwise, for some tangible object - where the claim was more or less certain, in so far as there is ever certainty in any litigation". If anything, this would suggest that O'Flaherty J would have preferred Mareva relief to be confined to actions commenced by summary summons.[41]

Special Summons

[8.17] Where proceedings are issued using a special summons the RSC provide that they are also summary, without pleadings and are heard on affidavit, with or without oral evidence.[42] The special summons procedure may be adopted in twenty two separate classes of claims.[43] These include claims arising in the administration of a deceased's estate, trusts, the construction of wills and deeds, the determination of questions under the Vendor and Purchaser Act 1874, the sale, delivery of possession by a mortgagee and redemption, reconveyance or delivery of possession by a mortgagee. In addition, a special summons is appropriate for proceedings required or authorised by either the RSC or by statute to be brought by special summons or to be brought in a summary manner where there is no other specific procedure prescribed by the RSC. It is submitted that injunctive relief, including Mareva relief, may also be sought in the special indorsement of claim on a special summons.

Plenary Summons

[8.18] Where proceedings are commenced by plenary summons the proceedings require the delivery of pleadings and the hearing of oral evidence, as opposed to evidence on affidavit. All claims commenced by summons, other than those referred to in Ord 2 (for summary summonses) and Ord 3 (for special summonses) of the RSC, are instituted by plenary summons. Examples of causes of action which are commenced by plenary summons include actions for breach of contract and actions in tort for negligence, conversion etc. By their very nature claims which are commenced by plenary summons are more contentious and will involve more conflicting evidence than claims commenced

---

40. [1995] 2 IR 411 at 422.
41. In *Deutsche Bank AG v Murtagh and Murtagh* [1995] 2 IR 122 a worldwide Mareva injunction was granted by Costello J where the plaintiff's proceedings were commenced by summary summons. See further, Ch 7, *The Defendant's Assets*, para **[7.37]**.
42. Ord 1, r 4.
43. Ord 3 (1)-(22).

by summary or special summons. In practice, Mareva relief is usually granted in cases commenced by plenary summons.

Originating Notice of Motion

[8.19] Notwithstanding that most proceedings must be commenced by summons, certain claims must be commenced by an originating notice of motion.[44] Examples of such claims are many actions commenced under the Companies Acts 1963-1990; this is by virtue of Ord 74, Ord 75A[45] and Ord 75B of the RSC.[46] During the course of the winding up of a company[47] a liquidator may uncover evidence of inappropriate activity by a company's directors or others which may indicate that such persons may be found to be personally liable for all or part of such company's debts. Where there has been an apprehended risk that such persons would remove their assets from the State or otherwise dispose of them with the intention of frustrating the liquidator's future judgment, liquidators have frequently sought Mareva relief. Order 74, r 136[48] of the RSC provides:

> In any winding up, an application under sections 234, 236, 237, 243, 244A, 256, 261, 286, 287(3), 297, 297A, 298, 299, 322B, 347 or 348 of the Companies Act 1963 or under sections 139, 140, 141, 148, 204 or 255 of the Companies Act 1990 or under any other section of the Acts not herein expressly provided for, shall, in the case of a winding up by the Court, be made by motion on notice and in the case of a voluntary winding up by originating notice of motion.

From this it can be seen that claims for, *inter alia*, fraudulent trading, (s 297 of the Companies Act 1963 ("the 1963 Act")) reckless trading (s 297A of the 1963 Act) and misfeasance (s 298 of the 1963 Act) must all be commenced by notice of motion as opposed to originating summons. In an official liquidation, where proceedings are already in train, a notice of motion is used to bring an application under the sections listed in Ord 74, r 136; in a voluntary winding up, where no proceedings will be in train, an *originating* notice of motion will be used. It will almost invariably be the case that such actions will be instigated by official liquidators and experience shows that on numerous occasions over the

---

[44.] See O'Floinn, *op cit*, p 1 where, *inter alia*, the author instances, by way of example, applications under the Registration of Title Act 1964 (Ord 96, r 2); applications under the Solicitors' Acts (Ord 53, r 12); applications under the Companies (Amendment) Act 1990 (Ord 75A) and Companies Act 1990 (Ord 75B); applications for judicial review (Ord 84, r 22); applications under s 27 of the Local Government (Planning and Development) Act 1977 (Ord 103).

[45.] Inserted by SI 147/1991.

[46.] Inserted by SI 278/1991.

[47.] See generally, Courtney, *The Law of Private Companies*, (1994) Butterworths, para [19.029].

[48.] This was inserted by article 2(3) of SI 278/1991 which also inserted Ord 75B of the RSC.

last number of years, liquidators have successfully sought Mareva relief against the directors and other officers of insolvent companies.[49]

[8.20] In *Re Greendale Developments Ltd*[50] Keane J questioned the availability of Mareva relief in proceedings commenced otherwise than by means of a plenary summons. In the course of his judgment he said:

> "... the notice of motion issued ... claimed, in addition to an order under s 298(2) [of the Companies Act 1963] and other orders, an injunction in the Mareva form. No issue appears to have been raised as to the Court's jurisdiction to grant such an injunction, although as a general rule it is only in proceedings commenced by a plenary summons that relief in the form of an injunction may be granted, but no argument was addressed to us on this point ... [B]ecause of this there may have been some uncertainty as to the liquidator's right to claim a Mareva injunction ...".[51]

In that case the Mareva relief sought by the liquidator was ancillary to a claim for misfeasance brought under s 298 of the 1963 Act which had been commenced by originating notice of motion.[52] At the outset one may observe that it was ironic that this question should have been raised in respect of proceedings brought under s 298 of the 1963 Act because it is well established that that section creates no new cause of action and because "it simply provides a more expeditious remedy"[53] for recovering damages from directors and other officers in respect of established causes of action[54] which would ordinarily be commenced by plenary summons.

[8.21] Notwithstanding the doubts raised by Keane J, it is respectfully submitted that his reservations are misplaced and that Mareva relief is available in all suitable causes of action, howsoever commenced. Whilst it is undoubtedly the case that injunctions are generally granted in cases commenced by plenary summons, it is thought that there is no rule of law or practice which precludes a court from granting Mareva or, indeed, other injunctive relief where a claim is

---

[49.] See, eg, *Re Unitas Investments Ltd*, *The Irish Times*, 26 October 1991 (Carroll J); *Re Holbern Investments Trust Ltd*, *The Irish Times*, 9 October 1991 (Barron J); *Re STC Ltd; M v F*, *The Irish Times*, 25 August 1995 (Barr J) and the celebrated *Re Mark Synnott (Life and Pensions) Brokers Ltd*, *The Irish Times*, 3 July 1991 (Carroll J) - Mark Synnott has the dubious distinction of being the first person to be imprisoned in Ireland for the offence of fraudulent trading.

[50.] Supreme Court, unrep, 20 February 1997 (Keane J) *nem diss*.

[51.] At p 43 of the transcript.

[52.] Pursuant to Ord 74, r 136 as inserted by SI 278/1991.

[53.] Keane, *Company Law in the Republic of Ireland*, (2nd ed, 1991) Butterworths, para 38.88.

[54.] In *Re Irish Provident Assurance Company Ltd* [1913] IR 352 Cherry J said of a previous form of the misfeasance provision that: "it applies only to cases where a cause of action would, independently of the section, exist, at the suit of the company". See also *Cavendish-Bentinck v Fenn* [1887] 12 AC 652.

grounded on a summary or special summons, a petition or an notice of motion (whether or not orginating). Neither s 28(8) of the Supreme Court of Judicature (Ireland) Act 1877 nor Ord 50 of the RSC, which governs the legal jurisdiction and practice to grant injunctive relief, contain any suggestion that injunctive relief is confined to cases which are commenced by plenary summons. Nowhere do the RSC say that interlocutory relief pursuant to Ord 50, r 6 can only be granted if the substantive proceedings are commenced by plenary summons.

Indeed, although Ord 50, r 7 refers to proceedings which are commenced by way of a summons, it does so only in the context of interlocutory orders under Ord 50 r 3 and r 4 - not r 6, pursuant to which a Mareva injunction is granted. Order 50 r 7 provides:

> An application for an order under rules 3, 4 or 6 may be made to the Court by any party. If an application be by the plaintiff for an order under rule 6 it may be made either *ex parte* or on notice, and if for an order under rules 3 or 4 it may be made on notice to the defendant at any time after the issue of the summons, and if it be by any other party, then on notice to the plaintiff, and at any time after appearance by the party making the application, provided that, where the exigencies of the case require it, any such application may be made *ex parte*.

The only types of injunctive relief in respect of which r 7 even distinguishes proceedings being issued by summons as opposed to being issued by any other means are applications for an order for the sale of goods, wares or merchandise of a perishable nature liable to injury from keeping (Ord 50, r 3) and applications for an order for the detention, preservation or inspection of property (Ord 50, r 4). An injunction made pursuant to Ord 50, r 4 will be made ancillary to a proprietary claim, not a Mareva injunction[55] and so it can be seen that Ord 50, r 7 makes no reference as to how proceedings are commenced in the context of a Mareva injunction the application for which will always be brought pursuant to Ord 50, r 6 of the RSC. Even if there were reference to "summons" in Ord 50 r 6 it is thought that such would not be conclusive as it is far from likely that the framers of Ord 50 would have had in mind an intention to distinguish proceedings commenced by "summons" from those commenced by other means.

[8.22] The permissive wording of Ord 50, r 6 also leads one to conclude that the High Court has indeed got jurisdiction to grant an injunction as relief ancillary to a claim commenced by a petition or an notice of motion. Order 50, r 6 provides, *inter alia*, that "the court may grant ... an injunction ... *in all cases* in which it appears to the court to be just or convenient so to do".[56] Why should

---

[55.] See Ch 1, *The Mareva Injunction in Context*, para **[1.16]** *et seq.*

[56.] Italics added. See generally Ch 2, *The Jurisdiction to Grant Mareva Relief*, para **[2.02]** *et seq.*

that be construed as referring only to proceedings commenced by plenary summons? It is undoubted that the RSC envisage that civil proceedings will normally be commenced by summons; however, since the current RSC came into existence in 1986, it has subsequently been provided that a whole series of claims are to be commenced by notice of motion; it is submitted that the widely drafted and permissive wording of Ord 50, r 6 is sufficiently clear and unambiguous as to permit the granting of interlocutory injunctive relief, and in particular, Mareva relief in all causes, *howsoever originated*, where such appears to the court to be just or convenient.[57]

Originating Petition

[8.23] The fifth means of commencing a High Court action is by originating petition. It has been noted that it appears from Ord 125, r 1 of the RSC that a petition is the appropriate method of commencing proceedings where there is no defendant.[58] The RSC do, however, provide that a petition is the appropriate means of commencing proceedings in a number of other specific instances. For the commercial lawyer, the most obvious and commonly recognised circumstances where a petition is the appropriate means of instituting proceedings is a petition to have a company wound up under s 213 of the 1963 Act; this is facilitated by Ord 74 of the RSC. In addition petitions are the appropriate means of commencing proceedings in cases, *inter alia*, of applications under certain sections of the Companies Acts 1963-1990 (Ord 75, r 4); matrimonial causes (Ord 70); wards of court (Ord 67); petitions in bankruptcy (Ord 76); patents (Ord 94). In the case of Ord 75, r 4 one of the nineteen instances cited therein is an application for relief relating to minority shareholder oppression under s 205 of the 1963 Act. Notwithstanding the reservations expressed in *Re Greendale Developments Ltd* [59] it is thought that Mareva relief is available in any cause of action commenced by petition.

Issuing the Originating Summons, Motion or Petition

[8.24] An originating summons is prepared by a plaintiff's solicitor and counsel and an indorsement of claim made thereon.[60] In the case of a plenary summons the indorsement is a "general indorsement" and in the case of a summary or special summons it is a "special indorsement". In the case of the latter, the indorsement will set out details of the plaintiff's claim in more detail than the

---

57. In *Re Kelly's Carpetdrome Ltd*, High Court, unrep, 9 May 1983 Costello J granted Mareva relief against the respondent in an action for fraudulent trading under the original s 297 of the Companies Act 1963.
58. O'Floinn, *op cit*, p 1.
59. See para **[8.20]** *supra*.
60. Order 4, r 1 of the RSC, 1986.

former.[61] Except in cases where proceedings have already been commenced, Mareva relief should be sought in the originating document. Once prepared, the summons must be issued.[62] The summons is stamped in the Stamps Office and issued in the Central Office of the High Court where it is dated, sealed,[63] assigned a record number and logged on their computer.[64] The summons will then be deemed to be issued.[65] One or more duplicates of every originating summons is sealed and marked with a record number on the application of a plaintiff's solicitor.[66] Where proceedings are commenced by way of originating notice of motion or petition the motion or petition will also be issued in the Central Office of the High Court.[67] At the end of a working day the registrar in charge of the Central Office of the High Court will examine the endorsement on all plenary summonses lodged during the day and assign those which are chancery matters to *Chancery 1* or *Chancery 2* (formerly known as Courts 5 or 6). After being issued, the originating document, be it summons, petition or motion is then served on the defendant in accordance with the provisions of Ord 9 of the RSC.[68]

[C] THE GROUNDING AFFIDAVIT FOR A MAREVA INJUNCTION[69]

[8.25] In an application for a Mareva injunction, as with all applications for interim and interlocutory injunctions, direct oral evidence is not usually[70] heard by the court. Consequently, the fundamental importance of a plaintiff's initial grounding affidavit cannot be overstressed.[71] The grounding affidavit should set out, in as comprehensive a manner as possible, the plaintiff's grievance and the

---

61. Order 5, r 2.
62. Order 5, r 1.
63. Order 5, r 11.
64. The current stamp duty is £60.
65. Order 5, r 8 and 9. A summons cannot be served until it has been sealed and marked with the record number.
66. On presenting a summons for sealing the plaintiff's solicitor must give a copy of the summons, signed by the plaintiff or his solicitor, to the Central Office and this will be marked with the record number, filed and recorded: see Ord 5, r 10 and r 12.
67. The current stamp duty payable in respect of an originating motion is £10.
68. As to service see Ch 12, *Enforcing Injunctions and Other Orders*, para **[12.11]** *et seq.*
69. For affidavits generally, see O'Floinn, *Practice and Procedure in the Superior Courts* (1996) Butterworths, pp 310-319 for a commentary on Ord 40; 17 *Halsbury's Laws of England* (4th ed, 1991) Butterworths, para 312 and 24 *Halsbury's Laws of England* (4th ed, 1991 reissue) para 968; Goldrein & Wilkinson, *Commercial Litigation: Pre-Emptive Remedies*, (2nd ed, 1991) Sweet & Maxwell, pp 20-24.
70. See para **[8.08]** *supra.*
71. It may be noted that where the application is *inter partes* there will be at least two affidavits, the plaintiff's and the defendant's. Where the application is strongly defended there will usually be several affidavits. See, for example, *Countyglen plc v Carway* [1995] 1 IR 208 at 213 and 217.

facts which support his application for an injunction. In cases of extreme urgency application may be made for an *ex parte* application based on a draft affidavit.[72] This section analyses the following aspects of affidavits which ground Mareva injunctions:

1.   The Form and Contents of Affidavits Generally.
2.   The Contents of an Affidavit Grounding Mareva Relief.
3.   The Duty to Make Full and Frank Disclosure.
4.   Full Particulars of the Plaintiff's Claim.
5.   The Risk of Removal or Disposal of the Defendant's Assets.
6.   The Defendant's Intention to Frustrate the Plaintiff's Judgment.
7.   The Existence of the Defendant's Assets.
8.   The Balance of Convenience.

The Form and Contents of Affidavits Generally

[8.26] The RSC prescribe the form which an affidavit should take. Affidavits should be drawn up in the first person and should be divided into consecutively numbered paragraphs which, as nearly as may be, must be confined to a distinct portion of the subject matter and must be written or printed bookwise.[73] The affidavit must state the description and true place of abode of the deponent.[74] Where an affidavit is made by two or more deponents all deponents' names must be inserted in the *jurat* except where the affidavit is sworn by all deponents at the same time before the same officer, in which case it is sufficient to state that it was sworn by all of the "above-named deponents".[75] Every affidavit must contain a note showing on whose behalf it is filed and an affidavit shall not be filed or used without such a note unless the court directs otherwise.[76]

[8.27] Once prepared, an affidavit should be sworn by the deponent before a commissioner for oaths or practising solicitor and should then be stamped.[77] A deponent is not permitted to swear an affidavit before his own solicitor or that solicitor's agent, correspondent, clerk or partner.[78] All exhibits (if any) which are referred to in an affidavit must be signed by the deponent and witnessed by the commissioner for oaths or practising solicitor. The time and the place where the affidavit is taken should be expressed by the commissioner or solicitor.[79] All

---

[72.]   See para **[8.05]** *et seq, supra.*
[73.]   Order 40, r 8.
[74.]   *Ibid,* r 9: see *Spaddacine v Treacy* 21 LR Ir 553 and *Harte v McCullagh* IR 5 CL 537.
[75.]   Order 40, r 10.
[76.]   *Ibid,* r 11.
[77.]   *Ibid,* r 5.
[78.]   *Ibid,* r 17 and r 18.
[79.]   *Ibid,* r 6.

interlineations, alterations or erasures to an affidavit must be authenticated by the initials of the commissioner or solicitor.[80] The commissioner or solicitor must, in the *jurat*, certify that he personally knows the deponent or some person named in the *jurat* who certifies his knowledge of the deponent.[81] It should be noted, however, that in exceptionally urgent *ex parte* applications, injunctive relief may be granted before the affidavit is sworn.[82]

[8.28] Generally, affidavits are concerned with matters of fact as opposed to law. In *Alfred Dunhill Ltd v Sunoptics SA*[83] Roskill LJ said:

> "Affidavits are designed to place facts, whether disputed or otherwise, before the tribunal for whose help they are prepared. They are not designed as a receptacle for or as a vehicle for legal arguments. Draftsmen of affidavits should not, as a general rule, put into the mouths of the intended deponents legal arguments of which those deponents are unlikely ever to have heard. Legal arguments, especially in interlocutory proceedings, should come from the mouths of those best qualified to advance them and not be put into the mouths of the deponents."

Although affidavits are essentially vehicles for the transmission of facts it would be naive to underestimate the importance of legal principles in drafting affidavits. Grounding affidavits are intended to convince a court that the deponent is entitled to the relief claimed and, accordingly, the contents of a grounding affidavit for Mareva relief should be structured so as to show that the facts upon which the application is based meet with the legal requirements for a Mareva injunction. Of course, where *ex parte* application is made, the plaintiff must make full and frank disclosure of all material facts.[84] Irrespective of whether application is made *ex parte* or on notice, a deponent to any affidavit should not deliberately mislead the court.

[8.29] Affidavits in interlocutory motions are peculiar vehicles for the transmission of facts, in that they may include certain hearsay evidence. Order 40, r 4 of the RSC provides that:

> Affidavits shall be confined to such facts as the witness is able of his own knowledge to prove, and shall state his means of knowledge thereof, except on interlocutory motions, on which statements as to his belief, with the grounds thereof, may be admitted. The costs of any affidavit which shall unnecessarily

---

[80.] *Ibid*, r 13.

[81.] *Ibid*, r 14 which also makes provision for cases where the deponent is illiterate or blind.

[82.] See *Jackson v Cassidy* (1841) 10 Sim 326 and *Elsey v Adams* (1863) 4 Giff 398, see para **[8.08]** *supra*.

[83.] [1979] FSR 337 at 352.

[84.] See para **[8.32]** *et seq.*

set forth matters of hearsay or argumentative matter, or copies of or extracts from documents, shall not be allowed.[85]

Accordingly, it is said that the rule against hearsay does not strictly apply to affidavits grounding interlocutory applications such as Mareva injunctions. As Moriarty J said in *MM v DD*,[86] in the context of the Proceeds of Crime Act 1996:

"Clearly also, the Act adopts a procedure broadly analogous to Mareva applications, and it is the established usage of the courts that some appreciable measure of hearsay evidence is considered acceptable in affidavits filed on behalf of parties."[87]

The rationale for this exception has been said to be the fact that interlocutory applications are frequently very urgent and all that a deponent may be able to say in evidence is that he has been informed of certain matters, believes them and believes that they can be proved.[88] Apprehension of harm is, after all, the hallmark of the Mareva jurisdiction. The inclusion of hearsay in an affidavit where there is no reference to the deponent's source of information and his grounds for believing it to be true is, however, inadmissible.[89]

In very exceptional cases a plaintiff's solicitor (as opposed to the plaintiff, or an authorised representative of the plaintiff) may swear a grounding affidavit. This is what happened in the Canadian case of *National Financial Services Corporation v Wolverton Securities Ltd*[90] and the comments of Henderson J are of interest to all legal practitioners:

"When it obtained the *ex parte* Mareva injunction, the applicant relied solely on the affidavit of one of its solicitors (who were not its current solicitors). Presumably, this was considered necessary because of the need for haste and because those who had more direct knowledge of the facts were located in other jurisdictions. The unfortunate result is that the only witness giving evidence in support of this motion had virtually no personal knowledge of what she was swearing to ... Having a solicitor to the applicant swear the affidavit in support raises the possibility that the respondents will seek to cross-examine the solicitor on matters that would otherwise be privileged: see for example

---

85. Note that Ord 40, r 12 empowers the court to strike out from any affidavit any matter which is scandalous.
86. High Court, unrep, 10 December 1996 (Moriarty J). For the Proceeds of Crime Act 1996, see generally, Ch 3, *Statutory Jurisdictions to Freeze Assets*, para **[3.31]** *et seq.*
87. At p 4 of the transcript.
88. *Savings and Investment Bank Ltd v Gasco Investments (Netherlands) BV* [1984] 1 WLR 271 at 282 (Peter Gibson J).
89. In *Re Young JL Manufacturing Co Ltd* [1900] 2 Ch 753 at 755 Rigby LJ said: "... when a deponent makes a statement on his information and belief, he must state the ground of that information and belief".
90. (1998) Supreme Court of British Columbia, 6 February 1998 (Henderson J).

United States v Friedland (1996) 6 CPC (4th) 29 (OntCJ(GD)). For this and other reasons the practice is to be avoided."

It is thought that extreme care should be exercised by a solicitor who is asked to swear a grounding affidavit in support of an application for a Mareva injunction.

The Contents of an Affidavit Grounding Mareva Relief

[8.30] It is now appropriate to consider what an affidavit grounding an application for a Mareva injunction should contain. In *Third Chandris Shipping Corporation v Unimarine SA*[91] Lord Denning laid down five criteria which have to be established before a Mareva injunction will be granted. These criteria were repeated by Murphy J in the High Court in *Re John Horgan Livestock Ltd* and endorsed by Hamilton CJ in the Supreme Court.[92] Those five criteria were said to be that:

"(i) The plaintiff should make full and frank disclosure of all material matters in his knowledge which are material for the judge to know.

(ii) The plaintiff should give particulars of his claim against the defendant, stating the grounds of his claims and the amount thereof and fairly stating the points made against it by the defendant.

(iii) The plaintiff should give some grounds for believing that the defendant had assets within the jurisdiction. The existence of a bank account is normally sufficient.

(iv) The plaintiff should give some grounds for believing that there is a risk of the assets being removed or dissipated.

(v) The plaintiff must give an undertaking in damages, in case he fails."

The foregoing formulation is not, however, sacrosanct and in the light of subsequent judicial developments of the Mareva injunction, they can be seen to have been expanded. Nevertheless, this formulation contains the essential points which must be addressed by the plaintiff in applying for Mareva relief and, accordingly, must be addressed in the plaintiff's grounding affidavit.

[8.31] The subsequent development of the Mareva injunction, suggests that, today, an applicant seeking Mareva relief ought to adduce evidence upon, and adhere to, the following matters:

[91.] [1979] 2 All ER 972 at 984; [1979] QB 645 at 668-669.

[92.] [1995] 2 IR 411 at 416 and 418; see also *Production Association Minsk Tractor Works and Belarus Equipment (Ireland) Ltd v Saenko*, High Court, unrep, 25 February 1998 (McCracken J), p 3, 4 of the transcript. These criteria have also been accepted in Canada in Ontario in *Liberty National Bank & Trust Co v Atkin* 121 DLR (3d) 160 at 165 (Montgomery J) and in the Northwest Territories in *BP Exploration Co (Libya) Ltd v Hunt* 114 DLR (3d) 35 at 62 (Tallis J).

1.   The plaintiff must make full and frank disclosure of all material matters in his knowledge which the court might find relevant;[93]

2.   The plaintiff must give full particulars of his substantive claim against the defendant and also satisfy the court that he has a "good arguable case" when it comes to the trial of that matter;[94]

3.   The plaintiff must adduce evidence that there is a real risk that the defendant intends to remove his assets from the State, dissipate them, secrete them or otherwise dispose of them;[95]

4.   The plaintiff must establish a likelihood that the foregoing risk or removal, disposal, dissipation etc is with a view, on the part of the defendant, to evade his obligation to the plaintiff and to frustrate the anticipated order of the court;[96]

5.   The plaintiff must satisfy the court that the defendant has assets; moreover, the plaintiff should give details of specific assets if he wishes to have them specifically mentioned in the order; where a worldwide Mareva is sought, details must be given of the defendant's assets which are situate outside of the State and evidence should be adduced that his "domestic" assets are insufficient to satisfy the plaintiff's future judgment;[97]

6.   The plaintiff must show that the balance of convenience favours the making of the Mareva injunction;

7.   In addition to any other undertakings as may be required in the circumstances of the application,[98] the plaintiff must give an undertaking in damages to the court in case he fails in his substantive action;[99]

8.   Additional undertakings must be given to the court where the plaintiff seeks a worldwide Mareva injunction.[100]

It will be seen that the matters required to be addressed in a plaintiff's grounding affidavit correspond largely to the legal requirements before a court will accede

---

[93.] See paras **[8.32]**-**[8.44]** *infra*.

[94.] See para **[8.47]** *et seq infra* and generally, Ch 4, *A Substantive Cause of Action* and Ch 5, *A Good Arguable Case*.

[95.] See para **[8.49]** *et seq infra* and generally, Ch 6, *The Risk of Removal or Disposal of Assets*, para **[6.29]**.

[96.] See para **[8.51]** *et seq infra* and generally, Ch 6, *The Risk of Removal or Disposal of Assets*, para **[6.16]** *et seq*.

[97.] See para **[8.53]** *et seq infra* and generally, Ch 7, *The Defendant's Assets*.

[98.] Such as, for example, undertakings in lieu of procedural formalities: see para **[8.73]** *infra*.

[99.] See para **[8.58]** *infra*.

[100.] See para **[8.81]** *et seq infra* and generally, Ch 7, *The Defendant's Assets*, para **[7.43]** *et seq*.

to an application for Mareva relief. It is now proposed to consider the first six requirements in turn, in the specific context of drafting a plaintiff's grounding affidavit. In Section [D], the various undertakings which a plaintiff may be asked to give are considered. Implicit in the treatment of the law and practice which follows is that application for a Mareva injunction should only be made in a proper case. As McCracken J said in *Production Association Minsk Tractor Works and Belarus Equipment (Ireland) Ltd v Saenko*:[101]

"I would emphasise that a Mareva injunction is an extremely drastic remedy. In some civil law countries there is provision for the freezing of assets pending the outcome of a claim. There is no such provision in our law, and a Mareva injunction cannot be used to attain this purpose. The court must look very carefully at any application to ensure that it is justified on the principles set out above."[102]

The basis of a Mareva plaintiff's application will be the grounding affidavit and it follows that great care must be given to its preparation.

The Duty to Make Full and Frank Disclosure[103]

[8.32] It has long been established that in any *ex parte* application there is a duty on the applicant to make full and frank disclosure of all material facts to the court. The principle of law which requires full and frank disclosure on an *ex parte* application is particularly necessary in an application for a Mareva injunction, an Anton Piller order or a Bayer order as these injunctions, if granted in a wrong case, can give rise to great injustice.[104] Here, the following aspects of this duty are considered:

(a) The golden rule;

(b) Disclosing "material facts" following "proper inquiry";

(c) The consequences of failing to disclose material facts;

(d) Deliberate non-disclosure of material facts;

(e) Defendants' duties of frankness in affidavits.

(a) The golden rule

[8.33] Affidavits grounding applications for *ex parte* injunctive relief must represent a full and frank disclosure of all material matters which are within the

---

101. High Court, unrep, 25 February 1998 (McCracken J).
102. At p 5 of the judgment.
103. See Goldrein & Wilkinson, *Commercial Litigation: Pre-Emptive Remedies*, (2nd ed, 1991), pp 27-32; 24 *Halsbury's Laws of England*, (4th ed reissue; 1991), pp 517; and Spry, *Equitable Remedies* (4th ed, 1990), pp 484-490.
104. As noted by O'Flaherty J in *Re John Horgan Livestock Ltd; O'Mahony v Horgan* [1995] 2 IR 411 at 422.

deponent's knowledge.[105] As has been considered above,[106] *ex parte* applications are heard without a defendant having any opportunity to rebut, in a replying affidavit, the evidence tendered by a plaintiff. In the case of Mareva injunctions, which are commonly sought on an *ex parte* basis, the courts have applied an exacting standard and the principle of full disclosure is sacrosanct. Sir Nicholas Browne-Wilkinson V-C in *Tate Access Floors Inc v Boswell*[107] identified full and frank disclosure as being "the golden rule" when he said:

> "No rule is better established, and few more important, than the rule (the golden rule) that a plaintiff applying for *ex parte* relief must disclose to the court all matters relevant to the exercise of the court's discretion whether or not to grant relief before giving the defendant an opportunity to be heard. If that duty is not observed by the plaintiff, the court will discharge the *ex parte* order and may, to mark its displeasure, refuse the plaintiff further *inter partes* relief even though the circumstances would otherwise justify the grant of such relief."[108]

In *The Niedersachen*[109] the plaintiff-deponent had averred that the defendant was a West German company which was selling both of its only two assets and that he was pessimistic about the prospects of recovering any award or judgment. Mustill J said that from this, "to the *ex parte* judge, there was nothing to detract from the impression of a defendant which had once been a two-ship foreign company, and was now a no-ship company, with a substantial claim against it". In truth, Mustill J found that the defendant companies were members of a long established group of companies and said that "plaintiffs who seek Mareva relief will do well to bear in mind that the same obligations of candour apply to these proceedings, as to any other form of *ex parte* application".[110] It should also be noted that a plaintiff's solicitor, as an officer of the court, has a personal responsibility to ensure that any affidavit prepared for his client-plaintiff complies with the "golden rule".[111]

[105.] Indeed, all *ex parte* applications must make full and frank disclosure of all material facts: *Atkin v Moran* (1871) IR 6 EQ 79, *McDonogh v Davies* (1875) IR 9 CL 300, *R v Kensington Income Tax Commissioners* [1917] 1 KB 486. See also, Clohessy, 'Mareva Injunctions', (1994) CLP 151.

[106.] See para **[8.05]** *supra*.

[107.] [1990] 3 All ER 303.

[108.] At 316c-d.

[109.] [1984] 1 All ER 398 at 403.

[110.] In *Bank of Mellat v Nikour* [1982] Com LR 158; [1985] FSR 87 Slade LJ observed: "I think it is of the utmost importance that on any *ex parte* application for an interim injunction the applicant should recognise his responsibility to present his case fully and fairly to the court and that he should support it be evidence showing the principle material facts upon which he relies. Most particularly, I think that this duty falls on an applicant seeking a Mareva injunction which, if granted, may have drastic consequences for the defendant."

[111.] *O'Regan v Iambic Productions* (1989) 139 NLJ 1378.

[8.34] The only Irish case (in which a written judgment has been given) to even touch upon the duty of full and frank disclosure in the context of an application for a Mareva injunction was *Production Association Minsk Tractor Works and Belarus Equipment (Ireland) Ltd v Saenko*.[112] In that case the first plaintiff (a body corporate under the laws of Belarus) and the second plaintiff (an Irish company which was a wholly owned subsidiary of the first plaintiff) successfully obtained an interim *ex parte* Mareva injunction which restrained the defendants (a married couple and their daughter) from *inter alia* dealing with their assets and bank accounts or dissipating them below £300,000. The second plaintiff was the distributing company in Ireland for the tractors produced by the first plaintiff. The first defendant, a citizen of Belarus, had been the managing director of the second plaintiff from 1 January 1993 to 31 July 1997. It was alleged that the first defendant had misappropriated moneys from the second plaintiff and that he had defrauded the second plaintiff. The plaintiffs' application for an interlocutory Mareva injunction came before McCracken J. After noting that the plaintiffs had made serious allegations of fraud, McCracken J said of the claim made by the plaintiffs:

> "The amounts concerned are very large, almost £300,000 according to the grounding affidavit of this motion. It is a matter of some concern to me that after the interim order was granted, it was conceded in a replying affidavit that over £95,000 of this was in fact paid into an account of the first named plaintiff. This must have been known to the plaintiffs when the original affidavit was sworn".[113]

In applying the first of the five criteria set out by Lord Denning MR in *Third Chandris Shipping Corporation v Unimarine SA*[114] - that the plaintiff should make full and frank disclosure of all matters in his knowledge which are material for the judge to know - McCracken J held:

> "... as I have said, I find it disturbing that the plaintiffs misled the court on the amount claimed by some £95,000. They now concede this money was paid to them on 27 March 1995 and therefore they must have known of it."[115]

This was one of the reasons why McCracken J refused the application for an interlocutory Mareva injunction.

[8.35] A further Irish example of where the duty to make full disclosure arose in the context of a Mareva injunction is provided by an application reported in *The Irish Times*. In *Allied Irish Banks plc v Two Solicitors*[116] Costello J was reported

---

[112] High Court, unrep, 25 February 1998 (McCracken J). See also *The Irish Times*, 27 February 1998 and the Supreme Court appeal reported in *The Irish Times*, 7 March 1998.

[113] At p 2 of the transcript.

[114] [1979] 2 All ER 972 at 984; [1979] QB 645 at 668-669.

[115] At p 4 of the transcript.

[116] *The Irish Times*, 3 June 1992 (Costello J).

as having granted an *ex parte* Mareva injunction against two solicitors, restraining them from disposing of their assets below £30,000. A representative of the plaintiff bank was reported as having alleged on affidavit that, *inter alia*, the defendants owed a sum of money on foot of a current account; that they did not have a *bona fide* defence to the claim; and that the deponent had learnt that the defendants had acted as solicitors for and were themselves part of a syndicate which had won a sum of money in the National Lottery draw held the previous Saturday. Two days later[117] it was reported that the Mareva injunction was discharged by Denham J who was reported in *The Irish Times* as having said that the information given by the applicant had proved to be incorrect and that such was a very serious matter, especially as it had been given by professional people and that the Court would not have given the interim injunction had it been aware of the true facts. *The Irish Times* reported that Denham J said that the applicant had acted on false information and that an injunction was a strong weapon: anyone coming before the court seeking such a lethal weapon must have taken all steps to ensure the information put before the Court is correct.[118]

(b) Disclosing "material facts" following "proper inquiry"

[8.36] In a number of cases it has been held that a plaintiff who applies *ex parte* for Mareva relief must not only disclose material facts within his actual knowledge, but also within his constructive knowledge. In *Brink's-Mat Ltd v Elecombe*[119] the Court of Appeal held that a plaintiff must disclose all facts which he would have known had he made proper enquiries. In this case, which arose out of the Brink's-Mat robbery at Heathrow in November 1983, the plaintiff had obtained an *ex parte* Mareva injunction restraining nine out of the eleven defendants from disposing of their assets. Subsequently, it was ordered that the injunction be discharged as against two of the defendants on the grounds that there had been an innocent, but material, non-disclosure of facts in the information put by the plaintiff to the judge at the *ex parte* hearing. In

---

[117.] *The Irish Times*, 5 June 1992 (Denham J).

[118.] The "golden rule" requiring full disclosure by an applicant in an *ex parte* application exists in all common law jurisdictions. In Australia, for example, in *Town & Country Sport Resorts (Holdings) Pty Ltd v Partnership Pacific Ltd* (1988) 97 ALR 315 the Federal Court of Appeal said (at 317): "A party who seeks the granting of an injunction on an *ex parte* basis has a duty to place before the court all relevant matters including such matters which would have been raised by the respondent in his defence if he had been present"; see also *Thomas A Edison Ltd v Bullock* (1912) 15 CLR 679 and, for a recent consideration of the duty to make full an frank disclosure in the context of a Mareva injunction, see *Hayden v Teplitzky* [1997] 230 FCA (9 April 1997).

[119.] [1988] 3 All ER 188.

addressing the question of non-disclosure, Gibson LJ said of the meaning of "material facts" that:

> "The material facts are those which it is material for the judge to know in dealing with the application as made; materiality is to be decided by the court and not by the assessment of the applicant or his legal advisers."[120]

And as to the question of the disclosure of material facts which are not within the plaintiff's actual knowledge, Gibson LJ continued:

> "The applicant must make proper inquiries before making the application: see *Bank Mellat v Nikpour* [1985] FSR 87. The duty of disclosure therefore applies not only to material facts known to the applicant but also to any additional facts which he would have known if he had made such inquiries ... The extent of the inquiries which will be held to be proper, and therefore necessary, must depend on all the circumstances of the case including:
>
> (a) the nature of the case which the applicant is making when he makes the application,
>
> (b) the order for which application is made and the probable effect of the order on the defendant ...
>
> (c) the degree of legitimate urgency and the time available for the making of inquiries: see *Bank Mellat v Nikpour* [1985] FSR 87 at 92-93 *per* Slade LJ."[121]

The plaintiff need not pursue every avenue of information, and is only obliged to make "proper inquiry". In a case of alleged fraud where time is of the essence and full and complete inquiry is thereby limited, a plaintiff's inquiries may be legitimately curtailed by reason of the urgency of the matter.

[8.37] It may be noted that an *ex parte* applicant's duty to make full and frank disclosure extends to disclosing any possible defence to his claim. In *Lloyds Bowmaker Ltd v Britannia Arrow Holdings plc (Lavens, third party)*[122] the Court of Appeal held that in complying with the duty to make full and frank disclosure, a plaintiff is obliged to disclose to the court any defence which he anticipates the defendant may advance. Similarly, in *Production Association Minsk Tractor Works and Belarus Equipment (Ireland) Ltd v Saenko*[123] McCracken J noted that the plaintiffs' grounding affidavit did not state any

---

[120.] At 192g-h: *R v Kensington Income Tax Commissioners* [1917] 1 KB 486 at 504 *per* Lord Cozens-Hardy MR citing *Dalglish v Jarvie* (1850) 2 Mac & G 231 at 238 and *Thermax Ltd v Schott Industrial Glass Ltd* [1981] FSR 289 at 295 *per* Browne Wilkinson J cited as authority.

[121.] At 192h-j. See also *Bank of Nova Scotia v Priority Corporate Services Inc* (1997) Supreme Court of British Columbia, 29 December 1997 (Morrison J) where it was found that a Mareva plaintiff had made a material non-disclosure, that significant information had been within the plaintiff's knowledge for some time and also that the application was not urgent.

[122.] [1988] 3 All ER 178.

[123.] High Court, unrep, 25 February 1998 (McCracken J). See para **[8.34]** *supra*.

points made against it by the defendant although these points were, at that point, before the court. Where a defendant has given notice of his intention to defend the proceedings, the plaintiff must also disclose this fact.[124]

(c) The consequence of failing to disclose material facts

[8.38] Where it is discovered that there has been non-disclosure of material facts or that the plaintiff has been less than full and frank in his disclosure, the general rule is that the injunction or order thereby obtained should be automatically discharged. In *R v Kensington Income Tax Commissioners*[125] it was said by Warrington LJ that where an *ex parte* application is granted on foot of an inaccurate grounding affidavit, the beneficiary of the court's relief "will be deprived of any advantage he may have already obtained by means of the order which has thus, wrongly, been obtained by him."[126]

[8.39] The old Irish cases of *Atkin v Moran*[127] and *McDonogh v Davies*[128] are authorities for the proposition that where an *ex parte* order is obtained without the plaintiff having made full and frank disclosure, the order will be automatically discharged. In *Atkin v Moran* the applicant for an *ex parte* order did not disclose the existence of a particular deed before getting the order, causing Lord O'Hagan LC to say:

> "... the party applying is not to make himself the judge of whether a particular fact is material or not. If it is such as might in any way affect the mind of the court, it is his duty to bring it forward. I do not think that in the present case there was any intention to deceive or mislead. I do not decide that the deed will make any real difference in the result of the case: all I say is, that this is a matter which ought to have been referred to in the affidavit upon which the order was obtained, and therefore I am obliged to set it aside."[129]

His lordship clearly did not consider that he had any discretion in the matter but that he was obliged to discharge the order. In *McDonough v Davies* the existence of an agreement and mortgage was not disclosed when the plaintiff obtained a charging order over stock. Palles CB said "[w]e think it of great importance that the utmost good faith should be always used towards the court, and, therefore, in discharging the order, on the ground of suppression of facts, discharge it with costs".[130]

---

124. *Mexican Co v Maldonado*[1890] WN 8.

125. [1917] 1 KB 486.

126. At 509. See also the Supreme Court of British Columbia's decision in *Gulf Islands Navigation Ltd v Seafarers International Union of North America (Canadian District)* [1959] 27 WWR 652.

127. (1871) IR 6 EQ 79.

128. (1875) IR 9 CL 300.

129. At 81. *Holcombe v Antrobus* 8 Beav 412, *De Feucheres v Daues* 11 Beav 46 and *St Victor v Devereaux* 6 Beav 584 cited in support.

130. At 304.

[8.40] The rule that an *ex parte* order obtained without making full and frank disclosure should be automatically discharged has been restated in more recent authorities. In *Bank Mellat v Nikpour*[131] Lord Donaldson found that a failure to make full and frank disclosure in an *ex parte* application was fatal even if the mistake was innocent. He said:

> "This principle that no injunction obtained *ex parte* shall stand if it has been obtained in circumstances in which there was a breach of the duty to make the fullest and frankest disclosure is of great antiquity. Indeed, it is so well enshrined in the law that it is difficult to find authority for the proposition; we all know it; it is trite law ...
>
> ... the court will be astute to ensure that a plaintiff who obtains an injunction without full disclosure - or any *ex parte* order without full disclosure - is deprived of any advantage he may have derived by that breach of duty ... The rule requiring full disclosure seems to me to be one of the most fundamental importance, particularly in the context of the draconian remedy of the Mareva injunction. It is in effect, together with the *Anton Pillar* order, one of the law's two 'nuclear' weapons. If access to such a weapon is obtained without the fullest and frankest disclosure, I have no doubt but that it should be revoked."[132]

It is important, however, that a balance be struck between stripping a party of an advantage wrongfully obtained and allowing some small latitude to an innocent omission of questionable materiality. As Lord Denning MR said in the same case:

> "... it is not for every omission that the injunction will be automatically discharged. A *locus poenitentiae* may sometimes be afforded."[133]

This was cited with approval by Ralph Gibson LJ in *Brink's-Mat Ltd v Elcombe*[134] where he said that the court has a discretion, notwithstanding proof of non-disclosure which justifies or requires the immediate discharge of the *ex parte* order, to nevertheless continue it or to make a new order.[135] Although the "golden rule" is that the fullest possible disclosure must be made by an *ex parte*

[131.] [1985] FSR 87.

[132.] At 90 and 91,92.

[133.] [1985] FSR 87 at 90.

[134.] [1988] 3 All ER 188. See also *High Speed Printing Ltd v Mendoza* Court of Appeal of 26 September 1986 (Lexis transcript) where Woolf LJ accepted (p 4 of the transcript) that there must remain in the court a discretion as to its decision with regard to whether it continues an injunction where there has been non-disclosure.

[135.] At 193. In *Dormeuil Freres SA v Nicolian International (Textiles) Ltd* [1988] 3 All ER 197, after setting out first principles, Browne-Wilkinson V-C said (at 199): "If such disclosure is not made by the plaintiff, the court may discharge the *ex parte* injunction on that ground alone. But if, in the circumstances existing when the matter comes before the court *inter partes*, justice requires an order either continuing the *ex parte* injunction or the grant of a fresh injunction, such an order can be made notwithstanding the earlier failure of the plaintiff to make such disclosure. Moreover, there is authority that, contrary to the law as it was originally laid down, there is no absolute right to have an *ex parte* order obtained without due disclosure set aside: there is a discretion in the court whether to do so or not".

applicant, the courts seem to have recognised also that, on occasion, legitimate haste may give rise to innocent inadvertent inaccuracies which should not invariably impel the court to discharge the order.[136] In the *Brink's-Mat* case Slade LJ said:

> "By their very nature, *ex parte* applications usually necessitate the giving and taking of instructions and the preparation of the requisite drafts in some haste. Particularly in heavy commercial cases, the borderline between material facts and the non-material facts can be a somewhat uncertain one. While in no way discounting the heavy duty of candour and care which falls on persons making *ex parte* applications, I do not think the application of the principle should be carried to extreme lengths. In one or two other recent cases coming before this court, I have suspected signs of a growing tendency on the part of some litigants against whom *ex parte* injunctions have been granted, or of their legal advisers, to rush to the *R v Kensington Income Tax Commissioners* principle as a *tabula in naufragio*, alleging material non-disclosure on sometimes rather slender grounds, as representing substantially the only hope of obtaining the discharge of injunctions in cases where there is little hope of doing so on the substantial merits of the case or on the balance of convenience."[137]

It is thought that most counsel and solicitors who have acted in preparing urgent cases for *ex parte* relief will empathise with the sentiments expressed by Slade LJ.[138]

[8.41] Should a court not wish to appear to countenance continuing an *ex parte* injunction which was obtained without the plaintiff making full disclosure of material facts, it is open to the court to discharge the first, tainted, injunction and to grant a second, fresh, injunction.[139] This is what happened in *Lloyd's*

[136.] In *Eastglen International Corp v Monpare SA* (1986) 136 NLJ 1087 Gatehouse J said, *obiter dictum*, that if an omission is innocent and the undisclosed fact is not of central importance, the court may decline to discharge the injunction. In that case a Mareva injunction was granted after the plaintiff's solicitor swore an affidavit which omitted a most material fact. The defendant sought to have the injunction discharged and when the plaintiff went to new solicitors they discontinued the action, started a fresh action, obtained a new Mareva injunction grounded by an affidavit which clearly disclosed the original non-disclosure. Notwithstanding his *obiter* finding, Gatehouse J discharged the injunction but the Court of Appeal (1987) 137 NJJ 56 allowed the appeal and continued the injunction because the fault was wholly that of the first solicitor.

[137.] [1988] 3 All ER 188 at 194, 195.

[138.] In *National Financial Services Corp v Wolverton Securities Ltd* (1998) Supreme Court of British Columbia, 6 February 1998 (Henderson J) the difficulty in striking a fair balance was put thus: "Disclosure must be full in the sense that it must be adequate to the demands of the particular application. It must also be fair to the absent defendant. On the other hand, an *ex parte* chambers application is not a trial and should not be turned into one by demands for an unrealistic standard of disclosure".

[139.] See *Yardley & Co Ltd v Higson* [1984] FSR 304.

Bowmaker Ltd v Britannia Arrow Holdings plc (Lavens, third party),[140] where both Gildewell and Dillon LLJ accepted that there was jurisdiction, in such circumstances, to grant a second, fresh, injunction if the court is so disposed. Gildewell LJ said:

> "Certainly on the more recent authorities it is my view that the High Court would have a discretion to grant a second Mareva injunction, and it may well be that this court would have a discretion to preserve the status quo in the mean time pending such an application, or a discretion itself to grant a second Mareva injunction."[141]

Dillon LJ adopted a more pragmatic approach. Whilst he accepted that there was jurisdiction[142] to make a second injunction he was sceptical of the practice of making second injunctions in such circumstances. He said:

> "I find it a cumberous procedure that the court should be bound, instead of itself granting a fresh injunction, to discharge the existing injunction and stay the discharge until a fresh application is made, possibly in another court, and the court which is asked to discharge the injunction should not simply, as a matter of discretion in an appropriate case, refuse to discharge it if it feels that it would be appropriate to grant a fresh injunction. That leads me to think that there is a discretion in the court on an application for discharge."[143]

This view appears to be more in accordance with common sense. Whilst of course the court must neither condone, nor be seen to condone, non-disclosure of material facts on *ex parte* applications, and while "he who seeks equity must come with clean hands", some discretion must surely remain in the court as to whether or not to discharge a Mareva or other injunction in such circumstances. It is submitted that the circumstances in which a court should consider it has a discretion to continue a Mareva injunction so obtained, should depend upon: the degree of materiality of the fact which was not disclosed; whether the non-disclosure was innocent or deliberate; the plaintiff's culpability in the entire matter; and whether or not it remains, on balance, just or convenient to continue the injunction.[144]

[140.] [1988] 3 All ER 178.
[141.] [1988] 3 All ER 178 at 185.
[142.] Each case will turn on its own facts: see *Behbehani v Salem* [1989] 2 All ER 143, where it was held that a failure to disclose that proceedings had been commenced in Spain and also the existence of a prior settlement were sufficiently serious matters which justified the court in not granting a fresh injunction. In that case it was also material that the defendants had agreed to undertake to the court not to dispose of their property assets within the jurisdiction.
[143.] [1988] 3 All ER 178 at 187.
[144.] In *Girocredit Bank Aktiengesellschaft Der Sparkassen v Bader* (1998) Court of Appeal for British Columbia of 25 June 1998, Goldie J accepted that it had been accepted in England that a reviewing judge had a discretionary scope to reinstate an injunction or order where the material non-disclosure was innocent. In that case, however, it was found that the non-disclosure was not innocent.

[8.42] The most far-reaching mitigation of the usual consequences of breaching the "golden rule" is seen in the judgment of Browne-Wilkinson V-C in *Dormeuil Freres SA v Nicolian International (Textiles) Ltd*[145] where he said that, save in exceptional cases, it is not the correct procedure to apply to discharge an *ex parte* injunction on the grounds of non-disclosure of material facts at the interlocutory stage and that the appropriate time to consider the matter was at the trial whereupon the plaintiff's undertaking as to damages[146] may be looked to. In the course of his judgment he said:

> "... applications to discharge the *ex parte* order are frequently made at the same time as the plaintiff's motion to continue the *ex parte* injunction comes before the court *inter partes*. The result of the joining of an application to discharge the *ex parte* order with the hearing of the *inter partes* motion for an injunction is almost invariably to increase both the duration and the complexity of the interlocutory proceedings to a substantial extent.
>
> To discover whether an *ex parte* order has been improperly obtained, the court first has to consider the evidence as it was at the time of the application for the *ex parte* order and then a mass of evidence designed to demonstrate that that evidence was misleading or failed to make full disclosure. The real question at the time of the *inter partes* hearing should not be what has happened in the past but what should happen in the future ...
>
> The cost in time and money to the parties in a complex case can become vast and the waste of court time quite unacceptable."[147]

The judge's misgivings about going into possibly complex issues at the interlocutory stage of proceedings are understandable. Indeed in *Re John Horgan Livestock Ltd*[148] O'Flaherty J referred to the Mareva application in that case as being a "side-show" to the main litigation. It is thought, however, that Browne-Wilkinson V-C's views are unlikely to be followed.[149] Where an *ex parte* order is wrongfully obtained on the back of a material non-disclosure there can be no doubt but that a defendant thereby affected has the right to apply immediately to have the order discharged. To suggest that a defendant, wrongly enjoined from using his own assets, must sit back and wait until the trial of the matter in the hope of relying upon the plaintiff's undertaking as to damages seems a preposterous distortion to the scales of justice which might encourage a

---

[145.] [1988] 3 All ER 197.

[146.] See para **[8.58]** *infra*.

[147.] At 199j-200c.

[148.] [1995] 2 IR 411 at 422.

[149.] It was not followed by Mervyn Davies J in *Ali & Fahd Shobokshi Group Ltd v Moneim* [1989] 2 All ER 404 who said "... it would not be right to require a defendant to wait until after trial to seek damages for non-disclosure. On the contrary, a defendant should be at liberty to require the discharge of an *ex parte* Mareva order (without its immediate reimposition) as soon as he can show non-disclosure of a substantial kind".

plaintiff to think that he had *carte blanche* to mislead the court on an *ex parte* hearing in the knowledge that he may not be deprived of the advantage thereby obtained for perhaps two years! If Browne-Wilkinson V-C's suggestion has any basis it can only apply where there has been a purely technical or accidental breach of the "golden rule", all other proofs for a Mareva injunction have been met and justice requires the injunction to continue to the trial of the substantive issues.

(d) Deliberate non-disclosure of material facts

[8.43] Different considerations should, however, apply in a case where a plaintiff's grounding affidavit is misleading by reason of the deliberate non-disclosure of material facts and it is submitted that an *ex parte* injunction so obtained should, upon the discovery of such non-disclosure, be automatically discharged. In *Ali & Fahd Shobokshi Group Ltd v Moneim* [150] the fact that there had been a deliberate suppression of material fact in the *ex parte* application was instrumental in Mervyn Davies J's decision to discharge the injunction. In that case the plaintiff had obtained a Mareva injunction following an *ex parte* application. In the grounding affidavit it was alleged, *inter alia,* that the defendant had obtained three specific sums of money by fraud during the course of his employment with the company. What was not disclosed was that the defendant's private account, into which the sums were allegedly paid, had been used openly and extensively for the company's business; that the defendant had given the directors of the plaintiff company a general power of attorney to operate the account; that substantial sums were paid into and out of the account over a number of years; and that statements on the account had been available to the plaintiff company *etc*. Following an analysis of these and other matters which had not been disclosed on the application for *ex parte* relief, the judge concluded that over the years the parties had conducted most complicated accounting transactions and that an account could well have shown that the defendant was owed money by the plaintiff. In discharging the Mareva injunction, Mervyn Davies J held:

> "... I cannot regard the non-disclosure as 'innocent' as that word is explained in the quotation above.[151] In fastening on three comparatively small sums as the

---

[150.] [1989] 2 All ER 404.

[151.] The judge had quoted from the judgment of Nourse LJ in *Behbehani v Salem* [1989] 2 All ER 143 who had quoted Ralph Gibson LJ in *Brink's Mat Ltd v Elcombe* [1988] 3 All ER 188 at 193 where he had said: "The court has a discretion, notwithstanding proof of material non-disclosure which justifies or requires the immediate discharge of the *ex parte* order, nevertheless to continue the order, or to make a new order...when the whole of the facts, including that of the original non-disclosure are before it, [the court] may well grant such a second injunction *if the original non-disclosure was innocent* and if an injunction could properly be granted even had the facts been disclosed." (Italics added).

principal foundation of the *ex parte* application one may, I think, readily infer that there was an intention not to disclose, at any rate at that stage, the fact that the group and the brothers and [the defendant] had been engaged together in the most complex financial transactions ... I doubt whether an order would properly have been granted if a better and truer picture of the parties' financial dealings had been painted. The whole story would have smacked of the need for an account rather than seeking to assert three specific claims."[152]

It seems certain that where non-disclosure is found by a court to have been deliberate (as opposed to innocent) an *ex parte* injunction thereby obtained should be automatically discharged. Whatever the subsequent merits of a plaintiff's case, the court must have regard to his prior conduct and where this shows that he has deliberately misled the court, he should be denied equitable relief in those and related proceedings.

(e) Defendants' duties of frankness in affidavits

[8.44] It may be noted that the duty to make full and frank disclosure applies equally to *ex parte* applications made by a Mareva defendant. Where a defendant applies *ex parte* to have a Mareva injunction varied or discharged it is also incumbent upon him to make full and frank disclosure to the court. In one of the few written Irish judgments in this context, *Re Kelly's Carpetdrome Ltd*[153] Costello J granted the liquidator of that company an interim Mareva injunction, being relief ancillary to the liquidator's action to pursue the respondents for fraudulent trading under s 297 of the Companies Act 1963. In a subsequent application to vary the terms of the order Costello J refused to do so, *inter alia*, on the ground that:

"The application *ex parte* this morning [by the defendant] was one which required the utmost *uberrimae fides*. I was told this afternoon that contrary to the impression given in Mrs Kelly's affidavit she is in fact now living with her husband and is not separated from him. I regard the breach of the applicant's duty to the court as a serious one justifying me in refusing the application".[154]

Full Particulars of the Plaintiff's Claim

[8.45] A plaintiff's duty to make full and frank disclosure as to all material facts is predicated upon a negative: a plaintiff must not, by omitting to disclose all material facts, mislead the court into believing that his case against the defendant is stronger than it is in truth. The converse to this is that it is in a plaintiff's interests to disclose in his grounding affidavit all material facts as are necessary to substantiate his claim against the defendant. This involves

---

[152.] [1989] 2 All ER 404 at 413.
[153.] High Court, unrep, 9 May 1983 (Costello J).
[154.] At p 3.of the transcript.

adducing evidence (a) that the plaintiff actually does have a currently actionable substantive cause of action against the defendant, and, (b) that the quality or strength of the plaintiff's claim is to the standard of a "good and arguable" case.

[8.46] Mareva relief can only ever be ancillary relief to a substantive right or cause of action[155] and, accordingly, it is necessary for a Mareva plaintiff to detail in his grounding affidavit the facts which establish his claim against a defendant which is set out in the indorsement to his originating summons or detailed in the affidavit grounding his originating notice of motion or petition. The factual circumstances necessary to satisfy this requirement should refer to a plaintiff's actual cause of action against a defendant, as distinct from the merits of his case for a Mareva injunction.

[8.47] Not only must a Mareva plaintiff establish that he has a substantive right or cause of action against the defendant, but so too must he establish that his claim against a defendant has the requisite *strength* and *quality* required before Mareva relief will be granted. The appropriate strength of a plaintiff's case must be that he has "a good arguable case" against the defendant in respect of his substantive claim. This standard is considered in detail in Chapter 5, *A Good Arguable Case*. The type of evidence which a plaintiff will need to adduce to satisfy this standard will obviously vary according to the particular claim asserted. So, for example, in a case where the substantive claim alleges breach of contract a plaintiff should adduce evidence of the contract which he claims has been breached, the facts which tend to show that the defendant is responsible for this breach, the facts which show that the plaintiff has suffered loss or damage and the facts which support the plaintiff's claim for damages against the defendant arising from this breach. In furtherance of a plaintiff's duty to make full and frank disclosure of all material matters, in an *ex parte* application a plaintiff must also disclose any possible defence which he has reason to believe may be advanced by a defendant.[156] Even on an *inter partes* application a plaintiff's affidavit should not mislead the court as to the veracity of the matters contained therein.

[8.48] In all claims, including claims for unliquidated damages, a Mareva plaintiff should make an attempt to value the amount of his claim against the defendant, in order to facilitate the making of a "maximum sum" Mareva order.[157]

---

155. *Caudron v Air Zaire* [1986] ILRM 10. See Ch 4, *A Substantive Cause of Action*, para **[4.06]** *et seq.*
156. See para **[8.37]** *supra.*
157. See Ch 9, *The Mareva Order and Its Effects*, para **[9.09]**.

The Risk of Removal or Disposal of the Defendant's Assets

[8.49] The very essence of Mareva relief is a plaintiff's apprehension that a defendant is likely to remove his assets from the State, dissipate them or otherwise dispose of them so as to put them beyond the reach of the plaintiff when he obtains judgment against the defendant. This basic requirement for Mareva relief is considered in detail in Chapter 6, *The Risk of Removal or Disposal of Assets*. Accordingly, it is axiomatic that the affidavit grounding an application for a Mareva injunction should adduce evidence that there is a likelihood that the defendant will make himself judgment-proof by removing his assets from the State or otherwise disposing of them.

[8.50] It is not sufficient that a Mareva plaintiff merely make a bald assertion that he believes it likely that a defendant will remove or dispose of his assets and so a plaintiff's grounding affidavit should advance reasonable grounds for the plaintiff's apprehension that assets will be disposed of or removed from the State.[158] Examples of the factual circumstances which might cause a plaintiff to apprehend that the defendant is likely to remove or dispose of his assets might include: an apparently sudden decision to liquidate real property; the advertisement of property for sale; and apparent preparations or plans to leave the jurisdiction. It may well be the case, however, that a plaintiff is unable to aver to any particular facts which ground his apprehension that the defendant is likely to remove or dispose of his assets. In such circumstances, a plaintiff could aver in his affidavit to indirect facts which lead him to believe that such is likely, such as the fact that the substantive cause of action alleges that the defendant defrauded the plaintiff, that the defendant is a disreputable person and that such makes it likely that the defendant might, if it suited him, remove, dispose or otherwise dissipate his assets. Evidence of a defendant's lifestyle has also been found to be relevant.[159]

The Defendant's Intention to Frustrate the Plaintiff's Judgment

[8.51] Of all of the proofs required before the court will exercise its discretion to make a Mareva injunction, in Ireland, the most pivotal is the proof that the defendant's removal or disposal of his assets is with the intention of evading his obligation to the plaintiff and to frustrate the anticipated order of the court. The legal basis for this requirement has been considered in detail in a previous chapter.[160]

[158.] See Ch 6, *The Risk of Removal or Disposal of Assets*, para **[6.29]** *et seq.*

[159.] Indeed, in *Countyglen plc v Carway* [1995] 1 IR 208 at 217 it was found to be significant that the defendant had moved to live from County Clare to the Isle of Man and that the nature of his business and lifestyle was such as would facilitate the transfer of assets on an international basis.

[160.] See Ch 6, *The Risk of Removal or Disposal of Assets*, para **[6.16]** *et seq.*

[8.52] Proving the existence of any "intention" on the part of another can be difficult; indeed, being subjective, in the absence of a direct admission it might be said that it can never be proved conclusively. It is useful to remember, however, that such an "intention" does not require to be proved conclusively in a Mareva application: it is sufficient that there is evidence which suggests a *likelihood* that the defendant possesses such an intention. Again, a mere "bald assertion"[161] by a plaintiff that the defendant possesses the requisite nefarious intent will not be sufficient and a plaintiff must establish that there is a likelihood that the assets will be removed or dissipated with a view to evading the defendant's obligations to the plaintiff and frustrating the anticipated order of the court.[162] In *Powerscourt Estates v Gallagher & Gallagher*[163] McWilliam J held that the requisite nefarious intent can be inferred from circumstantial evidence such as a reluctance to disclose assets, unexplained dispositions and proposed dispositions, conducting business through a group of companies etc. The factors from which the court may infer the requisite nefarious intent are considered in detail in Chapter 6, *The Risk of Removal or Disposal of Assets*.[164]

The Existence of the Defendant's Assets

[8.53] Equity does not act in vain; it stands to reason that a plaintiff seeking an order which restrains a defendant from dealing with his assets must show that the defendant actually has assets: if a defendant has no assets, any order would be useless. Moreover, various courts, including the Supreme Court in *Re John Horgan Livestock Ltd*,[165] have endorsed the requirement that a Mareva plaintiff must give some grounds for believing that a defendant has assets within the jurisdiction. It is thought, however, that this is not directed against the making of a worldwide Mareva injunction which affects assets outside the jurisdiction, as this requirement was first laid down by Lord Denning MR in *Third Chandris Shipping Corporation v Unimarine SA*[166] at a time when a worldwide Mareva jurisdiction had not been conceived of. It is thought that this requirement today means that where a domestic Mareva injunction is sought a plaintiff must adduce evidence that the defendant has assets within the jurisdiction; and where

---

[161.] *Ninemia Maritime Corp v Trave Schiffahrtgesellschaft mbH & Co KG; The Niedersachsen* [1984] 1 All ER 398.

[162.] *Re John Horgan Livestock Ltd* [1995] 2 IR 411 at 420 (Hamilton CJ). See further Ch 6, *The Risk of Removal or Disposal of Assets*, para **[6.18]** and generally, Courtney, 'Mareva Injunctions: Proving an Intention to Frustrate Judgment', (1996) CLP 3 at 8-10.

[163.] [1984] ILRM 123 at 126.

[164.] At para **[6.29]** *et seq*.

[165.] [1995] 2 IR 411. See also *Production Association Minsk Tractor Works and Belarus Equipment (Ireland) Ltd v Saenko* High Court, unrep, 25 February 1998 (McCracken J).

[166.] [1979] 2 All ER 972.

a worldwide Mareva injunction is sought, evidence as to the existence of assets outside of the jurisdiction must be adduced by a plaintiff.[167]

[8.54] Unless a Mareva injunction provides to the contrary it will have the effect of freezing all of a defendant's assets situate within the jurisdiction; where the order so directs it can also affect all of a defendant's assets which are situate outside of the jurisdiction. A plaintiff's grounding affidavit should, however, endeavour to give the fullest details of the defendant's assets known to the plaintiff. Frequently, applicants will give very specific details of a defendant's assets and where it is sought to freeze an account, details of the bank, branch and account number should, where available, be given. It is essential that some detail be given in relation to a defendant's assets, whether situate inside or outside of the jurisdiction. In *Intermetal Group Ltd and Trans-World (Steel) Ltd v Worslade Trading Ltd*,[168] O'Sullivan J refused to grant a worldwide Mareva injunction saying:

> "Even if the scope of a Mareva type injunction were limited, I do not think I have sufficient detail in relation to the defendant's assets to enable me to frame an order".[169]

It is, however, also in a Mareva plaintiff's own interests to give specific details of a defendant's bank accounts as he may be obliged to discharge the costs of a bank or other financial institutions served with a Mareva injunctions where they have to conduct a general trawl of their customers' accounts in order to comply with an order.[170]

Where application is made for a worldwide Mareva injunction it is necessary to show that the defendant has insufficient assets located in Ireland which could satisfy the plaintiff's future judgment; where a plaintiff does not establish this fact, he will not discharge the burden of showing that there are circumstances which justify the court in making such an extraordinary order.[171]

The Balance of Convenience

[8.55] In an ordinary interlocutory injunction application the applicable test is that a plaintiff must establish that he has a fair or serious question to be tried and that the balance of convenience is in his favour and supports the granting of the injunction. It is submitted that in Mareva applications the broad "balance of convenience" test is, to a large extent, superseded by the multi-requisite test

---

[167.] See Ch 7, *The Defendant's Assets*, para **[7.21]** *et seq.*
[168.] High Court, unrep, 12 December 1997 (O'Sullivan J).
[169.] At p 26 of the transcript.
[170.] See Ch 9, *The Mareva Order and Its Effects*, para **[9.46]**.
[171.] *Derby & Co Ltd v Weldon (No 1)* [1989] 1 All ER 469; [1989] 2 WLR 276. See Ch 7, *A Defendant's Assets*, para **[7.34]**.

which a plaintiff must satisfy in establishing that there is a risk of the defendant's assets being removed or otherwise disposed of with the intention of defeating the plaintiff's anticipated judgment. Clear evidence which tends to prove these matters will invariably determine the question of whether the "balance of convenience" lies in the plaintiff's favour. On occasions where it does not, the court may take a broader view of the matters in issue and in this regard the general observations on justice and the appropriateness of Mareva relief made by O'Flaherty J in *Re John Horgan Livestock Ltd*[172] are instructive:

> "... it needs to be emphasised that the Mareva injunction is a very powerful remedy which if improperly invoked will bring about an injustice, something that it was designed to prevent. It may put a person or a company out of business. It may contribute to delay in bringing litigation to a head. It may be used as a diversionary tactic and be a part of the skirmishes that increasingly occur in much litigation. It may - as is the case here - take on a life of its own while the main litigation is becalmed. I glean that a sense of urgency is not affecting the main litigation and will not do so while this side-show is running."

[8.56] Where the evidence in respect of the proofs for a Mareva injunction are somewhat weak or controverted, the question of where the balance of convenience lies may be considered by the courts. In *Countyglen plc v Carway*[173] the plaintiff's evidence on the question of the defendants' assets being removed or dissipated was acknowledged by Murphy J to be "extremely limited".[174] The judge went on to consider the balance of convenience in granting the Mareva injunction and, after noting that the first defendant had sworn three lengthy affidavits, he observed that it was striking that he had not dealt at all with the question of what assets he had within the jurisdiction or the allegation, suspicion or inference that same may be dissipated so as to frustrate an order of the court. Murphy J continued:

> "Even more surprising is the fact that Mr Carway does not claim that the interim order or the interlocutory order claimed has caused or will cause any particular difficulty for him. Counsel on behalf of the respondents asserts that a Mareva injunction must of necessity impinge upon a defendant's constitutional rights in relation to private property and his or her right to earn a livelihood. However, that argument merely relates to the existence of the rights and the likelihood of some measure of inconvenience. Whether that inconvenience has any degree of significance cannot be assessed without the assistance of the respondents."[175]

[172.] [1995] 2 IR 411 at 422.
[173.] [1995] 1 IR 208.
[174.] See generally Ch 6, *The Risk of Removal or Disposal of Assets*, para **[6.36]**.
[175.] [1995] 1 IR 208 at 217.

Accordingly, where a Mareva plaintiff establishes all of the pre-conditions required for a Mareva injunction, it is submitted that it will be apparent that the balance of convenience does favour the making of the injunction. Implicit in Murphy J's observation is that the balance of convenience may be raised by a defendant in contesting the plaintiff's application for Mareva relief. As to the factors which could be raised, the following passage from the judgment of Murphy J (which follows on from the last excerpt quoted) is instructive:

> "It may be that the assets of the respondents in the State far exceed the amount which the applicant seeks to freeze. At the other end of the scale the respondents may have no assets available to them within the jurisdiction. In either case, the actual hardship or inconvenience would be little or none. If the respondents disclose the existence of some asset within the jurisdiction of this court, then it might be anticipated in accordance with the guidelines indicated in the English cases and the practice adopted in this jurisdiction that the Mareva injunction, if granted, would be fine-tuned[176] to ensure that the interest of the applicant would be protected without any unnecessary hardship to the respondents. However, on the basis of the evidence presently available to the court, it seems to me that the proper inference to draw is that the respondents do have assets in the jurisdiction; that there is a real risk that those assets will be dissipated and that the respondents are not apprehensive of any real inconvenience to them as a result of a Mareva injunction being granted."[177]

In *Fleming v Ranks (Ireland) Ltd*,[178] McWilliam J said that the court should weigh the considerations for and against the granting of an injunction and that "the balance of convenience must be in favour of granting it".[179]

[D] UNDERTAKINGS REQUIRED ON APPLICATION FOR MAREVA RELIEF

[8.57] Applicants for all injunctive relief are required to provide undertakings to the court, this being the *quid pro quo* to being given equitable relief. In the first place, it has long been established that requiring an undertaking as to damages is a necessary safeguard for defendants as it can provide the basis for compensation in the event that it transpires that the injunction ought never to have been granted. In the second place, there are many general undertakings which will be implied, eg that a plaintiff will do (or will refrain from doing) a particular act. Moreover, the exigencies of a particular application might require

---

[176.] As to "fine-tuning", this is achieved by means of including provisos to the Mareva order which except the payment of legal, business and ordinary living expenses by the defendant: see Ch 9, *The Mareva Order and Its Effects*, para **[9.12]** *et seq*.

[177.] At 217, 218.

[178.] [1983] ILRM 541.

[179.] At 546.

the court to make an order without the necessary formalities (as to engrossing, stamping, issuing etc of documents) having been complied with; in these circumstances a plaintiff's undertaking is the oil which lubricates the interraction between formal requirements and practical exigencies. Thirdly, where the form of injunctive relief granted is particularly prone to abuse, as in the case of a worldwide Mareva injunction, a plaintiff's undertaking can temper the dangers inherent in making such extraordinary orders. In this section, these three distinct categories of undertakings are considered:

1. The Undertaking as to Damages.

2. General Undertakings which will be Implied.

3. Undertakings in Applications for Worldwide Mareva Injunctions.

The Undertaking as to Damages[180]

[8.58] An applicant for any interlocutory or interim injunction must give an undertaking as to damages to the court in case it is ultimately decided that the injunction was wrongly given, that the defendant has suffered loss and that the court considers it appropriate that the plaintiff pay compensation by way of damages to the defendant. The undertaking is directed to the court and not to the defendant; the defendant can ask the court to enforce the undertaking but has no right to its enforcement or to damages.[181] Although the court cannot compel an undertaking to be given, it can clearly make the grant of an injunction conditional upon the plaintiff giving an undertaking as to damages: no undertaking, no injunction. The High Court's power to do this is seen in Ord 50, r 6(2) of the RSC which provides, *inter alia*, that any injunction "may be made either unconditionally or upon such terms and conditions as the Court thinks just." In *Attorney General v Albany Hotel Company*[182] North J remarked that the requirement that "an applicant for an interlocutory injunction must give an undertaking to be answerable in damages as a condition of his obtaining the injunction" had "become a matter of course".[183] North J also said:

> "Upon drawing up an order for an interlocutory injunction the registrar invariably inserts such an undertaking on the part of the plaintiff, even though,

---

180. See generally, Goldrein & Wilkinson, *Commercial Litigation: Pre-Emptive Remedies* (2nd ed, 1991) Sweet & Maxwell, pp 80-93 for a most comprehensive yet lucid exposition of the principles. See also 24 *Halsbury's Laws of England*, (4th ed reissue; 1991), pp 524-527; Spry, *Equitable Remedies* (4th ed, 1990), pp 472-478; Baker & Langan, *Snell's Equity*, (29th ed, 1990), pp 666-667.

181. *Cheltenham and Gloucester Building Society v Ricketts* [1993] 4 All ER 276 at 285c-d *per* Peter Gibson LJ. See para **[8.69]** *infra*.

182. *Attorney General v Albany Hotel Company* [1896] 2 Ch 696.

183. At 699, citing *Graham v Campbell* 7 Ch D 490 where James J held that an undertaking in damages ought to be given on every interlocutory injunction.

as frequently happens, it has not been mentioned in court, but has been taken for granted. Of course such an undertaking must be voluntary: the court cannot compel a person to given an undertaking; and, if the plaintiff declines to give it, either in court or before the registrar, the order will not be made, or, if pronounced, will not be drawn up." [184]

The practice of requiring applicants to give undertakings as to damages in injunctions on notice dates from around 1860, although the practice of requiring such undertakings on *ex parte* applications dates many years back before that. [185]

[8.59] Undertakings as to damages are considered here under the following headings:

(a) The rationale for an undertaking as to damages;

(b) Circumstances when the court will not require an undertaking;

(c) The plaintiff's inability to give a worthwhile undertaking;

(d) Bonds in support of plaintiffs' undertakings;

(e) Capped plaintiffs' undertakings;

(f) Enforcing the undertaking as to damages.

(a) The rationale for an undertaking as to damages

[8.60] The basic rationale for requiring applicants who seek an interim or interlocutory injunction to give an undertaking as to damages was put thus by Peter Gibson LJ in *Cheltenham and Gloucester Building Society v Ricketts*: [186]

"The practice of requiring an undertaking in damages from the applicant for such an injunction as the price for its grant was originated by the Court of Chancery as an adjunct to the equitable remedy of the injunction. There is an obvious risk of unfairness to a respondent against whom an interlocutory injunction is ordered at a time when the issues have not been fully determined and when usually all the facts have not been ascertained. The order might subsequently prove to have been wrongly made but in the meantime the respondent by reason of compliance with the injunction may have suffered serious loss from which he will not be compensated by the relief sought in the proceedings. The risk of such injustice is the greater when the interlocutory injunction has been granted *ex parte*. The risk is particularly great with Mareva injunctions, granted as they are almost invariably *ex parte*, and frequently imposing severe restrictions on the respondents' right to spend their money or otherwise dispose of their assets...". [187]

In practice, the requirement means that an applicant for a Mareva injunction must put his money where his mouth is: an affidavit which grounds Mareva

---

[184] [1896] 2 Ch 696 at 699,700.
[185] See the judgment of Lindley LJ in the Court of Appeal in *Attorney General v Albany Hotel Company* [1896] 2 Ch 696 at 703; see also *Smith v Day* (1882) 21 Ch D 421 at 424.
[186] [1993] 4 All ER 276.
[187] At 284g-j.

relief must provide that, if it is subsequently found that the relief ought not to have been granted, the applicant agrees to pay whatever damages the court might so direct him to pay to the defendant. Typically, the form of the undertaking will be that the applicant undertakes to:

"... abide by any Order which this Honourable Court may hereafter make as to damages in the event that this Honourable Court forms the opinion that the Respondent shall have suffered any damage by reason of the Order which this Honourable Court may make which the Applicants ought to pay...".[188]

The plaintiff's undertaking in the foregoing form, or similar wording, will be given at the end of the grounding affidavit. In the case of an affidavit sworn for and on behalf of a plaintiff, typically a company or other body corporate, the deponent should aver to the fact that he has been authorised by the plaintiff to offer such an undertaking to the court or counsel will offer the undertaking.[189] Where a company is in liquidation the liquidator will usually seek to give the undertaking on behalf of the company and not his personal undertaking[190] unless he is indemnified by a large creditor such as the Revenue Commissioners.[191]

(b) Circumstances when the court may not require an undertaking

[8.61] The general rule is that the court will always require an applicant for an injunction to provide an undertaking as to damages. There are, however, circumstances in which the court will dispense with this requirement. In *Attorney General v Albany Hotel Company*[192] it was held that an undertaking as to damages from a plaintiff would only be dispensed with in "special circumstances". In that case the special circumstances were that the applicant for interlocutory relief was the Crown and it was held that the Crown would not ordinarily be required to give such an undertaking.[193] In Ireland the State is in no

---

[188.] The undertaking in the affidavit may take many different forms: *Moloney v Laurib Investments Ltd*, High Court, unrep, 20 July 1993 (Lynch J) where the undertaking given was an undertaking to give an undertaking "I further undertake to give such undertaking as to damages as to this Honourable Court shall seem fit".

[189.] *East Molesey Local Board v Lambeth Waterworks Ltd* [1892] 3 Ch 289.

[190.] *Rosling and Flynn Ltd v Law Guarantee and Trust Co* (1903) 47 Sol Jo 255. *Cf Re DPR Futures* [1989] BCLC 634, considered at para **[8.67]** *infra*.

[191.] See *Re John Horgan Livestock Ltd* [1995] 2 IR 411 at 416.

[192.] *Cf Kirklees Metropolitan BC v Wickes Building Supplies Ltd* [1992] 3 All ER 717 where the House of Lords held that there was no rule that the Crown was exempt from the requirement that an applicant for an interlocutory injunction give an undertaking as to damages, but that the court had a discretion not to insist upon such an undertaking and that this discretion extended to public authorities.

[193.] It is now the case in England that, generally, the Crown should be required to give an undertaking as to damages when applying for an interlocutory injunction "in an action brought against a subject to enforce or to protect its proprietary or contractual rights": *Hoffmann-La Roche & Co AG v Secretary of State for Trade and Industry* [1975] AC 295. This principle has also been accepted in Australia: *Commonwealth v John Fairfax & Sons Ltd* (1980) 147 CLR 39; it was recently applied in *Australian Competition & Consumer Authority v Giraffe World Australia Pty Ltd* [1998] 819 FCA (14 July 1998).

special position but there is authority to suggest that there still may exist special circumstances where an applicant for interlocutory relief may not be required to give such an undertaking. In *Keenan Brothers Ltd v CIE*[194] Budd J said that an applicant for interlocutory relief may not be required to provide an undertaking in a case of "clear fraud". He said:

> "The usual form of undertaking, which a party obtaining an order on an interlocutory application has to give, is one to abide any order as to damages which the court may make in case it is afterwards of opinion that the defendant has sustained any damage by reason of the order, which the plaintiff ought to pay. That the order to pay damages is made as a rule where it turns out eventually that the injunction should not have been granted and the defendant has sustained damage by reason of the injunction having been granted. *The undertaking is one which ought to be required on every interlocutory order save possibly in a case of clear fraud.*"[195]

It was held in *Securities and Investment Board v Lloyd-Wright*[196] that the court had a discretion not to require an undertaking as to damages from a "designated agency" (in that case the Securities and Investment Board) in return for making a worldwide Mareva injunction against the defendants. The rationale for this was because the plaintiff had a statutory cause of action[197] to claim monetary restitution for the benefit of those who suffered losses as a result of an unauthorised business and that this right of action was for the benefit of the public at large. It is thought that this decision should not be followed in this jurisdiction. Whilst the State and statutory authorities may well be fulfilling a public function, there can be no justification for failing to ensure that a defendant, enjoined at its request, is adequately protected. The fact that an applicant for interlocutory relief obtained such relief in furtherance of the public good is not a factor which should obviate the need to provide an undertaking as to damages although it may well be a highly relevant consideration if it comes to the court exercising its discretion in any subsequent inquiry as to damages.[198]

(c) The plaintiff's inability to give a worthwhile undertaking

[8.62] The (ordinarily just) general rule that an applicant for a Mareva injunction must give an undertaking as to damages has the potential to do injustice where an impecunious plaintiff has a just case. Can it be just and proper that a plaintiff with a fair case should be denied Mareva relief merely because any undertaking which he would give would be worthless on account of his impecuniosity? It is

---

[194.] (1963) 97 ILTR 54.
[195.] At 59. Italics added.
[196.] [1993] 4 All ER 210.
[197.] Under ss 6(1) and 61(1) of the UK's Financial Services Act 1986.
[198.] See para **[8.69]** *infra*.

submitted that the courts should not countenance such injustice and should grant Mareva relief where the basic requirements are met, even where a plaintiff is a "man-of-straw". Moreover, it is the view of the writer that evidence that a plaintiff's impecuniousity has been caused by the defendant's wrongdoing should be highly influential on the question as to whether the court will exercise its discretion and not insist upon the plaintiff's undertaking being "worthwhile".[199]

[8.63] Sometimes a plaintiff will be required to adduce evidence as to his means[200] to give the undertaking and where this is contained in his affidavit on an *ex parte* application, the "golden rule" will apply and his evidence should not mislead the court.

[8.64] One of the first cases in which the question of a Mareva plaintiff's inability to give a "worthwhile" undertaking as to damages arose was *Allen v Jambo Holdings Ltd.*[201] In that case, which is considered elsewhere,[202] the plaintiff was tragically widowed when her husband was decapitated by the propeller of the defendant's aircraft. Amongst other issues which arose for consideration in that case was the widowed-plaintiff's inability to give a "worthwhile" undertaking as to damages to the court. In the course of his judgment Lord Denning MR said:

"It is said whenever a Mareva injunction is granted the plaintiff has to give a cross-undertaking in damages. Suppose the widow should lose this case altogether. She is legally aided. Her undertaking is worth nothing. I would not assent to that argument...I do not see why a poor plaintiff should be denied a Mareva injunction just because he is poor, whereas a rich plaintiff would get it. One has to look at these matters broadly. As a matter of convenience, balancing one side against the other, it seems to me that an injunction should go to restrain the removal of the aircraft."[203]

[199.] In this regard it is thought that there is an obvious parallel between this situation and that of an insolvent company which is excused from having to give security for costs under s 390 of the Companies Act 1963 where it can be shown that its insolvency has been caused by the defendant's wrongs. See, generally, *Peppard and Co Ltd v Bogoff* [1962] IR 180, *SEE Company Ltd v Public Lighting Services Ltd* [1987] ILRM 255, *Campbell Seafoods Ltd v Brodene Gram A/S*, High Court, unrep, 21 July, 1994 (Costello J), *Jack O'Toole Ltd v MacEoin Kelly Associates* [1986] IR 277, *Harrington v JVC (UK) Ltd*, High Court, unrep, 16 March 1995 (O'Hanlon J), and, generally, Courtney, *The Law of Private Companies*, (1994) Butterworths, para [3.087].
[200.] In *Brigid Foley Ltd v Ellott* [1982] RPC 433 at 436 Megarry VC said that the plaintiff's ability to meet an undertaking in damages "should be dealt with by specific evidence and not left to be mentioned at the hearing of the motion by reference to an unaudited balance sheet which the other side has presumably not seen".
[201.] [1980] 2 All ER 502.
[202.] See Ch 4, *A Substantive Cause of Action*, para **[4.38]**.
[203.] [1980] 2 All ER 502 at 505d-f.

Shaw LJ agreed with this position saying that "questions of financial stability ought not to affect the position in regard to what is the essential justice of the case as between the parties".[204] Templeman LJ also agreed that the plaintiff's inability to give a worthwhile undertaking ought not to prevent the court from granting her the Mareva relief which she sought. He said:

> "In this case one factor which counsel for the first and second defendants very properly urged us (but it is only a factor which we must bear in mind) is the cross-undertaking in damages which must invariably be limited to the assets of the executors which I understand are no more than the present inflated value of a house. Nevertheless it seems to me that to deny an injunction in these circumstances would be to deny a measure of assurance to the widow which she is entitled to have."[205]

[8.65] A similar case was heard before the Irish courts. Again it involved very tragic circumstances. In *Moloney v Laurib Investments Ltd*[206] the fifteen year old plaintiff sustained a fall through an unguarded opening in a floor of an unfinished building situate at Mountjoy Square, Dublin. It was alleged that this had left her a paraplegic and that she was likely to be confined to a wheelchair for life. Here too, the plaintiff's inability to give a worthwhile undertaking as to damages was in issue. On this point Lynch J said:

> "This undertaking is, through no fault of the plaintiff, worthless. Even if the plaintiff's parents were to join in giving such an undertaking it would be of little value having regard to the potential losses of the defendant company in this case. If the interlocutory injunction is granted and the defendants win this case, I am satisfied that the defendants would suffer very serious loss and would have no remedy. On the other hand it is said that if the injunction is not granted and the plaintiff wins the case, she will have no prospect of recouping her award from the defendant company. This is undoubtedly true but it by no means follows that if the interlocutory injunction were granted and the plaintiff won the case, she would be in any significantly better position than if the injunction had been refused."[207]

Lynch J appears to have recognised the injustice of not granting a Mareva injunction simply because the plaintiff could not provide a worthwhile undertaking as to damages. Yet, he did cite this fact as one of the four reasons for refusing to grant the Mareva relief sought.[208] As this writer has stated

---

204. At 505h-j.
205. At 506h.
206. High Court, unrep, 20 July 1993 (Lynch J). See Ch 4, *A Substantive Cause of Action*, para **[4.42]**.
207. High Court, unrep, 20 July 1993 (Lynch J), p 5 of the judgment.
208. Lynch J referred, *inter alia* to: "... the absence of any worthwhile undertaking on behalf of the plaintiff as to damages", p 6 of the judgment.

elsewhere,[209] it is thought that the inadequacy of the plaintiff's undertaking as to damages was but one factor in the court declining to grant Mareva relief to the plaintiff in that case: it is felt that the most important reason was that the defendant's proposed disposal of its only asset was "not designed to be implemented for the purpose of defeating the plaintiff's claim".[210]

(d) Bonds in support of plaintiffs' undertaking

[8.66] Aside from a case where a plaintiff simply does not have available resources to support a worthwhile undertaking as to damages, cases do arise where the plaintiff is resident outside of the jurisdiction and where the court, on the defendant's application, seeks some tangible security from the plaintiff in support of his undertaking. In such cases the courts have sometimes required a plaintiff to provide a bond or bank guarantee in support of his undertaking.[211] An example of this, in a Mareva context, is provided by *Caudron v Air Zaire*[212] where Barr J held that, because the plaintiffs' undertaking was of little or no practical value because they had no connection with this jurisdiction, it was proper "that a bond should be posted on behalf of the plaintiffs in respect of loss which the [defendants] may have suffered if it is held ultimately that the injunction should not have been granted".[213] It will not be every case where the court will insist upon such a bond.

[209.] See Courtney, 'Mareva Injunctions in Personal Injuries Actions', (1995) Dli - the Western Law Gazette 107 at 109.

[210.] At p 5 of the transcript. Note that in *Production Association Minsk Tractor Works and Belarus Equipment (Ireland) Ltd v Saenko*, High Court, unrep, 25 February 1998 (McCracken J) it was observed by McCracken J that although the plaintiff had given an undertaking as to damages "... it is also clear that the second plaintiff is insolvent. Certain undertakings have been offered by the first plaintiff and a property which is not owned by either plaintiff has been offered as security. I have no way of knowing the validity of the undertakings or the power of the first plaintiff to give them. It in fact may well also be an insolvent company".

[211.] In *Ashtiani v Kashi* [1986] 2 All ER 970 at 978j-979a-b Dillon LJ said that the Iranian resident plaintiffs' undertakings were probably worthless and noted that a bank guarantee or deposit may be required. See also *Commodity Ocean Transport Corp v Basford Unicorn Industries Ltd, The Mito* [1987] 2 Lloyd's Rep 197 at 198 (Hirst J) a case involving an application for a Mareva injunction and, generally, *Jones v Pacaya Rubber and Produce Co Ltd* [1911] 1 KB 455 where money was required to be paid into court and *Harman Pictures NV v Osborne* [1967] 1 WLR 723 where security was required in support of the undertaking as to damages. In Ireland, see *Balkanbank v Taher, The Irish Times*, 18 October 1990 (Johnson J) where it was reported that a Mareva injunction against a co-defendant was discharged on condition that it provided an unconditional bank guarantee or bond in favour of the plaintiff for US$256,000 plus interest. See also the passage from *Production Association Minsk Tractor Works and Belarus Equipment (Ireland) Ltd v Saenko*, High Court, unrep, 25 February 1998 (McCracken J) quoted in fn 210, *supra*.

[212.] [1986] ILRM 10.

[213.] At 18. It may be noted that ultimately the Supreme Court upheld the defendant's appeal and held that there was no basis for granting a Mareva injunction in that case: see Ch 4, *A Substantive Cause of Action*, para **[4.06]** *et seq*.

(e) Capped plaintiffs' undertakings

[8.67] There is authority for the proposition that, in exceptional circumstances, the court may limit a plaintiff's undertaking as to the amount of damages which may be payable in the event of an inquiry. In *Re DPR Futures Ltd*[214] the company, which was ordered to be placed into official liquidation, had two liquidators appointed who instituted proceedings against the company's three former directors and shareholders for conspiracy to defraud. The liquidators obtained *ex parte* Mareva relief against the respondents and gave cross-undertakings as to damages, limited to a specific amount. The respondents claimed, *inter alia*, that the liquidators' undertaking should be unlimited. The liquidators argued that the undertakings should be limited to no more than £2m. It was held by Millett J that the court must estimate the likely loss to the respondents and that this was the main determining factor in deciding whether the liquidators' undertaking was sufficient. In that case the liquidators were prepared to give *personal* undertakings but were not prepared to give unlimited undertakings. In the circumstances of this case Millett J held:

> "In my judgment a liquidator cannot be criticised for refusing to risk his personal assets by giving an unlimited cross-undertaking. It is right to require him to give an undertaking of an amount commensurate with the size of the company's assets and to take the risk that he may not be authorised by the court to have recourse to them to meet his liability. If the value of such an undertaking is considered insufficient in any particular case he should be required to fortify it by obtaining a bond or indemnity from a substantial creditor, but in either case of a fixed amount. The court cannot avoid the need to make an intelligent estimate of the likely amount of any loss which may result from the grant of the injunction. There is nothing unusual in this. It is so in every case where the balance of convenience has to be considered. A plaintiff's resources are not infinite, But any such estimate can be reviewed from time to time and further fortification required if necessary. If fortification cannot be required this will affect the balance of convenience between granting or refusing the injunction. but the court cannot abdicate its responsibility for deciding where the balance of convenience lies."[215]

Millett J went on to mitigate the effect of the Mareva injunction in that case by providing that the respondents were at liberty to vary or transpose assets with the liquidators' prior consent and then held:

> "In my judgment, and in the absence of wholly unforeseen circumstances, a cross-undertaking of £2m is more than sufficient to cover any realistic estimate

---

[214.] [1989] BCLC 634.
[215.] At 640.

330

of the loss likely to be suffered by the respondents from the continuation of the injunctions."[216]

That the liquidators were giving the undertakings personally and that they had tried unsuccessfully to extend their firm's professional indemnity cover to permit them to give unlimited undertakings clearly influenced Millett J.

[8.68] This issue arose for partial consideration in *Re John Horgan Livestock Ltd*.[217] In that case Murphy J had, in the High Court, granted a Mareva injunction to the liquidator of the company against its directors as relief ancillary to the liquidator's claim against them under s 297 of the Companies Act 1963. The Mareva injunction restrained the second respondent director from disposing of, dissipating or charging a policy of insurance in respect of which £71,000 was due. The liquidator's undertaking as to damages was limited by Murphy J to £25,000. The judgment of the High Court is not reported but in the appeal to the Supreme Court Hamilton CJ quoted from counsel's note of the *ex tempore* judgment of Murphy J where he had said:

> "[The liquidator] has, perhaps surprisingly, agreed to [give the undertaking] because his personal liability will be indemnified by the Revenue Commissioners ... It seems to me that the injunction should be granted in the specific circumstances of the case. The undertaking as to damages, however, should be limited to £25,000".[218]

In his short concurring judgment wherein he held that the Mareva injunction should be discharged, O'Flaherty J said:

> "As regards the undertaking as to damages, I know of no case where a limit has been put on the amount that may be required to be paid, if it is held that the injunction was improperly obtained, nor do I think it right in principle that such a limit should be placed in view of the far-reaching implications involved in any restraint that is imposed on a party by reason of such an injunction prior to judgment."[219]

In his leading judgment Hamilton CJ was equally cautious but more circumspect than O'Flaherty J on this point. He said:

> "... it is not necessary for me to consider whether or not the learned trial judge was entitled to place a limit of £25,000 on the undertaking required to be given by the liquidator and I will reserve for future consideration the powers of the court in this regard should it arise in the future. I incline however to the views

---

216. At 641.
217. [1995] 2 IR 411.
218. At 416, 417.
219. At 422.

in this regard expressed in the judgment about to be delivered by Mr Justice O'Flaherty."[220]

It is submitted that the general rule must be that a Mareva plaintiff's undertakings as to damages should be unlimited. That said, there may be circumstances when the court would accept a limited undertaking as to damages, in the same way as a court is sometimes justified in making a Mareva injunction against a defendant on the application of an impecunious plaintiff who has a fair case. Where a bond or guarantee is accepted in support of an undertaking as to damages as in the case, say, of a non-resident plaintiff, the court is implicitly accepting a limited undertaking: whilst the plaintiff will have an unlimited liability as to damages, it is accepted that only a minimum limited sum will be available to meet any order of the court following an inquiry as to damages. The principle may be accepted in theory, but the reality is that any award of the court in a defendant's favour will be limited. Where, for example, as in the case of an official liquidator, a Mareva applicant is fulfilling a statutory duty, it can be argued that it is open to the court to accept a limited undertaking as to damages.

(f) Enforcing the undertaking as to damages

[8.69] As has been stated earlier, a plaintiff's undertaking as to damages is given to the court and not to the defendant; the undertaking will not ground a claim by the defendant in contract or tort against the plaintiff.[221] Where a court decides it proper to enforce a plaintiff's undertaking as to damages it will order *an enquiry as to damages.* An undertaking as to damages will become enforceable in either of the three circumstances identified by Plowman J in *Ushers Brewery Ltd v PS King & Co Finance Ltd,*[222] ie, (a) where a plaintiff's substantive cause of action fails; (b) where it is established before the trial of the substantive cause of action that the injunction ought never to have been granted; or (c) where a plaintiff is successful in his substantive cause of action but the defendant establishes that the plaintiff ought not to have been given an injunction.

[8.70] A point of fundamental importance to the understanding of the nature of an undertaking as to damages is that it lies entirely within the court's discretion as to whether or not to order an enquiry. In *Financiera Avenida v Shiblaq*[223] Lloyd LJ said, in circumstances where the plaintiff's substantive claims against the defendant were abandoned or failed:

[220.] At 421.

[221.] *Fletcher Sutcliffe Wild Ltd v Burch* [1982] FSR 64 *per* Gibson J at 70; *Digital Equipment Corp v Darkcrest Ltd* [1984] Ch 512.

[222.] [1971] 2 All ER 468; [1972] Ch 148.

[223.] (1991) *The Times* 14 January 1991 (CA), cited by Peter Gibson J in *Cheltenham and Gloucester Building Society v Ricketts* [1993] 4 All ER 276.

"Two questions arise whenever there is an application by a defendant to enforce a cross-undertaking in damages. The first question is whether the undertaking ought to be enforced at all. This depends on the circumstances in which the injunction was obtained, the success or otherwise of the plaintiff at the trial, the subsequent conduct of the defendant and all the other circumstances of the case. It is essentially a question of discretion. The discretion is usually exercised by the trial judge since he is bound to know more of the facts of the case than anyone else. If the first question is answered in favour of the defendant, the second question is whether the defendant has suffered any damage by reason of the granting of the injunction. Here ordinary principles of the law of contract apply[224] both as to causation and as to quantum ... In a simple case the trial judge may be able to deal with causation and quantum himself as soon as he has exercised his discretion. But in a more complicated case it may be necessary for him to order an inquiry as to damages either before himself, or before some other judge or before the master or registrar. Very occasionally he may find it necessary to leave over the exercise of the discretion."

This case was relied upon by Peter Gibson J in *Cheltenham and Gloucester Building v Ricketts*[225] as support for the proposition that the court has an inherent discretion as to whether or not to enforce the plaintiff's undertaking as to damages. In that case the plaintiff building society had obtained an *ex parte* Mareva injunction against the defendants, whom it had been claimed, had perpetrated a "mortgage fraud" by overvaluing properties and obtaining mortgages in false names. The plaintiff's affidavit had stated that its information was based on information received from the police and disclosed that it believed that it had lost between £1m and £2m although its investigations were incomplete. A Mareva injunction was granted to the plaintiff on its undertaking as to damages. The defendants were subsequently successful in having the Mareva injunction discharged and the trial judge ordered an inquiry as to damages suffered by the defendants as a result of having been enjoined from dealing with certain of their assets. The plaintiff appealed to the Court of Appeal which held that the matter should be adjourned until after the determination of the substantive cause of action. In the course of his judgment Peter Gibson LJ concluded that:

"... with all respect to the learned trial judge, he erred in principle in holding that on the discharge of the *ex parte* injunctions he should order enforcement of the undertaking in damages. He was bound to consider all the circumstances in exercising his discretion and he could not properly, in advance of the trial, treat the allegations of fraud as bound to fail. In these circumstances we are free to

---

[224.] Whilst analogous to contractual situations, there is no contract between the plaintiff and the defendant: see *Smith v Day* (1882) 21 Ch D 421 at 428.

[225.] [1993] 4 All ER 276.

exercise the discretion afresh. In my judgment the appropriate course is to adopt what I believe to be the usual practice of adjourning to the trial judge the application to enforce the undertaking, to be determined by him at the conclusion of the trial when all the facts are known."[226]

The appropriate time, therefore, for an inquiry as to damages to be held is when the presiding judge is in such a position as to have all relevant facts at his disposal. This will usually be after the substantive cause of action has been determined, although it may sometimes be before the trial of the substantive cause of action.[227]

[8.71] There is old authority for the proposition that the fact that a plaintiff is without fault in obtaining the injunction is irrelevant to the court's decision as to the inquiry as to damages.[228] It is not inevitable, however, that upon application being made, a court will invariably order an inquiry as to damages. The court has an inherent discretion and whilst it has been said that there is a presumption that the court will order an inquiry as to damages, this is most certainly a rebuttable presumption.[229]

[8.72] As stated by Lloyd LJ in *Financiera Avenida v Shiblaq*,[230] once a court exercises its discretion and orders an inquiry as to damages, the second question will be the *quantum* of damages. In this regard the principles applicable to breach of contract will apply. This is the established position and in *Hoffman-La Roche v Secretary of State for Trade and Industry*[231] Lord Diplock said:

"The assessment is made upon the same basis as that upon which damages for breach of contract would be assessed if the undertaking had been a contract between the plaintiff and the defendant that the plaintiff would *not* prevent the defendant from doing that which he was restrained from doing by the terms of the injunction ...".[232]

In appropriate cases, such as, for example, where a plaintiff has acted fraudulently or has deliberately misled the court in obtaining an injunction, the court may award aggravated or exemplary damages.[233]

[226.] At 290c-d.

[227.] See *Ushers Brewery v King & Co* [1972] Ch 148; *Smith v Day* (1882) 21 Ch D 421.

[228.] *Griffith v Blake* (1884) 27 Ch D 474.

[229.] See Goldrein & Wilkinson, *Commercial Litigation: Pre-Emptive Remedies*, (2nd ed, 1991) Sweet & Maxwell, p 88.

[230.] (1991) *The Times* 14 January 1991 (CA), cited by Peter Gibson J in *Cheltenham and Gloucester Building Society v Ricketts* [1993] 4 All ER 276.

[231.] [1975] AC 295 at 316.

[232.] See also *Smith v Day* (1882) 21 Ch D 421.

[233.] *Columbia Picture Industries Inc v Robinson* [1986] 3 WLR 542; *Digital Equipment Corporation v Darkcrest Ltd* [1984] Ch 512.

General Undertakings which will be Implied

[8.73] It is usual for the court to grant injunctive relief on certain implied, if not express, terms and conditions;[234] the form which such terms and conditions take is by the order of the court being made on the plaintiff's undertaking to do or refrain from certain action:

(a) To notify the defendant and any other parties affected by the order of its terms;

(b) To pay the reasonable costs and expenses incurred by third parties in complying with the order;

(c) To notify third parties of their right to seek a variation of the order;

(d) To notify third parties in the event of the order being discharged;

(e) Not to use information obtained for a collateral purpose;

(f) To stamp and issue the originating writ or motion or even to swear and lodge the grounding affidavit.

Many of these will be implied, even if they are not expressly given by a plaintiff.[235] Moreover, some of the general undertakings required of an applicant for injunctive relief will be designed to mitigate procedural formalities.

(a) To notify the defendant and other parties of the terms of the order

[8.74] The order will usually require the plaintiff, "as soon as practicable" to:

> "give notice of the terms of this order to the defendants and any other parties affected by the order".

It is obvious that if a defendant is expected to be bound by the order of the court he must have notice of its terms.

(b) To pay third parties' costs in complying with the order

[8.75] Mareva orders, in particular, should provide that the plaintiff must undertake:

> "to pay any third party served with or given notice of this order their reasonable costs and expenses (including costs and expenses incurred in ascertaining whether they hold any of the defendant's assets) and to indemnify them against any liability incurred for the purposes of complying with this order".

[234.] Order 50, r 6(2) provides: "Any such order may be made either conditionally or upon such terms and conditions as the court thinks fit.

[235.] The reader is referred to the precedent orders contained in the *Appendices* where extensive express undertakings are expressed to be given by the applicant for injunctive relief.

Such an undertaking will only apply to costs incurred by third parties, not to the costs incurred by *the defendant* upon whom the order is served.[236] Where third parties, such as banks, are served with notice of a Mareva injunction purporting to affect a customer, and are expected to act on foot of such order and refuse to pay out funds from that customer's account, they will invariably incur some cost and expense in diverting resources to attend to this. It has long been recognised that the costs involved in complying with a Mareva order are the responsibility of the party who procured the order. In *Z Ltd v A*[237] Lord Denning MR said:

> "In so far as the bank, or other innocent third party, is asked to take any action, or the circumstances require them to take any action and they are put to expense on that account, they are entitled to be recouped by the plaintiff; and insofar as they are exposed to any liability they are entitled to be indemnified by the plaintiff. This is because when the plaintiff gives notice of the injunction to the bank or innocent third party, he implicitly requests them to freeze the account or otherwise do whatever is necessary or reasonable to secure the observance of the injunction. This implicit request gives rise to an implied promise to recoup any expense and to indemnify against any liability ... In addition, in support of this implied promise, so as to ease the mind of the third party, the judge, when he grants the injunction, may require the plaintiff to give an undertaking in such terms as to secure that the bank or other innocent third party does not suffer in any way by having to assist and support the course of justice prescribed by the injunction."[238]

Where notice of an order is served on a bank or other financial institution it is important that details of the defendant's account be provided. Without an account, customer number and branch it will generally not be possible to identify the particular account without some difficulty.[239] Where such an undertaking is given it is clearly in the plaintiff's interests to delimit the bank's inquiries to a minimum to avoid having to pay perhaps unnecessary costs and expenses.[240]

[8.76] A plaintiff who gives such an undertaking may not, however, be liable to compensate third parties for *all* loss which they might suffer.[241] In *Guinness Peat Aviation (Belgium) NV v Hispania Lineas Aereas SA*[242] Webster J

---

[236]. *Searose Ltd v Seatrain Ltd* [1981] 1 WLR 894 at 896H.

[237]. [1982] 1 All ER 556 at 564.

[238]. See also the judgment of Kerr LJ in the same case at 572, 572.

[239]. See further, Ch 9, *The Mareva Order and Its Effects*, para **[9.46]**.

[240]. See also *Searose Ltd v Seatrain Ltd* [1981] 1 WLR 894 and *Clipper Maritime Co Ltd v Mineralimportexport* [1981] 3 All ER 664.

[241]. See generally, Ough and Flenley, *The Mareva Injunction and Anton Piller Order*, (2nd ed, 1993) Butterworths, pp 26-29.

[242]. [1992] 1 Lloyd's Rep 190.

distinguished between losses caused to third parties by the *grant* of a Mareva injunction from losses caused through *complying* with a Mareva injunction. In that case the plaintiff had obtained an injunction which enjoined the defendant from removing an aircraft from the jurisdiction, the effect of the injunction being to cause loss to third parties who had to make alternative arrangements as a result. Webster J held, however, that the third party's loss flowed from the actual grant of the injunction, not from the third party's compliance with the injunction and that, accordingly, the plaintiff's undertaking to "indemnify any person ... to whom notice of this order is given against any costs, expenses, fees or liabilities reasonably incurred in complying with or seeking to comply with the terms of this order" did not impose an obligation to make good the third party's losses. This must surely be the correct approach as, otherwise, no plaintiff could safely apply for any injunction.

(c) To notify third parties of their right to seek a variation of the order

[8.77] A Mareva plaintiff should be required to undertake to notify third parties of their right to seek a variation of the court's order. The case of *Guinness Peat Aviation (Belgium) NV v Hispania Lineas Aereas SA* demonstrates the effect of a plaintiff's undertaking:

> "to notify and inform any third parties affected by this order of their right to apply to have the order varied or discharged in so far as it affects them".

A similarly worded undertaking had been given by the plaintiff in that case and Webster J held that the plaintiff's failure to advise the third party that it could apply to have the order varied could be construed as a contempt of court which would have made the plaintiff liable to compensate the third party.

(d) To notify third parties in the event of the order being discharged

[8.78] Mareva orders should also contain an undertaking from the plaintiff:

> "to forthwith take all reasonable steps to inform in writing any person or company whom the plaintiff has given notice of the order or who he has reasonable grounds for supposing may act upon the order, if for any reason the order ceases to have effect that it has ceased to have effect".

The purpose of this undertaking is to minimise, so far as possible, the effects on third parties of an order which is later discharged.

(e) Not to use information obtained for a collateral purpose

[8.79] Where an asset-disclosure order[243] is made ancillary to a Mareva injunction it is particularly important that the order be granted on the plaintiff's

---

[243.] See Ch 10, *Ancillary Orders*, para **[10.03]** *et seq.*

undertaking not to misuse the information thereby obtained. A form of wording for such an undertaking might be:

> "not without the leave of the court, to use all or any of the information obtained by reason of this Order, except for the purposes of these proceedings".

Such an undertaking is similar to the undertakings required in the case of worldwide Mareva orders, considered below. Even where such an undertaking is not expressly given, it is likely that there will be an implied undertaking from the plaintiff not to use any information learned from the execution of the injunction for any collateral purpose.[244]

(f) To stamp and issue the originating document, affidavit etc

[8.80] Sometimes, in the case of *ex parte* order, there will not be time, prior to making application to court for the order, for a plaintiff to have the writ or other originating document, stamped and issued or, in cases of extreme emergency, to even have the grounding affidavit engrossed, sworn and stamped. In such cases, any order granted will be on the plaintiff's undertaking to, for example:

> "as soon as practicable, to issue and serve on the defendant the writ or motion in the form of the draft produced to the court together with this order"

and/or

> "to cause an affidavit to be sworn, stamped and filed substantially in the same terms as the draft produced to the Court confirming the substance of what was said to the court by the plaintiff's counsel/solicitors".

The importance of such an undertaking was demonstrated in *Siporex Trade SA v Comdel Commodities Ltd*[245] as in that case no such undertaking had been given. Bingham J discharged a Mareva injunction which had been obtained two months previous where no originating summons had been issued and no order had ever been formally drawn up and perfected.

Undertakings in Applications for Worldwide Mareva Injunctions

[8.81] Where the court accedes to a plaintiff's request to grant worldwide Mareva relief it is normal for the plaintiff to be required to provide further undertakings over and above those provided in the case of domestic Mareva injunctions. Such undertakings should ideally be expressly given, although it

---

[244] See O'Floinn, 'Implied Undertakings - Valuable Safeguard or Unnecessary Obstacle?', (1997) CLP 200.
[245] [1986] 2 Lloyd's Rep 428.

has been held that they will in any event be implied.[246] These undertakings, the legal basis for which has been considered in a previous chapter[247] are:

(a) Not to commence foreign proceedings or use information disclosed about foreign assets in foreign proceedings;

(b) Not to seek foreign enforcement;

(c) Not to transfer a defendant's assets without the consent of the court.

Each of these shall now be looked at briefly.

(a) Not to commence foreign proceedings or use information disclosed about foreign assets in foreign proceedings.

[8.82] It has been recognised as an important safeguard for a defendant that the plaintiff specifically undertake not to commence foreign proceedings or use information disclosed about foreign assets in foreign proceedings.[248] The wording for such an undertaking might provide:

> "the plaintiff will not without the leave of the court begin proceedings against the defendant in any other jurisdiction or use information obtained as a result of an order of the court in this jurisdiction for the purpose of civil or criminal proceedings in any other jurisdiction".

A similar undertaking which may be required from the plaintiff is to the following effect, namely:

> "that the plaintiff will not issue fresh proceedings in a foreign court arising out of the same subject matter without first obtaining leave of this Honourable Court".[249]

(b) Not to seek foreign enforcement

[8.83] Again, the plaintiff should undertake not to commence foreign proceedings without the leave of the national court which makes the worldwide Mareva injunction.[250] Such an undertaking might provide:

> "the plaintiff will not without the leave of the Court seek to enforce this order in any country outside of the State or seek any order of a similar nature including orders conferring a charge or other security against the defendants or the defendant's assets".

---

246. *Tate Access Floors Inc v Boswell* [1990] 3 All ER 303. See Ch 7, *The Defendant's Assets*, para **[7.43]**.

247. See Ch 7, *The Defendant's Assets*, para **[7.43]**.

248. *Tate Access Floors Inc v Boswell* [1990] 3 All ER 303.

249. *Morris v Mahfouz* (1993) *The Times Law Reports* 605.

250. *Derby & Co Ltd v Weldon (No 1)* [1989] 1 All ER 469.

(c) Not to transfer assets without the consent of the court

[8.84] Where the defendant is ordered to transfer his foreign assets to a receiver with a view to transferring those assets from one jurisdiction to another, there is a danger that financial ruin, in the guise of an unexpected taxation liability, might be visited upon the defendant.[251] Accordingly, it has been said that where the defendant in an action is ordered to transfer his assets to a receiver, it is appropriate that the plaintiff and the receiver undertake not to cause the defendant's assets to be transferred between jurisdictions without the prior consent of the defendant or the court.[252]

---

[251] See Ch 7, *The Defendant's Assets*, para **[7.52]**.
[252] *Mooney v Orr* [1994] BCJ No 2322; noted by Cook, [1995] 2 JIBL N-54.

Chapter 9

The Mareva Order and Its Effects

[9.01] Where a plaintiff satisfies the court that it is appropriate to exercise its discretion and grant a Mareva injunction, the operative instrument which will give effect to the injunction will be the formal order of the court. This chapter is divided into two sections: Section [A] considers the grant and content of Mareva injunctions and also their subsequent variation and discharge. Section [B] considers the effect of Mareva injunctions, particularly on third parties.

[A] THE MAREVA ORDER: GRANT, CONTENTS AND VARIATION

[9.02] In this section it is proposed to examine in close detail the operative parts of a Mareva order. Specimen Mareva injunctions are given in the *Appendices* to this book. The following specific matters are now considered:

1. Drafting the Order.
2. The Subject of the Order: The Defendant.
3. The Operative Part of the Order: A Prohibition.
4. General Freezing Orders.
5. Maximum Sum Orders.
6. Orders Restraining the Disposal of Specific Assets.
7. Provisos to Mareva Orders.
8. Penal Notices.
9. Service of the Order.
10. Defendants' Undertakings and Consent Orders.
11. Appealing Mareva Orders.
12. Variation and Discharge of Mareva Orders.

Drafting the Order

[9.03] In an *ex parte* application a draft of the Mareva order may be prepared by a plaintiff's counsel and submitted to the court's registrar either engrossed (ready for signing) or in draft (awaiting engrossment) in anticipation of the judge granting the application for relief.[1] In *Ashtiani v Kashi*[2] Dillon LJ

[1.] On *ex parte* applications generally, see Ch 8, *Applying for a Mareva Injunction*, para **[8.05]** *et seq.*
[2.] [1986] 2 All ER 970 at 974h-j.

recognised the potential which this practice has for Mareva orders, in result, to be "pro-plaintiff". In the course of his judgment he said:

> "One has to remember that, as applications for Mareva injunctions are almost invariably made *ex parte* in the first place, the form of order tends to be dictated by the form of draft minute of order which the plaintiff's counsel has prepared. Not surprisingly, therefore, one finds the forms of order being progressively tightened up so as to be more and more beneficial to the plaintiff, and, conversely, more and more onerous to the defendant."

In *Z Ltd v A*[3] Kerr LJ encouraged Mareva plaintiffs' counsel to have a draft order to hand for consideration by the judge which "contains all the undertakings[4] on the part of the plaintiff ... and which gives effect to the appropriate injunction in terms which are adapted to the particular circumstances of the case". In the case of Mareva orders obtained in England and Wales, following an *inter partes* hearing, the registrar of the court making the order will have precedent orders to hand which will be engrossed and signed by the judge making the order.[5]

[9.04] In Ireland, unlike England, there is no practice direction as to the form which a Mareva injunction should take. Accordingly, such precedent orders as exist in Ireland tend to be the result of the collective wisdom and experience of the Law Library, English text books and past orders which have been retained by court registrars. An example of a "domestic" Mareva order and a "worldwide" Mareva order are set out in the *Appendices* to this book. These are largely based upon the form of orders which are known to have been granted by the Irish High Court and also upon the wording of the most recent practice direction issued for England and Wales,[6] suitably modified.

The Subject of the Order: The Defendant

[9.05] Mareva orders operate *in personam* and so are directed at a person, ie the defendant and not a thing, eg his assets.[7] Injunctions are usually directed at a "defendant, his servants or agents or any person acting on his behalf" and may also include "any person having notice of this order".[8] Moreover, in the case of a defendant which is a body corporate, the order may also specifically reference

---

[3.] [1982] 1 All ER 556 at 574i.

[4.] As to which, see Ch 8, *Applying for a Mareva Injunction*, para **[8.57]** *et seq.*

[5.] *Third Chandris Shipping Corporation v Unimarine SA; The Pythia, The Angelic Wings, The Genie* [1979] 2 All ER 972.

[6.] Referenced in *Practice Direction* [1997] 1 All ER 288. Copies of the orders provided for in the Practice Direction can be obtained from The Court Service, Supreme Court Group, Chancery Order & Accounts, Enquiry Office, Room TM 5.10, Royal Courts of Justice, WC2A 2LL, England.

[7.] See para **[9.36]** *infra.*

[8.] The effects of a Mareva order on third parties is considered at para **[9.44]** *infra.*

its "officers".[9] The important point to remember here, in the context of a Mareva injunction, is that the only person who is restrained from disposing of his assets is the defendant. A defendant's servants or agents (or, in the case of a defendant which is a body corporate, its directors[10] and other officers) are not directly restrained[11] from doing the prohibited acts, and are merely restrained from acting as a conduit by which the defendant could do such acts. So in the context of a Mareva injunction, the effect of restraining a defendant company, its servants, agents or officers from disposing of the company's assets would be that a defendant cannot dispose of its own assets nor can its servants, agents or officers dispose of *its* assets; the injunction does not, however, restrain the servants or agents or officers from disposing of *their own personal* assets. Such persons are, *per se*, true "third parties" against whom a plaintiff could never hope to obtain a judgment and so can have no valid reason for restraining them from dealing with their *personal assets*.[12]

The case of *Brydges v Brydges and Wood*[13] is instructive in answering the question as to why the practice arose of inserting reference in injunctions to "servants and agents". In that case Farwell LJ observed, in a passage which was quoted with approval by the Supreme Court in *Moore v Attorney General*,[14] that the practice of mentioning a defendant's servants and agents "probably arose to give them [servants and agents] warning" of the fact that if they aid and abet the breach of an injunction they are rendered liable for contempt of court. Where there are two or more defendants it has been said that it is advisable to refer to them as "the defendants or either/any of them".[15]

The Operative Part of the Order: A Prohibition

[9.06] Mareva injunctions are prohibitory as opposed to mandatory in operation and so the wording of the operative part of a Mareva order is a form of

---

9. As to the circumstances when a company's officers can be made amenable for breach of a Mareva injunction, see Ch 12, *Enforcing Mareva Injunctions and Other Orders*, para **[12.06]** *et seq* and, generally, Courtney, *The Law of Private Companies* (1994) Butterworths, paras [3.099]-[3.106].

10. In *Dublin County Council v Elton Homes Ltd* [1094] ILRM 297 Barrington J said: "There may be many cases particularly in the case of small companies where the most effective way of ensuring that the company complies with its obligations is to make an order against the directors as well as against the company itself. But in such a case the order against the directors would be a way of ensuring *that the company* carried out its obligations ...". Italics added.

11. *Marengo v Daily Sketch and Sunday Graphic Ltd* [1948] 1 All ER 406.

12. See Ch 4, *A Substantive Cause of Action*, para **[4.14]** and Ch 7, *The Defendant's Assets*, para **[7.17]**.

13. [1909] P 187 at 191.

14. [1930] IR 471.

15. See *Lenton v Tregoning* [1960] 1 WLR 333, cited by Bean, *Injunctions*, (6th ed, 1994) Longmans Practitioner Series, p 83.

"prohibition" or "restraint" on dealing with, disposing of or removing from the State a defendant's assets; the actual wording of the prohibition can vary considerably from order to order. It is well established that all injunctions ought to be framed in such a manner as to leave a defendant in no doubt as to what he can or cannot do.[16] In Ireland the form of words used in Mareva orders tends to be drafted in terms as broad as possible, enjoining every conceivable means of alienating property. Typically, an Irish Mareva order will prohibit a defendant, his servants, agents or any persons acting on their behalf from:

> "... removing from the State[17] or in any way disposing of, reducing, transferring, charging, diminishing the value thereof, or otherwise dealing with all or any of his assets which are in[18] the State ...".

This is in contrast to the operative prohibition contained in the most recent *Practice Direction* for England and Wales[19] which simply (and succinctly) provides that the defendant "... must not remove from England and Wales or in any way dispose of or deal with or diminish the value of his assets...". One wonders, however, whether practitioners in this jurisdiction would risk such brevity without some sort of judicial sanction for such wording? In this regard it is submitted that clarity and precision ought never be sacrificed for economy of wording.

[9.07] Where there is any suspicion that a defendant holds assets jointly with a third party it is important that the order specifically reference assets "whether in the defendant's own name or not and whether solely or jointly owned".[20] Unless specifically referred to in the Mareva order, money which is held in a bank account by a defendant and a third party jointly may not be affected by the order.[21] Where the suggested wording is used and a joint owner of assets feels aggrieved, he can make application to court to vary the order.[22]

General Freezing Orders

[9.08] Early Mareva orders were very broadly drafted, containing a general, all-embracing, total prohibition on the removal of assets from the jurisdiction and, subsequently, on the disposal of assets within the jurisdiction.[23] General

---

[16.] See *Redland Bricks Ltd v Morris* [1970] AC 652; *Lawrence David Ltd v Ashton* [1991] 1 All ER 385.

[17.] Or, "Ireland" or "the jurisdiction of this court".

[18.] Obviously, this will be modified in the case of a worldwide Mareva injunction.

[19.] [1997] 1 All ER 288.

[20.] See Ch 7, *The Defendant's Assets*, para **[7.16]** *et seq.*

[21.] *Z Ltd v AZ & AA-LL* [1982] 2 WLR 288 at 299, [1982] 1 All ER 566 at 577 *per* Kerr LJ. See also *SCF Finance Co Ltd v Masri* [1985] 2 All ER 747.

[22.] See *infra* para **[9.31]** *et seq.*

[23.] See the comments of Denning MR in *Z Ltd v A* [1982] 1 All ER 556 at 565a.

prohibitions on the removal and disposal of assets have been almost entirely displaced by the use of "maximum sum" orders, considered next, which prevent defendants dealing with their assets save insofar as they exceed a specific sum. In *Z Ltd v A*[24] Kerr LJ said that general freezing orders cannot be justified save in wholly exceptional cases where it is clear that (a) the defendant's assets within the jurisdiction are insufficient to meet the plaintiff's claim *and* (b) the defendant is neither resident not carries on business within the jurisdiction. Following the Supreme Court's decision in *Re John Horgan Livestock Ltd*[25] it is thought that this would generally be followed in Ireland too.

Maximum Sum Orders

[9.09] If a general prohibition on the removal or disposal of assets was to be described as a "general anaesthetic" which freezes all of a defendant's assets, a maximum sum order would be analogous to a "local anaesthetic" which is selective in freezing only certain of the defendant's assets. In *Z Ltd v A*[26] Kerr LJ said in the course of his judgment:

> "... I must deal with the vexed problem whether it is better in the first instance to freeze the defendant's assets in the jurisdiction generally, or to make what have been referred to as 'maximum sum' orders, ie injunctions which only freeze the defendant's assets up to the level of the plaintiff's *prima facie* justifiable claim, leaving him free to deal with the balance. As to this, it seems to me to be plain that the latter alternative must be preferred, unless the case is exceptional, like the present one. There are two obvious reasons for this preference. First, it represents no more than what a plaintiff can justifiably request from the court. Second, an order which freezes all assets is, in the ordinary case, bound to lead to an outcry from the plaintiff[27] and to the need for an adjustment, at any rate if he is resident or carries on business within the jurisdiction ... It therefore follows, in my view, that the norm should be the 'maximum sum' order, and that an order applying to all assets should be the exception."[28]

The "maximum sum" order has indeed become the norm and it is notable that in all of the reported Irish judgments on Mareva injunctions, the order sought by the plaintiff was a maximum sum order.

---

24. [1982] 1 All ER 556 at 575b-c.
25. [1995] 2 IR 411.
26. [1982] 1 All ER 556.
27. It is thought that the reference to the "plaintiff" was in error and should be to the "defendant".
28. [1982] 1 All ER 556 at 575a-c. The exceptional circumstances referenced by Kerr LJ were those mentioned in para **[9.08]**.

[9.10] The typical wording of a maximum sum order will be to prevent a defendant, his servants, agents or any person acting on his behalf from removing or disposing of his assets:[29]

> "... save in so far as the value of said assets shall exceed the sum or value of IRL£___ ..."

The "maximum sum" specified in the order should represent the maximum amount of money which a plaintiff could hope to recover at the trial of the substantive cause of action together with the plaintiff's costs.[30] Great care should be taken not to overestimate the value of the plaintiff's claim against a defendant because a material overestimate could lead to the plaintiff being liable to compensate the defendant following an inquiry as to damages based on the plaintiff's undertaking.[31] The specific difficulties which maximum sum orders could pose to banks and other third parties are considered below.[32]

Orders Restraining the Disposal of Specific Assets

[9.11] The Mareva order may specifically enjoin a defendant from disposing of or otherwise dealing with specific assets, whether of real or personal property. The order may, for example, clarify the prohibition or restraint in the order on a defendant "removing and disposing" of assets up to a particular maximum sum by providing:

> This prohibition includes the following assets in particular:
>
> (a) the property known as [address] or the net sale proceeds thereof; and/or
>
> (b) all and any money standing to the credit of the defendant in account no(s). [a/c number] at the [branch address] branch of the [name of bank, building society or other financial institution]; and/or
>
> (c) [specific chattels] ....

[29.] As to the form of words in which the prohibition may be expressed, see para **[9.06]** *supra*.

[30.] As to the maximum sum including the plaintiff's costs: see *Charles Church Developments plc v Cronin* [1990] FSR 1. *Cf IC Ltd v CC Ltd, The Irish Times*, 26 February 1991 (Keane J) where it was reported that Keane J was not disposed to giving an order which would secure costs and that he confined the maximum sum order to the amount of a deposit paid together with estimated damages for breach of contract.

[31.] In *Jet West Ltd v Haddican* [1992] 2 All ER 545 at 549 Lord Donaldson MR said whilst the counsel for the applicant in that case "... will bear in mind that, while it is permissible and indeed sensible, in deciding what sum he wished to put forward as being the limit below which assets cannot be reduced in accordance with the injunction, to take account of claim, interest and costs, and perhaps even take a slightly optimistic view as to what may be at stake, there comes a point at which, if your open your mouth too wide, you run a substantial risk that there may be a claim against your client under the counter indemnity." As to the plaintiff's undertaking as to damages see, generally, Ch 8, *Applying for a Mareva Injunction*, para **[8.58]**.

[32.] See para **[9.53]** *et seq, infra*.

As has been previously noted it is important to recognise that although a court order may specify particular assets this is not to imply that a plaintiff has a proprietary interest in them.[33] The purpose of describing specific assets in a Mareva order is simply to further the certainty of that order and assist its enforcement. Where, for example, specific details of a defendant's assets are given the order becomes easier to enforce against third parties who will find it difficult to claim subsequently that they were unaware that specific assets belonging to a defendant, which were under their control, were caught by the order. Similarly, where it is sought to freeze a defendant's bank account the plaintiff should provide as much detail as possible to facilitate the bank in question in identifying the particular defendant's account because of the fact that the plaintiff will have to indemnify the bank for its costs in locating the account so as to comply with the order.[34]

Provisos to Mareva Orders

[9.12] Mareva injunctions are an extraordinarily powerful remedy not least because they prevent a defendant from dealing with *his own assets* in cases where a plaintiff claims no proprietary interest in those assets.[35] The only possible justification for restraining a person from dealing with his own assets is where there is evidence that he is likely to dispose of them with, in the words of Hamilton CJ in *Re John Horgan Livestock Ltd*[36]:

> "... an intention on the part of the defendant to dispose of his assets with a view to evading his obligation to the plaintiff and to frustrate the anticipated order of the court. *It is not sufficient to establish that the assets are likely to be dissipated in the ordinary course of business or in the payment of lawful debts.*"[37]

It follows that any disposal of assets by a defendant which is unaccompanied by a nefarious intent, such as a disposal to discharge living, legal or business expenses should never be restrained by court order. The strong emphasis placed by the Supreme Court on the need to establish a likelihood that the anticipated disposal of assets by a defendant is with a view to "evading" his obligation to the plaintiff and of "frustrating" the anticipated order of the court has been discussed at length in Ch 6, *The Risk of Removal or Disposal of Assets*.[38] This is

---

33. A Mareva injunction does not give rise to any "interest" in such "specific assets" as might be specified in the order: see generally para **[9.40]** *infra* and Ch 7, *The Defendant's Assets*, para **[7.03]**.
34. See para **[9.46]** *infra*.
35. See Ch 1, *The Mareva Injunction in Context*, para **[1.16]**.
36. [1995] 2 IR 411. See generally, Ch 6, *The Risk of Removal or Disposal of Assets*, para **[6.18]**.
37. At 419. Italics added.
38. See para **[6.16]** *et seq.*

the primary means used by the Irish courts to ensure that the Mareva jurisdiction is not abused and to prevent injustice being perpetrated upon a defendant. A complementary, if not alternative, means of achieving this end is by inserting provisos into Mareva orders which derogate from the general restraint order by permitting the defendant to make certain disbursements out of his assets. In this way a Mareva injunction can specifically permit a defendant to make certain disbursements from his assets, notwithstanding the general prohibition on disposing of assets up to a maximum amount. As Kelly J said in *Director of Public Prosecutions v EH*,[39] an application for a variation of a restraint order made under s 24 of the Criminal Justice Act 1994:[40]

> "The Mareva orders were always subject to being varied by the Court so as to allow a defendant to draw down from the frozen fund or assets, moneys sufficient to discharge legal and living expenses".

Those parts of a Mareva order which mitigate the ordinary effects of the order by exempting certain payments from the ambit of the order, are referred to as "provisos". Three such provisos have been clearly established:

(a) The ordinary living expenses proviso

(b) The legal expenses proviso

(c) The ordinary business expenses proviso

It could be argued that where these three provisos are inserted in a Mareva order, the strictness of the test promulgated by the Supreme Court may be somewhat unnecessary since little *de facto* injustice can be visited upon a defendant who is enjoined from dealing with his assets, subject to the three usual provisos being inserted into the Mareva order.[41]

[9.13] It may be noted that a fourth, more general, proviso may be inserted into a Mareva order, the effect of which is, notwithstanding the general prohibition on removal or disposal of a defendant's assets, to permit any disbursement which has first been authorised in writing by a plaintiff's solicitors.[42] This is an extremely useful provision because it presents the parties themselves with an opportunity to reach agreement on a disbursement without having to make

---

[39.] High Court, unrep, 22 April 1997 (Kelly J); note of judgment delivered *ex tempore* at p 1 of the transcript.

[40.] See further, Ch 3, *Statutory Jurisdictions to Freeze Assets*, para **[3.20]**.

[41.] See Courtney, 'Mareva Injunctions: Proving an Intention to Frustrate Judgment', (1996) CLP 3 at 10.

[42.] Where defendants give an undertaking not to dispose of assets, such a proviso may also be included: see, eg, *Balkanbank Ltd v Taher, The Irish Times*, 9 October 1990 (Costello J) where it was reported that Mareva injunctions were discharged in return for the defendants' undertakings not to dispose of assets covered by an interim order without prior notification to the plaintiff's solicitor for written consent, such consent not to be unreasonably withheld.

application to court for a variation of the original order. Notwithstanding Staughton LJ's acceptance in *Channel Tunnel Group Ltd v Balfour Beatty Construction Ltd*[43] of the fact that there was a relaxation of the rule in commercial cases that injunctions should be framed with precision on the grounds that the parties can easily apply to the court for variation or clarification, it is submitted that it is preferable, where possible, for parties to be able to settle such issues themselves, without having recourse to the court.

[9.14] Where a defendant's assets are expended pursuant to a proviso to a Mareva order there can be no question of a Mareva plaintiff tracing those assets into the hands of a third party. This is because, to apply for a Mareva injunction, implies that a plaintiff does not have the necessary proprietary interest as would be required to base a claim to trace.[44] The converse does, however, apply and where[45] a defendant is permitted to expend moneys (which he is otherwise restrained from disposing of by an ordinary injunction) a plaintiff with a proprietary interest may be able to trace those moneys into a payee's hands.

[9.15] The case of *United Mizrahi Bank Ltd v Doherty and Ors*[46] serves as an example of this point, although there the court purported to grant Mareva relief (as opposed to an ordinary interlocutory injunction) to a plaintiff who would appear to have had a proprietary claim. In that case the first defendant, a former employee with the plaintiff bank who had been dismissed for breach of duty, was alleged to have procured customers to enter into transactions with the bank to make payments, for his benefit, to third parties. The plaintiff also claimed that the moneys thus obtained had been spirited overseas and had ended up in the hands of the first defendant's wife (herself the fifth defendant) and certain companies. The funds were ultimately used to acquire properties in respect of which the plaintiff claimed a constructive trust, which it claimed, had arisen

---

[43]. [1992] QB 656: "Injunctions of the Mareva type are not infrequently framed without any high degree of precision, for example, by allowing money to be spent on living costs or ordinary business expenses. On occasion the courts are asked to vary an injunction so as to clarify what is within that licence ... Commercial concerns have ready access to lawyers, and are well able to apply to the court if they are in doubt as to what they must or must not do".

[44]. See Ch 1, *The Mareva Injunction in Context*, para **[1.21]** *et seq.*

[45]. In *Polly Peck International plc v Nadir (No 2)* [1992] 4 All ER 769 Scott LJ said that, ordinarily, the three provisos would not be inserted into an injunction which restrained a defendant from dealing with assets to which a plaintiff had a proprietary (as opposed to personal) claim. *Cf Sundt Wrigley & Co Ltd v Wrigley* [1993] CA Transcript 685 where Bingham said that it was only in an exceptional case, where a court was satisfied that the plaintiff's proprietary claim was well founded, that a defendant would not be permitted to draw on enjoined funds to finance his defence; and see *Cala Cristal SA v Emran Al-Borno (Mubarak Abdulaziz al Hassawi, third party)* (1994) *The Times* 6 May 1994. See further Ch 1, *The Mareva Injunction in Context*, para **[1.24]**.

[46]. [1998] 2 All ER 230.

from the breach of trust. The plaintiff sought to trace into the properties. Strangely,[47] on the plaintiff's application for relief, the court purported to grant a worldwide "Mareva" injunction, subject to living expenses and legal expenses provisos. The first and fifth defendants then sought a declaration that they would not be in breach of the Mareva order by utilising certain assets to fund their legal expenses of defending the action. In particular they expressed concern that by their expending money (as permitted by the proviso) it might subsequently be claimed that they were spending the proceeds of the plaintiff's property and that their solicitors might be alleged to be in breach of constructive trust through their knowing receipt or dishonest assistance. The judge confirmed that they would not be in breach of the Mareva injunction if they liquidated certain assets to fund their reasonable legal costs but he added a proviso that nothing in the order would operate to deprive the plaintiff of any proprietary claim it might have to those assets. The defendants issued a fresh notice of motion, seeking court confirmation that the utilisation of the assets would not be a continuation or perpetuation of a breach of trust or constructive trust as against the bank. The case raised a very interesting and far from academic point, particularly as far as the defendants' solicitors and counsel were concerned. Unless the court confirmed that the payment of the legal expenses (derived from the proceeds of sale of the specified property to which the plaintiff claimed a proprietary interest) would not be a continuation or perpetuation of a breach of trust or constructive trust, all moneys paid by way of fees, costs and expenses to the defendants' solicitors and counsel might be recoverable by the plaintiff. It was held by Michael Burton QC (sitting as a deputy judge of the High Court) that the defendants would not be in breach of the Mareva injunction by liquidating the specified property and expending its proceeds on reasonable legal expenses. He went on to hold, however, that should the plaintiff be successful in its action, the permission given to the defendant to pay legal expenses would be no guarantee that the recipients of that disbursement would be protected from a possible future claim in constructive trust for knowing receipt of the proceeds of the trust.

(a) The ordinary living expenses proviso

[9.16]. The purpose of an "ordinary living expenses" proviso is to permit a defendant, notwithstanding anything contained in the order, to expend money on his and his family's ordinary living expenses. Irrespective of a plaintiff's rights to recover damages from a defendant, a defendant will need to feed, clothe and

---

[47.] This is particularly strange in the light of the Court of Appeal's decision in *Polly Peck International plc v Nadir (No 2)* [1992] 4 All ER 769 where Lord Donaldson MR made it clear that in the context of relief ancillary to a proprietary claim, the principles to be applied are those set out in *American Cyanamid v Ethicon Ltd* [1975] 1 All ER 504 - and not those applicable to a Mareva injunction. See Ch 1, *The Mareva Injunction in Context*, para **[1.23]**.

keep a roof over his family's head and must be allowed to pay for such matters pending final judgment. The usual form of an ordinary living expenses proviso, which will follow on from the operative prohibition, is:

> "**PROVIDED THAT** the Defendant is at liberty to spend a sum not exceeding £___ per week for ordinary living expenses."

[9.17] In *PCW (Underwriting Agencies) Ltd v Dixon*[48] Lloyd J recognised that it would be unjust for a Mareva order to reduce a defendant's standard of living pending the determination of the plaintiff's substantive claim. He said:

> "I would regard it as unjust in the present case if the defendant were compelled to reduce his standard of living, give up his flat or to take his children away from school, in order to secure what is as yet only a claim by the plaintiffs."[49]

In that case the Court of Appeal subsequently[50] allowed living expenses of £1,000 per week to a well-to-do defendant who worked as a Lloyd's underwriter. In *TDK Tape Distributor (UK) Ltd v Videochoice Ltd*[51] it had been argued that the payment of legal fees came within the scope of a living expenses proviso. This was rejected by Skinner J who defined what he meant by living expenses:

> "I have to adopt a reasonable interpretation of the order. In my judgment it is certainly possible to aggregate expenses like a monthly account with the grocer, rates' bills and fuel bills, recurrent expenses of that sort: but I think it is impossible to argue that a bill to a lawyer for a defence against a serious criminal charge amounting to £10,000 is an ordinary living expense. Ordinary living expenses, in my judgment, mean ordinary, recurrent expenses involved in maintaining the subject of the injunction in the style of life to which he is reasonably accustomed. It does not include exceptional expenses like ... the purchase of a Rolls Royce or the equivalent in legal terms of the private employment of a Queen's Counsel to defend you against a serious criminal charge. That is not an ordinary living expense, and if it had been desired to create an exception from the injunction to cover that sort of expense, then an application to the court was necessary to effect it."[52]

Accordingly, where it is proposed to pay legal expenses from a defendant's assets, a specific legal expenses proviso must be inserted into the order either *ab initio* or following an application for a variation.

[48.] [1983] 2 All ER 158. See also *Xylas v Khanna* [1992] CA Transcript 1036.

[49.] At 164h. At 165b-c he said: "... justice and convenience require that he should be able to pay his ordinary bills and continue to live as he has been accustomed to live heretofore."

[50.] [1983] 2 All ER 697.

[51.] [1985] 3 All ER 345.

[52.] At 349, 350.

[9.18] Ideally, an ordinary living expenses proviso ought to be inserted into a Mareva order at the time the order is made so as to minimise unnecessary inconvenience to a defendant. However, this will not always be practical, especially on an *ex parte* application where a plaintiff may be entirely unaware of a defendant's personal circumstances and will, in particular, be unable to estimate a specific sum sufficient to meet a defendant's reasonable living expenses. In such circumstances it will be appropriate for the defendant to make an application by motion on notice to have the original order varied to insert such a proviso. This occurred in the case of *Re Kelly's Carpetdrome Ltd*[53] where a Mareva order had been made in a liquidator's favour against certain company directors against whom the liquidator was proceeding for fraudulent trading. With regard to both legal and living expenses, Costello J said of one of the defendants:

> "If he applies on affidavit giving particulars of the legal expenses which he has to meet and the living expenses he faces I will consider whether the injunction should be lifted in part."

Although there are no other reported judgments of the Irish courts inserting living expenses provisos in Mareva orders,[54] such can be seen to be commonplace from reports in the newspapers. In *Irish Press Newspapers Ltd v Malocco and Killeen*[55] an application for the variation of a Mareva order made by the second defendant was reported in *The Irish Times*. It was said that Blayney J acceded to a request to vary the Mareva order so as to permit the withdrawal of £200 per week from a bank account which was specifically frozen by the order. A figure of £300 per week had been sought but the court had heard argument from the plaintiff's counsel which took issue with some of the expenses claimed. The newspaper report stated that in allowing £200 per week as living expenses Blayney J had said that the second defendant was entitled to draw some reasonable sum to support himself and his family.[56]

[9.19] In *Director of Public Prosecutions v EH*,[57] Kelly J held that the applicable test for determining whether a restraint order made pursuant to the Criminal Justice Act 1994[58] should be varied was that applicable to a Mareva injunction

---

[53.] High Court, unrep, 16 May 1983 *ex tempore* decision; notes initialled (Costello J).
[54.] *Cf* in respect of restraint orders made pursuant to the Criminal Justice Act 1994. See para **[9.19]** *infra*.
[55.] *The Irish Times*, 10 December 1991 (Blayney J).
[56.] See also *Re Holbern Investments Trust Ltd*, *The Irish Times*, 9 October 1991 (Barron J) where a sum of £200 per week was allowed to be drawn in respect of ordinary living expenses and also an unspecified sum in respect of mortgage repayments.
[57.] High Court, unrep, 22 April 1997 (Kelly J); note of judgment delivered *ex tempore* at p 1 of the transcript.
[58.] See further, Ch 3, *Statutory Jurisdictions to Freeze Assets*, para **[3.20]**.

as prescribed by Robert Goff J in *A v C (No 2)*.[59] Kelly J expressly adopted the following passage:

> "In order to satisfy the burden placed upon a defendant who seeks such a variation he has to go further than merely to state that he owes money to someone, he has to show that he does not have other assets available out of which the debt would be paid".

In this case the defendant - against whom a restraint order had been made - had sought a variation of that order so as to permit him to draw living expenses from the frozen fund in the amount of £735 per month. Kelly J noted that there was evidence that since the defendant had been released from Garda custody sums amounting to £17,500 had been withdrawn by him from accounts under his control and of that sum, £12,000 was unaccounted for, save the defendant's explanation that he had used the money to repay a business associate. Kelly J said that he found "the evidence of the defendant in this regard to be unsatisfactory" and that the payment to the third party remained a mystery.[60] In these circumstances Kelly J held that the defendant had failed to meet the necessary test required in order to have a variation made in his favour.

(b) The legal expenses proviso

[9.20] Where appropriate, a legal expenses proviso will follow the operative part of the order with words to the following effect:

> "**PROVIDED THAT** the Defendant is at liberty to spend a sum not exceeding £___ per week for reasonable legal expenses."

In both *PCW (Underwriting Agencies) Ltd v Dixon*[61] and *TDK Tape Distributor (UK) Ltd v Videochoice Ltd*[62] the court inserted legal expenses provisos into the Mareva orders. The basic rationale for the proviso is that in the absence of any claim that a plaintiff has a proprietary interest in a defendant's assets, justice and convenience requires that a defendant should be allowed to defend himself by utilising his own money.

[9.21] In *Atlas Maritime Co SA v Avalon Maritime Ltd; The Coral Rose (No 3)*[63] the defendant company sought to have a Mareva injunction, which restrained it from dealing with all of its assets, varied in order to permit it to expend funds on its legal expenses. The Court of Appeal refused to vary the order on the grounds that the defendant was a wholly-owned subsidiary of another company which appeared to have used the defendant for the transaction which gave rise to the

---

[59] [1981] 2 All ER 126.
[60] At p 4 of the transcript.
[61] [1983] 2 All ER 158.
[62] [1985] 3 All ER 345.
[63] [1991] 4 All ER 783.

substantive claim and that it was open to the holding company to pay the subsidiary's legal expenses. Lord Donaldson MR said:

> "... the fact that the variation of the injunction to enable legal costs to be paid would be likely to render any award in favour of [the plaintiff] less effective is not of itself a fatal objection because of the proviso built into what I have described as the fundamental principle.[64] But this proviso only applies in cases in which the operation of the injunction would impede the person enjoined from defending himself against the claim."[65]

It is submitted that this case should not be followed by the Irish courts. Unless there is evidence that in discharging its legal expenses itself, as opposed to procuring their discharge through its holding company, a subsidiary is doing so with a view to frustrating the anticipated order of the court and the plaintiff's claim it should be entirely free to expend its own assets on its own legal defence. Perhaps, therefore, *Atlas Maritime* should be distinguished from other cases involving a group of companies on the grounds that it was a "special case" which can be distinguished on its own peculiar facts.[66]

(c) The ordinary business expenses proviso

[9.22] It has been consistently stated by the Irish courts that a Mareva injunction should not prevent a defendant from paying his ordinary business expenses. The rationale for this is that the only legitimate purpose of a Mareva injunction is to prevent a defendant from disposing of his assets with a view to defeating the plaintiff's claim and frustrating the anticipated order of the court.[67] Where a plaintiff seeks a Mareva injunction to prevent a defendant from making a particular disposal which is discovered to be the payment of a lawful debt, the court will refuse to grant any relief as there is nothing which can legitimately be frozen.[68] A Mareva injunction acts *in personam* against a defendant, not *in rem* against his assets and so provides no security to a plaintiff over a defendant's

---

[64.] The reference to the "fundamental principle" was to an earlier passage from *Derby & Co Ltd v Weldon (No 2)* [1989] 1 All ER 1002 at 1006-1007 where it was, *inter alia*, said: "The fundamental principle underlying this jurisdiction is that, within the limits of its powers, no court should permit a defendant to take action designed to ensure that subsequent orders of the court are rendered less effective than would otherwise be the case."

[65.] [1991] 4 All ER 783 at 791f.

[66.] A point made by Nicholls LJ at 793g, where he noted the unusual way in which the parent and subsidiary carried on their mutual dealings: the subsidiary did not operate its own bank account at all, did not have any funds of its own save those which the parent chose it to have and that, in relation to money matters, the subsidiary "seems not to have exercised any mind of its own, even in the attenuated sense in which that frequently is the case with wholly-owned subsidiary companies" (at 793j).

[67.] *Re John Horgan Livestock Ltd; O'Mahony v Horgan* [1995] 2 IR 411.

[68.] *Moloney v Laurib Investments* High Court, unrep, 20 July 1993 (Lynch J); see also *B v SFC Ltd, The Irish Times*, 31 August 1982 (Murphy J) where it was reported that the plaintiff's application for a Mareva injunction was refused by Murphy J on the grounds that there was nothing wrong in disposing of the assets of the defendant company provided the requirements of the Companies Act and the general requirements of law were abided by.

assets.[69] Therefore, a defendant cannot be prohibited from paying other creditors over the plaintiff and must be allowed to pay his normal business expenses as they become due.

[9.23] Where there is a case for granting Mareva relief[70] against a defendant who is in business, the court may recognise that a defendant will have certain normal business expenses which he should not be prevented from discharging. In such circumstances it will be appropriate to insert a proviso into the order along the following lines:

> "**PROVIDED THAT** the Defendant is at liberty to spend a sum not exceeding £ ___ per week for ordinary business expenses."

Such provisos are relatively more unusual than ordinary living expenses provisos. This is because it will generally be very difficult to determine the quantum of business expenses in advance of their being incurred and charged. Only where it is possible to make provision for regular expenses within reasonable parameters, will such a proviso be appropriate. Where extraordinary business expenses arise after a Mareva injunction has been made and a defendant seeks to discharge these from his assets, it is both necessary and appropriate that the defendant make application to vary the existing Mareva injunction.[71] In *Polly Peck International plc v Nadir (No 2)*[72] a defendant bank, which had been made the subject of a Mareva injunction, was permitted to make payment of up to £6 million in traunches of £1 million each, subject to the plaintiff's administrators' consent to such drawings.

Penal Notices[73]

[9.24] A penal notice is an endorsement on a court order the purpose[74] of which is to draw a defendant's attention to the fact that breach of the terms of the order will have penal consequences, eg that he may be imprisoned.[75] Strictly speaking, the endorsement of a penal notice is only required in the case of a mandatory injunction, it is, however, common practice amongst Irish practitioners to seek to include a penal notice in prohibitory injunctions such as Mareva injunctions.

[69.] See para **[9.35]** *infra, The Effects of Mareva Injunctions.*

[70.] As opposed to where, say, the relief is sought to prevent the defendant making one large disbursement which is in the ordinary course of his business or in discharge of a lawful debt as considered in the preceding paragraph.

[71.] See para **[9.31]** *et seq, infra, Variation and Discharge of Mareva Injunctions.*

[72.] [1992] 4 All ER 769.

[73.] See generally, Lowe & Sufrin, *Borrie & Lowe, The Law of Contempt*, (3rd ed, 1996) Butterworths, pp 562 - 565.

[74.] See *Prior v Johnston* (1893) 27 ILTR 108 and *Wallace v Graham* 11 LR Ir 369.

[75.] See *Iberian Trust Ltd v Founders Trust and Investment Co Ltd* [1932] 2 KB 87 at 97 *per* Luxmoore J.

The penal endorsement in Mareva injunctions and other ancillary orders is considered in a later chapter.[76]

Service of the Order

[9.25] After an order is made by the court it must be dated and, unless the court directs otherwise, it takes effect accordingly.[77] Here it is important to distinguish giving a defendant *notice* of the granting of an injunction from the *service* of an injunction on a defendant. In order for a defendant to be bound by an injunction all that is necessary is that he be given notice of the injunction. In order for parties to be bound by an injunction the general rule is that a person will not be bound unless and until they have *notice* of the order.[78] Accordingly, it is generally sufficient to serve a defendant personally with notice of the court's order; whilst it is preferable for this to be done in writing, the court will usually, on request, direct that notice of an *ex parte* order can be conveyed to a defendant (and any third party) by telegraph,[79] fax or telephone.[80] A defendant will, invariably, have first hand notice of an *inter partes* order.

[9.26] The difficulty with purporting to put a defendant on notice of an injunction which has been made against him, without *serving* him with the order, is in subsequently proving beyond all reasonable doubt that he had actual notice of the injunction's terms in proceedings for civil contempt arising from an alleged breach of the injunction. The general rule is that all injunctions should be served personally[81] and so, by Ord 121, r 6 of the RSC, service of a Mareva injunction should be effected as nearly as may be in the manner prescribed for the personal service of an originating summons.[82] Where, however, it is not practicable to personally serve a defendant, a plaintiff should seek an order for substituted service from the court to serve the order on the defendant, and other third parties such as banks, by telephone[83] or fax[84] or

---

[76.] See Ch 12, *Enforcing Mareva Injunctions and Other Orders*, para **[12.15]** *post*.

[77.] Order 115 of the Rules of the Superior Courts 1986.

[78.] *Duff v Devlin* [1924] 1 IR 56.

[79.] See, for example, *Re Bryant* 4 Ch D 98; *Re Bishop; Ex parte Langley*,(1879) 13 Ch D 110; and *Curtice v London City and Midland Bank* [1908] 1 KB 297.

[80.] As, for example, on the defendant in *Columbia Picture Industries Inc v Robinson* [1987] Ch 38 and as recommended in the case of third parties such as banks, by Lord Denning MR in *Z Ltd v A* [1982] 1 All ER 556 at 565h-j. See also *PPHS Ltd v vonK, The Irish Times*, 31 May 1995 (Circuit Court; Judge Kelly) where it was reported that the court allowed notice of a Mareva injunction to be made by telephone and fax.

[81.] *Vansandau v Rose* 22 RR 214; *Gooch v Marshall* 8 WR 410.

[82.] See further, Ch 12, *Enforcing Mareva Injunctions and Other Orders*, para **[12.11]** *et seq*.

[83.] The practice of allowing service of an order by telephone is not all that new: in *The National Bank Ltd v Barry* 100 ILTR 185 at 186 it was reported that the Supreme Court allowed service of an order of attachment to be effected by telephone on the solicitors for the defendants, to be confirmed by personal service.

[84.] See *Ralux v Spencer Mason, The Times*, 18 May 1989 and Hall, 'Service of Documents by FAX', (1989) Gazette ILSI 318.

otherwise. Such an order will usually be made on a plaintiff's undertaking to follow this up by sending a copy of the order and other relevant documents, such as the grounding affidavit, to a defendant by post. In such circumstances it may also be necessary to get leave from the court to serve notice of the order out of hours.[85] Service and notice of injunctions in the context of civil contempt of court are considered in detail in Ch 12, *Enforcing Mareva Injunctions and Other Orders*.

Defendants' Undertakings and Consent Orders

[9.27] On an *inter partes* hearing it is open to a defendant to compromise the proceedings by offering his undertaking to refrain from doing that which the plaintiff requires, in order to avoid having a court order made against him. As one author has commented:

> "... if the plaintiff consents, the court may accept an undertaking by counsel or solicitor on behalf of the defendant in lieu of an injunction in the terms of the interlocutory injunction sought."[86]

Implicit in this statement is that a plaintiff is entitled to refuse to accept a defendant's undertaking and may insist upon a formal injunction.[87] It should be noted, however, that there is a practice in Ireland for the court to accept a defendant's undertaking unless a plaintiff can satisfy the court that, owing to the particular circumstances of the case, the defendant's undertakings are insufficient.

[9.28] A plaintiff who accepts a defendant's undertaking in lieu of a formal injunction ought to be particularly careful in satisfying himself that it is adequately worded because of the rule that a plaintiff cannot apply to have an undertaking varied. In *Cutler v Wandsworth Stadium Ltd*[88] it was held that an undertaking which was given voluntarily by the defendant may not be varied, but application may be made for the release or discharge of a defendant's undertaking. This was found to be the position on account of the fact that litigants are not ordered by the courts to give such undertakings, but do so of their own volition. In *Butt v Butt*[89] it was said by Mustill LJ that:

---

85. Order 122, r 9 of the RSC provides, *inter alia*, that service of orders shall be effected before 5 pm, Monday to Friday; before 1 pm, Saturday.
86. Goldrein & Wilkinson, *Commercial Litigation: Pre-Emptive Remedies*, (2nd ed, 1991) Sweet & Maxwell, pp 18, 19.
87. *Royal Insurance Co v G & s Assured Investment Co Ltd* [1972] 1 Lloyd's Rep 267; see also Bean, *Injunctions*, (6th ed, 1994) Longman Practitioner Series, p 83 and p 91.
88. [1945] 1 All ER 103.
89. [1987] 3 All ER 657.

"If there is an *inter partes* hearing on which an undertaking is given in lieu of an injunction, and if it is made plain and understood by all concerned in the hearing, that the undertaking is given in the contemplation that the defendant may subsequently wish to apply for the discharge of the undertaking when his evidence is in order, there would, in my judgment, be something wrong with the law if that common understanding were to be frustrated simply because the relief takes the form of an undertaking rather than an injunction."[90]

The effect of an undertaking entered into or given by a defendant to the court is equivalent to an injunction and it is prudent to have a defendant's undertaking recorded in an order of the court.[91] The newspaper reports indicate that a great many applications for Mareva relief are compromised by defendants offering their undertakings *in lieu* of the court making a formal order or by making an order on consent.[92]

Appealing a Mareva Order

[9.29] Where a plaintiff is successful in obtaining a Mareva injunction it is open to a defendant to appeal the order of the court to the High Court (in the case of a Circuit Court order) or the Supreme Court (in the case of a High Court order). Where, however, the injunction has been obtained on foot of an *ex parte* application, the more usual course of action will be for a defendant to invoke his rights under the order to apply to have it varied or discharged and only exercise his right of appeal if unsuccessful. Even here, defendants in practice seldom apply to discharge interim orders, preferring to concentrate their resources on defending the application for interlocutory relief, reserving their right to appeal against an unfavourable interlocutory hearing. Equally, where a Mareva injunction is refused, it is open to the plaintiff to appeal the decision to refuse the relief sought.

[9.30] Where an injunction is granted on foot of an *ex parte* application the RSC provide that, in the case of an appeal to the High Court from a Circuit Court refusal, application shall be on two days' notice without the need to serve anyone,[93] and in the case of an appeal to the Supreme Court from a High Court refusal, application shall be within four days from the date of the refusal or such enlarged time as the Supreme Court allows.[94]

---

[90] At 660c-d.
[91] See *Hussain v Hussain* [1986] 1 All ER 961.
[92] One example of each will suffice: in *B v C & JPC & Co Ltd, The Irish Times*, 27 June 1991 (Barron J) it was reported that the defendant gave his undertaking not to dispose of a list of properties in lieu of a formal Mareva order being made against him; in *Re Mark Synnott (Life and Pensions) Brokers Ltd, The Irish Times*, 4 July 1991 (Carroll J) the court made an order on consent restraining Mr Synnott from reducing his assets below £2.3m and also restraining him from leaving the jurisdiction.
[93] Order 61, r 9. This can be enlarged or abridged pursuant to Ord 122, r 7.
[94] Order 58, r 13.

Variation and Discharge of Mareva Orders

[9.31] At any time after a Mareva injunction has been made it is open to a defendant to make application to the court, on notice to the plaintiff, to have the original order varied or discharged.[95] Clerical mistakes in orders or errors arising therein from any accidental slip or omission may at any time be corrected by the court on motion without an appeal.[96] Applications to vary a Mareva injunction, as opposed to discharge one, will very often arise where no, or inadequate, provision has been made in the original order for ordinary living expenses and/ or legal expenses and/or ordinary business expenses provisos.[97] All such applications to vary or discharge a Mareva injunction should be made by the defendant on notice of motion, and grounded upon affidavit. A defendant's case to have the order varied or discharged will invariably involve one or other of the following claims: that the plaintiff did not in law or in fact satisfy the proofs required before Mareva relief can be granted; or, in the case of an *ex parte* order, that there was a failure to disclose all material facts;[98] or that the plaintiff failed to comply with an undertaking which he was required to give to the court in return for the relief sought.[99]

[9.32] Application to have an existing order varied may be made for a more specific reason: that the defendant, is either desirous or obliged to make a payment to a third party in circumstances where there is no question of the disposal being made with a view to frustrating the plaintiff's future judgment. Sometimes the application for a variation will be at the behest of the third party, and in this respect the case law on variation of Mareva injunctions overlaps with the case law on the effects of Mareva injunctions, which is considered below.[100] The basis of such an application is that in these circumstances the disposal of a defendant's assets is not in conflict with the policy underpinning the Mareva jurisdiction. So, in *Iraqi Ministry of Defence v Arcepey Shipping Co SA (Gillespie Brothers & Co Ltd intervening); The Angle Bell*,[101] on the application of the interveners who claimed to be owed certain moneys by the defendant to have a Mareva injunction varied, Robert Goff J acceded to the request, rejecting the contention that:

[95.] As to appealing the order, see Ord 58 considered in para **[9.30]** *supra*.

[96.] Order 28, r 11. See *Concorde Engineering v Bus Atha Cliath* [1996] 1 ILRM 533. In *Belville Holdings Ltd v The Revenue Commissioners* [1994] 1 ILRM 29 it was held by the Supreme Court that an order may be amended in special or unusual circumstances although it had been perfected in accordance with Order 115.

[97.] See para **[9.12]** *et seq, supra*.

[98.] See Ch 8, *Applying for a Mareva Injunction*, para **[8.31]** for the proofs required to be established and para **[8.36]** for the basis for claiming material non-disclosure.

[99.] *Ibid*, para **[8.57]** *et seq*.

[100.] See para **[9.35]** *infra*.

[101.] [1980] 1 All ER 480.

"having established the injunction, the court should not thereafter permit a qualification to it to allow a transfer of assets by the defendant if the defendant satisfies the court that he requires the money for a purpose which does not conflict with the policy underlying the Mareva jurisdiction".[102]

It would seem that this must also be the position in Ireland following the Supreme Court's decision in *Re John Horgan Livestock Ltd.*[103]

[9.33] Not every application to vary a Mareva injunction for the purpose of authorising the discharge of a "business debt" allegedly owed by a defendant to another party will be successful. In *Atlas Maritime Co SA v Avalon Maritime Ltd; The Coral Rose (No 1)*[104] it was held by the Court of Appeal that a Mareva injunction made against a subsidiary company would not be varied to allow it to repay a loan made to it by its parent company. In that case the defendant subsidiary company had been advanced funds by its parent to purchase and repair a damaged vessel. A dispute had arisen between the plaintiff and the defendant whereby the plaintiff had claimed that there was an oral contract to sell the vessel and had instituted proceedings seeking a declaration to this effect and damages for wrongful repudiation. The plaintiff had obtained a Mareva injunction over the defendant's assets in the sum of US$3m. The defendant subsequently sold the vessel in question to a third party and transferred the proceeds, less the amount covered by the injunction, to its parent company. At trial, the declaration sought by the plaintiff was made but proceedings stayed and the Mareva injunction continued pending the outcome of the claim for damages which was being arbitrated. In these circumstances the defendant applied to have the Mareva injunction varied to enable it to pay the remaining funds to its parent on the grounds that they constituted a business debt. The judge refused the defendant's application for variation/discharge on the ground that the relationship between the defendant and its parent was not one of debtor and creditor but rather of agent and principal and also on the ground that the court was not obliged to vary a Mareva injunction for the purpose of permitting an agent to transfer its assets to its principal.

[9.34] The Court of Appeal upheld the decision to refuse the variation, but on different grounds. Although it did find that the defendant owed US$3m to its

---

[102.] At 486a. See also *Investment and Pensions Advisory Service Ltd v Gray* [1990] BCLC 38 where a Mareva injunction was varied to allow the defendant to fund the opposition of petitions to wind up a company of which he was a member and a partnership in which he was a partner.

[103.] *Cf A v C (No 2)* [1981] 2 All ER 126 where *The Angel Bell* [1980] 1 All ER 480 was distinguished on the grounds that the defendants failed to adduce evidence to show that they did not have assets, other than those which were frozen, with which to discharge legal costs. Also, see *Atlas Maritime Co SA v Avalon Maritime Ltd; The Coral Rose (No 3)* [1991] 4 All ER 783, considered at para **[9.21]** *supra.*

[104.] [1991] 4 All ER 769.

parent, the Court of Appeal nonetheless refused to vary the Mareva injunction. Neill LJ gave two reasons for not allowing the defendant's application:

> "In the first place the sum owed to [the parent] is not a debt incurred in the course of ordinary trading but represents moneys advanced in effect as trading capital. In the second place the close link between [the defendant] and [the parent] is a factor to be taken into account when deciding how, as a matter of discretion, the interests of the ultimate holding company should be balanced against those of [the plaintiff]".[105]

Neill LJ went on to look behind the corporate veil in order to examine all of the circumstances of the case.[106] Staughton LJ said:

> "In my judgment, it is wholly proper, in deciding whether to permit payment by [the defendant] at this stage of the moneys claimed by [the parent], to have regard to the fact that [the parent] is the ultimate parent of [the defendant] as to 100%. It is also right to regard the moneys sought to be repaid as in effect the loan capital of [the defendant]. This is not a case of repayment 'in the ordinary course of business' (see *Iraqi Ministry of Defence v Arcepey Shipping Co SA (Gillespie Brothers & Co Ltd intervening); The Angle Bell* [1980] 1 All ER 480 at 487) or of 'carrying on business in the ordinary way' (see *Derby & Co Ltd v Weldon (No 2)* [1989] 1 All ER 1002 at 1007), or of a payment to 'trade creditors in the ordinary course' (see *K/S A/S Admiral Shipping v Portlink Ferries Ltd* [1984] 2 Lloyd's Rep 166 at 167, *Avant Petroleum Inc v Gatoil Overseas Inc* [1986] 2 Lloyd's Rep 236 at 242, *SFC Finance Co Ltd v Masri* [1985] 2 All ER 747 at 750). On the contrary, it is a case of a defendant who is 'seeking to avoid his responsibilities to the plaintiff if the latter should ultimately obtain a judgment' (see *The Angel Bell* [1980] 1 All ER 480 at 487), or taking action 'designed to ensure that subsequent orders of the court are rendered less effective than would otherwise be the case' (see *Derby v Weldon (No 2)* [1989] 1 All ER 1002 at 1006-1007), or of a desire to use assets caught by the injunction 'merely to evade its underlying purpose' (see *A v B (X intervening)* [1983] 2 Lloyd's Rep 532 at 534)."[107]

It is thought that the repayment of a debt in the context of a parent-subsidiary relationship will not invariably lead to a refusal to vary or discharge a Mareva injunction so as to permit its payment.[108] Each case will turn upon its own facts and the courts will only "lift the corporate veil" in established circumstances.[109]

---

[105]. At 776c-d.

[106]. Neill LJ relied upon *Merchandise Transport Ltd v British Transport Commission* [1961] 3 All ER 495 at 518 and *Adams v Cape Industries plc* [1991] 1 All ER 929 at 1024. On piercing and lifting the corporate veil generally, see Courtney, *The Law of Private Companies*, (1994) Butterworths, para [4.014] *et seq.*

[107]. [1991] 4 All ER 769 at 780c-f.

[108]. It should be noted that in *Moloney v Laurib Investments Ltd* High Court, unrep, 20 July 1993 Lynch J refused to grant Mareva relief to the plaintiff where, *inter alia*, the defendant company intended to dispose of its only asset and use the proceeds to repay its indebtedness to one of its two directors.

[109]. See Courtney, *The Law of Private Companies*, (1994) Butterworths at Ch 4.

[B] THE EFFECTS OF MAREVA INJUNCTIONS

[9.35] It is a misnomer, albeit an understandable one, to refer to a Mareva injunction as "freezing a defendant's assets". Mareva injunctions only ever affect a defendant's assets *indirectly* by operating on the defendant, making him personally accountable to the court to ensure that his assets are not removed, disposed of or otherwise dealt with contrary to the court's order. This section is concerned with the nature and effects of Mareva injunctions which are considered here under the following headings:

1.   A Mareva Injunction Operates *In Personam* Against a Defendant.

2.   A Mareva Injunction Confers No Security on a Plaintiff.

3.   The Position of Banks and Other Third Parties.

A Mareva Injunction Operates *In Personam* Against a Defendant

[9.36] Mareva injunctions operate *in personam*[110] by directly restraining or prohibiting a defendant from removing, disposing of or otherwise dealing with his own assets, save as may be permitted by the terms of the injunction. In this way a defendant's assets may be said to be "frozen". The assets themselves, however, are not directly affected by the order: they are only indirectly affected by a Mareva injunction because their owner (the defendant) is restrained in his full and unfettered use and ownership of his assets. In this way the Mareva jurisdiction is manifestly different from other jurisdictions which operate *in rem* whereby a person's assets can be directly "frozen".[111] The fact that the Mareva jurisdiction operates *in personam* has actually assisted its development in that its *in personam* basis has provided the rationale for making worldwide Mareva injunctions: provided that a defendant is amenable to the jurisdiction of the court making the order, it matters not that his assets are situate outside of the jurisdiction.[112]

[9.37] The fact that Mareva injunctions *indirectly* affect a defendant's assets led Lord Denning MR to confuse the operation of a Mareva injunction with an *in rem* remedy in *Z Ltd v A*[113] when he said:

[110.] See the judgment of Hamilton CJ in *Re John Horgan Livestock Ltd; O'Mahony v Horgan* [1995] 2 IR 411 at 418. On the jurisdiction of equity acting *in personam* see 16 *Halsbury's Laws of England* (4th ed, reissue, 1991), para 742; Keane, *Equity and the Law of Trusts in the Republic of Ireland*, (1988) Butterworths, para 3.06; and Delany; *Equity and the Law of Trusts in Ireland*, (1996), p 33.

[111.] As, for example, the arrest of ships in admiralty law: see Ch 1, *The Mareva Injunction in Context*, para **[1.30]**.

[112.] See Ch 7, *The Defendant's Assets*, para **[7.21]** *et seq*.

[113.] [1982] 1 All ER 556.

"... a Mareva injunction is a method of attaching the asset itself. It operates *in rem* just as the arrest of a ship does. Just as a debtor gets the ship released on giving of security, so does the debtor get an aircraft released (see *Allen v Jambo Holdings Ltd* [1980] 2 All ER 502 at 505) or any other asset ... It operates just as the process of foreign attachment used to do in the City of London, and still does in the United States of America. It operates so as to attach any effects of the defendant, whether money or goods, to be found within the jurisdiction of the court."[114]

Certainly, the effect of a Mareva injunction may be to "attach" a defendant's assets, but only indirectly through the operation of equity on the defendant's person. Insofar as this passage is authority for the proposition that Mareva injunctions operate *in rem* it is submitted that it is clearly wrong[115] and that attempts to defend Lord Denning MR's suggestion that a Mareva injunction "operates *in rem* just as the arrest of a ship does" are totally misplaced.[116] The truth of the matter is that Mareva injunctions neither create rights *in rem* nor operate *in rem*.

[9.38] The effect of a Mareva order is that a defendant is legally obliged to comply with its terms. The fact that a Mareva injunction operates *in personam* is borne out by the fact that where a defendant disobeys the court's order, it is he, and not his assets who is liable to be attached. Wilful disobedience of a Mareva injunction is a contempt of court which may give rise to committal proceedings against a disobedient defendant (and any third party who aids and abets him or knowingly acts in a manner that obstructs or frustrates the objects of the order).[117]

A Mareva Injunction Confers No Security on a Plaintiff

[9.39] The purpose and intention of the Mareva jurisdiction is not to "rewrite the law of insolvency".[118] It has been consistently stated and restated that a Mareva

---

[114.] At 562e-g.

[115.] See the comments of Buckley LJ in *Cretanor Maritime Co Ltd v Irish Marine Management Ltd* [1978] 3 All ER 164 at 170b-e. As to the *in rem* type "effect" of Mareva injunctions, see *Babanaft International Co SA v Bassatne* [1989] 1 All ER 433 at 438g-h.

[116.] Hoyle, *The Mareva Injunction and Related Orders*, (3rd ed, 1997) Lloyd's of London Press, p 83 says: "Lest this should be misunderstood, Lord Denning later said that: 'It enables the seizure of assets so as to preserve them for the benefit of the creditor; but not to give a charge in favour of any particular creditor'." In the next paragraph following Hoyle says: "This latter qualification is vital to the effect of a Mareva injunction. It operates against the assets of the defendant, and so can be said to be *in rem*, but it does not create rights *in rem*".

[117.] See Ch 12, *Enforcing Mareva Injunctions and Other Orders*, para **[12.31]** *et seq.*

[118.] *Iraqi Ministry of Defence v Arcepey Shipping Co SA (Gillespie Brothers & Co Ltd intervening); The Angle Bell* [1980] 1 All ER 480 at 486 *per* Robert Goff J; *Investment and Pensions Advisory Service Ltd v Gray* [1990] BCLC 38 at 43f-g *per* Morritt J; *Atlas Maritime Co SA v Avalon Maritime Ltd; The Coral Rose (No 1)* [1991] 4 All ER 769 at 781b *per* Staughton LJ; *AJ Bekhor & Co v Bilton* [1981] 2 All ER 565 at 577c *per* Achner LJ.

injunction creates no rights in the nature of security in a plaintiff's favour.[119] As Hamilton CJ said in *Re John Horgan Livestock Ltd*:[120]

> "A Mareva injunction is an *in personam* order, restraining the defendant from dealing with assets in which the plaintiff claims no right whatsoever. A Mareva order does not give the plaintiff any precedence over other creditors with respect to the frozen assets."

As shall be considered below, however, the *effect* of a Mareva injunction may be to cause a defendant to provide security for the plaintiff's claim by agreeing to give a bond or similar security in return for the discharge of the injunction.

[9.40] The leading English case - with an Irish connection - which is authority for the proposition that a Mareva injunction creates no security rights in a plaintiff's favour is *Cretanor Maritime Co Ltd v Irish Marine Management Ltd*.[121] In that case the plaintiff owned a vessel which it chartered to the defendant Irish company. The defendant subsequently created a debenture in favour of Ulster Bank Ltd which contained a first floating charge on the defendant's property, a negative-pledge clause, and which also entitled the bank to appoint a receiver, acting as the defendant's agent, over the defendant's assets. A dispute arose in respect of the charterparty, the dispute was submitted to arbitration and the plaintiff obtained a Mareva injunction against the defendant. The arbitration was later compromised and it was agreed that after the defendant made a first payment and gave five post-dated cheques for the balance of the settlement amount, the plaintiff would apply to have the Mareva discharged. Although the judgment is unclear on this point it appears that M, who had guaranteed the defendant's loan from Ulster Bank Ltd, repaid that loan, that in return, Ulster Bank Ltd assigned the debenture to M, whereupon M appointed a receiver to collect in the defendant's assets. When the defendant

---

[119.] In *Jackson v Sterling Industries Ltd* (1987) 162 CLR 612 (FC 87/022) Gaudron J said in the High Court of Australia that "The development of the law and practice relating to the making of orders in restraint of dealing with assets has made it clear that such an order creates no right in the plaintiff in the assets the subject of the order ... The practice has developed that such orders may and should be varied to allow payment of debts incurred in the ordinary course of business even if not legally enforceable (*Iraqi Ministry of Defence v Arcepey Shipping Co SA; The Angle Bell* (1981) QB 558; *Bakarim v Victoria P Shipping Co Ltd; The Tatiangela* (1980) 2 Lloyd's Rep 193; and *Riley McKay Pty Ltd v McKay* [1982] 1 NSWLR 264), to allow the defendant sufficient funds to meet reasonable living expenses (*PCW (Underwriting Agencies) Ltd v Dixon* [1983] 2 All ER 158), and to prevent interference with the rights of third parties (*Galaxia Maritime SA v Mineralimportexport; The Eleftherios* [1982] 1 All ER 796; *Clipper Maritime Co Ltd v Mineralimportexport; The Maria Leonhardt* [1981] 3 All ER 664; and *Searose Ltd v Seatrain (UK) Ltd* [1981] 1 All ER 806). The practice is thus inconsistent with acquisition by a plaintiff of rights in respect of assets the subject of such order".
[120.] [1995] 2 IR 411 at 418.
[121.] [1978] 3 All ER 164.

only paid some of the moneys due under the compromise the plaintiff obtained a judgment in respect of the balance. The defendant had over £70,000 in a UK bank and the receiver appointed by M was successful in having the Mareva injunction varied to enable him remove the funds to Ireland. The plaintiff appealed this decision on the following grounds: that as the defendant's agent the receiver was in no better a position than the defendant and was bound by the Mareva injunction; that the plaintiff's right to maintain the injunction had priority over the debenture-holder's right to the moneys; that the Mareva injunction operated as a pre-trial attachment of the defendant's assets and conferred a partial security analogous to a lien; and that the equitable assignment of the moneys to the debentureholder should not be recognised because it took place after the date when the injunction came into force.

[9.41] The Court of Appeal accepted the first point, namely, that the receiver[122] was not entitled to apply for the discharge of the Mareva injunction as being the defendant's agent under the terms of the debenture, he could only realise the defendant's assets subject to any third party rights. It was held, however, that he debenture holder (M) was entitled to apply to have the Mareva discharged, and treating the application as having been made by the debenture holder, the Court of Appeal discharged the Mareva injunction and ordered the release of the moneys. In rejecting the suggestion that Mareva relief operated as a form of "attachment", Buckley LJ said[123]:

> "A Mareva injunction ... even if it relates only to a particularised asset ... is relief *in personam*. It does not effect a seizure of any asset. It merely restrains the owner from dealing with the asset in certain ways. The asset ... might be said to have been in a sense arrested, but only in a loose sense. All that the injunction achieves is in truth to prohibit the owner from doing certain things in relation to the asset. It is consequently, in my judgment, not strictly accurate to refer to a Mareva injunction as a pre-trial attachment."

On the question of whether a Mareva injunction conferred any security rights Buckley LJ said:

> "It seems to me ... that it is not the case that any rights in the nature of a lien arise when a Mareva injunction is made. Under such an injunction the plaintiff has no rights against the assets. He may later acquire such rights if he obtains

---

122. *Cf Capital Cameras Ltd v Harold Lines Ltd (National Westminster Bank plc, intervening)* [1991] 3 All ER 389 where Harman J varied an order on the application of administrative receivers on the grounds that the facts which supported the grant of the injunction had changed by reason of the appointment of a reputable licensed insolvency practitioner which meant that there was no risk of the company's assets being dissipated.
123. At 170d-e.

judgment and can thereafter successfully levy execution on them, but until that event his only rights are against the defendant personally."[124]

It was fundamental to the debenture holder's success that he had acquired security over all of the defendant's assets. The security in this case was by virtue of the equitable assignment of the moneys in favour of the debenture holder and this was in contrast to the plaintiff's rights which were completely unsecured.

[9.42] Although a Mareva injunction does not create any security interest in a plaintiff's favour, it may have the *effect* of prompting a defendant to offer to provide security for the plaintiff's claim to avoid a Mareva being granted or to have it discharged. This "side-effect" was recognised by Lord Donaldson MR in *Polly Peck International plc v Nadir (No 2)*[125] when he said:

> "It is not the purpose of a Mareva injunction to render the plaintiff a secured creditor, although this may be the result if the defendant offers a third party guarantee or bond in order to avoid such an injunction being imposed."[126]

The tendency to provoke an offer of security for a plaintiff's claim, after application has been made for a Mareva injunction, has been recognised in a number of English cases.[127] Moreover, there is evidence that the Irish High Court has, on a number of occasions, discharged or varied Mareva injunctions in return for defendants paying moneys into court.[128]

The Position of Banks and Other Third Parties

[9.43] When making a Mareva injunction, the court must take care to ensure that the rights of third parties are not prejudiced and also to ensure that third parties themselves are not unnecessarily exposed to being found to be in contempt of court. The position of banks and other third parties may usefully be considered under the following headings:

    (a) Third parties on notice must comply with Mareva injunctions;

    (b) Putting banks and third parties on notice of the order;

    (c) Freezing a Mareva defendant's account.

[124.] At 172g-h.

[125.] [1992] 4 All ER 769.

[126.] At 785j-786a. In *AJ Bekhor & Co v Bilton* [1981] 2 All ER 565 at 577 Ackner LJ said: "The purpose of the Mareva jurisdiction was not to improve the position of claimants in an insolvency ... It is not a form of pre-trial attachment but a relief *in personam*".

[127.] See, for example, *Rasu Maritima SA v Perusahaan Pertambangan Minyak Dan Gas Bumi Negara (Pertamina)* [1977] 3 All ER 324 at 335b-c *per* Lord Denning MR and *Cretanor Maritime Co Ltd v Irish Marine Management Ltd* [1978] 3 All ER 164 at 170h-j *per* Buckley LJ.

[128.] In *P v MM Ltd, The Irish Times*, 23 March 1991 (Blayney J) it was reported that a Mareva injunction against ten defendant companies was discharged upon their paying £2.3m into court to facilitate the plaintiff executing any judgment obtained by him against the ten defendants or any one of them.

(a) Third parties on notice must comply with Mareva injunctions

[9.44] Mareva injunctions, like all injunctions, are primarily directed at a defendant and direct him to refrain from removing his assets from the State or disposing of his assets within the State in accordance with the terms of the order. Third parties are in a peculiar position. Although it is well established that an injunction will only be granted *in personam* and will not be granted against a person who is a "true" third party to the action between a plaintiff and a defendant,[129] nevertheless, Mareva injunctions in particular can cause serious problems for third parties, especially banks who hold a defendant's cash or other assets. In *Z Ltd v A*[130] Eveleigh LJ said:

> "I think that the following propositions may be stated as to the consequences which ensue when there are acts or omissions which are contrary to the terms of an injunction. (1) The person against whom the order is made will be liable for contempt of court if he acts in breach of the order after having notice of it. (2) A third party will also be liable if he knowingly assists in the breach, that is to say if knowing the terms of the injunction he wilfully assists the person to whom it was directed to disobey it. This will be so whether or not the person enjoined has had notice of the injunction."

A defendant or a third party who wilfully breaches an injunction will be liable for contempt of court and this is considered in detail in Chapter 12, *Enforcing Mareva Injunctions and Other Orders*. Perhaps it is more correct to say that it is the *consequences* for third parties, as opposed to the direct effects of a breach of a Mareva injunction, which is the concern of this section. What are the duties and obligations of banks in particular, and third parties in general, when they are served with notice of a Mareva injunction, what information can a bank or other third party expect to be provided with when a Mareva injunction is granted against its, or his, customer?

[9.45] In *Z Ltd v A*[131] the Court of Appeal enumerated a series of principles by way of guidelines for banks and other third parties. This was an unusual judgment on account of the fact that the substantive issues which arose in that case had been dealt with by the court of first instance and so the entire judgment

---

[129.] See *Moore v Attorney General* [1930] IR 471. See generally, Ch 4, *A Substantive Cause of Action*, para **[4.14]** where Mareva injunctions and third parties are considered.

[130.] [1982] 1 All ER 556 at 566. The effect on third parties of a Mareva injunction was succinctly put by Lord Donaldson MR in *Derby & Co Ltd v Weldon (No 2)* [1989] 1 All ER 1002 at 1011h-j which, although in the context of worldwide Mareva injunctions, has equal relevance to domestic injunctions: "Court orders only bind those to whom they are addressed. However, it is a serious contempt of court, punishable as such, for anyone to interfere with or impede the administration of justice. This occurs if someone, knowing of the terms of the court order, assists in the breach of that order by the person to whom it is addressed."

[131.] [1982] 1 All ER 556.

of the Court of Appeal must be considered to be *obiter dictum*.[132] The case had involved an enormous international fraud where Mareva relief had been granted to the plaintiff, which was mysteriously allowed to remain anonymous. A number of banks which held the defendants' accounts were notice parties to the action and after the action settled, the five major clearing banks and another defendant applied for leave to appeal with a view to obtaining clarification of the law as to the obligations of banks and other third parties upon whom such injunctions were served.

Lord Denning MR said that the "juristic principle" raised where Mareva injunctions affect third party banks is that:

> "As soon as the bank is given notice of the Mareva injunction, it must freeze the defendant's bank account. It must not allow any drawings to be made on it, neither by cheques drawn before the injunction nor by those drawn after it. The reason is because, if it allowed any such drawings, it would be obstructing the course of justice, as prescribed by the court which granted the injunction and would be guilty of a contempt of court."[133]

Lord Denning MR made it clear that his observations applied not only to bank accounts, but also to chattels such as jewellery, stamps etc held by a bank and said that third parties should not dispose of any assets belonging to a defendant where there was a Mareva injunction in force.[134] In the same case, Kerr LJ said that in the absence of such chattels being specifically identified and valued a bank should not be prevented from releasing such chattels to the defendant.[135]

(b) Putting banks and third parties on notice of the order

[9.46] A Mareva plaintiff will frequently encounter difficulties in locating a defendant's assets. The temptation to serve every bank in town with notice of a Mareva injunction obtained against a defendant will usually be resisted by the plaintiff because every bank put on notice of a Mareva injunction will be obliged to trawl through all of its accounts in all of its branches to ascertain whether it holds an account for that particular defendant and the plaintiff will (whether expressly, or implicitly) be liable to indemnify the bank for the cost of such an extensive search. For a plaintiff, the cheapest and most cost-effective means of achieving the end of freezing a defendant's account is for the Mareva

---

[132] See Keane, *Equity and the Law of Trusts in the Republic of Ireland*, (1988) Butterworths at 15.38.

[133] [1982] 1 All ER 556 at 563g.

[134] In *Law Society v Shanks* (1987) 131 Sol Jo 1626 Donaldson MR, in a judgment which appears in conflict with that of Lord Denning MR in *Z Ltd v A*, said that a third party who had notice of a Mareva injunction against a defendant would not necessarily be in contempt of court unless there existed special circumstances in which the third party knew that "the sole purpose of requiring the asset to be handed over to the defendant is to facilitate a dissipation of that asset". See further Ch 12, *Enforcing Mareva Injunctions and Other Orders*, para **[12.35]**.

[135] At 576.

order to specify a particular named account by number, in a particular branch of a particular bank or other financial institution.[136] If this information is not readily available, a plaintiff may consider applying for an order of disclosure or discovery in respect of his defendant's assets.[137]

(c) Freezing a Mareva defendant's account

[9.47] The primary effect of a Mareva injunction will be to restrain a defendant from disposing of his property. Where his property comprises of or includes money held in a bank account he will be restrained from operating that account and, where it is on notice of the order, a bank cannot knowingly assist a defendant to breach the order. Here the following specific situations are considered:

    (i)   Deposit accounts and current accounts;

    (ii) Credit cards and cheque guarantee cards;

    (iii) Bank guarantees, letters of credit and performance bonds;

    (iv) The operation of set-off;

    (v) The difficulties associated with "maximum sum" orders.

(i) Deposit accounts and current accounts

[9.48] Of the two traditional generic account types, deposit accounts and current accounts, deposit accounts which create a debt owed by the bank to the customer are the least problematic when it comes to compliance with the terms of a Mareva injunction against a defendant.[138] Provided that the bank has notice of the terms of the injunction and is provided with the account name (and number, where available) and branch where located[139] there will be a cost, but there should ordinarily be less difficulty, in complying with the order in the case of a deposit account than in the case of a current account. Current accounts are more problematic since another third party can be involved: current account customers are invariably provided with a cheque book and can write cheques to third parties who will in due course present them to the bank for payment. No cheques drawn on a defendant's account should be honoured by a bank[140] and it

---

[136.] In *Z Ltd v A* [1982] 1 All ER 556 at 574f-g Kerr LJ said: "To the extend to which the assets are known or suspected to exist, these should be identified even if their value is unknown; and if it is known or suspected that they are in the hands of third parties, in particular of banks, everything should be done to define their location to the greatest possible extent. Thus, to take the example of bank accounts, the plaintiff should make every effort to try to indicate (a) which bank or banks hold the account in question, (b) at which branches, and (c) if possible, under what numbers."

[137.] See Ch 10, *Ancillary Orders*, para **[10.03]** *et seq.*

[138.] As to where the defendant holds a joint account with another person who is not a co-defendant, see Ch 7, *The Defendant's Assets*, para **[7.16]**.

[139.] See para **[9.46]** *supra.*

[140.] *Cf* where payment of a cheque has been "guaranteed" by compliance with the terms of a cheque guarantee card which has been issued to a customer: see para **[9.53]** *infra.*

would seem that this general rule applies even to cheques drawn *before* the making of the Mareva order, in the absence of a specific proviso to the contrary being inserted into the order.[141]

[9.49] Ordinarily, where a cheque is not honoured by a bank in circumstances where there are funds to meet it in a customer's account, the bank will be exposed to an action in defamation.[142] Where a bank does not honour a cheque by reason of its compliance with a Mareva injunction[143] "refer to drawer" may not be the appropriate endorsement. It has been suggested that a more suitable endorsement might be "payment postponed pending clarification of court order"[144] or "funds sufficient, but injunction granted against the account".[145]

(ii) Credit cards and cheque guarantee cards

[9.50] Where a defendant has been issued with a cheque guarantee card or a credit card[146] by a bank it has been said that a Mareva injunction will not operate to prevent a bank from honouring its obligations to a third party retailer.[147] As Kerr LJ said in *Z Ltd v A*:

> "Any bank on whom a copy of the order is served must clearly be entitled, as indeed it is obliged, to honour such obligations to the third parties concerned. The only question, accordingly, is whether, having done so, the bank is then entitled to debit the defendant's account with the corresponding amount, even though such account is otherwise frozen by the terms of the order."[148]

Although a distinction has been made between credit card transactions made before and after notice of a Mareva order has been served on a bank[149] and it has been suggested that a Mareva order may contain a specific proviso permitting

---

[141.] See Hapgood, *Paget's Law of Banking*, (11th ed, 1996) Butterworths, p 491 where it is noted that the effect of such a proviso "might result in post-order cheques being deliberately ante-dated".

[142.] *Pyke v Hibernian Bank Ltd* [1950] IR 195 and, generally, Johnston, *Banking and Security Law in Ireland*, (1998) Butterworths, paras [5.23]-[5.29].

[143.] This would be because notice of a court's order will terminate a bank's authority to pay on a cheque: see Richardson, *Guide to Negotiable Instruments*, (8th ed) Butterworths, para 16.13.

[144.] O'Connor, *The Law and Practice in Ireland Relating to Cheques and Analogous Instruments*, (1993) Institute of Bankers in Ireland, p 145.

[145.] See Keane, *op cit*, para 15.37.

[146.] On credit cards generally, see Donnelly, 'Credit Cards: The Law Relating to 'Your Flexible Friend'', (1997) CLP 75.

[147.] *Z Ltd v A* [1982] 1 All ER 556 at 563 *per* Lord Denning MR.

[148.] [1982] 1 All ER 556 at 576,577.

[149.] In *Z Ltd v A* [1982] 1 All ER 556 at 577, Kerr LJ said: "[where] ... the defendant ... might avoid the incidence of the order freezing his bank accounts by means of cheque and credit cards, in relation to which he would not be able easily to antedate the transactions in question, then the order should make it clear that it will not preclude the debiting of his account in respect of any such transactions effected by the defendant prior to the date when the order is served on the bank. However, once the bank has been served, it will no doubt consider it prudent to take steps to withdraw such facilities from the defendant in so far as it is in its power to do so."

the debiting of accounts in respect of transactions effected before the Mareva order is served, it is thought that such a distinction is wrong in principle. Irrespective of whether transactions are effected before or after a bank or other third party has been put on notice of the terms of a Mareva injunction, it will usually be the case that the agreement between the bank, the customer and the third-party retailer will contractually provide that the bank must pay the retailer. Moreover, the Mareva order itself will normally provide that the injunction does not prohibit the operation of set-off[150] between a defendant customer's accounts and in such circumstances the bank must be able to debit the defendant's account with the amount paid by the bank under the credit card agreement. There is nothing surprising about this as the result is no different to where a defendant does not have a bank account: where a defendant holds all his assets or goods in cash the success of a Mareva injunction is entirely dependant upon his complying with the court's order; a plaintiff cannot take comfort that a third party bank will enforce his order for him.

(iii) Bank guarantees, letters of credit and performance bonds

[9.51] Where a bank has provided a guarantee in respect of a defendant's debts to a third party or where it has given a letter of credit or performance bond, a Mareva injunction should not operate so as to prevent the bank from making payment on foot thereof and thereafter debiting the defendant's account.[151] On the other hand, where a Mareva defendant is the beneficiary of a guarantee, bond or letter of credit and payment is made on foot of such instrument, then, in the absence of a stipulation to the contrary, that payment made will be subject to the Mareva injunction.[152]

(iv) The operation of set-off

[9.52] Mareva orders often provide that "nothing in this Order shall prevent any bank from exercising any right of set-off which it may have in respect of facilities given to the defendants before the date of this order".[153] The only limitation on set-off, therefore, is set-off into an account which has a debit balance where the facility to overdraw that account was given to the customer *after* the date of the Mareva order.[154] Notwithstanding the view expressed by

---

[150.] See para **[9.52]** *infra*.

[151.] *Z Ltd v A* [1982] 1 All ER 556 at 563; *Intraco Ltd v Notis Shipping Corp* [1981] 2 Lloyd's Rep 256 and *Power Curber International Ltd v National Bank of Kuwait SAK* [1981] 3 All ER 607.

[152.] See Hapgood, *Paget's Law of Banking*, (11th ed, 1996) Butterworths, p 489-491.

[153.] Such was provided, for example, in the order made in *Clonmeen Manor House Ltd v Royal Lodge Ltd* High Court, unrep, 9 May 1994 (Costello J). See generally the specimen orders in Appendix 1.

[154.] Whilst "set-off provisos" typically reference "the date of the order", it is submitted that it is clear that a bank which sets off a credit account against a debit balance on an account where the facility to overdraw was only given after the making of the Mareva injunction cannot be prejudiced until such time as it has *notice* of the order.

Lloyd J in *Oceanica Castelana Armadora SA of Panama v Mineralimportexport*[155] that in the absence of this proviso a bank could not exercise set-off, it is thought that this was wrongly decided. It is submitted that where, in furtherance of its own interests, a bank or other financial institution exercises a contractual set-off or set-off by operation of law, in respect of a debit which predates the Order it could not be said that such a "disposal" of a defendant's funds was with a view to frustrate a future judgment or evade a defendant-customer's obligations to the plaintiff. It is thought in fact that set-off by a bank in these circumstances is not "a disposal" by a defendant at all, but rather the unilateral act of a defendant's creditor. Unilateral acts of a defendant's creditors are not within the rationale of the Mareva jurisdiction.

(v) The difficulties associated with "maximum sum" orders

[9.53] The widespread preference of the courts for maximum sum orders over general freezing orders has been considered earlier.[156] Notwithstanding that such orders operate to limit the hardship caused to a defendant by a Mareva injunction (and are more desirable than general freezing orders) compliance, by a bank, with a maximum-sum order is not without its complications. The problem for a bank when faced with a maximum sum order is that it will not know what other assets a defendant may have or the value of those assets so as to be able to say with confidence whether a particular withdrawal will have the effect of reducing a defendant's assets below the requisite amount.[157]

[9.54] Banks which are served with notice of a maximum sum Mareva injunction should, it is submitted, simply act without having regard to any other assets which the defendant may have eg if the maximum sum is say £100,000, a bank should not permit withdrawals from the defendant's account where such would reduce the amount in credit on that account to be less than £100,000. If a defendant has other assets worth say £50,000 it is open to him to apply to court for a variation of the order which would permit the bank to allow the credit on his account to be reduced to £50,000. Where a bank knows that at some time in the future it will acquire a right of set-off against a defendant's bank account it cannot "make provision" for this future eventuality by freezing in excess of the amount stated to be the maximum sum in the Mareva order.[158]

---

[155] [1983] 2 All ER 65.

[156] See para **[9.09]** *supra*.

[157] This matter was considered in *Z Ltd v A* [1982] 1 All ER 556 at 565a-e (Lord Denning MR) and at 574i-575f (Kerr LJ).

[158] In *Oceanica Castelana Armadora SA of Panama v Mineralimportexport* [1983] 2 All ER 65 this issue was considered by Lloyd J and it was found that, even where future set-off was likely, the Mareva order should only specify the lower amount. For comment, see Hapgood, *Paget's Law of Banking*, (11th ed, 1996) Butterworths, p 488,489.

Chapter 10

Ancillary Orders

[10.01] Although a Mareva injunction itself will always be relief ancillary to a substantive right or cause of action,[1] a Mareva plaintiff may sometimes need to apply for another ancillary order so as to make the Mareva injunction more effective. Perhaps the most obvious supplementary or ancillary orders are discovery and disclosure orders which oblige a defendant to disclose his assets to the plaintiff. The means may be by affidavit, interrogatories or cross-examination of a defendant. Sometimes the only effective means of preventing a defendant from disposing of his assets will be by taking action *in rem* against the assets and applying to appoint a receiver over the assets, as opposed to applying for an *in personam* Mareva order. It may, however, be possible to rely upon an *in personam* order, such as an Anton Piller order, whereby it is ordered that certain assets in a defendant's possession are to be delivered up. Where a plaintiff has already obtained judgment it may be appropriate to apply for a garnishee order or the appointment of a receiver by way of equitable execution.[2]

[10.02] In this chapter the following ancillary orders are considered:

1. Disclosure and Discovery Orders.
2. Disclosure by Interrogatories.
3. Cross-Examination of the Defendant.
4. Anton Piller Orders.
5. Delivery Up of Chattels.
6. Receivers.
7. Garnishee Orders.

Disclosure and Discovery Orders

[10.03] An order for discovery has long been available to a plaintiff who requires information from a defendant (and in some cases, a third party) in relation to matters which relate to the issues in the plaintiff's substantive cause of action against the defendant.[3] In the absence of voluntary discovery,[4]

[1.] See generally, Ch 4, *A Substantive Cause of Action*.

[2.] The remedy of civil arrest and injunctions to prevent defendants from leaving the jurisdiction are considered separately in Ch 11, *Restraining Defendants from Leaving the State*.

[3.] See Cahill, *Discovery in Ireland*, (1996) Roundhall Sweet & Maxwell, p 1 where "discovery" is defined as "a process generally available in civil proceedings whereby one party may, by way of certain pre-trial devices, obtain information in writing and on oath from the opposite party in the proceedings".

application for an order for discovery can be brought under Ord 31, r 12(1) of the Rules of the Superior Courts 1986 ("the RSC").[5] The difficulty for a Mareva plaintiff who wishes to compel a defendant to disclose the identity, value and whereabouts of his assets, is that discovery within the contemplation of the RSC is confined to documents "relating to any matter in question therein".[6] The particulars of a defendant's assets are not matters which relate to the matter in question: the matter in question is a plaintiff's substantive cause of action; particulars of a defendant's assets relate to the ancillary[7] Mareva injunction.[8] This point was made by Griffiths LJ in *AJ Bekhor & Co Ltd v Bilton*[9] when he said:

> "The phrases 'matters in question in the action' and 'matters in question ... in the cause or matter' have for generations been understood to refer to the issues to be decided in the litigation. The present existence and whereabouts of the defendant's wealth are not such an issue; they are relevant only to the defendant's ability to satisfy judgment if the 'matters in question in the action' are resolved in the plaintiff's favour. I therefore conclude that the judge had no power to order discovery pursuant to the rules of court and in so far as *A v C*[10] was founded on such a power it was wrongly decided."

Were it the case that the only authority for making an order for discovery was contained in Ord 31 of the RSC, then it is thought that to make an order for discovery to force a Mareva defendant to disclose his assets would involve straining the language used in Ord 31 to breaking point. At this point it is proposed to consider the following matters which arise in the context of discovery and disclosure of assets in aid of Mareva injunctions:

    (a) Disclosure in aid of proprietary claims distinguished;

    (b) Disclosure in aid of Mareva injunctions;

---

4. Under Ord 31, r 12(4), as inserted by SI 265/1993. A court order for compulsory discovery will not be made unless the applicant for same shall have previously requested voluntary discovery, provided that in any case where by reason of the urgency of the matter the court may order discovery.

5. See generally, O'Floinn, *Practice and Procedure in the Superior Courts*, (1996) Butterworths, pp 240-255.

6. See generally, Goldrein & Wilkinson, *Commercial Litigation: Pre-Emptive Remedies*, (2nd ed, 1991) Sweet & Maxwell, pp 238-242.

7. See *Caudron v Air Zaire* [1986] ILRM 10 considered in Ch 4, *A Substantive Cause of Action*, para **[4.06]** *et seq.*

8. *Cf* an injunction in respect of a proprietary claim of the sort considered in Ch 1, *The Mareva Injunction in Context*, para **[1.16]**. A distinction between Mareva claims and proprietary claims such as in a tracing action was made by Robert Goff J in *A v C* [1980] 2 All ER 347, considered in para **[10.04]** *infra.*

9. [1981] 2 All ER 565 at 582c.

10. [1980] 2 All ER 347.

(c) Disclosure of foreign assets;

(d) Disclosure orders against third parties;

(e) The privilege against self-incrimination;

(f) Orders under the Bankers' Books Evidence Acts 1879 to 1989.

(g) Section 908(3) of the Taxes Consolidation Act 1997

(a) Disclosure in aid of proprietary claims distinguished

[10.04] The application for an injunction where a plaintiff seeks to freeze assets to which he claims a proprietary interest has been distinguished[11] from an application for a Mareva injunction where a plaintiff will have no proprietary interest in the defendant's assets. Disclosure in aid of an injunction to protect a proprietary right or interest in assets can be brought under Ord 31 of the RSC where those assets are one of the matters in question. One of the first reported cases in which the matter arose was *A v C*,[12] the case mentioned in the extract of the judgment of Griffiths LJ in *AJ Bekhor & Co Ltd v Bilton* last quoted. In that case the plaintiffs alleged that they had been defrauded by the first five defendants who were all resident outside of the United Kingdom and, on foot of this, obtained an *ex parte* Mareva injunction. The plaintiffs also sued a sixth defendant - a bank - and sought to trace the sum of £383,872 which it was alleged the second plaintiff had paid into a third party's account with the bank. In addition to the Mareva relief and an ordinary injunction to restrain the disposal of the sum of £383,872, the plaintiffs obtained two disclosure orders from Robert Goff J. The first ordered the defendants to disclose the sums standing in accounts in their names or in the third party's name at the bank and the second ordered disclosure of the facts within the defendants' knowledge as to the whereabouts of the £383,872 if that sum was no longer in the third party's account at the bank. The two disclosure orders were subsequently suspended by a different judge but the plaintiffs reapplied to Robert Goff J who continued the injunctions and was left to consider whether the disclosure orders should be renewed. The defendants contended that the court had no power to make such disclosure orders for discovery or interrogatories ancillary to and in aid of a Mareva injunction.[13] In determining that the court had jurisdiction to make such

---

11. See Ch 1, *The Mareva Injunction in Context*, para **[1.16]**.
12. [1980] 2 All ER 347.
13. In the words of Robert Goff J (at 352), the defendants' counsel had contended "that to order discovery of documents or interrogatories in aid of the Mareva jurisdiction would constitute an unacceptable widening of that jurisdiction ... [and] ... an unwarranted invasion of the defendant's private affairs; it would really be taking what was no more than a first step in the process of execution; and it should be for the defendant to decide, not for the court to order, whether such information should be made available ...".

disclosure orders, the judge distinguished between a disclosure order in aid of a proprietary claim and a disclosure order in aid of a Mareva claim.

[10.05] In respect of the proprietary claim, Robert Goff J held that there was good authority for the proposition that the court may make an order for the purpose of ascertaining the whereabouts of a missing trust fund. Citing *London and County Securities Ltd v Caplan*[14] he noted that in that case an order was made which required a third party bank to produce the defendant's account statements to the plaintiff in order to enable the plaintiff to trace property which had been acquired by the defendant. Templeman J had said in that case that:

> "It is a case where, unless effective relief is granted, justice may well become impossible because the evidence and the fruits of crime and fraud may disappear."[15]

Robert Goff J went on to hold that:

> "... in an action in which the plaintiff seeks to trace property which in equity belongs to him, the court not only has jurisdiction to grant an injunction restraining the disposal of that property; it may, in addition ... make orders to ascertain the whereabouts of that property."[16]

Where it is sought to restrain a defendant from disposing of an asset at the centre of a proprietary claim, the appropriate application is for an injunction pursuant to Ord 50, r 4 of the RSC and not a Mareva injunction pursuant to Ord 50, r 6(1) of the RSC.[17] The juristic basis asserted by Robert Goff J in *A v C* for making a disclosure order in a proprietary claim was given as the inherent jurisdiction of the court. It is thought by the writer, however, that discovery as permitted by the RSC is available to a plaintiff pursuing a proprietary claim for breach of trust since there, the existence and whereabouts of the assets which the plaintiff is trying to trace, could surely be argued to be "relating to any matter in question therein".

Disclosure orders against third parties are also more readily granted in claims where a plaintiff seeks to protect a proprietary right or interest in, say, a trust fund. In *Re Murphy's Settlements; Murphy v Murphy*[18] Newberger J found that

---

14. English High Court, unrep, 26 May 1978, (Templeman J).
15. The case of *Mediterranea Reffineria Siciliana Petroli SpA v Mabanaft Gmbh* [1978] Court of Appeal Transcript 816 was also cited. There, the Court of Appeal upheld the validity of a disclosure order, Templeman LJ saying, *inter alia*,: "A court of equity has never hesitated to use the strongest powers to protect and preserve a trust fund in interlocutory proceedings on the basis that, if the trust fund disappears by the time the action comes to trial, equity will have been invoked in vain."
16. [1980] 2 All ER 347 at 351.
17. On the distinction between proprietary injunctions and Mareva injunctions, see Ch 1, *The Mareva Injunction in Context*, para **[1.16]**.
18. [1998] 3 All ER 1.

there was jurisdiction in equity to order a defendant, who was not otherwise an appropriate party in the proceedings, to identify the names and addresses of a third party, *inter alia*, in order to ascertain the whereabouts of a missing trust fund. The following passage is of interest:

> "However, even though no previous case has been found to show that the court has granted the relief of the sort claimed here to a potential beneficiary under a discretionary trust, no previous case has been cited, and no principle of equity has been invoked, to suggest that the court has no jurisdiction to grant such relief. Equity, it has been said, is not to be presumed to be of an age beyond child bearing (see (1951) 67 LQR 506). In so far as this case involved (as I accept that it does) extending the principle identified in *A v C*, I think that it is perhaps more a case of an existing child developing rather than a new child being born."[19]

(b) Disclosure in aid of Mareva injunctions

[10.06] In *A v C*[20] Robert Goff J also held that there was jurisdiction to make an order for discovery in aid of a Mareva injunction. After reviewing difficulties with the effectiveness of Mareva injunctions in the absence of specific information as to a defendant's assets he said that:

> "... the court should, where necessary, exercise its powers to order discovery or interrogatories in order to ensure that the Mareva jurisdiction is properly exercised and thereby to secure its objective which is ... the prevention of abuse. That the court has power to order discovery of particular documents and interrogatories at an early stage of proceedings is, I think, not in doubt ... If necessary, however, the court's power to make an appropriate order in aid of a Mareva injunction can be derived from the power to make mandatory orders conferred on the court by s 45 of the Supreme Court of Judicature (Consolidation) Act 1925 ... If the court were to deny itself the right to exercise this jurisdiction in aid of the Mareva injunction, it could prevent the Mareva jurisdiction from being effective to achieve its purpose...".[21]

While relying in part on the discovery provisions in the Rules, the judge also relied upon the power of the court to make such orders as it considers "just or convenient" as provided in Ireland by s 28(8) of the Supreme Court of Judicature Ireland Act 1877 and Ord 50, r 6 of the RSC to order the disclosure of a defendant's assets in aid of Mareva injunctions.

[10.07] The decision of Robert Goff J came in for some criticism by the Court of Appeal in *AJ Bekhor & Co Ltd v Bilton*.[22] There it was held that orders for

---

[19.] At 10d-e.
[20.] [1980] 2 All ER 347.
[21.] At 351, 352.
[22.] [1981] 2 All ER 565 at 582c.

discovery and interrogatories,[23] as an aid to Mareva injunctions, could not be made under the Rules of the Supreme Court because the orders could not relate to "matters in question in the action" or "matters in question in the cause or matter".[24] However, it was held that such orders could be made under s 45(1) of the English Supreme Court of Judicature (Consolidation) Act 1925[25] because since there was power to make a Mareva order, it implicitly followed that there was jurisdiction to make all ancillary orders which were necessary to ensure the effectiveness of a Mareva injunction.

[10.08] In *AJ Bekhor & Co Ltd v Bilton*[26] Ackner LJ said:

> "… it is now clearly established that the power of the High Court under s 45(1) includes the power to grant an interlocutory injunction to restrain a party to any proceedings from removing from the jurisdiction or otherwise dealing with assets located within the jurisdiction … To my mind there must be *inherent in that power* the power to make all such ancillary orders as appears to the court to be just and convenient to ensure that the exercise of the Mareva jurisdiction is effective to achieve its purpose."[27]

Stephenson LJ found that the jurisdiction to make a disclosure order lay in the court's inherent jurisdiction. However, like Griffith LJ he found that the trial judge, Parker J, had gone too far:

> "Parker J described the plaintiffs' application and his order for discovery as in aid or support of the Mareva injunction and so in a sense they were. But in so far as they relate to the defendant's assets at past dates as distinct from their present whereabouts their purpose seems to be not so much to help the court or the defendant to locate and 'freeze' particular assets now as to open the way to incriminating and ultimately punishing the defendant for contempt of court in formerly disobeying the Mareva injunction and/or breaking his undertaking … To that extent the order goes beyond the legitimate purpose of an order for discovery in aid of a Mareva injunction and Robert Goff J's order in *A v C* and is not necessary for the proper and effective exercise of the Mareva injunction."[28]

In *AJ Bekhor & Co Ltd v Bilton* the plaintiffs had obtained a Mareva injunction against the defendant, but later, on the defendant's undertaking not to remove £250,000 from the jurisdiction it was varied to allow him to remove his car, some personal possessions and £1,250 per month. In a subsequent application

---

[23.] See para **[10.36]** *infra*.

[24.] See the passage from the judgment of Griffiths LJ quoted at para **[10.03]** *supra*.

[25.] Which is in all material respects for these purposes identical to s 28(8) of the Supreme Court of Judicature (Ireland) Act 1877: see Ch 2, *The Jurisdiction to Grant Mareva Relief*, para **[2.02]**.

[26.] [1981] 2 All ER 565.

[27.] [1981] 2 All ER 565 at 576.

[28.] [1981] 2 All ER 565 at 586, 587.

for variation of the order, it was discovered that, contrary to his undertaking, the defendant had reduced his assets by £66,000 since the granting of the injunction and did not have assets which would produce an income of £15,000; the court had permitted him to remove funds from the jurisdiction for living expenses on the understanding that these funds would come from income as opposed to capital. It was against this background that the plaintiff applied for the disclosure orders and it can thus be seen that the order granted by Parker J was to enable the plaintiff to "police" the existing Mareva injunction.

[10.09] So what of the jurisdiction to make an asset disclosure order in aid of a Mareva claim in Ireland? It was recognised by Murphy J in *Countyglen plc v Carway*[29] that the Irish courts do indeed have the jurisdiction to make disclosure orders ancillary to Mareva injunctions. In that case he said:

> "With regard to discovery, there is no doubt as to the power of the Court to make an order for discovery as ancillary to a Mareva injunction. In my view, it is desirable that such an affidavit should be sworn in the present case. However, it seems to me that the order in that behalf should be restricted, like the injunction itself, to the assets of the defendants within the jurisdiction of this Court."[30]

In *MM v DD*[31] Moriarty J noted that *AJ Bekhor & Co Ltd v Bilton*[32] demonstrated that a court may be willing to grant an asset disclosure order (similar to the kind of order which can be made under s 9 of the Proceeds of Crime Act 1996) "... even in the absence of an express statutory power ...".[33]

[10.10] The practice of the Irish High Court, as gleaned from newspaper reports of successful applications clearly shows that disclosure orders are made in aid of Mareva injunctions, compulsory orders,[34] orders on consent[35] and even "policing" type orders.[36] As in the case of "traditional discovery", where it is ordered that a company or other body corporate make discovery, the order can

---

[29]. [1995] 1 IR 208.

[30]. At 218.

[31]. High Court, unrep, 10 December 1996 (Moriarty J).

[32]. [1981] 2 All ER 565.

[33]. At p 7 of the transcript.

[34]. In *Unitas Investments Ltd, The Irish Times*, 26 October 1991 (Carroll J) it was reported that a company and two directors were restrained from dealing with certain moneys and that there were orders for discovery of assets and documentation.

[35]. In *Irish Press Newspapers Ltd v Malocco & Killeen, The Irish Times*, 8 October 1991, it was reported that Mr Malocco consented to the making of a Mareva injunction and also that he agreed to discover on oath the whereabouts of all money paid to him by the plaintiff and to an order to discover on oath his assets.

[36]. In *Re Mark Synnott (Life and Pensions) Brokers Ltd, The Irish Times*, 27 June 1991 (Lardner J) it was reported that three directors of a company were directed by the High Court to swear an affidavit on the whereabouts of their assets for the purpose of "policing" Mareva injunctions which had been granted previously.

be directed at its directors or other officers and require them to make disclosure.[37]

(c) Disclosure of foreign assets

[10.11] The question of whether a court will order a defendant to make disclosure of his foreign assets is intrinsically linked to the court's power to make an *ex juris* or "worldwide" Mareva injunction.[38] In *Ashtiani v Kashi*[39] the plaintiffs had obtained an order which obliged the defendant to disclose the whereabouts of his assets both within and outside the jurisdiction. The plaintiffs, who had already obtained a domestic Mareva injunction in the United Kingdom, acted on the basis of what had been disclosed and obtained Mareva-type orders in those jurisdictions in which the defendant had disclosed he had assets. There, Dillon LJ said:

> "The disclosure of foreign assets cannot be regarded as ancillary to the making of a Mareva injunction limited to the English assets. It cannot stand on its own feet as a primary exercise of jurisdiction if the Mareva exercise is limited to English assets ...".[40]

Indeed, a similar view is seen in the extract from the judgment of Murphy J in *Countyglen plc v Carway*[41] quoted above. Of course, the reasoning of the Court of Appeal in *Ashtiani v Kashi* in the context of disclosure orders was coloured by their belief that there was no jurisdiction to make a worldwide Mareva order. Once it was accepted that, in appropriate circumstances, a worldwide Mareva injunction could be made,[42] the way was open to make disclosure orders

---

[37.] In *Re Holbern Investments Trust Ltd*, *The Irish Times*, 9 October 1991 (Barron J), it was reported that a person who it was claimed was the managing director of a company was ordered by the High Court to make a full discovery of both his own and the company's assets and liabilities; a Mareva injunction preventing the company, the managing director and his wife from reducing their assets below £300,000 had earlier been made.

[38.] See generally, Ch 7, *The Defendant's Assets*, para **[7.21]** *et seq*.

[39.] [1986] 2 All ER 970.

[40.] At 977, 978. Neill LJ said (at 980): "It seems to me that in the present state of the law the only basis for such an order is that it is made in aid of and ancillary to an injunction in the Mareva form. The power to order discovery exists, but it is a power which exists to make the injunction effective. It seems to me to follow that, at any rate *prima facie*, discovery should be limited, firstly, to the ascertainment of assets which will be covered by the Mareva order (in other words, the ascertainment of assets within the jurisdiction), and secondly, at a later stage, to enable the court to consider any application by the party enjoined to vary the Mareva injunction ... as the scope of a Mareva injunction is restricted to assets within the jurisdiction ... any discovery in aid of the Mareva should be similarly so restricted."

[41.] [1995] 1 IR 208 at 218; see para **[10.09]** *supra*.

[42.] In England: in *Babanaft International Co SA v Bassatne* [1989] 1 All ER 433; [1989] 2 WLR 232; *Republic of Haiti v Duvallier* [1989] 1 All ER 456, [1989] 2 WLR 261; *Derby & Co Ltd v Weldon (No 1)* [1989] 1 All ER 469, [1989] 2 WLR 276; and in Ireland: *Deutsche Bank Aktiengesellschaft v Murtagh & Murtagh* [1995] 2 IR 122 and *Taher v Balkanbank* (1995) High Court, unrep, 29 March 1995 (Barr J), *The Irish Times*, 30 March 1995; and *Clonmeen Manor House Ltd v Royal Lodge Ltd* (1994) High Court (Costello J), *The Irish Times*, 31 March 1994. See Ch 7, *The Defendant's Assets*, para **[7.51]** *et seq*.

regarding foreign assets in aid of such injunctions. So in *Deutsche Bank Aktiengesellschaft v Murtagh & Murtagh*[43] Costello J said:

> "In my opinion the court has jurisdiction to restrain the dissipation of extra-territorial assets where such an order is warranted by the facts. The basis on which a Mareva injunction is granted is to ensure that a defendant does not take action designed to frustrate subsequent orders of the court. It is well established in England that a Mareva injunction may extend to foreign assets and I believe that the Irish courts have a similar power in order to avoid the frustration of subsequent orders it may make. The court has ancillary power also and in suitable cases it may grant a disclosure order requiring a defendant to swear an affidavit in respect of assets outside the jurisdiction (see *Derby & Co Ltd v Weldon (Nos 3 and 4)*[44] [1989] 2 WLR 412."[45]

[10.12] On other occasions also the Irish High Court has ordered defendants to make disclosure of their foreign assets. Such an example is provided by *Balkanbank v Taher*[46] where, in making a worldwide Mareva injunction, Barr J's order[47] also provided:

> "That the plaintiff [against which the Mareva injunction was made] do forthwith disclose the full value of its assets within and without the jurisdiction of this court identifying with full particularity the nature of all such assets and their whereabouts and whether the same be held in its own name or by nominees or otherwise and the sum standing in such account such disclosures to be verified by affidavits to be made on the said plaintiff's behalf and served upon the solicitors for the defendants within 21 days."

Just as the court will exercise sparingly its jurisdiction to grant a worldwide Mareva injunction, so too will it be slow to order that a defendant disclose his assets which are situate outside of the jurisdiction.

(d) Disclosure orders against third parties

[10.13] It is one thing to say that a Mareva injunction should never be made against a true "third party",[48] it is another thing entirely to say that there is jurisdiction to compel third parties to disclose information. "Traditional discovery" against third parties is facilitated by Ord 31, r 29 of the RSC, a relatively new rule which was only introduced by the revision of the RSC in 1986.[49] The discretion to make third-party "traditional discovery" (ie in the

---

[43] [1995] 2 IR 122.
[44] *Sub nom Derby & Co Ltd v Weldon (No 2)* [1989] 1 All ER 1002.
[45] [1995] 2 IR 122 at 131.
[46] *The Irish Times*, 30 March 1995.
[47] The writer acknowledges with gratitude the assistance given by Mr Bryan F Fox, solicitor (who instructed Mr Connor Maguire SC) who made available a copy of Barr J's order.
[48] See Ch 4, *A Substantive Cause of Action*, para **[4.14]** *et seq*.
[49] See, generally, O'Floinn, *Practice and Procedure in the Superior Courts*, (1996) Butterworths, pp 254, 255 and Cahill, *Discovery in Ireland*, (1996) Roundhall Sweet & Maxwell, p 20-24.

course of normal proceedings) is exercised very sparingly;[50] and third party disclosure orders in aid of Mareva injunctions will only be made in exceptional circumstances. Where a defendant complies with an order for disclosure of his assets there will generally be little need for a disclosure order against third parties. One circumstance when a court might be persuaded to make a third party disclosure order in aid of a Mareva injunction is where the defendant refuses or claims some inability to comply with a disclosure order and make an affidavit disclosing the whereabouts of his assets. Equally, if a defendant is successful in invoking the privilege against self-incrimination as a defence to an application for disclosure, it may, in these circumstances, be appropriate instead to obtain from a third party the information necessary to make effective a Mareva injunction.

[10.14] In *Norwich Pharmacal Co v Customs and Excise Commissioners*[51] it was held by the House of Lords that there was jurisdiction to make a discovery order against a third-party for the purpose of identifying persons against whom a plaintiff might have a cause of action.[52] It was said by Hoffmann LJ in *Mercantile Group (Europe) AG v Aiyela*[53] that:

> "The effect of this decision, as expounded in later cases, is that jurisdiction to order disclosure against a third party exists when two conditions are satisfied. First, the third party must have become mixed up in the transaction concerning which discovery is required. Secondly, the order for discovery must not offend against the 'mere witness' rule, which prevents a party from obtaining discovery against a person who 'will in due course be compellable to give that information either by oral testimony as a witness or on a *subpoena duces tecum*'".[54]

The Supreme Court approved of the principle in the *Norwich Pharmacal* case in *Megaleasing UK Ltd v Vincent Barrett*,[55] although in that particular case it found that there were insufficient grounds to make such an order; it was held that such an order would only issue where there exists very clear proof of wrongdoing and where the purpose of the order is to discover the identities of wrongdoers as

---

50. See *Holloway v Belenos Publications Ltd* [1987] IR 405; *Allied Irish Banks plc v Ernst & Whinney* [1993] 1 IR 375; and *Fusco v O'Dea* [1994] 2 IR 93.
51. [1974] AC 133.
52. In *Re Murphy's Settlements; Murphy v Murphy* [1998] 3 All ER 1 Neuberger J held that there was jurisdiction to order a person, who was not otherwise an appropriate party to the proceedings, to identify the names and addresses of a third party, (a) where there was "wrongdoing" and (b) in equity, in order to ascertain the whereabouts of a missing trust fund: *Chaine-Nickson v Bank of Ireland* [1976] IR 393 cited.
53. [1994] 1 All ER 110.
54. At 115, quoting Lord Reid in the *Norwich Pharmacal* case at 173, 174.
55. [1993] ILRM 497.

opposed to evidence concerning the wrong they have committed. More recently in *IO'T v B; MH v Father Gerard Doyle and Rotunda Aid Girls School*[56] Hamilton CJ emphasised that it is "not a precondition to the granting of the relief that the persons against whom it is sought should themselves have been guilty of any wrongdoing."[57] It remains the case, however, that the defendant must be guilty of some "wrongdoing" in order to invoke the jurisdiction of the court to make a *Norwich Pharmacal* order. There is one exception to this in Ireland: Hamilton CJ found that the need to establish some wrongdoing was obviated in a case where a plaintiff sought to vindicate a constitutional right.[58]

[10.15] It would appear that different considerations may apply to third party asset disclosure orders in aid of post-judgment Mareva injunctions. In *Mercantile Group (Europe) AG v Aiyela and Ors*[59] the first defendant had admitted liability to the plaintiff and undertook to pay US$2.2m on foot of which the plaintiff abandoned actions against him, his wife and the other defendants; notwithstanding this, only US$388,000 was paid. The plaintiff then entered judgment for US$1.8m as it was entitled to do pursuant to the earlier agreement wherein the defendant admitted liability. The plaintiff then obtained a Mareva injunction which "froze" the first defendant's assets and also an order against his wife obliging her to disclose financial information about herself and her husband. After granting a worldwide Mareva injunction against the first defendant and also restraining the wife from disposing of her own assets, the wife applied to have the orders made against her discharged on grounds that there was no jurisdiction to make them since no judgment had been obtained against her. It was held, *inter alia*, by the Court of Appeal that there was jurisdiction to make a disclosure order against the first defendant's wife. Hoffmann LJ reviewed the *Norwich Pharmacal* case and the so-called "mere witness" rule, and said:

> "In the case of discovery against a third party in aid of a post-judgment Mareva, the mere witness rule can have no relevance. The trial, if any, will already have taken place. It follows that all that is necessary to found jurisdiction is that the third party should have become mixed up in the transaction concerning which discovery is required and, of course, that the court should consider it 'just and convenient' to make the order. The court will naturally exercise with care a jurisdiction which invades the privacy of an innocent third party. But this is a matter to be taken into account in the exercise of the discretion. It does not go to the existence of the jurisdiction."[60]

[56.] Supreme Court, unrep, 3 April 1998.
[57.] At p 57 of the transcript.
[58.] At p 58, 59 of the transcript.
[59.] [1994] 1 All ER 110.
[60.] At 115g-h.

[10.16] In *Bankers' Trust Co v Shapira*[61] a disclosure order was granted against a third party bank in aid of a proprietary tracing claim, as opposed to a Mareva claim. The Court of Appeal made it clear that such an order would only ever be justified where the evidence in favour of making it is very strong.[62] Where the third party is a bank, by reason of the long established relationship of confidentiality which exists between it and its customer, extreme prudence should be exercised when complying with any such order of the court and the wording of the order strictly construed.[63] In *Larkins v NUM*[64] Barrington J made an inspection order against a bank which, because it went further than would have been permitted by the Bankers' Books Evidence Acts 1879-1989, would appear to have amounted to the exercise of the court's inherent authority to make an order in aid of a Mareva injunction.[65]

(e) Privilege against self-incrimination

[10.17] The law has long recognised that an individual should not be obliged to answer questions which may tend to incriminate him in possible future criminal proceedings.[66] The privilege has been raised by Mareva defendants in Ireland against whom asset disclosure orders have been made.[67] Although some orders for the disclosure of a defendant's assets can be very widely drafted, it is thought that where no more than the nature and whereabouts of assets are sought, the privilege against self-incrimination should provide little defence to a defendant seeking to avoid such disclosure. In *Sociedade Nacional de Combustiveis de Angola UEE v Lundqvist*[68] the plaintiffs obtained Mareva injunctions, Anton Piller orders and disclosure orders, the latter which, *inter alia*, required the defendants to disclose on affidavit the value and whereabouts of their worldwide

---

[61.] [1980] 3 All ER 353. See also *A v C* [1980] 2 All ER 347.

[62.] Lord Denning MR said (at 356): "This new jurisdiction must, of course, be carefully exercised. It is a strong thing to order a bank to disclose the state of its customer's account and the documents and correspondence relating to it. It should only be done when there is a good ground for thinking the money in the bank is the plaintiff's money, as for instance when the customer has got the money by fraud, or other wrongdoing, and paid it into his account at the bank."

[63.] See, generally, Johnston, *Banking and Security Law in Ireland*, (1998) Butterworths at Ch 3.

[64.] [1985] IR 671.

[65.] See para **[10.31]** *infra*.

[66.] See Hogan & Whyte, *Kelly: The Irish Constitution*, (3rd ed, 1994) Butterworths, pp 593,594 where it is considered whether the privilege against self incrimination is a constitutional or common law right, the focus being on criminal law.

[67.] See, eg, *Bank of Ireland v K*, *The Irish Times*, 22 and 29 July 1997 (O'Sullivan J). There, the plaintiff had obtained a Mareva injunction restraining the defendant, a former employee, from reducing his assets below £500,000. It was reported that the defendant's counsel objected to certain asset disclosure orders on the grounds that such "might infringe upon his client's constitutional and legal rights".

[68.] [1990] 3 All ER 283.

assets. The plaintiffs' cause of action against the defendants alleged a conspiracy to defraud. It was held by the Court of Appeal that to require the defendants to disclose the *value* of their assets might assist in forming a link in the chain of proof of a criminal charge against them and to this extent struck down that aspect of the disclosure order. As Staughton LJ said:

> "Suppose, for example, that [the first-defendant] has US $88m worth of assets overseas. I do not doubt that a prosecutor would wish to prove this on a charge of conspiracy to defraud. No doubt he would wish to prove, if he could, that [the first defendant] was not a man of means before [the date of the alleged fraud], and did not have any other source of such wealth between [the date of the alleged fraud] and the present date. But his present assets, if of that order, would unquestionably be material for the jury to consider, as one link in the chain."[69]

However, Staughton LJ held that the privilege against self-incrimination would not be infringed by requiring the defendants to disclose the *nature* and *situation* of their assets because, the judge believed such information to be innocuous and did not see "reasonable grounds to apprehend danger to [the first defendant] if it is disclosed".[70] In *MM v DD*[71] Moriarty J rejected the view that the disclosure of assets could not amount to self-incrimination; it had been argued that the disclosure of assets merely facilitated an assessment of the amount to be recovered from a defendant who had benefited from drug trafficking. It is significant, however, that there it was the Proceeds of Crime Act 1996 which was in question: the very basis of which requires a strong suspicion that the defendant was engaged in criminal activity. In the case of civil asset disclosure orders in aid of Mareva relief it is opined that it is certainly not the case that the disclosure of the nature, whereabouts and even value of his assets will invariably lead to a defendant incriminating himself.

[10.18] It will often be possible to protect a defendant by requiring an undertaking from a plaintiff, which strictly delimits the use and circulation of information obtained about a defendant's assets. *Sociedade Nacional de Combustiveis de Angola UEE v Lundqvist*[72] demonstrates the importance of a plaintiff's undertakings not to use information obtained through disclosure of assets in any way as might infringe a defendant's privilege against self-incrimination. In that case, the plaintiffs' undertakings not to use the information thereby obtained to obtain further information by commencing proceedings in foreign courts against the defendants or third parties such as

---

[69] At 292g.
[70] At 292j. See also *Tate Access Floors Inc v Boswell* [1990] 3 All ER 303.
[71] High Court, unrep, 10 December 1996 (Moriarty J).
[72] [1990] 3 All ER 283.

banks, was highly relevant to disallowing the claim of privilege to the order for disclosure of the nature and situation of the defendants' assets.

[10.19] In Ireland, the use of a plaintiff's undertaking would also appear to be the primary means by which the privilege against self-incrimination can be reconciled with disclosure orders. In *MM v DD*[73] an application brought by the Criminal Assets Bureau for an asset disclosure order pursuant to s 9 of the Proceeds of Crime Act 1996[74] was met with the claim that, if granted, the relief would offend against the respondent's privilege against self-incrimination. Moriarty J noted the Court's inherent power to order disclosure of assets in aid of a civil Mareva injunction[75] and that it had been held in the United Kingdom that there was power to make such an order ancillary to a restraint order under s 77 of the UK's Criminal Justice Act 1988. By contrast, the Proceeds of Crime Act 1996 provided for an express statutory power to make a disclosure order. Moriarty J accepted,[76] in the context of a disclosure order made under the Proceeds of Crime Act 1996, that the disclosure of assets could amount to self-incrimination, but he found that the respondent could be protected by an undertaking from the office of the Director of Public Prosecutions. In this regard Moriarty J cited *Istel Ltd v Tully*[77] which concerned a civil disclosure order in aid of an Anton Piller order[78] and noted that there, the House of Lords had allowed a disclosure order to stand on the basis that the Crown Prosecution Service gave the plaintiff a letter confirming that it undertook not to profit from any disclosure in the civil proceedings and would only rely on evidence independently obtained.

[10.20] The stance taken by Moriarty J was followed by McGuinness J in *Gilligan v The Criminal Assets Bureau.*[79] There, the constitutionality of the Proceeds of Crime Act 1996 ("the 1996 Act") was challenged on the grounds, *inter alia*, that it infringed the privilege against self-incrimination or "the right to silence". McGuinness J quoted extensively from Moriarty J's judgment in *MM v DD* and also noted that it had been held by the Supreme Court in *Heaney v Ireland*[80] that the privilege was not absolute. McGuinness J indicated that it would always be necessary to require an undertaking not to profit from the disclosure when making an order under s 9 of the 1996 Act.[81] An undertaking

---

[73.] High Court, unrep, 10 December 1996 (Moriarty J).
[74.] See Ch 3, *Statutory Jurisdictions to Freeze Assets*, para **[3.31]** *et seq.*
[75.] As expounded in *AJ Bekhor Ltd v Bilton* [1981] 2 All ER 565: see para **[10.08]** *supra.*
[76.] Thereby refusing to follow the contrary view of Leggett LJ in *Re Thomas (Disclosure Order)* [1992] 4 All ER 814.
[77.] [1993] AC 45.
[78.] See para **[10.38]** *et seq, infra.*
[79.] High Court, unrep, 26 June 1997.
[80.] [1996] 1 IR 580.
[81.] See further Ch 3, *Statutory Jurisdictions to Freeze Assets*, para **[3.43]**.

from a plaintiff in whose favour a civil asset disclosure order is made, not to disclose the information thus obtained to any other person, would, it is submitted achieve the same end.

[10.21] The principles of law applicable to a claim of privilege against self-incrimination by a defendant against whom an order for discovery has been made were usefully set out by Staughton LJ in *Sociedade Nacional de Combustiveis de Angola UEE v Lundqvist*.[82] He considered that the discernible theme running through the cases on the privilege against self-incrimination was that stated by Cockburn CJ in *R v Boyes*[83] as being:

> "... the court must see, from the circumstances of the case and the nature of the evidence which the witness is called to give, that there is reasonable ground to apprehend danger to the witness from his being compelled to answer."

For Staughton LJ the substance of the test was that there must be *reasonable* grounds - as opposed to *fanciful* grounds - to apprehend danger of a criminal prosecution. He then observed[84] that the following points emerged from the authorities:

(i) "the affidavit claiming privilege is not conclusive ...";[85]

(ii) "the deponent is not bound to go into detail, if to do so would itself deprive him of protection ...";[86]

(iii) "... if the fact of the witness being in danger be once made to appear, great latitude should be allowed to him in judging for himself of the effect of any particular question ...";[87]

(iv) "the privilege is not available where the witness is already at risk, and the risk would not be increased if he were required to answer ...";[88] and

(v) "If it is one step, having a tendency to incriminate him, he is not compelled to answer"[89] "... as it is one link in a chain of proof".[90]

---

[82]. [1990] 3 All ER 283.

[83]. [1861-73] All ER Rep 172 at 174; (1861) 1 B & s 311 at 330.

[84]. [1990] 3 All ER 283 at 292a-e. In the interests of clarity the dictum is broken down into point form and the authorities for the points are footnoted.

[85]. *R v Boyes* [1861-73] All ER Rep 172 at 174; *Ex p Reynolds* [1881-5] All ER Rep 997, (1882) 20 Ch D 294; *Kahn v Kahn* [1982] 2 All ER 60.

[86]. *Short v Mercier* (1851) 3 Mac & G 205 at 217; *Rio Tinto Zinc Corp v Westinghouse Electric Corp* [1978] 1 All ER 434 at 465.

[87]. *R v Boyes* [1861-73] All ER Rep 172; *Rio Tinto Zinc Corp v Westinghouse Electric Corp* [1978] 1 All ER 434; *Kahn v Kahn* [1982] 2 All ER 60.

[88]. *Brebner v Perry* [1961] SASR 177; *Rio Tinto Zinc Corp v Westinghouse Electric Corp* [1978] 1 All ER 434.

[89]. *Paxton v Douglas* (1809) 16 Ves 239 at 242.

[90]. *Paxton v Douglas* (1812) 19 Ves 225 at 227.

Clearly, the circumstances of each case and, in particular the nature of the plaintiff's substantive cause of action against the defendant will be relevant to whether a plea of privilege against self-incrimination will succeed.[91] Where fraud underpins the cause of action such a plea may be more likely to succeed than where a disclosure order is sought in aid of a Mareva injunction in respect of, say, a breach of contract.

[10.22] Staughton LJ's judgment in *Sociedade Nacional de Combustiveis de Angola UEE v Lundqvist*[92] was considered by the English Court of Appeal in *Den Norse Bank ASA v Antonatos and Anor.*[93] In that case the Court of Appeal upheld the first-defendant's plea of privilege against self-incrimination in resisting disclosing certain of his assets. The facts were that the plaintiff had employed the first-defendant as manager of its Greek shipping finance business. Upon hearing allegations that the first-defendant had taken bribes and had induced the plaintiff by lies to make loans to third parties to buy ships at inflated prices, the plaintiff applied for and obtained an *ex parte* Mareva injunction and an order which required the first-defendant to disclose his assets to the plaintiff's solicitors. A "supervising solicitor" was appointed to assist in the enforcement of the order. The order also provided that the first defendant was to provide the requisite information to the plaintiff's solicitors and, if he claimed privilege to any other information, he was to supply this to the supervising solicitor who would hold it to the order of the court. The first defendant provided some information on sworn affidavit but resisted giving information on "specific assets" in respect of which he invoked the privilege against self-incrimination. The judge allowed the plaintiff's application to cross-examine the first-defendant, electing to deal with any questions of privilege as they arose. When the first defendant asserted his right of privilege against self-incrimination Steel J directed that he should answer the questions on the basis that where the court was concerned with whether a bribe has been taken, the offence was complete when the bribe was taken, and that what had happened to the money involved was immaterial and, therefore, nothing which was being asked would tend to increase the first-defendant's existing risk of prosecution. This finding was reversed by the Court of Appeal. After reviewing many of the

---

[91.] In *Bank of Ireland v K, The Irish Times*, 29 July 1997 an *ex parte* Mareva injunction, granted earlier, preventing the defendant bank official from reducing his assets below £500,000 was extended. The defendant's counsel is reported as having expressed his concern that certain disclosure orders might infringe his client's constitutional and legal rights and the plaintiff's counsel is reported as having said that such privilege should be claimed on affidavit. O'Sullivan J is reported as having made an order directing that there should be an affidavit in relation to the discovery.

[92.] [1990] 3 All ER 283.

[93.] [1998] 3 All ER 74.

established authorities on the privilege against self-incrimination Waller LJ held:

> "... it is not simply the risk of prosecution. A witness is entitled to claim the privilege in relation to any piece of information or evidence on which the prosecution might with to rely in establishing guilt. And, as it seems to me, it also applies to any piece of information or evidence on which the prosecution would wish to rely in making its decision whether to prosecute or not."[94]

It was, however, held that the appeal against Steel J's ruling to allow cross-examination should be dismissed as the plaintiff had justifiable concerns as to whether there had been breaches of the injunction.

[10.23] Where a defendant is likely to be charged with conversion under s 20 of the Larceny Act 1916, and the more obscure offences of conversion by trustee,[95] obtaining advances on the property of a principal, being a factor,[96] larceny of wills[97] or larceny of documents of title to land and other legal documents[98] regard should be had to s 43(2) of the Larceny Act 1916 in seeking any order for disclosure in aid of a Mareva injunction. That section provides that:

> No person shall be liable to be convicted of any offence against sections six, seven subsection (1), twenty, twenty-one, and twenty-two of this Act upon any evidence whatever in respect of any act done by him, if at any time previously to his being charged with such offence he has first disclosed such act on oath, in consequence of any compulsory process of any court of law or equity in any action, suit, or proceeding which has been bona fide instituted by any person aggrieved.

This does not mean that a straightforward disclosure of the existence and whereabouts of a defendant's assets will preclude his conviction of an offence mentioned in s 43(2). The effect of this provision is that a person shall not be convicted "upon any evidence whatever in respect of any act done by him, if at any time previously to his being charged with such offence he has first disclosed such act on oath." While it will clearly depend upon all surrounding circumstances, to merely disclose the location and amount of his assets, should not necessarily involve the disclosure of an "act done by him". It is submitted that the effect of s 43(2) of the 1916 Act is that a defendant may not invoke the privilege against self-incrimination where the likelihood is that the only offence which he will be charged with is conversion under s 20 of the 1916 Act or any of the other offences listed in s 43(2). Since, if he discloses the act on oath, he

---

94. [1998] 3 All ER 74 at 89a-b.
95. Section 21 of the Larceny Act 1916.
96. Section 22 of the Larceny Act 1916.
97. Section 6 of the Larceny Act 1916.
98. Section 7 of the Larceny Act 1916.

cannot be convicted of those offences, it follows that there is no risk of prosecution by making disclosure.

[10.24] The privilege against self-incrimination was comprehensively considered by Shanley J in *Re National Irish Bank Ltd (Under Investigation)*.[99] In that case two inspectors were appointed by the High Court on the application of the Minister for Enterprise, Trade and Employment pursuant to s 8(1) of the Companies Act 1990 to investigate and report on the affairs of National Irish Bank Ltd (NIB). The matter for decision was, *inter alia*, whether persons from whom information, documents or evidence was sought by the inspectors were entitled to refuse to answer questions or provide documents to the inspectors on the grounds that the answers or documents might tend to incriminate them. Although Shanley J's judgment was specifically concerned with s 10 of the Companies Act 1990 he found, *inter alia*, that even though a person might have answered self-incriminatory questions, it did not follow that his trial would be other than in due course of law. The following passage is very relevant to the assessment of any claim of this privilege in the context of any disclosure order:

> "When asked questions by an inspector, the witness does not stand as an accused person. If he becomes an accused person, having answered incriminating questions, the right to a fair trial may not even at that stage be infringed: it depends on whether the compelled testimony is tendered against him at his trial; if it is, he may, of course, object to it and it would be a matter for the trial judge to determine its admissibility. It is at that stage, and no sooner, that an adjudication on the admissibility of answers (or the fruits of such answers) is to be made. I therefore see no necessary connection between the occasion of questioning by an inspector and the occasion, at trial, of tendering compelled testimony."[100]

It is submitted that it is within a court's power to require a defendant to disclose information on his assets for the sole purpose of ensuring the effectiveness of a Mareva injunction while, at the same time, ensuring not only that such information is rendered inadmissible at any criminal trial, but not even disclosed to the gardaí or office of the Director of Public Prosecutions. When coupled with the use of suitable undertakings, it is thought that this may be a compelling reason to reject a defendant's plea of privilege to avoid disclosure of his assets.

(f) Orders under the Bankers' Books Evidence Acts 1879-1989[101]

[10.25] The Bankers' Books Evidence Acts 1879-1989, as amended, *inter alia*,[102] empower a court to make an order for the inspection and copying of

---

[99.] High Court, unrep, 13 July 1998 (Shanley J).

[100.] At p 28 of the transcript.

[101.] Section 141 of the Central Bank Act 1989 prescribes the title of these Acts.

[102.] The other main provision of the Bankers' Books Evidence Act 1879 concerns proof of contents of bankers' books: see Hapgood, *op cit*, pp 498-499.

entries in bankers' books by a party in any legal proceedings.[103] Section 7 of the 1879 Act provides:

> On the application of any party to a legal proceeding a court or judge may order that such party be at liberty to inspect and take copies of any entries in a bankers' book for any of the purposes of such proceedings. An order under this section may be made either with or without summoning the bank or any other party, and shall be served on the bank three clear days before the same is to be obeyed, unless the court or judge otherwise directs.[104]

"Bank" and "banker" are defined to include all holders of a banking licence;[105] ACC Bank plc;[106] ICC Bank plc;[107] the Trustee Savings Bank;[108] the Post Office Savings Bank;[109] building societies;[110] and others.[111] "Bankers' books" are defined by s 9 of the 1879 Act, as amended,[112] to *include*:

(a) any records used in the ordinary business of a bank, or used in the transfer department of a bank acting as registrar of securities, whether -

  (i) comprised in bound volume, loose-leaf binders or other loose-leaf filing systems, loose-leaf ledger sheets, pages, folios or cards, or

---

[103.] See Johnston, *Banking and Security Law in Ireland*, (1998) Butterworths, paras [3.07] *et seq*; Hapgood, *Paget's Law of Banking*, (11th ed, 1996) Butterworths, pp 498-502; Breslin, *Banking Law in the Republic of Ireland"* (1998) Gill & Macmillan, pp 287-292; Dunne & Davies, "The Bankers' Books Evidence Acts, 1879 and 1959", (1997) BLR 297; and Capper, *Mareva Injunctions*, (1988) SLS/Sweet & Maxwell, p 96-97.

[104.] Note that a new section, s 7A, was inserted by s 131(c) of the Central Bank Act 1989 and amended by s 14 of the Disclosure of Certain Information for Taxation and Other Purposes Act 1996 which allows a Superintendent of the Garda Siochana, in certain circumstances, to apply for liberty to inspect and take copies of entries: see Ch 3, *Statutory Jurisdictions to Freeze Assets*, para **[3.13]**.

[105.] Section 2 of the Bankers' Books Evidence Act 1959.

[106.] Section 10 of the ACC Bank Act 1992.

[107.] Section 7(1) of the ICC Bank Act 1992.

[108.] Section 59(a) of the Trustee Savings Bank Act 1989.

[109.] Section 2 of the Bankers' Books Evidence Act 1959.

[110.] Section 126(1) of the Building Societies Act 1989.

[111.] See s 13 of the Disclosure of Certain Information for Taxation and Other Purposes Act 1996 which provides that "bank" and "banker" shall include: any credit institution not being one authorised by the Central Bank which provides services in Ireland pursuant to Council Directive 89/646/EEC; a society registered as a credit union; a member firm for the purposes of the Stock Exchange Act 1995; an investment business firm for the purposes of the Investment Intermediaries Act 1995; a person authorised to carry on a moneybroking business under s 110 of the Central Bank Act 1989; a person providing foreign currency exchange services; certain life assurance undertakings; a person providing a service in financial futures and options exchanges within the meaning of s 97 of the Central Bank Act 1989; and, finally, any person prescribed by the Minister for Finance, following consultation with the Minister for Justice.

[112.] By s 2 of the Bankers' Books Evidence Act 1959 and s 131(d) of the Central Bank Act 1989.

(ii) kept on microfilm, magnetic tape or in any non-legible form (by the use of electronics or otherwise) which is capable of being reproduced in a permanent legible form, and

(b) cover documents in manuscript, documents which are typed, printed, stencilled or created by any other mechanical process in use from time to time and documents which are produced by any photographic or photostatic process.

Notwithstanding the apparent comprehensiveness of the foregoing definition, uncertainty surrounds what is and what is not within the definition of "bankers' books". So, it has been held that neither written correspondence (ie letters from a bank to its customer)[113] nor cheques or lodgment slips[114] are within the definition.

[10.26] Order 31, r 20(1) of the RSC facilitates the making of an order under the Bankers' Books Evidence Acts 1879-1989.[115] Section 7 of the 1879 Act allows any party to a "legal proceeding"[116] to apply for an order to inspect and take copies of bankers' books "for any of the purposes of such proceedings". The absence of any reference in such purpose to "in relation to any matter in question" and the width of the expressions used, clearly permits the use of s 7 in aid of execution, and so in aid of a Mareva injunction. In *Arnott v Hayes*[117] Cotton LJ said that the main object of s 7 of the 1879 Act was to enable evidence to be given at trial. He went on to say, however, that "I do not say that it cannot be used for any other purpose".[118] In *A v C*[119] it was said by Robert Goff J that it was open to a plaintiff to make application under s 7 of the 1879 Act for an order to inspect and take copies of any entries in bankers' books where the court has found that the plaintiff is entitled to discovery in aid of a Mareva injunction. The purpose of such an inspection would, it was said, be to know how much money was standing in an identified bank account and whether it was unencumbered

---

[113.] See *O'C v D* [1985] IR 265 and *R v Dadson* (1983) 77 Cr App Rep 91.

[114.] See *Williams v Williams; Tucker v Williams* [1987] 3 All ER 257.

[115.] Order 31, r 20(1) provides: "Where inspection of any business books is applied for, the Court may, instead of ordering inspection of the original books, order a copy of any entries therein to be furnished and verified by the affidavit of some person who has examined the copy with the original entries, and such affidavit shall state whether or not there are in the original book any and what erasures, interlineations, or alterations. Provided that, notwithstanding that such copy has been supplied, the Court may order inspection of the book from which the copy was made." Ord 63, r 1(17) authorises the Master of the High Court to hear such an application.

[116.] The expression "legal proceeding" is defined by s 10 of the 1879 Act as meaning "any civil or criminal proceedings or inquiry in which evidence is or may be given and includes an arbitration". As to criminal proceedings, see *Williams v Summerfield* [1972] 2 All ER 1334 and, generally, Ch 3, *Statutory Jurisdictions to Freeze Assets*, para **[3.13]**.

[117.] (1887) 36 Ch D 731.

[118.] At 737.

[119.] [1980] 2 All ER 347.

and in excess of the plaintiff's claim. Similarly, in *Chemical Bank v McCormack*[120] it was noted that the Irish High Court had, at an earlier hearing, made an order pursuant to the Bankers' Books Evidence Acts 1879-1989 in aid of a Mareva injunction.[121]

[10.27] On its face, s 7 of the 1879 Act provides that an order may be made either with or without summoning the bank and that the order must, unless the court orders otherwise, be served on the bank three clear days[122] before it is to be obeyed. In practice, the application should be grounded on affidavit.[123] While s 7 does not state that a bank should be a notice party to an application for inspection it was said, by Andrews J in *L'Amie v Wilson*[124] that:

> "[Section 7], no doubt gives the court, or Judge, a discretion to make an order for inspection of a bank account, either with or without notice to the Bank or any other party, but we are of opinion that, unless in very exceptional cases, notice of an application to inspect the bank account of a third party ought to be given, both to such third party and to the bank."

In *Staunton v Counihan*[125] Dixon J said in reference to the foregoing passage that:

> "it appeared to be an *obiter dictum*, and is not referred to elsewhere. The usual practice is to serve notice only on the party whose account is sought to be inspected and this, in my opinion, is sufficient."

While banks will not usually have a direct interest in the proceedings, they will have a direct interest in the outcome of an application under s 7 of the 1879 Act, because any order made will undermine the contractual confidentiality between

---

120. [1983] ILRM 350.
121. In *W v BI Ltd*, *The Irish Times*, 16 September 1989, 21 September 1989 and 6 October 1989 it was reported that the plaintiff in the action obtained from Costello J (as he then was) an order for discovery of books of account, ledgers and such other documentation as may relate to accounts in the name of certain of the defendants or companies controlled by them to which monies were lodged in a named branch of Bank of Ireland. Whilst unclear from the report, it would appear that the application was brought under the Bankers' Books Evidence Acts, 1879-1989.
122. Section 11 of the 1879 Act, as replaced by s 131(e) of the Central Bank Act 1989, provides that days which are "non-business days" as defined by the Bills of Exchange Act 1882 shall be excluded from the computation of time under the 1879 Act. Section 2 of the Bills of Exchange Act 1882, as amended by s 132 of the Central Bank Act 1989 defines "non-business days" as Saturday, Sunday, public holidays or any other specified day so deemed by the Minister for Finance in the national interest pursuant to s 134(1) of the Central Bank Act 1989.
123. As in *M'Gorman v Kierans* (1901) 35 ILTR 84; *cf Arnott v Hayes* (1887) 36 Ch D 731 where Cotton LJ said that an affidavit was not necessary although a court in its discretion may require the application to be made on affidavit.
124. [1907] 2 IR 130.
125. (1957) 92 ILTR 32 at 34.

banker and customer. By being put on notice, however, the bank may, in certain circumstances, be expected to vindicate its customer's confidentiality and so may not be too eager to be served with notice. In practice, especially where an order is made under s 7 of the 1879 Act in aid of a Mareva injunction, both applications may be made *ex parte* and in such circumstances a bank would only become aware of the order after it had been made.[126]

[10.28] Another issue which arises here is whether is it within the contemplation of s 7 of the 1879 Act to make an order relating to the bank account of a third party to the proceedings between a plaintiff and a defendant. The courts have adopted a cautious approach to all applications for inspection of third party accounts[127] and will generally only do so where the account in question is in form and substance that of a party to the action and each case will be assessed on its merits. So, in *Staunton v Counihan*[128] Dixon J refused to order inspection of the bank account of a third party company because although the defendant's son was a director and principal shareholder of the company, the defendant was found not to be so closely connected with the company that its bank account could be regarded in substance as her account. By contrast, in *M'Gorman v Kierans*,[129] Barton J did made an order for inspection of the defendant's husband's bank account.[130]

[10.29] In *Chemical Bank v McCormack*[131] it was held by Carroll J that an order for inspection and the making of copies under the Bankers' Books Evidence Acts 1879-1989 would not be made where it would involve an extension to branches of banks outside of the jurisdiction. In that case Carroll J held:

> "There are no clear words in the 1879 Act or the amending 1959 Act which would support an interpretation of an intention to have extra-territorial effect. I do not have power to order an inspection in a foreign country and the order

---

[126.] In *Arnott v Hayes* (1887) 36 Ch D 731 the Court of Appeal upheld the validity of an *ex parte* application under s 7 of the 1879 Act.

[127.] In *Staunton v Counihan* (1957) 92 ILTR 32 at 33 Dixon J said: "The jurisdiction to order inspection of entries in a banking account conferred by s 7 of the Bankers' Books Evidence Act 1879, must be exercised with extreme caution even where it is the account of a party to the action". See also *South Staffordshire Tramways Co v Ebbsmith* [1895] 2 QB 669; *Arnott v Hayes* (1887) 36 Ch D 731; *Pollock v Garle* (1898) 1 Ch 1; and *L'Amie v Wilson* [1907] 2 IR 130.

[128.] (1957) 92 ILTR 32.

[129.] (1901) 35 ILTR 84.

[130.] See also *L'Amie v Wilson* [1907] 2 IR 130 at 132 where Andrews J said "... before granting an inspection of a third party's account, the Court or Judge, ought to be satisfied that there are good grounds for believing that there are entries in the account material to some issue to be tried in the action, and which would be evidence at the trial for the party applying for the inspection."

[131.] [1983] ILRM 350.

which authorises inspection 'at' the Branch in New York is in excess of jurisdiction".[132]

In so finding Carroll J followed the English case of *R v Grossman*[133] where the Court of Appeal had set aside an inspection order made on Barclays Bank at its head office in London which required it to allow the Inland Revenue to inspect and take copies of an account of an Isle of Man company held at a branch of Barclays Bank in the Isle of Man.[134] While the Court has jurisdiction to order a person or company amenable to its jurisdiction to allow inspection it will not ordinarily make an order which would involve a conflict of jurisdiction out of deference to the comity of courts. It remains to be seen whether this remains the position in the light of the subsequent development of the worldwide Mareva jurisdiction.

[10.30] As in the case of a disclosure order or interrogatories, it is open to a defendant to seek to invoke the privilege against self-incrimination and, in such circumstances, the defendant's plea should be made on affidavit, setting out the grounds upon which it is claimed.[135] Where privilege is claimed, only the court is competent to decide whether it should stand or fall.[136]

[10.31] It should be remembered that in making any disclosure or inspection order against a bank, the court's discretion is *not* limited or circumscribed by the provisions of the Bankers' Books Evidence Acts 1879-1989. In *Larkins v NUM*[137] Barrington J made an inspection order in aid of a Mareva injunction, which was wider than any order which he could have made under s 7 of the Bankers' Books Evidence Acts 1879-1989. In that case Barrington J had made the following *ex parte* order against a bank in which funds which were the subject of a Mareva injunction were thought to be held:

> "That the [bank] do forthwith produce for the inspection of the intending plaintiffs or their solicitors the bankers' books including *correspondence or computer printouts from electronic recordings* relating to any account of the [NUM] held by the [bank] whether in the name of the [NUM], its officers, servants, agents or nominees or otherwise howsoever or in respect of which such persons have direct or indirect power to draw".[138]

By reason of the reference to the matters in italics, this order went beyond the scope of s 7 of the Bankers' Books Evidence Acts 1879-1989 because first, the

---

[132.] At 353.
[133.] [1981] Cr App Rep 302.
[134.] See also *MacKinnon v Donaldson, Lufkin and Jenrette Securities Corp* [1986] 1 All ER 653.
[135.] *Waterhouse v Barker* [1924] 2 KB 759.
[136.] *Murphy v Dublin Corporation* [1972] IR 215.
[137.] [1985] IR 671.
[138.] At 695. Italics added.

definition of "bankers' books" does *not* include "correspondence"[139] and secondly, at the time that order was made (November 1984) the definition of "banking' books" had not then been extended to include records kept in any non-legible form.[140] Nonetheless, the order was made by Barrington J who made the following comments in response to the bank's counsel's submissions:

> "Needless to say, this was a very far reaching order and was not lightly made. In the normal course a freezing order would have been sufficient to maintain the status quo and there would have been no justification for making an inspection order such as this, *ex parte*. The necessity for the *ex parte* order arose from the fear that portion of the funds had already been transferred to other financial institutions in Ireland, the identity of which was unknown to the sequestrators. In the event it transpired that the sequestrators' suspicion was correct but these financial institutions were not in Ireland. It is now possible to trace the funds, first to a bank in the Isle of Man, then to the defendant bank in Dublin and then to banks in New York, Luxembourg and Switzerland."[141]

Barrington J emphatically rejected the submission that any order for inspection should be limited to documents or books within the meaning of the Bankers' Books Evidence Acts 1878-1989 and found that there was nothing in either those Acts or the decision of Murphy J in *O'C v D*[142] which "circumscribed the power of the High Court, in an appropriate case, to order the production or inspection of any of a bank's books, documents or computer printouts".[143]

(g) Section 908(3) of the Taxes Consolidation Act 1997

[10.32] Where the plaintiff in an action happens to be the Revenue Commissioners, additional means of obtaining information are available. Section 908(3) of the Taxes Consolidation Act 1997 ("the 1997 Act")[144] confers on the High Court the power to order a financial institution to furnish the Revenue Commissioners with specified particulars and information relating to a taxpayer's bank accounts.[145] When taken in conjunction with s 908(4) of the 1997 Act[146] - which facilitates the freezing of a taxpayer's account in respect of which an order under s 908(3) is made - the effect of this provision is very far-reaching. As Murphy J said in *O'C v D*:[147]

---

139. In *O'C v D* [1985] IR 265 it was held by Murphy J that "banking' books" did not include bank correspondence; see para **[10.25]** *supra*.
140. This amendment was only made by s 131(d) of the Central Bank Act 1989.
141. [1985] IR 671 at 695.
142. [1985] IR 265.
143. [1985] IR 671 at 696.
144. Formerly, s 18(3) of the Finance Act 1983.
145. See Johnston, *Banking and Security Law in Ireland*, (1998) Butterworths, paras [3.16]-[3.18]; and Breslin, *Banking Law in the Republic of Ireland*, (1998) Gill & Macmillan, p 295.
146. See Ch 3, *Statutory Jurisdictions to Freeze Assets*, para **[3.74]**.
147. [1985] ILRM 123; [1985] IR 265.

"The section does have far-reaching effects and this is, I understand, the first application thereunder. Undoubtedly any order made under the section would involve an invasion of the traditional bond of confidentiality between a banker and his customer. Of necessity it would also impose a very considerable administrative and clerical burden on any bank to whom it was directed. On the other hand it is clear that such an order might be a very effective means of preventing and detecting tax evasion and assisting the revenue authorities in their task of ensuring that every taxpayer carries his fair share of the burden of taxation. It is for the legislature to find a proper balance between such conflicting interest."[148]

Indeed, it is interesting to note that in *Director of Public Prosecutions v W*,[149] after an order had been made under this section, the first custodial (albeit suspended) sentence for evading income tax in Ireland was handed down. This is one of a number of wide-ranging remedies in the Revenue Commissioners' arsenal.[150]

[10.33] Section 908(2) of the 1997 Act sets out the circumstances in which an authorised officer of the Revenue Commissioners can make such an application. It provides:

Where -

(a) a person who for the purposes of tax has been duly required by an inspector to deliver a statement of the profits or gains arising to that person from any trade or profession or to deliver to the inspector a return of income fails to deliver that statement or that return to the inspector, or

(b) the inspector is not satisfied with such a statement or return so delivered,

an authorised officer may, if he or she is of opinion that that person maintains or maintained an account or accounts, the existence of which has not been disclosed to the Revenue Commissioners, with a financial institution or that there is likely to be information in the books of that institution indicating that the said statement of profits or gains or the said return of income is false to a material extent, apply to a judge for an order requiring that financial institution to furnish the authorised officer -

(i) with full particulars of all accounts maintained by that person, either solely or jointly with any other person or persons, in that institution during a period not exceeding ten years immediately preceding the date of the application, and

---

[148] At 125.

[149] *The Irish Times*, 20 June 1998 (Circuit Court).

[150] See also the powers of attachment provided for by s 1002 of the Taxes Consolidation Act 1997 (which replaced s 73 of the Finance Act 1988 as amended by s 241 of the Finance Act 1992) and generally, Breslin, "Revenue Power to Attach Debts under Section 73 of the Finance Act 1988: Implications for Credit Institutions", (1995) CLP 167.

(ii) with such information as may be specified in the order relating to the financial transactions of that person, being information recorded in the books of that institution which would be material in determining the correctness of the statement of profits or gains or the return of income delivered by that person or, in the event of failure to deliver such statement or return would be material in determining the liability of that person to tax.

"Judge" means a judge of the High Court.[151] The meanings of "books", "financial institution" and "person" are assigned the same meanings respectively as in s 907(1) of the 1997 Act.[152] So, "books" means "bankers' books" as defined above[153] but extended also to include records and documents of persons referred to in s 7(4) of the Central Bank Act 1971; "financial institution" means a person who holds or has held a licence under s 9 of the Central Bank Act 1971 and a person referred to in s 7(4) of that Act; and "person" (other than in the definition of "financial institution") means an individual who is ordinarily resident in the State. From this definition of "person" it is clear that only the account of an individual (and not the account of a body corporate) can be the subject of an order under s 908.[154]

[10.34] As noted at the outset, the granting of orders made under s 908(3) of the 1997 Act must be balanced with conflicting interests. It is important to recognise that the High Court's power to grant an order under the section is entirely *discretionary*. On the question of balancing conflicting interests, in *O'C v D*[155] Murphy J said:

> "The solution provided in section 18 is to prescribe certain conditions precedent to the right of the authorised officer to apply to the court for relief under the section. There is then a further safeguard in that a judge of the High Court must be satisfied that there are reasonable grounds for making the application. Finally - in relation to the protection afforded by the section - the use of the word 'may' in section 18(3) is clearly designed to confer a discretion upon the Court as to whether or not in any particular case the order sought should be granted and even where granted the order is subject to such terms and conditions and indeed limitations as the Court in its order may direct."[156]

In that case Murphy J refused to make an order under s 18(3) of the Finance Act 1983 (which was materially similar to s 908(3) of the 1997 Act) on the grounds that the Revenue Commissioners had failed to prove that the pre-conditions in

---

[151.] Section 908(1) of the 1997 Act.

[152.] By s 908(1) of the 1997 Act.

[153.] See para **[10.25]** *supra.*

[154.] See Ch 3, *Statutory Jurisdictions to Freeze Assets*, para **[3.76]**. This is because only income tax is relevant to a s 908 order.

[155.] [1985] ILRM 123; [1985] IR 265.

[156.] At 125.

s 18(3)(a) and (b) had been fulfilled; specifically, they had not proved that the taxpayer had been "duly required" to produce a statement of profit or gains in the manner strictly provided for by the section. This finding was upheld by the Supreme Court.[157] In *Liston v O'C*[158] the Supreme Court stressed that the court's discretion extends to determining whether an applicant authorised officer had "reasonable grounds" for his belief and an order will only be made where it is found that there were such grounds. In that case it was held that there clearly were reasonable grounds for forming the opinion referred to in the fore-runner to s 908 of the 1997 Act

[10.35] Any order made by the High Court pursuant to s 908(3) of the 1997 Act should limit the information sought as closely as possible and the proper cost incurred by a financial institution in complying with an order will have to be borne by the Revenue Commissioners.[159]

Disclosure by Interrogatories

[10.36] The procedure of interrogatories involves the posing of a series of written questions and the answers thereto being given on affidavit. The grant of an order for "traditional interrogatories" ie in the course of a substantive cause of action is governed by Ord 31, r 1 of the RSC.[160] In *Mercantile Credit Company of Ireland and Highland Finance (Ireland) Ltd v Heelan*[161] Costello J reviewed the circumstances when an order for interrogatories would be granted and made the following general observations on Ord 31:

(i) interrogatories must relate to "any matter in question" in an action; this did not, however, permit a party to interrogate an opponent on every issue that might arise in the action; leave to deliver interrogatories will only be given where they are necessary for "disposing fairly" of the cause or matter or for saving costs and in the case of an action commenced by plenary summons, the use of affidavit evidence given in reply to interrogatories "is an exception which must be justified by some special exigency in the case which, in the interests of doing justice, requires the exception to be allowed";[162]

[157.] [1985] ILRM 131.
[158.] [1996] 1 IR 501.
[159.] *Per* Murphy J in *O'C v D* [1985] ILRM 123 at 130.
[160.] See O'Floinn, *Practice and Procedure in the Superior Courts*, (1996) Butterworths, p 236 and Cahill, *Discovery in Ireland*, (1996) Roundhall Sweet & Maxwell, p 62 *et seq.*
[161.] [1994] ILRM 406.
[162.] At 410.

(ii) interrogatories may be delivered for two distinct purposes: (a) to obtain information from the interrogated party about the issues that arise in the action and (b) to obtain admissions from the party interrogated;[163]

(iii) when information is sought the interrogatories must relate to the issues raised in the pleadings and not to the evidence which a party wishes to adduce to establish his case.

In the case of a company or other body corporate, application can be made for an order allowing the plaintiff to deliver interrogatories to any member or officer of the company or body corporate.[164] The jurisdictional basis of an order for disclosure by interrogatories, in the context of an order in aid of a Mareva injunction, is thought to be the same as an order for disclosure by discovery, which has already been considered.[165] In relation to the privilege against self-incrimination, the fact that the answer to interrogatories would or might tend to incriminate the defendant is no ground to objecting to leave being given to administer them; the objection to answer must be taken in the answer,[166] save where there is a penal notice attached which obliges the defendant to answer the interrogatories.[167] A Mareva plaintiff will only very rarely seek disclosure by interrogatories to assist in the enforcement of his injunction. Discovery (in the form of an asset disclosure order) will usually be sufficient for this purpose and interrogatories tend to be confined to issues requiring proof at trial which are either not within the plaintiff's direct means of proof or are going to be expensive or difficult to prove.

Cross-Examination of the Defendant

[10.37] Where evidence is given on affidavit Ord 40, r 1 of the RSC provides that the court may "order the attendance for cross examination of the person making any such affidavit".[168] Where a defendant is ordered to disclose his assets on affidavit in aid of a Mareva injunction and the plaintiff has legitimate grounds for believing that the information supplied on affidavit is incomplete,

---

[163.] *Attorney General v Gaskill* (1882) 20 Ch D 519 cited.

[164.] Order 31, r 5.

[165.] See para **[10.06]** *et seq, supra.*

[166.] *AJ Bekhor & Co Ltd v Bilton* [1981] 2 All ER 565 at 579 *per* Ackner LJ, citing *Fisher v Owen* (1878) 8 Ch D 645.

[167.] *Rank Film Distributors Ltd v Video Information Centre Ltd* [1980] 2 All ER 273.

[168.] Where a party has been delivered interrogatories, oral examination of a defendant is permitted by Ord 31, r 11 which provides: "If any party interrogated omits to answer, or answers insufficiently, the party interrogating may apply to the Court for an order requiring him to answer, or to answer further, as the case may be; and an order may be made requiring him to answer or answer further, either by affidavit of by *viva voce* examination, as the Court may direct."

he can make application to have the defendant cross-examined.[169] Normally, cross-examination on an affidavit of discovery *simpliciter* is not possible; however if it is not open to a Mareva plaintiff to apply under the Rules for an oral examination of a defendant on his affidavit (because the affidavit does not relate to the "matters in question" in the substantive cause of action) the court can still exercise its inherent authority and order that a defendant be examined orally. In *House of Spring Gardens Ltd v Waite*[170] Slade LJ said:

> "... cases, albeit perhaps rare cases, could arise where the court could properly take the view (1) that the defendant in an action appeared determined both to put or keep his assets beyond the reach of the plaintiff, and to conceal the true nature and extent of these assets from the court; and (2) that, in the particular circumstances of the case, an immediate order for oral examination or cross-examination of the defendant was the only 'just and convenient' way of ensuring that he would not deal with his assets so as to deprive the plaintiffs in the future of the fruits of any judgment. In such a case I consider it reasonably clear that section 37 would be wide enough to give the court the requisite power to make an immediate order obliging the defendant to give oral evidence, as 'just and convenient' relief ancillary to the Mareva order."

Even if Slade LJ's reliance upon the statutory power to grant an interlocutory order was misplaced, it could be argued on the authority of *AJ Bekhor & Co Ltd v Bilton*[171] that the court has an inherent authority to make any order which is necessary to give full effect to a Mareva injunction. The number of cases in which there will be an exercise of such inherent authority will be few.

Anton Piller Orders

[10.38] Anton Piller orders are worthy of a study in themselves.[172] The Anton Piller order is closely connected with the Mareva injunction, both owing their creation to the innovation of the English Court of Appeal presided over by Lord Denning MR. Sometimes Anton Piller orders are made *in support* of Mareva injunctions; and although rarely exercised, the courts have "pile[d] Piller on

---

[169.] See *AJ Bekhor & Co Ltd v Bilton* [1981] 2 All ER 565 at 580 where Ackner LJ said: "It is only in very exceptional cases that a judge ought to refuse an application to cross-examine a defendant on his affidavit"; citing *Comet Products UK Ltd v Hawkex Plastics Ltd* [1971] 1 All ER 1141.

[170.] *House of Spring Gardens Ltd v Waite* [1985] 11 FSR 173.

[171.] [1981] 2 All ER 565. See para **[10.08]** *supra*.

[172.] See generally, Ough & Flenley, *The Mareva Injunction and Anton Piller Order*, (2nd ed, 1993) Butterworths; Goldrein & Wilkinson, *Commercial Litigation: Pre-Emptive Remedies*, (2nd ed, 1991) Sweet & Maxwell; Keane, *Equity and the Law of Trusts in the Republic of Ireland*, (1988) Butterworths, p 241; Delany, *Equity and the Law of Trusts in Ireland*, (1996) Roundhall Sweet & Maxwell, p 426.

Mareva"[173] where this was considered necessary. Here, the following issues are considered:

(a) The nature and jurisdictional basis of the Anton Piller order;

(b) The proofs required on an Anton Piller application;

(c) The form and execution of Anton Piller orders;

(d) Safeguarding the defendant and the privilege against self-incrimination.

(a) The nature and jurisdictional basis of the Anton Piller order

(i) The nature of Anton Piller orders

[10.39] An Anton Piller order is almost invariably a mandatory *ex parte* order which, subject to certain conditions, directs a defendant to permit a plaintiff to enter upon and inspect the defendant's premises for the purposes of seizing evidence and assets in circumstances where it is apprehended that there is a likelihood that such evidence and assets would otherwise be destroyed by the defendant. The paradigm scenario where Anton Piller relief will be sought by a plaintiff is where he alleges that the defendant is infringing his copyright or other intellectual property rights by making unauthorised "bootlegged" or "pirated" copies of the plaintiff's goods.

[10.40] Although the first reported Anton Piller order was made in the case of *EMI Ltd v Pandit*[174] it was the case of *Anton Piller KG v Manufacturing Processes Ltd*[175] where the Court of Appeal pronounced upon the validity of such an injunction, which gave the relief its name. In that case the plaintiff was a foreign manufacturer which owned the copyright in the design of a high frequency converter used to supply computers and the defendant was its English agent who the plaintiff believed was planning to supply the plaintiff's competitors with information belonging to the plaintiff which would enable the competitors to produce a similar product. The plaintiff's most pressing concern was that before the matter would come to trial, or discovery, the defendant would take steps to destroy the documents or move them out of the jurisdiction so that they would no longer be available and the plaintiff would find it impossible to prove its case. It was in these circumstances that the plaintiff applied for an *ex parte* order to require the defendant to permit the plaintiff to enter the defendant's premises in order to inspect, remove or make copies of documents belonging to the plaintiff and when this was refused, appealed the

---

[173.] An expression used by Stephenson LJ in *AJ Bekhor & Co Ltd v Bilton* [1981] 2 All ER 565 at 586.

[174.] [1975] 1 WLR 302.

[175.] [1976] 1 All ER 779.

refusal to the Court of Appeal. In finding that the court did have an inherent jurisdiction to make such an order, Lord Denning MR said:

"Let me say at once that no court in this land has any power to issue a search warrant to enter a man's house so as to see if there are papers or documents there which are of an incriminating nature, whether libels or infringements of copyright or anything else of the kind ... But the order sought in this case is not a search warrant. It does not authorise the plaintiffs' solicitors or anyone else to enter the defendant's premises against their will. It does not authorise the breaking down of any doors, nor the slipping in by a back door, nor getting in by an open door or window. It only authorises entry and inspection by the permission of the defendants. The plaintiff must get the defendants' permission. But it does do this: it brings pressure on the defendants to give permission. It does more. It actually orders them to give permission - with, I suppose, the result that if they do not give permission, they are guilty of contempt of court."[176]

Just as a Mareva injunction does not give a plaintiff proprietary rights over the assets frozen, neither does an Anton Piller order operate as a "search warrant" - both operate *in personam*[177] against a defendant who will be in contempt of court if he disobeys the order.

(ii) The jurisdiction to make an Anton Piller order

[10.41] In *EMI Ltd v Pandit*[178] Templeman J had found the jurisdiction to make the order "from the terms of Ord 29 [of the English Rules of the Supreme Court] and from the authorities which I have quoted".[179] The basis of the jurisdiction to make such an order was found by Lord Denning MR in *Anton Piller KG v Manufacturing Processes Ltd*[180] to be the inherent jurisdiction of the court.[181] This basis was also necessary because the English Rules of the Supreme Court do not permit an *ex parte* order to be made for entry to a defendant's premises for the purpose of detention, custody and preservation of property which is the subject matter of a cause or matter. Lord Denning MR said:

"If the defendant is given notice beforehand and is able to argue the pros and cons, it is warranted by [*East India Co v Kynaston*] in the House of Lords and by RSC Ord 29, r 2(1) and (5). But it is a far stronger thing to make such an

---

176. At 782h-j, 783a.
177. See Ch 9, *The Mareva Order and Its Effects*, para **[9.36]**.
178. [1975] 1 WLR 302.
179. *East India Co v Kynaston* (1821) 3 Bli 153; *Lord Lonsdale's Case* (1799) 3 Bli 168; *Hennessy v Bohmann, Osborne & Co* [1877] WN 14.
180. [1976] 1 All ER 779.
181. Lord Denning MR relied upon a decision of the House of Lords in *East India Co v Kynaston* (1821) 3 Bli 153. For a critical analysis of the jurisdictional basis relied upon see Dockray, 'Liberty to Rummage - A Search Warrant in Civil Proceedings', (1977), Public Law 369.

order *ex parte* without giving him notice. This is not covered by the rules of court and must be based on the inherent jurisdiction of the court ... It seems to me that such an order can be made by a judge *ex parte*, but it should only be made where it is essential that the plaintiff should have inspection so that justice can be done between the parties; and when, if the defendant were forewarned, there is a grave danger that vital evidence will be destroyed, that papers will be burnt or lost or hidden, or taken beyond the jurisdiction, and so the ends of justice be defeated; and when the inspection would do no real harm to the defendant or his case."[182]

The absolute requirement that such an order under Ord 29, r 2[183] of the English Rules be *on notice* to a defendant stands in contrast to the Irish Ord 50, rr 4 and 7 of the RSC which provide:

Rule 4: The Court, upon the application of any party to a cause or matter, and upon such terms as may be just, may make any order for the detention, preservation, or inspection of any property or thing, being the subject of such cause or matter, or as to which any question may arise therein, and for all or any of the purposes aforesaid may authorise any person to enter upon or into any land or building in the possession of any party to such cause or matter and for all or any of the purposes aforesaid may authorise any samples to be taken or any observations to be made or experiment to be tried, which may be necessary or expedient for the purpose of obtaining full information or evidence.

Rule 7: An application for an order under [rules 3, 4, 6] may be made to the Court by any party. If the application be by the plaintiff ... for an order under [r 4] it may be made on notice to the defendant at any time after the issue of the summons, and if it be by any other party, then on notice to the plaintiff, and at any time after appearance by the party making the application, *provided that, where the exigencies of the case require it, any such application may be made ex parte.* (italics added).

Accordingly, it may appear unnecessary for an Irish court to have to rely upon its inherent authority to make an Anton Piller Order *ex parte*. If, however, the order does not fall exactly within the terms of Ord 50, r 4, then it is open to an Irish court to rely on its inherent jurisdiction and authority.

---

182. [1976] 1 All ER 779 at 783e-f.
183. RSC Ord 29, r 2(1) provided: "On the application of any party to a cause or matter the Court may make an order for the detention, custody or preservation of any property which is the subject matter of the cause or matter, or as to which any question may arise therein, or for the inspection of any such property in the possession of any party to the cause or matter; (2) For the purpose of enabling any order under paragraph (1) to be carried out the Court may by the order authorise any person to enter upon any land or buildings in the possession of any party to the cause or matter [and] (5) An application for an Order under this rule must be made by summons or by notice under Ord 25, r 7".

[10.42] There appears to be no written decision of an Irish court which rationalises the jurisdiction to make Anton Piller orders. The only written judgment which appears to touch upon Anton Piller orders is a decision of Costello J in *Orion Pictures Corporation v Hickey*[184] which concerned a motion to commit a defendant for contempt for breach of an earlier Anton Piller order.[185] That there have been no written decisions in this jurisdiction on the substantive issues raised by Anton Piller orders is indicative of the fact that the jurisdiction is exercised sparingly; it should not be taken as indicative that the Irish courts do not make such orders. On the contrary, such orders are regularly granted in copyright cases against video-pirates.

It is usually the case that, on the return date, a defendant will give an undertaking to the court not to infringe the plaintiff's copyright and, in these cases, the plaintiff will typically be satisfied that the piracy has ended and will not pursue a claim for damages. So, for example, in *House of Spring Gardens v Point Blank Ltd*,[186] an action for breach of confidence, there is passing reference to the Irish court having made such an order. Similarly, in *Re Mantruck Services Ltd; Mehigan v Duignan*, an action under ss 150 and 204 of the Companies Act 1990, an *ex tempore* Anton Piller order was made, the wording of which is noted below.[187]

(iii) The pre-conditions to the exercise of the jurisdiction

[10.43] In *Anton Piller KG v Manufacturing Processes Ltd*[188] Ormrod LJ said:

> "There are three essential pre-conditions for the making of such an order, in my judgment. First, there must be an extremely strong *prima facie* case. Secondly, the damage, potential or actual, must be very serious for the plaintiff. Thirdly, there must be clear evidence that the defendants have in their possession incriminating documents or things, and that there is a real possibility that they may destroy such material before any application *inter partes* can be made."

Although these three pre-conditions have remained intact, they have been bolstered in subsequent cases by additional rules, primarily for the protection of defendants. The "proofs required" to be established by an Anton Piller plaintiff are considered in detail below.[189]

[184.] High Court, unrep, 18 January 1991 (Costello J).

[185.] See Ch 12, *Enforcing Mareva Injunctions and Other Orders* para **[12.23]**.

[186.] [1984] IR 611.

[187.] High Court, unrep, 20 June 1996 (1993 No 4988P). The writer acknowledges with gratitude the assistance of Mr Hugh Garvey, of LK Shields, Solicitors, in providing a copy of the Anton Piller order made in that matter. See para **[10.55]** *infra*.

[188.] [1976] 1 All ER 779 at 784.

[189.] See para **[10.49]** *infra*.

(iv) Post-judgment relief in aid of execution

[10.44] While Anton Piller relief is essentially a pre-judgment relief, it can also be granted as post-judgment relief in aid of execution.[190] In such cases, the rationale behind the granting of the order will be for the "purpose of eliciting documents which are essential to execution and which would otherwise be unjustly denied to the execution creditor."[191] Although the proofs, as appropriately modified, remain strong, it is thought that a more lenient approach should be taken with a post-judgment Anton Piller plaintiff. In such cases, an Anton Piller order will frequently be relief additional, or ancillary to, a Mareva injunction.

(v) Worldwide Anton Piller orders

[10.45] The jurisdictional basis for making a "worldwide" Anton Piller order - to permit a plaintiff to enter upon a defendant's foreign premises and seize evidence - has its foundations in the court's *in personam* authority over those who are amenable to its jurisdiction.[192] The converse, where a defendant is not subject to the court's jurisdiction, is that such an order should never be made. This was confirmed by Scott J in *Altertext Inc v Advanced Date Communications Ltd*[193] where he said that an Anton Piller order ought not to be made "except against a party over whom the court does have jurisdiction." It is thought that the circumstances in which a court should make a worldwide Anton Piller order are extremely limited and that a court will only exercise its jurisdiction to make such an order in extraordinarily compelling circumstances.[194]

(vi) The constitutionality of Anton Piller Orders

[10.46] The jurisdiction to actually grant an Anton Piller order has never been judicially considered by the Irish courts, let alone the constitutionality of such an order. It is thought that in a contested case before the Irish courts, a defendant is likely to raise the constitutionality of a procedure which compels him, under pain of contempt of court, to permit a plaintiff and his solicitor to enter upon his premises to search for and seize evidence. Anton Piller orders are, *prima facie*,

---

[190.] *Distributori Automatici Italia SpA v Holford General Trading Co Ltd* [1985] 1 WLR 1066 applying *Orwell Steel (Erection and Fabrication) Ltd v Asphalt and Tarmac (UK) Ltd* [1985] 3 All ER 747.

[191.] *Per* Leggatt J in *Distributori Automatici Italia SpA v Holford General Trading Co Ltd* [1985] 1 WLR 1066 at 1073.

[192.] See generally, Ch 7, *The Defendant's Assets*, para **[7.21]** *et seq* where the jurisdiction to grant worldwide Mareva relief is considered.

[193.] [1985] 1 All ER 395 at 399.

[194.] See also *Cook Industries Inc v Galliher* [1978] 3 All ER 945 and *Protector Alarms Ltd v Maxim Alarms Ltd* [1978] FSR 442.

at variance with the principle of *audi alteram partem* and, possibly, the privilege against self-incrimination. Moreover, in the light of Art 40.5 of the Irish Constitution,[195] it would be of particular concern where an Anton Piller order directed a defendant to permit a plaintiff entry to his domestic residence. For the reasons set out in the following paragraph, it is thought that the outcome of any such hearing would be in favour of the constitutionality of the jurisdiction to grant an Anton Piller order; although, the *execution* of a particular Anton Piller order may be proven to be unconstitutional.

[10.47] Aside from the privilege against self-incrimination, which is considered below,[196] the main constitutional objection to the Anton Piller jurisdiction is that, before the substantive issues between the parties have been determined, the defendant is directed, under pain of being found to be in contempt of court, to permit his adversary, the plaintiff and his representatives, to enter his premises and to seize and take away, property which has not been proven to belong to anybody other than the defendant. These were some of the issues raised before the European Court of Human Rights in the *Chappell* case.[197] There, the complainant operated an exchange club for video cassettes with a membership of about 4,000. A substantial number of the videos were pirated and in breach of copyright. The plaintiffs were two film companies and two organisations for the protection of film producers and distributors; they employed a former policeman whose investigations indicated that the complainant had been in breach of their copyright. As a result the plaintiffs obtained an *ex parte* Anton Piller order which was supported by the plaintiffs' solicitor's and investigator's affidavits. One peculiarity of this case was that, while posing as a customer, the investigator has been shown an obscene video which, the former policeman thought might be of interest to the police, although it was of no interest to the plaintiffs. The police were informed and, having obtained a search warrant under the UK's Obscene Publications Act 1959, attended at the execution of the Anton Piller order at premises which included the complainant's home. The plaintiffs seized about 377 videos which they claimed were pirated and the police seized about 274 videos on the basis (it can only be presumed) that they were obscene. The complainant's only legal representation was a trainee solicitor. The complainant claimed that, because of the simultaneous searches, he was unable to supervise operations and take note of material seized; he also claimed that the plaintiffs' solicitors took a number of private, confidential and personal documents.

[195.] Article 40.5 provides: "The dwelling of every citizen is inviolable and shall not be forcibly entered save in accordance with law." See generally, Hogan & Whyte, *Kelly: The Irish Constitution*, (3rd ed, 1994) Butterworths, pp 914-920.

[196.] See para **[10.60]** *infra*.

[197.] (17/1987/140/194), judgment of the ECHR of 30 March 1989.

[10.48] The complainant alleged a breach of Article 8 of the European Convention on Human Rights.[198] It was held by the European Court of Human Rights that the making of an Anton Piller order was "in accordance with the law"; that the law on Anton Piller orders was "accessible" by reference to the published texts and case law and was also "foreseeable" as, notwithstanding variations between individual orders, "the basic terms and conditions for the grant of this relief were, at the relevant time, laid down with sufficient precision for the 'foreseeability' criterion to be regarded as satisfied."[199] If anything, this latter point illustrates a deficiency in the laws of Ireland insofar as there is not, to date, any written judgment - even one which simply accepts and adopts, in general terms, or accepts that the laws in Ireland are broadly similar to those across the channel! The European Court of Human Rights also found, in relation to the *grant* of the Anton Piller order, that:

> "The order made against Mr Chappell and his company was granted only after [the Court] had been supplied with evidence establishing that the requisite conditions were met ... Bearing in mind the nature and scope of the applicant's business ..., the Court - quite apart from any question of the United Kingdom's margin of appreciation - entertains no doubt that the actual grant of the order was a necessary step in the effective pursuit by the plaintiffs of their copyright action."[200]

In relation to the *execution* of the Anton Piller order in the *Chappell* case, the European Court of Human Rights considered that the manner of gaining entry (the complainant's employees had thought that the plaintiffs' solicitors were police officers) and the fact that two searches were conducted simultaneously by sixteen or seventeen people was "disturbing" and "unfortunate and regrettable". It held, however, that:

> "... the Court is of the opinion that the shortcomings in the procedure followed - which, by its very nature, was bound to cause some difficulties for the applicant - were not so serious that the execution of the order can, in the circumstances of the case, be regarded as disproportionate to the legitimate aim pursued."[201]

[198.] Article 8(1) provides that "Everyone has the right to respect for his private and family life, his home and his correspondence". Article 8(2) provides: "There shall be no interference by a public authority with the exercise of this right except such as is in accordance with the law and is necessary in a democratic society in the interests of national security, public safety or the economic well-being of the country, for the prevention of disorder or crime, for the protection of health or morals, or for the protection of the rights and freedoms as others."

[199.] At p 19 of the judgment.

[200.] At p 20 of the judgment.

[201.] At p 22 of the transcript.

Although it is acknowledged that an Irish court may apply different criteria to those employed by the European Court of Human Rights it is submitted that the essence of the analysis would not be markedly different. In distinguishing between the propriety of the jurisdiction to *grant* an Anton Piller order from the ultimate *execution* of an Anton Piller order, it is thought that the former is unassailable: where a plaintiff-citizen's property rights are violated, it beholds the court to vindicate these as best it can. Moreover, it is difficult to conceive that an Irish court exercising its discretion to make an order which it considers to be "just and convenient" could be found to have acted unconstitutionally. What is more likely is that an Anton Piller defendant might succeed in establishing that the *execution* of a particular Anton Piller order was conducted in an unconstitutional manner. It is for this reason that the English courts have sought to entrammel the granting of Anton Piller orders with undertakings and conditions to protect a defendant's rights.[202]

(b) The proofs required on an Anton Piller application

[10.49] Application for an Anton Piller Order will be made *ex parte* by motion supported by a grounding affidavit.[203] The matters which must be established to the satisfaction of the court are:

(i)   That the plaintiff has a "substantive cause of action" against the defendant;

(ii) That the plaintiff has an "extremely strong *prima facie* case" against the defendant;

(iii) That the actual or potential damage to the plaintiff if the evidence were destroyed would be "very serious";

(iv) That there is a "real possibility" that the defendant will destroy or otherwise dispose of the subject matter of the application before an *inter partes* hearing which justifies the court in exercising its discretion to make an *ex parte* order;

(v)   That the execution of the order will not infringe the defendant's right to claim privilege against self incrimination.[204]

As in the case of an application for a Mareva injunction, there must be full material disclosure of all relevant matters and the plaintiff will be required to give an undertaking as to damages.[205]

[202.] See para **[10.56]** *infra*.

[203.] See generally, Ch 8, *Applying for a Mareva Injunction*, para **[8.26]** *et seq* where the requirements for an affidavit grounding Mareva relief are considered.

[204.] For the privilege against self-incrimination in the context of Anton Piller orders, see para **[10.60]** *infra*.

[205.] See Ch 8, *Applying for a Mareva Injunction*, para **[8.32]** *et seq* and **[8.57]** *et seq* respectively.

(i) A substantive cause of action

[10.50] As in the case of a Mareva injunction or any other interlocutory injunction, an Anton Piller plaintiff must satisfy the court that he has a recognised and presently actionable cause of action against the defendant.[206] One of the earlier Anton Piller cases where this issue arose was *Ex parte Island Records Ltd*.[207] In that case the question was whether musicians and recording companies who did not own the copyright in their live performance could obtain an Anton Piller order against "bootleggers" who surreptitiously record a live performance and sell, often poor quality, recordings to the public. The Court of Appeal held that they had a sufficient cause of action from which to launch Anton Piller proceedings.[208] This decision was not followed in subsequent cases and was expressly disapproved of by the House of Lords in *Lonrho Ltd v Shell Petroleum Co Ltd*.[209] These cases merely underlie the general principle that the first obstacle which an Anton Piller-plaintiff must overcome is to establish that he has a substantive cause of action against the defendant. It should be noted, however, that where a plaintiff has a substantive cause of action in another Contracting State to the Brussels or Lugano Conventions he can rely upon s 11(1) of the Jurisdiction of Courts and Enforcement of Judgments Acts, 1988 and 1993 and is not required to have a substantive cause of action which is justicable against the defendant in Ireland.[210]

(ii) The "extremely strong prima facie case"

[10.51] This point was first made in *Anton Piller KG v Manufacturing Processes Ltd*[211] where Ormrod LJ said that one of the pre-conditions to granting an Anton

---

[206.] See generally, Ch 4, *A Substantive Cause of Action*.

[207.] [1978] 3 All ER 824. See Lord Denning, *The Due Process of Law*, (1980) Butterworths, p 127.

[208.] Lord Denning MR said: "In the present case both the performers and the recording companies have, to my mind, private rights and interests which they are entitled to have protected from unlawful interference. The recording companies have the right to exploit the records made by them of the performance. The performers have the right to the royalty payable to them out of those records. Those rights are buttressed by the contracts between the recording companies and the performers. They are rights in the nature of property. Both the recording companies and the performers suffer damage if those rights are unlawfully interfered with. Suppose that the bootlegger in the audience had in his hand or his pocket - instead of a recording device - a distorting device: and by it he could introduce a squeak or a screech into the musical performance: and thus ruin its commercial value. No one could doubt that the recording company and the performers could bring an action to stop him and claim damages. That illustration shows that they have a private right which they are entitled to have protected: and this is so, no matter whether the interference be by means of a tortious act or a criminal act."

[209.] [1981] 2 All ER 456. In *RCA Corp v Pollard* [1982] 3 All ER 771 the practice of "bootlegging" was again considered by the Court of Appeal and the House of Lords decision applied.

[210.] Reliance can also be placed on s 11(3) where a post-judgment Anton Piller order is sought in aid of execution. See Ch 4, *A Substantive Cause of Action*, para **[4.28]** *et seq*.

[211.] [1976] 1 All ER 779.

Piller order was that "there must be an extremely strong *prima facie* case".[212] The requirement that a plaintiff must have a "strong *prima facie* case" against the defendant refers to the *strength*, as opposed to the *existence*, of the plaintiff's substantive cause of action. Implicit in this requirement is that the jurisdiction to grant an Anton Pillar order was never intended to be used to conduct a "fishing expedition" in search of evidence which might support a plaintiff's cause of action.[213] In *Lock International v Beswick*[214] the defendants were former employees of the plaintiff who left its employment after it was taken over and new management installed and who joined a new company which intended to compete with the plaintiff in the manufacture of metal detectors. The defendants had made no secret of the fact that they were going to join the new company which had been started by a former managing director of the plaintiff company. While designing a new metal detector the new company bought three of the plaintiff's metal detectors and used or cannibalised them in order to test the new company's designs. The plaintiff issued a motion for an injunction to restrain the defendants from making use of its trade secrets and confidential information and also obtained an Anton Piller order. In executing the Anton Piller order, the new company's premises and three of the defendants' homes were searched and all of the new company's drawings, commercial documents, computer records and prototypes were seized. There was no evidence that the defendants had removed the plaintiff's records or that the defendants had used the plaintiff's confidential technical information. In discharging the Anton Piller order Hoffmann J said that the evidence against the defendants did not justify any form of *ex parte* relief, let alone an Anton Piller order and that "[t]he evidence came nowhere near disclosing an "extremely strong *prima facie* case"...".[215]

(iii) Very serious damage if evidence were destroyed

[10.52] This pre-condition was also first mooted by Ormrod LJ in *Anton Piller KG v Manufacturing Processes Ltd*[216] where he said, in reference to the destruction of the evidence sought to be preserved, that "the damage, potential or actual, must be very serious for the plaintiff". Equally, however, the damage

---

[212.] At 784d. In *Rank Film Distributors Ltd v Video Information Centre* [1981] 2 All ER 76 Lord Frazer said in the context of an action for breach of copyright that Anton Piller orders: "are only made when the plaintiff produces strong *prima facie* evidence of infringement of his copyright". This requirement was noted by the European Court of Human Rights in the *Chappell Case* (17/1987/140/194), p 5 of the transcript.

[213.] See *Hytrac Conveyors v Conveyors International Ltd* [1982] 3 All ER 415 at 418d where Lawton LJ said: "Those who make charges must state right at the beginning what they are and what facts they are based on. They must not use Anton Piller orders as a means of finding out what sort of charges they can make".

[214.] [1989] 3 All ER 373.

[215.] At 385j.

[216.] [1976] 1 All ER 779 at 784.

to a plaintiff must always be balanced against the actual or potential damage to a defendant. Where a defendant's own confidential trade secrets are likely to be jeopardised by the execution of an Anton Piller order, the courts should have regard to this and attempt to balance this risk against that of the plaintiff.[217]

(iv) A "real possibility" of destruction or disposal

[10.53] Again, it was in *Anton Piller KG v Manufacturing Processes Ltd*[218] that this pre-condition was first stated by Ormrod LJ. This is perhaps the most difficult proof as it implies the need to adduce evidence of a defendant's subjective intentions and, in this respect, is similar to the requirement that a Mareva plaintiff prove that the risk of disposal of assets by a defendant is with a view to frustrating a future judgment.[219] However, just as a Mareva plaintiff can adduce circumstantial evidence which is suggestive of a defendant's propensity to act in such a manner, so too can an Anton Piller plaintiff. A defendant's character and status may be used either to support or displace his propensity to destroy or dispose of material. In discharging an Anton Piller order in *Lock International plc v Beswick*[220] Hoffmann J noted that there:

> "... these defendants were no fly-by-night video pirates. They were former long-service employees with families and mortgages, who had openly said that there were entering into competition and whom the plaintiff knew to be financed by highly respectable institutions."

This approach is supported by *Yousif v Salama*[221] where a majority of the Court of Appeal acknowledged that the probability of destruction or disposal of evidence could be inferred from the fact that a defendant had been involved in nefarious dealings, eg forging a cheque.

(c) The form and execution of Anton Piller orders

(i) The form of Anton Piller orders

[10.54] An Anton Piller order is directed at a defendant *personally* and typically orders him (1) immediately[222] to permit the plaintiff (or a nominee) and the plaintiff's solicitor to enter a specified premises for the purpose of (2) allowing them to look for, inspect, copy and take into their custody certain specified items

---

[217.] See *Lock International plc v Beswick* [1989] 3 All ER 373 at 380 where Hoffmann J considered the disproportionate harm which could be caused the defendants by an Anton Piller order. See also *Thermax Ltd v Schlott Industrial Glass Ltd* [1981] FSR 289.

[218.] [1976] 1 All ER 779 at 784.

[219.] See Ch 6, *The Risk of Removal or Disposal of Assets*, para **[6.16]** *et seq*.

[220.] [1989] 3 All ER 373.

[221.] [1980] 3 All ER 405.

[222.] As to the circumstances when a defendant can delay entry pending his obtaining legal advice, see para **[10.65]** *infra*

and (3) disclosing forthwith to the plaintiff's solicitor the whereabouts of the specified items.[223]

[10.55] That the order should specify certain particular items is indicative of the fact that an Anton Piller order should not be used by a plaintiff to go on a fishing expedition for anything which might remotely be of interest to him. Where it is alleged that the defendant has taken property belonging to the plaintiff, eg, plans, designs, confidential memoranda, prototypes etc these should be specified in as detailed a manner as possible. The material may, on the other hand, be described generically. In *Re Mantruck Services Ltd; Mehigan v Duignan*[224] the liquidator of a company had brought proceedings against an officer of the company under ss 150 and 204 of the Companies Act 1990. In the course of the trial of the action the liquidator believed that he did not have in his possession all of the company's books and records and whilst the case was being heard he applied for, and was granted by Shanley J, an Anton Piller order in the following terms:[225]

> **"IT IS ORDERED** that [X] do permit the Solicitor for the Applicant herein, [the Liquidator's Solicitor] or a Solicitor nominated by him access to
>
> (a) [certain specified lands] on or before 5 pm on this 20 day of June 1996;
>
> (b) the company premises of Mantruck Services Ltd (in liquidation) at [address] on or before 6 pm this 20 day of June 1996;
>
> for the purposes of taking away any documents, books, records, computer discs or printouts relating to the said Mantruck Services Ltd (in liquidation) ..."[226]

In that case it was deemed to be appropriate that *any* "documents, books, records, computer discs or printouts" relating to the company in liquidation

---

[223.] See *Appendix 3*.

[224.] Judgment in the substantive matter was given by the High Court on 8 October 1996 (Shanley J). See generally, Garvey, 'Being Brought to Book Under Section 204 of the Companies Act 1990', (1997) CLP 27.

[225.] High Court, unrep, 20 June, 1996 (1993 No 4988P). The writer acknowledges with gratitude the assistance of Mr Hugh Garvey of LK Shields, Solicitors, in providing a copy of the Anton Piller order made in that matter.

[226.] The order went on to provide: "**AND IT IS ORDERED** that the liquidator ... or a person nominated by him be at liberty to accompany the said Solicitor [for the Liquidator] or his nominated assistant onto the aforesaid premises at [specified location] **AND IT IS ORDERED** that the ... Respondent herein together with his Solicitor (or a Solicitor nominated by said Solicitor) be at liberty to be present at such entry to said premises **AND IT IS ORDERED** that a member of An Garda Siochana do accompany the aforesaid persons onto said premises and the Court doth direct the appropriate Garda authorities to take all necessary steps forthwith to effect same **AND IT IS ORDERED** that the official liquidator herein shall within 48 hours of removal of the aforementioned property from said premises prepare and furnish to the Solicitor of [the Respondent] a complete list of said property and further shall make available to him if required and if appropriate copies of any document or item on said list."

should have been made available to the liquidator. In other cases, however, the order should specify the materials which are to be seized, eg specific "pirated" video tapes, *etc*.

(ii) Undertakings incorporated into the order

[10.56] When an Anton Piller order is granted, it will be subject to undertakings being given by both the plaintiff and his solicitor. The following undertakings should be included in the body of the order:

(i)   by the plaintiff, as to damages, in the event that the court decides that the defendant should be compensated for any loss or if the order is executed by his solicitor in contravention of his duties;[227] and security may be required in support of such undertakings;

(ii)   by the plaintiff, to cause a writ to be issued and swear and file a grounding affidavit (if these have not already been done);

(iii)   by the plaintiff, to serve with the order, on the defendant, a copy of the writ to be issued, copy original or grounding draft affidavit and any supporting evidence;

(iv)   by the plaintiff, not, without the leave of the court, to use any of the information or documents obtained through executing the Anton Piller order or to inform any third party of the order except for the purposes of the proceedings;

(v)   by the plaintiff's solicitor, to return all original documents to the defendant as soon as possible;

(vi)   by the plaintiff's solicitor, where the ownership of any article is in dispute, to return same to the defendant's solicitors for safe-keeping on their undertaking to retain them in safe place;

(vii)   by the plaintiff's solicitor, or if appointed, by a supervising solicitor, to explain the meaning of the order to the person upon whom it is served and to advise that the defendant may be entitled to claim the privilege against self-incrimination; and such solicitor may be required to provide a report to the court on the execution of the order.

The reference to a supervising solicitor is because such appears now to be the norm in England and Wales[228] following, in particular, the decision of Nicholls V-C in *Universal Thermosensors Ltd v Hibben*.[229] There, it was said:

[227.] As to a plaintiff's undertaking as to damages, see Ch 8, *Applying for a Mareva Injunction*, para **[8.58]**.

[228.] Reference to a supervising solicitor is contained in the *Practice Direction* [1997] 1 All ER 288. Copies of the orders provided for in the Practice Direction can be obtained from The Court Service, Supreme Court Group, Chancery Order & Accounts, Enquiry Office, Room TM 5.10, Royal Courts of Justice, WC2A 2LL, England.

[229.] [1992] 3 All ER 257.

"Anton Piller orders invariably provide for service to be effected by a solicitor. The court relies heavily on the solicitor, as an officer of the court, to see that the order is properly executed. Unhappily, the history in the present case, and what has happened in other cases, show that this safeguard is inadequate. The solicitor may be young and have little or no experience of Anton Piller orders. Frequently he is the solicitor acting for the plaintiff in the action, and however diligent and fair minded he may be, he is not the right person to be given a task which to some extent involves protecting the interests of the defendant."[230]

The solution proposed by Nicholls V-C was that:

"... when making Anton Piller orders judges should give serious consideration to the desirability of providing, by suitable undertakings and otherwise, (a) that the order should be served, and its execution should be supervised, by a solicitor other than a member of the firm of solicitors acting for the plaintiff in the action, (b) that he or she should be an experienced solicitor having some familiarity with the workings of Anton Piller orders, and with judicial observations on this subject ... (c) that the solicitor should prepare a written report on what occurred when the order was executed, (d) that a copy of the report should be served on the defendants and (e) that in any event and within the next few days the plaintiff must return to the court and present that report at an *inter partes* hearing, preferably to the judge who made the order."[231]

Notwithstanding the problem highlighted by Nicholls V-C it is thought that the vast majority of Anton Piller orders will be properly and adequately executed by the plaintiff's solicitor; and that comfort should be taken from a solicitor's status as an officer of the court.[232]

(iii) The execution of Anton Piller orders

[10.57] It is important to note that when executing an Anton Piller order a plaintiff is not entitled to effect a forcible entry to a defendant's premises: a plaintiff and his representatives must seek a defendant's permission to enter his premises. If, however, a defendant refuses to permit entry he is in contempt of court. This distinction was succinctly put by Scott J in *Bhimji v Chatwani*[233] who said:

---

[230] At 276e-f.

[231] At 276g-j. Nicholls V-C acknowledged the origin of this suggestion was in the "invaluable article" by Dockray & Laddie, 'Piller Problems', (1990) 106 LQR 601.

[232] In the *Chappell Case* (17/1987/140/194), judgment of the European Court of Human Rights, 30 March 1989 it was said (p 21 of the transcript) that: "It is true that a solicitor executing such an order may find himself faced with a conflict between his obligations to his client and his duty to the court, as one of its officers. However, a solicitor who fails to abide by an undertaking of his incorporated in the order lays himself open to heavy penalties, even to the point in some circumstances of putting his professional career in jeopardy".

[233] [1991] 1 All ER 705 at 708.

"... it is fundamental to the theory of Anton Piller type orders that a civil court in civil proceedings has no power to give one citizen the right to enter a house or premises of another citizen. These orders are *in personam* orders directed to the defendants. The defendants are ordered to allow entry and to allow search. The plaintiffs' right and their solicitors' right to enter and search is derived from the defendants' permission given to them to do so. It is not deprived from the power of the court to confer the right. The court does not have that power."

Where a defendant refuses to permit a plaintiff to execute the order the plaintiff can bring proceedings to have the defendant committed for contempt of court.[234]

[10.58] Anton Piller orders usually specify a particular number of people who may attend and enter the defendant's premises. Where, however, an order specifies a number of people but there are several premises to attend, it has been held by Scott J in *Columbia Picture Industries Inc v Robinson*[235] that, in the absence of an order providing to the contrary, the people who enter each premises may be different people.

[10.59] Another caution to those executing Anton Piller orders was sounded in *Universal Thermosensors Ltd v Hibben*[236] when Nicholls LJ said:

"If the order is to be executed at a private house, and it is at all likely that a woman may be in the house alone, the solicitor serving the order must be, or must be accompanied by, a woman. A woman should not be subjected to the alarm of being confronted without warning by a solitary strange man, with no recognisable means of identification, waving some unfamiliar papers and claiming an entitlement to enter her house and, what is more, telling her she is not allowed to get in touch with anyone (except a lawyer) about what is happening."[237]

Paternalistic and patronising to women? - yes; necessary in practice? - perhaps. Anton Piller orders frequently detail specified times when they are to be executed which, insofar as possible, are kept to between 9 am and 5 pm. While this is the ideal, circumstances may necessitate divergence from the ideal.

(d) Safeguarding the defendant and the privilege against self-incrimination

[10.60] The Anton Piller jurisdiction has the potential to be extremely draconian. To an observer of the development of the jurisprudence of Anton Piller orders in the English courts, it seems that, unlike the jurisdiction to grant Mareva relief which has continued to develop, the cases after *Anton Piller KG v Manufacturing Processes Ltd*[238] have attempted to claw-back the jurisdiction

---

[234.] See, generally, Ch 12, *Enforcement of Mareva Injunctions and Other Orders*.
[235.] [1986] 3 All ER 338.
[236.] [1992] 3 All ER 257.
[237.] At 275h.
[238.] [1976] 1 All ER 779 at 784.

and entrammel its exercise with conditions and undertakings in order to protect defendants. The reason is simple, "the procedure lends itself all too readily to abuse".[239] In the first case where an Anton Piller order had been granted which actually went to full trial, *Columbia Picture Industries Inc v Robinson*,[240] Scott J said:

> "... a decision whether or not an Anton Piller order should be granted requires a balance to be struck between the plaintiffs' need that the remedies allowed by the civil law for the breach of his rights should be attainable and the requirement of justice that a defendant should not be deprived of his property without being heard. What I have heard in the present case has disposed me to think that the practice of the court has allowed the balance to swing much too far in favour of plaintiffs and that Anton Piller orders have been too readily granted and with insufficient safeguards for respondents."

In that case the defendant had made a number of specific complaints against the plaintiffs in relation both to their obtaining, and enforcement of, the Anton Piller order. In relation to the *obtaining* of the order, Scott J noted, *inter alia*, the following complaints: insufficient consideration was given by the plaintiffs to whether an Anton Piller order should have been sought in view of the serious effects it had on the defendant and the plaintiffs' grounding affidavit was not sufficiently specific to the case in hand and had followed the plaintiffs' solicitors' precedents and was misleading in other respects; there had been certain material non-disclosure by the plaintiffs. In relation to the *execution* of the order, Scott J found, *inter alia*, the following defects: certain materials taken were not covered by the order and were not returned as expeditiously as possible; certain of the materials seized were lost by the plaintiffs' solicitors; and the plaintiffs' solicitors' had relied upon certain "consents" embodied in receipts, signed by the defendant. Certain other defects in the proper execution of the Anton Piller order were also acknowledged, but since they were not included in the order, the plaintiffs' solicitors could not be held responsible. These were the failure to provide detailed receipts of what was taken following the search and the failure to return the material seized as expeditiously as possible.[241]

The tendency for the courts to be more vigilant and attuned to the interests of the defendant is also apparent in other judgments, such as that of Hoffmann J in *Lock International plc v Beswick*[242] and Nicholls V-C in *Universal*

[239.] *Per* Nicholls V-C in *Universal Thermosensors Ltd v Hibben* [1992] 3 All ER 257 at 275d.

[240.] [1986] 3 All ER 338 at 371.

[241.] Scott J gave judgment for the plaintiffs for injunctions and for an inquiry as to damages for infringement of copyright but gave judgment for the defendant for £10,000 in lieu of inquiry on the plaintiffs' cross-undertaking in damages.

[242.] [1989] 3 All ER 373.

Thermosensors Ltd v Hibben.[243] These cases, along with others which vindicate defendants' rights to claim privilege against self-incrimination, now afford an Anton Piller defendant with more protection than heretofore. These protections are primarily concerned with the proper execution of Anton Piller orders but also demonstrate a more conservative approach to the grant of such orders. It is proposed to consider the following protections here:

(i)   The need for "proportionality" in granting relief;

(ii)   The privilege against self-incrimination;

(iii)   Defendants' pre-compliance opportunity to seek legal advice.

(i) The need for "proportionality" in granting relief

[10.61] In *Lock International plc v Beswick*[244] the plaintiff had obtained Anton Piller orders against its former employees who had joined another company which intended to compete with the plaintiff. Hoffmann J urged the following caution when granting Anton Piller relief:

> "Even in cases in which the plaintiff has strong evidence that an employee has taken what is undoubtedly specific confidential information, such as a list of customers, the court must employ a graduated response. To borrow a useful concept from the jurisprudence of the European Community, there must be *proportionality* between the perceived threat to the plaintiff's rights and the remedy granted. The fact that there is overwhelming evidence that the defendant has behaved wrongfully in his commercial relationships does not necessarily justify an Anton Piller order. People whose commercial morality allows them to take a list of the customers with whom they were in contact while employed will not necessarily disobey an order of the court requiring them to deliver it up. Not everyone who is misusing confidential information will destroy documents in the face of a court order requiring him to preserve them."[245]

In other words, the interference with a defendant's rights should be proportionate to the possible prejudice to a plaintiff. There is evidence that the courts in the United Kingdom are choosing to exercise their discretion to grant Anton Piller relief "more sparingly than previously",[246] but as Nicholls V-C also acknowledged in *Universal Thermosensors Ltd v Hibben*,[247] Anton Piller orders have both "virtues and vices". In that case he said the "virtue" was that the order enabled the plaintiff to recover documents which he strongly suspected would have been destroyed if less forceful steps had been taken; the "vice" involved the faulty execution of the order in that case.

[243.] [1992] 3 All ER 257.
[244.] [1989] 3 All ER 373. See para **[10.51]** *supra*.
[245.] At 384b-d.
[246.] [1992] 3 All ER 257 at 275.
[247.] [1992] 3 All ER 257.

(ii) The privilege against self-incrimination

[10.62] The privilege against self-incrimination has been considered above, in the context of disclosure orders in aid of Mareva injunctions.[248] The danger that an Anton Piller defendant will, in complying with the order, incriminate himself is more compelling than in the case of an asset disclosure order in aid of a Mareva injunction. The risk of self-incrimination for an Anton Piller-defendant was comprehensively addressed by the Court of Appeal in *Rank Film Distributors Ltd v Video Information Centre*.[249] That case, like most traditional Anton Piller order cases, had its origins in the pirating of films. The order in that case required the defendants to disclose the names and addresses of their suppliers of illicit films and customers and all invoices, letters and documents relating to the illicit films and the whereabouts of all copies and master copies of the illicit films. The defendants objected to this disclosure on the grounds that to comply with the order would leave them open to self-incrimination in possible criminal charges for breach of copyright under the UK's Copyright Act 1956. By majority,[250] the Court of Appeal upheld the claim of privilege. Templeman LJ said:

> "Discovery of correspondence between the defendants and third parties relating to infringing copies and answers to interrogatories which require the defendants to identify the suppliers and customers of infringing copies might well provide evidence of the knowledge which is an essential ingredient of an offence under s 21 of the 1956 Act and expose the defendants to criminal proceedings for an offence under that section or for the offence of conspiring to contravene that section."[251]

Having established that there existed a risk of self-incrimination for the defendants, Templeman LJ went on to find that the privilege against self-incrimination entitled the defendant to concealment and silence. As to what that meant in the context of an Anton Piller order which requires disclosure of such matters, he said:

> "In every case in which a defendant is faced with possible self-incrimination as a result of discovery or interrogatories and especially where the tort and crime are constituted by the same activity, the defendant has a choice. The defendant may choose to rely on the silence and concealment afforded by the doctrine of self-incrimination in order at one and the same time to hamper the plaintiff in the proof of his civil action and as a means of resisting or avoiding criminal prosecution or conviction. Alternatively the defendant may abandon his defence to the civil action in which case he will be immune from discovery and interrogatories and will not need to rely on the doctrine of self-incrimination

---

[248.] See para **[10.06]** *supra*.

[249.] [1980] 2 All ER 273.

[250.] Lord Denning MR dissented on the basis that to allow the defendants to claim privilege would be to allow them to take advantage of their wrongdoing (at 282).

[251.] At 288g.

unless and until he is confronted with an inquiry in damages. Failure to defend the civil action will not prejudice the defendant in any criminal proceedings. Alternatively again, if a defendant wishes to maintain a plausible defence to the civil suit, he will waive the privilege and give frank answers to interrogatories and full discovery."[252]

This decision, which was upheld in the House of Lords,[253] has severely curtailed the power of compulsion in most Anton Piller orders. While considerable latitude will be allowed a defendant who claims the privilege, his claim must not be fanciful and there must be reasonable grounds to apprehend a real danger of criminal prosecution.[254] In *Cobra Golf Ltd v Rata*[255] it was held by Rimer J that in the United Kingdom the privilege extended to a possible exposure to civil contempt.

[10.63] In the United Kingdom there are two statutory provisions which affect claims to the privilege against self-incrimination. Section 31(1) of the UK's Theft Act 1968 provides that a defendant in civil proceedings may not claim the privilege but goes on to provide that no statement made shall be admissible in evidence against a person under that Act. Section 72 of the UK's Supreme Court Act 1981 makes similar provision in relation to proceedings involving the infringement of intellectual property rights and passing off.

[10.64] In *Tate Access Floors Inc v Boswell*[256] an *ex parte* Anton Piller order and a worldwide Mareva injunction was granted against the defendants. The Anton Piller order directed the defendants to deliver up information and documents, permit the plaintiffs to enter, search and seize documents and disclose on oath the information and documents disclosed and delivered up. *Inter alia*, the defendants applied to have the Anton Piller order set aside on the grounds that to comply would infringe their privilege against self-incrimination. It was found that there was an appreciable risk of prosecution of the defendants. In distinguishing specific aspects of the Anton Piller order, Sir Nicholas Browne-Wilkinson V-C held that the privilege did not extend to that part of the order which authorised the plaintiff to enter and search the premises although it did preclude compelling the defendants to answer questions and produce documents. The rationale for this finding was:

"The basis of the privilege against self-incrimination is that a man is not bound to provide evidence against himself by being forced to answer questions or produce documents."

[252.] At 291h-j.
[253.] [1981] 2 All ER 76.
[254.] See para **[10.21]** *supra*.
[255.] [1997] 2 All ER 150.
[256.] [1990] 3 All ER 303.

This distinction was made in the context that the only compulsions on the defendants was to permit entry to the premises and not obstruct the search for documents.

(iii) Defendants' pre-compliance opportunity to seek legal advice

[10.65] The essence of Anton Piller relief is surprise; it is obtained by surprise on an *ex parte* basis and executed before a defendant has time to destroy the evidence which the plaintiff seeks to preserve. Nonetheless, it has been held that the requirement to permit a plaintiff to enter a defendant's premises "forthwith" should mean immediately after a reasonable period of time to obtain legal advice. In *Bhimji v Chatwani*[257] the plaintiffs sought to have the defendants committed to prison for contempt of court for refusing to permit the execution of an Anton Piller order. The order was served at 8 am but the defendants refused to permit the plaintiffs entry until they had obtained legal advice; by 11 am the defendants had obtained legal advice; in the afternoon the defendants applied to have it set aside and when, at 5 pm, they were unsuccessful in this (although some ameliorating variations were made) they permitted the plaintiffs to enter at 6 pm. Scott J found that the order was considerably complex and ran to some 14 pages. In these circumstances Scott J held that:

> "Respondents to Anton Piller orders who do not allow immediate entry and search in accordance with the terms of the orders are at risk. The defendants in the present case were, in my judgment, at risk from 11 am [onwards]. Respondents who choose to postpone a search for their own reasons should be warned, as these defendants were warned, that if they do so, they are at risk of committal. But when a committal application is made something more to justify an order under it must be shown than a mere technical breach of the obligation to allow entry forthwith."[258]

Of particular importance is the fact that a defendant is permitted to obtain legal advice and that, in the circumstances of that case, a period from 8 am to 11 am (when legal advice was actually obtained) was considered reasonable and that during that period the defendant was *not* in contempt of court, even though the plaintiffs were prevented, during that time, from entering the defendant's premises.[259]

Delivery Up of Chattels[260]

[10.66] The jurisdictional basis of an order for the delivery up of a defendant's chattels is s 28(8) of the Supreme Court of Judicature Ireland Act 1877, which

---

[257.] [1991] 1 All ER 705.

[258.] At 713e-f. See also *Wardle Fabrics Ltd v G Myristis Ltd* [1984] FSR 263.

[259.] See also *WEA Records Ltd v Visions Channel 4 Ltd* [1983] 2 All ER 589 and *Hallmark Cards Inc v Image Arts Ltd* [1977] FSR 150.

[260.] See generally, Ough & Flenley, *The Mareva Injunction and Anton Piller Order*, (2nd ed, 1993) Butterworths, p 74; Capper, *Mareva Injunctions*, (1988) SLS/Sweet & Maxwell, p 97.

empowers the court to make any order as appears just and convenient. Where the chattels which are ordered to be delivered up are the *subject matter* of the cause of action, Ord 50, r 4 of the RSC provides the procedure; where the chattels are not the actual subject matter of the cause of action, Ord 50, r 6 can be invoked. The order will be directed at a defendant and will require him to deliver up the specified chattels to the plaintiff's solicitor or a court appointed receiver for retention until final resolution of the substantive issues in dispute between the parties.

[10.67] This remedy is somewhere between a Mareva injunction and the appointment of a receiver. The case which is usually cited to demonstrate the court's willingness to grant such an order is *CBS (UK) v Lambert*[261] where Lawton LJ laid down a number of guidelines as to when it would be made. These include: (1) there should be evidence that the chattels were acquired through wrong-doing; (2) such chattels as a defendant might require to conduct his lawful business should be excluded from those chattels included in the order; (3) all chattels required to be delivered up should be specifically identified.

[10.68] An order for the delivery up of chattels is usually made following an *inter partes* hearing. The defendant is directed to deliver the specified chattels into the custody of the plaintiff's solicitors within a specified period of time. In this respect, while orders for the delivery up of chattels can be seen as very similar to Anton Piller orders, they are considerably less intrusive and less draconian than Anton Piller orders since they will not usually be made *ex parte* nor direct a defendant to permit a plaintiff to enter upon a defendant's premises. Hoffmann J recognised that an order for delivery up of chattels was a less severe order than an Anton Piller order in *Lock International plc v Beswick*[262] and suggested that in many cases it will be sufficient to make an order for delivery up.

Receivers[263]

[10.69] The appointment of a receiver to a person's property has been described as one of equity's oldest remedies.[264] At the outset it is important to distinguish

---

[261.] [1982] 3 All ER 237.

[262.] [1989] 3 All ER 373.

[263.] See generally, Picarda, *The Law Relating to Receivers, Managers and Administrators*, (2nd ed, 1990) Butterworths; Keane, *Equity and the Law of Trusts in the Republic of Ireland*, (1988) Butterworths, pp 288-290; Meagher, Gummow & Lehane, *Equity: Doctrines & Remedies*, (3rd ed, 1992) Butterworths, pp 689-732; Baker & Langan, *Snell's Equity*, (29th ed, 1990) Sweet & Maxwell, pp 689-699; and Black & Black, *Enforcement of a Judgment*, (8th ed, 1992) Longman Practitioner Series, pp 112-118.

[264.] *Hopkins v Worcester and Birmingham Canal Proprietors* (1868) LR 6 Eq 437 *per* Giffard V-C at 446, 447.

the types of receivership which are the subject of consideration here from a receivership following appointment by a debenture holder. A receiver appointed by a debenture holder over a company's assets will typically be deemed to be the agent of the company and will be appointed by deed, without recourse to the courts.[265] By contrast, the type of receivership considered here will result from a successful application to court to have a receiver appointed and in these cases the receiver will be an officer of the court and not the agent of any of the parties.[266] Although it has been observed by Keane J, writing ex-judicially,[267] that it is not usual to appoint one of the parties as receiver, where it is expedient an applicant's solicitor may be appointed receiver in aid of a Mareva injunction.[268]

[10.70] The jurisdiction to appoint a receiver has the same origins as the granting of an injunction and is given statutory force by s 28(8) of the Supreme Court of Judicature (Ireland) Act 1877 ("the 1877 Act") which provides, *inter alia*:

> A ... receiver [may be] appointed by an interlocutory order of the court in all cases in which it shall appear to the court to be just or convenient that such order shall be made; and any such order may be made either unconditionally or upon such terms and conditions as the court shall think just.

As in the case of an injunction, the court's discretion to appoint a receiver is also provided for by Ord 50, r 6(1) of the RSC which provides, *inter alia*:

> The court may ... appoint a receiver, by an interlocutory order in all cases in which it appears to the court to be just or convenient so to do.

As Keane J said, however, in *National Irish Bank Ltd v Graham*:[269]

> "[t]he appointment by the court of a receiver is a long established equitable remedy. The provisions to which I have referred afford a legislative basis for the granting of the remedy by way of an interlocutory order."

[10.71] For present purposes we are concerned with two distinct situations when the remedy of appointing a receiver may be availed of by a plaintiff in aid of or in substitution for a Mareva injunction: pre-judgment receivers and post-

---

[265] On receivers to companies, see, Courtney, *The Law of Private Companies*, (1994) Butterworths, Ch 16.

[266] *Bacup Corp v Smith* (1890) 44 Ch D 395 at 398 *per* Chitty J.

[267] Keane, *Equity and the Law of Trusts in the Republic of Ireland*, (1988) Butterworths, para [22.03].

[268] *Clonmeen Manor House Ltd v Royal Lodge Ltd*, *ex tempore* order of the High Court, unrep, 29 March 1994 (Flood J), which is considered at para **[10.75]** *infra*.

[269] [1994] 1 IR 215 at 221.

judgment receivers by way of equitable execution. In both situations it is s 28(8) of the 1877 Act which confers the formal jurisdiction to appoint a receiver.[270]

(a) Pre-judgment receivers

[10.72] Here, we consider the appointment of a receiver by the High Court on foot of an application by a plaintiff who has not at that point in time obtained a judgment against a defendant. The appointment of a receiver is a powerful remedy which goes further than an injunction since, although neither operate to confer proprietary rights in the assets which are "received", assets which are *prima facie* owned by a defendant, are taken out of his possession so as to ensure that they will be available to satisfy a plaintiff's claim. This is an extraordinary remedy and will usually only be granted where a plaintiff has a proprietary interest in the assets in question.

[10.73] The court's power to appoint a receiver is discretionary. As in the case of the granting of injunctive relief, however, the discretion to appoint a receiver should be exercised only in accordance with established criteria. In *Skip v Harwood*[271] Lord Hardwicke LC said of the court's power to appoint a receiver that it:

> "... is a discretionary power exercised by this court with as great utility to the subject as any sort of authority that belongs to them, and is provisional only for the more speedy getting in of a party's estate, and securing it for the benefit of such person who shall appear to be entitled and does not at all affect the right."

In *National Irish Bank Ltd v Graham*[272] Keane J said, albeit in the context of an application for the appointment of a receiver by way of equitable execution,[273] (which is a *post-judgment* remedy) that:

> "The most frequent ground for the appointment of a receiver by the court is the protection or preservation of property for the benefit of persons who have an interest in it."

In this passage lies the greatest obstacle to a Mareva plaintiff who wishes to have a court appoint a receiver: the traditional discretion has been underpinned by the requirement that a plaintiff has an *interest* in the property in question.[274]

---

270. The procedure governing the post-judgment appointment of a receiver is regulated by Ord 45, r 9 of the RSC: see para **[10.77]** *infra*.

271. (1747) 3 Atk 564.

272. [1994] 1 IR 215 at 221.

273. See para **[10.77]** *et seq, infra*.

274. *Cf Bond Brewing Holdings Ltd v National Australia Bank Ltd* (1990) 169 CLR; 92 ALR 49, cited by Meagher, Gummow and Lehane, *op cit*, para [2825] where the Australian Court of Appeal held that there was no principle which requires that an applicant for the appointment of a receiver have a proprietary interest in the property.

In a typical application for a Mareva injunction a plaintiff will *not* have a proprietary interest in the property which it is sought to receive. The absence of such a proprietary interest in the assets sought to be affected was, in 1976, the very novelty of the Mareva jurisdiction since it represented the main reason for the refusal of injunctive relief in *Lister & Co v Stubbs*[275] and is the distinction made in *Polly Peck International plc v Nadir (No 2)*[276] which differentiates Mareva injunctions from other injunctions where the plaintiff seeks to trace moneys. Where a plaintiff has a proprietary interest in the assets which it is sought to have "frozen" and he satisfies the other conditions, it will clearly be open to the court to exercise its discretion and appoint a receiver to those assets. Where, however, the plaintiff satisfies the conditions required for Mareva relief but does not have an interest in the property sought to be affected, should it be the case that he is not entitled to seek the appointment of a *pre-judgment* receiver?

[10.74] It is submitted that where, in the interests of justice, the circumstances of an application require a receiver to be appointed to protect or preserve a defendant's assets, the court has a discretion to make such an appointment notwithstanding that the plaintiff does not have an interest in the assets which are intended to be affected. Developments in the remedy of the injunction can, and where appropriate, should be reflected in other equitable remedies such as the appointment of a receiver. Indeed, in *Allied Irish Bank v Ashford Hotels Ltd; Ashford Hotels Ltd v Higgins*[277] the Court of Appeal held that on the appointment of a receiver by way of equitable execution, the court had jurisdiction to require a party to give a cross-undertaking in damages for the benefit of third parties and in so finding held that such a requirement was not confined to Mareva injunctions. Phillips LJ said:

> "The Mareva injunction is a comparatively recent addition to the armoury of the court. Having discovered the existence of, or some would say invented, this weapon, the court went on to invent the ancillary weapon of the cross-undertaking in damages for the benefit of third parties (see *Z Ltd v A* [1982] 1 All ER 556). In that case the cross-undertaking approved by the court was one designed to protect third parties from the consequences of compliance with the injunction but the scope of the protection of the undertaking has since been expanded to embrace third parties adversely affected by the injunction.
>
> For myself, I cannot accept that the jurisdiction of the court to require such an undertaking only exists where a Mareva injunction is ordered. Once the cross-undertaking for the benefit of third parties became a recognised feature of the court's jurisdiction in that context, it necessarily followed that the court could

---

[275.] (1890) 45 Ch D 1. See Ch 2, *The Jurisdiction to Grant Mareva Relief*, para **[2.04]**.
[276.] [1992] 4 All ER 769.
[277.] [1997] 3 All ER 309.

make use of it when granting other discretionary relief, at least where that relief was empowered under the same statutory provision."[278]

It is submitted that, by analogy, the remedy of the appointment of a receiver should be available, in *appropriate* cases, where the plaintiff does not have an interest in the assets thereby affected, ie where a plaintiff's claim is unsecured.

[10.75] Receivers have been appointed, pre-judgment, in aid of Mareva injunctions. In the Australian case of *Ballabil Holdings Pty Ltd v Hospital Products Ltd*[279] a receiver was appointed over the defendant's assets in circumstances where, notwithstanding the fact that a Mareva injunction had already been granted, assets continued to be disposed of and dissipated, with an apparent view to frustrating the plaintiff's future judgment. Those most critical observers of the Mareva jurisdiction, Meagher, Gummow and Lehane have referred to that case as "a (rare) proper case" for the grant of such an order.[280] In *International Credit and Investment Co (Overseas) Ltd v Adham*[281] Robert Walker J appointed a receiver over the defendants' assets because it was apparent that worldwide Mareva injunctions might not be obeyed. Pre-judgment receivers have also been appointed in aid of Mareva injunctions by the Irish High Court. So, for example, in *Clonmeen Manor House Ltd v Royal Lodge Ltd*[282] a receiver was appointed over the defendants' assets in aid of a pre-judgment Mareva injunction. It cannot be stressed enough that it will only be in the most exceptional of circumstances that a court will appoint a receiver over property where it has not been determined that a plaintiff is entitled to that property.

[10.76] It is submitted that where, before obtaining judgment, a plaintiff seeks to have a receiver appointed in aid of a Mareva injunction, he must establish the following proofs to the satisfaction of the court:

(a) that he has a substantive right (eg a cause of action) against the defendant;

(b) that he has a "good arguable case";

(c) that the defendant has assets which are available to be received;

[278.] At 317.

[279.] (1985) 1 NSWLR 155.

[280.] *Equity: Doctrines & Remedies*, (3rd ed, 1992), p 699.

[281.] [1998] BCC 134.

[282.] *Ex tempore* orders of the High Court, unrep, 29 March 1994 (Flood J) and 9 May 1994 (Costello J), referred to in Callanan, Strahan and Dempsey, 'The Obtaining of Mareva Injunctions in Ireland', [1994] 7 JIBL 273.

(d) that the defendant is likely to remove or dissipate his assets *with the intention of evading his obligations to the plaintiff and frustrating the anticipated order of the court*;

(e) that a Mareva injunction has been granted (or is being sought, or could be sought, in the same application) and there is compelling evidence that the defendant is likely to flout that order and that the only way of safeguarding the plaintiff's rights and of preventing the court's order from being frustrated is to appoint a receiver to take sufficient of the defendant's assets into his custody and possession and to hold same until the rights of the parties have been determined.[283]

It must be recognised that the appointment of a receiver over a defendant's assets where a plaintiff has not obtained judgment clearly has the potential to be draconian. If, in a particular case, justice dictates that Mareva relief is inappropriate, then this fact should, *per se*, also preclude the appointment of a pre-judgment receiver.[284]

(b) Post-judgment receivers by way of equitable execution

[10.77] The second situation when a receiver may be appointed by the court is where a plaintiff has obtained a judgment and the appointment of the receiver is by way of equitable execution against the defendant's property.[285] This particular remedy has long been available to judgment creditors; the circumstances, however, in which the court will grant such relief are strictly delimited by practice and precedent and it is not every judgment creditor who will succeed in having a receiver by way of equitable execution appointed. If the jurisdiction to appoint a pre-judgment receiver is developed and extended, there may well be a case for eschewing some of the existing restrictions on a post-judgment appointment of receiver by way of equitable execution.

---

[283] See, eg, *International Credit and Investment Co (Overseas) Ltd v Adham* [1998] BCC 134 where Robert Walker J appointed a receiver over property which had previously been made the subject of a worldwide Mareva injunction in circumstances where it appeared to the Court that there was a real risk that the Mareva orders might be breached.

[284] In *Bond Brewing Holdings Ltd v National Australia Bank Ltd* (1990) 169 CLR; 92 ALR 49 it was said by the Australian Court of Appeal that no proprietary interest in the property was required before a receiver would be appointed; however, it was stated that whilst it was available to "unsecured creditors" where there was no other adequate remedy it would be refused where a less severe remedy, such as an injunction, would remedy the problem.

[285] See generally, Black and Black, *Enforcement of a Judgment*, (8th ed, 1992) Longman Practitioner Series, pp 112-118; Keane, *Equity and the Law of Trusts in the Republic of Ireland*, (1988) Butterworths, para 22.05; Baker and Langan, *Snell's Equity*, (29th ed, 1990) Sweet & Maxwell, pp 697-699; Picarda, *The Law Relating to Receivers, Managers and Administrators*, (2nd ed, 1990) Butterworths, pp 293-295.

[10.78] In addition to the statutory basis for the appointment of a pre-judgment receiver, considered earlier,[286] Ord 45, r 9 of the RSC makes specific provision for the appointment of *post-judgment* receivers by way of equitable execution:

> In every case in which an application is made for the appointment of a receiver by way of equitable execution, the court in determining whether it is just or convenient that such appointment should be made shall have regard to the amount of the debt claimed by the applicant, to the amount which may probably be obtained by the receiver, and to the probable costs of his appointment, and may, if it shall so think fit, direct any inquiries on these or other matters, before making the appointment. The order shall be made upon such terms as the court may direct.

As in the case of a pre-judgment receiver, the appointment of a receiver by way of equitable execution is entirely at the court's discretion.

[10.79] Notwithstanding the development of the post-judgment Mareva injunction, the remedy to appoint a receiver by way of equitable execution remains a most useful tool for judgment creditors. Ordinarily, judgment creditors will have a judgment satisfied by execution at common law using the writ of *fieri facias*. The essence of the remedy of the appointment of a receiver by way of equitable execution is that it "enables a judgment creditor to capture an equitable interest in property which cannot be reached by the ordinary processes of execution eg an interest under a will".[287] In *Re Shephard*[288] Fry LJ explained the nature of equitable execution thus:

> "A receiver was appointed by the Court of Chancery in aid of a judgment at law when the plaintiff shewed that he had sued out the proper writ of execution, and was met by certain difficulties arising from the nature of the property which prevented his obtaining possession at law, and in these circumstances only did the Court of Chancery interfere in aid of a legal judgment for a legal debt."

Such distinctions between actions at law and in equity are today, anachronisms. Nevertheless and even today, this remedy is, technically, available only to capture *equitable interests* in property and for this and other reasons, where it is possible that a court will refuse to grant such relief, a plaintiff may simultaneously seek the alternative relief of a garnishee order,[289] or, indeed, a post-judgment Mareva injunction. The attraction to a plaintiff of the appointment of a receiver, as opposed to execution through the writ of *fi fa*, is that a receiver is, generally, perceived as being far more immediate and effective.

[286.] See para **[10.70]** *supra*.
[287.] See Keane, *op cit*, para 22.05.
[288.] (1889) 43 Ch D 131 at 138.
[289.] See para **[10.83]** *infra*.

[10.80] The prerequisites for an order appointing a receiver by way of equitable execution are:

  (a) that a plaintiff has obtained judgment against the defendant;

  (b) that a plaintiff has been unable at law to execute his judgment against the defendant; and

  (c) that the defendant is entitled to *an equitable interest* in property which could have been seized if he held the legal interest in the property.[290]

The big advantage which this procedure has over a post-judgment Mareva injunction is that there is no requirement that any nefarious intention on the part of the defendant be proved, to any degree. The courts have, *inter alia*, appointed receivers by way of equitable execution over the following property interests of defendants:[291] in a joint deposit receipt;[292] under a will;[293] an equitable interest in property;[294] policies of insurance;[295] salaries presently due;[296] and rents and profits deriving from property.[297] By contrast, the appointment of a receiver by way of equitable execution has been refused over the following property interests: assets of an insolvent defendant;[298] future assets;[299] and where the defendant's interest in the property is a legal interest,[300] although it was more recently stated in *Maclaine Watson & Co Ltd v International Tin Council*[301] that the remedy was not confined to cases where a defendant's interest in the subject assets is only equitable. It still appears to be the case in Ireland that the interest sought to be affected must be equitable. This appears from the judgment of Keane J in *National Irish Bank Ltd v Graham*[302] where he said:

[290.] See Keane, *op cit*.

[291.] See generally, Wylie, *Judicature Acts*, (Dublin 1906), pp 701, 702; Black and Black, *Enforcement of a Judgment*, (8th ed, 1992) Longman Practitioner Series, pp 114; Baker and Langan, *Snell's Equity*, (29th ed, 1990) Sweet & Maxwell, pp 697-698; Picarda, *The Law Relating to Receivers, Managers and Administrators*, (2nd ed, 1990) Butterworths, pp 293-295.

[292.] *O'Donovan v Goggin* 30 LR Ir 579.

[293.] *Sandford v King* (1900) 26 VLR 387.

[294.] *Re Pope* 17 QBD 743 (lands subject to an equitable mortgage); *Hills v Webster* 17 TLR 513 (a joint tenancy in property); *Salt v Cooper* 16 Ch D 544 (an equity of redemption).

[295.] *Beamish v Stephenson* 18 LR Ir 319.

[296.] *Picton v Cullen* [1900] 2 IR 612; *Smith-Barry v Hanley* 24 ILT&SJ 360.

[297.] *Cadogan v Lyric Theatre* 10 TLR 584; but not where the property is itself subject to a mortgage in another party's favour: *Walmsley v Mundy* 13 QBD 807.

[298.] *Harris v Beauchamp Bros* [1894] 1 QB 801.

[299.] See para **[10.81]** *infra*.

[300.] *Re Shephard* (1889) 43 Ch D 131; *Holmes v Millage* [1893] 1 QB 551.

[301.] [1987] 3 All ER 787.

[302.] [1994] 1 IR 215.

"Nor is this a case in which it would be appropriate to appoint a receiver by way of equitable execution over the milking herd. It is clear that the jurisdiction to appoint such a receiver is confined to cases in which a debtor enjoys an equitable interest in a property which cannot be reached by legal process ...

... The defendants are the legal owners, and not merely the owners in equity, of the milking herd. There is no impediment to the execution of the writ of *fieri facias* arising from the nature of the defendants' interest in the herd. There is in the result no ground for the appointment of a receiver by way of equitable execution."[303]

The problem for a plaintiff, as noted above, is that the appointment of a receiver will often have more teeth and be taken more seriously than involving the local sheriff in the execution of a writ of *fi fa*.

[10.81] The appointment of a receiver by way of equitable execution has traditionally been refused in applications concerning *future assets* which may become due to defendants.[304] The availability of this remedy in the case of future assets has, however, been upheld by Colman J in *Soinco SACA v Novokuznetsk Aluminium Plant and Ors*.[305] In that case the plaintiffs, which had obtained judgment for over US$10.5m, applied to have a receiver by way of equitable execution appointed; although a garnishee order *nisi* had been made against the fifth defendant in respect of sums due to the first defendant, difficulties were experienced in enforcing it. The plaintiffs' application sought the appointment of a receiver under s 37(1) of the English Supreme Court Act 1981 to effect execution of current and future debts arising under a supply contract between the fifth and first defendants. In rejecting the defendants' contentions that there was no jurisdiction to appoint a receiver over future debts, and refusing to follow earlier authorities,[306] Colman J said:

"Once it is accepted that availability of the property for execution by legal process is not a precondition to the appointment of a receiver by way of equitable execution, the question that has to be answered is whether future debts have intrinsic characteristics which would justify excluding them from this remedy.

In approaching this question it is necessary to keep in mind that the purpose of such a remedy would be to supplement legal process of execution by garnishee proceedings. Since that process does not apply to future debts and since it cannot be commenced in anticipation of debts becoming accruing due at a later

---

[303] At 222, citing *Re Shephard* (1889) 43 Ch D 131 and *Holmes v Millage* [1893] 1 QB 551 in support.
[304] *McCreery v Bennett* [1904] 2 IR 69; *Lyons v Harrison* 31 ILTR 180; *Maclaine Watson & Co Ltd v International Tin Council* [1987] 3 All ER 787.
[305] [1997] 3 All ER 523.
[306] Eg, *Holmes v Millage* [1893] 1 QB 551.

stage, there is much to be said for the availability of a remedy which would enable him to effect collection from third parties as and when they fell due".[307]

Colman J's reasoning as to why a receiver by way of equitable execution could be appointed was as follows:

"If pre-trial Mareva injunctions can apply, as in my judgment, they do,[308] to assets brought into the jurisdiction subsequently to the making of the order, there can be no reason, in principle, why post-judgment conservatory injunctions should not also be capable of applying to after-acquired assets, provided that they are within the overall monetary ceiling incorporated in the order. If that is correct, and there is jurisdiction to preserve for execution by injunction assets acquired and yet to be acquired after judgment, there would seem equally to be no reason in principle why a receiver should not also be appointed to preserve such assets. And if a receiver may be appointed to *preserve* such assets, why not to effect attachment of those assets for the benefit of the judgment creditor, provided that the court is satisfied that the debtor can be adequately protected against double jeopardy? In these circumstances I can see no reason whatever why, 124 years after the Judicature Acts, the court should deny to itself a jurisdiction which is self-evidently likely to be extremely useful as an ancillary form of execution. I would therefore hold that there is jurisdiction to appoint a receiver by way of equitable execution to receive future debts as well as debts due or accruing due at the date of the order."[309]

It is thought that the foregoing reasoning is both convincing and attractive and may be persuasive to an Irish court.[310]

[10.82] An application for the appointment of a receiver by way of equitable execution is by motion on notice under Ord 52 but it can also be made on an *ex parte* application.[311] Any receiver ultimately appointed may be required to give security in respect of his appointment.[312] It was recently established in *Allied Irish Bank v Ashford Hotels Ltd*[313] that by analogy with Mareva injunctions, the court had discretion to order that a cross-undertaking as to damages be given although in that case the Court of Appeal found that there was no justification to

---

[307.] At 537.
[308.] See Ch 7, *The Defendant's Assets*, para **[7.15]**.
[309.] [1997] 3 All ER 523 at 538.
[310.] Note that in *Ahern v Michael O'Brien & Co Ltd* [1991] 1 IR 421 O'Hanlon J appointed a receiver by way of equitable execution over ground rents which were payable at a future date which were not subject to disbursements in favour of third parties; he did, however, note that the remedy did not usually apply to future payments.
[311.] *Flannery v Ryan* [1919] 2 IR 338; *Mulhall v McCreery* 24 LR Ir 500.
[312.] *Fahey v Tobin* [1901] 1 IR 511; security is usually required where the value of the property exceeds the value of the judgment debt due: *Condon v Quilter* 32 ILTR 44.
[313.] [1997] 3 All ER 309.

make such an order. The appointment does not operate to confer any security on the plaintiff over the property received.[314] In *Clarke v Shephard*[315] an injunction was granted in aid of a receiver by way of equitable execution to restrain the defendant from endorsing over or otherwise dealing with promissory notes, the proceeds of which the receiver sought to seize. Were such an injunction to be granted today it is likely that it would be termed a post-judgment Mareva.

Garnishee Orders[316]

[10.83] Although it is beyond the scope of this book to treat garnishee orders in detail, it is thought that it is useful to consider briefly this remedy to judgment creditors which may also provide an alternative to a post-judgment Mareva injunction. Garnishee proceedings enable a judgment creditor to obtain an order, known as a garnishee order, against a third party (called a garnishee) which obliges that third party to pay to the judgment creditor sums which it owes to a judgment debtor. In *Choice Investments Ltd v Jeromnimon*[317] Lord Denning MR vividly described garnishee proceedings thus:

> "The word 'garnishee' is derived from the Norman French. It denotes one who is required to 'garnish', that is, to furnish a creditor with the money to pay off a debt. A simple instance will suffice. A creditor is owed £100 by a debtor. The debtor does not pay. The creditor gets judgment against him for the £100. Still the debtor does not pay. The creditor then discovers that the debtor is a customer of a bank and has £150 at his bank. The creditor can get a 'garnishee' order against the bank by which the bank is required to pay into court or direct to the creditor - out of its customer's £150 - the £100 which he owes to the creditor.
>
> There are two steps in the process. The first is a garnishee order *nisi. Nisi* is Norman-French. It means 'unless'. It is an order upon the bank to pay the £100 to the judgment creditor or into court within a stated time, *unless* there is some sufficient reason why the bank should not do so. Some reason may exist if the bank disputes its indebtedness to the customer for some reason or other ... If no sufficient reason appears, the garnishee order is made absolute - to pay to the judgment creditor - or into court: whichever is the more appropriate. On making the payment, the bank gets a good discharge from its indebtedness to its own customer - just as if he himself directed the bank to pay it. If it is a deposit on seven days' notice, the order *nisi* operates as the notice."

---

[314] *Re Whiteheart* (1971) 116 SJ 75.
[315] 4 NIJR 31.
[316] See generally, Hapgood, *Paget's Law of Banking*, (11th ed, 1996) Butterworths, pp 467-478; Black and Black, *Enforcement of a Judgment*, (8th ed, 1992) Longman Practitioner Series at Ch 14; Picarda, *The Law Relating to Receivers, Managers and Administrators*, (2nd ed, 1990) Sweet & Maxwell, pp 158-161; O'Floinn, *Practice and Procedure in the Superior Courts*, (1996) Butterworths, pp 353-356.
[317] [1981] QB 149.

As soon as the garnishee order *nisi* is served on the bank, it operates as an injunction. It prevents the bank from paying the money to its customer until the garnishee order is made absolute, or is discharged, as the case may be."[318]

Garnishee orders may be obtained in circumstances where a receiver by way of equitable execution is not available; moreover, where a debt is owed by a third party to a defendant, it may be a more attractive alternative to a post-judgment Mareva injunction because it can remove, entirely, a truculent defendant from the picture.

[10.84] Order 45, r 1(1) of the RSC contains the basic procedures which are involved when one seeks to invoke this remedy:

The court may, upon the *ex parte* application of any person who has obtained a judgment or order for the recovery or payment of money, either before or after any oral examination of the debtor liable under such judgment or order (hereinafter called the judgment debtor), and upon affidavit by himself or his solicitor stating that judgment has been recovered, or the order made, and that it is still unsatisfied, and to what amount, and that any other person is indebted to such debtor, and is within the jurisdiction, order that all debts owing or accruing from such third person (hereinafter called the garnishee) to such debtor shall be attached to answer the judgment or order; and by the same or subsequent order it may be ordered that the garnishee shall appear before the court or an officer of the court, as such court shall appoint, to show cause why he should not pay to the person who has obtained such judgment or order, the debt due from him to such debtor, or so much thereof as may be sufficient to satisfy the judgment or order.

Where the court agrees to make a garnishee order on an *ex parte* application, the order is provisional and is known as a *conditional order of garnishee*, or, an "order *nisi*", or, an order to show cause ie the garnishee must show cause why a garnishee order should not be made. The judgment creditor must disclose all matters material to the *ex parte* application and if it comes to light that the application was not *uberrimae fides* and an order *nisi* was obtained, the court may discharge it with costs at the hearing to have it made absolute.[319] Order 45, r 1(2) provides that at least seven days before the date of the *inter partes* hearing, the order *nisi* must be served[320] on the garnishee and (unless the court directs otherwise) and also on the judgment debtor and his solicitor. The effect of service of an order *nisi* for the attachment of debts on a garnishee is that such debts are bound in the garnishee's hands.[321]

---

[318] At 154-155.

[319] *Telford v Coady* 27 ILTR 7. See Ch 8, *Applying for a Mareva Injunction*, para **[8.32]** where the duty to make full and frank disclosure of all material facts on an *ex parte* application is considered.

[320] In the manner provided for by Ord 121 of the RSC.

[321] Order 45, r 2.

[10.85] The effects of a garnishee order depend upon whether the garnishee accepts or disputes the validity of the debt due by him to the judgment debtor. If the garnishee does not forthwith pay the monies owed into court, or an amount sufficient to pay the amount owed to the judgment creditor and if he does not dispute the debt due or claimed or does not appear, then the court may order execution to issue to levy the amount due by the garnishee or such amount equal to the judgment creditor's judgment or order together with the costs of the garnishee proceedings.[322] Where the garnishee disputes liability the court may, instead, order that any issue or question necessary to determine the garnishee's liability be tried[323] and where it is claimed that a third party is entitled to the debt or that he has a lien or charge on it, the court may order that third party to appear and state the nature and particulars of his claim to the debt owed by the garnishee to the judgment debtor.[324] After hearing the allegations of any third party, or if the third party does not appear, the court may order execution to issue to levy the amount due from the garnishee together with the costs of the proceedings; alternatively, the court may order any issue to be tried or determined and may bar the claim of the third party or make such order as the court thinks fit upon such terms with respect to any third party's lien, and as to costs, as the court shall think just and reasonable.[325] Protection is afforded a garnishee who makes payment or where execution is levied: Ord 45, r 7 provides that such is a valid discharge to him *vis-à-vis* the judgment debtor even if such proceedings may be set aside or the judgment or order is subsequently reversed. Costs for the garnishee proceedings are a matter for the discretion of the court and in relation to the costs of the judgment creditor shall, unless the court orders otherwise, be retained out of the money recovered by him under the garnishee order and in priority to the amount of the judgment debt.[326]

[10.86] What so are the pre-requisites to a judgment creditor obtaining a garnishee order? The judgment creditor must establish the following proofs:

(a) that he has obtained a judgment or order for the recovery or repayment of money;

(b) that the judgment or order is unsatisfied;

(c) that the judgment debtor is within the jurisdiction;[327]

(d) that debts are owing or accruing from any person, firm[328] or corporation (the intended garnishee) to the judgment debtor;

[322.] Order 45, r 3.
[323.] Order 45, r 4.
[324.] Order 45, r 5.
[325.] Order 45, r 6.
[326.] Order 45, r 8.
[327.] *Richardson v Richardson* [1927] P 228.
[328.] Order 45, r 1(3) provides that the garnishee shall include "... a firm, any member of which is resident within the jurisdiction ...".

(e) that the debt sought to be attached does not belong to a third person and that such third persons have no lien or charge on it.

Any unconditional debt may be attached; and whilst the debt must exist in law, it need not be immediately payable. Debts which may be made the subject of a garnishee order include: bank accounts;[329] the proceeds of fire insurance policies;[330] and instalments of a debt payable periodically as and when they fall due.[331]

[10.87] When an order *nisi* or order to show cause is made and served on a garnishee it binds attachable debts which are then held by the garnishee, but not debts which subsequently become due by the garnishee to the judgment debtor,[332] until the hearing of the application to make the order absolute. A garnishee order will not have priority over existing interests by way of security or otherwise. In *Fitzpatrick v DAF Sales Ltd and Allied Irish Finance Company Ltd*[333] the plaintiff had obtained judgment for £24,000 against the first defendant on foot of a hire-purchase agreement. The judgment was stayed on condition that two equal instalments of £12,000 were paid by specific dates. The second defendant counter-claimed against the plaintiff for £18,000 and succeeded, this judgment being stayed on condition that the plaintiff paid monthly instalments to the second defendant. When the plaintiff defaulted, the second plaintiff entered judgment and obtained a conditional order (*nisi*) of garnishee to attach the £12,000 still owing by the first defendant to the plaintiff. The plaintiff judgment-debtor resisted the garnishee order on the grounds that, first, he alleged that his solicitor had undertaken with another bank to discharge the plaintiff's liability under a subsequently negotiated loan out of the £12,000 due and that this was a prior security interest by way of equitable assignment in favour of the other bank; and secondly, that the plaintiff had agreed with his solicitor that the solicitor's costs would also be discharged out of these moneys. It was held by O'Hanlon J that the conditional order should be made an absolute order in favour of the second defendant *but subject to the bank's claim*. The question boiled down to one of evidence and O'Hanlon J held that in that case there was sufficient evidence of a specific agreement with the bank which gave rise to an equitable assignment in its favour. O'Hanlon J did not, however, allow the claim for solicitor's costs to take precedence on the authority of *James Bibby*

---

329. *Joachimson v Swiss Bank Corporation* [1981] 3 KB 110.

330. *Sinnott v Bowden* [1912] 2 Ch 414.

331. *Tapp v Jones* (1875) LR 10 QB 591.

332. *Webb v Stenton* (1883) 11 QBD 518. In *Tapp v Jones* (1875) LR 10 QB 591 Lord Blackburn said that the meaning of debt due or accrued debt is "*debitum in praesenti, solvendum in futuro*, but it goes no further, and it does not comprise anything which may be a debt, however probable, or however soon it may be a debt."

333. [1988] IR 464.

Ltd v Woods and Howard[334] where it had been held that a judgment creditor's claim took precedence over a solicitor's claim for costs where the solicitor had not applied for or obtained a charging order in respect of his claim for costs over the monies due by the judgment debtor on or before the hearing of the application to make the garnishee order absolute.

[10.88] A garnishee order does not operate to transfer the property in the debt to the judgment creditor. However, as Farwell LJ said in *Galbraith v Grimshaw and Baxter*[335] a garnishee order:

> "... is an equitable charge on [the debt], and the garnishee cannot pay the debt to any one but the garnishor without incurring the risk of having to pay it over again to the creditor."

There is old authority that an absolute garnishee order does not, however, create a debt between the garnishee and the judgment creditor for all purposes and so a judgment creditor cannot petition to have a garnishee, being a company, wound up.[336]

---

[334] [1949] 2 KB 449.

[335] [1910] 1 KB 339 at 343.

[336] *Re Combined Weighing and Advertising Machine Co* (1889) 43 Ch D 99 and *Re Steel Wing Co* [1921] 1 Ch 349.

Chapter 11

Restraining Defendants from Leaving the State

[11.01] In exceptional cases a plaintiff may seek a court order to restrain a defendant from leaving the State. A defendant's presence may be required for a number of distinct reasons: his absence may hinder a plaintiff's successful prosecution of his action against the defendant; it may hinder the execution of a judgment; or it may defeat a present or future court order against a defendant to make discovery or disclosure of his assets. The court's powers in equity to restrain a person from leaving the jurisdiction are of both ancient[1] and modern[2] ancestry; in addition, the power at law to have a person arrested in furtherance of civil proceedings is provided for in a number of statutes which are both Victorian[3] and modern day.[4] Although the remedies of civil arrest and injunctions to restrain persons from leaving the jurisdiction are given some prominence in a book such as this it must always be remembered that they are truly extraordinary and draconian remedies which greatly interfere with a defendant's personal liberty. In relatively few cases will these remedies be a proportionate response to the threatened harm to a plaintiff which is posed by a defendant leaving the State. Accordingly, the courts will only ever exercise such powers in clear and compelling cases where the facts are exceptional. In this chapter the following ways in which a person may be prevented from leaving the State are considered:

[A] Writ of *Ne Exeat Regno* and the Debtors Act (Ireland), 1872.

[B] Bayer Injunctions.

[C] Modern Powers of Civil Arrest

[A] WRIT OF *NE EXEAT REGNO* AND THE DEBTORS ACT (IRELAND), 1872

[11.02] In this section the equitable power of the court to issue a writ of *ne exeat regno* and the statutory power to order the civil arrest of a defendant under s 7 of

---

1. For example, the writ of *ne exeat regno*: see para **[11.02]** *et seq*, *infra*.
2. See *Bayer AG v Winter* [1986] 1 All ER 732, para **[11.23]** *infra*.
3. For example, the Debtors Act (Ireland) 1872: see para **[11.05]** *infra*.
4. For example, the Companies Acts 1963-1990 and the Bankruptcy Act 1988: see para **[11.41]** *et seq* and para **[11.51]** *et seq*, respectively, *infra*.

the Debtors Act (Ireland) 1872 are considered together as they are interrelated. The following issues arise for consideration:

1. The Historical Origins of the Writ of *Ne Exeat Regno*;

2. Section 7 of the Debtors Act (Ireland) 1872;

3. The Relationship between s 7 and the Writ of *Ne Exeat Regno*;

4. Order 69 of the Rules of the Superior Courts 1986;

5. The Requisite Conditions for the Issue of the Writ or s 7 Arrest.

The Historical Origins of the Writ of *Ne Exeat Regno*

[11.03] The writ of *ne exeat regno*, or command not to leave the realm, originated in the thirteenth century as a prerogative writ which was used by the English Crown for "great political objects and purposes of state, for the safety or benefit of the realm";[5] the writ of *ne exeat regno* could issue from the Lord Chancellor at the Crown's behest to prevent wayward subjects from going "beyond the seas"[6] in times of war and other civil crises. Over the centuries the remedy of civil arrest and of preventing a defendant from leaving the jurisdiction was extended beyond the Crown and came to be available to civil litigants.[7] In *Glover v Walters*[8] the similar writ of *ne exeat colonia* was described thus:

> "It is a prerogative writ for the purpose of preventing a subject quitting the country without giving bail or security to answer a money claim of an equitable nature. Formerly the writ was issued out of the High Court of Chancery. The writ is directed to the Marshal commanding him to cause the defendant personally to come before him and give sufficient bail or security in the sum mentioned in the order and adequate to the nature of the case; that the defendant will not go or attempt to go into parts beyond the seas without leave of the court, and in case the defendant shall refuse to give such bail or security then the Marshal is commanded to commit the defendant to prison, there to be kept in safe custody until he shall do it of his own accord and when the Marshal has taken such security he is to certify to the court".[9]

---

5.   *Story's Commentaries on Equity Jurisprudence*, (3rd ed, 1920), p 621. See generally, *Felton v Callis* [1968] 3 All ER 673 where Megarry J reviewed the origins of and conditions circumscribing the grant of the writ of *ne exeat regno*.

6.   *Fitzherbert's The New Natura Brevium*, (7th ed, 1790), pp 192-3, s 85 which is also referred to by Megarry J in *Felton v Callis* [1968] 3 All ER 673.

7.   In *Ex p Brunker* (1734) 3 P Wms 312 at 313, 314 Lord Talbot LC noted that whilst it was originally a "state writ", "it has been made use of in aid of the subjects for helping them to justice".

8.   [1949-50] 80 CLR 172.

9.   At 172, 173.

In the case of a writ of *ne exeat regno* the writ issued to the sheriff.[10] Up until 1872 (when the Debtors Act (Ireland) was passed) however, civil debtors were liable to be arrested on mesne process at law. The primary effect of that Act is contained in s 5 which provides that, subject to certain exceptions,[11] "no person shall after the commencement of this Act be arrested or imprisoned for making default in payment of a debt contracted after the passing of this Act". Prior to 1872, therefore, the equitable writ of *ne exeat* was not especially draconian; the writ only facilitated the arrest of persons who were about to leave the country, whereas at law, a civil debtor could be arrested and imprisoned even if there was no suggestion of his leaving the country. Quoting from Blackstone,[12] Megarry J said in *Felton v Callis*[13] that the use and object of the writ in the Courts of Chancery was:

> "... exactly the same as an arrest at law in the commencement of an action, *viz* to prevent the party from withdrawing his person and property beyond the jurisdiction of the court, before a judgment could be obtained and carried into execution; so where there is a suit in equity for a demand, for which the defendant cannot be arrested in an action at law, upon an affidavit made that there is reason to apprehend that he will leave the kingdom before the conclusion of the suit, the chancellor by this writ will stop him."

The need for an equitable remedy, as distinct from a remedy at law, was necessitated by the reason that it was not until the passing of the Supreme Court of Judicature Ireland Act 1877 that the common law and equity were fused. The purpose of the writ of *ne exeat regno* was to provide a plaintiff who had an *equitable* claim (and which, accordingly, the common law did not recognise) with an effective remedy against an absconding debtor.

[11.04] From its origins as a prerogative writ of State to a civil remedy in theory available to all, the purpose and objective of the writ of *ne exeat* was itself transformed. As Megarry J said in *Felton v Callis*[14]

> "... a process whereby the Crown, for reasons of state, prevented a subject from leaving the realm had become a process whereby an equitable creditor could have the debtor arrested and made to give security if, and only if, he was about to leave the realm. The threat of leaving the realm had ceased to be the objective which the writ sought to frustrate, and had instead become a

---

[10.] See Megarry J in *Felton v Callis* [1968] 3 All ER 673 at 676G.

[11.] As to which, see para **[11.05]** *infra* where the power under s 7 to order the arrest of a person "about to quit Ireland" is considered.

[12.] *Commentaries*, (15th ed, 1809) Vol 1, p 266, note 10.

[13.] [1968] 3 All ER 673 at 676.

[14.] At 676I.

condition precedent to enabling the plaintiff to coerce the defendant into giving security."

The prescribed purpose of the writ (and so the circumstances in which it can be issued) is of central importance in a court deciding whether it can be utilised in aid of a Mareva injunction; the purpose of the writ shall be considered in conjunction with the conditions which must be met before the writ will issue or an order is made under s 7 of the Debtors Act (Ireland), 1872.[15]

Section 7 of the Debtors Act (Ireland) 1872

[11.05] The enactment of the Debtors Act (Ireland) 1872, ("the 1872 Act") which followed the passing of the Debtors Act 1869 in England and Wales, marked "the general abolition of imprisonment for debt".[16] The 1872 Act did not, however, abolish the arrest and imprisonment of debtors in all circumstances and s 7 of the 1872 Act[17] empowered the court, in specified circumstances, to order the arrest and imprisonment of a debtor who is about to abscond from Ireland.[18] Section 7 provides, *inter alia*:

> Where the plaintiff in any action in any of Her Majesty's superior courts of law at Dublin, in which if brought before the commencement of this Act the defendant would have been liable to arrest, proves at any time before final judgment by evidence on oath, to the satisfaction of a judge of one of those courts, that the plaintiff has good cause of action against the defendant to the amount of twenty pounds or upwards, or has sustained damage to that amount, and that there is probable cause for believing that the defendant is about to quit Ireland unless he be apprehended, and that the absence of the defendant from Ireland will materially prejudice the plaintiff in the prosecution of his action, such judge may in the prescribed manner order such defendant to be arrested and imprisoned for a period not exceeding six months, unless and until he has sooner given the prescribed security, not exceeding the amount claimed in the action, that he will not go out of Ireland without the leave of the Court ...

Section 7 of the 1872 Act, therefore, confers a discretion on the court to order the arrest of a debtor upon certain conditions being satisfied. The court's power to order the arrest and imprisonment of a debtor was thereby confined to where a defendant was "about to quit Ireland" and so was made approximate to when the writ of *ne exeat regno* could issue.

[15.] See para **[11.10]** *infra*.

[16.] *Per* Cotton LJ in *Colverson v Bloomfield* (1885) 29 Ch D 341 at 342.

[17.] Section 7 of the Irish 1872 Act corresponds in most material respects with s 6 of the English Debtors Act 1869 ("the 1869 Act"); it is interesting to note, however, that whereas s 7 of the 1872 Act only applies where the cause of action against the defendant is worth £20 or upwards, s 6 of the 1869 Act provides that the cause of action must be worth £50 or upwards.

[18.] Imprisonment for debt is preserved in other circumstances too: s 6 of the Debtors Act (Ireland) 1872.

The Relationship between s 7 and the Writ of *Ne Exeat Regno*

[11.06] Prior to the enactment of the Supreme Court of Judicature Ireland Act 1877 ("the 1877 Act") the civil arrest of debtors to prevent them from leaving Ireland was possible in two distinct situations: under s 7 of the 1872 Act, where a plaintiff's cause of action was *at law* and by means of the writ of *ne exeat* where a plaintiff's cause of action was *equitable*. After the enactment of the 1872 Act (and especially after the enactment of the 1877 Act) the question arose as to whether the conditions contained in s 7 of the 1872 Act ought, by analogy, to be applied when exercising the court's equitable discretion to issue the writ of *ne exeat*.

[11.07] The intertwining of the conditions specified by s 7 for an arrest of an absconding debtor at law with the writ of *ne exeat* and the authorities on this point were examined extensively by Megarry J in *Felton v Callis*.[19] In that case, the facts of which are considered below,[20] counsel for the plaintiff had argued that the writ of *ne exeat regno* was not subject to the restrictions of s 6 of the English Debtors Act 1869; neither s 6 of the English Act of 1869 nor s 7 of the Irish Act of 1872 expressly refer to the writ of *ne exeat* and so the only way in which the writ could be interpreted as being conditioned by the statutory provision for civil arrest would be by applying the maxim that "equity follows the law".[21]

[11.08] The question as to whether the writ of *ne exeat* is subject to the shackles of s 6 of the English 1869 Act (and, by implication, the materially similar s 7 of the Irish 1872 Act) was conclusively addressed by the Court of Appeal in *Colverson v Bloomfield*.[22] In that case a trustee was ordered to pay a sum of money within seven days following service of the order, to a beneficiary of the trust. The beneficiary could not locate the trustee so as to serve the order and so applied for a writ of *ne exeat regno* on the grounds that he believed the trustee to be about to leave the jurisdiction. Chitty J had refused the application and this was affirmed by the Court of Appeal. There Bowen LJ said:

> "When the case is looked into it clearly is not within either section 4 or section 6 of the Debtors Act 1869. The granting of a *ne exeat* by the Court of Chancery was a kind of reflection of the common law process of arrest. It seems to me

---

[19.] [1968] 3 All ER 673.

[20.] See para **[11.11]** *infra*.

[21.] The case of *Drover v Beyer* (1879) 13 Ch D 242 is equivocal authority for the proposition that the writ is not fettered by s 6 of the English Debtors Act 1872: whereas Sir George Jessel MR did say that the writ was only to be applied in cases where arrest was permissible under s 6, James LJ, in the Court of Appeal, in an eight line judgment, seems to continue the distinction between arrest by way of *ne exeat regno* and arrest under s 6 of the 1872 Act.

[22.] (1885) 29 Ch D 341.

that the Court of Chancery never ordered arrest for an equitable debt except in cases where, if the debt had been legal, the courts of Common Law would have done so."[23]

Bowen LJ's judgment concurred with that of Cotton LJ. Cotton LJ found that the debt due by the trustee to the beneficiary was only payable in the future (ie seven days after service of the order) and that, accordingly, had the debt been a legal debt, as opposed to an equitable debt, arrest at common law would not have been permitted. He said:

"This is an application for a writ of *ne exeat regno* in a case where, if the debt had been legal, there could not have been any imprisonment at common law. The applicant's counsel says that the writ of *ne exeat regno* is not abolished by the Debtors Act 1869, and that the court ought to issue it in order to keep the defendant within the jurisdiction. But in my opinion, if the debt is not now due and payable a writ of *ne exeat* ought not to be issued. The Court of Chancery, in granting this writ, merely proceeded by analogy to the process at common law. At common law arrest on mesne process was only applicable to legal debts. The Court of Chancery, by analogy, issued a writ of *ne exeat regno* where the debt was equitable. In my opinion the objection is fatal, that if this had been a legal demand there could have been no arrest at common law, and by analogy we ought not to grant a writ of *ne exeat*. The debt is only payable *in fututro*, and in such a case the writ ought not to issue."[24]

This and other authorities[25] were cited by Megarry J in *Felton v Callis*[26] who concluded that:

"... in my judgment, the writ can issue in the present case only if the requirements of the Act of 1869 are satisfied. Authority binds me to this result, but even if it did not, I should reach the same conclusion myself. Today, if Parliament intends a statute to apply to some equitable right or remedy, one expects Parliament to say so. But in times past Parliament was frequently not so explicit, and equity often acted by analogy ... In the present case I am concerned with an Act nearly a century old; and it is the standards of those days, when the administration of law and equity was still separate, that must be applied for this purpose."[27]

[23.] At 343.

[24.] At 342.

[25.] For example, *Lewis v Lewis* (1893) 68 LT 198. There Stirling J said (at 199): "... in issuing such a writ, in execution of the jurisdiction formerly exercised in the Court of Chancery, the court by analogy should see that the circumstances which common law would require to justify the arrest under s 6 of the Debtors Act 1869 are established to its satisfaction."

[26.] [1968] 3 All ER 673.

[27.] At 697C-D.

The position may be summarised thus: the fetters on the civil arrest of absconding debtors contained in s 7 of the 1872 Act apply by analogy to the writ of *ne exeat*; the writ will only issue in respect of an equitable debt in circumstances where, were the debt a legal debt, arrest could be ordered under s 7 of the 1872 Act. Although there would seem to be a compelling case for saying that the effect of the 1877 Act was to do away with the writ of *ne exeat* by widening the scope of s 7 of the 1872 Act to include equitable causes of action, it would seem that both remedies continue to exist separately. It is thought that in those few cases where either remedy is sought, they should be pleaded in the alternative.

Order 69 of the Rules of the Superior Courts 1986

[11.09] Unlike the English Rules of the Supreme Court which, on being revised, removed the procedure applicable to civil arrest under s 6 of the English Debtors Act 1869, Ord 69 of the Irish Rules of the Superior Courts, 1986 ("RSC") continues to make provision for a civil arrest under s 7 of the 1872 Act.[28] Order 69 r 1 provides that an order to arrest under s 7 of the 1872 Act, shall be made upon affidavit and *ex parte* but the defendant may at any time after arrest apply to the court to rescind or vary the order or to discharge him from custody or for such other relief as may be just. An order for arrest must be indorsed with the registered place of business of a plaintiff's solicitor or with the address for service of the plaintiff in person.[29] The security which a defendant can give may be a deposit in court, a bond by the defendant and two sufficient sureties, or with the plaintiff's consent, any other security.[30] A debtor who is arrested is entitled to his release upon the provision of acceptable security.[31]

The Requisite Conditions for the Issue of the Writ or s 7 Arrest

[11.10] Before a court will make an order for the arrest of an absconding debtor under s 7 of the Debtors Act (Ireland), 1872 or, by analogy, issue the writ of *ne exeat*, the following conditions must be met:

    (a)   The plaintiff's action against the defendant must be one in which, prior to the passing of the 1872 Act, the defendant would have been liable to arrest;

[28.] The English Rules of the Supreme Court 1965 repealed without replacement Ord 69 which dealt with the writ of *ne exeat*. Despite this Megarry J in *Felton v Callis* [1968] 3 All ER 673 at 677E held that the omission did not in any way affect the validity of s 6 of the Debtors Act 1869.

[29.] Order 69, r 2.

[30.] *Ibid*, r 3.

[31.] *Ibid*, r 6.

(b) The plaintiff must have a good cause of action, at law or in equity, to the amount of £20 or upwards, or has sustained damage to that amount;

(c) There must be probable cause for believing that the defendant is about to quit Ireland unless he be apprehended;

(d) The absence of the defendant from Ireland must materially prejudice the plaintiff in the prosecution of his action.

Understandably, the standard of proof which the court will require before issuing a writ of *ne exeat* or ordering arrest under s 7 of the 1872 Act is high.[32] It must also be remembered that, even where all four conditions have been satisfied, the court's power to order arrest or issue the writ is discretionary.[33]

(a) Action must be one in which a defendant would, prior to 1872, have been liable to arrest

[11.11] This first condition was considered by Megarry J in *Felton v Callis*.[34] In this case the two plaintiffs were in partnership with the defendant, practising as chartered accountants. The partnership's bank account was overdrawn and an agreement was entered under seal whereby the two plaintiffs agreed to pay £900 to the bank and the defendant agreed to discharge the balance. The plaintiffs were fearful that the defendant would leave England with all of his assets without paying his share of the debt and issued proceedings for an order that he should pay his share of the debt to the bank. The writ was served but no appearance entered. Whereas, today, application might be made in these circumstances for a Mareva injunction, the plaintiffs there applied for a writ of *ne exeat regno* to prevent the defendant from leaving England. On the first condition for the writ of *ne exeat* (as opposed to arrest under s 7 of the Debtors Act (Ireland) 1872) Megarry J said:

> "The first condition requires that the action should be one in which the plaintiff would formerly have been liable to arrest at law. In applying this to the writ of *ne exeat regno*, what must be shown is that there exists the equitable equivalent of an action in which the plaintiff would previously have been liable for arrest at law. Debt is the obvious example. In the case before me the plaintiffs do not claim payment to them; they claim that the defendant should be ordered to pay the bank. It is, says counsel for the plaintiffs, a *quia timet* action whereby a surety who is liable as a principal debtor seeks to compel the principal debtor to pay the creditor the debt guaranteed ... A *quia timet* action is equitable in nature, he said, and, although the liability arose out of the contractual

---

32. See *Felton v Callis* [1968] 3 All ER 673; *Tomlinson v Harrison* (1802) 8 Ves 32; *Stones v Cooke* (1835) 8 Sim 321; *Re Underwood* (1903) 51 WR 335.
33. See *Hasluch v Lehman* (1890) 6 TLR 435; *Glover v Walters* [1949-50] 80 CLR 172.
34. [1968] 3 All ER 673.

obligations under the deed executed by the parties, and was not a mere equitable obligation such as the liability of a trustee to his beneficiary, nevertheless it was equitable enough to form the subject of the writ."[35]

Although the debt due by the defendant was a contractual debt, and therefore actionable at law, the plaintiffs were resorting to an equitable remedy in the form of *quit timet* proceedings. Megarry J said that the writ of *ne exeat* applied to cases within the exclusive jurisdiction of equity and that there was only one exception to this where, in the case of an account, it is applied in the concurrent jurisdiction; the writ has never been available in the auxiliary jurisdiction of equity. Megarry J said, *obiter dictum*, that even if the *quit timet* proceedings in that case came within the concurrent jurisdiction, there is only one type of case in that jurisdiction (namely, to account) where the writ has been issued.

[11.12] In the case of an application for an order under s 7 of the Debtors Act (Ireland) 1872, this first condition means that the debtor must have been liable to arrest at law in the cause of action in hand *before* the passing of that Act. Not all actions before 1872 entitled a plaintiff to seek a defendant's arrest. The paradigm cause of action in which a defendant was liable for arrest was an action for a liquidated debt. This is not to say that actions involving unliquidated claims are precluded: indeed s 7 of the Irish Act of 1872 provides that the claim against the defendant must be for an amount in excess of £20 or that the plaintiff has sustained damage to that amount. In the case of the writ of *ne exeat*, this first condition means that the plaintiff must have an equitable equivalent of an action at law which would have entitled him to seek the debtor's arrest.[36] To avoid being non-suited, it is thought that a claim for a s 7 arrest and a writ of *ne exeat* should, insofar as possible, be brought in the alternative.

(b) A good cause of action for £20 or upwards/damage to that amount

[11.13] In order to obtain a writ of *ne exeat* or an order for arrest under s 7 of the 1872 Act, the second condition which a plaintiff is required to show on affidavit is that he has a good cause of action against the debtor for an amount of £20 or upwards[37] or that the plaintiff has sustained damage to that amount.[38] It has been said by the court that "[t]he evidence as to the debt must be very clear".[39]

[35.] At 682C-E.

[36.] See *Allied Arab Bank Ltd v Hajjar* [1987] 3 All ER 739, considered at para **[11.14]** *infra*.

[37.] Note that s 6 of the English Debtors Act 1869 requires the plaintiff to show that he has a good cause of action for an amount of £50 or upwards.

[38.] Again, note that s 6 of the English Act of 1869 contains no reference to "or has sustained damage to that amount": see para **[11.14]** *infra*.

[39.] *Per* Romilly MR in *Thompson v Smith* (1865) 13 WR 422 at 423. In *Jackson v Petrie* (1804) 10 Ves 164 at 165 Lord Eldon said, in the context of a writ of *ne exeat*: "the affidavit must be as positive as to the equitable debt, as an affidavit of a legal debt to hold to bail".

However, in *Felton v Callis*[40] there was a discrepancy in the sum of £278 18s 5d between the amount claimed by the bank and the amount claimed by the plaintiffs, Megarry J held, *obiter*, that the discrepancy did not raise any real doubt as to the existence of the obligation and that, accordingly, this condition had been satisfied in that case.

[11.14] The fact that an Irish plaintiff can satisfy this condition by showing that he has sustained damage to the amount of £20 means that s 7 of the Irish Act of 1872 is slightly wider than s 6 of the English Act of 1869. This distinction was material in the case of *Allied Arab Bank Ltd v Hajjar*.[41] In that case Leggatt J said:

> "With regard to condition 1, it is plain that a debtor was never liable to arrest at law except for a debt certain, and equity followed the law in this respect: see *Colverson v Bloomfield* (1885) 29 Ch D 341. The plaintiffs are prosecuting their claim in this action for damages, having refrained from proceeding on the debt under the guarantees. In my judgment under condition 1 the first defendant would not have been liable to arrest at law, since the claim effectively being prosecuted is not the claim for debt ...".[42]

This raises an interesting question. If indeed it was the case that before 1872 a debtor could not be arrested at law in an action for damages, what is the significance of the reference to "or has sustained damage to that amount" in s 7 of the Irish Act of 1872? Leggatt J was correct in saying that a debtor was never liable to arrest in cases other than those involving a "debt certain". Indeed in *Alder v Ward*[43] the Irish Master of the Rolls, in refusing a writ of *ne exeat*, gave as one of the reasons for his refusal the nature of the plaintiff's claims because "that their being damages and unliquidated, forms in itself a distinct objection to the present application".[44] It is thought, however, that the position changed in Ireland after the passing of the 1872 Act. Indeed, in *Hester and Co v Byrne*,[45] Dowse B explained the reference to "has sustained damage" by saying "that is an action of tort". Accordingly, whilst s 7 of the 1872 Act purports to apply only to cases where a debtor "would have been liable to arrest", to come within s 7 a plaintiff need only show that he suffered damage to the amount of £20 or upwards and need not show a debt certain in that amount. Since, in the context of the writ of *ne exeat*, equity has consistently been held to "follow the law"[46] it

---

[40.] [1968] 3 All ER 673 at 683E.
[41.] [1987] 3 All ER 739.
[42.] At 744e-f.
[43.] (1843) 51 Ir Eq Rep 367 at 368.
[44.] See also *Etches v Lance* 7 Ves 417; *Cock v Ravie* 6 Ves 283 and *Blaydes v Calvert* (1820) 2 Jac & W 211.
[45.] (1874) 8 ILTR 53.
[46.] For example, in *Felton v Callis* [1968] 3 All ER 673.

is thought that in Ireland a writ of *ne exeat* can issue without proving that the plaintiff has a debt certain.

(c) Probable cause for believing that the defendant is about to quit Ireland

[11.15] There must be "probable cause" for believing that a defendant debtor is "about to quit Ireland" unless he is apprehended. In *Sichel v Raphael*[47] Sir William Page Wood V-C said that there must be evidence of a defendant's intentions to go abroad which is:

> "... corroborated by evidence as to his packing up his goods and making other arrangements consistent with such intention of going and not returning ... To found an order for so strong a remedy as the writ of *ne exeat*, or to hold a man to bail, there must be proof of a clear and distinct intention expressed by the defendant that he is going to leave the country permanently."

In so far as s 7 of the 1872 Act does not require it be shown that a defendant intends to leave Ireland "permanently", the foregoing quotation puts the matter too stringently, as Megarry J recognised in *Felton v Callis*.[48] In that case Megarry J said, *obiter*, that the evidence that the defendant had sold his house, was selling his furniture and intended to take up work in Thailand as a "part-time lecturer and accountant" was sufficient to satisfy this condition.

(d) Absence must materially prejudice the prosecution of the action

[11.16] This fourth condition has proved to be the most difficult to satisfy and, in particular, casts serious doubt on the availability of s 7 arrest or the writ of *ne exeat* in aid of a Mareva injunction. In order to procure an order for the arrest of a debtor under s 7 of the 1872 Act a plaintiff must show that a defendant's absence from Ireland will materially prejudice the plaintiff in the prosecution of his action. It is clear from s 7 that it is only envisaged that it will be used in the *prosecution* of an action and not as an aid to *execution*; indeed, all conditions in s 7 must, by its terms, be proved "at any time before final judgment". In *Yorkshire Engine Co Ltd v Wright*[49] a defendant who had been arrested under s 6 of the English 1869 Act and who had procured his release by paying £1,500 into court was held by the Court of Appeal to be entitled to the return of the money as soon as he submitted to final judgment. As Kelly CB said, the section:

> "... was intended only to secure the presence of the debtor during the progress of the suit, that it, before final judgment, and was not intended to allow him to be kept in prison after the plaintiff should have, by signing final judgment, established the validity of his claim against the defendant."[50]

[47.] (1861) 4 LT 114 at 115; cited by Megarry in *Felton v Callis* [1968] 3 All ER 673.
[48.] [1968] 3 All ER 673 at 683.
[49.] (1872) 21 WR 15.
[50.] At 16.

Moreover, the Irish case of *Hester & Co v Byrne*[51] makes it clear that a plaintiff is not permitted to delay unnecessarily the marking of judgment with the intention of keeping the defendant in prison.

[11.17] A bald statement that a defendant's presence is required within the jurisdiction is not sufficient. In *Comedy Opera Co v Carte*[52] Lopes J said:

> "A statement in an affidavit for arrest that the defendant is a material witness is not enough, but should shew why his presence is required, as for instance, that the case for the plaintiff cannot be proved without examining the defendant, or that he is in possession of documents material to it and discovery is necessary."

Accordingly, a plaintiff's requirement for a defendant's presence is not confined to cases where the defendant is required to give oral evidence as a witness; a defendant's presence may be required to facilitate discovery or interrogatories.[53] It must be remembered, however, that very often a defendant's absence will assist, not hinder, a plaintiff to obtain judgment, because judgment can be given in default of an appearance.[54]

[11.18] The greatest obstacle to the use of the writ of *ne exeat* in aid of a Mareva injunction (which is relief in aid of execution) is because it was only intended to assist in the prosecution of an action and not in its execution. In *Lipkin Gorman (a firm) v Cass*[55] a Mareva injunction was obtained against the defendant who, it was alleged, had been a partner in the plaintiff firm until some years previous when he had stolen over £200,000 of clients' money. Having been in Israel, the defendant was subsequently extradited to the UK. The plaintiff sought to recover the stolen money and needed an inquiry into the defendant's accounts. In February 1985 Harman J granted the plaintiffs a Mareva injunction, an order that the defendant disclose details of any accounts which he might have in banks and building societies and also a writ of *ne exeat* whereby his passport was impounded. When the defendant did not disclose the details of the accounts, the plaintiffs subsequently sought to have the defendant committed to Pentonville prison for disobeying the February order. In the course of these proceedings the defendant argued that the writ ought never to have issued because the writ was intended only to assist the plaintiff in obtaining judgment and not in executing it. The *Times*' law report of the judgment of Walton J states that the judge considered that the defendant's attractive submission rested upon a fallacy: the plaintiff had sought an order that the defendant deliver up all moneys and properties as represented the £200,000 and so any order would be "in the air"

---

51. (1874) 8 ILTR 53.
52. [1879] WN 210.
53. *Felton v Callis* [1968] 3 All ER 673; *Hasluck v Lehman* (1890) 6 TLR 435.
54. As noted by James LJ in *Drover v Beyer* (1879) 13 Ch D 242.
55. *The Times*, 29 May 1985.

until the plaintiff had obtained an inquiry as to what precisely should be contained in the order. It was found by Walton J that, until the plaintiff had obtained an order in a form which could be properly executed, the plaintiff was still prosecuting the action and not proceeding to execution thereon. It is significant that in this case the plaintiffs' claim was really in the nature of a tracing claim;[56] the moneys sought to be recovered had once belonged to the plaintiffs and so formed the subject matter of the action. It is arguable that this distinguishes this case from a case involving a genuine Mareva injunction where a plaintiff will have no proprietary claim to a defendant's assets and where the assets sought to be frozen are not themselves the subject matter of the proceedings.

[11.19] Again, in *Al Nahkel for Contracting and Trading Ltd v Lowe*,[57] it was found that the requirement that the defendant's absence should materially prejudice the prosecution of a plaintiff's action did not prevent the writ from issuing in aid of a Mareva injunction. There, the defendant who was alleged to have stolen $14,000 from the plaintiff in Saudi Arabia, flew to London with the intention of leaving for Manila on the following day. The plaintiff applied for a Mareva injunction and also sought leave to issue the writ of *ne exeat* unless the defendant gave security for the $14,000 claimed by the plaintiff. Tudor Price J granted the application for a Mareva injunction and held that there was jurisdiction to issue a writ of *ne exeat* in support of the Mareva injunction "to prevent a defendant fleeing the jurisdiction with assets in order to frustrate a lawful claim before the court".[58]

[11.20] The most detailed consideration of the "fourth condition" in the context of the issue of a writ of *ne exeat* in aid of Mareva relief is to be found in *Allied Arab Bank Ltd v Hajjar and Ors*.[59] The facts in that case are worth setting out in some detail. The first defendant was a Jordanian citizen who was one of the guarantors of a large loan made by the plaintiff to a company which subsequently went into liquidation. The plaintiff sued the first defendant and others claiming damages for fraudulent conspiracy and also claiming that they had procured a number of companies to dissipate the borrowed funds. When the first defendant came to England the plaintiff obtained and served on him a writ of *ne exeat* which ordered him to be detained unless £36m was lodged as security; as he was unable to do this he was jailed for the night. The following morning he appeared in court, undertook not to leave the jurisdiction and also undertook to disclose his own assets, the assets of other defendants within the

---

[56.] See Ch 1, *The Mareva Injunction in Context*, para **[1.21]**.
[57.] [1986] 1 All ER 729.
[58.] At 732h.
[59.] [1987] 3 All ER 739.

jurisdiction and certain inter-company dealings. The court also granted a Mareva injunction which restrained him from dealing with his assets until trial. The first defendant then filed affidavits making certain disclosures and subsequently applied for the discharge of the writ of *ne exeat*, claiming that it ought never to have issued; an inquiry as to damages and the variation or discharge of the Mareva injunction. The plaintiff sought an order requiring the first defendant to disclose his assets outside of the jurisdiction and also for leave to cross-examine on earlier affidavits on the grounds that such were necessary and reasonable to achieve the purpose of the Mareva injunction. The plaintiff also argued that the conditions required for the issue of the writ of *ne exeat* had been met.

In his judgment, Leggatt J noted that the plaintiff's counsel had argued that the "fourth condition" was satisfied in that case because the "prosecution" of the action may include obtaining discovery, interrogatories and a Mareva injunction, that he accepted that the writ must be subordinate to some other part of the claim, but that he contended that the writ may issue to make an injunction effective. As to the plaintiff's reliance upon the decision of Tudor Price J in *Al Nahkel for Contracting and Trading Ltd v Lowe*,[60] Leggatt J said:

> "His conclusion that the writ can issue in support of a Mareva injunction may have been intended to refer only to those cases in which both remedies may properly issue, with the result that the arrest of the debtor may incidentally prevent him from breaching the Mareva injunction. But, if it was intended to go further and to suggest that the writ may be ordered for the purpose of enforcing a Mareva injunction, I disagree: for that purpose the appropriate remedy is an injunction to restrain the defendant from leaving the jurisdiction".[61]

Injunctions to restrain defendants from leaving the jurisdiction, or *Bayer* injunctions as they are sometimes called, are considered below.[62] In support of his contention that a writ of *ne exeat* was an inappropriate means of preventing a defendant from leaving the jurisdiction where the purpose of preventing him from absconding was to facilitate a Mareva injunction, Leggatt J said:

> "A Mareva injunction issues for the purpose of preserving within the jurisdiction of the court assets against which a creditor may have recourse, provided that he is successful in obtaining judgment. The remedy is in aid of execution, and constitutes an exception to the principle enunciated in *Lister & Co v Stubbs* (1890) 45 Ch D 1. It is not part of the prosecution of the action. If the claim is a proprietary claim, or a tracing claim, it may well be appropriate for a writ to issue as well as a Mareva injunction. But in every case the question must be asked: for what purpose is the issue of the writ required? Here the

---

[60.] [1986] 1 All ER 729. See para **[11.19]** *supra*.
[61.] At 744a.
[62.] At para **[11.22]**, *infra*.

primary purpose suggested is to require the first defendant to identify assets in relation to which the Mareva injunction would operate. That is not part of the *prosecution* of the action. It follows that condition (iv) is not satisfied."[63]

On balance, it is thought that the reasoning of Leggatt J is correct. In particular, his differentiation between proprietary or tracing claims and true Mareva claims where the plaintiff has no legal or equitable interest in the assets frozen by the order, seems particularly well founded. Indeed, as noted earlier, the nature of the plaintiff's claim in *Lipkin Gorman (a firm) v Cass*,[64] (where the writ did issue) was essentially a tracing claim.

[11.21] In conclusion, even where all other conditions have been met, the writ of *ne exeat* or an order for arrest under s 7 of the 1872 Act will not, *per se*, be granted in aid of a Mareva injunction. The writ or an order under s 7 of the 1872 Act should only be granted where, *inter alia*, a defendant's absence from Ireland would materially prejudice the prosecution of a plaintiff's action. The writ or an order under s 7 may be required in a contested case in order to serve interrogatories or make discovery in relation to the substantive cause of action; the writ may be required to make effective an injunction in defence of proprietary rights over assets frozen.[65] These latter injunctions must, however, be distinguished from a case where the purpose is to make effective a Mareva injunction or an order for disclosure of assets where the plaintiff has no proprietary rights in the assets the subject matter of the injunction; in these cases a writ of *ne exeat* will not be appropriate, but, where satisfied that a defendant's presence is required within the jurisdiction, the court may grant an injunction which prevents him from leaving Ireland. It is to such injunctions that next we turn.

[B] BAYER INJUNCTIONS

[11.22] The courts in Ireland and the United Kingdom have occasionally granted injunctions which have restrained defendants from leaving the jurisdiction and/ or to deliver up their passports. Such injunctions have come to be known as Bayer injunctions,[66] although this term has not attained the same degree of accepted usage as, say, the Mareva injunction or Anton Piller order. The basis for this jurisdiction is the general power to grant an injunction "in all cases in which it appears to the court to be just and convenient to do so".[67] Although

---

63. At 744b-c.
64. *The Times*, 29 May 1985. See para **[11.18]** *supra*.
65. For such injunctions where the plaintiff has proprietary rights in the assets which are the subject matter of the injunction, see Ch 1, *The Mareva Injunction in Context*, para **[1.16]**.
66. In *Bayer AG v Winter* [1986] 1 All ER 733.
67. In England, pursuant to s 37(1) of the Supreme Court Act 1981; in Ireland the comparable statutory provision is to be found in s 28(8) of the Supreme Court of Judicature (Ireland) Act 1877 as applied to the present High Court by ss 8(2) and 48(3) of the Courts (Supplemental Provisions) Act 1961.

there is no written judgment on Bayer injunctions in aid of the civil process, such injunctions have also been made by the Irish High Court. Any order which restrains a defendant from leaving the jurisdiction - for no matter how short a time - is essentially draconian and will only ever be made in exceptional and compelling circumstances. Even though the jurisdiction to make such injunctions will only be exercised sparingly, and in exceptional cases, this means of preventing a defendant from leaving the jurisdiction is not entrammeled by the anachronistic conditions required for a writ of *ne exeat regno* to issue.

In this section, the following matters are considered:

1.   The Jurisdictional Basis for Bayer Injunctions;

2.   The Constitutionality of Restraining the Right to Travel;

3.   The Circumstances when Bayer Injunctions may be Granted.

The Jurisdictional Basis for Bayer Injunctions

[11.23] The case in which the Court of Appeal decided that there was jurisdiction under s 37(1) of the English Supreme Court Act 1981 to grant an injunction to restrain a defendant from leaving the jurisdiction, gave its name to this "new" form of injunction: *Bayer AG v Winter and Ors*.[68] The facts of that case were that the plaintiff-pharmaceutical company had instituted proceedings against the defendants for damages for the alleged worldwide distribution and sale of counterfeit insecticide. The plaintiff successfully applied for a Mareva injunction against the defendants and an Anton Piller order[69] which required the defendants to (a) disclose the whereabouts of documents relating to transactions worldwide in which the counterfeit insecticide had been supplied or offered for sale; (b) swear an affidavit, detailing such transactions; and (c) deliver up the relevant documents to the plaintiff's solicitors. The plaintiff was, however, fearful that the defendant would leave the jurisdiction and thereby evade the effect of the Mareva injunction and Anton Piller order. Accordingly, the plaintiff applied for an order that the first defendant deliver up his passports and sought an injunction to restrain him from leaving the jurisdiction until after the Anton Piller order had been served. Walton J declined to make these orders and it was against this refusal that the plaintiff appealed to the Court of Appeal.

[11.24] The main judgment of the Court of Appeal was delivered by Fox LJ. After reviewing the factual background to the application, Fox LJ noted that the court was being asked to grant the injunction to restrain the first defendant from leaving the jurisdiction under s 37(1) of the English Supreme Court Act 1981, ie

---

[68.]   [1986] 1 All ER 733.
[69.]   See Ch 10, *Ancillary Orders*, para **[10.38]** *et seq*.

on the grounds that such an injunction was "just and convenient". Fox LJ took comfort from the judgment of Jessel MR in *Smith v Peters*[70] in accepting that the court has a wide discretion. There, Jessel MR said, *inter alia*:

> "I have no hesitation in saying that there is no limit to the practice of the court with regard to interlocutory applications so far as they are necessary and reasonable applications ancillary to the due performance of its functions, namely, the administration of justice at the hearing of the cause. I know of no other limit. Whether they are or are not to be granted must of course depend upon the special circumstances of the case."[71]

Fox LJ continued:

> "The court has to exercise that discretion according to established principles, and the particular matter with which we are concerned at the moment, namely of an injunctive restraint on a person leaving the jurisdiction, is not one on which there appears to be previous authority. It is clear, however, that the law in relation to the grant of injunctive relief for the protection of a litigant's rights pending the hearing of an action has been transformed over the past ten years by the Anton Piller and Mareva relief which has greatly extended the law on this topic as previously understood so as to meet the needs of justice.
>
> Bearing in mind we are exercising a jurisdiction which is statutory, and which is expressed in terms of considerable width, it seems to me that the court should not shrink, if it is of opinion that an injunction is necessary for the proper protection of a party to the action, from granting relief, notwithstanding it may, in its terms, be of novel character."[72]

In assessing the harm which such an injunction would do to the defendant, Fox LJ said that if it causes him any hardship or embarrassment he can apply to have the injunction varied or, if necessary, discharged. As for the plaintiff, he found that if the defendant failed to answer the matters contained in the order or failed to be frank, the plaintiff could seek an order for cross-examination but that the court's order would be frustrated if the defendant left the jurisdiction. Fox LJ concluded:

> "For the reasons which I have indicated, therefore, I would be prepared to grant the order which counsel for the plaintiffs now seeks; that is to say, an injunction restraining the first defendant from leaving the jurisdiction, and secondly, that he deliver up his passports. The orders are, in my view, in Jessel MR's words, 'necessary and reasonable orders which are ancillary to the due performance of the court's functions'."[73]

---

[70]. (1875) LR 20 Eq 511.

[71]. At 512. This passage was part of a passage from the judgment of Jessel MR quoted in the decision of Fox LJ. It was also noted that this passage was approved of in *Astro Exito Navegacion SA v Southland Enterprise Co Ltd* [1982] 3 All ER 335.

[72]. [1986] 1 All ER 733 at 737e-f.

[73]. At 738a-b.

Both Fox and Ralph Gibson LJJ referenced the decision of Cumming-Bruce LJ in *House of Spring Gardens Ltd v Waite*[74] and Ralph Gibson LJ quoted the following passage as authority for the proposition that the court has power to injunct a defendant from leaving the jurisdiction:

> "The court has the power (and, I would add, the duty) to take such steps as are practicable upon an application of the plaintiff to procure that where an order has been made that the defendants identify their assets and disclose their whereabouts, such steps are taken as will enable the order to have effect as completely and successfully as the powers of the court can procure."

Having found that there was jurisdiction to grant such an injunction, the Court of Appeal went on to find that the case at bar was an appropriate case in which to exercise that jurisdiction. Acknowledging that such an injunction was "an interference with the liberty of the subject", Fox LJ said that it should be of "very limited duration" and "should be no longer than is necessary to enable the plaintiffs to serve the Mareva and Anton Piller orders which they have obtained and endeavour to obtain from the defendant the information which is referred to in those orders."[75]

[11.25] As can be seen from the reliance placed upon *House of Spring Gardens Ltd v Waite* by the Court of Appeal in *Bayer AG v Winter*, the jurisdictional basis for making a "Bayer injunction" is because it is necessary to make other orders of the court effective and therefore that such an injunction is "just and convenient". As such, the jurisdiction can be seen to flow from the same root source as asset "disclosure orders" in aid of Mareva relief.[76]

[11.26] Application for a Bayer injunction will invariably be by way of an *ex parte* application to the High Court under Ord 50, r 6(1) of the RSC grounded upon a plaintiff's affidavit. One peculiarity of an injunction or any order which has the effect of restraining a person from leaving the jurisdiction is found in Ord 40, r 21 which provides:

> Where an injunction or order not to leave the jurisdiction has been granted or made, the party applying for such injunction or order shall furnish copies of the affidavits grounding the same to any party affected thereby upon demand and payment therefor at the rate specified in Order 117.

[74.] (1985) 11 FSR 173 at 183.

[75.] [1986] 1 All ER 733 at 738c. See also the judgment of Leggatt J in *Allied Arab Bank Ltd v Hajjar* [1987] 3 All ER 739 where he said (at 746): "... an injunction not to leave the jurisdiction should run, since it constitutes an interference with the liberty of the subject, for no longer than is necessary to give effect to the orders of the court".

[76.] See Ch 10, *Ancillary Orders*, para **[10.03]** *et seq*.

This rule of court applies to injunctions and orders not to leave the jurisdiction and so applies equally to where a writ of *ne exeat* issues or an order for civil arrest is made, eg, under s 7 of the Debtors Act (Ireland) 1872.

The Constitutionality of Restraining the Right to Travel[77]

[11.27] In *Ryan v Attorney General*[78] it was first held that there is a constitutional right to travel, this being an unenumerated right contained in Article 40.3 of the Constitution. This finding was later developed by Finlay P in *State (M) v Minister for Foreign Affairs*[79] where he said:

> "... I have no doubt that a right to travel outside the State in the limited form in which I have already defined it (that is to say, a right to avail of such facilities as apply to the holder of an Irish passport at any given time) is a personal right of each citizen which, on the authority of the decisions to which I have referred, must be considered as being subject to the guarantees provided by Article 40."[80]

Hence it can be seen that the right to travel is inextricably intertwined with the right to a passport.[81]

[11.28] Any injunction or order which restrains a person from leaving the jurisdiction or orders a person to deliver up his passport is in *prima facie* conflict with the constitutional right to travel. As Finlay CJ said in *Attorney General v X*:[82]

> "That [the right to travel] exists as an important and, in a sense, fundamental right closely identified with the characteristics of any free society, cannot be challenged. The making of an order by way of injunction restraining a person from travelling out of the jurisdiction of the State, whether confined to travelling for a particular purpose or for a particular period, constitutes a major restriction of such right to travel, placing the right in actual abeyance."[83]

---

[77] See generally, Hogan & Whyte, *Kelly: The Irish Constitution*, (3rd ed, 1994) Butterworths, pp 777-778, Casey, *Constitutional Law in Ireland*, (2nd ed, 1992) Sweet & Maxwell, pp 337-339, and Courtney, 'Civil Arrest and Injunction to Restrain an Absconding Defendant from Leaving the Jurisdiction - Part II', (1990) ILT 222 at 225-226.

[78] [1965] IR 294.

[79] [1979] IR 73.

[80] At 81.

[81] Usually, the defendant may be ordered to deliver up his passport. Where a defendant has not got a passport, the Court could order him not to apply for a passport: see para **[11.40]** *infra*. The question of whether the Court could direct the Minister for Foreign Affairs to cancel a passport was addressed, but reserved for future consideration, in *PI v Ireland* [1989] ILRM 810.

[82] [1992] ILRM 401.

[83] At 428.

However, it has been recognised by the courts that there are circumstances where it is proper and just to curtail the right to travel. Indeed, in *State (M) v Minister for Foreign Affairs*[84] Finlay P said:

> "... it appears to me that, subject to the obvious conditions which may be required by public order and the common good of the State, a citizen has the right to a passport permitting him or her to avail of such facilities as international agreements existing at any given time afford to the holder of such a passport. To that right there are obvious and justified restrictions, the most common of which being the existence of some undischarged obligation to the State by the person seeking a passport or seeking to use his passport - such as the fact that he has entered into a recognisance to appear before a criminal court for the trial of an offence."[85]

In *Lennon v Ganley & Fitzgerald*,[86] where it was sought to restrain the defendant officers of the Irish Rugby Football Union from travelling to the Republic of South Africa to play rugby on account of its policy at that time of apartheid, O'Hanlon J said that the defendants:

> "... should only be restrained from exercising such right [to travel] if it was in some way *unlawful* for them to act in the manner in which they seek to act."[87]

Having accepted that the authorities have established that there is a constitutional right to travel, the question which then arises is, in what circumstances ought the right to travel be curtailed? From the foregoing passage it seems clear that a person can be restrained from going abroad if acting *unlawfully*; it is interesting to note that leaving the State with the intention of defrauding one's creditors is an unlawful act.[88]

[11.29] In *Attorney General v X*[89] the conflict of rights in question was whether the right to travel could be subordinated to the right to life of the unborn child. Both are protected constitutional rights. In the *X Case* Finlay CJ said, *obiter*, that where there is a conflict, or interaction of constitutional rights, the first objective of the court is to seek to harmonise them but, failing that, it may be necessary to apply a priority of rights. He then said:

[84.] [1979] IR 73.

[85.] At 81.

[86.] [1981] ILRM 84.

[87.] Italics added.

[88.] Leaving the State to evade one's creditors can be "unlawful": s 124 of the Bankruptcy Act 1988 provides: "If any person with intent to defraud his creditors leaves the State and takes with him, or attempts or makes preparation to leave the State and take with him, any part of his property to the amount of £500 or upwards, he shall be guilty of an offence."

[89.] [1992] ILRM 401.

"Notwithstanding the very fundamental nature of the right to travel ... if there were a stark conflict between the right of a mother of an unborn child to travel and the right of the unborn child, the right to life would necessarily have to take precedence over the right to travel. I therefore conclude that the submission made that the mother of the unborn child had an absolute right to travel which could not be qualified or restricted, even by the vindication or defence of the right to life of the unborn, is not a valid or sustainable submission in law."[90]

Where it is sought to restrain by injunction a person from leaving the jurisdiction and/or to deliver up his passport in the course of a *civil cause of action*, the right to travel may conflict with a plaintiff's rights to litigate and to defend his property rights, and perhaps more importantly, the authority of the court and the administration of justice. It is submitted that a defendant's right to travel can be subordinated to a plaintiff's right to litigate effectively a just cause against the defendant and to vindicate his property rights in the civil courts and also to preventing the administration of justice from being frustrated by the defendant's deliberate absence. As shall be seen the Irish High Court has, on a number of occasions, enjoined a defendant (to a civil cause of action) from leaving the State.

[11.30] While there is jurisdiction, in appropriate cases, to restrain a defendant from leaving the State it is submitted that such an injunction should only be granted where:

1. The court is satisfied that there is probable cause for believing[91] that the defendant is about to absent himself from the jurisdiction *with the intention* of frustrating the administration of justice and/or an order of the court;[92]

2. The jurisdiction should not be exercised for *punitive* reasons; a defendant's presence should be required in order to prevent a court hearing or process or existing order from being rendered nugatory;

[90.] At 429. Although in this case O'Flaherty J found that there was no jurisdiction to enjoin an individual from leaving the jurisdiction in the case in hand, his reasoning was that a person cannot lawfully be prevented from leaving a country so as to prevent them from committing an act which is criminal in the country he is in but lawful in the country where he intends to travel.

[91.] "Probable cause for believing" is the traditional standard of proof required by statutes which permit a person's civil arrest: see s 7 of the Debtors Act (Ireland), 1872, para **[11.15]** *supra*; s 247 of the Companies Act 1963, para **[11.44]** *et seq infra*; s 9(1) of the Bankruptcy Act 1988, para **[11.52]** *et seq infra*; and s 23(1) of the Bankruptcy Act 1988, para **[11.54]** *et seq infra*. Note, however, that in s 245(8) of the Companies Act 1963 (as inserted by s 126 of the Companies Act 1990) the standard of proof required there for civil arrest is described as "reasonable grounds for believing": see para **[11.50]** *infra*.

[92.] The purposes which have been recognised as appropriate for making Bayer injunctions are considered at para **[11.31]** *infra*.

3.   The injunction ought not to be granted where a lesser remedy would suffice;[93]

4.   The injunction should be *interim* in nature and limited to the shortest possible period of time;

5.   The defendant's right to travel should be out-balanced by those of the plaintiff and the proper and effective administration of justice;

6.   The grant of the injunction should not be futile.[94]

Where these conditions are fulfilled, it is submitted that a person's right to travel may be temporarily abridged by injunction or other order of the High Court.

The Circumstances in which Bayer Injunctions may be Granted

[11.31] Injunctions, which have restrained persons from leaving the jurisdiction and orders which have required the delivery up of passports, have been granted in diverse circumstances: in aid of Mareva injunctions and Anton Piller orders;[95] in aid of the statutory power to examine officers of insolvent companies;[96] in child abduction cases;[97] in other family law cases involving obligations to make financial provision to a spouse;[98] and to prevent a woman from travelling abroad to procure an abortion.[99] In *B v B (injunction: restraint on leaving jurisdiction)*,[100] after noting some of the foregoing circumstances, Wilson J said:

> "It is clear from the above that there are a number of circumstances in which under s 37(1) it is possible to restrain a party from leaving the jurisdiction and to make a consequential order for the surrender of his or her passport. The jurisdiction exists where the other party has established a right to interlocutory relief (such as an Anton Piller order) which would otherwise be rendered nugatory. It exists where a hearing is shortly to take place, the efficacy of which would be frustrated by his absence. In my view, it exists in principle in aid of all the court's procedures leading to the disposal of the proceedings".[101]

[93.] *Cf Brott v Drew* (1993) FLC 92-358 (Family Court of Australia). In that case Kay J granted an injunction to restrain the defendant from leaving Australia where "the effect of that would be if she leaves the jurisdiction and takes with her the fruits of her litigation and leaves no other fruits behind, that Mr Brott's action may well be defeated". Amazingly, Kay J declined to grant a Mareva injunction against the defendant because "there is no evidence before me on which I would place any reliance that would indicate that the fruits of any litigation which Mrs Drew obtains were she to remain in the jurisdiction would not be available to meet Mr Brott's claim if it has any substance at all."

[94.] See para **[11.40]** *infra*.

[95.] *Bayer AG v Winter* [1986] 1 All ER 733.

[96.] *Re Oriental Credit Ltd* [1988] 1 All ER 892. See also *Re J Ellis Pharmaceuticals, The Irish Times*, 13 August 1988, both of which are considered *infra*.

[97.] *Re A-K (minors) (foreign passport: jurisdiction)* [1997] TLR 123.

[98.] *Re S (financial provision: non-resident)* [1996] 1 FCR 148.

[99.] *Attorney General v X* [1992] ILRM 401. See para **[11.29]** *supra*.

[100.] [1997] 3 All ER 258.

[101.] At 264f.

The only legitimate purposes for which a Bayer injunction should be granted in civil proceedings[102] may be distilled into two generic sets of circumstances: namely, where a defendant's absence from the State would either:

(i) render nugatory another order of the court (eg an Anton Piller order, a disclosure order in aid of a Mareva injunction etc); or,

(ii) frustrate a judicial hearing which is shortly due to take place.

It is appropriate to examine next the case law where Bayer injunctions have been granted and been refused. These can be conveniently grouped under four headings:

(a) To facilitate a judicial hearing;

(b) To facilitate compliance with a court order;

(c) In aid of "established procedures" for the enforcement of a judgment;

(d) In defence of the Constitution.

(a) To facilitate a judicial hearing

[11.32] In *Re Oriental Credit Ltd*[103] an injunction to restrain a person from leaving the UK was granted in circumstances where the purpose of the injunction can be seen as having been designed both to prevent an order of the court from being rendered nugatory and to prevent a judicial hearing from being frustrated. The facts in that case were that shortly before a company was placed into creditors' voluntary liquidation a director left the jurisdiction and was, thereafter, uncontactable. The liquidator discovered that the director intended to return to England on 29 June 1987 for a short period. On 26 June 1987 the liquidator obtained an order under s 561 of the English Companies Act 1985 for the examination of the director, 21 July 1987 being the date set for such. The liquidator also successfully applied for an injunction to restrain the director from leaving the jurisdiction until after the examination had taken place. On 1 July 1987 the applicant director applied to have the injunction discharged on the ground that the court had no jurisdiction to make such an order. The basis of the applicant director's contention was that before an injunction could be granted, it was a condition that a plaintiff have a legal or beneficial right which the injunction sought to enforce or protect.[104] After quoting with approval from the

---

[102.] Note, different considerations apply to where such an injunction is granted to protect a constitutional right: see para **[11.39]** *infra*.

[103.] [1988] 1 All ER 892.

[104.] The authorities cited in support of this were *Gouriet v Union of Post Office Workers* [1977] 3 All ER 70; *Bremer Vulkan Schiffbau Und Maschinenfabrik v South India Shipping Corp* [1981] 1 All ER 289; *The Siskina* [1977] 3 All ER 803; *North London Rly Co v Great Northern Rly Co* (1883) 11 QBD 30; *Malmesbury Rly Co v Budd* (1876) 2 Ch D 113; *Beddow v Beddow* (1879) 9 Ch D 89; and *South Carolina Insurance Co v Assurantie Maatschappij "de Zeven Provincien" NV* [1986] 3 All ER 487.

judgment of Fox LJ in *Bayer AG v Winter*[105] and of Cumming-Bruce LJ in *House of Spring Gardens Ltd v Waite*[106] Harman J held that:

> "In my view, despite the observations in the House of Lords in *The Siskina*, I had power to make my order although it is not an order made in aid of a legal right or for the protection of an equitable interest. It is an order made and, in my view, one which must necessarily, under s 37 of the Supreme Court Act 1981, be available to be made in aid of, and ancillary to, the order made by the registrar under s 561 of the 1985 Act. And, though it is, I think, a novel application of it, it is an example of the jurisdiction mentioned in *House of Spring Gardens Ltd v Waite*, namely where an order has been made the court must have powers under the stature, here the Supreme Court Act 1981, which give it authority to make sure that its orders are performed and carried into effect."[107]

In this case, the obstacle to granting an injunction did not lie in the principle of enjoining a person from leaving the jurisdiction *per se*. Rather, the problem lay in the fact that the liquidator did not appear to have a legal right or equitable interest to protect. Section 561(4) of the English Companies Act 1985 provided for the immediate arrest of a person against whom an order to be examined had been made where they defied the order; the section did not, however, expressly provide any remedy in cases where the time for examination had not yet arrived, but where the person said they would not attend. Harman J said that such a situation would be astonishing :

> "... if the court, on being told, before the time for performance has arrived, 'Oh, I have no intention of complying and I shall absent myself the day before your order is due to come into effect', were to have to hold up its hands and say, 'Oh dear, oh dear, how very awkward, there is nothing we can do'."[108]

Although the applicant director had proffered an unsecured undertaking to return for his examination, Harman J considered this inadequate in view of the director's status.[109] He did, however, vary his order by providing that he would accept the director's undertaking to return for the examination if it was supported by a bond or similar obligation in the sum of £250,000 which would be liable for forfeiture on failure to comply with the undertaking.

[105.] [1986] 1 All ER 733: see para **[11.23]** *supra*.

[106.] (1985) 11 FSR 173: see para **[11.24]** *supra*.

[107.] [1988] 1 All ER 892.

[108.] At 895g-h.

[109.] At 896c-d, Harman J described the director as "a gentleman who is a foreigner, with no allegiance to this country, whose company in this country is insolvent and who, although he says he may come to visit his wife here, declares that neither his wife nor he himself have any substantial assets here".

[11.33] The Irish High Court has also granted, in similar circumstances, an injunction to a liquidator which ordered a director of an insolvent company not to leave the jurisdiction. In *Re J Ellis Pharmaceuticals*[110] Blayney J granted the liquidator of a company an injunction which restrained a director of the company from leaving the jurisdiction until he had been examined pursuant to s 245 of the Companies Act 1963. The newspaper report of the liquidator's application says that the liquidator stated on affidavit that his investigations of the company's pharmacy business had made him want to examine the director on oath in respect of several aspects of the company's activities and property and that it was believed that the director was about to leave the jurisdiction. The report stated that Blayney J made an order under s 245 of the Companies Act 1963 summoning the respondent before the court in order that he be examined under oath concerning, *inter alia*, the affairs and property of the company. In addition, an injunction was granted which restrained the director from leaving the jurisdiction until such time as his examination had been completed or until further order, the director having liberty to apply to the court for the injunction to be discharged. In view of the fact that an order for arrest under s 245 could not then have been made by reason of the fact that this power only arose,[111] where an order for examination had been disobeyed, the relief granted by Blayney J can only have been a Bayer injunction, made pursuant to s 28(8) of the Supreme Court of Judicature (Ireland) Act 1877.

(b) To facilitate compliance with a court order

[11.34] The court can take action to prevent its orders from being rendered nugatory or otherwise frustrated. In *Re Allan Joseph Brazel*,[112] a case where the judge ordered that the court retain the debtor's passport, Cooper J said:

> "Whether the passport ought to be retained pending the hearing of the creditors' petition is a question of balancing the public interest in ensuring that if the debtor's estate is sequestered, any order of the court or the operation of the Act is not rendered nugatory by the debtor's refusal to return to Australia against the debtor's common law right of freedom of movement and travel."

---

110. *The Irish Times*, 13 August 1988 (Blayney J). The writer acknowledges with gratitude the assistance of Mr Eugene McCague, partner, of Arthur Cox, for providing the writer with a copy of the actual order made by Blayney J.

111. As in *Re Oriental Credit Ltd* [1988] 1 All ER 892, in this case, an order for arrest could not be made under s 245 of the Companies Act 1963 by reason of the fact that such only applied to cases where an order to appear to be examined on oath had been defied. It should be noted that this has now been amended by s 126 of the Companies Act 1990 and an arrest may be ordered where there are reasonable grounds for believing that a person is *about to abscond* with a view to avoiding or delaying his examination: see generally, Courtney, *The Law of Private Companies*, (1994) Butterworths, para [19.022] and para **[11.48]** *infra*.

112. [1995] FCA 404/95 Bankruptcy.

Bayer-type injunctions have also been granted by the High Court, apparently, in aid of Mareva injunctions and disclosure orders incidental to Mareva injunctions. While all of these cases have been *ex tempore* orders of the High Court they, nevertheless indicate that the court is prepared to make such extraordinary injunctions, albeit in extraordinary circumstances. In *Re TSD Ltd; D v O'D & O'D*[113] the liquidator of three companies successfully applied to the High Court for injunctions restraining two directors from leaving the State. The newspaper report of the application stated that the liquidator had claimed that, from a perusal of the records of two of the companies, there was an overall deficit of more than £5m and no assets or no apparent uncharged assets to meet its liabilities. It was reported that some days previous the liquidator had obtained a Mareva injunction which restrained the directors from reducing their assets within the jurisdiction below £5m and that an interim injunction preventing the directors from leaving the jurisdiction had also been obtained at that time. It was also reported that the liquidator claimed that the companies appeared to have been involved in a system of obtaining finance in respect of non-existent vehicles.

[11.35] In *Re Mark Synnott (Life and Pensions) Brokers Ltd* it was reported[114] that the liquidator of this company which acted as investment broker was given leave to apply on short notice for an injunction to compel a director of the company to deliver up his passport so as to prevent him from leaving the jurisdiction. It was reported that the liquidator believed that the director intended to go to Spain and was apprehensive that he might not return. It was subsequently reported[115] that Carroll J made an interim order by consent[116] restraining the director, Mr Mark A Synnott,[117] from reducing his assets below

---

113. *The Irish Times*, 4 February 1992 and *Irish Independent* of 4 February 1992 (Murphy J). For background, see *The Irish Times*, 21 January 1992, 31 January 1992 and 3 February 1992.

114. *The Irish Times*, 3 July 1991 and see also *The Irish Times*, 4 July 1991. For background to this matter, see *The Irish Times*, 15, 18, 19, 27 29 June, 2, 3, 4, 6, 9 July and 6, 7, 8, 9 November 1991.

115. *The Irish Times*, 4 July 1991.

116. In *K v L*, *The Irish Times*, 20 August 1988, it was reported that Lardner J made certain orders by consent of the parties, one of which was on the basis of the defendant's undertaking not to leave the jurisdiction; it was reported that the plaintiff believed that the defendant intended to emigrate to Australia. Here too, a Mareva injunction had been made and an order for discovery of the defendant's assets. In that case it was claimed that the defendant accountant had administered the plaintiff's husband's business after her husband had fallen ill and, it was reported that the plaintiff had claimed, that after an 18 month period the current account of the business changed from a credit to a debit of over £120,000. See also *D v H*, *The Irish Times*, 23 January 1996 where it was reported that the defendant sought to have a Mareva injunction discharged so as to enable him to sell his family home. During the course of the report it was noted that in 1985 the defendant had undertaken, *inter alia*, not to leave the State and to hand up his passport.

117. Mr Mark A Synnott has the dubious distinction of being the first person to be convicted and imprisoned in Ireland for fraudulent trading under s 297 of the Companies Act 1963: see *Editorial* 'Punishing Delinquent Directors' (1996) CLP 110.

£2.3m and also restraining him from leaving the jurisdiction. It would appear that in this case the purpose of seeking to prevent the defendant from leaving the jurisdiction was to prevent an earlier order that the directors of the company disclose their assets from being rendered nugatory.[118]

(c) In aid of "established procedures" for the enforcement of a judgment

[11.36] In *B v B (injunction: restraint on leaving jurisdiction)*,[119] the facts of which are given in the next paragraph, Wilson J held that there was jurisdiction under s 37(1) of the English Supreme Court Act 1981, to restrain by injunction a person from leaving the jurisdiction *after judgment* had been entered against him. Wilson J confined the use of the remedy in support of the enforcement of a judgment to where it was in aid of the court's *established procedures* for the enforcement of judgment. The examples he gave of "established procedures" for enforcement were a judgment summons and an oral examination to establish a defendant's means.[120] The only recognised purpose for such an injunction in aid of execution is to prevent the administration of justice from being frustrated; not to ensure that a debt is paid.

[11.37] *B v B (injunction: restraint on leaving jurisdiction)*[121] is, however, also a compelling authority for the proposition that the courts will not grant a Bayer injunction where to do so would amount to the reintroduction of imprisonment for non-payment of a debt. The facts in that case were that the parties were a wealthy estranged husband and wife and a previous order had, by consent, been made in the plaintiff-wife's favour, requiring the husband to pay her costs of £75,000 in a previous action. The husband failed to comply with this order, although the sale of some items of jewellery belonging to him meant that the total owed had been reduced to £68,099. Upon the husband leaving Nigeria (where he lived) and visiting London, the wife obtained an *ex parte* order that the husband be examined as to his means before a High Court judge under Ord 48 of the English Rules of the Supreme Court; moreover, the judge granted her an injunction, restraining the husband from leaving the jurisdiction until that hearing and ordering him to deliver up his passport to the tipstaff. At the hearing the wife then applied for an injunction under s 37(1) of the English Supreme Court Act 1981, to restrain the husband from leaving the jurisdiction until he had paid her the full sum owing under the order for costs. Although, as noted

---

[118] *The Irish Times*, 27 June 1991 it was reported that the three directors of the company were ordered to disclose on affidavit the whereabouts of their assets in aid of earlier Mareva injunctions; in *The Irish Times*, 29 June 1991 it was reported that Lardner J had made an order for interrogatories.

[119] [1997] 3 All ER 258.

[120] At 264j.

[121] [1997] 3 All ER 258.

above,[122] Wilson J acknowledged the considerable width of the remedy of restraining a person from leaving the jurisdiction, he held that there was no jurisdiction to make such an injunction "as a free-standing enforcement procedure in its own right" but only in aid of the court's established procedures for enforcement of a judgment."[123] In that case it had been argued that the husband should have been so restrained until such time as he actually paid the costs owing to the wife.

[11.38] Wilson J's conclusion that the husband could not be enjoined from leaving the jurisdiction until the wife's costs were paid was based in part on the fact that in England and Wales, a person can only be committed to prison for non-payment of debt in very limited circumstances and then only for a period of six weeks.[124] In effect, Wilson J applied these limitations by analogy to the exercise of the equitable remedy of an injunction. In particular he rejected the suggestion that civil arrest and restraining a defendant from leaving the jurisdiction were wholly unalike. After referring to the decision of Hobhouse LJ in *Re B (child abduction: wardship: power to detain),*[125] Wilson J said:

> "It is therefore legitimate to reflect that, had the order for costs been regarded by Parliament as sufficiently important for breach to be attended by committal to prison, the husband could have been committed for only six weeks; whereas [the wife's counsel] is asking me to detain him within the jurisdiction indefinitely ...
>
> Although I would have been pleased to make the order sought, I have come to the clear conclusion that I have no power under s 37(1) or otherwise to do so. Were the lights at amber I would drive through them; but they are at red. The jurisdiction under s 37(1) is ancillary to other powers of the court. To the limited extent that the ambit of the writ of *ne exeat regno* illuminates its proper use, it points directly away from deployment in execution."[126]

[122.] See para **[11.31]** *supra.*

[123.] At 264j.

[124.] Under the English Administration of Justice Act 1970 and s 5 of the Debtors Act 1869; see s 6 of the Debtors Act (Ireland) 1872.

[125.] [1994] 2 FLR 479. Hobhouse LJ had said there (at 488): "The use of ancillary powers which have the practical effect of restricting the liberty, or freedom of movement of an individual is recognised in the granting of injunctions, now under s 37 of the Supreme Court Act 1981. Thus a defendant may be ordered not to leave the jurisdiction until he has complied with an order requiring him to disclose information as directed by the court...There is an obvious difference in kind between an injunction and the arrest or physical detention of an individual, but such orders are analogous and illustrate the proper use of an ancillary power although it prima facie infringes the personal rights of the individual involved. Where a power of arrest or detention has been recognised other than as part of a punitive jurisdiction, it is ancillary to the exercise of another power of the court and is legitimate because it is necessary to the implementation of the order of the court."

[126.] [1997] 3 All ER 258 at 265e-h.

Therefore, acting by analogy, equity continues to follow the law. It is thought by the writer that to have restrained the husband in *B v B* from leaving the jurisdiction until such time as he had discharged a debt due to his estranged wife would have been an injunction too far and could have brought the entire jurisdiction into disrepute. Moreover, it is inconceivable that the legislature in Ireland or the United Kingdom, would countenance the effective reintroduction, by the back-door, of imprisonment for non-payment of debt.

(d) In defence of the Constitution

[11.39] In very limited cases an injunction may properly issue to prevent a person from leaving the jurisdiction for the purpose of defending and vindicating the Constitution. In *Attorney General v X*[127] Costello J granted an injunction that restrained a 14 year old girl, who was pregnant, having been raped, from leaving the State in an attempt to prevent her from having an abortion in England. On appeal to the Supreme Court it was held by Finlay CJ that the Constitution did not contain an *absolute* prohibition on abortion and that on a true interpretation of Article 40.3.3°, if it is established as a matter of probability that there is a real and substantial risk to the life, as distinct from the health, of the mother which can only be avoided by the termination of her pregnancy, such termination is permissible.[128] The Supreme Court went on to find that there was indeed a real and substantial risk to the life of the girl and, for that reason, she should not have been restrained from leaving the State. Because of this finding, the propriety of an injunction to restrain a person from leaving the jurisdiction did not need to be addressed by the Supreme Court. Nevertheless, Finlay CJ acknowledged, expressly *obiter dictum* and in the context of travelling abroad to procure an abortion, that the court could grant an injunction to prevent a person from leaving the jurisdiction in an attempt to vindicate and defend the right to life of the unborn.

Delivery up of Passports to Aid the Enforcement of Bayer Injunctions

[11.40] It is an established maxim of equity that "equity will not act in vain"[129] and so, an order of the court should not be made if it cannot be enforced. The difficulties associated with the enforcement of an injunction restraining a person from leaving the jurisdiction were considered by the Supreme Court in *Attorney General v X*.[130] There, Finlay CJ said:

> "I would accept that in a great number of instances, living in a country which has a land frontier and in an age which has such wide and varied facilities of

---

[127] [1992] ILRM 401.
[128] At 425.
[129] See Wylie, *Irish Land Law*, (3rd ed, 1997) Butterworths, para [3.067].
[130] [1992] ILRM 401.

travel, the making of orders restraining an individual from travelling out of the jurisdiction either for a specified time or for a specified purpose would be impossible to supervise and impossible to enforce except in the negative sense or possible imposition of punishment or sanctions after the order has been disobeyed. The imposition of such penalties, except to the extent that they might provide a deterrent, would not be an effective defence to the right of the unborn to life."

It is thought that whilst there might be particular difficulties with injunctions designed to prevent a woman going abroad for an abortion, in general, an injunction to restrain a person from leaving the jurisdiction is subject to no particular difficulties. Like all injunctions, a Bayer injunction will act *in personam* against a defendant who is amenable to the jurisdiction of the Irish court and disobedience is subject to the ultimate sanctions of committal, fine and sequestration for a contempt of court.[131] The fact that an injunction to restrain a pregnant woman from leaving the State might not be obeyed will not *per se* be a reason to refuse injunctive relief. As Finlay CJ said:

"Having regard, however, to the obligation of the courts to vindicate and defend [the right to life of the unborn] and to use every power which they may have in an attempt to achieve that object I do not consider that it can be said that a mere expectation that a significant number of people may be unwilling to obey the orders of a court could deprive that court from attempting, at least, in appropriate cases to discharge its constitutional duty by the making of an injunction restricting, to some extent, the right to travel of an individual".[132]

One very practical way in which the courts have made it more difficult for a defendant to breach such an injunction is to order him to deliver up his passport.[133] Although this does not, in theory, restrict movement within the European Union it does pose a practical obstacle for would-be fugitives. Arguably, unless and until a defendant has specific plans to go abroad, ordering him to deliver up his passport does not, *per se*, affect his rights. This was found to be the case by the Federal Court of Australia in *Re Allan Joseph Brazel*[134] where Cooper J said:

"In the instant case, there is before the court no specific proposal in relation to overseas travel. There is therefore, with the passport being held by the court, no present impediment of any common law right of travel. The position may be

---

[131.] See Ch 12, *Enforcing Mareva Injunctions and Other Orders*.

[132.] [1992] ILRM 401 at 430.

[133.] See, eg, *Re Mark Synnott (Lifge & Pensions) Brokers Ltd, The Irish Times*, 3 July 1991 noted at para **[11.35]** *supra*; see also *Re Bishopgate Investment Management Ltd, The Irish Times*, 10 December 1991 where it was reported that both Kevin and Ian Maxwell were ordered by the English High Court to deliver up their passports.

[134.] [1995] FCA 404/95 Bankruptcy.

different should a specific occasion arise where the debtor wishes to exercise his right of travel for business or any other purpose and in order to do so needs his passport, or access to his passport as a document of international travel, to allow him to leave the country. If and when that occasion arises the question will then be whether or not there are circumstances which would enable the passport to be withheld notwithstanding that the withholding of the passport impinged or abrogated the debtor's common law right of travel."

In that case the court had refused to grant an injunction to restrain a debtor (who had not as then been declared bankrupt) from leaving the jurisdiction. It was held, however, that the debtor's passport was the property of the commonwealth and would be held by the court.[135]

[C] MODERN POWERS OF CIVIL ARREST

Civil Arrest under the Companies Acts 1963-1990

[11.41] Civil arrest is permissible in two distinct circumstances under the Companies Acts 1963-1990. Although both remedies are not specifically related to the Mareva jurisdiction, they are considered here in the interests of providing as complete a picture as possible of the basis for restraining persons from leaving the State.

(a) Section 247 of the Companies Act 1963[136]

[11.42] Section 247 of the Companies Act 1963 ("the 1963 Act") makes provision for the civil arrest of an absconding contributory. It provides:

> The court, at any time either before or after making a winding-up order, on proof of probable cause for believing that a contributory is about to quit the State or otherwise to abscond or to remove or conceal any of his property for the purpose of evading payment of calls or of avoiding examination about the affairs of the company, may cause the contributory to be arrested, and his books and papers and movable personal property to be seized and him and them to be detained until such time as the court may order.

Applications for the arrest of absconding contributories will usually be brought by an official liquidator. The application should be made by motion *ex parte*.[137] The matters which must be proved, before an order for arrest can be made under s 247 of the 1963 Act, are now considered.

---

135. It may be noted that Irish passports provide that "This passport remains the property of the Minister for Foreign Affairs of Ireland".
136. See also, Courtney, *The Law of Private Companies*, (1994) Butterworths, para [19.025].
137. Order 74, r 135(2) of the Rules of the Superior Courts 1986.

(i) "Contributories" defined

[11.43] Only "contributories" may be arrested under s 247, such persons being defined by s 208 of the 1963 Act as "every person liable to contribute to the assets of a company in the event of its being wound up" and any person alleged to be a contributory. Those persons who are deemed to be "liable to contribute" to the assets of a company on its liquidation are past and present members of the company, directors who have unlimited liability,[138] and a deceased contributory's personal representatives.[139] It is thought that a person will be a contributory even if they do not have an *actual* liability to contribute to the assets of a company being wound up; all that is required is that they are liable to contribute, which they will be if they are one of the persons detailed above. Officers, such as directors, of a company will not *per se* be liable to arrest; the arrest of a company director under s 247 can only be ordered where that director also happens to be a contributory.[140]

(ii) Probable cause for believing contributory about to quit the State

[11.44] Before a contributory can be arrested, there must be probable cause for believing that he is about to quit the State. This is a high standard of proof, because civil arrest under s 247 of the 1963 Act is a most stringent remedy. In *Re Imperial Mercantile Credit Company*[141] the official liquidators of the company sought an order for the arrest of a contributory under s 118 of the Companies Act 1862, which was identical in all material respects to s 247 of the 1963 Act. It was heard that a letter had been received by one of the liquidators from a solicitor which stated that the contributory had advertised his property for sale and that it was "well known in the neighbourhood that he was about to proceed to Lisbon". This hearsay evidence did not impress Sir W Page Wood VC who said:

> "I am not disposed to take the very strong step of arresting this gentleman without some more definite information upon oath as to his being about to abscond; but I think there is enough to induce me to stop the sale of his property until further notice".[142]

The official liquidators' subsequent application (grounded upon the actual affidavit of the solicitor referred to in the previous affidavit) to have the contributory arrested was also unsuccessful, although an order was made to seize his books, papers, moneys, securities for moneys, goods and chattels; in so

---

138. Section 207 of the Companies Act 1963.
139. Section 210 of the Companies Act 1963.
140. As, eg, in the case of *Re The Ulster Land, Building and Investment Company Ltd* (1887) 17 LR Ir 591, considered at para **[11.46]** *infra*.
141. (1867) LR 5 Eq 264.
142. At 265.

ordering Sir W Page Wood VC thought it had been sufficiently proved that the contributory was about to remove his goods from the jurisdiction and held that while the section contemplates arrest at the same time as seizure of goods, one can be ordered without ordering the other.[143]

[11.45] It is thought that the first successful application for civil arrest of an absconding contributory under s 247 of the 1963 Act was brought in the case of *Re Central Trust Investment Society*, which is only recorded in *The Irish Times*.[144] There, the liquidator of the society was anxious to examine a director, who must also have been a contributory, in view of the fact that the society's money had been used to purchase properties in Ireland and abroad; only one set of annual accounts had been prepared in five years; about £1.75m of depositors' money was credited to the society; and there was evidence that a great deal of the society's paperwork was kept in the boot of the director's car. An order for arrest was made but subsequently lifted on the contributory's undertaking not to leave the country, to attend at the liquidator's office and to give all relevant information concerning the liquidation, attend court for re-examination and to notify the liquidator of his intention to change address. Murphy J also ordered that the man hand his passport into the court registrar.

(iii) Purpose being to evade payment of calls/avoid examination

[11.46] In addition to having to show that there is probable cause for believing that a contributory is about to quit the State, otherwise abscond or to remove or conceal any of his property, it must be shown that such is to be done for the *purpose* of evading payment of calls or of avoiding examination about the affairs of the company. In an old Irish case, *The Ulster Land, Building and Investment Company Ltd*,[145] the official liquidator of the company in liquidation applied for an order for the arrest of two contributories and the seizure of their goods under s 118 of the Companies Act 1862. The company had been ordered to be wound up by the court, it having been proved that its directors had been guilty of many breaches of trust and irregularities. The liquidator claimed in his affidavit that one contributory - who was also a director of the company - had given up his house, sent his furniture to auction, transferred shares he had held in other companies, was endeavouring to dispose of all of his property and was believed by the liquidator to be "actually negotiating for his passage" to

---

[143.] The requirement that there be "probable cause" was also considered in the context of s 7 of the Debtors Act (Ireland), 1872, para **[11.15]** *supra*; the similarities between civil arrest under s 118 of the Companies Act 1862 and the writ of *ne exeat* resulted in the remedies being referred to interchangeably in *Re Cotton Plantation Company of Natal* [1868] WN 79.

[144.] *The Irish Times*, 31 August 1982 (Murphy J). This case was first noted by Ussher, *Company Law in Ireland*, (1985) Sweet & Maxwell, p 494.

[145.] (1887) 17 LR Ir 591.

America. The liquidator also claimed that the reason for his quitting the country was in order to avoid payment of a call and to evade his other responsibilities to the company".[146] The other contributory was allegedly preparing to leave the country and had actually taken his passage to San Francisco, had transferred his shares in other companies and was also allegedly disposing of his other property. The liquidator claimed that it was necessary, for the full elucidation of the company's affairs, to examine both contributories. On foot of this the contributories were arrested and their goods seized; however, on *inter partes* hearing conflicting evidence was heard from the contributories and as a result both were released on recognizances of £400 and £500.

[11.47] In *Re O'Shea's (Dublin) Ltd*,[147] a case which has also only been reported in *The Irish Times*, Keane J is reported as having made an order for the arrest of a contributory (who was also managing director) of a tractor and car distribution company which had liabilities of £9.2m. The official liquidator said that he believed that the contributory, who had accommodation in Ibiza, was deliberately evading him; that he had been unable to contact the contributory; that the contributory had sold his Irish home; that the contributory had been abroad; that the liquidator had only learnt of his return on being told that he had been seen in a Dublin night-club; and that in the light of the foregoing it was his belief that the contributory would quit the State or otherwise abscond unless arrested. The official liquidator is reported as having said that the circumstances surrounding the company's trading prior to going into liquidation had given rise to "very considerable suspicion". It was also reported that he said that during his inspection of the company's business records, he had come across a number of situations which clearly called for further investigations but which he could not carry out without the contributory's assistance; in both of these respects we can surmise that this evidenced that the purpose of the contributory absconding was to avoid an examination as to the affairs of the company. It is interesting to note that Keane J directed that the order for arrest be issued for execution to the Garda Commissioner and he directed that the contributory be arrested and brought before the court at the earliest opportunity. As it happened, the earliest opportunity turned out to be almost three years later, when on 2 April 1987 the contributory was arrested in Dublin on his return from Spain but was subsequently released on the basis that his passport be impounded for three weeks, which was, on application being made, subsequently extended by two weeks upon Murphy J hearing that he had given minimal co-operation to the official liquidator.[148]

[146.] At 592.

[147.] *The Irish Times*, 6 July 1984 (Keane J). See Ussher, *op cit*.

[148.] *The Irish Times*, 5 May 1987.

(b) Section 245(8) of the Companies Act 1963[149]

[11.48] Section 245(8) of the 1963 Act, as amended by s 126 of the Companies Act 1990 ("the 1990 Act"), facilitates civil arrest in aid of the court's power to order the examination of officers (and certain other persons) of insolvent companies. Under s 245(1) of the Companies Act 1963 the court can at any time after the appointment of a provisional liquidator or the making of a winding up order, summon before it any officer of a company (ie director or secretary) or person known or suspected to have company property in his possession or supposed to be indebted to the company, or any person whom the court deems capable of giving information relating to the promotion, formation, trade, dealings, affairs or property of the company. The definition of those liable to be examined is, therefore, cast very widely and is not limited to a company's contributories or even to its officers.

[11.49] Until the coming into force of s 126 of the 1990 Act, a person ordered to appear for examination could not be arrested until the time for his appearance in court had arrived and he had defied that summons. This was the reason why in *Re J Ellis Pharmaceuticals*[150] (the same position prevailed in England: *Re Oriental Credit Ltd*[151]) the court granted a Bayer injunction to restrain a person required to be examined from leaving the jurisdiction because the court could not order his arrest under s 245 of the 1963 Act by reason of the fact that such could only be ordered after the summons to be examined had been defied. Section 126 of the 1990 Act amended s 245 of the 1963 Act and now s 245(8) provides:

> In a case where a person without reasonable excuse fails at any time to attend his examination under this section or there are reasonable grounds for believing that a person has absconded, or is about to abscond, with a view to avoiding or delaying his examination under this section, the court may cause that person to be arrested and his books to be seized and him and them to be detained until such time as the court may order.

Therefore, it is now the law that an order for arrest can be made of any of the persons described in para **[11.48]** as being liable to be examined where they fail to attend an examination, or they have absconded, or they are about to abscond with a view to avoiding or delaying their examination. It is likely that this provision will be of more practical use to liquidators than s 247 of the 1963 Act which is artificially restricted by the reference to "contributories".

[149.] See Courtney, *The Law of Private Companies*, (1994) Butterworths, para [19.013] *et seq.*
[150.] *The Irish Times*, 13 August 1988: see para **[11.33]** *supra.*
[151.] [1988] 1 All ER 892: see para **[11.32]** *supra.*

[11.50] It is interesting that the standard of proof required to be shown to the court in this, the most recent statutory provision which facilitates civil arrest, departs from the traditional formula of "probable cause for believing". Although it is thought to be of minimal significance, the use of the expression "reasonable grounds for believing" in s 245(8) of the Companies Act 1963 is a slightly lesser standard of proof that "probable cause for believing".

Civil Arrest under the Bankruptcy Act 1988

[11.51] Civil arrest may be ordered under the Bankruptcy Act 1988 ("the 1988 Act") in two distinct conditions: (a) under s 9(1) of the 1988 Act where a debtor, whom it is intended to have declared bankrupt, is about to abscond, and (b) under s 23 of the 1988 Act where a person who has been actually declared bankrupt is about to abscond. Each of these shall now be considered.

(a) Section 9 of the Bankruptcy Act 1988

[11.52] Section 9(1) of the 1988 Act facilitates the arrest of a debtor whom it is sought to make bankrupt, although he has not as yet been declared bankrupt. It provides:

> Where, after a bankruptcy summons has been granted against a debtor and before a petition to adjudicate him bankrupt can be presented against him, it appears to the court that there is probable cause for believing that he is about to leave the State or to otherwise abscond with a view to avoiding payment of the debt for which the bankruptcy summons was issued or avoiding examination in respect of his affairs or otherwise avoiding or delaying proceedings in bankruptcy the court may cause such debtor to be arrested and brought before the court.

An arrest will not be lawful unless before, or at the time or his arrest, the debtor is served with a bankruptcy summons.[152] A bankruptcy summons may be granted by the court in accordance with s 8 of the 1988 Act where a creditor proves that the debtor owes him at least £1,500 for a liquidated sum and notice in the prescribed form has been served on the debtor.[153] In practice, the High Court usually requires the creditor to have obtained judgment against the debtor before issuing a bankruptcy summons. The requirements of bankruptcy legislation must be strictly complied with and the summons must be served in the prescribed manner.[154]

[152.] Section 9(2) of the 1988 Act.

[153.] See generally, Sanfey & Holohan, *Bankruptcy Law and Practice in Ireland*, (1991) Roundhall Press.

[154.] *Re O'M Bankrupt* High Court, unrep, 21 September 1988 (Hamilton P).

[11.53] Before ordering a debtor's arrest under s 9(1) of the 1988 Act the court must be satisfied that, to the time honoured evidential standard for ordering a person's civil arrest, there is "probable cause for believing that he is about to leave the state or to otherwise abscond": see para **[11.44]** above. Moreover, the court must be satisfied that the debtor's purpose in leaving the State is "with a view to avoiding payment of the debt for which the bankruptcy summons was issued or avoiding examination in respect of his affairs or otherwise avoiding or delaying proceedings in bankruptcy". Only where these conditions are met can the court order a debtor's arrest;[155] even when these conditions are met, the making of an order for arrest lies entirely within the court's discretion.[156]

(b) Section 23 of the Bankruptcy Act 1988

[11.54] A second provision for civil arrest in contained in s 23(1) of the 1988 Act. This empowers the court to order the arrest of a person who has actually been declared bankrupt, as opposed to merely having been served with a bankruptcy summons. Section 23(1) provides:

> Where it appears to the court, at any time after making an adjudication order, on proof of probable cause for believing that a bankrupt is about to leave the State or otherwise to abscond or has removed or concealed or is about to remove or conceal any of his property with a view to avoiding payment of his debts or avoiding examination in respect of his affairs, or is keeping out of the way and cannot be served with a summons, the court may cause him to be arrested and brought before it for examination.

In addition, s 23(2) facilitates the arrest of a bankrupt who has been summoned before the court for examination[157] and who does not come at the time appointed without having an excuse. It may be noted that the court may also order the arrest of any other person[158] who is summoned for examination and, who having been tendered a reasonable sum for his expenses, does not, without an excuse, come at the time appointed.[159]

[155.] Where the debtor offers such security, or upon making such payment or composition as the Court thinks reasonable, the debtor shall be discharged from custody unless the Court otherwise orders: s 9(3) of the 1988 Act.

[156.] As to whether the Court can grant an injunction to restrain a debtor from leaving the jurisdiction (in circumstances where the power of civil arrest has not arisen) see *Re Allan Joseph Brazel* [1995] FCA 404/95 (bankruptcy).

[157.] Pursuant to s 21 of the 1988 Act.

[158.] Persons who can be summoned to be examined under s 21(1), other than a bankrupt, are: any person who is known or suspected to have in his possession or control any property of a bankrupt; or who has disposed of any property of a bankrupt; or who is supposed to be indebted to a bankrupt; or who the Court deemed capable of giving information relating to a bankrupt's trade, dealings, affairs or property.

[159.] Section 23(3) of the 1988 Act.

Chapter 12

Enforcing Mareva Injunctions and Other Orders

[12.01] Mareva injunctions, like all injunctions, are orders of the court and as such must be obeyed. Where a defendant refuses to obey an order of the court, he is *prima facie* in contempt of court.[1] "Contempt of court" is a generic concept which is sub-divided into two broad classes of contempt, namely, civil contempt and criminal contempt. The disobedience of a court order, such as a Mareva injunction, by a defendant or a third-party, is classified as "civil contempt".[2] This chapter is concerned with civil contempt of court.

The vast majority of court orders are obeyed, since we are fortunate to live in a society where the rule of law is generally respected by its citizens. In those few cases where injunctions made by the courts are disobeyed, it is essential to the administration of justice that swift action is taken against the contemnor.[3] As O'Leary J said in the Canadian case of *Canadian Metal Co Ltd v Canadian Broadcasting Corporation (No 2)*:[4]

> "To allow court orders to be disobeyed would be to tread the road towards anarchy. If orders of the court can be treated with disrespect, the whole administration of justice is brought into scorn ... Loss of respect for the courts will quickly result in the destruction of our society."[5]

"Anarchy" is a very forceful term; but what other word can sufficiently convey the consequences which might follow where the orders of a nation's courts are flouted? In civil causes of action, a plaintiff's primary reason for litigating, apart from having an independent arbitrator determine the rights and wrongs of the matter, is to be afforded an enforceable remedy against his defendant. If a defendant does not comply with an order of the court, he must be subject to

---

[1.] See generally, Borrie & Lowe, *The Law of Contempt*, (3rd ed, 1996) Butterworths; Hoyle, *The Mareva Injunction and Related Orders*, (3rd ed, 1997) Lloyd's of London Press, pp 131-140; Capper, *Mareva Injunctions*, (1988) SLS/Sweet & Maxwell, pp 76-91.

[2.] See para **[12.06]** *infra*.

[3.] In this chapter "contemnor" is interchanged with "defendant".

[4.] (1975) 48 DLR (3d) 641 at 669; cited in Lowe & Sufrin, *op cit*, p 558.

[5.] As Borrie & Lowe, *The Law of Contempt*, (3rd ed, 1996) Butterworths, p 4 say, in a passage cited in *AMIEU v Mudginberri Station Pty Ltd* (1986) 161 CLR 98 at 107: "The rationale of both criminal and civil contempt is therefore essentially the same: upholding the effective administration of justice. If a court lacked the means to enforce its orders, and its orders could be disobeyed with impunity, not only would individual litigants suffer, the whole administration of justice would be brought into disrepute".

some sanction. As was recently stated by the Supreme Court of New South Wales in *Registrar Court of Appeal v Pelechowski*[6] in the context of a Mareva injunction:

> "The public is entitled to expect that a court injunction will be obeyed. If injunctions were to be disobeyed with any frequency, the civil justice system would suffer a serious loss of public confidence and credibility. This court must safeguard and vindicate the integrity and effectiveness of injunctive orders. The purposes of punishment for contempt include deterring both the contemnor and others from committing like contempts and denouncing in an emphatic way the conduct concerned."

Injunctive relief, such as a Mareva injunction, is at the very cutting edge of justice; it seeks to preserve a plaintiff's rights pending judgment; a plaintiff goes to court to have his rights defended and vindicated and where they are so defended and vindicated, by injunction of the court, a defendant's disrespect of the court's order will be a *prima facie* contempt of court and will be punishable accordingly.[7]

[12.02] The purpose of this chapter is first, to distinguish civil contempt from criminal contempt; secondly, to consider the circumstances which constitute civil contempt of court for the breach of an injunction or order by a defendant; thirdly, to consider the circumstances which constitute contempt of court by a third party; fourthly, to consider the consequences where a defendant acts in breach of an undertaking which he gave *in lieu* of the court making an order directing him to do or refrain from doing a particular act; and fifthly, to examine the sanctions which civil contempt of court may attract: fine, sequestration of the contemnor's assets, attachment and committal to prison of the contemnor. The following issues are considered in this chapter:

1. Civil Contempt and Criminal Contempt Distinguished.
2. Breach of Injunctions by Defendants.
3. Breach of Injunctions by Third Parties.
4. Breach of an Undertaking Given in lieu of an Injunction.
5. Sanctions: Attachment, Committal, Sequestration and Fine.

Civil Contempt and Criminal Contempt Distinguished[8]

[12.03] The law of contempt of court, civil and criminal, is primarily designed to protect and vindicate the effective administration of justice in the courts. In

---

6. [1998] NSWSC 2 (3 February 1998), p 4 of the internet transcript. In *A & McA v MM*, *The Irish Times*, 6 August 1988 (Murphy J), it was reported that in warning a couple who had managed an hotel but who had been ordered to vacate the premises, Murphy J had said: "You must realise that litigation is a troublesome and expensive business but if orders are not obeyed, all we stand for is nonsense."
7. See para **[12.51]** *et seq, infra.*
8. See generally, Hogan & Whyte, *Kelly: The Irish Constitution*, (3rd ed, 1994) Butterworths, pp 390-395.

Keegan & Keegan v De Burca[9] McLoughlin J said that the jurisdiction to deal with contempt of court:

> "is a necessary ancillary power to enable that court to exercise its jurisdiction by suppressing an interference with its exercise."

Contempt of court is, however, divided into two broad classes of transgression: contempt by *interference* and contempt by *disobedience*.[10] The former - contempt by interference - is broadly classified as criminal contempt and the latter - contempt by disobedience - can be broadly classified as civil contempt.[11]

[12.04] Civil contempt of court has been distinguished from criminal contempt of court in a number of Irish cases. Perhaps the most authoritative of these was *Keegan & Keegan v De Burca*[12] where O'Dalaigh CJ said, first, of criminal contempt:

> "The distinction between civil and criminal contempt is not new law. Criminal contempt consists in behaviour calculated to prejudice the due course of justice, such as contempt *in facie curiae*,[13] words written or spoken or acts calculated to prejudice the due course of justice or disobedience to a writ of *habeas corpus* by the person to whom it is directed - to give but some examples ... Criminal contempt is a common-law misdemeanour and, as such, is punishable by both imprisonment and fine at discretion, that is to say, without statutory limit, its objective is punitive."[14]

These examples of "conduct prejudicial to the due course of justice" can largely[15] be seen to be examples of *interference* with a court order.[16]

---

9. [1973] IR 223 at 236.
10. Lord Donaldson MR in *AG Newspaper Publishing plc* [1987] 3 All ER 276 preferred this approach over the "criminal v civil contempt" classification; it is thought, however, that in Ireland the criminal v civil distinction will not be displaced by the "interference v disobedience" distinction by reason of the constitutional distinction between criminal matters and civil matters: see *Keegan & Keegan v De Burca* [1973] IR 223.
11. Lowe & Sufrin, *Borrie & Lowe The Law of Contempt of Court*, (3rd ed, 1996) Butterworths, pp 2-3.
12. [1973] IR 223.
13. Ie disrupting the court process itself.
14. [1973] IR 223 at 227.
15. The "interference"/ "disobedience" distinction and its juxtaposition onto the categories of "criminal" and "civil" contempt respectively is a broad classification, disobedience to a writ of *habeas corpus* being an exception.
16. Another example of criminal contempt of court, not mentioned by O'Dalaigh CJ, is "scandalising the court": see *The State (Director of Public Prosecutions) v Walsh* [1981] IR 412. In that case criminal contempt of court was further classified into two categories: "... contempt in *facie curiae* which consists of conduct which is obstructive or prejudicial to the course of justice, and which is committed during court proceedings; or contempts committed outside court (known as constructive contempts) where pending proceedings may be interfered with or prejudiced by what is said or done."

[12.05] In *Keegan & Keegan v De Burca*[17] O'Dalaigh CJ went on to define civil contempt of court, saying:

> "Civil contempt usually arises where there is a disobedience to an order of the court by a party to the proceedings and in which the court has generally no interest to interfere unless moved by the party for whose benefit the order was made ... Civil contempt ... is not punitive in its object but coercive in its purpose of compelling the party committed to comply with the order of the court, and the period of committal would be until such time as the order is complied with or until it is waived by the party for whose benefit the order was made. In the case of civil contempt only the court can order release but the period of committal cannot be commuted or remitted as a sentence for a term definite in a criminal matter can be commuted or remitted pursuant to Article 13.6[18] of the Constitution."[19]

Disobedience to injunctions, such as Mareva injunctions, or other court orders (such as those considered in Chapter 10, *Ancillary Orders*) will therefore fall to be classified as civil contempt of court.[20]

[12.06] On first reading the definition of civil contempt of court, set out in *Keegan & Keegan v De Burca*,[21] would seem to exclude the breach of an injunction by a person who is not "a party to the proceedings" ie a third party. In many cases this issue will not arise by reason of the fact that a Mareva plaintiff will join third parties who are known to hold the defendant's assets - such as banks - as notice parties in the proceedings. Even where third parties are not joined in the action, they may still be in civil contempt of court where they are found to be "aiding and abetting a breach of an injunction or otherwise obstructing or frustrating a court order".[22] The contempt by those who aid and abet a defendant to be disobedient to a court order is best classified as civil, and

---

17. [1973] IR 223.
18. Article 13.6 of the Constitution provides: "The right of pardon and the power to commute or remit punishment imposed by any court exercising *criminal jurisdiction* are hereby vested in the President, but such power of commutation or remission may, except in capital cases, also be conferred by law on other authorities." Italics added.
19. [1973] IR 223 at 227.
20. *Cf McEnroe v Leonard*, High Court, unrep, 9 December 1975 (Parke J) where Parke J held: "I am therefore of opinion that failure to obey a court order is a crime. It is not a "minor offence" within Article 38(2) of the Constitution. I am therefore of opinion that the determination of the issue as to whether or not a person is guilty of such contempt comes within Article 38(5) of the Constitution and must be determined by a jury" (at page 2 of the transcript). It is respectfully submitted that this is an incorrect statement of the law and, moreover, is one which has not been followed by the Irish courts.
21. [1973] IR 223.
22. See Borrie & Lowe, *The Law of Contempt*, (3rd ed, 1996) Butterworths, p 573.

not criminal, contempt.[23] These points are amongst those considered below, in the discussion of *Breach of Injunctions by Third Parties*.[24]

Breach of Injunctions by Defendants

[12.07] The operative part[25] of a Mareva injunction will typically prohibit a defendant from:

> "... removing from the State[26] or in any way disposing of, reducing, transferring, charging, diminishing the value thereof, or otherwise dealing with all or any of his assets which are in[27] the State ...".

The order may go on to "freeze" all of the defendant's assets, but will usually be capped at a "maximum sum" ie the paragraph last quoted may go on to provide "save insofar as the defendant's assets exceed eg £250,000", in which case the defendant can dispose of his assets provided that at all times he retains assets to the value of £250,000.[28] Where a defendant disposes of his assets so as to reduce their value below the specified maximum amount he will be in breach of the court's order and will have committed a contempt of court.

[12.08] Here, it is proposed to consider the prerequisites which must be satisfied if a defendant is to be found to be in breach of an injunction or other order of the court:

   (a) Binding the defendant through notice of the injunction;

   (b) Service of injunctions;

   (c) Endorsing a penal notice in mandatory injunctions;

   (d) The terms of the order must be unambiguous;

   (e) The requisite standard of proof for contempt of court;

   (f) Proving breach by defendant companies.

[23.] See Borrie & Lowe, *op cit*, p 657 where it is said of "aiding and abetting" a breach of injunction that: "It can be argued that such an act amounts to a criminal contempt since the offence is not committed by a party to the action and the act clearly impedes the due course of justice. On the other hand, it can equally well be argued that the act amounts to a civil contempt, the punishment of the offender being an indirect means of enforcing the court order for the benefit of the plaintiff. Although support can be found for both views, the weight of modern authority is that it is a criminal contempt". The authorities cited for this latter proposition by the authors are *AG v Newspapers Publishing Plc* [1988] Ch 333, *AG v Times Newspapers Ltd* [1991] 2 All ER 398 and Miller, *Contempt of Court*, (2nd ed), p 430. See *Scott v Scott* [1913] AC 417 cited in 9 *Halsbury's Laws of England* (4th ed), para 85ff for authority that aiding and abetting is civil contempt.

[24.] See para **[12.31]** *infra*.

[25.] See the Appendices to this book.

[26.] Or, "Ireland" or "the jurisdiction of this court".

[27.] Obviously, this will be modified in the case of a worldwide Mareva injunction.

[28.] See further, Ch 9, *The Mareva Order and Its Effects*, para **[9.09]** *et seq*.

(a) Binding the defendant through notice of the injunction

[12.09] Where a court makes a Mareva injunction or other order, the order must be dated and, unless the court directs otherwise, it will take effect accordingly.[29] The general rule is that a defendant will only become bound by an injunction upon his being notified of the terms of the injunction.[30] As Lyell J said in *Husson v Husson*,[31] a person:

> "... cannot be held guilty of contempt in infringing an order of the court of which he knows nothing."

As has been emphasised in an earlier chapter,[32] it is important to distinguish the act of giving a defendant *notice* that an injunction has been made from the act of *serving* a defendant with the actual injunction. It is well settled that a defendant will be bound by an injunction where he has *notice* that it has been made[33] and, accordingly, while notice is best given by personal service of the injunction, a defendant will be bound by an injunction of which he has notice whether by means of a telegraph,[34] a fax, a telephone call[35] or orally in person. An example of the latter is seen in *Vansandau v Rose*.[36] In that case an injunction had been obtained which restrained the defendant from cutting down timber on the plaintiff landlord's farm and from carrying away timber which had been already cut down. Notwithstanding that notice of the injunction had been given orally to the defendant, together with a full verbal explanation of its effect, the defendant had acted in breach of the injunction. Lord Eldon held that the defendant was in contempt of court because although there had not been service of the injunction itself, notice was sufficient. He said: "... in many cases all the mischief would be done, and that you might as well grant no injunction at all, unless notice of it was held sufficient".[37] More recently, in *Z Ltd v A*[38] Eveleigh LJ said "the person against whom the order is made will be liable for contempt of court if he acts in

---

[29.] Order 115 of the Rules of the Superior Courts 1986.

[30.] *Duff v Devlin* [1924] 1 IR 56. In *R v The Freeman's Journal Ltd* [1902] IR 82 Gibson J said (at 91) in the context of the violation of an express order by the court "[s]uch order cannot be treated as disobeyed if its substance is not known".

[31.] [1962] 3 All ER 1056.

[32.] See Ch 9, *The Mareva Order and Its Effects*, para **[9.25]** *et seq*.

[33.] *Duff v Devlin* [1924] 1 IR 56.

[34.] See, for example, *Re Bryant* 4 Ch D 98; *Re Bishop, ex p Langley, ex p Smith* (1879) 13 Ch D 110; and *Curtice v London City and Midland Bank* [1908] 1 KB 297.

[35.] As, eg, on the defendant in *Columbia Picture Industries Inc v Robinson* [1987] Ch 38 and as recommended in the case of third parties such as banks, by Lord Denning MR in *Z Ltd v A* [1982] 1 All ER 556 at 565h-j. See also *PPHS Ltd v von K, The Irish Times*, 31 May 1995 (Circuit Court; Kelly J) where it was reported that the court allowed notice of a Mareva injunction to be made by telephone and fax.

[36.] 2 J & W 264.

[37.] At 265.

[38.] [1982] 1 All ER 556.

breach of the order *having notice of it*".[39] In the Irish case of *The Century Insurance Co Ltd v Larkin*[40] Meredith MR accepted that where the defendant was in court and a restraining or prohibitory order was made, the proof that the defendant had notice of the injunction could be dispensed with.[41]

[12.10] Notice of the terms of an undertaking which is embodied in a court order will also suffice to bind a defendant. In *D v A & Co*[42] the defendants, who had given an undertaking which had been embodied in a court order of which they had notice, objected to the fact that the order had not been served personally on them. The inter-relationship between *service* of an order and *notice* of an order was succinctly put by Cozens-Hardy J who held:

> "It is settled law that an order granting an injunction may be enforced by committal, although the order has not been *served*. It is sufficient if it be shewn that the defendant had *notice* of the order. Service of the order is a convenient mode of giving notice, but that is all. Notice may be given by telegram or otherwise: see *United Telephone Co v Dale* 25 Ch D 778."[43]

The difficulty with purporting to put a defendant on notice of an injunction which has been made against him, without serving him with the order, is in subsequently proving beyond all reasonable doubt,[44] in committal proceedings for contempt, that the defendant had actual notice of the injunction's terms. This is borne out by the case of *Re Bishop, ex p Langley, ex p Smith*[45] where the Court of Appeal found that there were reasonable grounds for believing that the defendants, who had merely been given notice of an injunction by telegram and had not been served with the injunction, *bona fide* believed that no injunction had been granted and, therefore, were not in contempt although the injunction had been disobeyed. Where a solicitor, being an officer of the court, informs a defendant of the making of an injunction, he is under a duty to ensure that what he says is accurate.[46]

---

39. At 566g-h. Italics added.
40. [1910] 1 IR 91.
41. At 94. See para **[12.16]** *infra* where the relevant passage is quoted.
42. [1900] 1 Ch 484.
43. At 486, 487. Italics added. On the particular question of an undertaking, Cozens-Hardy J went on to say: "If this holds good where a hostile order has been made, it must equally hold good where the defendant has voluntarily given an undertaking. Indeed in such a case I think no notice at all is requisite, for, in the words of Chitty J in *Callow v Young* 55 LT 544, 'it is not necessary to shew that the person sought to be attached had knowledge of his undertaking. He must be presumed to have known that he had given his undertaking'."
44. See *Churchman v Joint Shop Stewards' Committee of Workers of the Port of London* [1972] 3 All ER 603 at 606 per Lord Denning MR. See para **[12.19]** *et seq, supra*.
45. (1879) 13 Ch D 110.
46. In *Kimpton v Eve* 2 V & B 349 Lord Eldon LC noted that the ultimate safeguard against a solicitor falsely claiming that an injunction had been granted when it had not was that he could be struck off the roll of solicitors. He said (at 352): "... the solicitor, so intimating without foundation, that an injunction had been granted, would unquestionably be liable to be struck off the Roll, to make satisfaction to the party injured, and to an indictment for so acting".

(b) Service of injunctions

(i) Service of injunctions on individuals

[12.11] The general rule is that all injunctions should be served *personally*.[47] Accordingly, by Ord 121, r 6 of the RSC, service of an injunction should be effected as nearly as may be in the manner prescribed for the personal service of an originating summons ie in accordance with Ord 9, r 3 of the RSC. Personal service of an originating summons is effected:

> ... by delivering a copy of the summons to the defendant in person, and showing him the original or duplicate original.[48]

By analogy, personal service of an injunction or other order is effected by delivering a copy of the order to the defendant in person and showing him the original injunction or order or duplicate original.[49] Moreover, Ord 9, r 2 provides:

> ... Where it shall appear by affidavit that such defendant is personally within the jurisdiction and that due and reasonable diligence has been exercised in endeavouring to effect such personal service, service of such summons may be effected by delivering a copy thereof at the defendant's house or place of residence, or at his or her office, warehouse, counting house, shop, factory, or place of business, to the wife, husband, child, father, mother, brother, or sister of the defendant, or to any servant or clerk of the defendant (the person to whom such copy shall be delivered being of the age of sixteen years and upwards) and showing to such person the original or duplicate original of such summons.[50]

Again, by analogy, an injunction or order can similarly be served by reason of Ord 121, r 6 of the RSC. The difficulty with Ord 9, r 2 is that if an injunction is left at, say, a defendant's place of residence, it is open to the defendant to claim that service was not effected and that he did not have notice of the injunction. So, where personal service cannot be effected on the defendant in person, it is wise to consider making application for substituted service.

(ii) Substituted service of injunctions on individuals

[12.12] Just as personal service of originating summonses can be dispensed with and replaced by substituted service,[51] so too can service of an injunction or other

---

[47.] *Vansandau v Rose* 2 J & W 264; *Gooch v Marshall* 8 WR 410.

[48.] Order 9, r 3 of the RSC.

[49.] Order 41, r 7 of the RSC provides that: "... wherever any rule, or order, or the practice of the court, requires the production or service of the original judgment or order, it shall be sufficient to produce or serve the duplicate."

[50.] For commentary on the salient points see O'Floinn, *Practice and Procedure in the Superior Courts*, (1996) Butterworths, pp 49-51.

[51.] On substituted service of originating summonses, see Ord 10.

order be effected by alternative or substituted service. The appropriate rule to make application under is Ord 121, r 7 of the RSC which provides:

> Where personal service of any document is required by these Rules or otherwise, and it appears to the court that prompt personal service cannot be effected, the court may make an order for substituted or other service, or for the substitution for service of notice by letter, advertisement or otherwise.

In an attempt to ensure that a defendant has been served with notice of the terms of the court's order it is common practice, following the grant of an *ex parte* order, to seek leave from the court under Ord 121, r 7 to serve notice of the order on the defendant and or third parties by telephone[52] or fax[53] on the plaintiff's undertaking to follow this up by sending a copy of the order and other relevant documents, such as the grounding affidavit, to the defendant as soon as possible. In certain circumstances it may also be necessary to get leave from the court to serve notice of the order out of hours.[54]

(iii) Service of injunctions on companies

[12.13] Service of documents on companies is governed by s 379(1) of the Companies Act 1963 ("the 1963 Act") which provides:

> A document may be served on a company by leaving it at or sending it by post to the registered office of the company or, if the company has not given notice to the registrar of companies of the situation of its registered office, by registering it at the office for the registration of companies.

Section 379(2) of the 1963 Act provides that where any document is left at or sent by post to a company's registered office as recorded by the registrar of companies, it shall be deemed to have been left at or sent by post notwithstanding that the situation of the registered office may have changed.[55] As last noted, Ord 121, r 6 of the RSC provides that service of a court order or injunction is to be effected as nearly as may be in the manner prescribed for an originating summons; Ord 9, r 7 provides a procedure whereby corporations

---

[52.] *Columbia Picture Industries Inc v Robinson* [1987] Ch 38. See also *PPHS Ltd v von K, The Irish Times*, 31 May 1995 (Circuit Court; Kelly J) where it was reported that the court allowed notice of a Mareva injunction to be made by telephone and fax. The practice of allowing service of an order by telephone is not all that new: in *The National Bank Ltd v Barry* 100 ILTR 185 at 186 it was reported that the Supreme Court allowed service of an order of attachment to be effected by telephone on the solicitors for the defendants, to be confirmed by personal service.

[53.] See *Ralux v Spencer Mason, The Times* of 18 May 1989 and Hall, 'Service of Documents by FAX', (1989) Gazette ILSI 318.

[54.] Order 122, r 9 of the RSC provides, *inter alia*, that service of orders shall be effected before 5 pm, Monday to Friday; before 1 pm, Saturday.

[55.] See Courtney, *The Law of Private Companies*, (1994) Butterworths, para [3.080] *et seq*; and O'Floinn, *Practice and Procedure in the Superior Courts*, (1996), Butterworths pp 53, 54.

aggregate are to be served with an originating summons, but this will only apply "in the absence of any statutory provision regulating service". Since s 379 of the 1963 Act "regulates service" of documents on a company registered under the Companies Act 1963-1990 (a type of body corporate), it overrides Ord 9 of the RSC and so governs the service of court orders and injunctions on a "company" as defined by s 2 of the 1963 Act.

[12.14] Unlike England and Wales, there is no Irish equivalent to Ord 45, r 7 of the Rules of the Supreme Court 1965 which provide, *inter alia*, for the personal service of a court order, such as an injunction, on an officer of a defendant company. In Ireland, it is thought to be prudent to serve a company in accordance with s 379 of the 1963 Act and to put its directors and other officers *on notice* of the injunction and indicate to them that, if the injunction is breached, they may be attached and fined and their property sequestrated.[56] The indication that a person is liable to be imprisoned for breach of an order is termed a "penal notice" and is considered next.

(c) Endorsing a penal notice in mandatory injunctions

[12.15] Where a penal notice is attached to a court order its purpose[57] is to draw a defendant's attention to the fact that disobedience of the terms of the order will have penal consequences.[58] Strictly speaking, the endorsement of a penal notice in an injunction or other order is only required in the case of a *mandatory* injunction or order (ie an order made in any cause of matter which requires a person to do an act thereby ordered); however, it is common practice amongst Irish practitioners to include a penal notice in all injunctions and orders, including those which are *prohibitory* or *restrictive* in nature (eg a Mareva injunction which restrains or prohibits a defendant from removing, dissipating, disposing of or otherwise dealing with the his assets). Order 41, r 8 of the RSC provides, *inter alia*, that every mandatory order shall state the time, or the time after the service of the order, within which the act is to be done and an endorsement "in the words or to the effect" that:

> "If you the within named A.B. neglect to obey this judgment or order by the time therein limited, you will be liable to process of execution including imprisonment for the purpose of compelling you to obey the same judgment or order".

[56.] For an instance of where directors were fined where their company breached the terms of an injunction (not a Mareva) see *Irish Shell Ltd v Ballylynch Motors Ltd*, Supreme Court, unrep, 5 March 1997.

[57.] See *Prior v Johnston* (1893) 27 ILTR 108 and *Wallace v Graham* 11 LR Ir 369.

[58.] See *Iberian Trust Ltd v Founders Trust and Investment Co Ltd* [1932] 2 KB 87 at 97 per Luxmoore J.

This endorsement *must* be used in the case of a mandatory order ie where a defendant is obliged, by the order, to do something by a particular time (eg an order to disclose the extent and whereabouts of the defendant's assets made ancillary to a Mareva injunction).

[12.16] In *The Century Insurance Co Ltd v Larkin*[59] it was held that where a penal notice is not endorsed on a mandatory injunction or order the court will not attach the defendant for disobedience of the order, even where the defendant was personally present in court when the order was made. Distinguishing *mandatory* orders from *restraining* orders, Meredith MR said:

> "... it seems clear that the authorities in which the presence in court of the party sought to be attached has been held to dispense with notice of the order have been cases of injunctions to restrain a man from doing something, he having been present in court, and told by the court not to do the act. For some reason or another the rule-making authority in this country, and in England also, considered that the order of a court compelling a man to do a certain act stood in a different position from other orders. The rule in Ireland requires the time, or time after service of the order, within which the act is to be done to be stated, and requires a memorandum to be indorsed warning the person of the consequences of not doing the act ... If you want to sent a man to gaol for contempt of court for not doing a certain act, you must serve the order which compels him to do the act upon him, and it must contain a proper indorsement upon it."[60]

It is crucial that an Anton Piller order, which is mandatory in nature, be indorsed with a penal notice in accordance with Ord 41, r 8 of the RSC. Although it has been said that it is common practice to indorse a penal notice on prohibitory and restraining orders (which the writer believes to be a good practice) it may be noted that in *Murphy v Willcocks*[61] Barton J held that the predecessor to Ord 41, r 8 had "no application to prohibitive orders". Where a Mareva injunction incorporates an asset disclosure order[62] it will be in the nature of both a prohibitory and a mandatory order and a penal notice must, accordingly, be endorsed.

[12.17] Other mandatory orders which have been considered in an earlier chapter, such as disclosure orders in relation to assets in aid of Mareva injunctions should also contain a penal notice. Although Ord 31, r 22 of the RSC provides that service of an order for interrogatories or discovery or inspection on a party's solicitor shall be "sufficient service to found an application for an

---

[59.] [1910] 1 IR 91.
[60.] At 94.
[61.] [1911] 1 IR 402.
[62.] As it does in both Appendix 1 and Appendix 2, *post*.

attachment for disobedience to the order", it is thought that r 22 does not apply to such orders where made *ancillary* to Mareva relief under s 28(8) of the Supreme Court of Judicature Ireland Act 1877;[63] it is thought that Ord 31, r 22 of the RSC should be confined to situations where interrogatories, discovery or inspection relate to the "matters in question" in a cause of action.

(d) The terms of the order must be unambiguous

[12.18] If a defendant is to be found to be in breach of an injunction or other court order, it must be shown that the terms of the injunction or order were clear and unambiguous.[64] In the case of a Mareva injunction, which contains the standard prohibitory words,[65] it will usually be the case that the order will be relatively unambiguous. Regard must, however, be had to the monetary amount which it is sought to restrain a defendant from parting with, although here too, practice would suggest that a monetary limit, prefaced by "save where the amount exceeds" will render the operative part of the injunction clear and unambiguous.

(e) The requisite standard of proof for contempt of court

[12.19] It is well established that a defendant's liability for breach of an injunction or other court order is strict. Provided that a defendant is aware of the terms of the order,[66] it is irrelevant that he "did his best" to comply with the order if in fact it was not complied with;[67] or that the injunction or order ought not to have been made in the first place;[68] or that a defendant was motivated by good intentions;[69] or that a defendant's non-compliance was not intentionally contumacious nor did he intend to interfere with the administration of justice.[70]

[63.] For the jurisdiction to make disclosure orders in aid of Mareva injunctions, see Ch 10, *Ancillary Orders*, para **[10.03]**.

[64.] See generally, Borrie & Lowe, *The Law of Contempt*, (3rd ed, 1996) Butterworths, p 560 where Luxmoore J in *Iberian Trust Ltd v Founders Trust and Investment Co Ltd* [1932] 2 KB 87 at 95 is quoted: "If the court is to punish anyone for not carrying out its order the order must in unambiguous terms direct what is to be done."

[65.] See para **[12.07]** *supra*.

[66.] See *R v Freeman's Journal Ltd* [1902] 2 IR 82 at 91 where Gibson J said in connection with the violation of an express order of the court: "Such an order cannot be treated as disobeyed if its substance is not known." See also para **[12.09]** *et seq, supra*.

[67.] See *Howitt Transport v Transport and General Workers' Union* [1973] ICR 1 at 10 *per* Sir John Donaldson.

[68.] See *Hadkinson v Hadkinson* [1952] P 285 *per* Romer LJ, *Johnson v Walton* [1990] 1 FLR 350 *per* Lord Donaldson MR and *Isaacs v Robertson* [1984] 3 All ER 140 *per* Lord Diplock.

[69.] *R v Poplar Borough Council (No 2)* [1922] 1 KB 95.

[70.] See Borrie & Lowe, *The Law of Contempt*, (3rd ed, 1996) Butterworths, p 567 citing *Knight v Clifton* [1971] Ch 700 and *Stanbridge v Trowbridge UDC* [1910] 2 Ch 190, the latter authority being endorsed in *Heatons Transport* [1973] AC 15 and *Re Supply of Ready Mixed Concrete (No 2)* [1995] 1 All ER 135.

What must, however, be proved is that a defendant actually did the act which the order prevented him from doing or that he failed to do the act which the order obliged him to do.

[12.20] The standard of proof required to find that a defendant has breached an injunction or other order of the court - and thereby committed civil contempt of court - could either be the usual criminal standard of "beyond reasonable doubt" or the usual civil standard of "on the balance of probabilities". In England[71] it has been established that the standard of proof required to be shown in order that a defendant be found to be in contempt of court is that applicable to criminal cases, namely, "beyond all reasonable doubt".

[12.21] In *Re Bramblevale Ltd*[72] a company director had been ordered to produce the company's books to its liquidator. The director failed to comply with the order, claiming that the books of the company had been inadvertently thrown away after being soaked in petrol following a car accident. Megarry J refused to believe the defendant director's explanation and committed him indefinitely for contempt of court. The defendant director successfully appealed to the Court of Appeal where Lord Denning MR said:

> "A contempt of court is an offence of a criminal character. A man may be sent to prison for it. It must be satisfactorily proved. To use the time-honoured phrase, it must be proved beyond all reasonable doubt. It is not proved by showing that, when the man was asked about it, he told lies. There must be further evidence to incriminate him. Once some evidence is given, then his lies can be thrown into the scale against him. But there must be some other evidence."[73]

The reason why the appeal was successful was because it had not been proved beyond all reasonable doubt that the defendant director, either (a) had the company's books in his possession and refused to deliver them up or (b) had got rid of the books to avoid having to comply with the order. The finding in this case that the requisite standard of proof is that of "beyond all reasonable doubt" has been followed in subsequent English cases.[74]

[12.22] It is thought that, in Ireland, the appropriate standard of proof required to find that a defendant is in civil contempt of court is also "beyond all reasonable

---

71. See generally, Borrie & Lowe, *op cit*, p 565-569.
72. [1970] Ch 128.
73. At 137.
74. See *Knight v Clifton* [1971] 2 All ER 378; and *Dean v Dean* [1987] 1 FLR 517 where the Court of Appeal overruled the case of *West Oxfordshire District Council v Beratec Ltd* (1986) *The Times* of 30 October 1986 which had held that the balance of probabilities was the appropriate test in a case of civil contempt of court.

doubt". This is supported by *Cooke v Cooke & Cooke*[75] where O'Connor LJ said:

> "The rules and, so far as I know, the cases are silent as to the nature and degree of proof necessary to carry an application for committal or attachment. Common sense seems to suggest that, having regard to the consequences of making the order asked for - the imprisonment of the party for a term that may be limited or not - the degree of proof should approximate to that which is required to ensure a conviction in an ordinary criminal case. In most cases there is no serious controversy of fact; the probabilities and evidence are either all the one way or so overwhelmingly the one way that no doubt arises".

[12.23] "Beyond a reasonable doubt" was the standard of proof which Costello J found to have been met in *Orion Pictures Corporation v Hickey*,[76] a case concerning the breach of an Anton Piller order. There, a number of orders had been made against the defendant, the first order made on 26 February 1990 being an *ex parte* Anton Piller order, whereby the defendant was ordered to permit the plaintiffs' representatives to attend at the defendant's premises and to take away the records that were available and any of the video cassettes referred to in the order. The order had been made following an allegation of video piracy. Subsequently, on 28 May 1990, an interlocutory injunction was made against the defendant restraining him from infringing the plaintiffs' copyright in certain video cassettes; and on 3 October 1990 a search warrant was issued under the Copyright Act 1963 and was executed by the Gardai. The search under the search warrant produced 38 counterfeit videos which the defendant had in his possession. On 4 October 1990 a motion to commit the defendant for contempt for breach of the orders made on 26 February 1990 and 28 May 1990 was brought by the plaintiffs. Costello J held that he was:

> "... satisfied beyond a reasonable doubt that Mr Hickey was in very serious contempt of both of these orders."[77]

Costello J went on to instance five breaches of the orders:

(1) The plaintiffs' representative who executed the Anton Piller order had been technically assaulted and placed in apprehension of a battery;

(2) When the plaintiffs' representatives were at the defendant's home the defendant went to his video library in another part of town and secreted counterfeit videos there;

---

[75] [1919] 1 IR 227 at 249.
[76] High Court, unrep, 18 January 1991 (Costello J).
[77] At p 2 of the transcript.

(3) When the plaintiffs' representative went to the defendant's video library the defendant refused to hand over videos being returned by his customers (as he was required to do by the order) and held them back and put them in his car because they were counterfeit;

(4) The defendant had refused to hand over all computer records and a desk diary in the video library; and

(5) When the plaintiffs' representative proceeded to take the desk diary, the defendant was extremely aggressive and physically assaulted him.

Although the question of whether the "beyond all reasonable doubt" test was the appropriate test in a case of civil contempt of court was not canvassed by Costello J, it is significant that he expressed himself to be satisfied as to the defendant's breaches of the earlier orders "beyond a reasonable doubt".[78]

(f) Proving breach by defendant companies

[12.24] In Ireland it is a prerequisite to a company, or its directors or other officers, being sanctioned for contempt of court that the order of the court is shown to have been "wilfully disobeyed".[79] The precise meaning of the word "wilful" has proved to be contentious and perhaps it was for this reason that, when the English Rules of the Supreme Court were changed in 1965, different phraseology was employed and there is now no mention of the word "wilfully" in the most recent English Rules.[80] The difficulties associated with the expression "wilfully", are illustrated by three cases. In *AG v Walthamstow UDC*,[81] where a corporation had been ordered to abate a nuisance, Chitty J seemed to state that a defendant corporation's conduct which led to the breach of an order did not have to be "contumacious" or "obnoxious";[82] in *Fairclough & Sons v Manchester Ship Canal Co (No 2)*[83] the Court of Appeal seemed to

---

78. It is thought that there is little difference between "all" reasonable doubt and "a" reasonable doubt, the latter expression being used by Costello J. In particular it is thought that Costello J was not importing a different standard of proof to cases of civil contempt of court, nor differentiating the standard of proof applied to the "beyond all reasonable doubt" standard.
79. Order 42, r 32 of the RSC, see para **[12.61]** *et seq, infra*.
80. In England and Wales the words "wilfully disobeyed' have been dropped and do not appear in Ord 45, r 5 of the Rules of the Supreme Court 1965: see *Z Ltd v A* [1982] 1 All ER 556 at 567 *per* Eveleigh LJ.
81. [1895] 11 TLR 533.
82. The report of the case provided: "... the word "wilful" did not involve obstinacy in cases of this kind. What was meant was the refusal of the corporation to do those things which it had been ordered to do to remedy the injury. He held that in the present case there had been within the meaning of the order a wilful default, although he did not mean by that to cast on the defendants any imputation of an obnoxious kind."
83. [1897] WN 7.

require "contumacious disobedience" (ie stubborn and intentional disobedience) by a defendant corporation;[84] and subsequently, in *Stancomb v Trowbridge UDC*[85] Warrington J said:

> "In my judgment, if a person or a corporation is restrained by injunction from doing a particular act, that person or corporation commits a breach of the injunction, and is liable for process for contempt, if he or it in fact does the act, and it is no answer to say that the act was not contumacious in the sense that, in doing it, there was no direct intention to disobey the order ...
>
> ... I think the expression 'wilfully' ... is intended to exclude only such casual or accidental and unintentional acts ...".

[12.25] All three of the cases last mentioned were considered by Stirling J in 1964 in *Worthington v Ad-Lib Club Ltd*,[86] who concluded that he was bound to follow the Court of Appeal decision in *Fairclough & Sons v Manchester Ship Canal Co (No 2)*.[87] He said:

> "... in considering myself so bound, I interpret the words 'contumacious disregard' in an unlimited and ordinary sense. I can easily conceive that disobedience to an order or failure to obey it may be contumacious even when it does not connote deliberate consideration of the order and a conscious intention to disobey it. It may well be that in special facts a person or a company accused of disobedience might bother so little or take so little trouble to see what could be done or should be done, or have such slender ground for belief that steps had proved or would prove effective, that failure to obey the order could be said to be a deliberate disregard of the order in the sense that no real trouble was taken to obey it."[88]

In that case the defendant company had been restrained by an order on consent from causing a nuisance by noise from its nightclub. The plaintiffs subsequently sought liberty to issue a writ of sequestration in respect of the defendant company's goods and also to commit a director of the defendant company to prison for contempt. There was evidence that the defendant company had tried to abate the noise by retaining sound experts for advice, double glazing the

---

[84.] There it is reported that the Court of Appeal held: "The principles on which the court acts when it is asked to sequestrate the property of a company upon the ground of disobedience to one of its orders are the same as those applicable where it is sought to commit a private individual to prison for contempt. In these cases, casual, or accidental and unintentional disobedience to an order of the court is not enough to justify either sequestration or committal; the court must be satisfied that a contempt of court has been committed - in other words, that its order has been *contumaciously disregarded*." Italics added.

[85.] [1910] 2 Ch 190.

[86.] [1964] 3 All ER 674.

[87.] [1897] WN 7. Stirling J refused to follow the decision of Warrington J in *Stancomb v Trowbridge UDC* [1910] 2 Ch 190.

[88.] [1964] 3 All ER 674 at 682A-C.

premises and carrying out alterations. While Stirling J found that the steps taken by the defendant company to abate the noise were ineffective, and that the tests carried out after alterations might not have been sufficiently thorough, he held that neither the defendant company nor its director "had allowed it to occur contumaciously or in any sense in defiance of the order."[89] Stirling J did, however, find that if the noise continued thereafter, it would "be virtually impossible to contend, after today, that such continuance would not be contumacious."[90]

[12.26] Stirling J's interpretation of the word "wilful" in *Worthington v Ad-Lib Club Ltd*[91] was not followed in a number of subsequent cases.[92] In *Heatons Transport (St Helens) Ltd v Transport and General Workers' Union*[93] Lord Wilberforce endorsed the statement of Warrington J in *Stancomb v Trowbridge UDC*[94] quoted at para **[12.24]** above. Lord Wilberforce said that Warrington J's view as to the meaning of "wilful":

> "... has thus acquired high authority. It is also the reasonable view, because the party in whose favour an order of a court has been made is entitled to have it enforced, and also the effective administration of justice normally requires some penalty for disobedience to an order of a court if the disobedience is more than casual or accidental or unintentional."

In that case the House of Lords was not actually interpreting the meaning of "wilfully" because the last English order to make reference to such, Ord 42, r 31, had by then been replaced by Ord 45, r 5(1). Nevertheless, this case is strong authority for the proposition that the only significance attaching to the word "wilfully" is to exclude casual, accidental and unintentional acts which constitute disobedience. It is submitted that this is the correct interpretation of the meaning and significance of "wilful" and that Ord 42, r 32 of the RSC would be so construed by the Irish courts. Indeed, support for this can be taken from the Supreme Court's decision in *Irish Shell Ltd v Ballylynch Motors Ltd and Morris Oil Company Ltd*[95] where Ord 42, r 32 was in issue. There, Costello P

---

[89] At 682G-H.
[90] At 682I.
[91] [1964] 3 All ER 674.
[92] *Re Agreement of the Milage Conference Group of the Tyre Manufacturers' Conference Ltd* [1966] 2 All ER 849; *Knight v Clifton* [1971] 2 All ER 378 and *Steiner Products Ltd v Willy Steiner Ltd* [1966] 2 All ER 387. In the latter case Stamp J (at 390) said: "I do not think that the Court of Appeal intended to use the word "contumaciously" as meaning something different from "wilfully", for to do so would be to put a gloss on the words of the Order, which they will not, in my judgment, tolerate."
[93] [1972] 3 All ER 101.
[94] [1910] 2 Ch 190.
[95] Supreme Court, unrep, 5 March 1997 (Lynch J) *nem diss*.

had found three of the directors of the second defendant company to be in contempt of court and had fined each of them £1,000. Their contempt arose from an injunction made by the High Court which restrained the second defendant company from providing to the first defendant company or any other persons, motor fuels for resale from premises bearing the plaintiff's livery, trademark and logo and which were also under contract to the plaintiff for the exclusive sale of "Shell" brand motor fuels. In breach of the injunction the second defendant had supplied motor fuels to a third party whose premises was also under contract with the plaintiff for the exclusive sale of "Shell" products. The defence tendered was that the third party who had been supplied by the second defendant had represented that it was out of contract with the plaintiff. On appeal to the Supreme Court the counsel for the second defendant's directors argued that none of the directors were wilfully in breach of the injunction, as was required by Ord 42, r 32.[96] The plaintiff's counsel contended that the directors had a duty to be aware of what was being done by their company and that because they had taken no steps in that behalf, they were, accordingly, answerable for the breach of the injunction.[97] In his judgment for the Supreme Court Lynch J held that Costello P was entitled to conclude that the second defendant had wilfully disobeyed the order and that the directors were liable to attachment or fine in lieu thereof. He said that once the second defendant had been requested to supply motor fuels to a premises which bore the plaintiff's "Shell" logo then:

> "... they must as a matter of common sense make all necessary and proper enquiries to ensure that the premises are no longer tied to the plaintiffs and are free to accept the second defendant's motor fuels. If a company operating tied premises in the plaintiff's livery, trademark and logo requests the second defendants to supply motor fuels to them for resale it is wholly inadequate to rely solely upon that company's assurances that they are not tied ...
>
> ... Nothing whatever was done by the [appellant-directors] to check the accuracy and reliability of the assurances given to them by the consignee company...and to ensure that a delivery of motor fuels to them did not contravene the order ...".[98]

A breach of an injunction will be "wilful" if it is anything other than casual, accidental or unintentional. "Wilful" is not to be construed as intentional; a careless disregard as to whether a court order is respected or breached can amount to a wilful breach. On the contrary, the applicable test is objective.

[96.] Relying upon *Ronson Products Ltd v Ronson Furniture Ltd* [1966] 2 All ER 381 and 9 *Halsbury's Laws of England* (Simmonds Edition), p 26.

[97.] Relying upon Borrie & Lowe, *The Law of Contempt*, Butterworths, p 567 and *Biba Ltd v Stratford Investments Ltd* [1972] 3 All ER 1041.

[98.] At p 5, 6 of the transcript.

[12.27] Where it is found that an injunction or other court order, directed at a company, is "wilfully disobeyed", it must also be shown that the conduct which led to the breach was the *act of the company* and not, say, the act of an employee of the company acting outside of the scope of his employment or, to use the colloquial favoured in this context, "on a frolic of his own".[99] Although a company can only act through its directors, officers and employees, not every act of its directors, officers or employees can be attributed to the company.[100] It seems reasonably straightforward that where a company's board of directors cause a company to act in breach of an injunction or other court order, the company itself will be found to have been in breach of the order and in contempt of court.[101] What is less clear is where the breach of an injunction or other court order is occasioned by the actions of persons, such as employees, who may not have authority to bind the company. Here, and in the paragraphs which follow, the question of a company's liability for contempt for the acts of its employees in circumstances where the company is the defendant in the action is specifically addressed; the position of corporate third parties' liability in contempt is considered below.[102] Moreover, the legal consequences which follow where a company's shareholders vote in such a manner so as to cause their company to breach a court order or undertaking is considered below.[103]

[12.28] Where the act or omission which amounts to a breach of the injunction or other court order is caused by a company's employee, as opposed to a director or senior manager with power to bind the company, difficult questions are raised. Should a company be found to be in contempt of court because of the actions of its employees if its directors or other senior management expressly instruct the company's employees not to act in breach of a court order? This was the question in issue in *Director General of Fair Trading v Smiths Concrete Ltd*.[104] In that case the company was subject to orders of the Restrictive Practices Court which restrained it from, *inter alia*, "giving effect to or enforcing or

---

99. *Cf Stancomb v Trowbridge UDC* [1910] 2 Ch 190. In the course of his judgment in that case Warrington J had said of a body corporate that: "Such a body can only act by its agents or servants, and I think, if the act is in fact done, it is no answer to say that, done, as it must be, by an officer or servant of the council, the council is not liable for it, even though it may have been done by the servant through carelessness, neglect, or even in dereliction of his duty."

100. See generally, Courtney, *The Law of Private Companies*, (1994) Butterworths, para [6.027] *et seq*.

101. A company's directors or other officers may also be liable for the breach: see para **[12.61]** *infra*.

102. See para **[12.28]** *infra*.

103. See *Northern Counties Securities Ltd v Jackson & Steeple Ltd* [1974] 2 All ER 625 and generally, at para **[12.47]** *infra*.

104. [1991] 4 All ER 150. See Courtney, *The Law of Private Companies*, (1994) Butterworths, para [3.101].

purporting to enforce, whether by itself, its servants or agents or otherwise", agreements with other companies relating to the supply of ready-mixed concrete in contravention of s 35(1) of the English Restrictive Practices Act 1976. It was held by the Court of Appeal that the company itself did not breach the order because, *inter alia*, there should be a *mens rea* on the part of the contemnor. There, Lord Donaldson MR said:

> "It is an essential prerequisite to a finding of contempt that the factual basis shall have been proved beyond all reasonable doubt and that there shall have been *mens rea* on the part of the alleged contemnor. *Mens rea* in this context does not mean a wilful intention to disobey the court's order, but an intention to do the act which constitutes the disobedience with knowledge of the terms of the order, although not necessarily an understanding that the act is prohibited."[105]

In relation to a company's employees, the Court of Appeal, *per* Lord Donaldson MR said:

> "Whether X is doing an act by the instrumentality of its servants or agents will depend upon the scope of their mandate. This will be judged in the light of reality rather than form. If X should have appreciated that the servant or agent would be likely to do the prohibited act unless dissuaded by X, the act will be regarded as being within the scope of that mandate if X has not taken all reasonable steps to prevent it. Such steps may in appropriate cases involve far more than express prohibition and extend to elaborate monitoring and compliance machinery and procedures and the creation of positive incentives designed to dissuade the servant or agent.
>
> If the mandate of the servant or agent has been effectively restricted, ie all reasonable steps have been taken to achieve this objective, X may nevertheless be answerable to third parties for damage suffered in consequence of the acts of the servant or agent, if it can be said that X put him in a position to do them. This is to be distinguished from answerability for acts done by X personally through the instrumentality of his servants or agents and does not involve a disobedience by X of the court's orders or any liability in contempt."[106]

[12.29] This decision of the Court of Appeal was, however, overruled by the House of Lords in *Re The Supply of Ready Mixed Concrete (No 2); Director General of Fair Trading v Pioneer Concrete (UK) Ltd.*[107] Following the Court of Appeal's decision, certain other companies which had at first instance been found to be in contempt of court for breach of the order, were given leave to appeal out of time and were successful before the Court of Appeal.[108] The matter

---

[105] At 168.
[106] *Ibid*.
[107] [1995] 1 All ER 135.
[108] [1994] ICR 57.

eventually came before the House of Lords. After reviewing the authorities against[109] and for[110] finding the companies liable for contempt of court, the House of Lords held that where a breach of a court order is committed by an employee, a company will be liable for the breach even though the employee was expressly forbidden by the company to do the act prohibited by the court order, provided that the employee was acting within the scope of his employment. In so holding, Lord Nolan expressly endorsed the decision of Warrington J in *Stancomb v Trowbridge UDC*[111] and held that Lord Wilberforce's judgment in *Heatons Transport (St Helens) Ltd v Transport and General Workers' Union*[112] was not inconsistent with Warrington J's decision. Lord Nolan said:

> "Given that liability for contempt does not require any direct intention on the part of the employer to disobey the order, there is nothing to prevent an employing company from being found to have disobeyed an order 'by' its servant as a result of a deliberate act by the servant on its behalf. In my judgment, the decision in *Stancomb v Trowbridge UDC* is good law and should be followed in the present case."

It is thought by the writer that to find a company liable for contempt for its employees' acts or omissions, in circumstances where there is clear evidence that the company expressly prohibited those employees from doing such acts, is wrong in principle and it is further submitted that the decision of the House of Lords in *Re The Supply of Ready Mixed Concrete (No 2)* ought not in this respect be followed in Ireland.

[12.30] The following criticisms may be made of the House of Lords decision in *Re The Supply of Ready Mixed Concrete (No 2)*. In the first place, the *Stancomb* case is only authority for the proposition that the sole significance attaching to the word "wilfully" is to exclude casual, accidental and unintentional acts which constitute disobedience.[113] Secondly, Warrington J did not say that a company or other body corporate would be in contempt of court where its employees acted in breach of a court order in circumstances where those in authority expressly prohibited such employees from doing such acts. Thirdly, it is thought that there is much sense in the following statement of the law by Slade J in *Hone v Page*[114]

[109.] The earlier Court of Appeal decision in *Smith's* case [1994] 4 All ER 150; *Tesco Supermarkets Ltd v Natrass* [1971] 2 All ER 127.

[110.] *Rantzen v Rothchild* (1865) 14 WR 96; *Stancomb v Trowbridge UDC* [1910] 2 Ch 190; *Heatons Transport (St Helens) Ltd v Transport and General Workers' Union* [1972] 3 All ER 101.

[111.] [1910] 2 Ch 190.

[112.] [1972] 3 All ER 101. See para **[12.26]** *supra*.

[113.] See paras **[12.24]**-**[12.26]** *supra*.

[114.] [1980] FSR 500.

(a passage cited with approval by the Court of Appeal in *Attorney General for Tuvalu v Philatelic Distribution Corp Ltd*[115]):

> "I think that a man must be deemed to do a relevant act 'by his servants or agents' ... if (a) the persons who did the acts were his servants or agents, (b) the acts were done in the course of the service or agency, and (c) he either (i) authorised the acts or (ii) could reasonably have foreseen the possibility of such acts and failed to take all reasonable steps to prevent them".

It would seem that the House of Lords paid no regard at all to basic agency principles.[116] Fourthly, the "deliberate act" of a company's employee cannot, in justice, be the sole determinant for holding that company to have been in contempt of court. Matters such as whether the employee was acting within the course of his employment, his or her "apparent competence"[117] and whether the company *genuinely* exhorted the employee not to act in breach of an injunction or other order of the court *must* be material considerations. It is thought therefore that where these circumstances are found to exist, the appropriate finding is that the company as principal is not in contempt of court, although the employee personally may well be in contempt of court as a third party who knowingly obstructs or frustrates the object of the injunction or other order.

Breach of Injunctions by Third Parties

[12.31] Third parties (ie persons who are not directly enjoined by a court's order) will be liable for contempt of court where they either:

(a) aid and abet the defendant in breaking the order, or,

(b) knowingly act in a manner that obstructs or frustrates the object of the order.[118]

Where a third party acts in a manner which breaches an injunction or other court order, he may be liable in contempt under either, or perhaps both, (a) and (b). If a defendant (ie a person to whom an order is directed) does not himself have notice of the order,[119] or does not himself cause the order to be breached, a third

---

[115.] [1990] 2 All ER 216 at 222.

[116.] See generally Wickins & Ong, 'Confusion Worse Confounded: The End of the Directing Mind Theory?', [1997] JBL 524.

[117.] Where a firm of solicitors employed an "apparently competent" solicitor it was found that they had taken all reasonable care and that they were not in contempt of court: see the decision of Skinner J in *TDK Tape Distributor (UK) Ltd v Videochoice Ltd* [1985] 3 All ER 345; see para **[12.36]** *infra*.

[118.] See *Lord Wellesley v Earl of Mornington* (1848) 11 Beav 181; *Seaward v Paterson* [1897] 1 Ch 545; *Z Ltd v A* [1982] 1 All ER 556; *AG v Times Newspapers Ltd* [1991] 2 All ER 398 and the treatment thereof in Borrie & Lowe, *The Law of Contempt*, (3rd ed, 1996) Butterworths, pp 573-578.

[119.] As to notice of injunctions, see para **[12.09]** *supra*.

party cannot be said to have "aided and abetted" the defendant because, in such circumstances, there was no primary act of disobedience to which the third party could be an accessory. Where, however, a defendant has notice of an order and causes the order to be breached, a third party may be liable in contempt where he "aids and abets" the defendant in breaking the order. In circumstances where a defendant does *not* have notice of the court's order, a third party may still be liable for contempt of court under (b) where he knowingly acts in a manner which obstructs or frustrates the object of the order.[120]

[12.32] The liability of a third party for contempt of court in the context of Mareva injunctions was comprehensively considered by the English Court of Appeal in *Z Ltd v A*.[121] There, Eveleigh LJ said:

> "(1) the person against whom the order is made will be liable for contempt of court if he acts in breach of the order after having notice of it. (2) A third party will also be liable if he *knowingly assists in the breach*, that is to say if knowing the terms of the injunction he wilfully assists the person to whom it was directed to disobey it. This will be so whether or not the person enjoined has had notice of the injunction."[122]

In this section third parties' liability for contempt of court is considered under the following headings:

    (a) "Aiding and abetting" and obstructing/frustrating a court order;

    (b) The special position of banks.

(a) "Aiding and abetting" and obstructing/frustrating a court order

[12.33] A third party can be found to be in contempt of court where he "aids and abets" a defendant in breaching an injunction or other order of the court. As noted above,[123] in theory, this can only be a ground for finding a third party in contempt of court where the defendant has notice of the court order and causes the order to be breached eg in the case of a Mareva injunction, where, knowing

---

[120.] In *Z Ltd v A* [1982] 1 All ER 556, Eveleigh LJ said (at 566, 567): "It was argued that the liability of a third party arose because he was treated as aiding and abetting the defendant (*ie* he was an accessory) and as the defendant could himself not be in breach unless he had notice it followed that there was no offence to which the third party could be an accessory. In my opinion this argument misunderstands the true nature of the liability of the third party. He is liable for contempt of court committed by himself. It is true that his conduct may be very often seen as possessing a dual character of contempt of court by himself and aiding and abetting the contempt by another, but the conduct will always amount to contempt of court by himself. It will be conduct which knowingly interferes with the administration of justice by causing the order of the court to be thwarted".

[121.] [1982] 1 All ER 556.

[122.] At 566g.

[123.] See para **[12.31]** *supra*.

of the existence of a court order, a defendant seeks a third party's assistance in removing his assets from the State or otherwise disposing of his assets. So, where a defendant himself breaches the court's order, any third party aiding and abetting him to do this will be an accessory.

[12.34] One of the leading authorities on a third party aiding and abetting the breach of a court order is *Seaward v Paterson*.[124] In that case the defendant had leased a premises from the plaintiff and the lease contained a covenant, *inter alia*, that the defendant would not do or suffer to be done anything on the premises which might be noisy, noisome, offensive or inconvenient to the landlord, his tenants or adjoining occupiers. The plaintiff successfully obtained an injunction which restrained the defendant from using the premises for boxing displays which had caused a serious nuisance to the owners and occupiers of adjoining premises. It was subsequently alleged that the defendant had breached the order by allowing boxing matches upon the premises and that two other individuals (Sheppard and Murray) had assisted the defendant in disobeying the injunction. The plaintiff sought to have the defendant and Sheppard and Murray committed to prison or for liberty to issue writs of attachment against all three for their contempt. In this case there was evidence (which North J accepted) that both Sheppard and Murray had notice of the terms of the injunction before they aided and abetted its breach. Sheppard had been "master of the ceremonies" at the boxing entertainment; Murray had been present at the boxing match and was found by North J not to be a mere spectator, but was there as one of the persons interested in the club. The third parties' counsel had argued that there was no jurisdiction to commit, for breach of an injunction, a person who is not enjoined by the injunction. This was rejected by North J who held that all three persons should be committed and this decision was upheld on Murray's appeal by the Court of Appeal. There, Lindley LJ said of Murray:

> "There is no injunction against him - he is no more bound by the injunction granted against Patterson than any other member of the public. He is bound, like other members of the public, not to interfere with, and not to obstruct, the course of justice; and the case, if any, made against him must be this - not that he has technically infringed the injunction, which was not granted against him in any sense of the word, *but that he has been aiding and abetting others in setting the Court at defiance, and deliberately treating the order of the Court as unworthy of notice.* If he has so conducted himself, it is perfectly idle to say that there is no jurisdiction to attach him for contempt as distinguished from a breach of the injunction, which has a technical meaning."[125]

---

[124] [1897] 1 Ch 545. The case was cited by Kennedy CJ in *Moore v Attorney General* [1930] IR 471 at 486, 487.
[125] At 554. Italics added.

Lindley LJ went on to distinguish between a defendant's liability for contempt of court from a third party's liability, saying:[126]

> "A motion to commit a man for breach of an injunction, which is technically wrong unless he is bound by the injunction, is one thing; and a motion to commit a man for contempt of court, not because he is bound by the injunction by being a party to the cause, but because he is conducting himself so as to obstruct the course of justice, is another and a totally different thing. The difference is very marked. In the one case the party who is bound by the injunction is proceeded against for the purpose of enforcing the order of the court for the benefit of the person who got it. In the other case the court will not allow its process to be set at naught and treated with contempt. In the one case the person who is interested in enforcing the order enforces it for his own benefit; in the other case, if the order of the court has been contumaciously set at naught the offender cannot square it with the person who has obtained the order and save himself from the consequences of his act. The distinction between the two kinds of contempt is perfectly well known, although in some cases there may be a little difficulty in saying on which side of the line a case falls. As to the jurisdiction ... I cannot bring myself to entertain any difficulty about it."

Seaward v Paterson is clear authority for the proposition that a third party can be in contempt of court for aiding and abetting a breach by a defendant. The case also demonstrates, though, that for a third party to be in contempt in these circumstances, he must (a) have notice of the court's order and (b) must take an active part in assisting a defendant: were the third parties in *Seaward v Patterson* found to have been "mere spectators", they would not have been found to have been in contempt.[127]

[12.35] In *Z Ltd v A*[128] Eveleigh LJ considered that the decision in *Seaward v Patterson* went wider than simply "aiding and abetting". There, he said:

> "I think it is clear from the judgments of the Court of Appeal that the conduct of the other two respondents was regarded from the standpoint of interference with the course of justice, rather than simply that of aiding and abetting another to do an act which was wrongful in that other as being a disobedience by him of a court order."

That a third party can be found to be in contempt of court for "obstructing or frustrating" a court order was conclusively decided by the House of Lords in *AG*

---

126. At 555, 556.
127. See also *Johnston v Moore* [1964] NILR 128 where Lowry J said (at 135): "It is of course clear that a person may be in contempt through aiding and abetting the disregard of an order ... just as surely as if he were the party named in the order; and in this the Irish practice is the same as that in England: *Smith-Barry v Dawson* (1891) 27 LR Ir 558.
128. [1982] 1 All ER 556 at 568.

v Times Newspapers Ltd.[129] In that case the British government obtained injunctions against the *Observer* and *Guardian* newspapers, which prevented them from publishing extracts from *Spycatcher* (written by Peter Wright). Acting independently of the *Observer* and the *Guardian*, the *Sunday Times* (which was not a party to the injunctions) published extracts from the book; in these circumstances the *Sunday Times* was not "aiding and abetting" the other two newspapers and so could not have been found to be in contempt of court on this ground. It was, nevertheless, held unanimously by the House of Lords that the *Sunday Times* was in contempt of court. The grounds for this finding were expressed by Lord Jauncey to be:

> "... a person who knowingly acts in a way which will frustrate the operation of an injunction may be guilty of contempt even although he is neither named in the order nor has he assisted the person who is named to breach it.".[130]

[12.36] Applying the principles established in these cases to breach of a Mareva injunction, the following appears to be the case:

(a) Where it is believed that a person (who is not a party to an injunction) holds assets which belong to a defendant, it is prudent for a plaintiff to put that person on notice of the terms of the injunction as soon as possible.[131]

(b) Making a third party aware of the terms of the injunction will have the effect of binding him, even if the injunction has not yet been served on the defendant and the defendant has not been put on notice of the injunction.[132]

(c) Where a third party, who holds a defendant's assets, succumbs to a defendant's representations and assists him to dissipate or otherwise dispose of his assets, such third party is liable to be found to have "aided and abetted" the defendant in breaching the order and may be found to be in contempt of court.[133]

(d) Even where a defendant does not actively seek a third party's assistance in breaching a Mareva injunction, a third party who, being aware of the terms of the Mareva injunction, moves or disposes of a

---

[129.] [1991] 2 All ER 398.

[130.] At 426.

[131.] *Seaward v Patterson* [1897] 1 Ch 545.

[132.] In *Z Ltd v A* [1982] 1 All ER 556 Eveleigh LJ said (at 569a): "... there is no need for the defendant himself to have had notice of the injunction before the third party can be guilty of contempt". Extreme care should be exercised in conveying the precise terms of the order to the third party and, in particular, their attention should be drawn to any provisos, such as an ordinary living expenses proviso which might be included.

[133.] *Seaward v Patterson* [1897] 1 Ch 545.

defendant's funds, is liable to be found to have "obstructed or frustrated" the injunction and the administration of justice and may be found to be in contempt of court.[134]

Third parties who are solicitors need to be especially careful. This is clear from the case of *TDK Tape Distributor (UK) Ltd v Videochoice Ltd*[135] which concerned the breach of a Mareva injunction. In this case, which has been considered previously,[136] one of the defendants, who had been obliged by court order to disclose the nature, location and value of his assets, did not disclose the existence of an endowment policy which secured a mortgage on his house. The defendant's solicitor had not included the policy in the affidavit of disclosure because at that time, the policy had not matured. After the policy matured the solicitor paid the proceeds (£10,000) to the defendant's counsel for defending the defendant against fraud charges; in this regard the solicitor believed that such expenditure was permitted because of an ordinary living expenses proviso in the Mareva order. It was held by Skinner J that the policy ought to have been disclosed in the affidavit of disclosure and also that the solicitor was in contempt for paying the proceeds of the policy to the defendant's counsel because those fees were not ordinary living expenses. Skinner J held that the individual solicitor was in contempt but he refused to find that his firm or its partners were in contempt because:

> "... it seems to me that, on the evidence before me, they took all reasonable care by employing an apparently competent solicitor to do work which was, or should have been, within his competence and therefore I am not prepared to make a serious finding such as I am asked to do against them."[137]

The finding of contempt against the solicitor in this case seems harsh and the case provides a stark reminder to all solicitors of their potential liability for contempt of court.

[12.37] In the case of an Anton Piller order, the same general principles will apply. Any obstruction by a third party of a plaintiff's representatives in gaining entry to a defendant's premises will be a contempt of court; similarly destroying, or assisting the defendant to destroy, any of the evidential items referred to in the Anton Piller order will be contempt. Again, in the case of a Bayer injunction or other order restraining a person from leaving the jurisdiction, it will be a contempt of court for any third party to "aid and abet" a defendant to leave the jurisdiction.[138]

[134.] *AG v Times Newspapers Ltd* [1991] 2 All ER 398; *Z Ltd v A* [1982] 1 All ER 556.

[135.] [1985] 3 All ER 345.

[136.] See Ch 7, *The Defendant's Assets*, para **[7.15]**.

[137.] At 350.

[138.] See, eg, the basis upon which the defendant was found by Costello J to be in breach of an Anton Piller order in *Orion Pictures Corporation v Hickey*, High Court, unrep, 18 January 1991 (Costello J).

(b) The special position of banks

[12.38] One of the most effective ways of enforcing a Mareva injunction is to serve notice of the injunction on a bank where a plaintiff knows that a defendant has funds; whereas a defendant may be tempted to breach the terms of a court order, banks and other financial institutions will not knowingly breach an order of the court, as they have nothing to gain and all to lose. As has been considered in an earlier chapter,[139] it is in a plaintiff's interests to ensure that every care is taken to identify a defendant's account as precisely as possible since he will be liable to indemnify the bank for its costs incurred in complying with the Mareva injunction. Once a bank has notice of the terms of a Mareva injunction, it is obliged to comply with such order. In a large organisation, such as a bank, an extensive communications exercise is required in order to ensure that all of the staff in its various branches and departments have notice of the terms of the injunction. Moreover, a further difficulty for a third party, such as a bank, is the fact that in complying with a Mareva injunction which has been granted against its customer, it must balance its obligation to comply with the court order against its contractual obligations to, and business relationship with, its customer.

[12.39] The circumstances when a bank will be liable in contempt for the acts of an employee who knowingly assists in the breach of the terms of an injunction was considered by Eveleigh LJ in *Z Ltd v A*.[140] He said:

> "What is the position ... when a bank clerk who has no notice of the terms of an injunction pays out a cheque after notice of an injunction freezing the account has been given to another person employed by the company? The position could be said to depend upon the status of the person receiving notice and the relationship between him and the person making the payment. In my opinion, however, in all cases it should be necessary to show that the person to whom notice was given authorised the payment or, knowing that the payment was likely to be made under a general authority derived from him, deliberately refrained from taking any steps to prevent it. I do not think that it should be possible to add together the innocent state of mind of two or more servants of the corporation in order to produce guilty knowledge on the part of the corporation."[141]

Eveleigh LJ cited *Armstrong v Strain*[142] and referred to the strong criminal element in such a case, ie interfering with the course of justice, and the

---

[139.] See Ch 9, *The Mareva Order and Its Effects*, para **[9.46]** *et seq.*
[140.] [1982] 1 All ER 556.
[141.] At 569c-d.
[142.] [1952] 1 All ER 139.

consequent need to prove *mens rea* before a third party company could be found liable in contempt.[143]

[12.40] Accordingly, banks will only be liable for contempt of court where it is proved that the person to whom notice was given actually authorised the payment or, knowing that the payment was likely to be made under a general authority derived from him, deliberately refrained from taking any steps to prevent the payment. This is because, in order to prove that there has been contempt of court (by interfering with the course of justice) a bank must be shown to have a *mens rea*. Eveleigh LJ said:

> "I therefore do not think that the fact that one of the bank's officials is given notice of the terms of an injunction obliges the bank to undertake searches in order to discover whether or not at any of its branches the bank holds the defendant's account. On the other hand, it will obviously be prudent and in its own interests for the bank to take some steps in the matter. If it does nothing and a cheque is cashed or some other transaction completed, the bank may find it difficult to resist an inference that there was complicity or connivance at the breach. It will be a question of fact and degree in every case. The greater the difficulty in discovering the account and consequently controlling it, the less likely the risk of contempt of court."[144]

The following propositions concerning the liability of a bank for contempt of court arise:

(a) if a bank does not have notice of a Mareva injunction and allows a defendant's funds to be reduced, that bank cannot be found to be in contempt of court;

(b) even if one representative of a bank has notice of a Mareva injunction, it may not be liable for contempt if a defendant reduces his funds with the bank with the assistance of a different representative provided that the first representative took all reasonable steps to communicate notice of the injunction throughout the organisation.

[143.] [1982] 1 All ER 566 at 569. In *Atkinson v Strain* the Court of Appeal approved the judgment of Atkinson J in *Anglo-Scottish Beet Sugar Corp v Spalding* [1937] 3 All ER 335. There, Atkinson J said: "I am not satisfied that a company can be saddled with fraud unless some agent has guilty knowledge with reference to the representation complained of. Therefore, even if the principles applicable to fraud apply to mistake (and I am far from laying it down as a matter of law that they do), there is nothing to prevent my giving relief in this case, and holding that the mistake by an agent is the mistake of the principal ... In my opinion, the mere fact that some agent of the company knew of the second agreement is immaterial, so long as he had no idea that it was not being acted on."

[144.] *Z Ltd v A-Z and AA-LL* [1982] 1 All ER 556 at 570a-b.

In practice, it is often difficult, even in these highly computerised times, to locate an account by reference to a customer's name alone. In the first place, the bank must ensure that it does not freeze the account of a different customer who happens to have the same name as the defendant - to do this could leave the bank open to an action for breach of contract and/or defamation were a cheque to be stopped or a direct debit returned. In the second place, without details of the branch of the bank where the account is supposed to be held, a bank may have to trawl all of its branches to determine whether it holds a defendant's funds. It is therefore very important that a plaintiff provides a third party bank with as much detail relating to the account sought to be frozen as is possible.

[12.41] Maximum sum orders provide particular difficulties. How is a bank to know whether or not the defendant has other funds elsewhere which he claims have been set aside to cover the maximum amount required to be preserved by a Mareva injunction. In *Z Ltd v A*[145] Eveleigh LJ said:

> "The need to establish *mens rea* on the part of the bank is of particular importance in considering a breach of a maximum order injunction. I think that only very rarely will it be possible to show that a bank is in contempt. It is a fundamental requirement of an injunction directed to an individual that it shall be certain. This is particularly so in the case of a mandatory injunction. If a person to whom the injunction is addressed is entitled to certainty, how much more so should this apply to a person who is not even a party to the proceedings. From the point of view of the bank that has notice of an injunction, it has elements of a mandatory order even though directed against the defendant himself in negative terms; for it is not simply a question of the bank refraining from doing something but of taking positive steps to see that someone else, namely the defendant, does not act in defiance of the court's order. If it were the duty of the bank to ensure compliance, it would have to make extensive enquiries to ascertain the existence of an account and whether or not it held property on behalf of the defendant and then, in the case of a maximum order injunction, to make inquiries and to liase between different accounts and possible with other banks in order to avoid making a payment or releasing property in contravention of the order. It is an impossible situation...if a bank refuses to pay out on the grounds that a payment would contravene the maximum sum order, the bank might be faced with a claim from the defendant who can prove that he was preserving assets in other hands."[146]

Because of these difficulties, Eveleigh LJ held:

> "... the need to prove guilty knowledge against the bank is all the more essential. Carelessness or even recklessness on the part of the banks ought not in my opinion to make them liable for contempt unless it can be shown that

---

[145.] [1982] 1 All ER 556.
[146.] At 570c-e.

there was indifference to such a degree that was contumacious. A Mareva injunction is granted for the benefit of an individual litigant and it seems to me to be undesirable that those who are not immediate parties should be in danger of being in contempt of court unless they can be shown to have been contumacious."

This last quotation best sums up the court's view to finding banks or other third parties liable for contempt of court in these circumstances. Only in the most explicit circumstances will a person who is not a party to an action be found to be in contempt of court and thereby liable for the attendant sanctions.[147] Even if the views of the House of Lords in *Re the Supply of Ready Mixed Concrete (No 2)*[148] were somehow to be followed in Ireland, it is submitted that the principles of law established therein should be confined to where a body corporate is a defendant in an action and not to where a body corporate is a third party, such as a financial institution.

[12.42] Banks are faced with another difficulty where they are given notice that a Mareva injunction affects a customer who has been issued with a cheque guarantee card. In such circumstances, a bank will have contractual obligations which were entered into before the Mareva injunction was made. Again, in *Z Ltd v A*[149] Eveleigh LJ said:

> "Thus to honour a cheque drawn with the support of a banker's card should not be treated as contempt because before the order is made the bank will have made it known, as banks already have, that they will honour cheques up to a certain amount when supported by such a card. Where after the order is made some positive step from the bank is necessary before it incurs liability to a third party, then, of course, it should refrain from taking that step because the court would not then regard its obligation to a third party as an excuse for contributing to the disobedience of the court's order."[150]

Most cheque guarantee cards only guarantee payment of a cheque up to £100. Where the terms of the guarantee is so limited there is a strong arguable case that a bank should only honour a cheque, presented for payment after the making of a Mareva injunction, up to this amount. Moreover, it is opined that a bank cannot demand the return of a cheque guarantee card from its customer otherwise than (a) in accordance with the terms of the contract between the bank and its customer, and/or, (b) in the unusual case where the court order expressly directs the bank to demand the return of the card. In reality, the amount of most guarantees is so small as to be insignificant to a defendant's overall finances.[151]

[147.] See para **[12.51]** *et seq, infra.*
[148.] [1995] 1 All ER 135. See para **[12.29]** *supra.*
[149.] [1982] 1 All ER 556.
[150.] At 570j, 571a.
[151.] For the effects of a Mareva injunction on cheque guarantee cards, credit cards, bank guarantees and performance bonds, see generally, Ch 9, *The Mareva Order and Its Effects*, para **[9.47]** *et seq.*

Breach of an Undertaking Given in lieu of an Injunction[152]

[12.43] A plaintiff's application for an injunction or other court order may be compromised where a defendant gives his undertaking or do or refrain from doing that which is the subject of the plaintiff's application, *in lieu* of a formal order being made.[153] It is well established that a defendant's undertaking *in lieu* of an injunction is "as solemn, binding and effective as an order of the court in like terms".[154] As in the case of an injunction or other court order,[155] an undertaking to the court should be made in clear and unambiguous terms.[156]

(a) Undertakings by companies

[12.44] Undertakings given on behalf of companies raise particular issues. Insofar as it is accepted that an undertaking by a company has the same effect as a court order, it was held in England in *Biba Ltd v Stratford Investments Ltd*[157] that the Rules of the Supreme Court should be construed as applying to undertakings. As has been considered above,[158] in Ireland under the RSC it is a prerequisite to a company, or its directors or other officers, being sanctioned for contempt of court that the order of the court has been "wilfully disobeyed".[159] On this basis it is thought that the same principles apply to a breach of an undertaking.

[12.45] An undertaking given by or on behalf of a company must be properly authorised by those with authority in the company. In most private companies the board of directors will be the most appropriate organ to authorise (by resolution of the board of directors) the giving of an undertaking. A company's board may, however, delegate the actual authority to any person to give such an undertaking. It is thought by the writer, albeit without authority, that a director of a private company, present in court, at the hearing of an application may be said to have ostensible (if he does not, in fact, have actual) authority to bind his company.[160] By contrast, an ordinary employee would not have ostensible authority, although if properly authorised, he may have the actual authority to

---

[152.] See generally, Borrie & Lowe, *The Law of Contempt*, (3rd ed, 1996) Butterworths, pp 578-582.

[153.] See Ch 9, *The Mareva Order and Its Effects*, para **[9.27]** *et seq.*

[154.] *Hussain v Hussain* [1986] 1 All ER 961 at 963 *per* Sir John Donaldson MR. See also *Biba Ltd v Stratford Investments Ltd* [1972] 3 All ER 1041.

[155.] See para **[12.18]** *supra*.

[156.] See *Redwing Ltd v Redwing Forest Products Ltd* (1747) 177 LT 387; *O'Neill v Murray* (1990) *The Times* 15 October 1990.

[157.] [1972] 3 All ER 1041.

[158.] See para **[12.24]** *supra*.

[159.] Order 42, r 32 of the RSC, see para **[12.53]** *infra*.

[160.] On actual and ostensible authority of corporate officers see generally, Courtney, *The Law of Private Companies*, (1994) Butterworths, paras [6.027]-[6.054].

give an undertaking. An undertaking given by a company's solicitor or counsel is enforceable against a company because they are the company's agents in the cause or matter.

[12.46] Notwithstanding English authority, apparently to the contrary,[161] it is thought that a company will not be liable in contempt for breaching an undertaking *in lieu* of an injunction or other court order where breach is occasioned by employees acting contrary to express instructions. It is thought that the situation whereby a company fails to take "adequate and continuing steps to ensure"[162] that its obligations under an undertaking are complied with, must be distinguished from a situation whereby a company's employees cause an undertaking to be breached when acting outside the scope of their employment.[163]

[12.47] It has been held that where a company's shareholders cause a company to act in breach of an undertaking they, the shareholders, will not be liable in contempt of court.[164] In *Northern Counties Securities Ltd v Jackson & Steeple Ltd*[165] the defendant company undertook to court to use its best endeavours to apply for a stock exchange quotation, within 28 days of such quotation being obtained, to allot and issue shares to the plaintiff and not to increase the authorised share capital of the company or to do any other thing requiring the shareholders' authority in general meeting. Subsequently, the defendant company discovered that the stock exchange required that the issue of shares be subject to the consent of the "company in general meeting". The defendant company's directors initially failed to give notice of an extraordinary general meeting. At the plaintiff's prompting, they did eventually convene the meeting. Contrary to the company's undertaking the resolutions proposed (i) that the company's share capital be increased by 370,000 ordinary shares ranking pari passu as to dividend with the existing ordinary shares; and (ii) that the directors be authorised to issue those shares fully paid to the plaintiff. The text of the proposed resolutions was accompanied by a circular which stated that having

---

[161.] In *Re Garage Equipment Associations' Agreement* (1964) LP 4 RP 491 Megaw J said (at 504): "The court is prepared to accept that none of the officers of the company individually knew or realised that an undertaking given to the court was being broken or had been broken. But that does not in any way detract from the fact that the company - and this motion is only concerned with the company - was in contempt of court by these things being done when an undertaking had been given on behalf of the company and the company was aware of the existence of that undertaking."

[162.] *Re Galvanised Tank Manufacturers' Association's Agreement* [1965] 2 All ER 1003.

[163.] *Cf Re The Supply of Ready Mixed Concrete (No 2)* [1995] 1 All ER 135. See also para **[12.30]** *supra* where the House of Lord's decision in this case is criticised.

[164.] The principle here is equally applicable to a court order made against a company.

[165.] [1974] 2 All ER 625. See further Courtney, *The Law of Private Companies*, (1994) Butterworths, para [3.104].

taken a leading counsel's advice on the court order and the company's undertaking, the shareholders were free to vote as they wished. The directors also said that they were making no recommendation to the shareholders and were leaving the decision on how to vote to their individual judgment. Moreover, the directors advised that if the resolutions were passed the company would have to pay £300,873 for an asset it had acquired from the plaintiff but that if they were not passed, the cost would be *circa* £183,873. The plaintiff objected to the terms of what was circulated by the directors to the shareholders. Walton J held that the circular did not comply with the undertaking of the company to use its best endeavours to have the shareholders pass a resolution to issue shares to the plaintiff and that it ought to have been couched in more positive terms; he also held, *inter alia*, that the resolution to increase the company's share capital was a breach of the company's undertaking. More significantly for present purposes, however, was the finding by Walton J that the shareholders would *not* be in contempt of court if they voted against the resolution to issue shares to the plaintiff. In distinguishing the position of a director who votes, at a *directors' meeting*, against his company complying with a court order or undertaking to court, Walton J rejected the submission that a shareholder who votes, at a *members' meeting*, against a course of action required to comply with a court order or undertaking would be "a step taken by him knowingly which would prevent the company from fulfilling its undertaking to the court".[166] Walton J said:

"When a director votes as a director for or against any particular resolution in a directors' meeting, he is voting as a person under a fiduciary duty to the company for the proposition that the company should take a certain course of action. When a shareholder is voting for or against a particular resolution he is voting as a person owing no fiduciary duty to the company who is exercising his own right of property to vote as he thinks fit. The fact that the result of the voting at the meeting (or subsequent poll) will bind the company cannot affect the position that in voting he is voting simply as an exercise of his own property rights.

... a director is an agent, who casts his vote to decide in what manner his principal shall act through the collective agency of the board of directors; a shareholder who casts his vote in general meeting is not casting it as an agent of the company in any shape or form. His act, therefore, in voting as he pleases cannot in any way be regarded as an act of the company."[167]

In so finding he concluded:

166. [1974] 2 All ER 625 at 635a.
167. At 635e-g.

"It is, I think, equally clear that the shareholders are not abetting the company to commit a contempt of court; the company is, indeed, by convening the requisite meeting and putting a positive circular before the members duly complying with the obligations which rest on it. It will have done its best, and the rest is in the lap of the gods in the shape of the individual decisions of the members.

It would, of course, be otherwise if one could envisage any circumstances in which an order was made by the courts on a company to do something, for example, to increase its capital (as distinct from using its best endeavours to increase its capital), which must of necessity involve the shareholders voting in a particular manner. But I at any rate cannot envisage any ordinary resolution (as distinct from, for example, a situation where all the shareholders were before the court and bound by the order) where such an order would ever be made."[168]

This decision might at first appear to be at odds with the general principle that a third party will be in contempt of court for aiding and abetting the breach of a court order or obstructing or frustrating a court order.[169] All other things being equal, however, it is thought that there is no conflict between these two principles. First, an individual shareholder who casts his vote in such a manner as to *indirectly* cause a company to act in breach of a court order is acting in furtherance of his own property rights - it would be unjust to expect a shareholder who is not directly party to the matter which gave rise to the court order or undertaking by the company to sacrifice his own interests in favour of another party's interests. Secondly, it may be considered that a court order or undertaking in such circumstances *implicitly* acknowledges that the company will abide by same to the extent that such is within its own remit - because it must be acknowledged that a shareholder can act in his own interests, to so act cannot be a contempt of court.

[12.48] In circumstances where a company's shareholders are different persons to a company's directors, the foregoing seems to the writer to represent good law. What may be seen as less clear is where the directors and shareholders are one and the same persons, as may be the case in a small, closely held private company, which may even be run on the basis of a "quasi-partnership". In such a case it may be argued that it would somehow be unconscionable for the directors, wearing their shareholders' hats, to cast their vote in such a manner as to cause the company to breach a court order or undertaking. To that extend, the finding by Walton J in *Northern Counties Securities Ltd v Jackson & Steeple*

[168.] At 636a-b.
[169.] See para **[12.31]** *supra*.

Ltd[170] that a director may, wearing his shareholder's hat, vote as he pleases, may be doubted. He said there that:

> "I think that a director who has fulfilled his duty as a director of a company by causing it to comply with an undertaking binding on it is nevertheless free, as an individual shareholder, to enjoy the same unfettered right of voting at general meetings of the members of the company as he would have if he were not also a director."

Where, on the facts of a case, the directors' conduct is found to be fraudulent or unconscionable, it is thought that it is open to a court to disregard which particular "hat" a person is wearing on the same grounds as a court can disregard a company's separate legal personality. In so finding that a director/shareholder is in contempt of court, the court would, in effect, be lifting the corporate veil on grounds of fraud or circumvention of an existing legal obligation.[171]

[12.49] Another possible situation where a company's shareholders may conceivable be found to be in contempt of court might be where they vote to cause a company to breach a court order or undertaking, without any personal gain, and where the dominant purpose of their action was spiteful or malicious. Were this basis to be found sufficient to deem shareholders to be in contempt of court, it could apply to large companies with unconnected membership and not be confined to small closely-held companies. One practical problem with this ground as a basis for finding shareholders in contempt of court is that it is notoriously difficult to establish a "dominant intention", this being such a subjective concept.

(b) Third parties' liability for breaching an undertaking

[12.50] An interesting question is whether a third party can be liable for aiding and abetting the breach of an undertaking *in lieu* of an injunction or obstructing or frustrating an undertaking *in lieu* of an injunction? It is thought that in certain circumstances he can, but that in every case he must be on notice of the terms of the defendant's undertaking. Where an undertaking, which has an equivalent effect to a Mareva injunction, is procured from a defendant, a plaintiff would be well advised to notify all third parties who hold the defendant's assets of the terms of the undertaking and in this regard would be advised to seek to have the court make an order by consent on the basis of the undertaking.[172]

[170.] [1974] 2 All ER 625.

[171.] On the grounds for lifting the veil and disregarding a company's separate legal personality, see Courtney, *The Law of Private Companies*, (1994) Butterworths at Ch 4.

[172.] As to orders by consent, see Ch 9, *The Mareva Order and Its Effects*, para **[9.28]**.

Sanctions: Attachment, Committal, Sequestration and Fine

[12.51] Here it is proposed to consider the consequences for a defendant and others, such as a third party, who breach an injunction or other court order and are found to be in contempt of court. The following structure is adopted:

(a) Attachment and committal;

(b) Sequestration;

(c) Fine.

Where appropriate, the position of individuals and companies who are found to be in contempt of court shall be distinguished. At the outset, it may be noted that where a defendant is in breach of a court order, the court has an alternative to proceeding against him for contempt. Order 42, r 31 of the RSC provides that where, *inter alia*, an injunction is not complied with:

> "... the court, besides or instead of proceedings against the disobedient party for contempt, may direct that the act required to be done may be done so far as practicable by the party by whom the judgment or order has been obtained, or some other person appointed by the court, at the cost of the disobedient party ...".

Whilst this will be of little or no use in the context of a restraining or prohibitory order, such as a Mareva injunction, it may be of assistance to a party who has obtained a mandatory order, such as an asset disclosure order, in circumstances where a third party has knowledge of a defendant's assets which would aid the enforcement of a Mareva injunction.

(a) Attachment and committal

(i) Individuals: The jurisdiction to attach and commit

[12.52] Attachment and committal of an individual defendant who fails to comply with a court order is dealt with in Ord 42, r 7 of the RSC which provides:

> A judgment requiring any person to do any act other than the payment of money, or to abstain from doing anything, may be enforced by order of attachment or by committal.

Although r 7 is expressly confined to "judgments", Ord 42, r 25 provides that every *order* of the court, which of course includes an injunction, in any cause or matter "may be enforced against all persons bound thereby in the same manner as a judgment to the same effect". Rule 7 restricts the remedy of attachment and committal to judgments and orders "other than the payment of money" because imprisonment for non-payment of debt has been abolished generally.[173]

(ii) Companies: The jurisdiction to attach corporate officers

[12.53] In the case of a company which breaches an injunction or other court order, Ord 42, r 32 of the RSC provides:

> Any judgment or order against a company wilfully disobeyed may, by leave of the court, be enforced by sequestration against the corporate property, or by attachment against the directors or other officers thereof, or by order of sequestration[174] of their property.[175]

It will be noticed that r 32 only makes provision for "attachment" and not the "more stringent remedy"[176] of committal.[177] The attachment of a company's directors and other officers is considered in detail, *post*.[178]

(iii) "Attachment" and "committal" distinguished

[12.54] An order for *attachment* directs the person against whom the order is directed to be brought before the court to answer the contempt in respect of which the order is issued.[179] An order for *committal* directs that upon the arrest of the person against whom the order is directed, he "shall be lodged in prison until he purge his contempt and is discharged pursuant to further order of the court".[180] The distinction between "attachment" and "committal" was considered in *Cooke v Cooke & Cooke*.[181] There, Sir James Campbell C said:

> "It has been said in *Callow v Young*[182] that committal was the proper remedy where a prohibited act was done, while attachment was the proper remedy for neglecting to do some act ordered to be done. In practice, however, it is certain that both forms of redress have been treated as substantially the same, though it is equally certain that, ever since the passing of the Judicature Acts of England and Ireland, a distinction has been made in the rules of procedure applicable to each."[183]

[173.] See s 7 of the Debtors Act (Ireland), 1872 and, generally, Ch 11, *Restraining Defendants from Leaving the State*, para **[11.02]** *et seq*. As to the circumstances when a defendant may be committed for non-payment of debts, see s 6 of the Debtors Act (Ireland), 1872 and Ord 44, rr 9-14 of the RSC.

[174.] Sequestration in these circumstances is not "of right" and the leave of the court must be obtained: as to "sequestration", see para **[12.68]** *infra*.

[175.] See Courtney, *The Law of Private Companies*, (1994) Butterworths, para [3.099] *et seq*.

[176.] *Per* Ronan LJ in *Cooke v Cooke & Cooke* [1919] 1 IR 227 at 241.

[177.] As to the distinction between "attachment" and "committal" see para **[12.54]** *infra*.

[178.] See para **[12.61]** *et seq, infra*.

[179.] Order 44, r 1.

[180.] Order 44, r 2.

[181.] [1919] 1 IR 227.

[182.] 56 LT 147.

[183.] [1919] 1 IR 227 at 238.

It has been said that the only practical difference between attachment and committal concerns the manner of enforcement: attachment was enforced by the sheriff and committal was enforced by the tipstaff.[184] Even this distinction no longer holds true in Ireland, since the RSC provide that every order of attachment or committal shall be directed to the Commissioner and members of the Garda Siochana.[185] "Attachment" as a distinct redress has fallen into complete disuse in the United Kingdom because now committal is available in all cases of contempt.[186]

(iv) The effect of attachment and committal

[12.55] In the case of an application for an order of either "attachment" or "committal" the effect may be the same: the contemnor may be committed to prison. Order 44, r 4 of the RSC concerns *attachment*. It provides:

> When the person against whom an order of attachment is directed is brought before the court on his arrest, the court may either discharge him on such terms and conditions as to costs or otherwise as it thinks fit or commit him to prison for his contempt either for a definite period to be specified in the order, or until he shall purge his contempt and be discharged by further order of the court.

Rule 5 of the same order concerns *committal*. It provides:

> A person against whom an order of committal is directed may apply to the court to discharge such order. Every such application shall be by motion on notice to the party at whose instance the order of committal was made, and where on the hearing of such motion the court discharges the order of committal, the court may do so on such terms and conditions as to costs or otherwise as it thinks fit.

In the case of an order of attachment, an alleged contemnor is brought before the court to answer his contempt. He is thereby given an opportunity, prior to being incarcerated, to explain his actions or omissions which are alleged to have caused the court's order to have been breached.[187] An order of committal directs that a contemnor be summarily lodged in prison: he will not have an opportunity

---

[184.] *R v Lambeth County Court Judge and Jonas* (1887) 36 WR 475.

[185.] Order 44, r 7.

[186.] Order 52, r 1 of the English Rules of the Supreme Court 1965.

[187.] See, eg, *M Ltd v T, The Irish Times*, 19 September 1991 (Johnson J). There Johnson J ordered that the defendant be brought to court to explain why he should not be sent to prison for failing to comply with an order of Carroll J which directed him to make discovery on oath concerning various goods within 14 days from the making of the order. The plaintiff claimed that it had never been paid by the defendant or the company of which he was manager for tea and coffee-making equipment which it had supplied and which was valued at over Stg£99,000. It appears from the newspaper report that the plaintiff had obtained the order from Carroll J as ancillary relief to either a Mareva application or a claim for a proprietary injunction and *The Irish Times* report said that Carroll J had also made an order restraining the sale of or disposing of any interest in goods which had been supplied by the plaintiff.

to answer his contempt unless he applies to vary the order. Although it may well transpire to be the prelude to committal, an "attachment" order can therefore be considered to be a lesser order than a "committal" order.[188] An order for either committal or attachment for contempt of court requires the leave of the court which is applied for by motion on notice, save in the case of a criminal contempt "in the face of the court".[189]

(v) The purpose of attachment and committal

[12.56] Where, following an order of attachment or committal, a person is imprisoned for civil contempt, it was said by Finlay P in *The State (Commins) v McRann*[190] that:

> "... the purpose of the imposition of imprisonment is primarily coercive; for that reason it must of necessity be in the form of an indefinite imprisonment which may be terminated either when the court, upon application by the person imprisoned, is satisfied that he is prepared to abide by its order and that the coercion has been effective or when the party seeking to enforce the order shall for any reason waive his rights and agree, or consent, to the release of the imprisoned party."

On this analysis, the purpose of a contemnor's imprisonment is considered only to be *coercive*: the court has made an order which the contemnor has not obeyed and, in these circumstances, the contemnor is liable to be visited with an indefinite term of imprisonment until he agrees to comply with the order or the plaintiff agrees to his release.

[12.57] In respect of some breaches of injunctions and other court orders the purpose of attachment or committal of a defaulting defendant will more properly be characterised as being *retributive* or *punitive*.[191] As O'Hanlon J said in *Ross Co Ltd & Shorthall v Swan*:[192]

> "I am of opinion that the court must exercise its jurisdiction to commit for contempt, not merely for the primary coercive purpose of compelling obedience to its orders, but in order to vindicate the authority of the court whose order has been disobeyed."[193]

[188.] See *Piper v Piper* [1876] WN 202.

[189.] Order 44, r 3.

[190.] [1977] IR 78 at 89.

[191.] *Cf Keegan and Keegan v de Burca* [1973] IR 223 at 227 where the Supreme Court (*per* O'Dalaigh CJ) said: "Civil contempt ... is only punitive in its object but coercive in its purpose of compelling the party committed to comply with the order of the court, and the period of committal would be until such time as the order is complied with or until it is waived by the party for whose benefit the order was made".

[192.] [1981] ILRM 416.

[193.] At 417.

If a defendant removes his assets from the State or otherwise deals with them in a manner which is in breach of a Mareva injunction and he is subsequently committed to prison it cannot be said that the purpose of this imprisonment is coercive. The deed is done and it may not be possible to undo it. In such circumstances the purpose of the imprisonment can only be to punish the defendant. Similarly, a one month prison sentence for failing to fully comply with an Anton Piller order, as in the case of *Orion Pictures Corporation v Hickey*,[194] can only have the purpose of punishing the defendant. Indeed, the fact that a fixed term of imprisonment can be imposed is illustrative of the purpose of imprisonment in such cases.[195]

[12.58] Imprisonment for contempt following the breach of a Mareva injunction will almost invariably be retributive or punitive and in this regard the Australian case of *Registrar Court of Appeal v Pelechowski*[196] is instructive. There, it had earlier[197] been found that the defendant had committed wilful breaches of a Mareva injunction by creating a second mortgage over a house which secured advances which were used to pay creditors other than the plaintiff and or to fund litigation in which he was engaged. In sentencing the contemnor, the court[198] noted that the damage which had been done was irretrievable:

> "Here, of course, the damage is done. The contempt cannot be remedied by obedience to the order which has already been broken by the borrowings from HFS of $45,000. Nor is Mr Pelechowski offering to make any reparation to the judgment creditor. Imposition of a fine would be a wholly inappropriate response to the wilful and deliberate flouting of the Mareva injunction, even assuming that the contemnor had the means to pay a substantial fine."[199]

In sentencing the contemnor to 6 months' imprisonment, the court said:

> "The breaches are of a most serious nature. The authority of the court can only be protected and vindicated by the imposition of a custodial sentence, indeed a not insubstantial one. We are cognisant that not all wilful and deliberate interferences with the administration of justice should attract a custodial

---

[194.] High Court, unrep, 18 January 1991 (Costello J); see para **[12.23]** *supra*.

[195.] In *Lightfoot v Lightfoot* [1989] 1 FLR 414 (at 416, 417) Lord Donaldson MR distinguished between a "purely punitive sentence where the contemnor is being punished for a breach of an order which has occurred but which was a once and for all breach" and a "coercive sentence where the contemnor has been ordered to do something and is refusing to do it". In the case of a breach of a Mareva injunction or Anton Piller order the sentence will usually be of the former, "purely punitive" category; the breach of an order for disclosure of assets may be visited by a coercive sentence.

[196.] [1998] NSWSC 2 (3 February 1998).

[197.] *Registrar of Court of Appeal v Pelechowski* (28 February 1997).

[198.] Handley JA, Beazley JA and Stein JA.

[199.] At p 4 of the internet transcript.

sentence ... This is obviously so. But here the court is faced with a particularly blatant and determined threat to the integrity of the civil justice system."

The imprisonment of the defendant in that case was not to ensure that he complied with the order for that was no longer possible; the sole reason for his imprisonment was to punish him and to vindicate the court's authority.

(vi) The courts' attitude to attachment and committal

[12.59] By any standard, imprisonment is a severe punishment. It is, however, absolutely necessary that the courts of justice have the right to imprison a person who commits a civil contempt of court. As O'Connor LJ said in *Cooke v Cooke & Cooke*:[200]

> "The power to commit or attach is highly salutary and beneficial, for without it the administration of justice in many cases would be paralysed. It is, likewise, a power of an extraordinary drastic character, for it concerns that which our law holds most sacred, the liberty of the subject. Obviously, therefore, it should be exercised with great care and circumspection, and certainly not without giving the party impeded the fullest opportunity, consistent with the interests of justice, or making his case."[201]

In that case O'Connor LJ went on to say that the foregoing principles of justice meant that if "a reasonable[202] adjournment be asked for" it should be given. In the same case Sir James Campbell C said of attachment that:

> "... having regard to its punitive consequences, [it is] a jurisdiction to be exercised with scrupulous care and caution upon convincing evidence, and only after the fullest and fairest opportunity has been given to the person sought to be attached of making his defence".[203]

More recently in *Ross Co Ltd and Shorthall v Swan*[204] O'Hanlon J reiterated the sentiment expressed in both of the foregoing judgments saying that imprisonment for "an indefinite period for what is known as civil contempt of court is one which is exercised sparingly for a number of reasons".[205] Citing with approval the Court of Appeal's decision in *Danchevsky v Danchevsky*,[206] O'Hanlon J said:

[200.] [1919] 1 IR 227.

[201.] At 248.

[202.] As to what would be "reasonable" O'Connor LJ said (at 248, 249): "... good faith is the essence of the application; the respective degrees of diligence shown by the party asking for and the party resisting the adjournment; and the possibility of mischief should it be granted, are material elements in determining whether the application is reasonable or not".

[203.] At 235.

[204.] [1981] ILRM 416.

[205.] At 417.

[206.] [1974] 3 All ER 934.

"It is undesirable that the High Court should commit to prison for an indefinite period a person who has no intention of obeying the order of the court, and who may even welcome the publicity he gains by the making of such an order as a means of furthering his own cause. If no other reasonable course is open, then the order may have to be made to vindicate the authority of the court. If some other reasonable course is open, then it is preferable that it should be adopted."[207]

In *Ross Co Ltd and Shorthall v Swan* certain defendants in the action (two being members of a trade union) were deliberately disobeying an order of the court which restrained them from trespassing on a property. Although satisfied that there was a sufficient case for attachment and imprisonment for contempt O'Hanlon J found that there was another course of action open, namely, under the Prohibition of Forcible Entry and Occupation Act 1971. In the circumstances he awarded the costs of the application for attachment against the defendants. In practice, civil contemnors will only be sent to prison in exceptional circumstances and even then the intention will often be to engender a "short, sharp shock". At a time when our prisons are over-crowded with criminals, many convicted of heinous crimes against the person, it is easy to see why punishments, other than prison, will be explored before the step is taken of imprisoning a civil contemnor. In commercial litigation it has been said, by Colman J in *Belgolaise SA v Purchandani*[208] that proceedings to commit for contempt should only be brought where there had been a flagrant refusal to disclose assets or respond to further requests for more detailed accounts of assets or disclosure of documents relevant to the location of them.

[12.60] Sometimes the very threat of attachment and committal will have the desired effect. In *Mercantile Credit Company of Ireland v K*[209] it was reported in *The Irish Times* that Costello J had made certain Mareva injunctions (which froze up to £7m) against a number of individual defendants and also against a company which was owned by two of the individual defendants. One of the individual defendants and the company undertook to execute an immediate charge in favour of the plaintiff over certain properties in Dublin. It was reported that the nature of the plaintiff's claim was that it alleged that it had been defrauded by a series of fictitious transactions and the creation of false records. Subsequently, it was reported in *The Irish Times* that an order for attachment was granted against two of the defendants for their failure to comply with the undertaking; it was alleged that a solicitor of the defendants had approved the deed of charge, had travelled to the defendants home but had been unsuccessful

---

[207.] At 417.

[208.] [1998] TLR 490.

[209.] *The Irish Times*, 1 August 1990 (Costello J) and 8 and 11 August 1990 (Lavin J). On threats of imprisonment, see also *PP(I) Ltd v G, The Irish Times*, 25 August 1994.

in having the deed of charge executed.[210] When, however, the matter again came before the court it was reported that the undertaking had by then been complied with and that, in those circumstances, the plaintiff would not be proceeding with the application for attachment and committal.

(vii) Attachment of defaulting companies' directors and officers

[12.61] Order 42, r 32 of the RSC, which has been considered *ante*,[211] provides *inter alia* that a judgment or order against a company which is wilfully disobeyed[212] may, by leave of the court, be enforced by *attachment against the directors or other officers* of the company. This is a necessary rule which merely reflects reality: a company, being an artificial legal person, can neither be attached nor committed.[213]

[12.62] Where a company wilfully disobeys an injunction or other court order those persons liable to be attached are its directors and other officers. "Officer" of a company is defined by s 2 of the Companies Act 1963 to include its directors and the company secretary.

[12.63] Where a director or other officer of a company actively assists the company in disobeying an injunction or other court order he will be in contempt of court, as would any third party, on the basis that he has either aided and abetted the breach of the court's order or that he obstructed or frustrated the court's order.[214] This much is clear from cases such as *Ronson Products Ltd v Ronson Furniture Ltd*[215] and *Biba Ltd v Stratford Investments Ltd.*[216]

[12.64] The circumstances in which a director or other officer can be attached for his company's breach of a court order must, however, be distinguished from cases where the director or other officer does not actively participate in the breach of the order or undertaking[217] given by the company. The question here is whether a director or other officer who has not actively participated in the breach of a court order and who has adopted a purely passive role will be liable to be attached. The English authorities are equivocal on this point. On the one hand, in *Director General of Fair Trading v Buckland*[218] Anthony Lincoln J held

---

[210.] It was also reported that the plaintiff was fearful that charges over the property might be executed in favour of some third party and that it had obtained an injunction preventing certain of the defendants from creating any such other charge.

[211.] See para **[12.53]** *supra.*

[212.] See para **[12.24]** *et seq, supra.*

[213.] *Re Hibernia National Review Ltd* [1976] IR 388 at 392; *R v Freeman's Journal Ltd* [1902] 2 IR 82 at 89.

[214.] See generally, para **[12.31]** *et seq supra.*

[215.] [1966] 2 All ER 381.

[216.] [1972] 3 All ER 1041 at 1045c.

[217.] As to attachment of directors and other officers following the breach of an undertakings by a company see *Biba Ltd v Stratford Investments Ltd* [1972] 3 All ER 1041.

that a person is not liable in contempt merely by virtue of his office ie by simply being a director. In so finding he said:

> "... I reach the conclusion that Ord 45, r 5 does not render an officer of a company liable in contempt by virtue of his office and his mere knowledge that the order sought to be enforced was made. Resort can be had to r 5 only if he can otherwise be shown to be in contempt under the general law of contempt. In the circumstances set out in the preliminary issue neither Mr Buckland not Mr Stone could be liable in contempt in the absence of *mens rea* or an *actus reus*".[219]

On the other hand, in *Biba Ltd v Stratford Investments Ltd*,[220] the director whom it was sought to be found in contempt was a solicitor who had taken only a superficial interest in the day to day affairs of the defendant company and had nothing to do with staffing, advertising, selling or stocking. There, although it was accepted that he had, as director, played a "purely passive role" Brightman J held that he was liable to proceedings for contempt, although he failed to support his finding with reasons.

[12.65] The decision of Anthony Lincoln J in *Buckland* was, however, distinguished by Woolf LJ in the Court of Appeal decision in *Attorney General for Tuvalu v Philatelic Distribution Corp Ltd*.[221] In that case the defendant company had contracted with the plaintiff government to design, produce and sell Tuvalu postage stamps. The plaintiff government subsequently suspected that the security printer company (which was owned by the defendant's managing director) had deliberately printed flawed stamps; the plaintiff government obtained injunctions restraining the managing director and his companies from producing any more Tuvalu stamps or selling or dealing in stamps or other articles of philately or printing materials bearing the name Tuvalu. The injunction was subsequently varied and the managing director and the defendant both undertook not to make use of the printing materials. Prior to the variation of the injunction, an employee of the defendant company gave an order to the security printer to produce stamps and the printing materials were used to this end. The plaintiff government proceeded against a number of persons, including the managing director of the defendant company for contempt of court and the employee who ordered the stamps. The managing director was found to be in breach of the injunction by, *inter alia*, causing or permitting the further production of Tuvalu stamps after the injunction was made and also in giving the later undertaking without making sure than no

---

[218.] [1990] 1 All ER 545.
[219.] At 549j.
[220.] [1972] 3 All ER 1041.
[221.] [1990] 2 All ER 216.

prohibited stamps were on order or were in the process of being printed. The managing director was fined £3,000 and committed to prison for three months. It was against this that he appealed to the Court of Appeal.

In the Court of Appeal, judgment was delivered by Woolf LJ who held that:

> "In our view where a company is ordered not to do certain acts or gives an undertaking to like effect and a director of that company is aware of the order or undertaking he is under a duty to take reasonable steps to ensure that the order or undertaking is obeyed, and if he wilfully fails to take those steps and the order or undertaking is breached he can be punished for contempt. We use the word 'wilful' to distinguish the situation where the director can reasonably believe some other director or officer is taking these steps."[222]

Later, it was said:

> "There must, however, be some culpable conduct on the part of the director before he will be liable to be subject to an order of committal under Ord 45, r 5; mere inactivity is not sufficient."[223]

In this regard the Court of Appeal distinguished *Buckland* on the grounds that, there, no finding of culpable conduct on the part of the director had been found and the decision should not be taken as meaning that a director must actively participate in the breach before he is liable in contempt. A director's failure to supervise or investigate or his deliberate blindness will be regarded as being "wilful" and he may be found to be in contempt.[224]

[12.66] An undertaking given to the court is equivalent to a formal court order and its breach will be a contempt of court which can result in the contemnor being attached or committed. In *AG v Wheatley & Co Ltd*[225] Warrington J said:

> "The practice of the Court of Chancery was not to treat an undertaking as distinct from an injunction with regard to breach, and for the purpose of enforcing an undertaking that undertaking is equivalent to an order - that is to say, an undertaking, if broken, would involve the same consequences on the persons breaking the undertaking as would their disobedience to an order for an injunction."[226]

[222.] At 222c.

[223.] At 223e.

[224.] *Re Galvanized Tank Manufacturers' Association's Agreement* [1965] 2 All ER 1003 cited.

[225.] (1903) 48 Sol Jo 116. Applied in *Biba Ltd v Stratford Investments Ltd* [1972] 3 All ER 1041.

[226.] Warrington J went on to cite *London and Birmingham Railway Co v Grand Junction Canal Co* (1835) 1 Ry & Can Cas 224 where it was said that: "... an undertaking is equivalent to an injunction, and, if violated, may be the subject of an application to this court."

(b) Sequestration

(i) The jurisdiction to sequester assets

[12.67] Sequestration is "essentially penal in effect."[227] It is a "process of contempt"[228] by which a person or persons known as *sequestrators* are empowered to take a contemnor's property into their possession until such time as the contemnor purges his contempt. Sequestration of an individual defendant's assets is facilitated by Ord 43, r 2 of the RSC which provides:

> Where any person is by any judgment or order directed to pay money into court or to do any other act in a limited time, and after due service of such judgment or order refuses or neglects to obey the same according to the exigency thereof, the person prosecuting such judgment or order shall, at the expiration of the time limited for the performance thereof, be entitled, without obtaining any order from the court for that purpose, to issue an order of sequestration in the Form No 17 in the Appendix F, Part II, against the estate and effects of such disobedient person.

Sequestration is primarily available as a remedy to a plaintiff where a defendant or other person breaches a *mandatory* court order or injunction. Sequestration is also available to enforce a judgment or order for the recovery of property other than land.[229] Although sequestration in these circumstances is "of right" ie without the leave of the court, before issuing an order for sequestration against a contemnor, the plaintiff must apply to the Master of the High Court to approve one or more sequestrators and to obtain directions as to his or their security and accounting.[230]

(ii) Sequestration of corporate assets and corporate officers' assets

[12.68] Where a company "wilfully disobeys"[231] a judgment or order of the court Ord 42, r 32 of the RSC provides that the judgment or order may, by leave of the court, be enforced, *inter alia*, by sequestration against the corporate property or by order of sequestration of its directors' or other officers' property. Again, sequestration is not "of right" and must be by leave of the court.

(iii) The purpose of sequestration

[12.69] A person appointed a sequestrator is an officer of the court. As a process, sequestration can only ever be effective against a contemnor of substance. Upon his appointment, a sequestrator will take possession of a contemnor's real and personal estate and collect, receive and get into his hands

---

[227.] *Larkins v NUM* [1985] IR 671 at 688.
[228.] *Pratt v Inman* (1889) 43 Ch D 175 at 179; *Romilly v Romilly* [1963] 3 All ER 607 at 609F-G.
[229.] Order 42, r 6.
[230.] Order 43, r 3.
[231.] See para **[12.24]** *supra.*

the rents and profits of the real estate and personal estate and keep same in his possession until such time as the contemnor purges his contempt. Unlike a fine, which is considered below,[232] sequestration does not permit the indefinite retention of a contemnor's assets. This was made clear in *Con-Mech Ltd v Amalgamated Union of Engineering Workers*[233] where Sir John Donaldson MR said:

> "If someone is fined the money is lost to him for ever. If his assets are sequestrated the money remains his but he cannot use it. The money stays in the sequestrator's possession until the court orders what shall be done with it. The man can come to court at any time and ask for the money to be returned to him, but if he does so the court will require some explanation of his conduct."[234]

While a sequestrator has possession of a contemnor's assets, he owes the contemnor a duty of care in respect of those assets.[235]

[12.70] Sequestration will normally only be available where a defendant fails to comply with a mandatory order; sequestration as a means of enforcing a prohibitory order is only appropriate where a particular order lends itself to multiple future breaches. As considered in the preceding paragraph, once a contemnor purges his contempt, his assets will ordinarily be returned. Accordingly, sequestration as a remedy will rarely, if ever, be a suitable remedy for the breach of a Mareva injunction. This was noted by the English Court of Appeal in *Inland Revenue Commissioners v Hoogstraten*.[236] In that case the English revenue authorities had obtained a Mareva injunction against the defendant which restrained him from disposing of his assets up to £2.5m. In breach of this order, the defendant had made certain dispositions of his property and, on learning of this, the revenue authorities brought proceedings for committal or, alternatively, sequestration. The defendant subsequently admitted that he had breached the Mareva injunction and agreed to his assets being sequestered on the revenue authority's agreement not to seek his committal. In the Court of Appeal Dillon LJ held that the defendant's assets ought not to have been sequestered:

[232.] See para **[12.71]** *infra*.

[233.] [1973] ICR 620 at 627.

[234.] See further Borrie & Lowe, *The Law of Contempt*, (3rd ed, 1996) Butterworths, p 606 *et seq* where this and other cases such as *Australian Consolidated Press Ltd v Morgan* (1965) 112 CLR 483 are considered.

[235.] *Inland Revenue Commissioners v Hoogstraten* [1984] 3 All ER 25.

[236.] [1984] 3 All ER 25.

"Sequestration is one of the court's remedies by way of execution to ensure compliance with its orders ... It is a particularly stringent remedy in that it can only be exercised against a person who is in contempt of court.

In the present case, however, Mr Hoogstraten was no longer in contempt of court. He had made good his breaches of the Mareva injunction and had apologised (as his affidavit shows). There was nothing else for him to do. A Mareva injunction is a notoriously stringent remedy. There can be no jurisdiction to commit a man to prison merely for fear that he will in future dispose of his assets in breach of a Mareva injunction and there can equally be no jurisdiction to sequester his assets for fear of future breaches of a Mareva injunction."[237]

Even in the case of a mandatory order, such as an Anton Piller order, sequestration will rarely be an appropriate remedy for breach of the order since the defendant may have destroyed the evidence which was the subject of the order and, accordingly, apart from purging his contempt, there will be nothing left for him to do. In such cases, attachment, committal or fine will be the more appropriate sanctions for the contempt of court.

(c) Fine

[12.71] The RSC are silent as to the jurisdiction to fine a person or a company who or which is found to be in contempt of court. It is, however, accepted practice that the High Court has jurisdiction to impose a fine where it considers attachment, committal, or sequestration to be inappropriate. The jurisdiction to impose a fine *in lieu* of attachment or committal was considered by Cross J in *Phonographic Performance Ltd v Amusement Caters (Peckham) Ltd*.[238] There, he said:

"I cannot for myself see the logic of saying that in a case of civil contempt the court has no alternative to sending the defendants to prison ... I think that the court must have power, if there has been contumacious behaviour, to impose the lesser penalty of a fine".[239]

Where a company's directors are being fined for their company's contempt of court it has been said by the English Court of Appeal in *McMillan Graham Printers v RR (UK) Ltd*[240] that each individual director's circumstances should be examined separately and that the directors should not be fined jointly and severally.

[237.] At 27g-h.
[238.] [1963] 3 All ER 493.
[239.] At 497.
[240.] [1993] TLR 152.

[12.72] One of the more recent Irish cases where the court fined persons who were found to be in contempt was in *Irish Shell Ltd v Ballylynch Motors Ltd and Morris Oil Company Ltd*[241] where the Supreme Court, *per* Lynch J, held that the President of the High Court had power to fine a defaulting company's directors *in lieu* of attachment.[242] Furthermore, Ord 44, rules 4 and 5 of the RSC, provide that with regard to attachment and committal, the court may discharge a person "on such terms and conditions as to costs *or otherwise* as it thinks fit". It is thought that this contemplates a fine *in lieu* of imprisonment.[243]

[241.] Supreme Court, unrep, 5 March 1997 (Lynch J; *nem diss*). See also *Phonographic Performances Ltd v Amusement Caterers (Peckham) Ltd* [1963] 3 All ER 493.

[242.] At p 6 of the transcript. See para **[12.26]** *supra*.

[243.] Order 36, r 22 of the RSC provides that the officer having the management of the Central Office of the High Court is the proper officer to make entries and render accounts of all fines or penal sums imposed by the court.

APPENDICES

Appendix 1[1]

Mareva Injunction Restraining the Disposal of Assets in Ireland Removing them from the State and Requiring the Defendant to Disclose his Assets

THE HIGH COURT
199 ___ No. XXXXP

Monday _____ day of _____ 199 ___

BEFORE MR JUSTICE

BETWEEN

PLAINTIFF

DEFENDANT

Upon Motion of Counsel for the Plaintiff[2] and upon reading the Affidavit sworn on the _____ day of _____ 199__ by _____, the Plaintiff, and the exhibits referred to therein and upon hearing Counsel for the Plaintiff[3]

AND the Plaintiff by his Counsel giving the following undertakings:

1. To abide by any Order as to damages should the Defendant suffer by reason of this Order which in the opinion of the Court the Plaintiff ought to pay;[4]

2. To pay to any Third Party served with or given notice of this Order his or their reasonable costs and expenses and to indemnify them against all and

---

[1] The writer acknowledges the kind assistance of Mr Brendan Reedy, Senior Chancery Registrar of the High Court for reading and approving in principle the form of Orders contained in these Appendices. *NB* the Orders contained in these Appendices are merely intended as sample examples and must always be tailored to the specific needs of an individual case.

[2] It is assumed that the application for the Order will have been made *ex parte*; in the case of an *inter partes* application, the hearing will be on foot of a Notice of Motion and the Order may say here "made pursuant to Notice dated the day of _____ 199__ ". For *ex parte* and *inter partes* applications, see Ch 8, *Applying for a Mareva Injunction*, at para **[8.05]** *et seq*.

[3] In the case of an *inter partes* application, the recitals to the Order may provide here "and upon hearing Counsel for the Defendants and upon reading the replying Affidavit of the defendant ...".

[4] As to the undertaking as to damages, see Ch 8, *Applying for a Mareva Injunction*, at para **[8.58]** *et seq*.

any liability reasonably incurred by any such Third Party for the purposes of ascertaining whether any assets to which this Order applies are within his or their power, possession, custody or control and in particular, in complying with the terms of this Order;

3.   In the event of this Order being discharged or the terms hereof being varied, to forthwith take all reasonable steps to inform in writing any person or company whom the Plaintiff has given notice of the Order or who he has reasonable grounds for supposing may act upon the Order;[5]

4.   Not, without the leave of the Court, to use any of the information obtained by this Order except for the purposes of these proceedings and for no other purpose;[6]

5.   To give a copy of this Order to the Defendant[7] and to any other person who is notified of the terms of this Order;[8]

6.   As soon as practicable, to issue and serve on the Defendant the Plenary Summons[9] in the form of the draft produced to the Court claiming the appropriate relief together with a copy of this Order;[10]

7.   As soon as practicable, to cause an Affidavit to be sworn, stamped and filed in substantially the same terms as the draft affidavit produced to the Court;[11]

IT IS ORDERED as follows:

1.   That the Defendant, his servants or agents or any person acting on behalf of them and any person having knowledge of the making of this Order or otherwise be restrained until [after the _____ day of _____ 199___][12] [or further order] from removing from the State[13] or in any way disposing of, reducing, transferring, charging, diminishing the value thereof, or otherwise dealing with all or any of his

---

[5]   As to the undertaking to notify third parties in the event of the Order being discharged or varied, see Ch 8, *Applying for a Mareva Injunction*, para **[8.78]** *et seq*.

[6]   This undertaking refers to the disclosure order contained in point 3 of the operative part of the Order.

[7]   It is assumed that the Order is obtained on foot of an *ex parte* application.

[8]   In appropriate cases, the Order may go on to provide "... by facsimile, telephone or by courier service".

[9]   Or Summary Summons or Special Summons or Notice of Motion, as the case may be: see Ch 8, *Applying for a Mareva Injunction*, para **[8.14]** *et seq*.

[10] Such an undertaking would only be appropriate in an *ex parte* application where the proceedings have not yet issued.

[11] Or "confirming the substance of what was said to the court by the Plaintiff's Counsel or Solicitor"; again, such an undertaking would only be appropriate in an *ex parte* application.

[12] This is appropriate in the case of an *ex parte interim* Order; in the case of an interlocutory Order - which will invariably be *inter partes* - alternative wording might be "... until judgment in the substantive cause of action between the Plaintiff and the Defendant ...".

[13] Or, "Ireland" or "the jurisdiction of this Court".

assets which are in the State[14] save in so far as the value of said assets shall exceed the sum or value of IRL£ ___, subject to the provisos hereunder;

2. In particular, and without prejudice to the generality of the foregoing prohibition, the Defendant, his servants or agents or any person acting on behalf of him or them and any person having knowledge of the making of this Order or otherwise be restrained until [after the _____ day of _____ 199 ___] [or further order] from:

   (a) drawing on, assigning, charging or otherwise debiting or dealing with any money in the Account No. _____ at the _____ branch of the _____ Bank; or

   (b) removing from the State, or in any way disposing of, reducing, transferring, charging, diminishing the value thereof, or otherwise dealing with the net proceeds of sale[15] of the property known as _____ at _____ in the County of _____.

   subject to the provisos hereunder;

3. The Defendant do disclose to the Plaintiff, in writing, forthwith of all of his assets within the State whether in his own name or by nominees or otherwise and whether solely or jointly owned detailing the value, location and specific descriptions of all such assets, and, without prejudice to the generality of the foregoing, that the Defendant shall identify all Accounts with banks or other financial institutions held in his own name or by nominees or otherwise and whether solely or jointly owned; said disclosure to be confirmed by Affidavit which must be served on the Plaintiff's Solicitors within _____ days after this Order has been served on the Defendant;

PROVIDED THAT the Defendant:

1. is at liberty to spend a sum not exceeding IRL£ _____ per week for ordinary living expenses, and,

2. is at liberty to spend a sum not exceeding IRL£ _____ per week for reasonable legal expenses, and,

3. is at liberty to spend a sum not exceeding IRL£ _____ per week for ordinary business expenses;

AND not otherwise than, in each case aforesaid, without first notifying the Plaintiff's Solicitors in advance, in writing, of the source or the Account or Accounts from which such sums are to be drawn

---

[14] A "general" freezing Order would stop after "... State"; as considered in Ch 9, *The Mareva Order and Its Effects*, para **[9.08]** by far the most common and appropriate restriction is the inclusion of a "maximum sum" Order.

[15] Here the Order might detail precisely what is meant by "net proceeds of sale", eg after the discharge of a mortgage or charge affecting the property etc.

AND PROVIDED that this Order does not prevent any bank or other financial institution from exercising any right of set-off it may have in respect of any facility which it gave to the Defendant before it was notified of this Order

AND no bank or other financial institution need to inquire as to the application or proposed application of any money withdrawn by the Defendant if the withdrawal appears to be permitted by this Order

AND IT IS ORDERED that the Plaintiff's Solicitors be at liberty to notify forthwith the terms of this Order by telephone and facsimile [or courier service] to:[16]

    (a) the Defendant, and

    (b)

AND IT IS ORDERED THAT the Plaintiff be at liberty to service Notice of Motion for an Interlocutory Order returnable on Monday _____ day of _____ 199___;[17]

AND the parties hereto and all parties having notice of or being affected by this Order have liberty to apply on 48 hours' notice to the Plaintiff's Solicitors and the Court to vary the terms or discharge this Order[18]

AND the Court doth reserve the costs of this application and Order.

_____
REGISTRAR

If you the within named A.B. neglect to obey this Order by the time therein limited, you will be liable to process of execution including imprisonment for the purpose of compelling you to obey the same Order.[19]

Signed: _____

    Solicitor for the Plaintiff

_____

[16] It will often be considered useful for the terms of the actual Order to expressly permit liberty to notify, forthwith by modern means, the Defendant and other parties (such as banks) whom the Plaintiff believes may hold assets on the Defendant's behalf.

[17] It is assumed that this is an *interim* Order.

[18] On "variation" and "discharge" of a Mareva injunction, see Ch 9, *The Mareva Order and Its Effects*, para **[9.31]**.

[19] This 'penal endorsement' is usually endorsed vertically in the margin on the front page of the Order. A penal endorsement is not strictly required by the *Rules of the Superior Courts 1986* in the case of an Order which is solely *restrictive* or *prohibitive*; in the case of the sample Order here a penal endorsement is, however, required as the requirement that the Defendant disclose his assets is in the nature of a *mandatory* order. See Ch 12, *Enforcing Mareva Injunctions and Other Orders*, at para **[12.15]**.

Appendix 2

Mareva Injunction Restraining the Worldwide Disposal of Assets and Requiring the Defendant to Disclose His Assets Wherever Situate[20]

THE HIGH COURT
199 __ No. XXXXP

Monday _____ day of _____ 199 ___

BEFORE MR JUSTICE

BETWEEN

PLAINTIFF

DEFENDANT

Upon Motion of Counsel for the Plaintiff[21] and upon reading the Affidavit sworn on the _____ day of _____199___ by _____, the Plaintiff, and the exhibits referred to therein and upon hearing Counsel for the Plaintiff[22]

AND the Plaintiff by his Counsel giving the following undertakings:

1. To abide by any Order as to damages should the Defendant suffer by reason of this Order which in the opinion of the Court the Plaintiff ought to pay;[23]

2. To pay to any Third Party served with or given notice of this Order his or their reasonable costs and expenses and to indemnify them against all and any liability reasonably incurred by any such Third Party for the purposes

---

[20] On worldwide Mareva injunctions, see generally Ch 7, *The Defendant's Assets*, para **[7.21]** *et seq.*

[21] It is again assumed that the application for the Order will have been made *ex parte*; in the case of an *inter partes* application, the hearing will be on foot of a Notice of Motion and the Order may say here "made pursuant to Notice dated the day of _____ 199__".

[22] In the case of an *inter partes* application, the recitals to the Order may provide here "and upon hearing Counsel for the Defendants and upon reading the replying Affidavit of the defendant ...".

[23] As to the undertaking as to damages, see Ch 8, *Applying for a Mareva Injunction*, para **[8.58]** *et seq.*

of ascertaining whether any assets to which this Order applies are within his or their power, possession, custody or control and in particular, in complying with the terms of this Order;

3.   In the event of this Order being discharged or the terms hereof being varied, to forthwith take all reasonable steps to inform in writing any person or company whom the Plaintiff has given notice of the Order or who he has reasonable grounds for supposing may act upon the Order;[24]

4.   Not, without the leave of the Court, to use any of the information obtained by this Order except for the purposes of these proceedings and for no other purpose;[25]

5.   To give a copy of this Order to the Defendant[26] and to any other person who is notified of the terms of this Order;[27]

6.   As soon as practicable, to issue and serve on the Defendant the Plenary Summons[28] in the form of the draft produced to the Court claiming the appropriate relief together with a copy of this Order;[29]

7.   As soon as practicable, to cause an Affidavit to be sworn, stamped and filed in substantially the same terms as the draft affidavit produced to the Court;[30]

8.   Not without the leave of the Court to begin proceedings against the Defendant in any other jurisdiction or use any of the information obtained as a result of this or any other Order of a Court in this jurisdiction for the purpose of civil or criminal proceedings in any other jurisdiction;

9.   Not without the leave of the Court to seek to enforce this Order in any country outside the State or seek an Order of a similar nature including Orders conferring a charge or other security against the Defendant or the Defendant's assets;

IT IS ORDERED as follows:

That the Defendant, his servants or agents or any person acting on behalf of them and any person having knowledge of the making of this Order or otherwise be restrained until [after the _____ day of _____199__][31] [or

---

[24]   As to the undertaking to notify third parties in the event of the Order being discharged or varied, see Ch 8, *Applying for a Mareva Injunction*, para **[8.78]** *et seq.*

[25]   This undertaking refers to the disclosure order contained in point 3 of the operative part of the Order.

[26]   It is assumed that the Order is obtained on foot of an *ex parte* application.

[27]   In appropriate cases, the Order may go on to provide "... by facsimile, telephone or by courier service".

[28]   Or Summary Summons or Special Summons or Notice of Motion, as the case may be: see Ch 8, *Applying for a Mareva Injunction*, para **[8.14]** *et seq.*

[29]   Such an undertaking would only be appropriate in an *ex parte* application where the proceedings have not yet issued.

[30]   *Ibid.*

further order] from removing from the State[32] or in any way disposing of, reducing, transferring, charging, diminishing the value thereof, or otherwise dealing with all or any of his assets which are within or without the State save in so far as the value of said assets shall exceed the sum or value of IRL£ ___, subject to the provisos hereunder;

In particular, and without prejudice to the generality of the foregoing prohibition, the Defendant, his servants or agents or any person acting on behalf of them and any person having knowledge of the making of this Order or otherwise be restrained until [after the_____ day of_____199__] [or further order] from:

(a) drawing on, assigning, charging or otherwise debiting or dealing with any money in the Account No._____at the_____ branch of the_____ Bank; or

(b) removing from the State, or in any way disposing of, reducing, transferring, charging, diminishing the value thereof, or otherwise dealing with the net proceeds of sale[33] of the property known as_____ at_____in the County of _____.

subject to the provisos hereunder;

3. The Defendant do disclose to the Plaintiff, in writing, forthwith of all of his assets within or without the State whether in his own name or by nominees or otherwise and whether solely or jointly owned detailing the value, location and specific descriptions of all such assets, and, without prejudice to the generality of the foregoing, that the Defendant shall identify all Accounts with banks or other financial institutions held in his own name or by nominees or otherwise and whether solely or jointly owned; said disclosure to be confirmed by Affidavit which must be served on the Plaintiff's Solicitors within _____ days after this Order has been served on the Defendant;

PROVIDED THAT the Defendant:

1. is at liberty to spend a sum not exceeding IRL£_____ per week for ordinary living expenses, and,

2. is at liberty to spend a sum not exceeding IRL£_____ per week for reasonable legal expenses, and,

---

[31] This is appropriate in the case of an *ex parte interim* Order; in the case of an interlocutory Order - which will invariably be *inter partes* - alternative wording might be "... until judgment in the substantive cause of action between the Plaintiff and the Defendant ...".

[32] Or, "Ireland" or "the jurisdiction of this Court".

[33] Here the Order might detail precisely what is meant by "net proceeds of sale", eg after the discharge of a mortgage or charge affecting the property etc.

3. is at liberty to spend a sum not exceeding IRL£_____ per week for ordinary business expenses;

AND not otherwise than, in each case aforesaid, without first notifying the Plaintiff's Solicitors in advance, in writing, of the source or the Account or Accounts from which such sums are to be drawn

AND PROVIDED that this Order does not prevent any bank or other financial institution from exercising any right of set-off it may have in respect of any facility which it gave to the Defendant before it was notified of this Order

AND PROVIDED that insofar as this order purports to have any extra-territorial effect, no person shall be affected thereby or concerned with the terms thereof until it shall be declared enforceable or be enforced by a foreign court and then it shall only affect them to the extent of such declaration or enforcement, **UNLESS** they are:

(a) a person to whom this order is addressed or an officer of or an agent appointed by power of attorney of such a person, or,

(b) persons who are subject to the jurisdiction of this court and

  (i) have been given written notice of this order at their residence or place of business within the jurisdiction, and,

  (ii) are able to prevent acts or omissions outside the jurisdiction of this court which assist in the breach of the terms of this order.[34]

AND no bank or other financial institution need to inquire as to the application or proposed application of any money withdrawn by the Defendant if the withdrawal appeals to be permitted by this Order

AND IT IS ORDERED that the Plaintiff's Solicitors be at liberty to notify forthwith the terms of this Order by telephone and facsimile [or courier service] to:[35]

(a) the defendant, and

(b)

AND IT IS ORDERED THAT the Plaintiff be at liberty to service Notice of Motion for an Interlocutory Order returnable on Monday _____ day of _____ 199__;[36]

AND the parties hereto and all parties having notice of or being affected by this Order have liberty to apply on 48 hours' notice to the Plaintiff's Solicitors and the Court to vary the terms or discharge this Order[37]

---

[34] This is the so-called '*Babanaft* proviso'. See Ch 7, *The Defendant's Assets*, para **[7.46]** *et seq.*

[35] It will often be considered useful for the terms of the actual Order to expressly permit liberty to notify, forthwith by modern means, the Defendant and other parties (such as banks) whom the Plaintiff believes may hold assets on the Defendant's behalf.

[36] It is assumed that this is an *interim* Order.

AND the Court doth reserve the costs of this application and Order.

———————————

REGISTRAR

If you the within named A.B. neglect to obey this Order by the time therein limited, you will be liable to process of execution including imprisonment for the purpose of compelling you to obey the same Order.[38]

Signed: _____

      Solicitor for the Plaintiff

---

[37] On "variation" and "discharge" of a Mareva injunction, see Ch 9, *The Mareva Order and Its Effects*, para **[9.31]**.

[38] This "penal endorsement" is usually endorsed vertically in the margin on the front page of the Order. A penal endorsement is not strictly required by the Rules of the Superior Courts 1986 in the case of an Order which is solely *restrictive* or *prohibitive*; in the case of the sample Order here a penal endorsement is, however, required as the requirement that the Defendant disclose his assets is in the nature of a *mandatory* order. See Ch 12, *Enforcing Mareva Injunctions and Other Orders*, para **[12.16]**.

Appendix 3

Anton Piller Order[39]

THE HIGH COURT
199 __ No. XXXXP

Monday _____ day of _____ 199 ___

BEFORE MR JUSTICE

BETWEEN

PLAINTIFF

DEFENDANT

Upon Motion of Counsel for the Plaintiff[40] and upon reading the Affidavit sworn on the _____ day of_____199___ by _____ , the Plaintiff, and the exhibits referred to therein and upon hearing Counsel for the Plaintiff

AND the Plaintiff by his Counsel giving the following undertakings:

1. To abide by any Order as to damages should the Defendant suffer by reason of this Order or by reason of any breach of the terms of this order or otherwise in a manner inconsistent with the Plaintiff's Solicitors' duties as Officers of the Court which in the opinion of the Court the Plaintiff ought to pay;

2. Not, without the leave of the Court, to use any of the information obtained by this Order except for the purposes of these proceedings and for no other purpose;

3. As soon as practicable, to issue and serve on the Defendant the Plenary Summons[41] in the form of the draft produced to the Court claiming the appropriate relief together with a copy of this Order;

---

[39] On Anton Piller orders, see generally Ch 10, *Ancillary Orders*, para **[10.38]** *et seq.*

[40] Anton Piller order will almost invariably be granted following an *ex parte* application. *Cf Re Mantruck Services Ltd; Mehigan v. Duignan,* High Court, unrep, 20 June, 1996 (1993 No. 4988P); see Ch 10, *Ancillary Orders*, para **[10.55]**.

[41] Or Summary Summons or Special Summons or Notice of Motion, as the case may be: see Ch 8, *Applying for a Mareva Injunction*, para **[8.14]** *et seq.*

4. As soon as practicable, to cause an Affidavit to be sworn, stamped and filed in substantially the same terms as the draft affidavit produced to the Court;

5. Not without the leave of the Court to begin proceedings against the Defendant in any other jurisdiction or use any of the information obtained as a result of this or any other Order of a Court in this jurisdiction for the purpose of civil or criminal proceedings in any other jurisdiction;

6. Not without the leave of the Court to seek to enforce this Order in any country outside the State or seek an Order of a similar nature including Orders conferring a charge or other security against the Defendant or the Defendant's assets;

AND the Plaintiff's solicitors undertake as follows:

1. To offer to explain to the person served with the Order its meaning and effect in simple everyday language and to inform the person served of his or her right to seek legal advice, such advice to include an explanation that the Defendant may be entitled to avail himself of the privilege against self-incrimination or legal professional privilege and apply to vary or discharge the Order;[42]

2. To answer at once to the best of their ability any question whether a particular item is a Listed Item as defined herein;

3. To return the originals of all documents obtained as a result of this Order (except original documents which belong to the Plaintiff) as soon as possible and in any event within five working days of their removal;

4. Where the ownership of any item obtained as a result of this Order is in dispute, to deliver the article into the keeping of the Solicitors acting for the Defendant within five working days from receiving a written undertaking from them, in terms satisfactory to the Plaintiff's Solicitors, to retain the article in safe keeping and to produce it to the Court when required so to do;

5. To retain in their own safe keeping all other items obtained as a result of this Order until the Court directs otherwise;

6. Not to remove any item from the Defendant's premises until a list of the items to be removed has been prepared and a copy of the list has been supplied to the person served with the Order and he has been given a reasonable opportunity to check the list;

7. Not to search the Defendant's premises or remove any items therefrom save in the presence of the Defendant or a person appearing to be a responsible partner, associate, employee or relation of the Defendant or a person in control of the Defendant's premises.

---

[42] In the United Kingdom it is usual that a Supervising Solicitor would be appointed who would give this undertaking; in the absence of the appointment of Supervising Solicitors in Ireland, it is thought appropriate that the Plaintiff's Solicitor would give such an undertaking.

IT IS ORDERED as follows:

1. That the Defendant, his servants, agents or persons acting on his behalf do allow Mr/Ms_____, the Plaintiff's Solicitor, and up to _____ persons who are employed by the Plaintiff's Solicitor or his firm ("the Plaintiff's Legal Representatives"), accompanied by two (2) servants or agents of the Plaintiff, between the hours of 8.00 am and 6.00 pm, to enter the Defendant's premises at_____("the Defendant's Premises") and any other premises disclosed pursuant to this Order and any vehicles under the Defendant's control on or around the premises so that they can search for, inspect, photograph or photocopy, and deliver into the safekeeping of the Plaintiff's Solicitors all the documents and articles which are listed in the Schedule to this Order ("the Listed Items") or which Mr _____ believes to be Listed Items;

2. That the Defendant do allow the Plaintiff's Legal Representatives and such servants or agents to remain on the Defendant's Premises until the search is complete, and to re-enter the premises on the same or the following day in order to complete the search;

3. This Order must be complied with immediately upon its being served either by the Defendant himself or by an employee of the Defendant or by any other person who appears to be in control of the Defendant's Premises and having authority to permit the Defendant's Premises to be entered and the search to proceed;

4. The Defendant do immediately hand over to the Plaintiff's Legal Representatives all or any of the Listed Items which are in his possession or under his control save for any computer or hard disk integral to any such computer;

5. If any of the Listed Items exist only in computer readable form, the Defendant do immediately give the Plaintiff's Solicitors effective access to the computers, with all necessary passwords, to enable them to be searched, and cause the Listed Items to be printed. A print out of the items must be given to the Plaintiff's Solicitors or displayed on the computer screen so that they can be read and copied. All reasonable steps shall be taken by the Plaintiff's Legal Representatives to ensure that no damage is done to any computer or data;

6. The Defendant do, immediately upon being requested so to do, inform the Plaintiff's Legal Representatives of the location and whereabouts of all or any of the Listed Items and to the best of his knowledge, information and belief, of the names and addresses of every person who has supplied the Defendant (or who has been supplied by the Defendant) with the Listed Items together with full particulars of the dates and quantities of each and every such supply to or from the Defendant of the Listed Items and within five working days from the service of this Order the Defendant must swear an affidavit setting out the foregoing information;

Appendix 4

Bayer Injunction Restraining the Defendant from Leaving the State and Ordering him to Deliver Up the Defendant's Passport

THE HIGH COURT
199 __ No. XXXXP

Monday _____ day of _____ 199 __

BEFORE MR JUSTICE

BETWEEN

PLAINTIFF

DEFENDANT

Upon Motion of Counsel for the Plaintiff[45] and upon reading the Affidavit sworn on the _____ day of_____ 199__ by _____, the Plaintiff, and the exhibits referred to therein and upon hearing Counsel for the Plaintiff[46]

AND the Plaintiff by his Counsel giving the following undertakings:

1. To abide by any Order as to damages should the Defendant suffer by reason of this Order which in the opinion of the Court the Plaintiff ought to pay;

2. To pay to any Third Party served with or given notice of this Order his or their reasonable costs and expenses and to indemnify them against all and any liability reasonably incurred by any such Third Party for the purposes of complying with this Order;

3. In the event of this Order being discharged or the terms hereof being varied, to forthwith take all reasonable steps to inform in writing any person or

---

[45] It is assumed that the application for the Order will have been made *ex parte*; in the case of an *inter partes* application, the hearing will be on foot of a Notice of Motion and the Order may say here "made pursuant to Notice dated the _____ day of _____ 199__". On *ex parte* and *inter partes* applications, see Ch 8, *Applying for a Mareva Injunction*, para **[8.05]** *et seq*.

[46] In the case of an *inter partes* application, the recitals to the Order may provide here "and upon hearing Counsel for the Defendants and upon reading the replying Affidavit of the defendant ...".

company whom the Plaintiff has given notice of the Order or who he has reasonable grounds for supposing may act upon the Order;

4. To give a copy of this Order to the Defendant and to any other person who is notified of the terms of this Order;

5. As soon as practicable, to issue and serve on the Defendant the Plenary Summons[47] in the form of the draft produced to the Court claiming the appropriate relief together with a copy of this Order;

6. As soon as practicable, to cause an Affidavit to be sworn, stamped and filed in substantially the same terms as the draft affidavit produced to the Court;

7. To give a copy of the affidavit grounding this Order to the Defendant and, on demand to any party affected thereby;[48]

AND the Plaintiff's solicitors undertake as follows:

1. To keep all passports and other travel documents (if any) delivered up into the Plaintiff's Solicitor's custody by the Defendant pursuant to this Order until further Order of the Court

IT IS ORDERED as follows:

1. That the Defendant be restrained from leaving the State until the [date] or until further Order of the Court;

2. That the Defendant do immediately hand up to the person serving this Order upon him all passports or other travel documents in his name or on which he has the right to travel out of the State

AND IT IS ORDERED that the Plaintiff's Solicitors be at liberty to notify forthwith the terms of this Order by telephone and facsimile [or courier service] to:[49]

(a) the Defendant, and

(b)

AND IT IS ORDERED THAT the Plaintiff be at liberty to service Notice of Motion for an Interlocutory Order returnable on Monday _____ day of_____199___;[50]

AND the parties hereto and all parties having notice of or being affected by this Order have liberty to apply on 48 hours' notice to the Plaintiff's Solicitors and the Court to vary the terms or discharge this Order[51]

---

[47] Or Summary Summons or Special Summons or Notice of Motion, as the case may be: see Ch 8, *Applying for a Mareva Injunction*, para **[8.14]** *et seq.*

[48] In accordance with Ord 40, r 21 of the RSC. See further Ch 11, *Restraining Defendants from Leaving the State*, at para **[11.26]**.

[49] It will often be considered useful for the terms of the actual Order to expressly permit liberty to notify, forthwith by modern means, the Defendant and other parties who may be able to assist in enforcing the order.

[50] It is assumed that this is an *interim* Order.

AND the Court doth reserve the costs of this application and Order.

——————————
REGISTRAR

If you the within named A.B. neglect to obey this Order by the time therein limited, you will be liable to process of execution including imprisonment for the purpose of compelling you to obey the same Order.

Signed: _____

        Solicitor for the Plaintiff

---

[51] On "variation" and "discharge" of a Mareva injunction, see Ch 9, *The Mareva Order and Its Effects*, para **[9.31]**.

Index